Welcome to

McGraw-Hill's

Praxis I and II

*C*ongratulations! You have chosen the Praxis guide from America's leading educational publisher. You probably know us from many of the textbooks you used in school and college. Now we're ready to help you take the next step — and become a licensed teacher.

This book gives you everything you need to succeed on the Praxis test. You will get in-depth instruction and review of every topic tested, tips and strategies for every question type, and plenty of practice exams to boost your test-taking confidence. To get started, go to the following pages where you'll find:

- **How to Use This Book:** Step-by-step instructions to help you get the most out of your test-prep program.

- **50 Fast Tips for Test Day:** The most important things you need to know to get a top score.

- **The 10 Most Common Praxis Writing Topics:** a preview of the kinds of writing prompts you're most likely to encounter on test day.

- **Praxis Writing Checklist:** Handy tips to help you evaluate your practice PPST essays.

ABOUT THE AUTHOR Dr. Laurie Rozakis taught high school for more than a decade and is now a full professor of English and Humanities in the State University of New York. A master teacher, Dr. Rozakis was awarded the highly prestigious New York State Chancellor's Award for Excellence in Teaching.

ABOUT McGRAW-HILL EDUCATION

This book has been created by a unit of McGraw-Hill Education, a division of The McGraw-Hill Companies. McGraw-Hill Education is a leading global provider of instructional, assessment, and reference materials in both print and digital form. McGraw-Hill Education has offices in 33 countries and publishes in more than 65 languages. With a broad range of products and services — from traditional textbooks to the latest in online and multimedia learning — we engage, stimulate, and empower students and professionals of all ages, helping them meet the increasing challenges of the 21st century knowledge economy.

Learn more. Mc Graw Hill **Do more.**

How to Use This Book

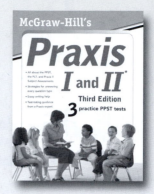

You lead a hectic life. Most likely you're in school and perhaps even working at the same time. You want to devote a lot of time to studying for the Praxis, but you just don't have the time to do so. As a result, you need to make the most of the study time that you do have. You need a book and a study plan that work for you.

There are many different ways to approach a test review book. As a result, it's not as easy as it might appear to know how to use this book to your best advantage. We've designed this book to make it as easy for you as possible to earn your highest possible score on the Praxis. Follow these guidelines to make the most of your study time.

1 Read This Section
This section gives you hands-on advice for doing your best on this all-important test. The advice in this part of the book will help you get your studying off to a great start no matter which Praxis tests you take.

2 Read *Chapter 1: The Ten-Step Power Study Plan*
Follow the suggestions described in this section. For instance, set up a personal study center, choose a test strategy, and set up a study routine. Familiarize yourself with the Praxis test, too, and boost your reading comprehension by reading high-quality novels and nonfiction for pleasure. Be especially vigilant about dealing with any special needs that you may have, as described in Step 8. By the time you finish reading this section, you'll have the tools you need to power up your studying.

3 Take the Three Diagnostic Pretests in Part 2
Take these tests under the exact test conditions you will have on the day of the Praxis. Sit in a quiet room and time yourself. Be sure to use only the amount of time you are allocated for each section. Then analyze the results to determine your strengths and weaknesses. List these so you know where to spend the most time as you study.

4 Review Parts 3 through 6
Here's where you'll fill in the gaps in your knowledge. As you read these sections, refer to the list of your strengths and weaknesses. Use this analysis to decide how to allocate your time. Spend the most time on the areas in which you are most deficient and the least time on the areas where you are proficient.

5 Complete Part 7, the Practice Tests
Take the practice tests one at a time. After each practice test, carefully analyze the questions you missed. Go back to the book and review the sections that cover these topics before you move on to another practice test. Always focus on the topics that will gain you the most points.

6 Go Over *50 Fast Tips for Test Day*
On the day of the Praxis exam, review *50 Fast Tips for Test Day*. Not only will these suggestions help boost your score, but they will also help you relax. You'll feel fully equipped to do your very best on the Praxis.

50 Fast Tips for Test Day

Three, two, one…The countdown is over and it is test day! You know that you are well-prepared because you have read this book, completed all the exercises, and worked through the practice tests. You have checked your answers and reviewed the most challenging concepts, too. Now is the time to put the final polish on your preparations to take Praxis I or II. The best way to do that is to study these 50 Fast Tips. They are designed to help you identify the key elements to remember as you take Praxis I or II so you can earn your highest possible grade.

These pages are designed to give you a convenient last-minute reminder of the key concepts you need to succeed on test day. Use this review to check your test readiness to ensure you're prepared to do your best and get your best score.

Overall Test-Taking Tips

Here are some useful tips to help you maximize your Praxis I or II score on test day.

USE THE TEST-TAKING SKILLS YOU HAVE LEARNED FROM THIS BOOK

1   **Have a test strategy**. Since you can complete the test in any order you wish, decide beforehand how you will attack the questions. As you learned in this book, you can work from the beginning of the test to the end, but you might just as well decide to complete all the easiest questions first and then return to the more difficult ones. Select the strategy that works best for you, the one that you have practiced while taking the sample tests in this book.

2   **Make notes**. If you are taking the paper-and-pencil version, write in your test booklet. Underline main ideas and key points, do calculations, make notes, and so on.

3   **Use process of elimination**. Always try to cross out incorrect choices. The more choices you can eliminate, the better your chances of choosing the right answer. This is especially important if you have to guess. Remember that there is no penalty for guessing, so don't leave any answers blank.

4   **Double-check your work**. If you are taking the paper-and-pencil version, be sure to bubble in the correct choices.

5   **For the computerized version**. Take advantage of the computer tutorial that is offered before you begin the actual test. At any point during the test, you may return to the tutorial by clicking your mouse on the "HELP" box at the bottom of the screen. Also be aware of scroll bars. Some images and text are too big to fit on your screen and require you to scroll down to view them.

PACE YOURSELF

6   **Watch the time**. Be sure to bring a watch. Don't count on the test room having a clock. If you take the computer version of Praxis I, there is a clock on the screen, but you should still bring a watch. You will NOT be able to use your cell phone as your watch.

7 **Stick to your plan**. Decide beforehand how much time to allot for each test question, and stick to your plan. Remember that on average, you should allow no more than 90 seconds per question.

8 **Stay on track**. Don't get stuck on any one question; if you can't answer a question, leave it and move on.

9 **Stay focused**. Ignore how quickly or slowly other test-takers are working.

10 **Check your work**. Be sure to leave time to check your answers.

STAY COOL

11 **Reread**. The questions on Praxis I and II are designed to be clear, not tricky. If a question seems confusing, read it again.

12 **Don't second-guess yourself**. Doing so can make you feel tense.

13 **Don't look for traps**. Remember that the test does not contain trick questions.

14 **Use relaxation techniques**. If you feel yourself tensing up, take a few deep breaths and visualize a peaceful scene. Then return to the test.

15 **Stay calm**. Even if you're having a hard time answering the questions, keep cool. Recall that you don't have to answer all of the questions correctly to get a good score.

Tips for the Praxis I Reading Test

16 **Read the passage first**. Read it thoroughly and carefully, all the way through.

17 **Identify the main idea and key details**. If you are taking the pencil-and-paper version of the test, underline these or mark them in some other way.

18 **Predict the answers**. Read each question in turn. Cover the answer choices and predict each answer. Then look at the choices to find which one (if any) matches. Chances are good that the answer you predicted will be correct.

19 **Refer to the passage to check your answers**.

20 **Use strategy**. If you can't find the answer, use process of elimination. Then skim the passage to find information you need to find literal details or make inferences.

21 **Categorize**. If you are having difficulty answering a question, try to identify it as a literal detail or making inference question. Then you will know whether you can find the actual fact you need or if you'll have to draw a conclusion from stated and unstated information.

22 **Use ONLY the information contained in the passage**. Do not use information that you already know.

23 **Paraphrase**. Put difficult questions and answer choices into your own words to make them easier to understand.

24 **Don't get sidetracked by unfamiliar words**. Chances are they are not critical to your understanding. If you do need to define the word, use context clues as well as roots, prefixes, and suffixes to figure out what unfamiliar words mean.

25 **Work in sections.** Try to complete every question in a reading set, even if you have to make an educated guess. You will lose a lot of time if you have to go back and reread the passage to answer one or two questions.

Tips for the Praxis I Writing Test

USAGE QUESTIONS

26 **Know the format.** These questions have four underlined parts; the fifth choice (E) is always "No error."

27 **Be thorough.** Even if you think you have identified the answer early on, read the sentence all the way through.

28 **Know which changes to make.** When you find an error in an underlined part, you can delete it, change its form (such as tense or spelling), replace it, or add a mark of punctuation.

29 **Keep it simple.** If you have to guess, keep it simple. Go for the answer that creates the most direct, least complex and convoluted sentence.

SENTENCE CORRECTION QUESTIONS

30 **Know the format.** These questions have one underlined part. The first choice (A) will always repeat the original part; the other four choices offer different revisions.

31 **Read the sentence all the way through.** Even if you think you have figured out the answer immediately, read the entire sentence.

32 **Read the sentence "aloud."** Of course, do this in your head so you don't disturb other test-takers. Often, "hearing" the sentence can help you figure out the answer.

33 **Make predictions.** Cover the answers, predict the correction, and then look for your revision among the answer choices.

34 **Avoid traps.** If you can't find your choice, use process of elimination. Length is not a good predictor of correctness: a long answer may be better than a short one, and vice-versa. As a result, have a reason for your choice. (See tip #35 for reasons.)

35 **Consider the basics.** The test-makers go for the most common sentence errors rather than esoteric writing problems. As a result, look for problems with sentence boundaries (run-ons and fragments), parallel structure, pronoun case ("who" and "whom," for instance), pronoun reference, agreement of subject and verb, agreement of pronoun and antecedent, degree of comparison, misplaced and dangling modifiers, and so on.

36 **Make predictions.** Predict the correction and then look for your revision among the answer choices.

37 **Avoid traps.** If you can't find your choice, use process of elimination. Length is not a good predictor of correctness: a long answer may be better than a short one, and vice-versa, so go for logic rather than length.

38 **Look for logic.** Your choice must be logical and fit with the rest of the sentence as well as grammatically correct.

THE ESSAY

39 **Stay on topic.** You must address the specific topic, not a topic of your own choice. No matter how well-written your essay, you will not receive any credit if it is off topic. Always choose the position that you can most strongly support.

40 **Start with a topic sentence.** State your position in the first paragraph, organize your ideas clearly, and use ample specific details and examples. Follow the rules of standard written English and be sure to leave sufficient time to proofread your essay.

Tips for the Praxis I Math Test

41 **Do a "memory dump."** Jot down key formulas when you begin working on this part of Praxis I and II. Even if you don't use these formulas, having written them down will give you confidence.

42 **Check the operation.** Make sure you do the correct operation, such as addition or subtraction. Look for key words such as *sum, more than, increased* (addition) and *minus, difference,* and *less than* (subtraction).

43 **Draw a picture on your scratch paper.** This will help you visualize the problem. Also create a number line to help you visualize and figure out "less than" and "greater than." This strategy is especially helpful for word problems.

44 **Base your response only the data given.** Do not include any outside information you may have.

45 **Make a number line.** Remember that negative numbers have less value than positive numbers.

46 **Consider working backwards.** To do so, start with the possible answers and work backward through the problem. This technique is especially helpful with algebra-based problems, where you are trying to find a variable. Use each possible answer choice in place of the variable to see which one works.

47 **Estimate the answer.** This will help you to make sure that your conclusion is reasonable.

48 **Consider charts.** Do not let a chart or graph daunt you. Figure out what the data mean before you look at the question and the answer choices.

49 **Make educated guesses.** Do so after you have used process of elimination.

50 **Check your calculations.**

The 10 Most Common Praxis Writing Topics

To earn your best possible score on the PPST: Writing Test essay, you must know what to expect. Although you can't know exactly what writing prompt will be on your exam, you *can* familiarize yourself with the kinds of prompts that have appeared on previous tests. The following list shows the ten most common types of PPST: Writing Test essay prompts, based on prior exams.

Try writing at least one multiple-paragraph essay for each of the prompts below. Organize your ideas logically and include examples and clear explanations. When you have completed each essay, use the checklist on the next page to evaluate your efforts.

1. Success and Goals

Erma Bombeck once said: "Don't confuse fame with success. Madonna is one; Helen Keller is the other." Define "success" and explain what you hope to achieve that will make you a success.

2. Values

The United States should remain an island of plenty in a sea of hunger. The future of humanity is at stake. We are not responsible for the rest of the world. Agree or disagree.

3. Government and Laws

To date, eighteen states and the District of Columbia have banned text messaging for all drivers. Texting while driving should be illegal in the entire United States. Agree or disagree.

4. Education and Educational Reform

Same-sex schools provide a better education than co-ed schools. Take a stand on this issue and argue your point with specific examples and details.

5. Personal Responsibility

Athletes have an enormous influence on children. As a result, they have a responsibility to act as positive role models. Agree or disagree.

6. Technology

Television is more interesting and educational than most people. Agree or disagree.

7. Multiculturalism

Currently, the United States does not have an "official" language, although English is generally accepted. English should be the official U.S. language. Agree or disagree.

8. Maturity

All students should be required to take a year off between high school and college, a "gap year," to work and assess their future plans. Take a stand on this issue and argue your point with specific examples and details.

9. Censorship

The Internet should be censored, its objectionable content filtered, to protect everyone, but especially children. Take a stand for or against censoring the Internet. Persuade your readers by using convincing evidence.

10. The Influence of Society on the Individual

Everyone is influenced in significant ways—both good and bad—by the area in which they grow up. Agree or disagree with this statement. Convince your audience by using specific evidence.

Praxis Writing Checklist

Use this checklist to evaluate your practice essays on the **PPST: Writing Test**.

Overall: Did I...

___ take a clear and logical side of the argument?

___ clearly state my thesis in the opening paragraph?

___ include the opposition but show that my view has more merit?

___ end with a strong conclusion that sums up my main points and makes my case?

Organization: Did I...

___ organize my ideas in a logical way?

___ present the opposition first and then argue my side?

___ make my method of organization clear?

___ link related ideas with parallelism, transitions, and repetition of key words?

Logic: Did I...

___ back up my opinions with facts, statistics, and expert opinions?

___ use specific and correct information?

___ analyze cause and effect correctly?

___ make sense?

Diction: Did I...

___ correctly understand the connotation of the words I selected?

___ use diction appropriate to my audience?

___ use nonbiased language?

___ use idioms and idiomatic phrases correctly?

___ use Standard Written English, not substandard usage?

Grammar: Did I...

___ write complete and correct sentences? Did I check for run-ons and fragments?

___ make sure that all verbs agree with their subjects and pronouns with their antecedents?

___ use the active voice to make my writing more direct and effective?

___ correct misplaced and dangling modifiers?

Style: Did I...

___ begin my essay in a compelling way, such as with an interesting fact or anecdote?

___ use the correct word, not its close cousin?

___ use vivid words, especially verbs?

___ revise and edit to eliminate wordiness?

___ use a variety of sentence structures—including simple, compound, complex, and compound-complex sentences?

Mechanics: Did I...

___ use all end punctuation correctly? Did I avoid overusing exclamation marks?

___ use apostrophes correctly, especially with contractions?

___ spell every word correctly? If I wasn't sure how a word is spelled, did I substitute a correctly spelled synonym?

___ use commas, semi-colons, and colons correctly?

___ capitalize proper nouns?

___ proofread my essay and correct all careless errors?

McGRAW-HILL's

PSAT/NMSQT

McGRAW-HILL's

PSAT/NMSQT

Second Edition

CHRISTOPHER BLACK

MARK ANESTIS

and the TUTORS of COLLEGE HILL COACHING™

New York / Chicago / San Francisco / Lisbon / London / Madrid / Mexico City
Milan / New Delhi / San Juan / Seoul / Singapore / Sydney / Toronto

7 8 9 QVS/QVS 1 5 4 3

ISBN: 978-0-07-174211-5
MHID: 0-07-174211-5

McGraw-Hill books are available at special quantity discounts to use as premiums and sales promotions, or for use in corporate training programs. To contact a representative please e-mail us at bulksales@mcgraw-hill.com.

PSAT is a registered trademark of the College Entrance Examination Board, which does not endorse this book.

College Hill Coaching® is a registered trademark under the control of Christopher F. Black.

Library of Congress Cataloging-in-Publication Data

Black, Christopher.
   McGraw-Hill's PSAT/NMSQT/Christopher Black, Mark Anestis, and the tutors of College Hill coaching.
      p. cm.
   ISBN-13: 978-0-07-174211-5
   ISBN-10:   0-07-174211-5

   1. PSAT (Educational test)—Study guides. 2. National Merit Scholarship Qualifying Test—Study guides. I. Anestis, Mark. II. College Hill Coaching (Organization) III. Title.
   LB2353.56.B53 2010
   378.1′662—dc22
                                        2010010443

CONTENTS

ACKNOWLEDGMENTS

We would like to gratefully acknowledge the help of those who have contributed to this enormous project and have been committed to its success. This project would not have been the same without the help of so many of our close friends and relatives: Elizabeth Black, the world's greatest teacher of mathematics, for her many years of patience, wisdom and gracious support; Sarah and Anna Black for their constant inspiration and marvellous good humor; Stephanie Anestis for her invaluable efforts in reading and editing the text and for her incredible love and support; Robert, Janice, Michael, and Matthew Anestis who also gave their insight on the work in progress; and Andrew Hathaway, the legendary and inspirational Mr. Zip-Zap-Zup. We would also like to thank Brigid Barry, Aulden Kaye, Peter Obourn, Kristoffer Shields and the brilliant tutors of College Hill Coaching for their thoughtful and valuable assistance. We appreciate the hard work of those at McGraw-Hill who made this project work and the thoughtful help of our agent, Grace Freedson. Finally, we would like to thank all the students of College Hill Coaching who have contributed to the growth of these materials over the years; their insight and experiences have thoroughly inspired and informed this book.

CHAPTER 1

WHAT YOU NEED TO KNOW ABOUT THE PSAT/NMSQT

1.   Questions and Answers about the PSAT/NMSQT

I QUESTIONS AND ANSWERS ABOUT THE PSAT/NMSQT

What is the PSAT/NMSQT?

The PSAT/NMSQT (Preliminary SAT and National Merit Scholarship Qualifying Test) is a 2 hour and 10 minute-long test administered each October to high school sophomores and juniors throughout the country. It consists of three parts: Critical Reading, Math, and Writing. It is essentially an abbreviated form of the SAT (which is just under 4 hours long) without the essay.

PSAT scores are not used for college admission, but they are used to select National Merit Scholars. However, since only the top 4% of test takers actually earn National Merit honors, most students take the PSAT primarily as a "practice run" for the SAT, which they will take in the spring of junior year.

How is the PSAT scored, and what do the scores mean?

You will receive three scores on your PSAT—Critical Reading, Math, and Writing—each ranging from 20 to 80. The sum of these three scores is your NMSQT selection index, which can range from 60 to 240. The "scaled" scores are based on the "raw" scores for each section. Every correct answer increases your raw score for that section by 1 point, and every wrong answer decreases your raw score for that section by 1/4 point, except for wrong answers on math "grid-in" questions, which do not decrease your raw score. Unanswered questions are worth 0 points to your raw score.

PSAT scores are scaled so that a 50 represents roughly the median of all scores. In other words, a score of 50 on any section of the PSAT will outscore about 50% of all students taking the test. Also, a score of 55 on any section outscores about 66% of all students, a 60 outscores about 85% of all students, and a score of 70 outscores about 97% of all students. Of course, these numbers vary slightly from year to year and from state to state.

Will colleges see my PSAT scores?

No. Don't worry about colleges judging you on your PSAT scores. When you register for the PSAT, however, you will have the option of giving colleges permission to send you information about their schools. These schools will simply receive your profile and, if they are interested in having you apply, send you brochures and other information in your junior year. Also, if you qualify as a National Merit Scholar, you will be given the opportunity to notify two colleges or universities that you have received this honor.

What skills does the PSAT assess?

Like the SAT, the PSAT is designed to assess a number of reasoning skills that are an important part of college success, namely, mathematical reasoning, analytical reading, vocabulary, and writing. It is not, as many "test-prep" companies claim, an assessment of how well you've memorized some secret test-taking tricks. Of course, it's important to know what the test is (and is not) testing, how the test is structured, and how to budget your time wisely on the test, but any big improvements in your scores will most likely come from improving the specific academic skills it assesses.

How are National Merit Scholars determined?

Each year, about 50,000 students of the 1.3 million who take the PSAT/NMSQT as juniors receive National Merit honors on the basis of high PSAT index scores. Your PSAT index score is simply the sum of your three PSAT scores. The qualifying scores for National Merit honors vary from year to year and from state to state. There are three levels of National Merit Scholar: Commended Scholar, Semifinalist, and Finalist. Those students who qualify will be notified in April of their junior year. In September of their senior year, about 34,000 of these students will be notified that they are Commended Scholars and will not continue in competition for National Merit scholarships. The remaining 16,000 of these students will qualify as Semifinalists and will be invited to submit their academic records, an essay, a school recommendation, and information about their extracurricular activities and their school's standards and curriculum. Most of these students, about 15,000 of them, will qualify for Finalist standing, and from these, about 8,000 will be chosen to receive National Merit Scholarships.

If you are interested in learning more about the National Merit Scholarship program, go to its web site at www.nationalmerit.org.

How does the PSAT differ from the SAT?

In a nutshell, the PSAT is shorter (2 hours 10 minutes versus 3 hours 45 minutes for the SAT), doesn't require you to write an essay, and doesn't test some of the more advanced concepts from second-year algebra. Other than that, the two tests are very similar.

How do I register for the PSAT?

You can register for the PSAT only at your high school or at a high school in your community. You cannot register for the PSAT online. If you attend high school, your school will likely inform you when and how to register. If not, feel free to ask your guidance counselor how to register. If you are home-schooled, contact a local high school to get this information. While doing so, be sure to pick up the *PSAT/NMSQT Student Bulletin*, which contains important information as well as a full practice test.

Can I take the PSAT with extended time?

Some students with special needs can qualify to take the PSAT with extended time. These administrations are only available to students with a formal rec-ommendation, which must be submitted to the College Board more than one month prior to the test administration. If you have a learning disabi-lity that has been diagnosed by a psychologist and you feel that an extended-time PSAT would benefit you, talk to your guidance counselor about how to qualify and register. You may also find more information about special accommodations online at www.collegeboard.com/disable/students/html/psat.html.

When should I take the SAT and SAT Subject Tests?

The SAT Subject Tests are the subject-area tests administered by the College Board. Plan to take an SAT Subject Test in June for any course you've fin-ished successfully. If you do well in freshman biology, for instance, take the SAT Subject Test in biology in June of your freshman year. Likewise, con-sider taking the Math Level 1 after completing algebra II successfully, the Math Level 2 after precal-culus, etc. You will want to take any SAT Subject Test in a subject when you feel you are at your peak in that subject. Learn which SAT Subject Tests your colleges require, and try to complete them by June of your junior year. You can take up to three SAT Subject Tests on any one test date.

After you take the PSAT in October of your junior year, you can take the SAT in late January, late March (or early April), or early May of your junior year and in early November, early December, and late January of your senior year. To give yourself ample time to prepare, you may wish to take the SAT in March and May of your junior year and again in October of your senior year if necessary. Remember, you can take the SAT more than once, and colleges will only use your top scores.

Are my SAT and SAT Subject Test scores the most important part of my college application?

In most cases, no, but these scores are becoming more important as college admissions becomes more selective. Without exception, high SAT scores will provide you with an admission advantage regardless of what kind of school you are applying to. Most colleges are also very interested in your high school curriculum, your high school grades, your essay, your teacher recommendations, your special talents or experiences, and your extracurricu-lar activities. Generally, the more selective a college is, the more important the personal factors are, such as extracurricular activities and special talents. Some large or specialized schools will weigh the SAT or ACT scores more heavily than others and even declare a cutoff score for applicants. If you have any questions about how heavily a certain college weighs your SAT or ACT scores, call the admissions office and ask.

Should I guess if I don't know the answer to a question?

On any PSAT, SAT, or SAT Subject Test multiple-choice question, if you get the question right, your raw score increases by 1 point. If you get it wrong, your raw scores decreases by 1/4 point. If you skip it, your raw score remains the same. Therefore, on multiple-choice questions, blind guessing will likely harm your score in the short run. If you are guessing on no more than five questions, be conservative and only guess when you can eliminate two or more choices. If you are guessing on more than ten ques-tions, though, be more aggressive and just try to elim-inate at least *one* choice before guessing.

On any math question in which you must "grid in" a numerical answer, if you get the question right, your raw score increases by 1 point. If you get it wrong or skip it, your raw score remains the same. Therefore, on grid-in questions, blind guessing won't harm you any more than leaving the question blank. This means that if you have any kind of guess, you should fill it in.

CHAPTER 2

SMART TRAINING FOR THE PSAT/NMSQT AND BEYOND

1. The College Hill Coaching Plan for Success on the PSAT and SAT

▌ THE COLLEGE HILL COACHING PLAN FOR SUCCESS ON THE PSAT AND SAT

If you are beginning now to prepare for the PSAT, you have plenty of time (probably many months) before the big test, the SAT. You have the advantage of being able to make a smart, relaxed, long-term study plan, which is always much more effective than cramming just before the test. Both the PSAT and SAT are tests of academic reasoning. You will improve your scores most dramatically by immersing yourself in varied and interesting college-level reading, studying those words and word roots that are linked to college success, improving your writing skills through careful practice, becoming more fluent in key mathematical concepts, and improving your reasoning and problem-solving skills.

Here are some of the principles behind College Hill Coaching's Smart Training for the PSAT and SAT:

Step 1: Get a good reading list, make a reading plan, and stick to it. Read at least one good book every few weeks.

The PSAT and SAT emphasize college-level critical reasoning skills more than ever. One of the best ways to be successful on the Critical Reading portion of the PSAT and SAT is to read and analyze college-level prose as often as possible. As you do so, focus on the reading skills discussed in Chapter 5: Critical Reading Skills. **Read actively, ask the three key questions, visualize, and summarize**. These skills will translate into success not only on the PSAT and SAT, but in college as well.

Read a wide variety of interesting college-level prose in all areas of the curriculum. Keep in mind that only about one-third of the passages on the SAT or PSAT will be narratives, so don't restrict yourself to novels and stories. Challenge yourself by reading plenty of good nonfiction books about history, the arts, the sciences, and philosophy, like those from the list below. **As you read, make flashcards for any new vocabulary words you come across, using the strategies discussed in Chapter 4**.

Here is part of the College Hill Coaching reading list for our students taking the SAT:

Narrative

One Hundred Years of Solitude, G. Garcia-Marquez
Candide, Voltaire
The Wall, John Hersey
The Best American Short Stories of the Century, John Updike, Editor
Frankenstein, Mary Wollstonecraft Shelley
The Color Purple, Alice Walker
Metamorphosis (and other stories), Franz Kafka
The Autobiography of Frederick Douglass
The Painted Bird, Jerzy Kozinsky
Macbeth, William Shakespeare
Growing Up, Russell Baker
Baby, It's Cold Inside, S. J. Perelman
Pride and Prejudice, Jane Austen
Atlas Shrugged, Ayn Rand
The Life of Pi, Yann Martel
Crime and Punishment, Fyodor Dostoevsky

Argument

The Op-Ed pages of *The New York Times*
Essays from *Harper's, The Atlantic Monthly*, and *The New Yorker*
Lanterns and Lances, James Thurber
Drift and Mastery, Walter Lippmann
The Best American Essays, Robert Atwan, Editor
Walden, Henry David Thoreau
The Chomsky Reader, Noam Chomsky

Analysis

A Brief History of Time, Stephen Hawking
The Mismeasure of Man, Stephen J. Gould
The Republic, Plato
Civilization and Its Discontents, Sigmund Freud
A People's History of the United States, Howard Zinn
How the Mind Works, Steven Pinker
QED, Richard Feynman
The Lives of a Cell, Lewis Thomas
Democracy in America, Alexis de Tocqueville
The Language Instinct, Steven Pinker

Step 2: Figure out which tests you will take and when you will take them.

After you take your PSAT, you will probably take your SAT once or twice in the spring of your junior year, and two or three of your SAT Subject Tests in June of your junior year. Even though these tests may be months away, mark down the important dates now on your calendar so that you can plan around them. Find out more about registration at www.collegeboard.com.

Step 3: Diagnose your skills by taking the diagnostic test in Chapter 3.

A key to success on the PSAT and SAT is taking realistic practice tests. Use your first test as a diagnostic test. This might be a PSAT you've already taken (perhaps in your sophomore year) or the Diagnostic PSAT in Chapter 3 of this book. Don't worry about acing it, but rather, consider it as a guide to your strengths and weaknesses. Set aside about 2 1/2 hours to take the Diagnostic PSAT in Chapter 3. Follow the guidelines at the beginning of the test: time yourself strictly, or, better yet, have someone else time you. The test is followed by a detailed answer key that includes references to chapters in the book that teach the skills and knowledge you may need to review.

Step 4: Use the results from your diagnostic PSAT to plan your review.

The answer key to the diagnostic PSAT in Chapter 3 is a great starting point for your PSAT study plan. Whenever you miss a question, read the answer explanation carefully and write down the lesson or lessons that are mentioned after the explanation. After reviewing the entire diagnostic test, you may notice that some lessons showed up on the list more than once. Use this list to draw up a plan to review the lessons. Start with those lessons that showed up most frequently on the list.

Step 5: Review key concepts with the College Hill Lessons in this book.

College Hill Coaching has spent 15 years developing the most effective self-guided lessons in test preparation. The College Hill Lessons found throughout this book are enormously effective, but only if you use them properly. Follow the instructions below carefully to make your work as productive as possible.

Each College Hill Lesson is designed to be completed in about 30 minutes. This should allow you enough time to check your work thoroughly and be sure that you understand the key concepts. College Hill Lessons in this book discuss important concepts, key examples, sample problems, and explanations. Always read each lesson and examples completely and carefully and take notes before moving on to the worksheet that follows. The worksheets are designed to review the concepts and show you how they will be presented on the PSAT. Work through each problem first without looking back at the lesson. As you work, circle the difficult questions. Only after completing the entire worksheet, go to the answer key and check your work. Mark your wrong answers and try to understand what mistakes you made and how to avoid them in the future.

Every lesson is followed by an answer key, either immediately after the worksheet or at the end of the chapter. This provides detailed explanations of the answers and often shows different ways to approach the questions. Read the answer key solution to every question, even for those questions you answered correctly. Often it will provide options for solving questions even more efficiently than you did, or it might remind you of a way to approach the question that you hadn't thought of.

Step 6: Follow up your review with realistic practice tests.

The best way to keep motivated in your studies is to see your progress on realistic practice tests. This book provides three complete, full-length practice tests in Chapter 14 and more online. Take them in regular intervals, at least a week apart. Take them in the morning, as you will the real test, under strictly timed conditions in a quiet setting. Set an aggressive but realistic score goal for yourself, and use the feedback from each test to help you adjust your review or the way you approach the next test.

After you take and score a practice test, think about the following questions:

1. Were you satisfied with your score? If not, which concepts, skills, or test-taking strategies do you need to improve?
2. Did your nerves affect your performance? If so, what can you do to improve your anxiety, focus, and confidence?
3. Did you budget your time well? If not, how could you improve your use of time?
4. Did you get many more questions wrong than you left unanswered? If so, you may benefit from slowing down and being more selective. Remember, you can get an above-average score on the PSAT if you get just over half of the questions right. And you can get 600 on a section by getting only about two-thirds of the questions right.

CHAPTER 3

DIAGNOSTIC PSAT

I. A Complete Diagnostic PSAT to Assess Your Strengths and Weaknesses

A COMPLETE DIAGNOSTIC PSAT TO ASSESS YOUR STRENGTHS AND WEAKNESSES

ANSWER SHEET

Last Name: _____ First Name: _____

Date: _____ Testing Location: _____

Administering the Test

- Remove this answer sheet from the book and use it to record your answers to this test.
- This test will require 2 hours and 10 minutes to complete. Take this test in one sitting.
- Use a stopwatch to time yourself on each section. The time limit for each section is written clearly at the beginning of each section. The first four sections are 25 minutes long, and the last section is 30 minutes long.
- Each response must completely fill the oval. Erase all stray marks completely, or they may be interpreted as responses.
- You must stop ALL work on a section when time is called.
- If you finish a section before the time has elapsed, check your work on that section. You may NOT move on to the next section until time is called.
- Do not waste time on questions that seem too difficult for you.
- Use the test book for scratchwork, but you will only receive credit for answers that are marked on the answer sheets.

Scoring the Test

- Your scaled score, which will be determined from a conversion table, is based on your raw score for each section.
- You will receive one point toward your raw score for every correct answer.
- You will receive no points toward your raw score for an omitted question.
- For each wrong answer on a multiple-choice question, your raw score will be reduced by 1/4 point. For each wrong answer on a numerical "grid-in" question (Section 4, questions 29–38), your raw score will receive no deduction.

SECTION 1 — Critical Reading — 25 minutes

Questions 1–24, answer choices A B C D E

Time: 25 minutes Start: _____ Stop: _____

SECTION 2 — Math — 25 minutes

Questions 1–20, answer choices A B C D E

Time: 25 minutes Start: _____ Stop: _____

SECTION 3
Critical Reading
25 minutes

25. Ⓐ Ⓑ Ⓒ Ⓓ Ⓔ   33. Ⓐ Ⓑ Ⓒ Ⓓ Ⓔ   41. Ⓐ Ⓑ Ⓒ Ⓓ Ⓔ
26. Ⓐ Ⓑ Ⓒ Ⓓ Ⓔ   34. Ⓐ Ⓑ Ⓒ Ⓓ Ⓔ   42. Ⓐ Ⓑ Ⓒ Ⓓ Ⓔ
27. Ⓐ Ⓑ Ⓒ Ⓓ Ⓔ   35. Ⓐ Ⓑ Ⓒ Ⓓ Ⓔ   43. Ⓐ Ⓑ Ⓒ Ⓓ Ⓔ
28. Ⓐ Ⓑ Ⓒ Ⓓ Ⓔ   36. Ⓐ Ⓑ Ⓒ Ⓓ Ⓔ   44. Ⓐ Ⓑ Ⓒ Ⓓ Ⓔ
29. Ⓐ Ⓑ Ⓒ Ⓓ Ⓔ   37. Ⓐ Ⓑ Ⓒ Ⓓ Ⓔ   45. Ⓐ Ⓑ Ⓒ Ⓓ Ⓔ
30. Ⓐ Ⓑ Ⓒ Ⓓ Ⓔ   38. Ⓐ Ⓑ Ⓒ Ⓓ Ⓔ   46. Ⓐ Ⓑ Ⓒ Ⓓ Ⓔ
31. Ⓐ Ⓑ Ⓒ Ⓓ Ⓔ   39. Ⓐ Ⓑ Ⓒ Ⓓ Ⓔ   47. Ⓐ Ⓑ Ⓒ Ⓓ Ⓔ
32. Ⓐ Ⓑ Ⓒ Ⓓ Ⓔ   40. Ⓐ Ⓑ Ⓒ Ⓓ Ⓔ   48. Ⓐ Ⓑ Ⓒ Ⓓ Ⓔ

Time: 25 minutes

Start: _____

Stop: _____

SECTION 4
Math
25 minutes

21. Ⓐ Ⓑ Ⓒ Ⓓ Ⓔ   25. Ⓐ Ⓑ Ⓒ Ⓓ Ⓔ
22. Ⓐ Ⓑ Ⓒ Ⓓ Ⓔ   26. Ⓐ Ⓑ Ⓒ Ⓓ Ⓔ
23. Ⓐ Ⓑ Ⓒ Ⓓ Ⓔ   27. Ⓐ Ⓑ Ⓒ Ⓓ Ⓔ
24. Ⓐ Ⓑ Ⓒ Ⓓ Ⓔ   28. Ⓐ Ⓑ Ⓒ Ⓓ Ⓔ

Time: 25 minutes

Start: _____

Stop: _____

29.   30.   31.   32.   33.

34.   35.   36.   37.   38.

SECTION 5
Writing Skills
30 minutes

1. Ⓐ Ⓑ Ⓒ Ⓓ Ⓔ   14. Ⓐ Ⓑ Ⓒ Ⓓ Ⓔ   27. Ⓐ Ⓑ Ⓒ Ⓓ Ⓔ
2. Ⓐ Ⓑ Ⓒ Ⓓ Ⓔ   15. Ⓐ Ⓑ Ⓒ Ⓓ Ⓔ   28. Ⓐ Ⓑ Ⓒ Ⓓ Ⓔ
3. Ⓐ Ⓑ Ⓒ Ⓓ Ⓔ   16. Ⓐ Ⓑ Ⓒ Ⓓ Ⓔ   29. Ⓐ Ⓑ Ⓒ Ⓓ Ⓔ
4. Ⓐ Ⓑ Ⓒ Ⓓ Ⓔ   17. Ⓐ Ⓑ Ⓒ Ⓓ Ⓔ   30. Ⓐ Ⓑ Ⓒ Ⓓ Ⓔ
5. Ⓐ Ⓑ Ⓒ Ⓓ Ⓔ   18. Ⓐ Ⓑ Ⓒ Ⓓ Ⓔ   31. Ⓐ Ⓑ Ⓒ Ⓓ Ⓔ
6. Ⓐ Ⓑ Ⓒ Ⓓ Ⓔ   19. Ⓐ Ⓑ Ⓒ Ⓓ Ⓔ   32. Ⓐ Ⓑ Ⓒ Ⓓ Ⓔ
7. Ⓐ Ⓑ Ⓒ Ⓓ Ⓔ   20. Ⓐ Ⓑ Ⓒ Ⓓ Ⓔ   33. Ⓐ Ⓑ Ⓒ Ⓓ Ⓔ
8. Ⓐ Ⓑ Ⓒ Ⓓ Ⓔ   21. Ⓐ Ⓑ Ⓒ Ⓓ Ⓔ   34. Ⓐ Ⓑ Ⓒ Ⓓ Ⓔ
9. Ⓐ Ⓑ Ⓒ Ⓓ Ⓔ   22. Ⓐ Ⓑ Ⓒ Ⓓ Ⓔ   35. Ⓐ Ⓑ Ⓒ Ⓓ Ⓔ
10. Ⓐ Ⓑ Ⓒ Ⓓ Ⓔ   23. Ⓐ Ⓑ Ⓒ Ⓓ Ⓔ   36. Ⓐ Ⓑ Ⓒ Ⓓ Ⓔ
11. Ⓐ Ⓑ Ⓒ Ⓓ Ⓔ   24. Ⓐ Ⓑ Ⓒ Ⓓ Ⓔ   37. Ⓐ Ⓑ Ⓒ Ⓓ Ⓔ
12. Ⓐ Ⓑ Ⓒ Ⓓ Ⓔ   25. Ⓐ Ⓑ Ⓒ Ⓓ Ⓔ   38. Ⓐ Ⓑ Ⓒ Ⓓ Ⓔ
13. Ⓐ Ⓑ Ⓒ Ⓓ Ⓔ   26. Ⓐ Ⓑ Ⓒ Ⓓ Ⓔ   39. Ⓐ Ⓑ Ⓒ Ⓓ Ⓔ

Time: 30 minutes

Start: _____

Stop: _____

Section 1

Time—25 minutes
24 Questions (1–24)

Each of the sentences below is missing one or two portions. Read each sentence. Then select the choice that most logically completes the sentence, taking into account the meaning of the sentence as a whole.

Example:

Rather than accepting the theory unquestioningly, Deborah regarded it with ------.

(A) mirth
(B) sadness
(C) responsibility
(D) ignorance
(E) skepticism

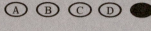

1. Hillary opened the door quietly and sneaked into her seat in order to remain as -------- as possible.

(A) inconspicuous
(B) coincidental
(C) tolerant
(D) inspired
(E) offensive

2. The speech began with focused and riveting vignettes about the life of a diplomat, but then deteriorated into a -------- list of unrelated facts.

(A) reflexive
(B) declining
(C) spellbinding
(D) superb
(E) rambling

3. The clothing stores in the new mall cater to the -------- and ever-changing tastes of their clientele, and so have a much more -------- inventory than typical boutiques.

(A) modest .. expensive
(B) diverse .. eclectic
(C) subtle .. permanent
(D) conservative .. extravagant
(E) redundant .. corporate

4. Some languages have very rigid rules of --------, while others allow many different possible arrangements of words to convey the same idea.

(A) pronunciation
(B) emphasis
(C) syntax
(D) acceptance
(E) symbolism

5. The ex-mayor's reputation has become so tainted that even members of his own party -------- at the mere mention of his name.

(A) recoil
(B) applaud
(C) defer
(D) pontificate
(E) calculate

6. Although few voters pay close attention to a presidential candidate's -------- policies, it is such -------- the economy that often affect citizens' lives most dramatically.

(A) foreign .. differences about
(B) political .. deliberations on
(C) domestic .. retreats on
(D) corporate .. indifference to
(E) fiscal .. stances on

GO ON TO THE NEXT PAGE ▶▶▶

7. When the editor learned that much of the information in the news article was --------, she quickly -------- the story and reprimanded the journalist who wrote it.

    (A) verifiable .. published
    (B) improbable .. marketed
    (C) refutable .. compensated
    (D) spurious .. retracted
    (E) polished .. disowned

8. Many developing nations face the choice of, on the one hand, cultivating -------- and self-sufficient economy or, on the other hand, creating an international system of trade that renders them -------- the industries of many other nations.

    (A) a free .. tolerant of
    (B) an impoverished .. ignorant of
    (C) an unregulated .. pursued by
    (D) an isolated .. dependent on
    (E) a robust .. superior to

The passages below are followed by questions based on their content and the relationship between the passages. Answer each question based on what is stated or implied in the passages.

Questions 9–12 are based on the following passages.

Passage 1

The currently fashionable criticism of the media as "liberal" is an interesting one. The
Line term derives from the Latin *liber*, meaning free. A free-thinking press, independent of a self-
5 serving government, is central to American values as embodied in the Constitution. So why do right-wing pundits use it so derisively? The answer to this question goes to the heart of what it means to be a conservative as well as
10 what it means to be a good journalist. Conservatism depends, in large measure, on verifying that the status quo is working, so that the current power structure can remain in place. It is founded on a need for comfort and a
15 disdain for change. Good journalism, on the other hand, requires a divestment from governmental and corporate ideologies. Conservatives are wary of those who would

look closely at things with a mind open to
20 changing them if necessary. Good journalists, however, examine worldly issues with a free and open mind. All good journalists are proud to be called liberals.

Passage 2

Those who debate whether the media are too
25 "liberal" or too "conservative" fundamentally misconstrue the problem with the way news is presented to the American public. The very fabric of the media is corporate. The object of the major news enterprises is not impartial
30 analysis. Even if they employ the most capable and scrupulous journalists, the corporate goal is to make a profit. This inescapable fact molds the "news" in myriad important ways. The issues, be they liberal or
35 conservative, must be packaged for the least common consumer. Deep analysis or, God forbid, instruction, only causes consumers to tune out. The media have mastered the formula
40 of "scare, titillate, and reassure" in twenty words or less. Television and newspaper editors are essentially marketing executives, responsible not to the tenets of journalism but to what sells.

9. The primary purpose of Passage 1 is to

    (A) examine the history of a term
    (B) criticize a social policy
    (C) propose a means of educating journalists
    (D) recast a criticism into a compliment
    (E) analyze a phenomenon objectively

10. Unlike Passage 1, Passage 2 focuses on

    (A) conservatism
    (B) the profit motive
    (C) the rights of journalists
    (D) the liberal nature of the media
    (E) the need for social change

GO ON TO THE NEXT PAGE ▶▶▶

11. In line 28, the word "object" most nearly means

(A) criticism
(B) instrument
(C) goal
(D) insight
(E) obstacle

12. The authors of the two passages differ in their analysis of journalists in that the author of Passage 1 focuses on their

(A) freedom, while the author of Passage 2 focuses on their constraints
(B) incompetence, while the author of Passage 2 focuses on their skills
(C) political affiliations, while the author of Passage 2 focuses on their education
(D) appeal to consumers, while the author of Passage 2 focuses on their professionalism
(E) cynicism, while the author of Passage 2 focuses on their optimism

> The questions that follow are to be answered on the basis of what is stated or implied in the passage below or the introductory material that precedes the passage.

Questions 13–18 are based on the following passage.

The following is an excerpt from a biography of Paul Erdös, an eccentric and prolific mathematician of the late twentieth century.

It was dinnertime in Greenbrook, New Jersey, on a cold spring day in 1987, and Paul Erdös,
Line then seventy-four, had lost four mathematical colleagues, who were sitting fifty feet in front of
5 him, sipping green tea. Squinting, Erdös scanned the tables of the small Japanese restaurant, one arm held out to the side like a scarecrow's. He was angry with himself for letting his friends slip out of sight. His mistake
10 was to pause at the coat check while they charged ahead. His arm was flapping wildly now, and he was coughing. "I don't understand why the SF has seen fit to give me a cold," he wheezed. (The SF is the Supreme Fascist, the
15 Number-One Guy Up There, God, who was always tormenting Erdös by hiding his glasses,

stealing his Hungarian passport, or, worse yet, keeping to Himself the elegant solutions to all sorts of intriguing mathematical problems.)
20 "The SF created us to enjoy our suffering," Erdös said. "The sooner we die, the sooner we defy his plans."

Erdös still didn't see his friends, but his anger dissipated—his arm dropped to his
25 side—as he heard the high-pitched squeal of a small boy, who was dining with his parents. "An epsilon!" Erdös said. (*Epsilon* was Erdös's word for a small child; in mathematics that Greek letter is used to represent small quantities.)
30 Erdös moved slowly toward the child, navigating not so much by sight as by the sound of the boy's voice. "Hello," he said, as he reached into his ratty gray overcoat and extracted a bottle of Benzedrine. He dropped
35 the bottle from shoulder height and with the same hand caught it a split second later. The epsilon was not at all amused, but perhaps to be polite, his parents made a big production of applauding. Erdös repeated the trick a few
40 more times, and then he was rescued by one of his confederates, Ronald Graham, a mathematician at AT & T, who called him over to the table where he and Erdös's other friends were waiting.
45 The waitress arrived, and Erdös, after inquiring about each item on the long menu, ordered fried squid balls. While the waitress took the rest of the orders, Erdös turned over his placemat and drew a tiny sketch vaguely
50 resembling a rocket passing through a hula-hoop. His four dining companions leaned forward to get a better view of the world's most prolific mathematician plying his craft. "There are still many edges that will destroy chromatic
55 number three," Erdös said. "This edge destroys bipartiteness." With that pronouncement Erdös closed his eyes and seemed to fall asleep.

Mathematicians, unlike other scientists, require no laboratory equipment–a practice
60 that reportedly began with Archimedes, who, after emerging from his bath and rubbing himself with olive oil, discovered the principles of geometry by using his fingernails to trace figures on his oily skin. A Japanese restaurant,
65 apparently, is as good a place as any to do mathematics. Mathematicians need only peace of mind and, occasionally, paper and pencil. "That's the beauty of it," Graham said. "You can lie back, close your eyes, and work. Who knows
70 what problem Paul's thinking about now?"

GO ON TO THE NEXT PAGE ▶▶▶

"There was a time at Trinity College, in the
1930s I believe, when Erdös and my husband,
Harold, sat thinking in a public place for more
than an hour without uttering a single word,"
75 recalled Anne Davenport, the widow of one of
Erdös's English collaborators. "Then Harold
broke the long silence, by saying, 'It is not
nought. It is one.' Then all was relief and joy.
Everyone around them thought they were mad.
80 Of course, they were."

13. In the first paragraph, Erdös is characterized
primarily as

(A) domineering
(B) playful
(C) disoriented
(D) charismatic
(E) stoic

14. The passage suggests that Erdös's extended
arm indicates his

(A) desire for silence
(B) illustration of a mathematical concept
(C) attempt to entertain children
(D) anger
(E) efforts to signal a waitress

15. The quotations from Erdös in the passage
demonstrate that he feels most keenly
oppressed by

(A) his fellow mathematicians
(B) his waitress
(C) God
(D) small children
(E) scientists

16. In line 53, the word "craft" most nearly means

(A) skill
(B) creation
(C) means of transportation
(D) deception
(E) artwork

17. The reference to Archimedes in lines 60–64
serves primarily to emphasize Erdös's

(A) use of tricks to entertain small
children
(B) prolific mathematical output
(C) ability to do mathematical work almost
anywhere
(D) disregard for his surroundings
(E) lack of self-consciousness

18. The story in the final paragraph (lines
71–80) characterizes Erdös as

(A) impatient
(B) reclusive
(C) jocular
(D) distractible
(E) focused

The questions that follow are to be answered
on the basis of what is stated or implied in
the passage below or the introductory
material that precedes the passage.

**Questions 19–24 are based on the
following passage.**

*The following passage discusses the principles
of aesthetics, the study of the nature and meaning
of art.*

Since it is our purpose to develop an adequate
idea of art, it might seem as if a definition were
Line rather our goal than our starting point; yet we
must identify the field of our investigations and
5   mark it off from other regions; and this we can
do only by means of a preliminary definition,
which the rest of our study may then enrich and
complete.
    We shall find it fruitful to begin with the
10 definition recently revived by Crocc: art is
expression, and expression we may describe,
for our own ends, as the putting forth of
purpose, feeling, or thought into a sensuous
medium, where they can be experienced again
15 by the one who expresses himself and
communicated to others. Thus, in this sense, a
lyric poem is an expression—a bit of a poet's
intimate experience put into words; epic and

Excerpt from *The Man Who Loved Only Numbers* by Paul
Hoffman. © 1998 Paul Hoffman. Reprinted by permission of
Hyperion. pp. 3–5.

GO ON TO THE NEXT PAGE ▶▶▶

dramatic poetry are expressions—visions of a
20   larger life made manifest in the same medium.
Pictures and statues are also expressions, for
they are embodiments in color and space-forms
of the artists' ideas of visible nature and man.
Works of architecture and the other industrial
25   arts are embodiments of purpose and
the well-being that comes from purpose
fulfilled.

This definition, good so far as it goes, is,
however, too inclusive, for plainly, although
30   every work of art is an expression, not every
expression is a work of art. Automatic
expressions, instinctive overflowings
of emotion into motor channels, like
the cry of pain or the shout of joy, are not
35   aesthetic. Practical expressions also, all such
as are only means or instruments for the
realization of ulterior purposes—the command
of the officer, the conversation of the market
place, a saw—are not aesthetic. Works
40   of art—the *Ninth Symphony*, the *Ode
to the West Wind*—are not of this character.

No matter what further purposes artistic
expressions may serve, they are produced and
valued for themselves; we linger in them; we
45   neither merely execute them mechanically, as
we do automatic expressions, nor hasten
through them, our minds fixed upon some
future end to be gained by them, as is the
case with practical expressions. Both for
50   the artist and the appreciator, they are ends
in themselves. Compare, for example, a love
poem with a declaration of love. The poem is
esteemed for the rhythmic emotional
experience it gives the writer or reader; the
55   declaration, even when enjoyed by the suitor,
has its prime value in its consequences, and
the quicker it is over and done with and its
end attained the better. The one, since it has
its purpose within itself, is returned to and
60   repeated; the other, being chiefly a means to
an end, would be senseless if repeated, once the
end that called it forth is accomplished. The
value of the love poem, although written to
persuade a lady, cannot be measured in terms
65   of its mere success; for if beautiful, it remains of
worth after the lady has yielded, nay, even if it
fails to win her. Any sort of practical purpose
may be one motive in the creation of a work
of art, but its significance is broader than the

70   success or failure of that motive. The Russian
novel is still significant, even now, after the
revolution. As beautiful, it is of perennial
worth and stands out by itself. But practical
expressions are only transient links in the
75   endless chain of means, disappearing as
the wheel of effort revolves. Art is indeed
expression, but free or autonomous
expression.

19.   The purpose of the passage as a whole is to

(A)   contrast several different modes of
artistic expression
(B)   discuss the effects of art on modern
society
(C)   establish the importance of defining
terms as a prelude to philosophical
discourse
(D)   distinguish between artistic expression
and nonartistic expression
(E)   compare modern definitions of art with
definitions from the past

20.   As it is used in line 14, "medium" most
nearly means

(A)   moderate position
(B)   environment
(C)   prediction
(D)   artist
(E)   mode of creation

21.   According to the passage, "the cry of pain
or the shout of joy" (line 34) is

(A)   a potential reaction to a moving work
of art
(B)   something that could hinder creativity
(C)   an expression of emotion that can inspire
a great work of art
(D)   an action that in itself lacks meaning
as art
(E)   an outburst that could interfere with the
appreciation of a work of art

This passage is in the public domain.

22. The author mentions the *Ninth Symphony* in line 40 primarily as an example of

    (A) an underappreciated masterpiece
    (B) a work that was inspired by an instinctive expression of emotion
    (C) an expression that has a purpose in itself, rather than as a means to something else
    (D) a piece of art that was intended as a declaration of love
    (E) a musical piece that is not held in high regard by critics

23. The "success" mentioned in line 65 refers to the ability of

    (A) a sentimental expression to influence a particular person
    (B) an artist to sell a work of art at a high price
    (C) an artwork to remain popular after many years
    (D) an artist to maintain high aesthetic standards
    (E) a society to appreciate the meaning of art

24. The sentence beginning on line 67 ("Any sort of … of that motive") conveys the author's opinion that

    (A) every work of art must have an ulterior motive
    (B) few works of art have any significant effect on historical events
    (C) a work of art has meaning beyond its intended purpose
    (D) art does not need a wide audience in order to be successful
    (E) a musical piece that is not held in high regard by critics

STOP

You may check your work, on this section only, until time is called.

Section 2

Time—25 minutes

20 Questions

Directions for Multiple-Choice Questions

In this section, solve each problem, using any available space on the page for scratchwork. Then decide which is the best of the choices given and fill in the corresponding oval on the answer sheet.

- You may use a calculator on any problem. All numbers used are real numbers.
- Figures are drawn as accurately as possible EXCEPT when it is stated that the figure is not drawn to scale.
- All figures lie in a plane unless otherwise indicated.

Reference Information

$A = \pi r^2$ $A = \ell w$
$C = 2\pi r$ $A = \frac{1}{2}bh$ $V = \ell wh$ $V = \pi r^2 h$ $c^2 = a^2 + b^2$ Special Right Triangles

The arc of a circle measures 360°.
Every straight angle measures 180°.
The sum of the measures of the angles in a triangle is 180°.

---

1. If $x = 5$ and $y + 2 = 10$, what is the value of xy?

(A) 13
(B) 17
(C) 40
(D) 50
(E) 60

2. The average (arithmetic mean) of four numbers is 10. If three of the numbers are 8, 9, and 10, what is the fourth number?

(A) 10
(B) 11
(C) 12
(D) 13
(E) 17

3. Two of the angles in a triangle measure 70° and 60°. What is the measure of the third angle?

(A) 40°
(B) 50°
(C) 60°
(D) 80°
(E) 230°

4. The ratio of 5 to 6 is equal to the ratio of 30 to what number?

(A) 25
(B) 31
(C) 36
(D) 38
(E) 40

5. If $k = 2m \neq 0$, what is the value of $\frac{m}{k} \times 16$?

(A) 4
(B) 8
(C) 16
(D) 32
(E) 64

GO ON TO THE NEXT PAGE ▶▶▶

VOTING RESULTS FOR CLASS ELECTION

	Student A	Student B	Total
Boys	19		
Girls			40
Total	35		67

6. The table above represents the results of a vote for a class election between Student A and Student B. How many girls voted for Student B?

(A) 8
(B) 16
(C) 24
(D) 27
(E) 32

7. Caroline and Mark together own 36 DVDs, but Caroline owns 6 more than Mark does. How many DVDs does Caroline own?

(A) 12
(B) 15
(C) 18
(D) 21
(E) 24

8. How many ounces of nuts must be added to 12 ounces of raisins if the resulting mixture is to be 25% nuts, by weight?

(A) 3
(B) 4
(C) 8
(D) 36
(E) 48

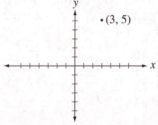

9. The point $(3, 5)$ undergoes three consecutive transformations: first, a reflection over the x-axis, then a reflection over the y-axis, and then a reflection over the x-axis. What are the coordinates of the resulting point?

(A) $(3, -5)$
(B) $(-3, -5)$
(C) $(-3, 5)$
(D) $(-5, 3)$
(E) $(-5, -3)$

10. If $m + 6n = 40$ and m and n are positive integers, then what is the least possible value of m?

(A) 1
(B) 4
(C) 6
(D) 8
(E) 10

11. If k is divisible by both 27 and 36, it must also be divisible by which of the following?

(A) 8
(B) 10
(C) 16
(D) 54
(E) 72

$$1, 1, 2, 3, 5, 8, \ldots$$

12. Each term in the sequence above, except the first, is the sum of the previous two terms. How many of the first 60 of these terms are even?

(A) 18
(B) 20
(C) 30
(D) 40
(E) 42

13. At a certain store, the price of a sweater is discounted by 10% after each week that it is on the shelf. What is the price of a sweater after 4 weeks on the shelf if its original price was $100?

(A) $59.05
(B) $60.00
(C) $65.61
(D) $72.90
(E) $93.44

14. If $9x^2 - 9y^2 = 36$ and $x + y = 2$, then how much greater is x than y?

(A) 2
(B) 4
(C) 6
(D) 8
(E) 10

GO ON TO THE NEXT PAGE ▶▶▶

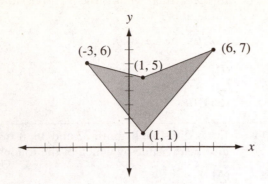

15. What is the area, in square units, of the shaded region above?

(A) 22
(B) 21
(C) 20
(D) 19
(E) 18

---

16. Points A, B, C, and D lie on a line, in that order. If $AC = 6BC$ and $BD = 5AB$, then $\dfrac{CD}{AC} =$

(A) $\dfrac{1}{4}$

(B) $\dfrac{1}{3}$

(C) $\dfrac{3}{4}$

(D) 3

(E) 4

---

17. If some aggles are iggles and all aggles are uggles, then which of the following statements must be true?

   I. All iggles are uggles.
  II. Some uggles are iggles.
 III. There are no uggles that are not aggles.

(A) I only
(B) II only
(C) III only
(D) I and II only
(E) II and III only

---

18. If x gallons of paint cost d dollars, and each gallon of paint covers 500 square feet, how much would it cost, in dollars, to purchase enough paint to cover m square feet?

(A) $\dfrac{md}{500x}$

(B) $\dfrac{500md}{x}$

(C) $\dfrac{500x}{md}$

(D) $\dfrac{500m}{dx}$

(E) $\dfrac{m}{500dx}$

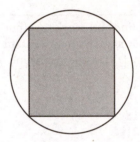

19. In the figure above, a square is inscribed in a circle. If the circle has an area of 16π, what is the area of the square?

(A) 12
(B) 16
(C) 32
(D) 36
(E) 38

---

20. Let $r \diamond t \diamond s$ be defined by the equation $r \diamond t \diamond s = r^s + t^s$. If m and n are positive integers and $m \diamond n \diamond 2 = 100$, what is the value of $m + n$?

(A) 10
(B) 11
(C) 12
(D) 13
(E) 14

STOP

You may check your work, on this section only, until time is called.

Section 3

Time—25 minutes
24 Questions (25–48)

Each of the sentences below is missing one or two portions. Read each sentence. Then select the word or words that most logically complete the sentence, taking into account the meaning of the sentence as a whole.

Example:

Rather than accepting the theory unquestioningly, Deborah regarded it with - - - - -.

(A) mirth
(B) sadness
(C) responsibility
(D) ignorance
(E) skepticism

Correct response: (E)

25. As activists, they knew that they could not remain - - - - - while their most precious values were being attacked.

(A) repetitive
(B) passive
(C) memorable
(D) confrontational
(E) generalized

26. Although he was - - - - - by a strained tendon, Schilling did not allow this - - - - - to keep him from pitching a masterful game.

(A) hobbled .. impediment
(B) weakened .. inspiration
(C) disabled .. aid
(D) deterred .. promotion
(E) consoled .. hurdle

27. Martin Gardner is considered one of the most - - - - - writers in science and mathematics, having authored over 65 books and countless magazine articles.

(A) conservative
(B) ingenuous
(C) obscure
(D) prolific
(E) desperate

28. Normally a sympathetic person, Jerry surprised his supporters by attacking his opponent with seemingly - - - - - remarks.

(A) stoic
(B) delicate
(C) synthetic
(D) venerable
(E) callous

29. The - - - - - display advertising the new video game, which included a garish neon sign, was a marked departure from the more - - - - - promotions that the company had used in the past.

(A) listless .. lethargic
(B) dynamic .. insightful
(C) ostentatious .. subdued
(D) beguiling .. volatile
(E) nondescript .. mutable

GO ON TO THE NEXT PAGE ▶▶▶

Each passage below is followed by questions based on its content. Answer each question based on what is stated or implied in the passage or the introductory material that precedes it.

Questions 30–31 are based on the following passage.

Passage 1

Line The American Revolution overspread
Nantucket like a pall. Trade and
communication with the outside world were
reduced to a trickle. Vessels arriving home were
5   necessarily laid up, as there was too much risk
of life and property to venture out again.
Moreover, the Provincial Congress of
Massachusetts and later the Continental
Congress restricted such voyages. Some people
10   resorted to surreptitious trade in swift, light
vessels designed to outrun a pursuer, but this
often proved disastrous since they carried such
a press of sail that they were frequently
swamped and their crews drowned. Because
15   the majority of the islanders were members of
the Society of Friends, they were opposed to
war and thus took no active part in the conflict;
but this did not keep its consequences from
their shores.

30.   The passage characterizes the effects of the
American Revolution primarily as

(A) political
(B) restrictive
(C) triumphant
(D) bloody
(E) hopeful

31.   The passage suggests that, during the
American Revolution, members of the Society
of Friends were

(A) patriots
(B) pacifists
(C) adventurers
(D) entrepreneurs
(E) conservatives

First passage: *The Architecture of Historic Nantucket*, Lancaster, Clay.
Second passage: *Quarks, the Stuff of Matter*, Fritzsch, Harald.
© 1983 Basic Books Inc.

Questions 32–33 are based on the following passage.

Passage 2

Line About 500 years ago, a new dimension was
added to man's age-old attempt to satisfy his
insatiable curiosity about the nature of the
universe—people began to verify their scientific
5   hypotheses by stringent tests. It was Galileo
Galilei who ushered in the era of modern
science 400 years ago when he conducted the
first verifiable experiments during his
investigation of freely falling bodies. Compared
10   to Galileo's throwing rocks off the leaning tower
of Pisa, our using gigantic particle detectors to
penetrate to the heart of matter seems to
represent something of an entirely different
order. Yet the principle behind both kinds
15   of experiments, and the excitement of discovery
they engender, remains the same: when we
conduct an experiment we put a question to
nature, and nature is forced to yield an answer.
Frequently the answer is rather complicated
20   and we have enormous difficulty understanding
it. Sometimes, however, the answer is simpler
than anticipated. When insights suddenly
appear and new ideas are born—these are the
great moments of science, when it becomes as
25   sublime as a great work of art.

32.   The author compares one of Galileo's
experiments with a modern one primarily to
make the point that

(A) Galileo's experiments did not yield
accurate results
(B) modern equipment is often inordinately
expensive
(C) stringent scientific tests are a recent
development
(D) the scientific method has endured many
centuries
(E) modern physicists are much more
knowledgeable than the scientists of
centuries ago

33.   The passage suggests that "insights" (line 22)
are produced primarily through

(A) imagination
(B) experimentation
(C) re-examination of traditional texts
(D) the use of systematic logic
(E) synthesizing divergent viewpoints

GO ON TO THE NEXT PAGE ▸▸▸

Questions 34–48 are based on the following passages.

The following passages examine the issue of global warming. The first was written in 1997, the second in 2004.

Passage 1

Line A small, vocal minority of skeptics claims there is no scientific evidence to support the theory that man-made emissions of greenhouse gases will alter the Earth's climate. They claim that
5 global warming is liberal, left-wing, claptrap science and a ploy by the scientific community to ensure funding for yet another "Chicken Little" scare. Others suggest that attempts to reduce greenhouse-gas emissions by changing
10 energy or land use policies would needlessly cost the American taxpayer tens to hundreds of billions of dollars annually and that it is really part of an international conspiracy to undermine America's competitiveness in the
15 global marketplace.

The truth, however, is quite different. The overwhelming majority of scientific experts believes human-induced climate change is inevitable. The question is not *whether* climate
20 will change in response to human activities, but rather *where*, *when* and by *how much*.

We must keep in mind the following points about current scientific understanding of the climate system:
25 First, human activities undoubtedly are increasing atmospheric concentrations of greenhouse gases, which tend to warm the atmosphere. The most important greenhouse gas directly affected by human activities is
30 carbon dioxide, which has increased by nearly 30 percent since 1700, primarily because of changes in land use and the burning of coal, oil and gas.

Second, there is no doubt that the Earth's
35 climate has changed during the last 100 years. The global mean air-surface temperature over the land and ocean has warmed between 0.6° and 1.1 °F, glaciers have retreated globally, and sea level has risen by 10 to 25
40 centimeters.

Third, comparing the observed changes in global mean temperature with model simulations that incorporate the effect of increases in greenhouse gases in aerosols
45 suggests that the observed changes during the last century are unlikely to be due entirely to natural causes. In addition, the increase in the frequency of heavy rains in the United States is yet another signal consistent with human-
50 induced global warming.

Many people, especially those in colder climes, question whether we should care if the climate becomes warmer. The answer is quite simple: a warmer climate will be accompanied
55 by changes in precipitation, floods, droughts, heat waves and rises in sea level.

Policymakers are faced with responding to the risks posed by human-induced emissions of greenhouse gases. Decisions made during the
60 next few years are particularly important because climate-induced environmental changes cannot be reversed for decades, if not millennia.

Passage 2

We live in an age in which facts and logic have a
65 hard time competing with rhetoric—especially when the rhetoric is political alarmism over global warming.

We continue to hear that "the science is settled" in the global warming debate, that we
70 know enough to take significant action to counter it. Those who hold this view believe emissions of carbon dioxide are the primary cause of any change in global temperature and inevitably will lead to serious environmental
75 harm in the decades ahead.

In 1997, for instance, Vice President Al Gore played a leading role in the negotiation of the Kyoto Protocol, the international agreement to deal with the fears about global warming. He
80 was willing to embrace severe reductions in United States' emissions, even though the Clinton administration's own Department of Energy estimated that Kyoto-like restrictions could cost $300 billion annually. Then, when it
85 became clear that the Senate would not agree to a treaty that would harm the economy and exempt developing countries like China and India, the Clinton administration did not forward it for ratification. Since then, the
90 treaty's flaws have become more evident, and too few countries have ratified it to allow it to "enter into force."

The Bush administration, as an alternative to such energy-suppressing measures, has
95 focused on filling gaps in our state of knowledge, promoting the development of new technology, encouraging voluntary programs

GO ON TO THE NEXT PAGE ▶▶▶

and working with other nations on controlling the growth of greenhouse gas emissions.

100 Collectively, these actions involve spending more than $4 billion annually, and the United States is doing more than any other nation to address the climate-change issue.

Of these efforts, filling the gaps in our
105 knowledge may be the most important. What we know for sure is quite limited. For example, we know that since the early 1900s, the Earth's surface temperature has risen about 1°F. We also know that carbon dioxide, a greenhouse
110 gas, has been increasing in the atmosphere. And we know that the theory that increasing concentrations of greenhouse gases like carbon dioxide will lead to further warming is at least an oversimplification. It is
115 inconsistent with the fact that satellite measurements over 35 years show no significant warming in the lower atmosphere, which is an essential part of the global-warming theory.

120 Much of the warming in the twentieth century happened from 1900 to 1940. That warming was followed by atmospheric cooling from 1940 to around 1975. During that period, frost damaged crops in the Midwest during summer months,
125 and glaciers in Europe advanced. This happened despite the rise in greenhouse gases. These facts, too, are not in dispute.

And that's just our recent past. Taking a longer view of climate history deepens our
130 perspective. For example, during what's known as the Climatic Optimum of the early Middle Ages, the Earth's temperatures were 1 to 2 degrees warmer than they are today. That period was succeeded by the Little Ice Age,
135 which lasted until the early nineteenth century. Neither of these climate periods had anything to do with man-made greenhouse gases.

The lessons of our recent history and of this longer history are clear: It is not possible to
140 know now how much of the warming over the last 100 or so years was caused by human activities and how much was because of natural forces. Acknowledging that we know too little about a system as complicated as the planet's
145 climate is not a sign of neglect by policymakers or the scientific community. Indeed, admitting

that there is much we do not know is the first step to greater understanding.

Meanwhile, it is important that we not be
150 unduly influenced by political rhetoric and scare tactics. Wise policy involves a continued emphasis on science, technology, engagement of the business community on voluntary programs and balancing actions with
155 knowledge and economic priorities. As a nation, by focusing on these priorities, we show leadership and concern about the well-being of this generation and the ones to follow.

34. The main purpose of the first paragraph of Passage 1 is to

(A) describe the author's perspective on global warming
(B) present an objective viewpoint
(C) rally support for a little-known cause
(D) outline a scientific theory
(E) present positions to be refuted

35. The argument described in lines 8–15 appeals to the reader's

(A) love of nature
(B) fear of rising sea levels
(C) fiscal responsibility
(D) sense of humor
(E) political loyalties

36. The "minority" mentioned in line 1 and the "others" mentioned in line 8 agree that

(A) global warming is a serious concern
(B) greenhouse gas emissions have not been increasing
(C) efforts to counteract global warming are ill-conceived
(D) the costs of curbing gas emissions are much less than most people think
(E) scientists should do more to study global warming

37. Which of the following, if true, would most directly weaken a claim made in the sixth paragraph of Passage 1 (lines 41–50)?

   (A) The activities of many factories and power plants are regulated by the government.
   (B) The emission of greenhouse gases has greatly accelerated in the last 50 years.
   (C) The effects of global warming are more pronounced near the Earth's poles.
   (D) The computer models used to simulate climate changes do not account for significant environmental variables.
   (E) Scientists have been analyzing climate changes for over 100 years.

38. The author discusses "changes in precipitation" in line 55 primarily in order to

   (A) persuade those who doubt that global warming is a serious concern
   (B) demonstrate the effectiveness of a particular scientific model
   (C) show that a prediction is incorrect
   (D) explain a potential benefit
   (E) describe a way to slow global warming

39. Which of the following does the author of Passage 1 specifically cite as a potential result of global warming?

   I. widespread extinctions
   II. rising sea levels
   III. longer growing seasons

   (A) II only
   (B) I and II only
   (C) I and III only
   (D) II and III only
   (E) I, II, and III

40. With which of the following statements would the author of Passage 2 most likely agree?

   (A) The belief that global surface temperatures have risen in the last 100 years is false.
   (B) The U.S. Senate should ratify the Kyoto Protocol.
   (C) Research indicates that Americans should immediately reduce greenhouse emissions.
   (D) We do not yet know enough about the science of climate change to base environmental policy on it.
   (E) The United States is not addressing the issue of climate change to the degree that other nations are.

41. The author of Passage 2 regards the statement that "the science is settled" (lines 68–69) with

   (A) reluctant acceptance
   (B) skepticism
   (C) urgent agreement
   (D) indifference
   (E) surprise

42. The author of Passage 2 objects to the Kyoto Protocol chiefly because it

   (A) does not cut carbon dioxide emissions sufficiently
   (B) does not incorporate current climatological research
   (C) is too costly and unfairly applied
   (D) does not promote new technology
   (E) has not been ratified by the U.S. Senate

43. In lines 123–125, the author of Passage 2 mentions damage done to crops primarily to make the point that

   (A) global warming has hurt American agriculture
   (B) the effects of global warming seem to be localized, rather than global
   (C) more must be done to protect American farmlands
   (D) increased carbon dioxide emissions can have a positive effect
   (E) the climate has not been consistently warming over the last 50 years

44. The author of Passage 2 discusses the "Climatic Optimum" (line 131) because it

(A) illustrates the effects of unbridled carbon dioxide emmissions
(B) shows a general cooling trend over the centuries
(C) is an example of political alarmism
(D) demonstrates a defect in the Kyoto Protocol
(E) seems to contradict a widely held theory

45. In line 144, the term "system" refers to a

(A) complex scientific phenomenon
(B) way of making environmental policy decisions
(C) means by which scientists can work together
(D) method of communication
(E) governmental bureaucracy

46. The author of Passage 2 suggests that the "scientific community" (line 146) should

(A) be active in publicizing its findings
(B) become more involved in policymaking
(C) be more cautious in making claims
(D) work more closely with industry
(E) change the focus of its study

47. With which of the following statements would the authors of BOTH passages likely agree?

I. Global surface temperatures have increased over the last 100 years.
II. The atmospheric concentration of greenhouse gases has been increasing.
III. The extent to which human activities have contributed to global warming is well known.

(A) I only
(B) I and II only
(C) I and III only
(D) II and III only
(E) I, II, and III only

48. The author of Passage 2 would most likely respond to the observation noted in Passage 1 that "global mean air-surface temperature . . . has warmed" (lines 36–37) by noting that this observation is

(A) false
(B) inconsistent with other measured trends in atmospheric temperature
(C) based on political dogma rather than scientific study
(D) not addressed in the Kyoto Protocol
(E) the result of increased carbon dioxide emissions

STOP

You may check your work, on this section only, until time is called.

Section 4

Time—25 minutes
18 Questions (21–38)

Directions for Multiple-Choice Questions

In this section, solve each problem, using any available space on the page for scratchwork. Then decide which is the best of the choices given and fill in the corresponding oval on the answer sheet.

- You may use a calculator on any problem. All numbers used are real numbers.
- Figures are drawn as accurately as possible EXCEPT when it is stated that the figure is not drawn to scale.
- All figures lie in a plane unless otherwise indicated.

Reference Information

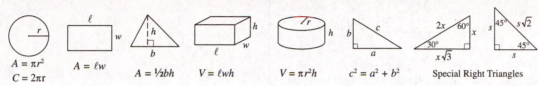

$A = \pi r^2$
$C = 2\pi r$
$A = \ell w$
$A = \frac{1}{2}bh$
$V = \ell w h$
$V = \pi r^2 h$
$c^2 = a^2 + b^2$
Special Right Triangles

The arc of a circle measures 360°.
Every straight angle measures 180°.
The sum of the measures of the angles in a triangle is 180°.

$$2a + 3b + c = 20$$
$$3b + c = 24$$

21. If a, b, and c satisfy the equations above, what is the value of a?

(A) -8
(B) -4
(C) -2
(D) 2
(E) 4

---

22. If $0.00035 = 3.5 \times 10^n$, then $n =$

(A) -5
(B) -4
(C) -3
(D) 3
(E) 4

---

23. What is 25 percent of $\left(12x + \frac{1}{2}\right)$?

(A) $3x + \frac{1}{8}$

(B) $3x + \frac{1}{2}$

(C) $3x + \frac{1}{6}$

(D) $4x + \frac{1}{2}$

(E) $6x + \frac{1}{8}$

$$\begin{array}{ccccccccc} & & a & & & & b & & \\ \hline -1.5 & -1.0 & -0.5 & 0 & 0.5 & 1.0 & 1.5 \end{array}$$

24. If a and b are the coordinates of the points on the number line above, then which of the following best describes the location of ab on the number line?

(A) between -1.5 and -1.0
(B) between -1.0 and -0.5
(C) between -0.5 and 0
(D) between 0 and 0.5
(E) between 0.5 and 1.0

---

25. The greatest of 4 consecutive positive even integers is k. If the average (arithmetic mean) of these integers is m and the median of these integers is n, which of the following must be true?

    I. m is odd
   II. $k - m = 3$
  III. $m = n$

(A) I only
(B) II only
(C) I and II only
(D) II and III only
(E) I, II, and III

GO ON TO THE NEXT PAGE ▸▸▸

26. $2^{2x} \cdot 4^{3x} =$

(A) 2^{8x}
(B) 2^{12x^2}
(C) 4^{3x^2}
(D) 8^{5x}
(E) 8^{6x^2}

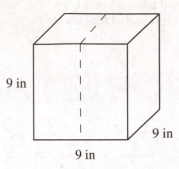

9 in

9 in

9 in

27. The solid cube of wood shown above is to be cut into two congruent pieces with a cut that is parallel to two of the faces. What is the surface area (in square inches) of <u>one</u> of these two pieces?

(A) 243
(B) 283.5
(C) 324
(D) 364.5
(E) 445.5

28. For all positive integers n, let $\{n\}$ be defined as follows:

$\{n\} = \dfrac{n}{2}$ if n is a multiple of 4

$\{n\} = 4n$ if n is <u>not</u> a multiple of 4

Which of the following is equivalent to $\{\{6\}\}$?

(A) $\{3\}$
(B) $\{6\}$
(C) $\{12\}$
(D) $\{20\}$
(E) $\{22\}$

Directions for Student-Produced Response Questions

Each of the questions in this section requires you to solve the problem and enter your answer in a grid, as shown below.

- If your answer is 2/3 or .666..., you must enter **the most accurate value the grid can accommodate**, but you may do this in one of four ways:

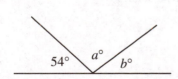

- In the example above, gridding a response of 0.67 or 0.66 is **incorrect** because it is less accurate than those above.
- The scoring machine cannot read what is written in the top row of boxes. You **MUST** fill in the numerical grid accurately to get credit for answering any question correctly. You should write your answer in the top row of boxes only to aid your gridding.
- Do **not** grid in a mixed fraction like $3\frac{1}{2}$ as $\boxed{3}\,\boxed{1}\,\boxed{/}\,\boxed{2}$ because it will be interpreted as $\frac{31}{2}$. Instead, convert it to an improper fraction like 7/2 or a decimal like 3.5 before gridding.
- None of the answers will be negative, because there is no negative sign in the grid.
- Some of the questions may have more than one correct answer. You must grid only one of the correct answers.
- You may use a calculator on any of these problems.
- All numbers in these problems are real numbers.
- Figures are drawn as accurately as possible EXCEPT when it is stated that the figure is not drawn to scale.
- All figures lie in a plane unless otherwise indicated.

54° $a°$ $b°$

Note: Figure not drawn to scale.

29.   In the figure above, if $a = 2b$, what is the value of a?

$m, 12, m + 10$

30.   In the sequence above, each term after the first is equal to the previous term plus a constant. What is the value of m?

31.   If $p + r = 5$, what is the average (arithmetic mean) of 5, 3p, 12, and 3r?

---

32.   How many integers between 1 and 100 contain at least one 3 or at least one 5?

GO ON TO THE NEXT PAGE ▶▶▶

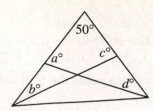

Note: Figure not drawn to scale.

33. In the figure above, what is the value of $a + b + c + d$?

34. On each of four cards, a different positive integer greater than 1 but less than 20 is written. Exactly three of the numbers are multiples of 3, exactly two of the numbers are multiples of 5, and none of the numbers is even. What is the sum of these four numbers.

35. At a certain store, employees may buy clothing at a 20% discount from the original price, but must pay a 6% sales tax. If the final cost of a sweater purchased by an employee is $55.12, what is the original price of the sweater, before the discount and tax? (Disregard the $ symbol when gridding.)

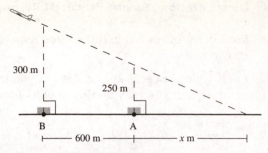

Note: Figure not drawn to scale.

36. Two detectors, located 600 meters apart on a flat airport runway, measure the altitude of airplanes as they pass overhead. Detector A determines that, when a certain plane passes directly above it, the plane has an altitude of 250 meters. A short time later, detector B determines that, when the same plane passes over it, the plane has an altitude of 300 meters, as shown in the diagram above. If the plane follows a straight path once it leaves the ground, how many meters from detector A did the plane first leave the ground?

37. If pump A, working at a constant rate, can fill a tank in 6 hours, and pump B, working at a constant rate, can fill the same tank in 2 hours, how many hours should it take them to fill the tank if they work together?

38. In a group of 500 students, 150 are studying physics, 220 are studying biology, and 100 are studying chemistry. At least 25 students are studying more than one of these sciences. What is the greatest possible number of these students that might NOT be studying any of these sciences?

STOP

You may check your work, on this section only, until time is called.

Section 5

Time—30 minutes
39 Questions (1–39)

Directions for Improving Sentences Questions

Each of the sentences below contains one underlined portion. The portion may contain one or more errors in grammar, usage, construction, precision, diction (choice of words), or idiom. Some of the sentences are correct.

Consider the meaning of the original sentence, and choose the answer that best expresses that meaning. If the original sentence is best, choose (A), because it repeats the original phrasing. Choose the phrasing that creates the clearest, most precise, and most effective sentence.

EXAMPLE:

The children <u>couldn't hardly believe their eyes</u>.

(A) couldn't hardly believe their eyes
(B) would not hardly believe their eyes
(C) could hardly believe their eyes
(D) couldn't nearly believe their eyes
(E) could hardly believe his or her eyes

1. <u>Despite having received</u> a majority of the votes, few people regarded Mark Lemann as the best candidate for the office.

    (A) Despite having received
    (B) Although having received
    (C) Although he had received
    (D) While receiving
    (E) In his receiving

2. The radiation from naturally occurring carbon-14 atoms <u>are used to determine</u> the age of many ancient artifacts.

    (A) are used to determine
    (B) determining
    (C) are what are used to determine
    (D) is used to determine
    (E) are determining

3. Nelson has written and directed many acclaimed films, <u>but he is</u> best known as a character actor.

    (A) but he is
    (B) is
    (C) but being
    (D) so is
    (E) although

4. Although Magnus was clearly inspired by the romance novelists of the early nineteenth century, <u>they were deliberately not imitated by him</u>.

    (A) they were deliberately not imitated by him
    (B) he deliberately avoided imitating them
    (C) the imitation was deliberately avoided by him
    (D) he was avoiding the imitation of them by deliberation
    (E) his avoidance to imitate them was deliberate

5. Many economists believe that, when used judiciously, <u>you can stimulate a stagnant economy with deficit spending</u>.

    (A) you can stimulate a stagnant economy with deficit spending
    (B) one can stimulate, with deficit spending, a stagnant economy
    (C) deficit spending can, for a stagnant economy, stimulate it
    (D) a stagnant economy can be stimulated by deficit spending
    (E) deficit spending can stimulate a stagnant economy

GO ON TO THE NEXT PAGE ▶▶▶

6. When a nation is at war, the military conflict tends to override <u>what controversies, if any, that may exist</u> within the government.

   (A) what controversies, if any, that may exist
   (B) the controversies, if there are any, that are
   (C) any controversies
   (D) the controversies, if any exist
   (E) what the controversies are that are

7. The vast landscape of the Bonneville Salt Flats in Utah is utterly devoid of plant life and geographical irregularities <u>and hence is an ideal location for racing</u> high-speed vehicles.

   (A) and hence is an ideal location for racing
   (B) which are ideal for racing
   (C) providing the ideal location for racing
   (D) that are ideal to race
   (E) making these ideal for racing

8. Weighed down by an overloaded backpack, <u>David's search for a place to rest was urgent</u>.

   (A) David's search for a place to rest was urgent
   (B) David's urgent search was for a place to rest
   (C) a place to rest was what David urgently needed
   (D) a place to rest for which David urgently searched
   (E) David searched urgently for a place to rest

9. The small breach in the hull of the ship soon became a gaping hole, quickly flooding the hold and <u>it made the possibility of repairing the damage almost impossible</u>.

   (A) it made the possibility of repairing the damage almost impossible
   (B) it made repairing the damage almost impossible
   (C) making it almost impossible to repair the damage
   (D) this fact made it almost impossible to repair the damage
   (E) rendering the possibility of repairing the damage almost impossible

10. Yearning for a new challenge in college, <u>the forensics team provided me with a strong sense of camaraderie and teamwork</u>.

    (A) the forensics team provided me with a strong sense of camaraderie and teamwork
    (B) I found a strong sense of camaraderie and teamwork in the forensics team
    (C) a strong sense of camaraderie and teamwork was what I found in the forensics team
    (D) providing me with a strong sense of camaraderie and teamwork was the forensics team
    (E) I was by the forensics team provided with a strong sense of camaraderie and teamwork

11. <u>The base camp had an insufficient supply of oxygen tanks, which were not enough for those climbers who required them as a necessity</u>.

    (A) The base camp had an insufficient supply of oxygen tanks, which were not enough for those climbers who required them as a necessity.
    (B) The insufficient supply of oxygen tanks at the base camp was not enough for those climbers who needed them.
    (C) Lacking a sufficient supply of oxygen tanks, the base camp did not have enough for the climbers who needed them.
    (D) The base camp did not have enough oxygen tanks for the climbers who needed them.
    (E) The climbers' need for oxygen tanks was not met by the insufficient supply of them at the base camp.

12. Today's political campaigns rely so much on scare tactics and superficial sound bites <u>that voters rarely get any substantial perspective</u> on policy issues.

    (A) that voters rarely get any substantial perspective
    (B) so voters get rarely any substantial perspective
    (C) and the substantial perspective is hardly gotten by voters
    (D) and they don't give voters any substantial perspective
    (E) that the substantial perspective is not really received by voters

GO ON TO THE NEXT PAGE ▶▶▶

13. In medieval times, many doctors believed that <u>if you had a disease it was because of an imbalance in your bodily "humours."</u>

    (A) if you had a disease it was because of an imbalance in your bodily "humours"
    (B) diseases were caused because you had an imbalance in your bodily "humours"
    (C) diseases were caused by the fact of your bodily "humours" not being in balance
    (D) diseases were being caused by imbalances in the "humours" in your body
    (E) diseases were caused by imbalances in the bodily "humours"

14. <u>The charity finally reaching its goal through a pledge drive, it</u> did not want to neglect to thank its many benefactors.

    (A) The charity finally reaching its goal through a pledge drive, it
    (B) It reached its goal through a pledge drive, the charity
    (C) To reach its goal through a pledge drive, the charity
    (D) The charity reaching its goal through a pledge drive
    (E) Having finally reached its goal through a pledge drive, the charity

15. In some ostensibly democratic countries, elections rarely take place, <u>unlike every year in the United States</u>.

    (A) unlike every year in the United States
    (B) where in the United States they take place every year
    (C) unlike in the United States, where they take place every year
    (D) unlike the United States' having them every year
    (E) unlike the elections that take place every year in the United States

16. To become a *Jeopardy!* champion requires not only a broad knowledge base, but also <u>you must have quick reflexes and be able</u> to decipher hidden clues.

    (A) you must have quick reflexes and be able
    (B) your reflexes must be quick and the ability
    (C) quick reflexes and the ability
    (D) to have quick reflexes and the ability
    (E) to have quick reflexes and to be able

17. A longstanding national tradition permits the monarch, regardless of his or her tribe of origin, <u>to be proclaimed as an honorary elder of every clan</u>.

    (A) to be proclaimed as an honorary elder of every clan
    (B) to have been proclaimed in every clan as an honorary member of it
    (C) being proclaimed as an honorary elder of every clan
    (D) as an honorary elder of every clan
    (E) for being proclaimed an honorary elder of every clan

18. The tests performed to assess the age of the painting have produced inconclusive <u>results, and</u> many historians continue to insist that it predated the Renaissance.

    (A) results, and
    (B) results because
    (C) results; thus
    (D) results for
    (E) results, but

19. Confident in its ability to hold on to its sizable lead, <u>the second half saw the team lose focus and allow its opponent to seize the momentum.</u>

   (A) the second half saw the team lose focus and allow its opponent to seize the momentum

   (B) the team allowed its opponent to seize the momentum in the second half because it lost its focus

   (C) the momentum was seized by the opponent when the team lost its focus in the second half

   (D) the team lost its focus in the second half and allowed its opponent to seize the momentum

   (E) its opponents seized the momentum in the second half because the team lost its focus

20. An increasing number of feature films are starting to be regarded not so much as works of art or even as commercial products, <u>but rather as</u> advertisements for embedded products.

   (A) but rather as
   (B) or even as
   (C) but not as
   (D) but also as
   (E) but are instead

Directions for "Identifying Sentence Error" Questions

The following sentences may contain errors in grammar, usage, diction (choice of words), or idiom. Some of the sentences are correct. No sentence contains more than one error.

If the sentence contains an error, it is in one of the parts that are underlined and lettered. The parts that are not underlined are correct.

If there is an error, select the part that must be changed to correct the sentence.

If there is no error, choose (E).

EXAMPLE:

By the time they reached the halfway point
     A
in the race, most of the runners hadn't hardly
 B   C   D
begun to hit their stride. No error
      E

Ⓐ Ⓑ ● Ⓓ Ⓔ

---

21. The twelve choral pieces that the choir sung
     A   B
in the spring concert were chosen for their
        C
vibrant melodies and intricate harmonies.
       D
No error
 E

22. The effects of the decision to invade Iraq
    A
has been felt not only in the Middle East but
 B
throughout the world as well. No error
  C   D E

23. Partisanship still divides the state
     A
legislature, with some representatives
     B
tenaciously demanding tax relief and others
  C
insist on balancing the budget. No error
 D   E

24. Ever since the university vowed to dedicate
         A
more of its resources to professional studies,

there have been less courses available
  B   C
in the arts and humanities. No error
   D   E

25. Although over 80 percent of citizens profess
           A
a strong opinion on the issue, a much lower
     B
percentage actually intend on voting on the
 C   D
referendum. No error
    E

26. This year's geography bee, which was the

first to be held on a college campus, drew
     A   B
nearly three hundred more participants than
       C
last year. No error
 D E

27. One of the first challenges that most
    A
first-year college students must address is
           B
coordinating his or her academic schedules
     C
with many new social opportunities. No error
 D   E

28. Our opponents in the debate had prepared
         A
very well for their opening presentation,

but they did not fare well with the
      B
challenging questions posed by Denitra and
        C
myself. No error
 D E

GO ON TO THE NEXT PAGE ▶▶▶

29. Although <u>they</u> deliberated for
   A
<u>over four full days</u>, the jury members could
   B
not <u>agree for</u> the verdict, because several key
   C
pieces of evidence had been <u>called into</u>
   D
question. <u>No error</u>
   E

30. By virtue of <u>its ability</u> to use echolocation,
   A
dolphins can, <u>even</u> while blindfolded,
   B
<u>retrieve</u> small objects that are
   C
<u>dozens of meters</u> away. <u>No error</u>
   D   E

31. If <u>expecting</u> a clever and comic masterpiece
   A
<u>like</u> Bryant's debut novel, the second
   B
installment <u>of this trilogy</u> is <u>likely</u> to
   C   D
disappoint you. <u>No error</u>
   E

32. Many in the embassy <u>believe</u> that, if
   A
negotiations <u>between</u> the two disputing
   B
factions <u>had been given</u> more of a chance,
   C
civil war might have been <u>averted</u>. <u>No error</u>
   D   E

33. The board soon <u>realized that</u>, in order to
   A
avoid the need <u>to declare</u> bankruptcy, the
   B
company would have to eliminate not only
<u>millions of dollars</u> in annual costs, but also
   C
<u>get rid</u> of hundreds of jobs. <u>No error</u>
   D   E

34. Many students who are <u>critics about</u> the
   A
current administration <u>remarked</u> that <u>their</u>
   B   C
greatest fear is that the president will
misinterpret his election <u>as a mandate</u> for
   D
his economic policies. <u>No error</u>
   E

Directions for Improving Paragraphs Questions

Below is an early draft of an essay. It requires revision in many areas.

The questions that follow ask you to make improvements in sentence structure, diction, organization, and development. Answering the questions may require that you understand the context of the passage as well as the rules of standard written English.

Questions 35–39 pertain to the following passage.

(1) *In the Copper Canyons of northwestern Mexico lives a remarkable people called the Tarahumara. (2) They are know by many as the Running Indians. (3) Running being such an integral part of their lifestyle, and so they are ready to take off on a long run at almost any time.*

(4) *You may never have heard of them because they rarely run in the big marathons around the world. (5) Believe it or not, this is because many of their runners think that such races are too short. (6) Where they excel is at the super-long races, many of which are well over 100 miles long. (7) Their economy is based on the trade of corn beer, which they make themselves. (8) Even over rocky and treacherous terrain, they often run barefoot, or with sandals handmade of old tires. (9) They do not use rigorous training methods, nor do they stretch or warm up before races.*

(10) *The Tarahumara may be among the best ultra marathoners in the world. (11) Although most runners consider their nontraditional running methods dangerous and unwise, it is because they have a very different perspective on the meaning of running. (12) One common ritual is the rarajipari, an all-out running race that pits one village against another. (13) After a night of drinking corn beer and betting, the two teams will run for 24 to 40 straight hours kicking a wooden ball over a predetermined course. (14) Often, the ball careens into a crevice and must be retrieved by one of the runners. (15) The race can easily cover over 100 miles. (16) Most runners would consider this an ordeal only to be endured for some personal victory, but to the Tarahumara it's just a heck of a lot of fun.*

35. Which of the following changes should be made to sentence 1?

(A) Change *of* to *to*.
(B) Insert a semicolon after *people*.
(C) Omit the phrase *called the*.
(D) Insert the phrase *which are* after *people*.
(E) Change *lives* to *live*.

36. Which of the following is the best revision of sentence 3 (reproduced below)?
Running being such an integral part of their lifestyle, and so they are ready to take off on a long run at almost any time.

(A) Because they are ready to take off on a long run at almost any time, and so running is an integral part of their lifestyle.
(B) Running is such an integral part of their lifestyle that they are ready to take off on a long run at almost any time.
(C) Being able to take off on a long run at almost any time, running is an integral part of their lifestyle.
(D) Running being such an integral part of their lifestyle, and being ready to take off on a long run at almost any time.
(E) Running being such an integral part of their lifestyle that they are ready to take off on a long run at almost any time.

37. The unity of the second paragraph can best be improved by deleting which of the following sentences?

    (A) sentence 4
    (B) sentence 5
    (C) sentence 7
    (D) sentence 8
    (E) sentence 9

38. In context, which of the following best replaces *"The Tarahumara"* in sentence 10?

    (A) Secondly, the Tarahumara
    (B) Cultures like that of the Tarahumara
    (C) Nevertheless, the Tarahumara
    (D) While the Tarahumara
    (E) In this sense, the Tarahumara

39. In context, which of the following is the best revision of the underlined portion of sentence 11 (reproduced below)?

    Although most runners consider their nontraditional running methods dangerous and unwise, it is because they have a very different perspective on the meaning of running.

    (A) Most runners consider the nontraditional running methods of the Tarahumara to be dangerous and unwise, but the Tarahumara
    (B) Because most runners consider their nontraditional running methods to be dangerous and unwise, the Tarahumara
    (C) Considering the nontraditional running methods of the Tarahumara to be dangerous and unwise, the Tarahumara, to most runners
    (D) Considered by most runners, the nontraditional running methods of the Tarahumara are dangerous and unwise, but they
    (E) Although most runners would consider the running methods of the Tarahumara to be nontraditional, dangerous and unwise, they therefore

STOP

You may check your work, on this section only, until time is called.

ANSWER KEY

Section 1 Critical Reading	Section 3 Critical Reading	Section 2 Math	Section 4 Math	Section 5 Writing
☐ 1. A	☐ 25. B	☐ 1. C	☐ 21. C	☐ 1. C
☐ 2. E	☐ 26. A	☐ 2. D	☐ 22. B	☐ 2. D
☐ 3. B	☐ 27. D	☐ 3. B	☐ 23. A	☐ 3. A
☐ 4. C	☐ 28. E	☐ 4. C	☐ 24. B	☐ 4. B
☐ 5. A	☐ 29. C	☐ 5. B	☐ 25. E	☐ 5. E
☐ 6. E	☐ 30. B	☐ 6. C	☐ 26. A	☐ 6. C
☐ 7. D	☐ 31. B	☐ 7. D	☐ 27. C	☐ 7. A
☐ 8. D	☐ 32. D	☐ 8. B	☐ 28. A	☐ 8. E
☐ 9. D	☐ 33. B	☐ 9. C	# Right (A):	☐ 9. C
☐ 10. B	☐ 34. E	☐ 10. B	_____	☐ 10. B
☐ 11. C	☐ 35. C	☐ 11. D	# Wrong (B):	☐ 11. D
☐ 12. A	☐ 36. C	☐ 12. B	_____	☐ 12. A
☐ 13. C	☐ 37. D	☐ 13. C	# (A) $-\frac{1}{4}$ (B):	☐ 13. E
☐ 14. D	☐ 38. A	☐ 14. A	_____	☐ 14. E
☐ 15. C	☐ 39. A	☐ 15. E	☐ 29. 84	☐ 15. C
☐ 16. A	☐ 40. D	☐ 16. E	☐ 30. 7	☐ 16. C
☐ 17. C	☐ 41. B	☐ 17. B	☐ 31. 8	☐ 17. A
☐ 18. E	☐ 42. C	☐ 18. A	☐ 32. 36	☐ 18. E
☐ 19. D	☐ 43. E	☐ 19. C	☐ 33. 260	☐ 19. D
☐ 20. E	☐ 44. E	☐ 20. E	☐ 34. 32	☐ 20. A
☐ 21. D	☐ 45. A		☐ 35. 65	☐ 21. B
☐ 22. C	☐ 46. C		☐ 36. 3000	☐ 22. B
☐ 23. A	☐ 47. B		☐ 37. 3/2 or 1.5	☐ 23. D
☐ 24. C	☐ 48. B		☐ 38. 280	☐ 24. C
				☐ 25. D
				☐ 26. D
				☐ 27. C
				☐ 28. D
				☐ 29. C
				☐ 30. A
				☐ 31. A
				☐ 32. E
				☐ 33. D
				☐ 34. A
				☐ 35. E
				☐ 36. B
				☐ 37. C
				☐ 38. C
				☐ 39. A

# Right (A):	# Right (A):	# Right (A):	# Right (A):	# Right (A):
_____	_____	_____	_____	_____
# Wrong (B):	# Wrong (B):	# Wrong (B):		# Wrong (B):
_____	_____	_____		_____
# (A) $-\frac{1}{4}$ (B):	# (A) $-\frac{1}{4}$ (B):	# (A) $-\frac{1}{4}$ (B):		# (A) $-\frac{1}{4}$ (B):
_____	_____	_____		_____

SCORE CONVERSION TABLE

How to score your test

Use the answer key on the previous page to determine your raw score on each section. Remember to add the raw scores from Sections 1 and 3 to get your Critical Reading raw score, and to add the raw scores from sections 2 and 4 to get your Math raw score. Write the three raw scores here:

Raw Critical Reading score (Section 1 + Section 3): _____

Raw Math score (Section 2 + Section 4): _____

Raw Writing score (Section 5): _____

Use the table below to convert these to scaled scores.

Scaled scores: Critical Reading: _____   Math: _____   Writing: _____

Raw Score	Critical Reading Scaled Score	Math Scaled Score	Writing Scaled Score	Raw Score	Critical Reading Scaled Score	Math Scaled Score	Writing Scaled Score
48	80			20	49	52	54
47	80			19	48	51	52
46	78			18	47	50	51
45	76			17	46	48	50
44	74			16	45	47	49
43	72			15	44	46	48
42	71			14	43	45	46
41	69			13	42	44	45
40	68			12	41	43	44
39	67		80	11	40	42	43
38	66	80	80	10	39	41	41
37	64	77	78	9	38	40	40
36	63	74	77	8	37	39	39
35	62	72	76	7	36	38	37
34	62	70	74	6	34	36	36
33	61	68	73	5	33	35	35
32	60	66	71	4	32	34	33
31	59	65	69	3	30	32	32
30	58	64	68	2	29	30	31
29	57	62	66	1	27	29	30
28	56	61	65	0	25	26	29
27	55	60	63	−1	22	23	28
26	54	59	62	−2	20	20	27
25	54	58	60	−3	20	20	25
24	54	57	59	−4	20	20	24
23	52	55	57	−5	20	20	22
22	51	54	56	−6	20	20	21
21	50	53	55	−7 or less	20	20	20

Detailed Answer Key

Section 1

1. A   The fact that Hillary opened the door *quietly* and *sneaked* into the room suggests that she was trying not to be noticed. *inconspicuous* = not readily noticed; *coincidental* = occurring together by chance

2. E   The word *but* indicates a contrast in tone from the description of the speech as *focused and riveting*. The missing word should mean something opposite to *focused*. *reflexive* = referring to an action that is automatic and unintentional; *spellbinding* = riveting; *rambling* = unfocused

3. B   If the stores *cater to* a clientele with *ever-changing tastes*, they must carry a wide variety of clothing. Both missing words should mean something like *varied*. *modest* = humble; *diverse* = varied; *eclectic* = deriving from a wide variety of sources; *subtle* = not obvious; *conservative* = traditional; *extravagant* = extremely abundant; *redundant* = characterized by needless repetition; *corporate* = appropriate to the business world

4. C   This sentence indicates a contrast between *rigid rules* on the one hand and more flexible rules on the other. The missing word must mean *rules for arranging words to convey an idea*. *emphasis* = the placement of stress or significance; *syntax* = the rules that govern word-order in a language; *symbolism* = the use of symbols to represent concepts

5. A   A *tainted* reputation is one that is damaged, usually by a scandal. If one's reputation is particularly tainted, the mention of one's name might cause even one's friends to *cringe*. *recoil* = cringe or shrink from; *applaud* = praise highly; *defer* = to submit to the wishes of another; *pontificate* = to speak haughtily; *calculate* = plan deliberately

6. E   Reading the whole sentence makes it clear that the subject of the sentence is a candidate's *economic policies*. Policies are positions on how an organization like the government should be run. *deliberations* = careful discussions to reach a decision; *domestic* = pertaining to one's own country rather than foreign ones; *retreats* = withdrawals from previous positions; *indifference* = apathy; *fiscal* = pertaining to financial matters; *stances* = official positions

7. D   If the editor *reprimanded* (scolded) the journalist, the journalist must have done something wrong. One common mistake in journalism is publishing incorrect information, which must later be withdrawn. *verifiable* = capable of being proved true; *marketed* = advertised for sale; *refutable* = capable of being proven incorrect; *compensated* = provided payment for a good or service; *spurious* = invalid, false; *retracted* = withdrew published material, usually because it contained erroneous information; *polished* = perfected; *disowned* = refused to claim as one's own

8. D   The sentence describes a contrast between two kinds of economy. The first is *self-sufficient*, so the second must *rely* on other nations. Such an economy is necessarily not *disconnected* with the outside world. *impoverished* = poor; *unregulated* = without rules designed to govern behavior; *pursued* = chased; *isolated* = set apart from the outside world, *robust* = vigorous and strong

9. D   The passage begins by describing a *currently fashionable criticism* (line 1), namely, that the press is *liberal*. It ends with the conclusion that *all good journalists are proud to be called liberals* (lines 22–23), so the overall purpose of the passage is to recast a criticism into a compliment. Although the origin of the term "liberty" is briefly discussed, it is not the main idea of the passage. It also does not discuss social policy or education. Lastly, it is not an *objective* analysis because it contains subjective evaluations of *good* journalism,

10. B   The main point of the second passage is that *the very fabric of the media is corporate* (lines 28–29) and that *the corporate goal* [of journalism] *is to make a profit* (lines 32–33).

11. C   In saying that *the object of the major news enterprises is not impartial analysis*, the author means that the *goal* of the media is not to give objective information.

12. A   The first passage focuses on the fact that journalists should be independent of *governmental and corporate ideologies* (line 17), while the second suggests that they cannot be independent of corporate ideologies and are constrained by the need *to make a profit*. Neither passage discusses the skill level, education, or optimism of journalists.

13. **C**   The first paragraph says that Erdös *had lost four mathematical colleagues* (lines 3–4), although they were sitting in front of him, so he was somewhat disoriented. There is nothing in the paragraph to suggest that he is *domineering* (overbearing and controlling), *playful* (although he certainly becomes more playful in the *second* paragraph), *charismatic* (showing natural leadership qualities), or *stoic* (deliberately unemotional).

14. **D**   At two points in the passage, the author suggests that Erdös's extended arm indicates his anger. In lines 8–9, the author states that Erdös *was angry with himself* immediately after stating that he had *one arm held out to the side like a scarecrow's* (lines 7–8). Later the author states that *his anger dissipated—his arm dropped to his side* (lines 23–24).

15. **C**   The passage states that *God . . . was always tormenting Erdös by hiding his glasses . . . or, worse yet, keeping to Himself the elegant solutions to all sorts of intriguing mathematical problems* (lines 15–19).

16. **A**   In this context, the phrase *plying his craft* means exercising his skill, since it is referring to Erdös's explanation of an obscure mathematical proof.

17. **C**   Archimedes is mentioned as an example of a mathematician who required *no laboratory equipment* and who could solve problems on his oil-drenched skin, much as Erdös was able to do complicated mathematics on a restaurant napkin.

18. **E**   The last paragraph is a short vignette about Erdös and a colleague *thinking . . . for more than an hour without uttering a single word* (lines 73–74). Clearly, this requires a good deal of focus, and so Erdös is clearly not portrayed as *impatient* or *distractible*. And although there was *joy* at the resolution of the problem, the joy was not the result of a joke, and so Erdös is not portrayed as *jocular*.

19. **D**   The first paragraph indicates that the author's purpose is to *develop an adequate idea of art* (lines 1–2) and to *identify the field of our investigation and mark it off from other regions* (lines 4–5). The essay then goes on to define art as a type of *expression* (line 11) that is distinct from nonartistic expression such as *automatic expressions* (lines 32–33) and *practical expressions* (line 36). Therefore, the main purpose of the essay is to distinguish artistic expression from nonartistic expression.

20. **E**   In saying that *expression* [is] *the putting forth of purpose, feeling, or thought into a sensuous medium* (lines 11–14), the author is saying that artistic expressions must be made through some means that is detectable by the senses. Such a means is a *mode of creation*.

21. **D**   The author refers to *the cry of pain or the shout of joy* (line 35) as an example of *automatic expression*, which are *instinctive overflowings of emotion* (lines 33–34). These, the author claims, are *not aesthetic* (lines 35–36); that is, they are not expressions of true art.

22. **C**   When the author states that a *work of art* such as the *Ninth Symphony* [is] *not of this character*, he indicates that it is not *only* [a means or instrument] *for the realization of ulterior purposes* (lines 37–38). That is, the *Ninth Symphony* has its purpose in itself.

23. **A**   The word *success* in this sentence refers to the ability of a *love poem . . . to persuade a lady* (lines 64–65). Therefore, it refers to the ability of a sentimental expression to influence a particular person.

24. **C**   This sentence states that a *work of art* has *significance* [that] *is broader than the success or failure of* [its] *motive*. That is, even if a piece of art was created for a specific purpose, such as to *persuade a lady* or to inspire a revolution, the work must still have meaning beyond the original purpose in order to be considered true art. This idea is summarized in choice (C). The sentence indicates that a work of art has meaning *despite* its ulterior motive, not *because* of it; therefore choice (A) is incorrect. The sentence does not refer to *historical events*, an *audience*, or *critics*; therefore choices (B), (D), and (E) are incorrect.

Section 2

1. **C**

$$y + 2 = 10$$
$$\text{Subtract 2:} \quad y = 8$$

Therefore $xy = (5)(8) = 40$
(Chapter 9 Lesson 1: Solving Equations)

2. **D**   If the average of 4 numbers is 10, then the sum of the four numbers must be $4 \times 10 = 40$. Since the other three numbers have a sum of $8 + 9 + 10 = 27$, the fourth number must be $40 - 27 = 13$.
(Chapter 10 Lesson 2: Mean/Median/Mode Problems)

3. **B** The measure of the angles in a triangle adds up to 180°, so

$$70 + 60 + x = 180$$

Simplify: $130 + x = 180$

Subtract 130: $x = 50$

(Chapter 11 Lesson 2: Triangles)

4. **C** Set up the proportion: $\dfrac{5}{6} = \dfrac{30}{x}$

Cross-multiply: $5x = 180$

Divide by 5: $x = 36$

(Chapter 8 Lesson 4: Ratios and Proportions)

5. **B** Simply substitute $2m$ for k (because they are equal) and simplify: $\dfrac{m}{k} \times 16 = \dfrac{m}{2m} \times 16 = \dfrac{1}{2} \times 16 = 8.$
(Chapter 9 Lesson 1: Solving Equations)

6. **C** Notice first that the column showing the votes for Student A contains two numbers, so you can easily find the missing number. Since a total of 35 students voted for Student A and 19 of these were boys, $35 - 19 = 16$ of them must have been girls. (Write this number into the table.) Since the "girls" row indicates that a total of 40 girls voted and since you just determined that 16 of them voted for Student A, then $40 - 16 = 24$ girls must have voted for Student B.
(Chapter 10 Lesson 5: Counting Problems)

7. **D** Start by saying that Caroline owns c DVDs. Since she owns 6 more than Mark does, Mark must own $c - 6$ DVDs. Since they own 36 altogether,

$$c + c - 6 = 36$$

Simplify: $2c - 6 = 36$

Add 6: $2c = 42$

Divide by 2: $c = 21$

(Chapter 9 Lesson 7: Word Problems)

8. **B** Start by saying that you will add x ounces of nuts. If the resulting mixture is to be 25% nuts, then

$$\frac{\text{ounces of nuts}}{\text{ounces of mixture}} = \frac{x}{x + 12} = \frac{25}{100}$$

Simplify: $\dfrac{x}{x + 12} = \dfrac{1}{4}$

Cross-multiply: $4x = x + 12$

Subtract x: $3x = 12$

Divide by 3: $x = 4$

(Chapter 8 Lesson 5: Percents)
(Chapter 8 Lesson 4: Ratios and Proportions)

9. **C** The figure below shows the three consecutive transformations. The resulting point is at $(-3, 5)$.

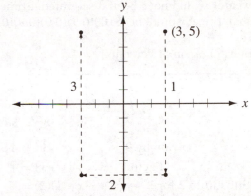

(Chapter 11 Lesson 4: Coordinate Geometry)

10. **B** Since the sum $m + 6n$ is fixed at 40, minimizing the value of m means <u>maximizing</u> the value of $6n$. Since both m and n are positive integers, $6n$ must be a multiple of 6. The greatest multiple of 6 less than 40 is 36, so the maximum possible value of n is 6. If n were 7 or greater, then m would have to be negative for the sum to equal 40, which would contradict the given information. Therefore, for the minimum value of m,

$$m + 36 = 40$$

Subtract 36: $m = 4$

(Chapter 10 Lesson 3: Numerical Reasoning Problems)

11. **D** The prime factorization of 27 is $3 \times 3 \times 3$, and the prime factorization of 36 is $2 \times 2 \times 3 \times 3$. The least common multiple of 27 and 36 is therefore $2 \times 2 \times 3 \times 3 \times 3 = 108$. Therefore, if an integer is divisible by both 27 and 36, it must also be divisible by 108. Any number that is divisible by 108 must also be divisible by 54, since 54 is a factor of

108 ($54 \times 2 = 108$).
(Chapter 8 Lesson 7: Divisibility)
(Chapter 9 Lesson 5: Factoring)

---

12. **B** Looking at the 6 given terms, notice that the sequence is:

odd, odd, even, odd, odd, even...

In other words, one out of every three consecutive terms is even. Since 60 is divisible by 3, the total number of even numbers in the first 60 is $60 \div 3 = 20$.
(Chapter 7 Reasoning Skill 3: Finding Patterns)

---

13. **C** Reducing a number by 10% is equivalent to multiplying that number by 0.9. After 4 weeks, the sweater would have been discounted 4 times, so the final price would be $100(0.9)(0.9)(0.9)(0.9) = $65.61.
(Chapter 8 Lesson 5: Percents)

---

14. **A**

$$9x^2 - 9y^2 = 36$$

Divide by 9: $\quad x^2 - y^2 = 4$

Factor: $\quad (x-y)(x+y) = 4$

Substitute 2 for $x+y$: $\quad (x-y)(2) = 4$

Divide by 2: $\quad x - y = 2$

This means that x is 2 greater than y.
(Chapter 9 Lesson 5: Factoring)
(Chapter 9 Lesson 1: Solving Equations)

---

15. **E** Divide the shaded regions into two triangles with a vertical line as shown here:

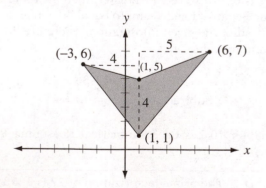

One triangle has a base of 4 and a height of 4, and the other has a base of 4 and a height of 5. The first triangle, then, has an area of $(4)(4)/2 = 8$, and the second has an area of $(4)(5)/2 = 10$. Altogether, then, the shaded region has an area of $8 + 10 = 18$.
(Chapter 11 Lesson 2: Triangles)

(Chapter 11 Lesson 4: Coordinate Geometry)
(Chapter 11 Lesson 5: Areas and Perimeters)

---

16. **E** Start by drawing a line segment with points labeled A, B, C, and D, in that order. You don't have to worry about drawing it perfectly to scale.

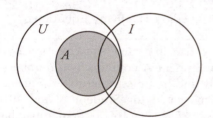

Assume, for simplicity's sake, that $BC = 1$. If $AC = 6BC$, then $AC = 6(1) = 6$. This means that $AB = 6 - 1 = 5$. If $BD = 5AB$, then $BD = 5(5) = 25$, and so $CD = 25 - 1 = 24$. Therefore, $CD/AC = 24/6 = 4$.
(Chapter 7 Reasoning Skill 2: Analyzing)

---

17. **B** A Venn diagram is very handy in a problem like this. If some aggles are iggles, then the circle representing the set of aggles must intersect the circle representing the set of iggles. If all aggles are uggles, then the circle representing the set of aggles must be *completely contained in* the circle representing the set of all uggles. Your diagram, then, should look something like this:

Now look at statement I: are all iggles also uggles? The diagram shows a lot of space inside the "iggles" circle that is not inside the "uggles" circle. Therefore, it is possible that there are iggles that are not uggles. So statement I is not necessarily true. [This lets you eliminate choices (A) and (D).] Now look at statement II: are some uggles also iggles? The diagram suggests yes, because part of the "uggles" circle must overlap the "iggles" circle in order to completely contain the "aggles" circle. This means that at least some uggles are necessarily iggles. Therefore, statement II is necessarily true. [And you can eliminate choice (C).] Now look at statement III: are all uggles also aggles? Not necessarily, because there is a lot of space within the "uggles" circle that is not inside the "aggles" circle, so there could be some uggles that are not aggles, and therefore statement III is not necessarily true, and the correct answer is (B).
(Chapter 10 Lesson 5: Counting Problems)

18. **A**   You can solve this problem numerically, by "plugging in" values for the unknowns, or algebraically, by "converting" m square feet to the corresponding number of dollars. To use the "plugging-in" method, just pick simple values for the unknowns, like $x = 2$, $d = 20$, and $m = 1000$. (Think about the problem situation and notice why these are particularly convenient choices for the unknown values.) This suggests that 2 gallons of paint cost $20, so 1 gallon must cost $10. This one gallon covers 500 square feet, so it costs $10 to buy enough paint to cover 500 square feet. Since 1,000 square feet is twice as much as 500 square feet, it must cost twice as much, or $20. Therefore, when you plug in $x = 2$, $d = 20$, and $m = 1,000$ to the answer choices, the correct answer must equal 20. Notice that only choice (A) has a value of 20 in this case.

Alternatively, you can solve this with simple algebra:

$$m \text{ square feet} \times \frac{1 \text{ gallon}}{500 \text{ square feet}} \times \frac{d \text{ dollars}}{x \text{ gallons}} = \frac{md}{500x} \text{ dollars}$$

Notice that here you convert m square feet into dollars by multiplying by two "conversion factors." Notice that the numerator and denominator in each conversion factor are equal, and that all of the units "cancel" except for the one you're looking for: dollars.
(Chapter 9 Lesson 6: Inequalities, Absolute Values, and Plugging In)
(Chapter 9 Lesson 7: Word Problems)

19. **C**   Use the circle area formula to find the radius of the circle:

$$16\pi = \pi r^2$$

Divide by π: $\qquad\qquad 16 = r^2$

Take the square root: $\qquad 4 = r$

Now write this information into the diagram. You might notice that the square can be divided up and reassembled as shown to form two squares that have an area of $4^2 = 16$. Therefore the entire shaded region has an area of $2(16) = 32$.

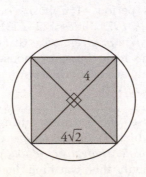
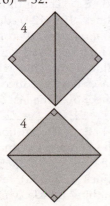

Alternatively, you might notice that each radius of the circle sketched in the diagram above is also a leg of a 45°-45°-90° triangle. Using the relationships among sides in this "special" triangle shows that each side of the inscribed square is $4\sqrt{2}$. Therefore the area of this square is $(4\sqrt{2})^2 = 32$.
(Chapter 11 Lesson 3: The Pythagorean Theorem)
(Chapter 11 Lesson 5: Areas and Perimeters)
(Chapter 11 Lesson 8: Circles)

20. **E**

$$m \diamond n \diamond 2 = 100$$

Translate using definition: $m^2 + n^2 = 100$
The fact that m and n must be positive integers and that $10^2 = 100$ suggests that m and n must each be an integer from 1 to 9. A small amount of trial and error should quickly show that the only possible solution is $6^2 + 8^2 = 100$. Therefore $m + n = 6 + 8 = 14$.
(Chapter 10 Lesson 1: New Symbol or Term Problems)

Section 3

25. **B**   *Activists* are people who take political action for causes that are important to them. As an activist, one could not remain *idle* while one's values were being attacked. *passive* = inactive; *confrontational* = inclined to starting fights

26. **A**   The word *although* indicates that it is surprising that Schilling was not kept from pitching a masterful game. Therefore, his strained tendon must have been a real *hindrance* to him. *hobbled* = caused to limp; *impediment* = hindrance; *deterred* = prevented from taking action

27. **D**   One who has *authored over 65 books* is very *productive*. *conservative* = resistant to change; *ingenuous* = lacking sophistication or worldliness; *obscure* = not well known; *prolific* = very productive

28. **E**   If someone is normally *sympathetic*, it would be surprising if he were suddenly *mean*. *stoic* = deliberately unemotional; *synthetic* = artificial or man-made; *venerable* = honorable; *callous* = emotionally hardened, insensitive

29. **C**   *Garish* means gaudy or excessively flashy. If such a display was a *departure*, their promotions must have previously been more *tame*. *listless* = lacking energy; *lethargic* = sluggish; *dynamic* = energetic; *ostentatious* = showy; *subdued* = modest; *beguiling* = charming in a deceitful way; *volatile* = explosive; *nondescript* = lacking in distinctive qualities; *mutable* = changeable

30. B   The passage states that, as a result of the Revolution, *trade and communication with the outside world were reduced to a trickle* (lines 2–4), and *the Continental Congress restricted* (line 8–9) voyages. This indicates that the revolution had a very restrictive effect on the people of Nantucket.

31. B   The passage states that, as members of the Society of Friends, islanders were *opposed to war*. This means that they were *pacifists*.

32. D   The overall purpose of the passage is to discuss briefly the effectiveness of experimentation and the scientific method over the last 500 years. The author compares one of Galileo's ancient experiments with a modern one primarily to make the point that *the principle behind both kinds of experiments, and the excitement of discovery they engender, remains the same* (lines 14–16). In other words, the scientific method has endured many centuries. Although the passage does suggest subtly that Galileo's experiments were cruder than modern ones, it does not state or even suggest that Galileo's experiments were inaccurate, that Galileo was less knowledgeable than modern scientists, or that modern scientific equipment is too expensive.

33. B   The *insights* mentioned in line 22 are part of the discussion of the results of well-conducted *experimentation*.

34. E   The viewpoints presented in the first paragraph are later refuted by the author, so they cannot represent the *author's perspective*. The fact that the author argues against these viewpoints indicates that they are not *objective*, nor are they part of a *scientific theory*. This paragraph is clearly presenting *positions to be refuted*.

35. C   The argument described in lines 8–15 suggests that *changing energy or land use policies would needlessly cost the American taxpayer tens to hundreds of billions of dollars annually*. Although the author clearly disagrees with this argument, it is also clear that this argument is appealing to the reader's concerns about money, or *fiscal responsibility*.

36. C   The two perspectives described in the first paragraph emphasize different points, but agree that *efforts to counteract global warming are ill-conceived*, either because there is no such thing as global warming or because the remedies would undermine America's competitiveness.

37. D   The claim in the sixth paragraph that *the observed changes during the last century are unlikely to be due entirely to natural causes* (lines 45–47) is based on *model simulations* (lines 42–43) of the environment. If these simulations are innacurate, or do not consider important variables, then this conclusion would be called into question.

38. A   The *changes in precipitation* and other effects of global warming are mentioned in order to convince those who *question whether we should care if the climate becomes warmer* (lines 52–53).

39. A   On line 56, the author mentions *rises in sea level* as one effect of global warming, but does not mention widespread extinctions or longer growing seasons anywhere in the passage.

40. D   The thesis of Passage 2 is that the belief that *we know enough to take significant action to counter [global warming]* (lines 69–71) is incorrect. Therefore, he would clearly agree with the statement that *we do not yet know enough about the science of climate change to base environmental policy on it*.

41. B   The overall purpose of the passage is to question some common conceptions about global warming and environmental policy. The claim that *the science* [about climate change] *is settled* is refuted throughout the passage by pointing out the *gaps in our state of knowledge* (lines 95–96). Thus, the author has clearly adopted a *skeptical* view of this statement.

42. C   The author of Passage 2 states that *Kyoto-like restrictions could cost $300 billion annually* (lines 83–84) and that the Kyoto Protocol *would harm the economy and exempt developing countries like China and India* (lines 86–88). This means that the author believes that the treaty is too expensive and unfair.

43. E   The author states that *frost damaged crops* (lines 123–124) during a period of *atmospheric cooling from 1940 to around 1975* (lines 122–123), which occurred *despite the rise in greenhouse gases* (line 126). This refutes the idea that greenhouse gases have produced a steady atmospheric warming effect over the last 50 years.

44. E   The author discusses the warming during the Climatic Optimum, in which *the Earth's temperatures were 1 to 2 degrees warmer than they are today* (lines 132–133), even though this warming had nothing *to do with man-made greenhouse gases* (line 138) in order to discredit the widely held assumption that there is a strong connection between greenhouse gases and atmospheric warming.

---

45. **A**   The *system* in line 144 is that of *the planet's climate*, which is a complex scientific phenomenon.

---

46. **C**   The overall thesis of Passage 2 is that we do not know enough about the science of global warming to base environmental policy on it. According to the author, the common claims about the science of global warming are suspect. The author states that the *scientific community* (line 146) should acknowledge that *we know too little about a system as complicated as the planet's climate* (lines 143–145) and therefore should be cautious in making claims about it.

---

47. **B**   Both authors acknowledge that the Earth's surface temperature has increased over the last 100 years: the author of Passage 1 in lines 34–35 and the author of Passage 2 in lines 107–109. They also both acknowledge that the atmospheric concentration of greenhouse gases has been increasing: the author of Passage 1 in lines 25–27 and the author of Passage 2 in lines 112–113. The author of Passage 2, however, clearly disagrees with statement III.

---

48. **B**   The author of Passage 2 acknowedges (in lines 107–110) that the global surface temperature has warmed, but says that this fact is *inconsistent with the fact that satellite measurements over 35 years show no significant warming in the lower atmosphere, which is an essential part of the global-warming theory* (lines 115–119). Although the author of Passage 2 does criticize *political alarmism* (line 67) surrounding global warming, he does not suggest that this statement is an example of it.

Section 4

21. **C**

$$2a + 3b + c = 20$$

Subtract the equations: $-(3b + c) = -24$

$$2a = -4$$

Divide by 2: $a = -2$

(Chapter 9 Lesson 2: Systems)

---

22. **B**   Remember that multiplying a number by 10^{-n} is the same as dividing that number by 10^n, which is the same as moving the decimal point

of the number n places to the left. Therefore $0.00035 = 3.5 \times 10^{-4}$.
(Chapter 9 Lesson 3: Working with Exponents)

---

23. **A**   25% is the same as 1/4.

Distribute: $\dfrac{1}{4}\left(12x + \dfrac{1}{2}\right) = 3x + \dfrac{1}{8}$

(Chapter 8 Lesson 2: Laws of Arithmetic)
(Chapter 8 Lesson 3: Fractions)

---

24. **B**   One simple approach to this problem is to estimate the values of a and b and then multiply them. a is approximately -1.1 and b is approximately 0.6, so ab is approximately $(-1.1)(0.6) = -0.66$, which is between -1.0 and -0.5.
(Chapter 8 Lesson 1: Numbers and Operations)
(Chapter 8 Lesson 6: Negatives)

---

25. **E**   Consider any 4 consecutive positive even integers, like 2, 4, 6, and 8. Notice that, in this case, the largest number, k, is 8. The average, m, is $(2 + 4 + 6 + 8)/4 = 20/4 = 5$. The median of the set, n, is the average of the two middle numbers, which is $(4 + 6)/2 = 5$ also. Is this just a coincidence? No: you should know that the median of any set of "evenly spaced" numbers is always equal to the average. In this example, and with any other example you choose, all three statements are true.
(Chapter 10 Lesson 2: Mean/Median/Mode Problems)

---

26. **A**   There are two basic approaches to this problem: plugging in for x and simplification. To plug in, choose a simple value for x, like 1. Thus $2^{2x} \cdot 4^{3x} = 2^2 \cdot 4^3 = 4 \cdot 64 = 256$. Next, plug in $x = 1$ to the choices and eliminate all that are not equal to 256:

(A) $2^8 = 256$ Yes
(B) $2^{12} = 4096$ No
(C) $4^3 = 64$ No
(D) $8^5 = 32768$ No
(E) $8^6 = 262144$ No

So the correct answer is clearly (A).
Alternatively, if you are confident with using the rules of exponents, simplifying this expression is fairly simple. The key is to notice that 4 is a power of 2:

$$2^{2x} \cdot 4^{3x}$$

Write 4 as 2^2: $2^{2x} \cdot (2^2)^{3x}$
Simplify the second exponential: $2^{2x} \cdot 2^{6x}$
Simplify the product of the exponentials: 2^{8x}
(Chapter 9 Lesson 3: Working with Exponens)
(Chapter 9 Lesson 6: Inequalities, Absolute Values, and Plugging In)

27. **C**   The resulting box will have 6 faces: two 9×9 faces and four 9×4.5 faces. The total surface area, then, is $2(9 \times 9) + 4(9 \times 4.5) = 162 + 162 = 324$.
(Chapter 11 Lesson 7: Volumes and 3-D Geometry)

28. **A**   Since 6 is <u>not</u> a multiple of 4, $[6] = 4(6) = 24$. Therefore, $[[6]] = [24]$. Since 24 <u>is</u> a multiple of 4, $[24] = 24/2 = 12$. If you've gotten this far, be careful not to jump to choice (C) $\{12\}$, because $\{12\}$ does not equal 12, but rather $12/2 = 6$. The only choice that is equal to 12 is (A) $[3] = 4(3) = 12$.
(Chapter 10 Lesson 1: New Symbol or Term Problems)

29. **84**   First remember that a straight angle measures $180°$, so $54 + a + b = 180$. Since $a = 2b$,

$$54 + 2b + b = 180$$

Simplify: $54 + 3b = 180$
Subtract 54: $3b = 126$
Divide by 3: $b = 42$
Substitute to find a: $a = 2b = 2(42) = 84$

(Chapter 11 Lesson 1: Lines and Angles)

30. **7**   Recall that an arithmetic sequence is one in which the difference between consecutive terms is always the same. Since the third term, $m + 10$, is 10 greater than the first term, m, the difference beween consecutive terms must be 5. Since the middle term is 12, the terms must be 7, 12, 17. Notice that each term is 5 more than the previous one.
(Chapter 7 Reasoning Skill 3: Finding Patterns)

31. **8**   Recall that the average (arithmetic mean) of a set of numbers is its sum divided by the number of numbers. So the average of this set is

$$\frac{5 + 3p + 12 + 3r}{4}$$

Recall given equation: $p + r = 5$
Subtract r: $p = 5 - r$
Substitute $5 - r$ for p: $\dfrac{5 + 3(5 - r) + 12 + 3r}{4}$
Distribute multiplication: $\dfrac{5 + 15 - 3r + 12 + 3r}{4}$
Simplify numerator: $\dfrac{32}{4} = 8$

(Chapter 10 Lesson 2: Mean/Median/Mode Problems)

32. **36**   There are 10 integers that with a 3 in the tens place (30-39), and 10 more integers that with a 5 in the tens place (50-59). Every other "decade" of integers contains one integer that ends in a 3 and one that ends in a 5. There are 8 such decades, accounting for 16 more integers, for a total of $10 + 10 + 16 = 36$.
(Chapter 10 Lesson 5: Counting Problems)

33. **260**   Notice that this figure contains two triangles with angles that add up to $180°$.

First triangle: $50 + a + d = 180$
Second triangle: $50 + b + c = 180$
Add two equations: $100 + a + b + c + d = 360$
Subtract 100: $a + b + c + d = 260$

(Chapter 11 Lesson 2: Triangles)

34. **32**   The four integers must be 3, 5, 9 and 15. Since none of the integers is even, the four numbers must be chosen from the set 3, 5, 7, 9, 11, 13, 15, 17, and 19. Since exactly three of the numbers are multiples of 3, the set must include 3, 9 and 15, since these are the only multiples of 3 remaining. Since the set must contain exactly two multiples of 5, it must contain 5, the only multiple of 5 remaining that has not already been chosen. (We've already chosen 15, which is a multiple of 5). This gives a sum of $3 + 5 + 9 + 15 = 32$.

35. **65**   Call the original price (in dollars) x. With a discount of 20% and a tax of 6%, the final price will be $(.80)(1.06)x$. Set up an equation:

$$(.80)(1.06)x = 55.12$$

Simplify: $.848x = 55.12$
Divide by .848: $x = 65$

(Chapter 8 Lesson 5: Percents)
(Chapter 9 Lesson 7: Word Problems)

36. **3000**   The key is seeing that the two triangles in the diagram are similar. This means that the corresponding sides are proportional.

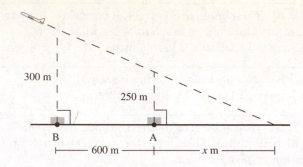

Set up the proportion: $\dfrac{x}{250} = \dfrac{x+600}{300}$

Cross-multiply: $300x = 250x + 150{,}000$

Subtract $250x$: $50x = 150{,}000$

Divide by 50: $x = 3{,}000$

(Chapter 11 Lesson 6: Similar Figures)

---

37. **3/2 or 1.5** Pump A works at a rate of 1/6 of a tank per hour, and pump B works at a rate of 1/2 of a tank per hour. Together, then, they work at a rate of $1/6 + 1/2 = 2/3$ of a tank per hour. This is equivalent to 3/2 of an *hour* per *tank*.
(Chapter 10 Lesson 4: Rate Problems)

---

38. **280** To maximize the number of students who do NOT take any of these sciences, you must minimize the number of students who DO take those sciences. The minimum possible number of students taking any of those sciences is 220, as this Venn diagram shows:

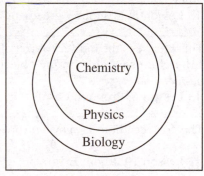

Entire Class

To minimize the number of science students, the sets of science students must be "nested" so that all the chemistry students also take physics, and all the physics students also take biology. This means that only 220 students in all take any kind of science, so there can be at most $500 - 220 = 280$ students who don't take any science class at all.
(Chapter 10 Lesson 5: Counting Problems)

Section 5

1. **C** In the original sentence, the participle *having received* is dangling because the noun that it modifies—*Mark Lemann* or *he*—does not immediately follow the comma. Since you cannot change the portion of the sentence that is not underlined, the only way to fix the problem is to incorporate the subject *he* into the opening phrase.
(Chapter 13 Lesson 7: Dangling and Misplaced Participles)

2. **D** The subject of the verb is *radiation*, which is singular, so the verb should be *is used*.
(Chapter 13 Lesson 1: Subject-Verb Disagreement)
(Chapter 13 Lesson 2: Trimming Sentences)

---

3. **A** The original sentence is correct, because it concisely shows the contrast between the two clauses. (Chapter 13 Lesson 15: Coordinating Ideas)

---

4. **B** The original sentence lacks parallel form and therefore reads very awkwardly. The two clauses have the same subject and so should both be in the active voice. Choice (B) accomplishes this most concisely.
(Chapter 13 Lesson 3: Parallelism)

---

5. **E** In the original sentence, the participle *used* dangles, and the usage of the pronoun *you* is unnecessary. Since *deficit spending* is what is *used*, it is what should follow the comma. (Chapter 13 Lesson 7: Dangling and Misplaced Modifiers)

---

6. **C** The original phrasing is redundant and hence needlessly wordy. Choice (C) provides the most concise phrasing without any loss of meaning.
(Chapter 13 Lesson 12: Other Problems with Modifiers)

---

7. **A** The original phrasing is the most concise and logical. Choices (B), (C), (D), and (E) suggest that the *irregularities* are ideal, rather than the *Salt Flats*.
(Chapter 13 Lesson 15: Coordinating Ideas)

---

8. **E** The participle *weighed down* modifies *David*, which must follow the comma.
(Chapter 13 Lesson 7: Dangling and Misplaced Participles)

---

9. **C** The underlined phrase must be parallel to the phrase *flooding the hold*. Choice (C) provides that parallelism by beginning with a gerund. Choice (E) provides this as well, but includes the absurdity of an *impossible possibility*.
(Chapter 13 Lesson 12: Other Problems with Modifiers).
(Chapter 13 Lesson 2: Trimming Sentences)

10. **B**   The participle *yearning* modifies *I*, which must follow the comma. Choice (E) does this, but contains a misplaced modifier, *by the forensics team*.
(Chapter 13 Lesson 1: Subject-Verb Disagreement)

11. **D**   The original phrase contains redundancies like *insufficient* and *not enough* as well as *required them as a necessity*. Choice (D) is the most concise of all the choices.
(Chapter 13 Lesson 12: Other Problems with Modifiers)

12. **A**   The original sentence is correct.

13. **E**   Since this sentence is about an ancient theory about diseases, it should not address the reader directly. The use of *you* and *your* is improper in the other choices.
(Chapter 13 Lesson 5: Pronoun Agreement)

14. **E**   Since the goal was reached before the benefactors could be thanked, the past perfect tense should be used with the past tense to show the proper sequence. Choice (E) is the only one that provides the proper sequencing.
(Chapter 13 Lesson 15: Coordinating Ideas)
(Chapter 13 Lesson 9: Tricky Tenses)

15. **C**   The contrast in this sentence is between what it is like *in some ostensibly democratic countries* and what it is like *in the United States*. Choice (C) is the only one that provides a logical and parallel contrast.
(Chapter 13 Lesson 4: Comparison Errors)

16. **C**   The sentence indicates two things that *Jeopardy! champions* need, the first being *a broad knowledge base*. The second item must be parallel in phrasing to the first, and so should be an impersonal common noun, as in (C).
(Chapter 13 Lesson 4: Comparison Errors)

17. **A**   The original sentence is correct.

18. **E**   The original sentence does not connect the clauses logically since there is a clear contrast between the ideas. Choice (E) provides the logical contrast.
(Chapter 13 Lesson 15: Coordinating Ideas)

19. **D**   The adjective *confident* modifies *the team*, so *the team* must follow the comma so that the modifier does not dangle. With choice (B), the adjective no longer dangles, but the pronouns *it* and *its* at the end have unclear antecedents.
(Chapter 13 Lesson 8: Other Misplaced Modifiers)
(Chapter 13 Lesson 5: Pronoun Agreement)

20. **A**   This sentence is correct. It completes the parallel structure *not so much as A but rather as B*.
(Chapter 13 Lesson 3: Parallelism)

21. **B**   The past tense of *sing* is *sang*.
(Chapter 13 Lesson 13: Irregular Verbs)

22. **B**   The subject of the verb *has been felt* is *effects*, which is plural. Therefore, the correct verb conjugation is *have been felt*.
(Chapter 13 Lesson 1: Subject-Verb Disagreement)
(Chapter 13 Lesson 2: Trimming Sentences)

23. **D**   The phrasing in choice (D) is not parallel with the previous phrasing. Since some are *demanding*, others are *insisting*.
(Chapter 13 Lesson 3: Parallelism)

24. **C**   The word *less* should only be used in a comparison of a quantity that is uncountable. Since *courses* are countable things, the word should be *fewer*
(Chapter 13 Lesson 4: Comparison Errors)

25. **D**   The correct idiom is *intend to vote*, not *intend on voting*.
(Chapter 13 Lesson 10: Idiom Errors)

26. **D**   This comparison is illogical. The comparison is to *this year's geography bee*, so the phrase should be *last year's bee*.
(Chapter 13 Lesson 4: Comparison Errors)

27. **C**   The antecedent is *students*, so the pronoun should be *they*.
(Chapter 13 Lesson 5: Pronoun Agreement)

28. **D**   This phrase is the indirect object of the verb *posed* and therefore should be in the objective case, *Denitra and me*.
(Chapter 13 Lesson 6: Pronoun Case)

29. **C**   The correct idiom is *agree on* (or *upon*) *the verdict*.
(Chapter 13 Lesson 10: Idiom Errors)

30. **A**   The antecedent of the pronoun is *dolphins*, so it should be the plural pronoun *their*.

31. **A**   As it is worded, the participle *expecting* dangles, because the noun it modifies does not follow the participial phrase. To correct this, the subject should be incorporated into the phrase: *If you are expecting*.
(Chapter 13 Lesson 7: Dangling and Misplaced Participles)

32. **E**   The sentence is correct.

33. **D**   In the phrase *not only A but also B*, the phrases *A* and *B* must be parallel. In order for this phrase to be completed in a parallel way, the phrase in (D) must be eliminated.
(Chapter 13 Lesson 3: Parallelism)

34. **A**   The correct idiom is *critics of*.
(Chapter 13 Lesson 10: Idiom Errors)

35. **E**   The subject of the verb is the plural noun *people*, so the verb form is *live*.
(Chapter 13 Lesson 1: Subject-Verb Disagreement)

36. **B**   Choice (B) is the only one that coordinates the two clauses logically.
(Chapter 13 Lesson 15: Coordinating Ideas)

37. **C**   In a paragraph about the running habits of the Tarahumara, sentence 7, about its beer-based economy, is out of place.
(Chapter 13 Lesson 15: Coordinating Ideas)

38. **C**   Since the previous sentences described the primitive nature of the Tarahumara's training and equipment, the statement that they are *among the best ultramarathoners in the world* is surprising. Therefore, this sentence should begin with a contrasting transition, as in choice (C).
(Chapter 13 Lesson 15: Coordinating Ideas)

39. **A**   The two clauses should be coordinated to contrast each other, as in choice (A). Choice (B) indicates an illogical cause and effect. Choice (C) contains a dangling participle. Choices (D) and (E) are awkward, and in both cases, the pronoun *they* has an ambiguous antecedent.
(Chapter 13 Lesson 15: Coordinating Ideas)

CHAPTER 4

HOW TO BUILD AN IMPRESSIVE VOCABULARY

1. Building an Impressive Vocabulary

2. Vocabulary Lessons 1–49

I BUILDING AN IMPRESSIVE VOCABULARY

Vocabulary building is one of the big challenges of preparing to take the PSAT. Building a vocabulary for college success requires discipline. Like all tough problems, it's best attacked by focusing on the eight reasoning skills: MAPS-CATCH.

Map the Problem: Build understanding; don't just memorize meanings

If you want to build a useful vocabulary, your goal should not be just to memorize the meanings of words. By only memorizing meanings, you are ensuring that your studies will be not only unsuccessful but very, very dull.

If you are a typical 16-year-old, then you have a 30,000- to 50,000-word vocabulary. How many of these words did you memorize with flashcards? How many did you look up in a dictionary? How many did you learn by using a memory trick? Only a tiny portion.

So how did you learn all those words so effortlessly? By using your mind's innate language-building system. This system is an "organ" very much as our hearts or kidneys are organs. In order to build a strong vocabulary, we have to keep that language-building system healthy with the right kinds of experiences and exercises.

Your mind's language-building system does not respond well to mere repetition of words and their meanings. **Don't try to build vocabulary simply by rote study of word meanings.** Infants don't learn the meaning of words merely by having them repeated over and over. Rather, they learn words by trying to understand and communicate with others. If the words are separated from real everyday communication, our mind's language-building system doesn't work very well.

So what do our minds need to build a great vocabulary?

- **A vocabulary-rich environment.** When you were a baby, you were surrounded by people with much stronger vocabularies than yours. This is why your vocabulary grew so rapidly when you were very young. As you have gotten older, however, you have probably surrounded yourself with people whose vocabularies are more on par with your own. So how do you improve your vocabulary? First, talk with smart people and read books with challenging vocabulary. Watch college-level documentaries on television rather than mindless entertainment. Listen to National Public Radio. Read the *New York Times* Op-Ed page and magazine. Read articles and stories from *Harper's*, The *Atlantic Monthly*, The *New Yorker*, The *Nation*, and *Scientific American*.

- **A willingness to use new vocabulary.** As we grow older, most of us become more and more self-conscious about our speech. We don't like to use words that our friends don't use, or to misuse words in front of our friends for fear of sounding stupid. This reluctance can hinder the growth of your vocabulary. **Find a friend or relative with whom you can practice your new vocabulary—perhaps someone who is also training for the SAT I.** Don't merely ask her or him to quiz you on meanings: talk about how to use and pronounce the words, about situations in which they are helpful, about related words, about their roots, and about creative ways to remember them.

- **A willingness to think about words as you read and speak.** Think about their roots, their origins, their synonyms, their antonyms, and their cognates (words that share a common root). Even when you are not *specifically* practicing your vocabulary, you can reinforce your new vocabulary by looking at everyday words in new ways.

Analyze: Break words apart

Analyzing means breaking a problem into its parts. Many words can be broken apart into **roots** and **affixes**. If you can recognize the parts of a new word, you can make good guesses about its meaning, part of speech, and usage. Consider the word *magnanimity*. This word has three parts: *magna-anima-ity*, which can help you to determine its meaning, part of speech, and usage. Its meaning derives from the roots *magna*, which means *great*, and *anima*, which means *spirit*. We can determine its part of speech from its suffix, *ity*, which is a *noun* suffix. We also can determine its usage because *ity* indicates a *quality*. Thus, a good guess is that *magnanimity* is *the quality of having a great spirit*.

Learning word roots and affixes is an important part of building an impressive vocabulary. But again, mere memorization is not enough: you must practice by analyzing the roots of the words you encounter every day. As you study the Vocabulary Lessons that follow, pay close attention to the roots and affixes that are indicated after many of the words, and think about the family of words that share each root or affix.

Find Patterns: Learn how words relate in sentences, forms, and cognates

A pattern is a rule that helps you to predict or understand another item in a sequence. Many patterns relate words to each other. One obvious pattern of words is a sentence or a phrase, in which the context gives you clues about the meanings of the individual words. Less obvious patterns of words are *form patterns* and *cognate patterns*. Let's use *magnanimity* as an example again. It can be part of a pattern of words in a sentence like:

> *The college is filled with examples of the magnanimity of its early founders.*

Here the sentence gives you important clues about the meaning of the word *magnanimity:* it is something that college founders can be considered to have, it is something whose effects can be seen in future generations, etc.

It can also be part of a **pattern of word forms** that derive from the same basic word:

> *magnanimous* (generous), *ultramagnanimous* (super-generous), *pseudomagnanimity* (fake generosity)

It can also be part of a **cognate pattern** of words that derive from a common root:

> *pusillanimous* (cowardly), *equanimity* (even temper), *unanimous* (of one mind)

The more we recognize how a word relates to others through usage rules, word-form rules, and cognate rules, the better we understand the word.

Simplify: Make word groups

Your brain doesn't store vocabulary words in the same way that a computer hard drive stores information, by making exact copies of "inputs." Your mind does not just record information, it processes it. To learn words efficiently, study **related groups of words**.

You can group words together as cognates, related forms, or words with similar or opposite meanings.

The Vocabulary Lessons that follow allow you to group words in many ways: into theme groups (like "words that relate to talking"), into **synonym groups**, into **antonym pairs**, and into **cognate groups** (words with a common root). When you think of words in groups, learning them is easier.

Connect to Knowledge: Connect new vocabulary to your own experiences

You don't really know a word until you are deeply familiar with the concept it represents. Don't treat word meanings as isolated facts to memorize. Rather, when you discover the meaning of a new word, think about how you could use that word right now. For instance, to learn the word *magnanimous*, you should ask: what people in my life are *magnanimous?* Who is the most *magnanimous* character I've read about in literature or seen in a movie? Do I want to be more *magnanimous*, and if so, what kinds of things would I do to become more *magnanimous?* The more you think about these questions, the more you build your understanding of *magnanimity*.

You learn words by communicating about the concepts that the words represent. Since communication is a very personal activity, learning new vocabulary should be a personal thing too. Think about how the concept behind a new word applies to your life and the people around you.

Find Alternatives I: Use College Hill's ALIVE System for tough words

When trying to learn an obscure word, like *polemic*, College Hill's ALIVE visual mnemonic system is a great tool. Visualization is perhaps the most effective mnemonic strategy for learning difficult information quickly. Here's how it works:

1. Break down the sounds of the word, and turn them into a picture. For example, break down *polemic* into *pole* and *lemon*, and imagine a lemon on the end of a pole. (You might break it down differently. That's okay!)

2. Imagine a picture for the meaning of the word. *Polemic* means an unpopular or controversial intellectual position or argument, so you might imagine someone with a crazy philosophy—a hippie, perhaps—arguing with a senator at a

debate. Try to picture someone you actually know, if possible. Get a vivid picture in your mind.

3.   Put the two pictures together into one: see the hippie hitting the senator with a pole with a lemon on the end. The crazier the picture, the better!

4.   Make your image come ALIVE. As you imagine your picture, check that it is:

Active: Make the picture move, like a wacky animated cartoon.

Linking: Be sure that one picture links both images: the image for the sound and the image for the meaning.

Illogical: Don't try to make a "sensible" picture. Instead, make it unique and bizarre.

Vivid: See the picture in 3-D, in vivid color, and in **rich detail**. Work at painting a picture in your mind.

Exaggerated: The image that represents the meaning of the word should "pop out" of your picture. Make that part bigger than the rest, even if it makes the picture crazier.

Find Alternatives II: Consider secondary meanings of words

Many words have more than one meaning. In *Webster's Collegiate*, for instance, the word *jack* has 23 meanings! **Don't always assume you understand a particular usage of a word just because you happen to know *one* meaning of the word.** Pay careful attention to how words are used, and realize that any word might mean something different than you assume!

The SAT I frequently tests your understanding of "secondary" meanings of words, particularly in "word-in-context" questions on the Critical Reading section, in which the test asks things like, *In context, the word "apprehension" most nearly means…* In these questions, the word has many possible meanings, and you must use the clues in the passage to determine which one is being used.

Think Logically: Practice drawing inferences about meaning from sentences

Imagine hearing some new words in a sentence like:

Heather said that Newton's laws are pedestrian and obvious, but I find them inscrutable.

Perhaps you don't know what *pedestrian* and *inscrutable* mean, but the logical structure of the sentence allows you to make some educated guesses. For

instance, since Heather said that Newton's laws are *obvious*, she finds them easy to understand. Since she also finds them *pedestrian*, then *pedestrian* cannot mean *hard to understand*. Furthermore, the word *but* signals a contrast between statements, so it is likely that *inscrutable* does mean something like *hard to understand*. Also, *pedestrian* and *inscrutable* must both be adjectives that can describe ideas.

It is this kind of logical work that our minds use to grasp the meanings of words when we hear or read them. To understand the function of a gear in a machine, we have to see and tinker with its connections to other parts of the machine, guided by the laws of physics. Likewise, to understand a word, we need to see and tinker with its connections to other parts of a sentence, guided by the laws of logic.

When you come across a new word in your reading, write it down in a notebook, and try to make a logical guess about its meaning. Then look it up to see if you're right.

Check: Test yourself continually as you speak and write

Education is what changes the way you think. Developing a good vocabulary means thinking carefully about your words as you use them. If you are truly to improve your verbal skills, *to educate yourself in language*, then you must practice by continually thinking about words in the ways we've discussed.

Check your understanding of the words you are learning by using them carefully as often as you can and by checking the way other people use the words. Make this practice more than just "test prep." Change the way you look at words. See them analytically, see their patterns, learn their histories, consider their alternatives, and see how they are used. As you gain more control over your vocabulary this way, you will become a more articulate, persuasive, and confident speaker and writer.

The College Hill Word Study System

Building vocabulary requires good practice. The College Hill Word Study System allows you to build your vocabulary through mindful, creative practice.

Each week, carefully study three to seven of the Vocabulary Lessons in this chapter, and from those words, make 30–40 flashcards for those words you

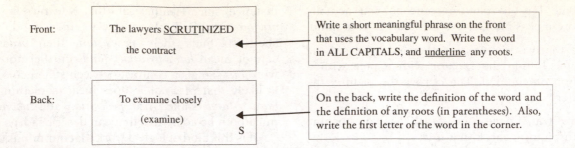

Front: The lawyers SCRUTINIZED   Write a short meaningful phrase on the front
          the contract   that uses the vocabulary word. Write the word
                                             in ALL CAPITALS, and underline any roots.

Back: To examine closely   On the back, write the definition of the word and
          (examine)   the definition of any roots (in parentheses). Also,
                                   S   write the first letter of the word in the corner.

need to study in depth. Your flashcards should look something like the example above.

After you've made a card for a word in the lesson, check off that word from the list.

You may also make cards for words you find in the lessons and worksheets in this book or in your practice SAT I tests. When you do this, you should look up the words and their roots in a good collegiate dictionary, like *Webster's Collegiate*. The roots can be found in the etymology of the word (the abbreviated history of the word), which usually appears in angle brackets just before the definition.

Study your cards **daily** for at least 10 minutes. Schedule this time with the rest of your homework. Review with a friend or relative whenever possible, using the following study techniques:

Study Method 1:   Have your friend read the word, and you create a new and meaningful sentence with it.

Study Method 2:   Have your friend read the word, and you give its roots and, for each root, give as many other words as you can that share the root.

Study Method 3:   Have your friend read the definition and the first letter, and you give the word.

Study Method 4:   Discuss appropriate uses of the word with your friend, and teach your friend how to apply the word in his or her own life.

Study Method 5:   Teach your friend any clever mnemonics you have created for your words using ALIVE.

Study Method 6:   Have your friend read the sentence, and you give the definition.

Study Method 7:   Post a bunch of flashcards around your room where you'll see them every day! Think of creatively appropriate places to post them, like *narcissist* on the mirror, *lethargic* on the bed, and so on.

Study Method 8:   Review your flashcards once before you go to sleep, as your brain will continue to work on them while you are sleeping.

After you finish a Vocabulary Unit (which consists of sixteen lessons), **complete the Exercise Sets** at the end of each unit, and check your work with the answer key. These activities provide a great way of reviewing and reinforcing your word knowledge.

When you are reading, for school or for pleasure, **write down any new vocabulary words** in a small notebook, and keep your dictionary handy. Guess the meanings of new words from their context; then check your guesses with the dictionary. **If it is a good SAT word, make a flashcard for it**. Also, read at a desk rather than on a couch or bed; your brain works better when you are sitting upright than when you are lying down.

Vocabulary Lessons 1-49

Vocabulary Lesson 1: Get to the Point!

Today's roots:	co-, con-	together, with	brev	brief
	cis	cut		

❏ **concise** (adj)   brief and to the point (*con-* altogether+*cis* cut) (***succinct, terse***)

Ricky, try to be a bit more **concise** in this paper; the assignment was for a three-page paper; yours was 106.

❏ **laconic** (adj)   disposed to using few words (***taciturn, reticent***)

I've known Lucy for 10 years, but she's so **laconic** that I hardly know anything about her past.

❏ **succinct** (adj)   spoken or written in a clear and precise manner (***concise, terse***)

Because commercial time during the Super Bowl runs over $3 million per minute, it's good to be **succinct**.

❏ **brusque** (adj)   rudely abrupt (***curt, abrupt***)

My girlfriend tends to be **brusque** when she's mad; she just tells me to "talk to the hand."

❏ **abridge** (v)   to shorten a written text (***abbreviate, curtail, prune, synopsize***)

The dictionary was 1,400 pages long before it was **abridged** by the publishers to 850 pages.

❏ **brevity** (n)   quality of succinct expression (*brev* brief + *ity* quality of) (***conciseness, pithiness, succinctness***)

Speeches at the Academy Awards are not known for their **brevity**; they often go on long past their allotted time.

Vocabulary Lesson 2: Think Before You Judge

Today's roots:	jud	judge	per	through, thoroughly
	jur	oath, law	scrut	to examine

❏ **judicious** (adj)   showing sound judgment; prudent (*jud* judge + *-ious* full of) (***wise, sagacious, prudent***)

After much thought, I decided that the most **judicious** thing to do was to avoid the swamp full of alligators.

❏ **adjudicate** (v)   to hear and judge a case (*jud* judge + *-ate* to do) (***judge, arbitrate***)

Sometimes when my two children fight, I feel like I'm **adjudicating** a capital crime rather than settling a quarrel.

❏ **astute** (adj)   shrewd; keen (***incisive, shrewd, canny, perspicacious***)

The young Sherlock Holmes was quite the **astute** investigator; he always unraveled even the toughest mystery.

❏ **scrutinize** (v)   to examine carefully (*scruta* examine + *-ize* to do) (***analyze, peruse, probe, inspect***)

Before buying an apple, **scrutinize** it to be sure that it has no bruises.

❏ **perjure** (v)   to lie under oath (*per-* through + *jur* oath)

The mobster told blatant lies while on the stand, **perjuring** to keep his partners out of jail.

❏ **prudent** (adj)   using good judgment (*prudentia* knowledge) (***judicious, sensible, politic, shrewd***)

It would not be **prudent** to sneak out of your room again tonight; your parents will ground you if they catch you!

Vocabulary Lesson 3: Let's Talk about It

Today's roots:	locu, loqu	talk	circum	around
	verb	word	e-, ex-	out

❏ **eloquent** (adj)   well spoken (*e-* out + *loqu* talk) (**articulate, expressive, fluent**)

She is an **eloquent** spokeswoman for animal rights; she conveys her ideas with great ease and fluidity.

❏ **loquacious** (adj)   very talkative (*loqu* talk + *-ious* full of) (**garrulous, voluble, expansive**)

That guy never stops talking; now I understand why they call him "**Loquacious** Larry!"

❏ **circumlocution** (n)   evasive speech; talking around the subject (*circum* around + *loqu* talk) (**evasion**)

The politician had perfected the art of **circumlocution**; he knew exactly how to avoid answering direct questions.

❏ **colloquial** (adj)   conversational; using everyday language (*co-* together + *loqu* talk)

I like Professor Thompson because she is so **colloquial**; yesterday she said my thesis idea was "really cool."

❏ **grandiloquent** (adj)   speaking in a pompous manner (*grand* great + *loqu* talk + *-ent* adjective) (**florid**)

His speech was pompous and **grandiloquent**; it seemed he was just trying to use as many big words as possible.

❏ **elocution** (n)   expressive delivery of public speech (*e-* out + *loqu* talk + *-tion* noun) (**enunciation**)

James is quite the **elocutionist**; his expressions and mannerisms add a new level of meaning to his words.

Vocabulary Lesson 4: "Good, Thanks."

Today's roots:	ben, bene	bon good	eu	good
	fact	to make	vole	wish

❏ **benefactor** (n)   one who supports or helps another (*bene* good + *fact* to make) (**philanthropist**)

Mr. King is the **benefactor** who generously donated the money for the new children's wing in the hospital.

❏ **benign** (adj)   harmless (*bene* good) (**innocuous, kindly**)

She was relieved to find out that her tumor was **benign**.

❏ **benevolent** (adj)   kind; considerate (*bene* good + *vole* wish) (**altruistic, munificent, gracious**)

The **benevolent** Cub Scout did his good deed for the day when he helped a motorist change a tire.

❏ **benediction** (n)   an expression of good wishes (*bene* good + *dictus* declaration) (**blessing**)

At the reception, the father of the bride offered a **benediction**, wishing the couple never-ending love and happiness.

❏ **euphemism** (n)   the substitution of an inoffensive term for an offensive one (*eu-* good + *pheme* speech)

A good journalist avoids the **euphemisms** of war, like "ordnance" for bombs and "collateral damage" for casualties.

❏ **eulogy** (n)   a praising tribute (*eu-* good + *logia* discourse) (**accolade, panegyric**)

His touching **eulogy** for his fallen friend left all the mourners weeping.

Vocabulary Lesson 5: Changes

Today's roots:	*rupt*	break	*morph form,*	shape
	mut	change	*meta*	change, beyond

❏ *immutable* (adj)   unchangeable (*im-* not + *mut* change) (***inveterate, steadfast, static***)

Emily is an **immutable** vegetarian. No matter how hard we try, we cannot get her to eat meat.

❏ *metamorphosis* (n)   a transformation (*meta-* change + *morph* form) (***transformation, transmutation***)

The old house underwent a **metamorphosis** from a rundown shack into a beautiful cottage.

❏ *rupture* (v)   to break open (*rupt* break) (***breach, fracture***)

When the vat of smelly liquid **ruptured**, we picked up our feet to avoid getting the stuff on our shoes.

❏ *transmute* (v)   to transform (*trans-* across + *mut* change) (***transform, metamorphose***)

Harry Potter was able to **transmute** a feather into a frog using a spell he learned in incantations class.

❏ *amorphous* (adj)   lacking shape, changeable in form (*a-* without + *morph* shape) (***nebulous, shapeless***)

Rather than marching in precise formation, the battalion broke down into an **amorphous** mass of charging soldiers.

❏ *mercurial* (adj)   erratic, subject to wild changes in character (from the speedy god Mercury) (***volatile***)

Molly is the most **mercurial** person in the office; we can never tell if she'll be the evil Molly or the sympathetic Molly.

Vocabulary Lesson 6: One Boring World

Today's roots:	*vac*	empty	*sapere*	taste
	mund	world		

❏ *hackneyed* (adj)   overused, trite (***clichéd, overused, vapid, banal***)

This film was a **hackneyed** remake with a story line that had been done a hundred times.

❏ *mundane* (adj)   ordinary, typical (*mund* world) (***monotonous, workaday, routine***)

Having worked for years behind a desk, she wanted to leave the **mundane** world behind for exotic adventures.

❏ *vacuous* (adj)   lacking substance (*vac* empty) (***inane, insipid, fatuous***)

His latest book is widely criticized as **vacuous** and unintelligent.

❏ *prosaic* (adj)   unimaginative, ordinary (***conventional, run-of-the-mill, trite***)

I don't understand why his oration was selected as the best; it was so **prosaic** that I nearly fell asleep.

❏ *insipid* (adj)   uninteresting, dull, without flavor (*in-* not + *sapere* taste) (***uninspired, inane, pedestrian***)

Christine is the life of the party, but Tom is as **insipid** as they come; hardly anyone wants to talk with him.

❏ *banal* (adj)   ordinary, trivial (***pedestrian, lackluster***)

That show used to be my favorite, but its story lines became so **banal** that I could no longer stand it.

Vocabulary Lesson 7: The Humours

Today's roots:	*sanguis*	blood	*melan*	black
	choler	bile	*re*	back

❑ **sanguine** (adj)   cheerfully optimistic (*sanguis* blood) (***optimistic, buoyant, bullish***)

After acing his final, David was **sanguine** about his prospects for a good overall course grade.

❑ **phlegmatic** (adj)   emotionally calm, sluggish (***impassive, stolid, imperturbable***)

His prolonged illness turned Julio from a spry, happy bon vivant to a morose and **phlegmatic** bore.

❑ **melancholy** (adj)   sad, depressed (*melan* black + *choler* bile) (***lugubrious, mournful, despondent***)

She has been so **melancholy** ever since she broke up with her boyfriend; sometimes she stays in her room all day.

❑ **choleric** (adj)   easily angered (*choler* bile + *-ic* characterized by) (***irascible, irritable, fractious***)

Gena's mom is really nice, but her dad is **choleric**; he freaks out about the smallest things.

❑ **recalcitrant** (adj)   stubbornly resistant to authority (*re-* back + *calcitrare* kick) (***obstinate, intractable***)

Christine is a talented volleyball player, but she's so **recalcitrant** that our coach often keeps her on the bench.

❑ **lethargic** (adj)   sluggish; dully apathetic (***indolent, languid, listless, torpid***)

After three weeks of factoring polynomials, my entire class became **lethargic**; we were bored to death!

Vocabulary Lesson 8: Sneaky Sneaky

Today's roots:	*sub*	secretly	*rapere*	seize
	strategos	army general		

❑ **spurious** (adj)   fake; counterfeit (***fraudulent, specious***)

The head of the FBI cursed the **spurious** lead that incorrectly led the investigators to an abandoned warehouse.

❑ **guile** (n)   trickery; deceit (***cunning, craftiness, artfulness***)

The Big Bad Wolf deceived Little Red Riding Hood with **guile** and cunning.

❑ **beguile** (v)   to deceive with charm (***enchant, charm, seduce, mesmerize***)

The con artist **beguiled** me out of my money, convincing me to play his game over and over.

❑ **strategem** (n)   a deceitful scheme (*strategos* army general) (***machination, ruse, subterfuge***)

The teenager devised an elaborate **strategem** to escape his parents' curfew.

❑ **surreptitious** (adj)   deceptive; sneaky (*sub* secretly + *rapere* seize) (***clandestine, furtive***)

The **surreptitious** lion was able to trick the gazelle into running directly at the other lions.

❑ **clandestine** (adj)   secret; hidden (***furtive, backstairs***)

The **clandestine** military facility in the capital city was unknown even to the President of the United States.

❑ **stealth** (n)   sneakiness; ability to avoid detection (***secretiveness, slyness***)

The "**stealth** bomber" is so effective because it is undetectable by most radars.

Vocabulary Lesson 9: Time Is of the Essence

Today's roots:	trans	across, through	vanecere	to disappear
	chronos	time	tempus	time

❑ *transient* (adj)   fleeting; short-lived (*transire* to go across) (**impermanent, short-lived, fleeting**)

We never understand the **transient** nature of childhood until we wake up one day and realize we're all grown up.

❑ *ephemeral* (adj)   short-lived (*hemera* day) (**transitory, transient**)

Critics wrote off the band as a fad, their success an **ephemeral** phenomenon.

❑ *sporadic* (adj)   irregular or unpredictable; infrequent (*sporas* scattered) (**occasional, intermittent**)

He has experienced **sporadic** success as an actor, with occasional big roles amid many unmemorable parts.

❑ *capricious* (adj)   whimsical; impulsive (**fickle, mercurial, whimsical**)

My English teacher runs her class **capriciously**, flitting from idea to idea with no reason or direction.

❑ *evanescent* (adj)   likely to vanish (*vanescere* to disappear) (**vanishing, fugitive, ephemeral**)

The aurora borealis is beautiful but **evanescent**, a curtain of cascading light that can disappear in a heartbeat.

❑ *extemporaneous* (adj)   done with little or no practice (*ex tempore* of time) (**spontaneous, improvised**)

The speech was all the more remarkable because Dr. Sherman gave it **extemporaneously**.

❑ *anachronism* (n)   something out of place in time (*ana-* backward + *chronos* time) (**archaism, antiquity**)

Her old-fashioned perspective on motherhood makes her an **anachronism** among her friends.

Vocabulary Lesson 10: If You Can't Say Anything Nice . . .

Today's roots:	de	down	dia	through, thoroughly
	monere	to warn		

❑ *censure* (n)   official condemnation; harsh criticism (**rebuke, reprimand, admonishment**)

Congress voted to declare **censure** on the representative who took money and gifts from a lobbyist.

❑ *diatribe* (n)   malicious criticism or abuse (*dia-* thoroughly + *tribein* to rub) (**tirade, harangue, polemic**)

A good debate must avoid vicious personal **diatribe** and focus on a respectful discussion of issues.

❑ *caustic* (adj)   corrosive; sarcastic (**abrasive, sardonic, scathing, mordant**)

James immediately regretted making such a **caustic** remark; he could tell his words truly hurt Vanessa.

❑ *derogatory* (adj)   disparaging; belittling (*de-* down, away) (**deprecatory, pejorative, libelous**)

Derogatory remarks are not allowed in class; discussions should criticize ideas, not people.

❑ *admonish* (v)   to reprimand mildly (*ad-* to + *monere* to warn) (**reprimand, scold, reprove, chide**)

The boy was **admonished** by his mom for spilling his soda on the brand-new rug.

❑ *repudiate* (v)   to cast off publicly (*repudium* divorce) (**renounce, disown, revoke**)

The newspaper **repudiated** the reporter's comments and retracted the story.

Vocabulary Lesson 11: Holy Cow

Today's roots:	*sacer*	sacred	*de*	down
	sanctus	holy	*vereri*	respect

❑ **sanctimonious** (adj)   falsely pious or self-righteous (*sanctus* holy) (**self-righteous, preachy**)

> I prefer ministers who are real people, not **sanctimonious** know-it-all preachers.

❑ **sacrosanct** (adj)   profoundly sacred (*sacer* sacred + *sanctus* holy) (**hallowed, inviolable**)

> To Hindus, the cow is a **sacrosanct** creature to be treated with the utmost respect.

❑ **sanctuary** (n)   a place of refuge; a sacred place (*sanctus* holy) (**haven, refuge**)

> The Notre Dame cathedral is a **sanctuary** to all; anyone in need of a safe place to rest is welcome.

❑ **sacrilegious** (adj)   grossly irreverent; disrespectful of something sacred (*sacer* sacred) (**profane**)

> To Hindus, to whom cows are sacred, the mass slaughter of cattle is considered **sacrilegious**.

❑ **revere** (v)   to regard with honor and devotion (*re-* intensive + *vereri* respect) (**esteem, lionize**)

> Every genre of music has its stars, whom fans **revere** like gods.

❑ **pious** (adj)   showing religious reverence (Latin *pious* devout) (**sanctimonious, religious**)

> Cotton Mather considered it his **pious** duty to hang anyone in Salem accused of witchcraft.

❑ **deference** (n)   respect for the wishes of others (*de-* away, down + *ferre* carry, bring) (**submissiveness**)

> It is important to show **deference** to your elders and treat them with respect.

Vocabulary Lesson 12: Power It Up

Today's roots:	*potens*	strong	*in-, im-*	not
	domit	lord	*via*	way

❑ **formidable** (adj)   awesome; hard to overcome; dreadful (*formido* fear) (**redoubtable, daunting**)

> The Yankees are a **formidable** team; we'll be lucky to win a single game against them this year.

❑ **potent** (adj)   strong and effective (*potens* strong) (**powerful, efficacious**)

> Although the drug is clearly the most **potent** treatment for depression, it also has the strongest side effects.

❑ **indomitable** (adj)   unable to be conquered (*in-* not + *domit* lord) (**invincible, unassailable**)

> The **indomitable** castle has been under the control of the Spaniards for 6,000 years, despite repeated attacks.

❑ **redoubtable** (adj)   arousing fear; formidable; awesome (*re-* intensive + *douter, dubitare* to doubt)

> The mob boss is a **redoubtable** figure who makes his enemies cower in fear.

❑ **robust** (adj)   full of vigor (**resilient, powerful**)

> The **robust** young men were able to run miles at a time through the rugged terrain without breaking a sweat.

❑ **impervious** (adj)   incapable of being penetrated or affected (*im-* not + *per* through + *via* road)

> Bulletproof vests are almost always **impervious** to bullets.

Vocabulary Lesson 13: Come Together

Today's roots:	co-, com-, con-	together	vocare	to call
	syn	same, together	legere	choose

❑ *coalesce* (v)   to blend or fuse together (*co-* together + *alere* to nourish) (**consolidate, amalgamate**)

Raindrops are usually formed when water vapor and microscopic particles in the atmosphere **coalesce**.

❑ *anthology* (n)   a collection of works (*anthos* flower + *legion* together) (**compendium, treasury**)

The *Beatles* **Anthology** is one of the best-selling greatest-hit albums of all time.

❑ *convoke* (v)   to call together (*con-* together + *vocare* call) (**summon, convene**)

The village elders **convoked** the citizens to discuss the sale of the ceremonial land.

❑ *synchronize* (v)   to arrange events to occur simultaneously (*syn-* same, together + *chronos* time) (**coordinate**)

Nothing is harder for a dance teacher than trying to **synchronize** 10 eight-year-old ballerinas.

❑ *synthesis* (n)   a fusion; a bringing together (*syn-* together + *tithenai* to put) (**fusion, amalgam**)

The **synthesis** of DNA occurs when many ribonucleic acids are joined together into one long double helix.

❑ *eclectic* (adj)   made up of parts from many different sources (*ec-* out + *legere* to choose) (**diverse**)

Rob Mathes's **eclectic** compositions reveal a subtle yet effective blend of blues, gospel, classical, and jazz styles.

❑ *yoke* (v)   to join different things (**harness, hitch, tether**)

Politicians often **yoke** unpopular legislation to popular bills so that they can sneak them through Congress.

Vocabulary Lesson 14: Cruel and Unusual

Today's roots:	homos	same	idios	peculiar
	super-	above, beyond	-less	without

❑ *ruthless* (adj)   cruel; merciless (*rue* regret + *-less* without) (**callous, sadistic, merciless**)

Torquemada is widely regarded as the most **ruthless** interrogator of the Spanish Inquisition.

❑ *contempt* (n)   scorn; disrespect (*temnere* to despise) (**scorn, disdain**)

Many eminent and successful scientists often show **contempt** for novel theories that question their own.

❑ *callous* (adj)   hardened; insensitive (*callum* hard skin) (**heartless, ruthless**)

Since they see so much suffering daily, emergency room doctors often struggle to avoid becoming **callous**.

❑ *supercilious* (adj)   full of haughty arrogance (*super* above + *cilium* brow) (**condescending, patronizing**)

Although he seems **supercilious** when you first meet him, Joe is actually a modest and down-to-earth guy.

❑ *idiosyncrasy* (n)   a peculiar trait or habit (*idio* peculiar) (**eccentricity, peculiarity, quirk**)

My history teacher has the **idiosyncrasy** of always squinting just before she asks a question of the class.

❑ *anomaly* (n)   unusual event (*an-* not + *homos* same) (**incongruity, aberration**)

The 90-degree day in Siberia was an **anomaly**; the temperature had only gone that high once before.

Vocabulary Lesson 15: Weak and Weaker

Today's roots:	batre	to beat	troph	nourishment
	ad	to	lassus	weary

❏ **atrophy** (v)   to weaken from disuse (*a-* without + *troph* nourishment) (**wither, deteriorate**)

After surgery, extended bed rest often causes muscles to **atrophy** unless it is accompanied by physical therapy.

❏ **abate** (v)   to subside; to decrease in intensity (*ad-* to + *batre* to beat) (**subside, ebb**)

The crews had to wait until the storm **abated** before they could begin to assess the damage to the coastal town.

❏ **porous** (adj)   filled with many holes (*porus* opening) (**pervious, permeable**)

The teenager's story was a **porous** one that her parents could easily see through.

❏ **wane** (v)   to grow smaller or less intense (**diminish, flag**)

As the size of the moon **wanes** over the next few nights, it will get harder to see when it is dark.

❏ **lassitude** (n)   a feeling of weakness (*lassus* weary) (**languor, lethargy, torpor**)

Although she tried valiantly to play through her illness, Danielle's **lassitude** overtook her in the second half.

❏ **undermine** (v)   to weaken or diminish something (**subvert, compromise**)

The continual setbacks to the project over many weeks **undermined** the morale of the workers.

Vocabulary Lesson 16: Chillin'

Today's roots:	status	position, standing	quies	rest
	plac	to please	serenus	calm

❏ **placid** (adj)   calm (*plac* to please) (**tranquil, unflappable**)

A relaxing day at the spa always makes me feel more **placid**.

❏ **inert** (adj)   sluggish; inactive (*in-* not + *ertem* active) (**dormant, indolent**)

After his final exams, Ricky sat **inert** on his couch for two days watching soap operas and game shows.

❏ **listless** (adj)   sluggish; without energy (*-less* without) (**enervated, lethargic, languid**)

I always feel **listless** on rainy days; sometimes I don't even want to get out of bed.

❏ **quiescent** (adj)   resting; quiet (*quies* rest) (**idle, passive**)

During the **quiescent** phase of cell division, the cell does not split or grow.

❏ **serene** (adj)   tranquil; calm; placid (*serenus* peaceful, calm) (**placid, equable, tranquil**)

There was not a single wave on the surface of the **serene** lake.

❏ **static** (adj)   stationary (*status* standing) (**immobile, constant**)

The patient's vitals have been **static** for an hour. We hope this means he can be moved from intensive care.

❏ **languid** (adj)   weak; sluggish (**listless, lethargic**)

The flu left me feeling **languid** even two days after my fever had broken.

Vocabulary Exercise Set 1

> **Time—7 minutes**
> For each question, select the best answer among the choices given.
> Note any vocabulary words to review on the Hit List below.

Each sentence below has one or two blanks, each blank indicating that something has been omitted. Beneath the sentence are five words or sets of words labeled A through E. Choose the word or set of words that, when inserted in the sentence, <u>best</u> fits the meaning of the sentence as a whole.

Example:
    Medieval kingdoms did not become constitutional republics overnight; on the contrary, the change was ------.

(A) unpopular   (B) unexpected
(C) advantageous   (D) sufficient   (E) gradual

Correct response: (E)

1. As a young boy, Miguel was ------; even as an adult he almost never stops talking.

    (A) ruthless   (B) loquacious
    (C) mercurial   (D) lethargic
    (E) formidable

2. The army's ability to ------ its efforts made the invasion a success; the opponents could not withstand the simultaneous attack from three sides.

    (A) abridge   (B) scrutinize
    (C) revere   (D) synchronize
    (E) transmute

3. The Indianapolis Colts' ------- offense, the most prolific in league history, cut through the holes in the ------ Kansas City Chiefs' defense with ease.

    (A) inert .. placid
    (B) redoubtable .. prudent
    (C) potent .. porous
    (D) colloquial .. benign
    (E) pious .. succinct

4. An anonymous ------ contributed enough money to the university to allow for the creation of six full scholarships.

    (A) benefactor   (B) strategem
    (C) anthology   (D) euphemism
    (E) sanctuary

5. Lydia's heart transplant surgery last fall left her in a state of ------; this lack of activity resulted in ------ of her leg muscles from which she has only recently recovered.

    (A) listlessness .. idiosyncracy
    (B) lethargy .. anomaly
    (C) lassitude .. atrophy
    (D) diatribe .. brevity
    (E) serenity .. evanescence

6. The teenager showed ------ beyond her years when she left the party because her friends were about to do something illegal.

    (A) elocution   (B) prudence
    (C) melancholy   (D) guile   (E) deference

7. The agony felt by Steelers fans was ------: just as it seemed the game was lost, their team somehow surged to victory in overtime.

    (A) capricious   (B) derogatory
    (C) astute   (D) concise   (E) ephemeral

8. Critics harshly condemned the play as ------ and ------; it lacked originality and employed outdated dramatical devices.

    (A) mundane .. anachronistic
    (B) amorphous .. robust
    (C) hackneyed .. extemporaneous
    (D) caustic .. eclectic
    (E) sanctimonious .. callous

_____   _____

_____   _____

_____   _____

_____   _____

Write the meaning next to each root. Then write as many words as you can that contain the root.

9. PER _____

_____

_____

_____

12. VAC _____

_____

_____

_____

15. BENE, BONUS _____

_____

_____

_____

18. EU _____

_____

_____

_____

21. LOQU _____

_____

_____

_____

10. RE _____

_____

_____

_____

13. EX-, E- _____

_____

_____

_____

16. IN-, IM- _____

_____

_____

_____

19. JUR _____

_____

_____

_____

22. VERB _____

_____

_____

_____

11. SACER _____

_____

_____

_____

14. VOCARE _____

_____

_____

_____

17. CO-, CON- _____

_____

_____

_____

20. DE- _____

_____

_____

_____

23. SUB _____

_____

_____

_____

24. Is a *stalwart* weak?　　　　　　　　　　　Y N

25. Is wearing a seat belt *prudent*?　　　　　Y N

26. Should a politician be *perspicacious*?　　Y N

27. Is a *diffident* person *haughty*?　　　　　Y N

28. Is a *beneficiary* one who gives?　　　　　Y N

Write the word with the given meaning

29. to change form　　　　　　m _____

30. lacking substance　　　　　v _____

31. even-temperedness　　　　 e _____

32. commonplace　　　　　　　p _____

33. overused　　　　　　　　　h _____

34. sluggish　　　　　　　　　p _____

35. resistant to authority　　　r _____

36. disposed to complain　　　q _____

37. rudely abrupt　　　　　　　b _____

38. talkative　　　　　　　　　g _____

39. a strong defense　　　　　b _____

40. place of refuge　　　　　　s _____

41. magical object　　　　　　t _____

42. extended in time　　　　　p _____

43. call on for inspiration　　 i _____

44. full of vigor　　　　　　　r _____

45. trickery; deceit　　　　　　g _____

46. falsely pious　　　　　　　s _____

47. to regard with honor　　　r _____

48. out of place in time　　　　a _____

Write the correct form of the italicized word

49. the state of feeling *lethargic*

_____

50. the quality of being *pusillanimous*

_____

51. to give *censure*

_____

52. the act of *adjudicating*

_____

53. like an *anomaly*

_____

Write the word with the given root

54. beyond comprehension (*scrut*)

_____

55. stubbornly resistant (*re*)

_____

56. uninteresting (*sapere*)

_____

57. to attack as untrue (*pugn*)

_____

58. speaking in a pompous manner (*loqu*)

_____

59. most important (*domit*)

_____

60. harmless (*ben*)

_____

61. blend or fuse together (*co-*)

_____

62. one who supports another (*bene*)

_____

63. weak (*potens*)

_____

64. sphere of legal authority (*jur*)

_____

Vocabulary Exercise Set 1 Answer Key

1. **B** The second sentence states that *even as an adult* Miguel almost *never stops talking*. This suggests that as a child he loved to talk as well. The missing word should mean talkative.
    ruthless = cruel
    loquacious = very talkative
    mercurial = subject to wild changes
    lethargic = lazy; sluggish
    formidable = hard to overcome

2. **D** *The invasion was a success* because the attack was *simultaneous*. The missing word should mean something like *coordinate*.
    abridge = shorten a written text
    scrutinize = examine carefully
    revere = regard with honor and respect
    synchronize = arrange events to occur simultaneously
    transmute = transform

3. **C** The Colts' offense was the most *prolific* (producing abundant results) in the league history, which means it was very good. The first missing word should mean *powerful*. That powerful offense cut holes through *a weak* Chiefs' defense *with ease*.
    inert = sluggish; inactive
    placid = calm
    redoubtable = arousing fear
    prudent = wise, showing good judgment
    potent = strong and effective
    porous = filled with holes
    colloquial = using everyday language; conversational
    benign = harmless
    pious = showing religious reverence
    succinct = spoken or written in a clear and precise manner

4. **A** Enough money was contributed to allow for the creation of *six scholarships*. That is a very kind gift and would come from someone who was generous.
    benefactor = one who supports or helps another
    strategem = deceitful scheme
    anthology = collection of works
    euphemism = the substitution of an inoffensive term for an offensive one
    sanctuary = a place of refuge

5. **C** Lydia underwent *heart transplant surgery*, which is a serious operation that causes much *fatigue*, which explains why she experienced a *lack of activity*. This caused a problem with her leg muscles, which required physical therapy to be corrected. A lack of activity can often lead to a weakening of muscle tissue.
    listlessness = sluggishness; without energy
    idiosyncrasy = a peculiar trait or habit
    lethargy = sluggishness
    anomaly = unusual event
    lassitude = a feeling of weakness
    atrophy = weakening caused by disuse
    diatribe = malicious criticism or abuse
    brevity = quality of succing expression
    serenity = tranquility
    evanescence = likely to vanish

6. **B** The teenager left the party when she realized *something illegal* was about to occur. That shows *good judgment*.
    elocution = expressive delivery of public speech
    prudence = using good judgment
    melancholy = sad, depressed
    guile = trickery
    deference = respect for the wishes of others

7. **E** Since the Steelers won the game *just as* the game seemed to be lost, the *agony* Steelers fans felt during that short time *did not last long*.
    capricious = whimsical
    derogatory = disparaging; belittling
    astute = shrewd
    concise = brief and to the point
    ephemeral = short-lived

8. **A** Critics were *harsh* and *condemned* (criticized) the play because *it lacked originality* and it *employed outdated dramatical devices*. The two missing words should fit those descriptions.
    mundane = ordinary
    anachronistic = out of place in time
    amorphous = lacking shape
    robust = full of vigor
    hackneyed = overused
    extemporaneous = done with little or no practice
    caustic = corrosive
    eclectic = made up of parts from many different sources
    sanctimonious = falsely pious
    callous = hardened; insensitive

9. PER: through, thoroughly
   perfunctory, permeate, perceive, perspicacious, perennial, peruse

10. RE: back
    recalcitrant, reiterate, remunerate, retract

11. SACER: sacred
    sacrilegious, sacrament, sacrosanct, consecrate

12. VAC: empty
    vacate, evacuate, vacuum, vacuous, vacation, vacant

13. EX-, E-: out
    emit, extract, exclaim, exit, egregious, enormous

14. VOCARE: to call
    invoke, provoke, vocation, voice, revoke

15. BENE: well, BONUS: good
    benevolent, beneficiary, bonus, bona fide, benediction

16. IN-, IM-: not
    intolerant, immoral, immodest, inconceivable

17. CO-, CON-: together, with
    cooperate, connect, correlate, committee, collect, conspire

18. EU: good
    euphemism, eulogy, euphony, euphoria, eugenics

19. JUR: oath, law
    jurisdiction, abjure, adjure, jury, jurisprudence

20. DE-: down, of
    descend, demoralize, demote, deride, decline

21. LOQU: talk
    loquacious, eloquent, ventriloquist, elocution, circumlocution

22. VERB: word
    verbatim, verbose, verbal, verbalize, proverb

23. SUB: under, secretly
    subterfuge, surreptitious, subjugate, subliminal, subvert

24. N

25. Y

26. Y

27. N

28. N

29. mutate

30. vacuous

31. equanimity

32. pedestrian

33. hackneyed

34. phlegmatic

35. recalcitrant

36. querulous

37. brusque

38. garrulous

39. bulwark

40. sanctuary

41. talisman

42. protracted

43. invoke

44. robust

45. guile

46. sanctimonious

47. revere

48. anachronistic

49. lethargy

50. pusillanimity

51. censure

52. adjudication

53. anomalous

54. inscrutable

55. recalcitrant

56. insipid

57. impugn

58. grandiloquent

59. predominant

60. benign

61. coalesce

62. benefactor

63. impotent

64. jurisdiction

Vocabulary Lesson 17: Wanna Fight?

Today's roots:	bellum	war	vola	to fly
	pugnare	fight	ire	anger

❑ **belligerent** (adj)   warlike; quarrelsome (*bellum* war + *gerere* to wage) (**bellicose, pugnacious**)

My brother is a **belligerent** guy; he picks his fair share of bar fights.

❑ **irascible** (adj)   easily angered (*ire* anger) (**cranky, petulant, fractious**)

Adam's **irascible** nature landed him in anger management therapy; he overreacts to the smallest things.

❑ **volatile** (adj)   explosive; tending to evaporate quickly (*vola* to fly) (**mercurial, capricious**)

The situation in the Middle East is a **volatile** one that must be handled with care.

❑ **rebuttal** (n)   refutation; opposing response to an argument (*re-* back + *bouter* to put) (**refutation**)

After the opponent made his remarks, the debate team captain approached the podium to deliver her **rebuttal**.

❑ **refute** (v)   to disprove; to rebut forcefully (*refutare* to drive back) (**debunk, discredit**)

The judge found no evidence to **refute** your claim that the car is yours, so you get to keep it for now.

❑ **incite** (v)   to urge into action (*citare* to cause to move) (**inflame, instigate, provoke**)

The rebels **incited** a revolt in the small city by convincing the citizens that their mayor was a crook.

❑ **pugnacious** (adj)   quarrelsome; warlike (*pugnare* fight) (**combative, belligerent, contentious**)

The **pugnacious** punk was happiest when his fists were pounding someone else's chin.

Vocabulary Lesson 18: Bad and Ugly

Today's roots:	acri	bitter	caco	ugly
	plorare	to cry out	phon	sound

❑ **acrimony** (n)   bitterness of feeling; harsh words (*acri* bitter + *monia* action or condition) (**rancor**)

Her toast was inappropriately **acrimonious**, and we could all tell that she had not forgiven her friend.

❑ **appalling** (adj)   shocking; causing dismay (*palir* to grow pale) (**abhorrent, ghastly**)

The way he yells at his wife is **appalling**; he treats her like she is his servant.

❑ **cacophony** (n)   discord; harsh sounds (*cacos* ugly + *phon* sound) (**din, clamor**)

How can this **cacophony** coming out of my son's room be today's popular music?

❑ **abysmal** (adj)   extremely bad; wretched (Gr *byssos* bottom of the sea) (**atrocious, dire**)

The food at this hospital is **abysmal**! Is this bread or cardboard?

❑ **acrid** (adj)   harsh smelling or tasting (*acri* bitter) (**pungent, caustic**)

Don't inhale too much of this chemical; it is known to be quite **acrid** and can make you pass out.

❑ **deplorable** (adj)   worthy of reproach or censure (*plorare* to cry out in sorrow) (**reprehensible**)

Although they claimed to love animals, the conditions at their run-down shelter were **deplorable**.

Vocabulary Lesson 19: Moving Right Along

Today's roots:	*ambulare*	walk	*flux*	flow
	pel, pul	force, drive	*peri-*	around

❑ *ambulatory* (adj) capable of moving around (*ambulare* walk) (*mobile, motile*)

   He must stay in bed for a week, and once he is **ambulatory**, he will need crutches.

❑ *deviate* (v) to swerve or deflect (*de-* away + *via* path) (*digress, diverge*)

   The tire sitting in the left lane of the highway casued the driver to **deviate** from her path.

❑ *influx* (n) a flowing in (*in-* in + *flux* flow) (*inundation*)

   The school saw quite an **influx** of new applicants once it increased the number of scholarships.

❑ *peripatetic* (adj) traveling from place to place (*peri-* around + *patein* to walk) (*itinerant, nomadic*)

   The nomads were a **peripatetic** clan; they never stayed in the same place very long.

❑ *impel* (v) to put into motion; to urge (*pel* force) (*coerce, compel, exhort, goad, spur*)

   The zoo visitors were **impelled** into action by the announcement that a lion was loose.

❑ *expedite* (v) to speed up the progress of (*ex-* out + *pes, pedis* foot: to free from entanglement) (*hasten*)

   The project was **expedited** once the CEO decided that its outcome reflected on him personally.

Vocabulary Lesson 20: Going, Going, Gone!

Today's roots:	*purgare*	cleanse	*ab-*	away
	deplere	to empty		

❑ *raze* (v) to destroy completely (*demolish*)

   The massive level-five hurricane **razed** the entire port city, crushing everything in its path.

❑ *jettison* (v) to throw overboard (*reject, spurn*)

   The killer **jettisoned** the murder weapon into the lake as he sailed to his hideout in the cove.

❑ *abort* (v) to terminate prematurely (*ab-* away + *oriri* to appear (*terminate*)

   The soldiers **aborted** their mission when they learned their cover was blown and it was no longer safe.

❑ *purge* (v) to cleanse of something unwanted (*purgare* to cleanse) (*cleanse, eradicate*)

   It is satisfying to **purge** your email inbox of unwanted junk messages.

❑ *forgo* (v) to give something up (*for-* away + *go* go) (*eschew, waive, abstain from, abjure*)

   The woman decided to leave the hospital early and **forgo** further treatment on her injured hip.

❑ *deplete* (v) to decrease the supply of (*deplere* to empty) (*expend, exhaust, diminish*)

   The run on gasoline **depleted** the gas station of its fuel reserves, and it was forced to shut down.

❑ *dearth* (n) lack; scarcity (*dear* greatly valued) (*paucity, deficiency, sparseness*)

   There has been a **dearth** of good will between the teams ever since the bench-clearing brawl.

Vocabulary Lesson 21: Mr. Nice Guy

Today's roots:	*amicus*	friend	*anthro*	mankind
	munus	gift, money, sharing	*phila*	brotherly love

❑ *altruism* (n)   selflessness (*alter* other) (*benevolence, philanthropy, charity, magnanimousness*)

Tom's **altruism** pushes him to spend 30 hours per week working with the needy.

❑ *amiable* (adj)   friendly; agreeable (*amicus* friend) (*affable, amicable, genial, cordial*)

Mr. Richards is such an **amiable** guy, always smiling and laughing as he interacts with his customers.

❑ *philanthropist* (n)   one who does good; lover of mankind (*phila* love + *anthro* mankind) (*benefactor, patron*)

It is amazing that a penny-pincher like Paul is a **philanthropist** who has donated millions to charity.

❑ *congenial* (adj)   friendly; pleasant (*con-* with + *genialis* pleasant) (*genial, amiable, convivial*)

After months of imagining her in-laws as monsters, Julia was surprised at how **congenial** they actually were.

❑ *munificent* (adj)   generous (*munus* sharing) (*magnanimous, beneficent, philanthropic, altruistic*)

Donating that outfit to charity is quite a **munificent** gesture, considering that it is your favorite.

❑ *decorum* (n)   propriety; good manners (*decorus* proper) (*propriety, seemliness, protocol, etiquette*)

While eating at the country club, you must behave with the utmost **decorum** and mind your manners.

Vocabulary Lesson 22: Show Off!

Today's roots:	*ped-, paedere-*	instruct	*grandis*	great, big
	ostentare	to display	*pomp*	splendor

❑ *pedantic* (adj)   showy about knowledge (*paedere* to instruct) (*dogmatic, pompous, bombastic*)

Kim's **pedantic** teaching style bothers her students; she uses bizarre vocabulary words nobody understands.

❑ *grandiose* (adj)   pretentious; ridiculously exaggerated (*grand* great + *osus* full of) (*resplendent, pompous*)

The castle's foyer was the most **grandiose** of its kind, adorned with crystal chandeliers and guilded banisters.

❑ *bombastic* (adj)   pompous; using inflated language (*pompous, turgid, verbose, ostentatious*)

The **bombastic** language in the mayor's campaign speech made her seem arrogant and disconnected from the public.

❑ *braggart* (n)   one who boasts; a showoff (*braguer* to show off) (*swaggerer, pedant*)

"No one likes a **braggart**, son; it's best to be modest and humble about your successes."

❑ *ostentatious* (adj)   showy; pretentious (*ostentare* to display + *-ious* full of) (*pretentious, gaudy, grandiose*)

That solid-gold statue is the most **ostentatious** display of wealth I have ever seen.

❑ *pompous* (adj)   possessing excessive self-esteem; pretentious (*pomp* splendor + *-ous* full of) (*haughty*)

His **pompous**, holier-than-thou attitude annoyed all of his classmates.

❑ *swagger* (v)   to walk or strut in an arrogant manner (*strut, gloat, bluster*)

Having beat their crosstown rivals handily, the players **swaggered** back to the locker room.

Vocabulary Lesson 23: Like a Pit Bull

Today's roots:	*tract*	pull	*tenax*	holding fast
	ob-	against	*per-*	very

❑ *dogged* (adj)   determined; unwilling to give up (think of "follow like a dog") (***tenacious, resolute, staunch***)

Outmanned and overmatched, the **dogged** fighters nevertheless refused to surrender the Alamo.

❑ *inexorable* (adj)   relentless (*in-* not+*exorabilis* able to be swayed) (***obdurate, relentless, intransigent***)

Inexorable in his wooing, Jason vowed to send Kathy roses every day until she accepted his prom invitation.

❑ *obstinate* (adj)   stubborn (*obstinatus* to stand stubbornly) (***intractable, recalcitrant, refractory***)

No matter what she tried, she could not make her **obstinate** husband change his mind.

❑ *intractable* (adj)   difficult to manage (*in-* not + *tract* pull) (***obstinate, intransigent***)

The **intractable** mule refused to pull the plow and instead sat in the field all day.

❑ *contentious* (adj)   quarrelsome (*contendere* to strive after + *-ious* full of) (***disputatious, pugnacious***)

Julia sighed as her excessively **contentious** husband started another unnecessary argument with their waiter.

❑ *pertinacity* (n)   stubbornness (*per-* very + *tenax* holding fast) (***obstinacy, willfulness, tenacity***)

Kyle showed incredible **pertinacity** after breaking his leg, making it back in time for the championship game.

❑ *steadfast* (adj)   unchanging; unswerving (*stede* stand + *foest* firmly fixed) (***resolute, staunch, unfaltering***)

Despite many hardships, the team was **steadfast** in its pursuit of the summit.

Vocabulary Lesson 24: You're Good at That!

Today's roots:	*apt*	fit	*summus*	highest
	para-	beyond	*dexter*	skillful

❑ *adroit* (adj)   dexterous; skillful (*à droit* rightly) (***adept, dexterous, astute, deft***)

An **adroit** con-man, Clarence knew how to fool even the most skeptical eye.

❑ *unerring* (adj)   committing no mistakes; perfect (*un-* not + *err* to make a mistake) (***infallible, impeccable***)

Her **unerring** sense of direction always puts her in the right place even if she has never been there before.

❑ *adept* (adj)   highly skilled (***adroit, proficient, consummate***)

Roberto, an **adept** mathematician, completed the outrageously difficult calculus final in just 25 minutes.

❑ *aptitude* (n)   a natural ability; intelligence (*apt* fit) (***capacity, faculty, facility***)

Kenneth showed a great **aptitude** for computers as a child, designing complex programs at the age of ten.

❑ *paragon* (n)   a model of excellence; perfection (*para-* beyond) (***epitome, quintessence, archetype***)

The head of several charities, Susan is the **paragon** of philanthropy.

❑ *consummate* (adj)   perfect in every respect; highly skilled (*summus* highest) (***superlative, preeminent***)

A **consummate** psychologist, Dr. Carter is often asked to lend his expertise on difficult cases.

Vocabulary Lesson 25: Bad and Worse

Today's roots:	*mal*	bad, evil	*vol*	wish
	facere	to do or make	*odium*	hate

❏ *nefarious* (adj) wicked; sinful (*ne-* not + *fas* lawful) (***iniquitous, heinous, diabolical***)

    Cinderella's **nefarious** step-sisters took joy in making her do their daily chores.

❏ *repugnant* (adj) offensive; repulsive (*re-* back + *pugnare* to fight) (***abhorrent, odious, execrable***)

    Christopher's mother found his superstition of not bathing after games **repugnant**.

❏ *infamous* (adj) famous for bad deeds; notorious (*in-* not + *famosus* celebrated) (***ignominious***)

    The **infamous** "El Hector" was remembered for the way he tortured the poor villagers of Santa Potula.

❏ *odious* (adj) worthy of dislike; arousing feelings of dislike (*odium* hate + *osus* full of) (***vile***)

    Jimmy was no longer afraid to go to school once the **odious** bully was suspended.

❏ *malevolent* (adj) wishing harm to others; evil (*mal* evil + *vol* wish) (***malicious, vindictive***)

    The **malevolent** dictator smiled as he ordered his soldiers to burn down the church.

❏ *malefactor* (n) an evil-doer (*mal* evil + *facere* to do or make) (***miscreant, culprit, transgressor***)

    Superman has found and stopped many a **malefactor** before the crime could actually be committed.

❏ *abominable* (adj) loathsome; unpleasant (***loathsome, odious, repugnant, execrable***)

    His **abominable** behavior at the game included excessive drinking, loud swearing, and the removal of his clothes.

Vocabulary Lesson 26: Ripped Off

Today's roots:	*sub, subter*	under, secretly	*fugere*	to flee

❏ *charlatan* (n) a fraud; a quack (It *chiarlatino* a quack) (***sham, quack, fraud, mountebank***)

    June's family warned her that Chaz was a **charlatan**, only pretending to be a successful lawyer.

❏ *ruse* (n) a crafty scheme (***ploy, stratagem, machination, gambit***)

    The clever criminal came up with a flawless **ruse** to steal the money from the bank.

❏ *subterfuge* (n) a scheme; an attempt to deceive (*subter* secretly + *fugere* to flee) (***duplicity***)

    It takes real **subterfuge** to sneak anything past Principal Guber; it's like he is able to see your every move.

❏ *pilfer* (v) to steal (***purloin, loot***)

    The looters **pilfered** countless items from the electronics store during the riot.

❏ *swindle* (v) to cheat (***defraud, bilk, hoodwink***)

    The street hustler **swindled** the unsuspecting man, tricking him into buying a fake designer watch.

❏ *gullible* (adj) easily deceived (***credulous, naive, dupable***)

    The **gullible** teenager was easily tricked by her friends into believing that one of them was a secret agent.

Vocabulary Lesson 27: Good Guys and Bad Guys

Today's roots:	archos	leader, government	theos	god
	a-, an-	without	pacis	peace

❏ **hedonist** (n)   a pleasure seeker (*hedone* pleasure) (***sybarite, epicure, voluptuary***)

The 1960s are often considered the age of the **hedonist**, a time when everyone felt she had the right to have fun.

❏ **ascetic** (n)   one who lives a holy life of self-denial (*asketes* monk) (***abstainer, puritan, hermit***)

Tim has spent years at a time as an **ascetic**, each time giving away all he owns and living on rice and prayer.

❏ **anarchist** (n)   one who opposes all political authority (*an-* without + *archos* leader) (***subversive***)

Before the coup d'etat, the dictator claimed to be an **anarchist**; that all changed once he was given power.

❏ **pacifist** (n)   an individual who is opposed to violence (*pacis* peace + *facere* to make) (***peace-monger***)

Forever a **pacifist**, Julie organized a rally protesting the war in the Middle East.

❏ **atheist** (n)   one who does not believe that God exists (*a-* without + *theos* god) (***skeptic, nonbeliever***)

Although she is an **atheist** and does not worship the Buddha, Cathy meditates with her Buddhist friends.

❏ **nihilist** (adj)   one who rejects moral distinctions and knowable "truths" (*nihil* nothing) (***negativist, disbeliever***)

Because she is a **nihilist**, Carrie likes to contend that the world may be a figment of her imagination.

❏ **despot** (n)   a tyrant; one who rules oppressively (Gr *despotes* absolute ruler) (***tyrant, oppressor, dictator***)

The **despot** rules with reckless abandon, doing only what he wants with no concern for the citizens.

Vocabulary Lesson 28: That's Better

Today' roots:	culpa	blame	placare	please
	ex-, e-	out	mollis	soft

❏ **vindicate** (v)   to clear from blame (***absolve, exonerate, exculpate, acquit***)

The adroit defense lawyer was able to **vindicate** her client of all charges, and he was set free.

❏ **assuage** (v)   to soothe anger or pain; to satistfy a hunger (*suavis* agreeable, sweet) (***mollify, placate***)

If your dog gets stung by a bee, place a wet washcloth on the area to **assuage** the pain.

❏ **mollify** (v)   to soothe the anger of (*mollis* soft) (***appease, pacify, conciliate, allay***)

The waiter attempted to **mollify** the angry customer by offering him a free dessert with his dinner.

❏ **exonerate** (v)   to clear from accusation (*ex-* out + *onus* burden) (***exculpate, vindicate, acquit***)

When the principal found the spray paint in Rex's locker, Timmy was **exonerated** of all graffiti charges.

❏ **placate** (v)   to soothe; to mollify (*placare* please) (***appease, mollify, propitiate***)

The mother attempted to **placate** her crying baby by handing him his favorite teddy bear.

❏ **exculpate** (v)   to free from blame (*ex-* out + *culpa* blame) (***absolve, vindicate, exonerate***)

Although the DNA evidence did not identify the killer, it did **exculpate** the police's primary suspect.

Vocabulary Lesson 29: Make Me!

Today's roots:	*legare*	**to bind**	*vocare*	**to call**
	ducere	**to lead**	*pro-*	**forth**

❑ *cajole* (v)   to persuade by using flattery (*coax, inveigle, entice*)

The clever eight-year-old girl successfully **cajoled** her parents into taking her to Disney World.

❑ *exhort* (v)   to urge strongly (*ex-* thoroughly + *hortari* to urge) (*entreat, implore, enjoin*)

The doctor **exhorted** his patient to stop smoking by explaining how dangerous a habit it really was.

❑ *coerce* (v)   to persuade through the use of force (*coercere* hold in, restrain) (*compel, browbeat*)

The bully **coerced** the smaller boy into handing over his lunch money with threats of wedgies and deadarms.

❑ *induce* (v)   to cause (*in-* in + *ducere* to lead) (*effect, instigate, engender*)

After 36 hours of labor, the doctors decided to **induce** the baby's birth with medication.

❑ *coax* (v)   to persuade by using flattery (*wheedle, cajole*)

The charming man used well-placed compliments to **coax** the pretty waitress into meeting him for a drink.

❑ *provoke* (v)   to stir up; to excite (*pro-* forth + *vocare* to call) (*goad, incite*)

Eric **provoked** his older brother into fighting by whacking him on the head with his action figure.

❑ *obligatory* (adj)   required (*ob-* to + *ligare* to bind) (*mandatory, compulsory, incumbent*)

The **obligatory** jumps in the skating competition must be performed or the competitor loses points.

Vocabulary Lesson 30: Come to Your Senses

Today's roots:	*audire*	**to hear**	*palpare*	**to touch**
	gustare	**to taste**	*cernere*	**to separate**

❑ *tactile* (adj)   able to be sensed by touch (*tactilis* touchable) (*palpable*)

The petting zoo provides a fun **tactile** experience for children, allowing them to touch dozens of animals.

❑ *olfactory* (adj)   relating to the sense of smell (*olere a* smell of + *facere* to make)

For those with a strong **olfactory** sense the spray of a skunk is extremely pungent.

❑ *gustatory* (adj)   relating to the sense of taste (*gustare* to taste)

The meal was a **gustatory** extravaganza; her taste buds were exploding from all the savory spices.

❑ *auditory* (adj)   relating to the sense of hearing (*audire* to hear) (*acoustic, auricular*)

Kris's **auditory** deterioration prevented him from appreciating the subtle tonality of the music.

❑ *discern* (v)   to perceive as separate; to sense keenly (*dis-* away + *cernere* distinguish, separate)

The fog made it difficult for me to **discern** how many people stood at the far end of the parking lot.

❑ *palpable* (adj)   detectable by touch (*palpare* to touch) (*tangible, discernable*)

As the tightrope walker attempted to regain his balance, the tension in the audience was nearly **palpable**.

Vocabulary Lesson 31: Stop It!

Today's roots:	*ab-, abs-*	from	*terrere*	to frighten
	tenere	hold	*ped*	foot

❑ *thwart* (v)   to stop something before it is able to succeed (*frustrate, stymie, foil, forestall*)

Thanks to inside information, the police department was able to **thwart** the bank robbery before it even began.

❑ *abstain* (v)   to refrain from action (*ab-* from + *tenere* to hold) (*refrain, forbear, eschew*)

An alcoholic of 20 years, Robert was unable to **abstain** from drinking when offered a beer.

❑ *deterrent* (n)   something that acts to discourage (*de-* away + *terrere* to frighten) (*curb, disincentive*)

The picture of the vicious lion baring his teeth was an effective **deterrent** against kids' reaching into the cage.

❑ *impede* (v)   to slow the progress of, to block (*impedire* to entangle the foot) (*obstruct, thwart*)

The orange cones did not do much to **impede** the progress of the cars; they just drove right over them.

❑ *hinder* (n)   to slow the progress of (*hamper, impede, thwart*)

The weed-killer sprayed on the garden successfully **hindered** the growth of the unwanted plants.

❑ *curtail* (v)   to make less (*curtus* to cut short) (*curb, retrench*)

In an effort to lose weight, Mark tried to **curtail** his ice cream consumption.

❑ *impediment* (n)   something that works to impede progress; a hindrance (*hindrance, handicap*)

Louise had a speech **impediment** that caused her to stutter, but that did not keep her from being a D.J.

Vocabulary Lesson 32: Must Be the Money!

Today's roots:	*pecunia*	money	*parsi*	to save
	pro-	ahead	*videre*	to see

❑ *destitute* (adj)   completely penniless (*destitutus* abandoned) (*impoverished, impecunious*)

The stock market collapse of 2000–2002 left many an adept investor **destitute**.

❑ *frugal* (adj)   economical; good with your money (*frux-* fruit, profit) (*thrifty, economical, austere*)

A **frugal** shopper does not make a purchase before checking many other places for a lower price.

❑ *remuneration* (n)   payment for services (*re-* back + *munerari* to give) (*compensation, reimbursement*)

The job is tedious, but the **remuneration** is worthwhile—over 50 dollars per hour!

❑ *impecunious* (adj)   without money (*im-* not + *pecunia* money) (*indigent, insolvent, destitute*)

You would never guess that Marisa was so **impecunious** if you watched her spend money at the mall.

❑ *improvident* (adj)   failing to provide for the future (*im-* not + *pro-* ahead + *videre* to see) (*spendthrift, prodigal*)

Despite once being a millionaire, Tom was now broke due to his **improvident** spending decisions.

❑ *parsimony* (n)   excessive thriftiness (*parsi-* to spare, save + *monium* an action, a condition) (*stinginess*)

Al's **parsimoniousness** reached an extreme when he hand-delivered a bill rather than spending money on a stamp.

Vocabulary Exercise Set 2

Time—7 minutes
For each question, select the best answer among the choices given.
Note any vocabulary words to review on the Hit List below.

Each sentence below has one or two blanks, each blank indicating that something has been omitted. Beneath the sentence are five words or sets of words labeled A through E. Choose the word or set of words that, when inserted in the sentence, best fits the meaning of the sentence as a whole.

Example:
Medieval kingdoms did not become constitutional republics overnight; on the contrary, the change was -------.

(A) unpopular   (B) unexpected
(C) advantageous (D) sufficient
(E) gradual

Correct response: (E)

1. Professional athletes who are ------- may receive more publicity, but they are usually not liked as much as those who are modest and humble.

(A) abysmal   (B) ostentatious
(C) altruistic (D) unerring   (E) frugal

2. The unexpectedly heavy snowfall in California has ------ the construction crew's attempts to complete the building on time; the machines can't get to the building because the roads are not yet plowed.

(A) expedited   (B) hindered
(C) pilfered   (D) exhorted (E) mollified

3. Many analysts point to the one-time millionaire's ------ spending habits as the cause for his now ------ lifestyle; had he been more frugal, he would not now be so impoverished.

(A) parsimonious .. amiable
(B) volatile .. peripatetic
(C) munificent .. pompous
(D) improvident .. destitute
(E) obstinate .. infamous

4. Members of the United Nations decried the Prime Minister's actions as ------, pointing out that his attempts to ------ the pacifist neighbors of his nation into war violated the peace accord.

(A) appalling .. refute
(B) philanthropic .. raze
(C) belligerent .. abort
(D) grandiose .. incite
(E) deplorable .. provoke

5. The climber showed incredible ------ in her quest to reach the top of Mount Everest; she was not willing to stop even though the driving blizzard dangerously reduced visibility.

(A) subterfuge   (B) congeniality
(C) doggedness   (D) malevolence
(E) despotism

6. The ------ of vegetarian options on the island forced Elena to ------ from her promise to avoid eating meat.

(A) preeminence .. jettison
(B) dearth .. deviate
(C) induction .. exonerate
(D) influx .. impel
(E) remuneration .. assuage

7. The video footage recovered from the security cameras was able to ------ the main suspect, and he was therefore released by the police.

(A) placate   (B) coax   (C) impede
(D) exculpate   (E) coerce

8. Michelle's ------ lifestyle was in stark contrast to Eric's ------ ways; she went to parties on a regular basis, while he denied himself even the simplest pleasures of life.

(A) hedonistic .. ascetic
(B) irascible .. ambulatory
(C) nihilist .. atheist
(D) pedantic .. intransigent
(E) bombastic .. nefarious

HIT LIST

Write the meaning next to each root. Then write as many words as you can that contain the root.

9. PED _____

_____

_____

_____

_____

10. AB- _____

_____

_____

_____

11. PURG- _____

_____

_____

_____

12. AM-, AMICUS _____

_____

_____

_____

13. ANTHRO _____

_____

_____

_____

14. BELLUM, BELLI- _____

_____

_____

_____

15. PERI- _____

_____

_____

_____

16. CULP _____

_____

_____

_____

17. SUB- _____

_____

_____

_____

18. MIS _____

_____

_____

_____

19. PLAC _____

_____

_____

_____

20. TRACT _____

_____

_____

_____

21. GRAND _____

_____

_____

_____

22. TENERE _____

_____

_____

_____

23. VOCARE _____

_____

_____

_____

24. Is a *deft* person good at what
    she does?   Y N

25. Is an *infamous* person known for
    kind things?   Y N

26. Can you be *parsimonious* with words?   Y N

27. Is a *philanthropist* generous?   Y N

28. Does someone *thrifty* waste money?   Y N

Write the word with the given meaning

29. a fraud   c _____

30. without money   i _____

31. nimbleness   a _____

32. to urge strongly   e _____

33. worthy of dislike   o _____

34. payment   r _____

35. a tyrant   d _____

36. to stop before it begins   t _____

37. to walk or strut   s _____

38. to put in motion   i _____

39. detectable by touch   p _____

40. to throw overboard   j _____

41. a pleasure seeker   h _____

42. capable of moving   a _____

43. to steal   p _____

44. to destroy completely   r _____

45. relating to taste   g _____

46. worthy of reproach   d _____

47. using inflated language   b _____

48. to perceive   d _____

Write the correct form of the italicized word

49. how someone who displays *altruism* behaves

    _____

50. that which an *anarchist* seeks

    _____

51. charcterized by *agility*

    _____

52. the act of *cajoling*

    _____

53. to act as a *deterrent*

    _____

Write the word with the given root

54. economical (*frux*)

    _____

55. difficult to manipulate (*tract*)

    _____

56. to soothe (*mollis*)

    _____

57. quarrelsome (*belli*)

    _____

58. stubbornness (*per*)

    _____

59. easily angered (*irasci*)

    _____

60. to free from blame (*culp*)

    _____

61. to swerve (*via*)

    _____

62. an evildoer (*facere*)

    _____

63. natural ability (*apt*)

    _____

64. model of excellence (*para*)

    _____

Vocabulary Exercise Set 2 Answer Key

1. **B** The structure of the sentence indicates a contrast. Athletes who are *modest* and *humble* are liked more than athletes who are *not modest* and who *receive more publicity* for these actions.

   abysmal = extremely bad
   ostentatious = showy
   altruistic = selfless
   unerring = committing no mistakes
   frugal = economical

2. **B** The crew's machines were unable to get to the building because the roads are *not yet plowed*. It is clear that the *unexpectedly heavy snowfall* has *interrupted* or *delayed* the completion of the building.

   expedited = sped up
   hindered = slowed the progress of
   pilfered = stole
   exhorted = urged strongly
   mollified = soothed

3. **D** The one-time millionaire is *now impoverished* (out of money). The sentence suggests that had he been a bit more *frugal* (economical) he would not be in this bind. It can be inferred that his spending habits were *wasteful* and that he now leads a *poor* lifestyle.

   parsimonious = excessively thrifty
   amiable = friendly
   volatile = explosive
   peripatetic = traveling from place to place
   munificent = generous
   pompous = pretentious
   improvident = failing to provide for the future
   destitute = completely penniless
   obstinate = stubborn
   infamous = famous for bad deeds

4. **E** The members *decried* (condemned openly) the actions of the Prime Minister, so they must be *worthy of censure*. The Prime Minister is attempting to push his *pacifist neighbors* into a war they do not want to fight. The second missing word should mean push.

   appalling = shocking
   refute = to disprove
   philanthropic = doing good
   raze = destroy completely
   bellligerent = warlike
   abort = to terminate prematurely
   grandiose = pretentious
   incite = to urge into action
   deplorable = worthy of censure
   provoke = to stir up; to excite

5. **C** The climber refused to stop even though the blizzard created dangerous conditions. This shows the climber's *determination*.

   subterfuge = a scheme
   congeniality = friendliness
   doggedly = determinedly
   malevolence = evil
   despotism = tyranny

6. **B** Elena did not want to eat meat. The sentence explains that she is *forced* to do something, which implies it is against her will. It can be inferred that she was forced to eat meat against her will because of a *lack* of vegetarian options.

   preeminence = outstanding
   jettison = throw overboard
   dearth = a lack
   deviate = swerve
   induction = cause
   exonerate = clear from accusation
   influx = a flowing in
   impel = put into motion
   remuneration = payment for services
   assuage = soothe

7. **D** If the suspect was released by the police due to the video footage, then he must have been *cleared of blame*.

   placate = soothe
   coax = persuade by using flattery
   impede = slow the progress of
   exculpate = free from blame
   coerce = persuade through use of force

8. **A** Michelle and Eric lead different lifestyles (*stark contrast*). The information in the second clause tells you what the missing words should be. The first word should relate to *partying*, and the second word should relate to *self-denial*.

   hedonistic = pleasure seeking
   ascetic = one who leads a life of self-denial
   irascible = easily angered
   ambulatory = capable of moving around
   nihilist = one who rejects moral distinctions and knowable "truths"
   atheist = one who does not believe that God exists
   pedantic = showy about knowledge
   intransigent = uncompromising
   bombastic = pompous
   nefarious = wicked

9. PED: foot
   impediment, pedestrian, expedient, quadruped, tripod

10. AB-: away
abdicate, abscond, abduct, aberration, absolve, abject, abscess

11. PURG-: to clean
expurgate, purge, purgatory, spurge

12. AM-, AMICUS: friend
amicable, amiable, enemy, inimical, amity

13. ANTHRO: mankind
anthropology, anthropocentric, philanthropist, misanthrope

14. BELLUM, BELLI-: war
belligerent, bellicose, rebel, rebellion

15. PERI-: around
peripatetic, perambulate, pericardium, period, perimeter, peripheral, peristalsis, periscope

16. CULP: blame
exculpate, inculpate, disculpate, culprit, culpable

17. SUB-: under, secretly
subtle, subcutaneous, subliminal, subterfuge, subservient, subconscious

18. MIS: bad, wretched, hatred
miserly, miserable, misanthrope, miser, misery, misogyny

19. PLAC: to please
placate, placid, placebo, complacent, complaisant, plea, please, displease

20. TRACT: to pull
subtract, abstract, attract, distract, contract, traction, intractable, tractor

21. GRAND: great, big
grandeur, grandparent, grandiose, grandiloquent

22. TENERE: to hold
sustain, abstain, contain, detain, entertain, tenable, tenacity, pertinacity, retain, obtain, pertain

23. VOCARE: to call
vocabulary, convocation, prevoke, revoke

24. Y

25. N

26. Y

27. Y

28. N

29. charlatan

30. impecunious

31. agility

32. exhort

33. odious

34. remuneration

35. despot

36. thwart

37. swagger

38. impel

39. palpable

40. jettison

41. hedonist

42. ambulatory

43. pilfer

44. raze

45. gustatory

46. deplorable

47. bombastic

48. discern

49. altruistically

50. anarchy

51. agile

52. cajolery

53. deter

54. frugal

55. intractable

56. mollify

57. belligerent

58. pertinacity

59. irascible

60. exculpate

61. deviate

62. malefactor

63. aptitude

64. paragon

Vocabulary Lesson 33: Saw That Coming

Today's roots:	pro-, pre-, fore-	before	scientia	knowledge
	monere	to warn	por-	forward

❏ **prophecy** (n)   a prediction of the future (*pro-* before + *phanai* to speak) (**prognostication, divination, augury**)

The **prophecy** told of a young boy who would soon be born to save the human race from extinction.

❏ **harbinger** (n)   a precursor (**herald, omen, portent**)

Many consider the robin to be a **harbinger** of spring.

❏ **augur** (v)   to predict the future (an *augur* in ancient Rome was an official who foretold events) (**bode, portend**)

The "psychic network" claims to **augur** what is to come for its callers, but most believe it to be a hoax.

❏ **premonition** (n)   a forewarning (*pre-* before + *monere* to warn) (**foreboding, presentiment**)

The traveler had a **premonition** of the upcoming disaster and refused to board the plane.

❏ **portend** (v)   to give advanced warning (*por-* forward + *tendere* to extend) (**presage, foreshadow, prophesy**)

The weather service looks for atmospheric signs that **portend** violent storms.

❏ **prescient** (adj)   having knowledge of future events (*pre-* before + *scientia* knowledge) (**clairvoyant**)

The seemingly **prescient** gambler made a fortune at the racetrack, always knowing which horse would win.

❏ **omen** (n)   a sign of something to come (**harbinger, portent, herald**)

The nervous bride took the death of the minister who was to marry them as an **omen** that her marriage was doomed.

Vocabulary Lesson 34: Old and Worn-Out

Today's roots:	arch	ancient	per-	through
	ante-	before	linguere	to leave

❏ **archaic** (adj)   ancient (*arch* ancient) (**obsolete, outmoded, anachronistic**)

The boat's **archaic** navigation system confused the young sailor who knew how to read only the newer consoles.

❏ **relic** (n)   an object from an ancient time (*re-* back + *linquere* to leave) (**artifact, antiquity**)

The **relic** found at the ancient burial site once served as a water pitcher for an Aztec family.

❏ **decrepit** (adj)   worn out from old age or use (*de-* down + *crepare* to break, to crack) (**feeble, rickety**)

The **decrepit** swing set in the schoolyard had been used by four generations of children.

❏ **antiquated** (adj)   obsolete; outdated (*antiquus* ancient) (**archaic, outmoded, anachronistic**)

The computer technology in rural Italy is quite **antiquated**; even Internet access is rare.

❏ **antediluvian** (adj)   very old (*ante-* before + *diluvian* a flood; in reference to the Biblical flood) (**obsolete**)

The piece of pottery they found was an **antediluvian** bowl that was made over 4,000 years ago.

❏ **perpetuate** (v)   to keep from dying out (*per-* through + *petere* to seek, go to) (**sustain, prolong**)

The myth that cigarettes don't harm you has been **perpetuated** by the cigarette companies.

Vocabulary Lesson 35: Feelings

Today' roots:	pathos	emotion	prehens	to grasp
	con-	with	solari	comfort

❏ **apathy** (n)   lack of feeling; lack of interest (*a-* without + *pathos* emotion) (***indifference***)

Mark was **apathetic** about Stephanie's desire to keep her laptop clean; he put his fingerprints all over the screen.

❏ **apprehensive** (adj)   anxious about what is to come (***anxious, agitated***)

It is normal to feel **apprehensive** on the morning of your driver's test; it is a nerve-wracking experience.

❏ **contrite** (adj)   repentant (*con-* with + *terere* to wear down) (***remorseful, penitent, rueful***)

The **contrite** murder suspect scored points with the judge, who appreciated her remorseful attitude.

❏ **lament** (v)   to mourn, to show sorrow (*lamentum* a wailing) (***deplore, bemoan, rue***)

The fans **lamented** the passing of John Lennon; they cried as if they had lost a brother.

❏ **console** (v)   to comfort (*con-* with + *solari* comfort) (***solace, comfort, reassure***)

Many family members were on hand to **console** the grieving widow at her husband's funeral.

❏ **impassive** (adj)   lacking emotion (*im-* not + *passivus* capable of feeling) (***stoic, indifferent***)

Joy's **impassiveness** about her grades upset her parents; they wanted her to care more about her work.

Vocabulary Lesson 36: What the Heck?

Today's roots:	vocare	to call	equi	same
	crypto	secret	nebula	mist

❏ **ambiguous** (adj)   unclear in meaning (*ambigere* to wander) (***equivocal, imprecise***)

The teacher's **ambiguous** instructions left us with no idea of what we were supposed to do.

❏ **obscure** (adj)   not easily understood; indistinct (*obscurus* to darken) (***abstruse, arcane***)

The comedian's jokes contained **obscure** references that left the audience confused and silent.

❏ **equivocal** (adj)   deliberately ambiguous or misleading (*equi* same + *vocare* to call) (***ambiguous***)

The defendant's **equivocal** answers made it hard for the prosecutor to prove his case.

❏ **convoluted** (adj)   intricate and hard to follow (*con-* together + *volvere* to roll) (***tortuous***)

The instructions in this manual are so **convoluted** that I don't know where even to begin.

❏ **cryptic** (adj)   enigmatic; mysterious (*crypto* concealed, secret) (***enigmatic, arcane***)

The soldier's **cryptic** reply over the radio to his captain suggested that something was amiss.

❏ **unfathomable** (adj)   impossible to comprehend (*un-* not + *fathom* to grasp) (***inscrutable***)

The idea that time slows as our speed increases is **unfathomable** to most of us.

❏ **nebulous** (adj)   vague; indefinite (*nebula* mist) (***amorphous, vague***)

Bill's memory of the car accident was **nebulous**; he remembered only bits and pieces of the ordeal.

Vocabulary Lesson 37: True or False?

Today's roots:	*verax*	true	*candere*	to shine
	genuinus	natural	*apo-*	away

❏ *candor* (n) honesty; straightforwardness (*candere* to shine) (***frankness, forthrightness, sincerity***)

I appreciated my doctor's **candor**; I prefer a straightforward approach when discussing my health.

❏ *affect* (v) to put on airs; to pretend (***feign, make a pretense of***)

Hoping to fit in while in London, Jules **affected** a British accent.

❏ *veracity* (n) truthfulness (*verax* true) (***probity, rectitude***)

Since we can't test the **veracity** of his statements, we will never know for sure if he was telling the truth.

❏ *debunk* (v) to expose something as fraudulent (***explode, quash, discredit, refute***)

The D.A. knew that the cop was crooked and made it his mission to **debunk** the officer's claims.

❏ *apocryphal* (adj) of doubtful authenticity (*apo-* away + *kryptein* hide) (***spurious, unauthenticated***)

Before they found out it was a fake, the **apocryphal** Van Gogh painting sold for over a million dollars.

❏ *forthright* (adj) honest; straightforward (***candid, frank, unsparing***)

The student's **forthright** admission of guilt was appreciated by the principal, who reduced his suspension.

❏ *disingenuous* (adj) insincere; crafty (*dis-* away from + *genuinus* natural) (***duplicitous, insincere***)

Daphne's expressions of remorse were clearly **disingenuous** because she did not feel any regret for her actions.

Vocabulary Lesson 38: Arts and Entertainment

Today's roots:	*curare*	to take care of	*aisthetikos*	perception
	jocus	joke	*satira*	a poetic melody

❏ *mirth* (n) merriment; laughter (***levity, jocularity, buoyancy, joviality***)

The little boy could not contain his **mirth** when playing with the bubbles.

❏ *aesthetic* (adj) relating to beauty or a theory of beauty (Gr *aisthetikos* perception) (***artistic, tasteful***)

The beautiful colors that emerged from the crystal when struck by the sunlight were **aesthetically** pleasing.

❏ *satire* (n) a mocking literary or dramatic work (*satira* a poetic medley) (***parody, burlesque, lampoon***)

Animal Farm by George Orwell is a **satire** that mocks socialism.

❏ *curator* (n) the individual in charge of a museum (*curare* to take care of)

The **curator** in charge of the Louvre in Paris controls the *Mona Lisa*, perhaps the world's most famous painting.

❏ *witticism* (n) a clever or funny remark (***quip, bon mot, wisecrack***)

Will Rogers is famous for his **witticisms** about American life.

❏ *jocular* (adj) done in a joking way (*jocus* joke) (***droll, witty, facetious***)

Jeff's **jocular** tone relaxed the visitors trapped in the elevator; he even made a few people laugh.

Vocabulary Lesson 39: You're in Trouble

Today's roots:	*culpa*	blame	*censura*	judgment
	dictare	to declare	*probus*	honest, worthy

❏ *censure* (v)   to express strong disapproval (*censura* judgment) (*admonish, scold, castigate*)

The congressman's illicit behavior was met with public **censure** in the media.

❏ *reprove* (v)   to scold (*re-* not + *probus* worthy) (*reproach, upbraid, chastise*)

The teacher **reproved** her students strongly for talking during her lecture.

❏ *reprehensible* (adj)   worthy of blame or censure (*deplorable, despicable, repugnant*)

The woman could not believe that her son would do something so **reprehensible** as torturing small animals.

❏ *culpable* (adj)   deserving blame (*culpa* blame) (*censurable, reproachable, blame worthy*)

Although the DNA evidence clearly proved he was **culpable**, the defendant continued to claim innocence.

❏ *indict* (v)   to accuse of an offense (*dictare* to declare) (*impeach, arraign*)

The mob boss was **indicted** on 10 cases of money laundering.

❏ *reproach* (v)   to blame; to express disapproval (*admonish, chide, berate, rebuke*)

After hitting the softball through the window, Ella was **reproached** by her mother for being so careless.

❏ *rebuke* (v)   to scold (*re-* back + *buke* to strike) (*castigate, admonish, censure*)

Because Belinda was **rebuked** the last time she left her toys out, she cleaned up thoroughly to avoid another scolding.

Vocabulary Lesson 40: Working Hard

Today's roots:	*fatigare*	tire	*sedere*	to sit
	metus	fear		

❏ *diligence* (n)   hard work and dedication (*diligentia* attentiveness) (*assiduousness, rigor*)

Ty's **diligence** paid off when his boss gave him a promotion and a raise.

❏ *scrupulous* (adj)   careful, ethical (*scruples* ethical standards) (*punctilious, meticulous*)

Always a **scrupulous** student, Simone made sure she got her assignments in on time.

❏ *meticulous* (adj)   extremely attentive to detail (*metus* timidity) (*painstaking, fastidious*)

The accountant was incredibly **meticulous**; no detail ever slipped by her.

❏ *indefatigable* (adj)   untiring (*in-* not + *fatigare* to tire) (*resolute, unrelenting, unflagging*)

Despite working 100 hours per week, the lawyer was **indefatigable**, remaining energetic about his job.

❏ *painstaking* (adj)   meticulous; paying great attention to detail (*meticulous, conscientious*)

After 11 **painstaking** hours in the operating room, the surgeon declared the brain surgery a complete success.

❏ *assiduous* (adj)   hard working (*sedere* to sit) (*diligent, meticulous, painstaking*)

Dave studied **assidously** for the bar exam, dedicating 12 hours of daily studying for over five weeks.

Vocabulary Lesson 41: The Faithful and the Unfaithful

Today's roots:	*orthos*	straight, strict	*sub-*	under
	surgere	to rise	*klas*	to break

❏ **conform** (v)   to do what one is expected to do (*com-* together + *formare* to form) (***acquiesce, yield***)

His desire to avoid punishment at all costs causes him to **conform** to his parents' many rules.

❏ **orthodoxy** (n)   strict adherence to tradition (*orthos* straight, strict + *doxa* opinion) (***dogma***)

The Amish are well known for their **orthodoxy**; tradition is very important to their culture.

❏ **iconoclast** (n)   one who challenges tradition (Gr *eikon* image + *klas* to break) (***renegade, infidel***)

Always an **iconoclast**, Michael did everything in his power to do the opposite of what was expected.

❏ **heresy** (n)   opinion or action that violates traditional belief (***dissent, heterodoxy, apostasy***)

In many villages in colonial New England, to question religious doctrine was considered **heresy**.

❏ **insurgent** (n)   rebel (*in-* against + *surgere* to rise) (***subversive, guerrilla, rebel***)

Gillian was an **insurgent** on the team; although she had a lot of talent, she couldn't tolerate authority.

❏ **convention** (n)   a practice that comports with the norms of a society (***custom, propriety, norm***)

Ms. Frazier's teaching style went against **convention** and thus angered the conservative school board.

❏ **insubordination** (n)   rebellion against authority (*in-* against + *sub-* under + *ordinare* arrange) (***insolence***)

By punishing all **insubordination**, the commander showed his troops that any act of rebellion would not be tolerated.

Vocabulary Lesson 42: How Rude!

Today's roots:	*pudere*	to cause shame	*vereri*	to respect
	solere	accustomed	*haut*	high

❏ **insolence** (adj)   brash disrespect (*in-* not + *solere* accustomed) (***impertinence, impudence***)

The despot punished the rebel's **insolence** with a lengthy prison sentence.

❏ **affront** (n)   an insult (Fr *afronter* to confront) (***indignity, insult, slight, outrage***)

When he found out that his dad had let him win, Frank took it as a personal **affront** to his tennis skills.

❏ **haughty** (adj)   overly proud (*haut* high) (***pompous, supercilious, condescending, vain***)

The **haughty** young goalie felt that he had no equal in the league.

❏ **impudent** (adj)   rudely bold (*im-* not + *pudere* to cause shame) (***impertinent, insolent, brash***)

The young soldier's **impudence** would be punished; it is not wise to undermine the authority of a superior officer.

❏ **boorish** (adj)   crude, barbaric (unrelated to *boar*, a wild pig, but *piggish* is a close synonym) (***uncouth***)

The **boorish** barbarians ripped at the meat with their bare hands and spit bones onto the table.

❏ **irreverence** (n)   disrespect (*ir-* not + *vereri* to respect) (***contempt, insolence, impudence***)

The **irreverence** with which he mocked his teachers showed he had no respect for their authority.

Vocabulary Lesson 43: Earth, Moon, and Sky

Today's roots:	*astrum*	star	*luna*	moon
	naus, nauticus	pertaining to ships	*kosmos*	universe

❑ *arid* (adj)   extremely dry (*arere* to be dry) (**barren, scorched**)

Some regions of Africa have become so **arid** that entire lakes have evaporated.

❑ *astral* (adj)   relating to the stars (*astrum* star) (**celestial, stellar**)

The supernova is perhaps the most dramatic of **astral** events.

❑ *nautical* (adj)   pertaining to sailing (*naus, nauticus* pertaining to ships or sailors) (**maritime**)

The southern tip of Africa poses many **nautical** challenges to even the most adept and experienced sailor.

❑ *lunar* (adj)   relating to the moon (*luna* moon)

The **lunar** vehicle can traverse some of the rockiest and most forbidding terrain on the moon.

❑ *fecund* (adj)   fertile; fruitful (*fecundus* fruitful) (**fertile, prolific, efficacious**)

Over the summer, our **fecund** vegetable garden provided us with an endless supply of wonderful salads.

❑ *fallow* (adj)   unused; plowed but not cultivated (**dormant, quiescent, inert**)

The **fallow** land would be replanted in two years once all the nutrients had been restored.

❑ *cosmic* (adj)   relating to the universe (Gr *kosmos* universe, order) (**celestial, extraterrestrial**)

The enormous and unprecedented meteor shower was being hailed as the **cosmic** event of the century.

Vocabulary Lesson 44: More or Less

Today's roots:	*facere*	to do	*plere*	to fill
	copia	abundance		

❑ *paucity* (adj)   lack, scarcity (*paucus* few, little) (**dearth, scarcity, want**)

I love good food, so I'm frustrated by the **paucity** of good restaurants in town.

❑ *surfeit* (n)   an excessive amount (*sur-* over + *facere* to do) (**superfluity, glut, abundance**)

The **surfeit** of food on the table for Thanksgiving dinner left us all with bulging stomachs.

❑ *copious* (adj)   abundant (*copia* abundance) (**abundant, profuse, lavish**)

The **copious** number of mistakes in Robert's final paper showed his lack of effort.

❑ *barren* (adj)   infertile (**sterile, unproductive, infertile**)

The **barren** land was so devoid of life that it was difficult to find even a weed.

❑ *scanty* (adj)   meager; barely enough (**sparse, paltry, deficient**)

The **scanty** portions the soldiers received left them hungry and weak.

❑ *replete* (adj)   completely filled (*re-* again + *plere* to fill) (**sated, gorged, satiated**)

The old storage facility was **replete** with decrepit furniture that had far outlived its usefulness.

Vocabulary Lesson 45: Tough Times

Today's roots:	*logia*	speaking	*dolus*	grief
	eu-	good	emia	blood

❑ *eulogy* (n)   an honorific speech at a funeral (*eu-* good + *logia* speaking) (**accolade, tribute, acclaim**)

Because Eric had been her best friend, he delivered an emotional **eulogy** at her funeral.

❑ *despondent* (adj)   lacking hope (*de-* without + *sperare* hope) (**disheartened, woebegone, crestfallen**)

With their team trailing by ten runs in the ninth inning, the fans became **despondent**.

❑ *doleful* (adj)   filled with grief (*dolus* grief + *-ful* full of) (**lugubrious, morose, melancholy, forlorn**)

The funeral for the child was a **doleful** affair; it is always so sad to see someone die at such a young age.

❑ *anemic* (n)   feeble; characterized by oxygen deficiency in the blood (*a-* without + *emia* blood) (**feeble**)

Our offense was so **anemic** that we didn't hit the ball out of the infield all game.

❑ *malady* (n)   a disease (*mal* bad) (**affliction, infirmity, ailment**)

The flu is a common **malady** that strikes millions of people each year.

❑ *anguish* (n)   extreme suffering (**agony, torment, angst**)

The **anguish** Walter felt when his dog died was unbearable; he could hardly stop crying for a week.

❑ *dirge* (n)   a funeral song (**elegy, lament, requiem**)

You may think all **dirges** are depressing until you've been to a New Orleans jazz funeral.

Vocabulary Lesson 46: Good Learnin'

Today's roots:	*graph*	write	*demos*	people
	logos	study, word, speech	*genea*	descent

❑ *etymology* (n)   the study of the origin of words (Gr *etymon* true sense + *logos* word)

A good understanding of **etymology** can help you succeed on the SAT I.

❑ *anthropology* (n)   the study of human cultures (*anthro* mankind + *logia* study)

Anthropologists are fascinated by the similarities between tribal rituals and modern social conventions.

❑ *ethics* (n)   the study of and philosophy of moral choice (*ethos* character) (**morality**)

The more deeply one studies **ethics**, the less one is able to think in terms of moral absolutes.

❑ *theology* (n)   the study of religion (*theos* god + *logia* study)

In Catholic school, we had many **theological** discussions about the role of God in daily life.

❑ *genealogy* (n)   the study of ancestry (*genea* descent + *logia* study) (**lineage, ancestry, pedigree**)

Sarah was so fascinated by **genealogy** that she compiled a three-volume guide to her family ancestry.

❑ *demographics* (n)   the study of statistics relating to human populations (*demos* people + *graph* write)

The **demographics** reveal that Democratic candidates typically perform better in urban areas than rural areas.

Vocabulary Lesson 47: All Alone

Today's roots:	*claudere*	to close	*solus*	alone
	insula	island	*ex-*	out

❑ *hermit* (n)   one who prefers to live alone (Gr *ermita* a person of solitude) (***recluse, ascetic***)

The **hermit** lived alone in a shack in the middle of the woods, more than 10 miles from the nearest road.

❑ *ostracize* (v)   to exclude from a group (***shun, exile, snub***)

Her comments to the others were so self-centered and cruel that she was **ostracized** for months.

❑ *exile* (n)   a banishment (*ex-* out) (***banish, expatriate, expel***)

After the dictator was overthrown, he lived a life of **exile** far away from his native country.

❑ *recluse* (n)   one who likes to live alone (*re-* away + *claudere* to close) (***hermit, ascetic, eremite***)

In *To Kill a Mockingbird*, the **recluse** Boo Radley is endlessly fascinating to Scout.

❑ *isolate* (v)   to place something apart from everything else (*insula* island) (***segregate, sequester***)

The patient with tuberculosis was **isolated** from the other patients so he could not infect them.

❑ *solitude* (n)   isolation; the quality of being alone (*solus* alone) (***seclusion, isolation***)

Before the two cosmonauts joined him, the lone astronaut on the space station had spent five months in **solitude**.

Vocabulary Lesson 48: Go Forth

Today's roots:	*seminare*	to sow	*dis-*	away
	vergere, vert	to turn	*undare*	to flow

❑ *disseminate* (v)   to spread information (*dis-* away + *seminare* to sow) (***promulgate, propagate***)

The members of the band **disseminated** flyers that advertised their debut concert this coming weekend.

❑ *diverge* (v)   to go apart (*dis-* away + *vergere* to turn) (***bifurcate, digress, veer, stray***)

After traveling together for nearly 100 miles, the two cars finally **diverged**.

❑ *proliferate* (v)   to grow rapidly; to produce offspring at a rapid pace (*proles* offspring) (***flourish***)

The bacteria **proliferated** at an alarming rate, multiplying tenfold in just 30 minutes.

❑ *amass* (v)   to accumulate; to gather together (***accumulate, accrue, gather***)

Over the years, Rick has **amassed** quite a collection of CDs, accumulating over one thousand of them.

❑ *distend* (v)   to swell; to increase in size (*dis-* away + *tendere* to stretch) (***swell, bloat, dilate***)

Malnutrition can cause the abdominal cavity to **distend** and produce a bloated look.

❑ *propagate* (v)   to cause to multiply; to publicize; to travel through a medium (*pro-* forth) (***proliferate***)

Plants of all sizes and shapes **propagate** by forming seeds, which develop into new seedlings.

❑ *inundate* (v)   to flood (*in-* into + *undare* to flow) (***swamp, deluge, engulf, besiege***)

After days without work, the lawyer was astonished to suddenly find himself **inundated** with paperwork.

Vocabulary Lesson 49: Even More

Today's roots:	ad-	to	scriber	to write
	post-	after	aug-	to increase

❏ *annex* (v) to attach; to acquire land to expand an existing country (*ad-* to + *nectare* to attach) (**seize**)

When Hitler **annexed** Poland, the dictator's imperialist designs should have been clear.

❏ *addendum* (n) something added; a supplement to a book (*ad-* onto) (**appendix, supplement**)

After he completed the story, the author wrote an **addendum** explaining why he finished it the way he did.

❏ *postcript* (n) a message added after the completion of a letter (p.s.) (*post-* after + *scriber* to write)

After my wife signed the postcard, she remembered something else she wanted to say and wrote a **postcript**.

❏ *epilogue* (n) an extra chapter added onto the end of a novel (Gr *epi-* in addition + *logia* words)

In the **epilogue**, the author described what the characters of the novel did 15 years after the main narrative.

❏ *append* (v) to affix something; to add on (*ad-* to + *pendere* to hang) (**affix, add**)

The publishers **appended** an index to the end of the text to help the reader find things more easily.

❏ *adjunct* (adj) added in a subordinate capacity (*ad-* to + *jungere* to attach) (**supplement**)

Although principally a biologist, Dr. Carter was also an **adjunct** professor in the zoology department.

❏ *augment* (v) to add onto; to make greater (*aug* to increase) (**amplify, escalate**)

One important way to **augment** your SAT I score is to study vocabulary.

Vocabulary Exercise Set 3

Time—7 minutes
For each question, select the best answer among the choices given.
Note any vocabulary words to review on the Hit List below.

Each sentence below has one or two blanks, each blank indicating that something has been omitted. Beneath the sentence are five words or sets of words labeled A through E. Choose the word or set of words that, when inserted in the sentence, <u>best</u> fits the meaning of the sentence as a whole.

Example:
   Medieval kingdoms did not become constitutional republics overnight; on the contrary, the change was ------

(A) unpopular   (B) unexpected
(C) advantageous   (D) sufficient   (E) gradual

Correct response: (E)

1. The student's refusal to ------ the headmaster's dress code led to her suspension; such acts of ------ would not be accepted.

   (A) debunk .. heresy
   (B) indict .. exile
   (C) rebuke .. orthodoxy
   (D) conform to .. sedition
   (E) propagate .. irreverence

2. Missy hoped that the gigantic snowstorm on the first day of winter was not a ------ of a long and brutal season to follow.

   (A) relic   (B) satire   (C) harbinger
   (D) surfeit   (E) postcript

3. After watching countless members of the tribe perish from the unidentified ------, the doctor decided to ------ anyone displaying symptoms in an effort to avoid an epidemic.

   (A) affront .. reprove
   (B) malady .. isolate
   (C) dirge .. ostracize
   (D) distension .. amass
   (E) inundation .. disseminate

4. Appearing in front of the press after the scandal was made public, the CEO was ------ in both word and appearance, expressing regret for his actions.

   (A) cryptic   (B) contrite   (C) insurgent
   (D) haughty   (E) fecund

5. After receiving many complaints about the organization of the material, the publishers ------ an index to the text to help readers find information more easily.

   (A) appended   (B) affected
   (C) proliferated   (D) augured   (E) diverged

6. It was difficult to determine the ------ of the suspected felon's comments; although his friends professed that he was forthright, many of his coworkers described him as ------.

   (A) diligence .. candid
   (B) obscurity .. meticulous
   (C) veracity .. disingenuous
   (D) etymology .. doleful
   (E) solitude .. copious

7. Tom broke his leg the last time he went skiing, so he was understandably ------ about the ski trip he was going to attend this weekend.

   (A) impassive   (B) convoluted
   (C) indefatigable   (D) anemic
   (E) apprehensive

8. Melina studied ------ for the MCAT, dedicating 10 hours of daily preparation for over a month.

   (A) assiduously   (B) nebulously
   (C) apathetically   (D) ambiguously
   (E) impudently

HIT LIST

Write the meaning next to each root. Then write as many words as you can that contain the root.

9. CANDERE _____

10. SOLARI _____

11. CRYPTO_____

12. ORTHOS _____

13. EU-_____

14. DOXA _____

15. APO- _____

16. LEV _____

17. CURARE_____

18. PONERE _____

19. EQUI_____

20. SCRIBERE _____

21. POST- _____

22. PLERE _____

23. LOGOS _____

24. Is it honest to *equivocate*?   Y N

25. Does an *iconoclast conform*?   Y N

26. Is a *pariah* popular?   Y N

27. Do people *germinate*?   Y N

28. Can a person be *capacious*?   Y N

Write the word with the given meaning

29. a disease   m _____

30. merriment   m _____

31. to shun   o _____

32. honest   f _____

33. study of ancestry   g _____

34. strong disapproval   c _____

35. abundant   c _____

36. to do what is expected   c _____

37. lacking hope   d _____

38. candid   o _____

39. able to be cultivated   a _____

40. insubordination   s _____

41. inadequate   m _____

42. clever remark   w _____

43. uncultivated   f _____

44. barbaric   b _____

45. excessive amount   s _____

46. overly submissive   s _____

47. extreme suffering   a _____

48. insult   a _____

Write the correct form of the italicized word

49. having the quality of *heresy*

_____

50. having the qualities of an *iconoclast*

_____

51. a person who is *culpable*

_____

52. the act of *proliferating*

_____

53. having *anemia*

_____

Write the word with the given root

54. deliberately ambiguous (*vocare*)

_____

55. an inscription (*taphos*)

_____

56. a scarcity (*paucus*)

_____

57. tiny (*minuere*)

_____

58. banishment (*ex*)

_____

59. to multiply (*pro*)

_____

60. to make greater (*aug*)

_____

61. to punish (*rate*)

_____

62. done in a joking way (*jocus*)

_____

63. untiring (*fatiga*)

_____

64. overly proud (*haut*)

_____

Vocabulary Exercise Set 3 Answer Key

1. **D** The student *refused* to do something, and it led to *her suspension*. It can be inferred that this must have been a *negative* or *inappropriate* act. If the act got her suspended, the first missing word should mean something like a refusal to *follow* or *obey*.

   debunk = expose as false
   heresy = opinion or action that violates traditional belief
   indict = accuse of an offense
   exile = a banishment
   rebuke = scold
   orthodoxy = strict adherence to tradition
   conform = do what one is expected to do
   sedition = insubordination
   propagate = cause to multiply
   irreverence = disrespect

2. **C** There was a *gigantic snowstorm* on the first day of winter. She was hoping this was not a *sign* of a long and brutal winter to follow.

   relic = an object from an ancient time
   satire = a mocking literary or dramatic work
   harbinger = a precursor
   surfeit = an excessive amount
   postscript = a message added after the completion of a letter

3. **B** An unidentified force was causing the tribe members to *perish* (pass away). It can be inferred that there was some form of *illness* since the doctor was attempting to *avoid an epidemic*. The doctor would *separate* or *quarantine* individuals displaying symptoms in order to do so.

   affront = an insult
   reprove = scold
   malady = an illness
   isolate = place something apart from everything else
   dirge = a funeral song
   ostracize = exclude from a group
   distension = swelling
   amass = accumulate
   inundate = flood
   disseminate = spread

4. **B** The CEO *expressed regret* for his actions. This would indicate that he was quite *remorseful*.

   cryptic = enigmatic; mysterious
   contrite = repentant
   insurgent = rebellious
   haughty = overly proud
   fecund = fertile

5. **A** The publishers received complaints about the organization of the material, which suggests that it was hard to navigate. The missing word should mean *added* since they clearly created something to put into the text to fix the problem pointed out by the complaints.

   appended = affixed something on
   affected = behaved unnaturally
   proliferated = grew rapidly
   augured = predicted
   diverged = parted

6. **C** The word *although*, which follows the semicolon, indicates a contrast in the sentence. It was difficult to determine something about the felon's comments. The missing word in the first blank should mean *truthfulness* because the contrast indicates that some friends *professed that he was forthright* (honest), whereas many of his co-workers described him as something else. It follows logically that the second missing word should mean *dishonest* since there is a contrast being made.

   diligence = hard work
   candid = honest
   obscurity = not easily understood
   meticulous = attentive to detail
   veracity = truthfulness
   disingenuous = insincere
   etymology = the study of the origin of words
   doleful = filled with grief
   solitude = isolation
   copious = in abundance

7. **E** Tom got hurt last time he went skiing, so it would make sense that he felt *nervous* or *anxious* about skiing again.

   impassive = lacking emotion
   convoluted = intricate and hard to follow
   indefatigable = untiring
   anemic = feeble
   apprehensive = anxious about what is to come

8. **A** To study for 10 hours a day for a month shows incredible dedication and hard work. The missing word should reflect that fact.

   assiduous = hard working
   nebulous = vague
   apathetic = lacking interest
   ambiguous = unclear
   impudent = rudely bold

9. CANDERE: to shine
   candid, candor,
   incandescent, candle

10. SOLARI: comfort
solace, console, inconsolable, consolation

11. CRYPTO: secret
cryptic, crypt, cryptogram, cryptography

12. ORTHOS: right, strict
orthography, orthodox, unorthodox, orthopedic, orthodontics, orthodoxy

13. EU-: good
eulogy, euphemism, eugenics, euphoria, euphon, euthanasia

14. DOXA: opinion
orthodox, paradox, heterodox

15. APO-: away from
apocalypse, aphorism, apostate, apoplexy, apostle, apocryphal, apology

16. LEV: light, lifted up
levity, relieve, elevate, elevator, levitate, alleviate, oblivion

17. CURARE: to take care of
procure, curator, curate, pedicure, manicure

18. PONERE: to place
impose, appropriate, interpose, opponent, proponent, opposite

19. EQUI: same
equinox, equivalent, equipotential, equanimity, equality, equitable, equator, equalize

20. SCRIBERE: to write
inscribe, circumscribe, conscription, description, inscription, subscription

21. POST-: after
posterior, posterity, posthumous, postpone, postscript

22. PLERE: to fill
accomplish, complement, deplete, replete, supplement

23. LOGOS: study of
psychology, anthropology, oncology, geology

24. N

25. N

26. N

27. N

28. N

29. malady

30. mirth

31. ostracize

32. forthright

33. genealogy

34. censure

35. copious

36. conform

37. despondent

38. outspoken

39. arable

40. sedition

41. meager

42. witticism

43. fallow

44. boorish

45. surfeit

46. servile

47. anguish

48. affront

49. heretical

50. iconoclastic

51. culprit

52. proliferation

53. anemic

54. equivocal

55. epitaph

56. paucity

57. diminutive

58. exile

59. propagate

60. augment

61. berate

62. jocular

63. indefatigable

64. haughty

CHAPTER 5

CRITICAL READING SKILLS FOR THE PSAT AND SAT I

What to Read For

Strong critical reading skills are essential to college success. For this reason, critical reading questions comprise one-third of the PSAT and SAT. Good professors, expect you to understand and use what you read. They will ask you to talk and write about the salient points in your reading. But what are good critical reading skills? Many of us think that good readers are sponges, memorizing as much information as possible from what they read. In fact, good readers are more like whittlers of prose, shaving big pieces down into tools. Good readers try to find something useful in everything they read. They always try to answer three key questions:

1. **What is the purpose of this passage?**
2. **What is the central idea of this passage?**
3. **What is the structure of this passage?**

These three questions are at the core of good academic reading, so they are also at the core of PSAT and SAT reading questions.

Master the Basics, Not the Tricks

Some SAT-prep books and classes tell you that the SAT doesn't assess your reading skills—it assesses your "test-taking skills." Then they teach you tricks and shortcuts to "crack" the test. (They do this because it's easier to teach tricks and shortcuts than to teach solid academic reading skills.) Perhaps, if you have weak reading skills and are paralyzed with fear about the SAT, these tricks will boost your self-confidence a bit. But they won't get you very far, particularly if you want more than a mediocre SAT score.

Ignore the tricks until you've mastered the basic critical reading skills in this chapter. Once you do, you'll find that you won't need the tricks, just your common sense. You can't ace the Critical Reading questions without being able to **determine why a passage was written**, **summarize its main point**, **and describe its basic structure**. Most SAT Critical Reading questions distinguish good readers from those who just know a few test-taking tricks.

Learn the good academic reading skills discussed in this chapter, and then use them on the SAT. Many of the test-taking tricks are actually very bad reading habits. For instance, a good reader would not read the SAT questions before trying to understand the gist of the passage. This strategy is like putting the cart before the horse.

Practice the reading skills in this chapter every day, as you're reading novels, newspapers, textbooks, and magazines; and answer the three key questions as you read, and not just when taking the PSAT or SAT.

At first, this process may seem like a chore when you are reading a book or article for fun, but after a while you will see that the key questions enhance your reading experience. You will get more out of what you read, and you'll do much better on the SAT.

Have the Right Attitude

When reading, your attitude means a lot. If you are intimidated or bored by a passage, you won't get much out of it. "But it's not my fault," many students say. "These SAT passages are so boring!" If that were true, then college would be a dreary experience, because PSAT and SAT reading passages represent typical college reading in the liberal arts.

But here's the good news: if a passage bores you, it probably has more to do with your approach than with the content of the passage. Most students don't believe me at first when I tell them this, but after a few weeks of practice in critical reading, they begin to find the challenging ideas, and to see that these challenging ideas make the passages interesting. The passages are no different, only the approach is.

Expectations of boredom are self-fulfilling prophecies. If you expect the reading to be dull and pointless, you won't look for the interesting points and so the passage will seem dull and pointless. Finding those interesting points is the key to good reading.

If you expect to learn something new from every passage, you become an active reader rather than a passive reader. You will read more like a whittler than like a sponge, and you'll come away with something useful.

SAT Questions vs. English Class Questions

SAT reading questions must be *objective* rather than *subjective*. They must be a matter of verifiable fact rather than opinion. In English class, your teacher may ask you subjective questions—connect this essay to your life, explore the symbolism in this novel, or explore the hidden meanings in this story. The SAT, however, won't do that. The answer has to be verifiable from the text so that there is no doubt about the correct answer.

This does not mean that English class questions are better or worse than SAT questions. Think of SAT reading questions as the foundation questions: they focus on the literal meaning of the passage, rather than the *speculative* meaning. Before you can answer English class questions very well, you must be able to answer the SAT-type reading questions.

- SAT reading questions don't ask about your outside knowledge, just about the information in the passage.

- SAT reading questions don't ask you to make creative connections to the material in the passage.
- SAT reading questions don't ask you to speculate, but might ask you to draw reasonable conclusions from information in the passage

The Three Purposes of Prose

The first key question a good reader asks is "What is the purpose of this passage?" Although SAT reading passages cover a wide range of topics in the liberal arts like philosophy, history, science, literature, literary criticism, psychology, and anthropology, every passage will have one of three purposes: to *tell you a story*, to *persuade you*, or to *teach you about an event or concept*.

Passages that tell stories are called **narratives**. These include not only fiction stories, but also biographies and memoirs. The purpose of every narrative is the same: to describe how a main character deals with a problem.

Passages that try to persuade you are called **arguments**. The purpose of every argument is the same: to present and justify the author's point of view. They are subjective, that is, largely a matter of opinion.

Passages that try to teach you something are called **analyses**. You should think of these as objective answers to essay questions, like "What is impressionism?" or "How was the telescope invented?" They are objective, that is, largely a matter of fact.

Always read the italicized introduction to each passage. It often gives important background information and clues about the purpose of the passage. Notice clues like the following.

Words that indicate narrative: *biography, story, autobiography, memoir, novel, fiction, account*

Words that indicate argument: *comment, argue, opinion, perspective, point of view, position*

Words that indicate analysis: *examine, analyze, scientific, historical, explore*

The Three Central Ideas

Every passage has a central idea that unifies and organizes the entire passage.

Every narrative is focused on a conflict. The conflict is the problem that the main character must deal with. Understanding a narrative begins with understanding the conflict. Nearly every narrative has the same basic structure: (1) the conflict is introduced, (2) the conflict is developed, and (3) the conflict is resolved.

Every argument is focused on a thesis. The thesis is simply what the writer is trying to persuade you to believe. A thesis must take a side, that is, state clearly whether something is good or bad or right or wrong. To understand a thesis, it is just as important to understand what an essay is arguing *against* as what it is arguing *for*.

Every analysis is focused on answering a question objectively. On the SAT, this question is always one that would interest a college professor of history, literature, geology, philosophy, anthropology, or literature, and so on.

Always find the central idea of the passage: the conflict, thesis, or question. Jot it down in the margin. Then check that every paragraph relates to this central idea. No paragraph should stray from the point of the passage. If a paragraph doesn't seem to fit with the central idea, reread it or rethink the central idea. Maybe it's not what you first thought.

Find the Basic Structure of the Passage

A good piece of writing is like a good painting. Its many different parts work together to make a meaningful whole. Looked at a different way, a good piece of writing is a unique journey through "narrative space," "argument space," or "analysis space." A good reader recognizes how a good piece of writing moves through this space.

Understanding an SAT passage means understanding its parts. Those parts have a sequence, like the stops on a journey. This journey can be summarized with a line through "prose space," just as a real trip can be summarized with a red line through a geographical map. There are many ways of planning a journey, so there are many possible paths through a "prose space." Usually, though, a piece of prose travels from left to right from task to task in the "spaces" shown below.

You might think of the boxes below as "cities" that must be visited in the journey, and the ovals as the optional sites you can visit within each city.

Narrative Space

This path describes the structure of a story in which a man's wife is murdered (crime), he pursues the criminal (adventure), he discovers that his wife only staged her own death and ran off with another man (revealing experience), and he becomes more aware of this vulnerability to deception (transformation).

Argument Space

This path describes the structure of an argument in which the author states that a particular philosopher's ideas are harmful (evaluation), explains why she believes this (explanation), gives an example of the potential harm of those ideas (example), and then discusses how this evaluation should affect how we think (implication).

Analysis Space

This path describes the structure of an analysis in which the author describes the discovery of a strange type of radiation from deep space (phenomenon), provides a theory to describe its origin (theory), gives data that support the theory (data), explains why the data support the theory (explanation), and discusses what this theory suggests about the composition of the universe (implication).

Simplify by Paraphrasing

When you read, your brain can't simply record the information for playback the way a CD records music. Rather, your brain must *consolidate* the information, that is, simplify it so that you can more easily recall and analyze it. The best way to *consolidate* information is by *paraphrasing*.

Consciously paraphrase each paragraph as you read. Reduce it to a simple sentence in your own words. Don't worry—this won't waste time. The opposite is true—those who *don't* paraphrase spend much *more* time answering critical reading questions, because they must spend more time rereading the passage to find the important points that they should have gotten the first time through.

Visualize

You probably first learned to read with picture books but moved away from them as you grew older. As you did, you may have found reading more of a challenge, not simply because the language and plots became more complex, but because the pictures disappeared. **Vivid pictures in your head are invaluable tools for consolidating information, and for enjoying what you read.** (The cliché *a picture is worth a thousand words* is probably an understatement.) Those who turn words into vivid pictures maintain a strong interest in reading. Those who don't, struggle.

Visualizing as you read increases your interest level as well as your ability to consolidate information. Like any skill, you must consciously practice to get good at it. If you have trouble staying interested in or remembering what you read, focus on painting vivid pictures—or even better, vivid *movies*—in your head as you read.

Practice visualization whenever you read.

- Visualize a narrative unfolding like a movie. Visualize the characters as vividly as possible. See the action clearly. See the conflict as a "battle" between characters, or within a character, or between a character and a situation, etc. See the development and resolution of the conflict and how they change the protagonist.

- Visualize an argument as a battle between the author's thesis on one hand and the opposing thesis on the other. See the explanations and examples as weapons against the enemy. Make sure that you can see *both* sides of the battle.

- Visualize an analysis as a schematic diagram unfolding before your eyes, with the central question in the middle of the diagram and the supporting points, explanations, or examples around it. This takes practice, because analytical prose is not as naturally visual as narrative prose is. You need to work harder to see an analysis in your mind's eye, but it will become easier with practice.

Review after Each Paragraph

Think of the start of each new paragraph as a "scene change" in your movie and a jump to a new place in "prose space." Let paragraphs help you to check your understanding of the passage; use paragraph breaks as "signposts."

Every paragraph contributes a new idea, so make sure to find it. At the end of each paragraph, ask:

- What was the main idea of that paragraph?
- How is this idea related to the previous paragraph? (What's the transition?)
- How does this paragraph contribute to the main idea of the passage?

It may help to write a quick summary of the paragraph in the margin. Practice doing this under timed PSAT conditions to make sure you can do it without rushing.

Now Attack the Questions

With practice, you will learn to extract the key information from a passage—the purpose, central idea, and structure—in just a few minutes, after which you are ready to attack the PSAT questions.

Know What Each Question Is Asking For

Read each question very carefully—several times, if necessary. Look for the key words or phrases that tell you what to look for in the passage. There are seven general kinds of critical reading questions.

- **Purpose** questions ask you to explain why the author wrote the passage or used a particular term or phrase. To answer these, first reflect on the purpose of the passage as a whole, as well as the purpose of the line mentioned.
  *The overall **purpose** of the passage is to…
  The author mentions the "depth of division" to suggest that…*

- **Central idea** questions ask you to describe the main idea of the passage. You should always be ready for these questions, because they are just rephrasings of the second key question.
  *Which of the following is the **best title** for this passage? What is the **main idea** of the passage?*

- **Secondary idea** questions ask you to identify the points made in individual paragraphs or sentences. To answer these, remember that secondary points must always support the central idea, so remind yourself of the overall main idea of the passage.
  The "problems" mentioned in line 56 are those of…

- **Inference** questions ask you to draw conclusions based on the main or secondary points of the passage. To answer these, you must understand not only what the reference means, but also what it **logically** implies.
  With which of the following statements would the author most likely agree? The author suggests that…

- **Tone** questions ask you to describe author's attitude toward an idea, or the tone of a characterization. To answer these, you must find the key words or ideas that convey a mood.
  *In the final paragraph, the author's cousin is **characterized** as… The first sentence conveys a tone of…*

- **Word- or phrase-in-context** questions ask you to give the meaning of a word or phrase as it is used in the passage. To answer these, you must read the sentence with the given word or phrase, think about its meaning, and then *replace* it with your *own* word or phrase and find the closest match.
  In line 41, the word "final" most nearly means…

- **Structure or device** questions ask you to describe the overall structure of the passage or identify certain devices, like similes, metaphors, anecdotes, etc. You should always be ready for these questions, because they are rephrasings of the third key question, which you should always answer as you read.
  *The **structure** of this passage is best described as… Which of the following **devices** is not used in the last paragraph?*

The SAT sometimes (but not too often) asks about the use of technical literary or rhetorical terms like those listed below, so it's a good idea to make sure you know what they mean. **Put them on flashcards and study them.**

Analyze—examine the parts of something. Analyzing a theory means examining its *origin, components, implications*, etc.

Anecdote—an illustrative story. An anecdote about an incident with a mean teacher can illustrate a critique of schooling.

Counterexample—an example to disprove a claim. One white rat is a counterexample to the claim "all rats are black."

Hyperbole—exaggeration for rhetorical effect. Saying *"everyone* knows that reality shows are staged" is hyperbolic.

Irony—a reversal of expectations. A firehouse burning down is ironic; it is the *last* building you would expect to burn.

Logic—systematic reasoning. Logical reasoning usually employs terms like *therefore, because, so*, etc.

Metaphor—saying one thing is another thing. "War is hell" is a famous metaphor.

Objective—using only indisputable facts, not opinion. A good reporter should be objective and never editorialize.

Simile—comparison using *like* or *as*. "The presentation went over like a lead balloon" is a vivid simile.

Subjective—based on personal opinion. Music and movie reviews are mostly subjective evaluations.

Think of Your Own Answer First

Top scorers on the PSAT and SAT Critical Reading always think of their own answers to the questions before checking the answer choices. They know that some choices are written to tempt students who aren't careful. These "distractors" contain information from the passage, but not the *right* information. If you've ever tried a critical reading question where more than one choice sounded correct, you probably didn't think carefully enough about *your own* answer to the question first. If you've answered the three key questions already, you should have no problem thinking of your own answers to most of the critical reading questions. If you do so, then the right choice will pop out at you when you scan the choices.

Practice "translating" critical reading questions to make them "open-ended" so you can think of your own answer:

Question: *The tone of the opening paragraph is best characterized as . . .*

Translation: *What is the tone of the opening paragraph?*

Find an answer to this, rereading if necessary; then look for a match among the choices.

Question: *The author implies that most people do not notice bias in the media because . . .*

Translation: *Why (according to this author) don't people notice bias in the media?*

Find an answer to this, rereading if necessary; then look for a match among the choices.

"Paired" Passages

Every SAT or PSAT contains two "paired" passages that share a common theme but that are written by different authors. They will be followed by normal questions about the individual passages and then questions comparing or contrasting the two passages with each other. For the most part, it's best to approach these passages just as you would any other passage, but there are a couple of points to keep in mind.

On paired passages, remember that the passages are written by different authors and will likely have different perspectives on the same theme. As you read, then, ask yourself, "What is the common theme?" and "How do these two perspectives differ from each other?"

After reading Passage 1, answer the first few questions before moving on to Passage 2. The first few questions will probably deal only with Passage 1, so it makes sense to tackle those questions first. Once you've finished the questions on Passage 1, read Passage 2 and then tackle the rest of the questions. This approach will help you to attack the questions more quickly and to avoid confusing the two passages.

Single and "Paired" Paragraphs

Every SAT or PSAT will contain several single paragraphs about 100 words long, each followed by one to three questions. These questions will be much like the questions on the longer reading passages. Each SAT or PSAT will also contain one set of "paired" paragraphs, each 70–200 words long, followed by four questions based on the two passages and the relationship between the passages.

> Approach the single-paragraph or paired-paragraph passages in the same way as you would approach the longer passages. These questions are of the same type and difficulty as the other critical reading questions.

Use the Line References Intelligently

> Questions on a critical reading section, unlike the questions on other SAT sections, don't necessarily get harder as you go along. **Instead, they are usually arranged chronologically**—the first question is about the *beginning* of the passage, and the last question is about the *end of the passage*. See for yourself—look at the critical reading questions on a PSAT or SAT and notice that the line references in the questions get later and later.

> Where should you look for the answer to a reading question if the question doesn't include line references? **Look for line references in the previous question and the following question.** The answer to the question is probably found between those two line references. For instance, if question 25 does not refer to a line, but question 24 refers to line 46 and question 26 refers to line 55, you should look for the answer to question 25 between lines 46 and 55!

Find Evidence in the Passage

> **Always make sure that you have clear, literal evidence from the passage to support every answer you give.** You will never need to recall information from your studies. All the information you need is in the passage or its introduction.

Logically Analyze the Questions and Answers

Solid test-taking logic can often help you decide among the answer choices on tough questions.

> **If two answers seem similar, the less extreme or less exclusive answer is more likely to be right.** Statements with "exclusive" words like *never* or *always* are less likely to be true than statements with "inclusive" words like *sometimes* or *often*. Also, "extreme" statements are less likely to be true than are banal, ordinary statements.

What is the author's attitude toward the "transgressions" mentioned in line 12?

(A) indifference
(B) vehement opposition
(C) ambivalence
(D) disapproval
(E) resignation

Of course, you must understand the passage to answer this question, but let's say you've thought about it, and you know it must be either (B) *vehement opposition* or (D) *disapproval*. Logically, since *vehement opposition* is a type of *disapproval* (but *disapproval* is not necessarily a type of *vehement opposition*), (B) cannot be the answer unless (D) is also correct, but of course two answers can't be right, so it must be (D).

> **Writers write about what they care about.** Don't forget this when answering critical reading questions. In the question above, for instance, choice (A) *indifference* is almost certainly not the right answer if the "transgressions" are a topic of discussion in the passage. Of course, it's remotely possible that the author is saying, "Here is something that some other people *think* is important, but it's really not; I'm not really interested in this idea." But even then, the author at least thinks it's important enough to discuss, right? So she's not really *indifferent* about it.

> **An author can do a lot in 400–800 words, but not too much.** An author can more easily "suggest a few political reforms" in 500 words than "delineate the history of European political reform." So when answering questions about the overall purpose of a passage, use common sense about what can be done in 400–800 words and what can't.

Which of the following best expresses the purpose of the passage as a whole?

(A) to describe the relationship between literature and history
(too big a task for 500 words—eliminate)
(B) to belittle modern literary critics
(possible, but a very petty purpose—eliminate)
(C) to refute a misconception
(very possible and a worthwhile purpose—keep)
(D) to delineate a new mode of literary analysis
(too big a task for 500 words—eliminate)
(E) to suggest several remedies for a problem
(very possible and a worthwhile purpose—keep)

The right answer won't always be what common sense alone says, but it will never *violate* common sense. The authors of SAT passages may sometimes have strange points of view, but none of the authors is clinically insane!

A Few Words about Reading Speed

On the SAT, you don't have to read very quickly. You just have to read intelligently. Many students make the mistake of racing through the reading passages without focusing on the three key questions. They think that reading fast saves them time. In fact, if you skim too quickly, you'll miss important points and get bogged down in the questions.

As you take the practice tests in Chapter 14, time yourself carefully and notice if you have much difficulty finishing the Critical Reading sections. **Don't panic, though, if you don't finish in time for the first couple of tests; you will probably improve your efficiency after a few tests, and the problem will go away.** If it doesn't, however, you have four options:

1. Change the way you're attacking the questions (as discussed below).
2. Use a stopwatch to budget your time: give yourself 2 minutes per 100 words to read and answer the questions.
3. Work on improving your reading speed (as discussed below).

4. Get tested to see if you qualify to take the SAT with extended time.

After taking a few practice tests, you may feel that the standard time is not enough for you to get through the readings. If so, talk to your guidance counselor about how to qualify for extended time on the SAT I. Be careful, though: extra time doesn't necessarily mean extra points. Some students actually score lower with extra time, because they don't use their time as effectively.

The "Attack the Questions as You Read" Approach

Most students do best by reading the whole passage before attacking the questions. However, you might want to experiment with **attacking the questions as you read.** With this method, you first read the introduction and the first paragraph, then immediately answer the first few questions on that section (skipping any "central idea or purpose" questions for now). When you reach a question about a part of the passage that you haven't read, read the next paragraph or two, and so on. **Always read whole paragraphs at a time: don't stop in the middle of a paragraph.**

Increase Your Speed Gradually

If you increase your reading speed the right way, your comprehension will increase as well. Imagine yourself driving a car when it suddenly accelerates beyond your control. What would you do? You'd pay very close attention to everything around you so you don't crash! Similarly, when you speed up your reading, you break yourself of the habit of mindlessly moving your eyes over the page. You will pay better attention to the ideas. **The key, though, is to increase your speed gradually.**

One barrier to fast reading is "subvocalization," or the tendency to "hear" in your head the words that you are reading. **To break this barrier, practice forcing your eyes to move over the words faster than you can speak them.**

Use Your Hand

If you want to read faster or improve your focus, you must "retrain" your eyes to move smoothly and quickly through the page. Use your hand to help. Let your fingers sweep smoothly across the page to guide and focus your eyes on the words near your fingers. Work on "pushing" your eyes through the passage. Practice with different sweep techniques. Good hand-eye coordination will boost your comprehension as well as your speed.

Practice, Practice, Practice

Daily "quick reading" exercises help you to hone your comprehension skills. Take out a stopwatch and try to get the key ideas of a newspaper or magazine article in 30 seconds. Try to get the key ideas of a book in only five minutes. "Quick reading" exercises will help you to locate important points in your reading and skim over unnecessary ones.

What to Do When You "Space Out"

Most everyone "spaces out" from time to time on the PSAT critical reading. Spacing out is when your eyes move across the page, but your mind doesn't really process the words. If this happens to you, don't panic. It's usually nothing to worry about. **Just calmly go back to where you left off, and reread normally.** Of course, it's a good idea to minimize space-outs, too.

The best way to minimize space-outs is to continually know what to look for. **When you have a conscious task, your mind stays focused and you're less likely to space out.** Constantly keep the three key questions in mind, and check your understanding at the end of each paragraph.

Sit Up Straight

When reading the PSAT, sit up straight and lean slightly forward, so that your eyes are directly over the page. This keeps your brain in "alert" mode and makes it easier to absorb information. Ever try to read while lying down? Hard to stay alert, isn't it? This is because your body is telling your brain that it's time for sleep, and so your brain begins to shut down, hardly what you want to do when taking the PSAT!

Practice Your Speed, If Necessary

If you consistently run out of time on the critical reading sections of the SAT, consider keeping a stopwatch with you as you practice. Budget about 2 minutes for every 100 words of the passage to read the passage and answer the questions. For instance, reading and answering the questions on an 800-word passage should take you about 16 minutes. Practice increasing your reading speed until you are comfortable working within that time limit, and practice maintaining that speed every time you read.

Keep Your Eyes on the Prize

Unless you have a good shot at a perfect 80 Critical Reading score, it's probably best not to answer every question. Don't get bogged down on tough questions. If you can't decide between two answers, make your best guess and move on. Make a small mark next to the question number on your answer sheet so you know what to come back to if you have time. Keep in mind that, in order to break 50, you need to get only about half of the questions right, and to break 60, you need to get only about two-thirds of the questions right. To break 70, though, you'll need to get more than 86% of the questions right.

Read, Read, Read!

Those who do the best on the SAT Critical Reading are those who read lots of college-level prose across the curriculum. The SAT I will include readings on history, philosophy, science, biography, and fiction in a wide variety of voices. It helps tremendously to be familiar with these kinds of passages. Good readers appreciate the work of a wide variety of writers. William Shakespeare, S. J. Perelman, Walter Lippmann, and Jane Austen all use the English language masterfully, but their writing styles are very different.

Don't restrict yourself to reading just a narrow range of prose that you've enjoyed in the past. Delve into works of different genres, different eras, and different styles. The following list represents some of the most influential books in the liberal arts, and they represent a wide variety of voices. Push yourself to read the books on this list that go beyond your conventional reading.

Also, read to expose yourself to the vast world of ideas. The readings you will likely see on the SAT I will span the liberal arts and touch on many ideas that interest current scholars in those areas. The more familiar you are with these ideas, the easier it will be to understand passages that discuss them.

The College Hill Reading List
Narrative

One Hundred Years of Solitude, G. Garcia-Marquez
Candide, Voltaire
The Wall, John Hersey
The Best American Short Stories of the Century,
    John Updike, Editor
Frankenstein, Mary Wollstonecraft Shelley
The Color Purple Alice Walker
Metamorphosis (and other stories), Franz Kafka
The Autobiography of Frederick Douglass
The Painted Bird, Jerzy Kozinsky
Macbeth, William Shakespeare
Growing Up, Russell Baker
Baby, It's Cold Inside, S. J. Perelman
Pride and Prejudice, Jane Austen
Atlas Shrugged, Ayn Rand
The Life of Pi, Yann Martel
Crime and Punishment, Fyodor Dostoevsky

Argument

The Op-Ed pages of The *New York Times*
Essays from *Harper's,* The *Atlantic Monthly*, and
    The *New Yorker*
Lanterns and Lances, James Thurber
Drift and Mastery, Walter Lippmann
The Best American Essays, Robert Atwan, Editor
Walden, Henry David Thoreau
The Chomsky Reader Noam Chomsky

Analysis

A Brief History of Time, Stephen Hawking
The Mismeasure of Man, Stephen J. Gould
The Republic, Plato
Civilization and Its Discontents, Sigmund Freud
A People's History of the United States Howard Zinn
How the Mind Works, Steven Pinker
QED, Richard Feynman
The Lives of a Cell, Lewis Thomas
Democracy in America, Alexis de Tocqueville
The Language Instinct, Steven Pinker
The Man Who Mistook His Wife for a Hat,
    Oliver Sacks

Critical Reading Practice 1

The *following is an essay regarding current knowledge of subatomic physics.*

Line   A tantalizing paradox peers out from every
basic physics textbook, but rarely do students
notice it or teachers exploit it. Despite the vast
knowledge that scientists have accumulated
5   about the subatomic realm, including
astonishingly accurate equations for predicting
the behavior of barely detectable particles, an
obvious conundrum persists that they are only
recently beginning to understand: protons stick
10   together in atomic nuclei.

All first-year physics students learn that the
atomic nucleus contains neutrons, which have
no charge, and protons, which are positively
charged. They also learn that while opposite
15   charges attract, all like charges repel each
other, just like the north poles of two magnets.
So what keeps all of those positively-charged
protons bound together in a nucleus? Physicists
have long postulated that there must be another
20   special force, called the nuclear force, that
counteracts the electrical repulsion between
protons. But where does it come from?

One theory, proposed by Nobel laureate
Hideki Yukawa in the 1930's, held that the
25   nuclear force is conveyed by a particle called a
pion, which, he claimed, is exchanged among
the neutrons and protons in the nucleus. Forty
years later, physicists discovered that pions,
not to mention the protons and neutrons
30   themselves, are actually composed of yet
smaller paticles called "quarks," which are held
together by aptly-named "gluons." The force
conveyed by gluons is called the "strong" force.
Although experiments had clearly
35   demonstrated that these gluons are responsible
for the force that binds quarks within protons
and neutrons, nothing suggested that gluons
are exchanged between protons and neutrons.
Nevertheless, by the early 1980's, most
40   physicists became convinced that some
combination of gluons and quarks—perhaps
the pion—must be responsible for the nuclear
force.

Professor Yukawa's theory, however, was
45   dealt a blow by a series of experiments that
were conducted at Los Alamos National
Laboratory in the early 1990's. These

experiments demonstrated that pions carry the
nuclear force only over distances greater than
50   half a fermi—the radius of a proton—yet the
distance between bound protons is far less than
that. The pion seemed to be a giant plumber's
wrench trying to do a tweezer's job.

In the years since, physicists have refined
55   Yukawa's theory to suggest that closely bound
protons or neutrons are held by a "residual"
force left over from the strong forces binding
quarks together into protons and neutrons, so
that pions don't need to be exchanged. If the
60   protons and neutrons are far enough apart
within the nucleus, however, perhaps pions
do the job.

1.   Which of the following best summarizes the
"paradox" mentioned in line 1?

(A) Teachers don't utilize educational
materials effectively.
(B) A law of physics appears to be violated.
(C) Scientists continue to test hypotheses
that they suspect are false.
(D) Hideki Yukawa's theory is incorrect.
(E) Scientists are increasingly reluctant to
explore the difficult field of nuclear
physics.

2.   In lines 35–36, the phrase "responsible for"
most nearly means

(A) guardians of
(B) guilty of
(C) representative of
(D) capable of conveying
(E) responsive to

3.   According to the passage, the nuclear force
cannot be completely explained in terms of the
exchange of pions because pions

(A) are not composed of quarks
(B) have little or no effect in the distances
between nuclear particles
(C) repel each other
(D) cannot coexist with the gluons that
convey the "strong" force
(E) are positively charged

Reproduced courtesy of the author, Christopher Black.

4. Which of the following best describes the purpose of the final paragraph (lines 55–62)?

(A) It resolves a problem indicated in the previous paragraph

(B) It provides an example of a concept introduced in the previous paragraph.

(C) It presents a counterexample to a misconception described in the previous paragraph.

(D) It provides an example that is similar to the one presented in the previous paragraph.

(E) It logically analyzes a claim made in the previous paragraph.

5. Which of the following best describes the organization of the passage as a whole?

(A) presentation of a theory followed by refutation

(B) description of a problem followed by a history of attempts to solve it

(C) statement of fact followed by logical analysis

(D) description of a scientific discovery followed by a discussion of its implications

(E) analysis of a theory and suggestions on how it should be taught

Critical Reading Practice 2

The following passage was written in 1911 by Wassily Kandinsky, a renowned abstract painter. Here he discusses the relationship between primitivism, an artistic movement that seeks to move away from technology and the divisions of modern society, and materialism, which denies that there is a spiritual component of reality.

Line Every work of art is the child of its age and, in many cases, the mother of our emotions. It follows that each period of culture produces an art of its own which can never be repeated.
5 Efforts to revive the art-principles of the past will at best produce an art that is still-born. It is impossible for us to live and feel as did the ancient Greeks. In the same way those who strive to follow the Greek methods in sculpture
10 achieve only a similarity of form, the work remaining soulless for all time. Such imitation is mere aping. Externally the monkey completely resembles the human being; he will sit holding a book in front of his nose, and turn
15 over the pages with a thoughtful aspect, but his actions have for him no real meaning.

There is, however, in art another kind of external similarity which is founded on a fundamental truth. When there is a similarity of
20 inner tendency in the whole moral and spiritual atmosphere, a similarity of ideals, at first closely pursued but later lost to sight, a similarity in the inner feeling of any one period to that of another, the logical result will be a
25 revival of the external forms which served to express those inner feelings in an earlier age. An example of this today is our sympathy, our spiritual relationship, with the Primitives. Like ourselves, these artists sought to express in
30 their work only internal truths, renouncing in consequence all considerations of external form.

This all-important spark of inner life today is at present only a spark. Our minds, which are
35 even now only just awakening after years of materialism, are infected with the despair of unbelief, of lack of purpose and ideal. The nightmare of materialism, which has turned the life of the universe into an evil, useless
40 game, is not yet past; it holds the awakening soul still in its grip. Only a feeble light glimmers like a tiny star in a vast gulf of darkness. This feeble light is but a presentiment, and the soul, when it sees it, trembles in doubt whether the
45 light is not a dream, and the gulf of darkness reality. This doubt and the still harsh tyranny of the materialistic philosophy divide our soul sharply from that of the Primitives. Our soul rings cracked when we seem to play upon it, as
50 does a costly vase, long buried in the earth, which is found to have a flaw when it is dug up once more. For this reason, the Primitive phase, through which we are now passing, with its temporary similarity of form, can only be of
55 short duration.

Concerning the Spiritual in Art, Wassily Kandinsky. © 1997 Dover Publications. Reprinted by permission of Dover Publications.

1. Which of the following is the best title for this passage?

   (A) The Art of the Early Twentieth Century
   (B) The Dangers of Materialism
   (C) Why Primitive Art Cannot Be Rekindled
   (D) The Similarities in Artistic Movements
   (E) The Lack of Purpose in Art

2. As it is used in line 15, the word "aspect" most nearly means

   (A) meaningful perspective
   (B) facial expression
   (C) configuration
   (D) contemplation
   (E) minor part

3. Which of the following is an example of the "fundamental truth" mentioned in line 19?

   (A) the inability of great artists like Vincent Van Gogh to achieve fame in their lifetimes
   (B) the tendency of artists from all cultures to eschew social conventions
   (C) the failure to reproduce artwork that was created in the fourth century BC
   (D) the ability of apes to create paintings that resemble abstract works by humans
   (E) the similarity between two paintings created a century apart, each in the midst of a great class war

4. In saying that the soul "trembles in doubt" (line 44) when it sees the "feeble light" (line 41) the author suggests that

   (A) artists have doubts about whether the era of materialism is truly past
   (B) the public is unsure that its hunger for art will be met
   (C) artists do not know from where their next inspiration will come
   (D) the Primitives found mysterious lights more frightening than modern people do
   (E) artists usually do not work well under the harsh light of scrutiny

5. How would the author characterize the effect of materialism on the artist's soul?

   (A) supportive
   (B) confusing
   (C) calming
   (D) oppressive
   (E) inspirational

Critical Reading Practice 3

The following passage is excerpted from a text on the principles of zoology.

Line From ancient times, people commonly believed that life arose repeatedly by spontaneous generation from nonliving material in addition to parental reproduction. For example, frogs
5 appeared to arise from damp earth, mice from putrefied matter, insects from dew, and maggots from decaying meat. Warmth, moisture, sunlight and even starlight often were mentioned as factors that encouraged
10 spontaneous generation of living organisms.
    Among the accounts of early efforts to synthesize organisms in the laboratory is a recipe for making mice, given by the Belgian plant nutritionist Jean Baptiste van Helmont
15 (1648). "If you press a piece of underwear soiled with sweat together with some wheat in an open jar, after about 21 days the odor changes and the ferment...changes the wheat into mice. But what is more remarkable is that the
20 mice which came out of the wheat and underwear were not small mice, not even miniature adults or aborted mice, but adult mice emerge!"
    In 1861, the great French scientist Louis
25 Pasteur convinced scientists that living organisms cannot arise spontaneously from nonliving matter. In his famous experiments,

Pasteur introduced fermentable material into a flask with a long s-shaped neck that was open to
30 air. The flask and its contents were then boiled for a long time to kill any microorganisms that might be present. Afterward the flask was cooled and left undisturbed. No fermentation occurred because all organisms that entered
35 the open end were deposited in the neck and did not reach the fermentable material. When the neck of the flask was removed, microorganisms in the air promptly entered the fermentable material and proliferated. Pasteur concluded
40 that life could not originate in the absence of previously existing organisms and their reproductive elements, such as eggs and spores. Announcing his results to the French Academy, Pasteur proclaimed, "Never will the doctrine of
45 spontaneous generation arise from this mortal blow."

All living organisms share a common ancestor, most likely a population of colonial microorganisms that lived almost 4 billion
50 years ago. This common ancestor was itself the product of a long period of prebiotic assembly of non-living matter, including organic molecules and water, to form self-replicating units. All living organisms
55 retain a fundamental chemical composition inherited from their ancient common ancestor.

1. Throughout the passage, the word "spontaneous" can best be taken to mean

(A) without reproductive elements
(B) in a medium
(C) unthinking
(D) free-spirited
(E) adult

2. In Pasteur's experiment, why was the neck of the flask removed?

(A) to allow the air to escape
(B) to provide access to microorganisms
(C) to kill any microorganisms that may be present
(D) to permit the heating of the flask
(E) to introduce fermentable material

3. In line 45, the word "mortal" most nearly means

(A) human
(B) impermanent
(C) fatal
(D) earthly
(E) malicious

4. If both Pasteur's conclusion that "life could not...eggs and spores" (lines 40–42) and the statement "This common ancestor...units" (lines 50–54) are true, then which of the following statements must also be true about "prebiotic assembly" (lines 51–52)?

(A) It is not a "spontaneous" process.
(B) It does not depend on sunlight.
(C) It produces molecules unlike those in current life-forms
(D) It occurs in the absence of water.
(E) It occurs very quickly.

5. In what sense is the use of the word "water" (line 53) ironic?

(A) It is a substance in which many living organisms thrive.
(B) It has a relatively low boiling point.
(C) Pasteur did not mention it specifically in his description of his experiment.
(D) It was not one of the ingredients in Helmont's recipe.
(E) It was earlier mentioned as a factor in a debunked theory of how life was generated.

Critical Reading Practice 4

The following passage discusses the philosophical distinction between two methods of explaining scientific phenomena.

Line
As our theories about the world around us have evolved and become more useful, they have become, almost without exception, less teleological and more mechanistic. A
5   teleological explanation of a phenomenon describes causes and effects in terms of desires or purposes: something happens simply because it serves a certain purpose, because it is "supposed" to happen or because someone or
10   something "wants" it to happen. Teleological explanations never survive as useful theories because they are backward: they place the cause after the effect. A ball falls to earth because, as it is in the air, it perceives that its
15   more proper place is on the ground, and not because anything pushes it.

A mechanistic explanation, on the other hand, requires that any discussion of causes and effects be restricted by the known laws of
20   how physical objects and substances interact as time moves *forward*. This is the language of the scientist. No right-minded chemist would say that trinitrotoluene explodes because it "wants to." It does so because the presence of heat and
25   oxygen releases the potential energy stored in its bonds.

Early scientific theories were almost exclusively teleological. If you could drive Socrates around in your SUV, he would be far
30   more likely to ask you about your vehicle's nature, or its desires, or its soul than about how the engine worked, how the odometer received its information, or how the different buttons on the CD player produced their effects. It would
35   seem to him that he was in the belly of a metallic animal, or at least a possessed machine.

Teleological explanations are convenient for explaining what people do, because most of us
40   understand the concepts of "wants" and "needs" far more deeply than we understand the mind's mechanisms for processing information. If you only have three minutes to explain to your friend why you're not going to a
45   party, you don't very well have the knowledge, not to mention the time or desire, to explain

how your cerebral cortex processed the information and concepts associated with the decision to stay home. You just give a reason
50   why you don't want to, and your friend understands.

This convenience persuades us that teleological explanations are the best for analyzing human behavior. Furthermore, we
55   resist mechanistic explanations of behavior because they seem to deny another preciously guarded concept: free will. If our decision to stay home from a party could be explained in the same way that the action of an internal
60   combustion engine can be explained, then doesn't that reduce us all to mindless machines?

No: the mind's understanding of the mind will always leave room for "free will," whatever
65   that really means. Full understanding of a phenomenon depends on the mind's ability to detach from and observe it, and the mind can never fully detach from itself. This complication may imply that a full understanding of
70   the human mind is impossible, but it does not imply that we must be satisfied with mere teleology. Perhaps this will require an entirely new conception of psychology, but if psychology is to remain relevant, we have no
75   other choice.

1. Which of the following is the best title for this passage?

    (A) Why Mechanism Should Replace Teleology
    (B) The Science of the Ancient Greeks
    (C) The Psychology of Wants and Needs
    (D) The Causes of Scientific Ignorance
    (E) Obstacles to a Full Understanding of the Mind

2. Which of the following is an example of a "teleological" explanation?

    (A) Water evaporates because it absorbs heat.
    (B) An engine works because it burns fuel.
    (C) A bird sings because it likes the sound.
    (D) A dog yelps because it perceives pain.
    (E) A ball falls because a gravitational field pulls it.

3. The discussion of Socrates in lines 28–37 emphasizes the fact that he was

(A) more influential than other Greek philosophers
(B) fearful of complicated machines
(C) concerned more with ethics than with physics
(D) aware of the mechanistic laws of physics
(E) inclined to explain phenomena in terms of purposes

4. In line 36, the word "possessed" most nearly means

(A) owned
(B) willful
(C) purchased
(D) determined
(E) spontaneous

5. The fourth paragraph suggests that teleological explanations persist chiefly because they

(A) are easier to use
(B) are more logically consistent
(C) agree with physical laws
(D) deny free will
(E) explain physical phenomena accurately

6. According to the author, which of the following describes the main difference between the "machine" in line 37 and the "machines" in line 62?

(A) The "machine" is modern, but the "machines" are ancient.
(B) The "machine" obeys mechanistic physical laws, but the "machines" do not.
(C) The "machine" cannot be explained teleologically, but the "machines" can.
(D) The "machine" is simple, but the "machines" are not.
(E) The "machine" is thought to have a soul, but the "machines" have had their souls attentuated.

Critical Reading Practice 5

The following is an excerpt from a recent book by two science writers on the evolution of human intelligence.

Line Where can freedom be found? Perhaps in a flock of estuary birds? Flying together at high speeds, thousands of birds maneuver with precise coordination. The flock flies this way
5 and then that. It turns as if a wave has passed through it. These "maneuver waves" start slowly in a few individuals but quickly spread. Unless the individual birds reacted together, the flock would disperse, exposing isolated
10 birds to predators. Sometimes it is "smart," in a survival sense, to give up your freedom and fit in with a group.

Once started, a wave travels through a flock at about 70 birds a second. Surprisingly, this is
15 much faster than a single bird's reaction time. Thus, individual birds cannot have seen their neighbors and said to themselves, "Hey, they've changed direction—I'd better copy them." Something else besides copying is
20 synchronizing the birds. Somehow they see themselves, if only for a short time, as part of a

whole. They see the wave maneuver and time their own change of flight with it.

Individuals cease to be individuals in many
25 ways—not just when flying together. Humans can react physically as a group; a wave of legs passes down a chorus line at roughly 10 dancers every second. As with birds taking off, this is too fast for movements made in reaction to
30 neighbors. A similar thing, no doubt at a deeper level, organizes a jazz jam or a basketball team. This suggests that people are good— surprisingly good—at synthesizing their actions into a larger whole. Soldiers marching
35 in step with each other are not doing so as individuals.

We all have a sense of "we" that identifies with "our" group and favors "us" against outsiders. We have our fraternities, sororities,
40 and other old boy and girl networks. We seek out people who share the same club, school tie, or accent. Much of this activity is harmless, but our loyalties also have their darker side. When loyal group members are found to be doing
45 wrong—committing sexual or physical abuse, faking data, or taking bribes—other group

members protect them. The bonds among group members may make them treat the whistle-blower, not the wrongdoer, as the
50   criminal. They do this especially if the whistle-blower is a member of their in-group—one does not squeal, tell tales, or inform on one's comrades.

Social psychologists find that we easily
55   become prejudiced. It takes the smallest hint that you belong to one group and other people to another for you to favor "your own" group. The reason you belong to one group rather than another may be no more than a preference for
60   abstract artists, Paul Klee rather than Wassily Kandinsky. You need not even meet and interact with the members of your own group, but prejudice will nonetheless rear its ugly head. It may be our football team, school, town
65   or nation or the color of our skin. Once fully identified with that "we," people become sensitive to the needs of their group and callous toward other groups. Outsiders cease to matter. The stronger our identification with the "we,"
70   the blinder we become to the humanity we share with "them." Out of this psychology comes the nasty side of history and the human race: the world of "ethnic cleansing," genocide, racial prejudice, and global terrorism. Thus, we
75   may be born alone, but we quickly learn to identify ourselves with a group, leading, in some cases, to barbaric consequences.

1.   The primary purpose of this passage is to

(A) examine a problem
(B) compare human behavior with bird behavior
(C) disprove a theory
(D) suggest an alternative
(E) analyze a phenomenon

2.   The authors refer to "estuary birds" (line 2) in their discussion of freedom in order to emphasize that

(A) birds are more physically free than humans
(B) something is not as it appears
(C) scientists do not yet understand how birds move in flocks
(D) the coordination of birds in flight is distinctly different from the coordination of human political movements
(E) birds do not appreciate the complexity of their actions

3.   By saying that soldiers do not march "as individuals" (lines 35–36) the authors suggest that the soldiers

(A) are compelled to march through coercion
(B) must obey the orders of their superiors
(C) react as a part of an organized whole
(D) lack leadership skills
(E) are reluctant

4.   Klee and Kandinsky (lines 60–61) are mentioned as examples of

(A) artists whose works are closely related
(B) people who do not act as individuals
(C) men whose followers may form distinct groups
(D) those who belong to a privileged group
(E) individuals who express prejudice

5.   On the whole, the authors' attitude toward group behavior is one of

(A) ambivalence
(B) disdain
(C) admiration
(D) skepticism
(E) fear

Critical Reading Practice 6

Passage 1

Line We have five senses in which we glory and
which we recognize and celebrate, senses that
constitute the sensible world for us. But there
are other senses—secret senses, sixth senses, if
5   you will—equally vital, but unrecognized, and
unlauded. These senses, unconscious,
automatic, had to be discovered. Historically,
indeed, their discovery came late: what the
Victorians vaguely called "muscle sense"—the
10   awareness of the relative position of trunk and
limbs, derived from receptors in the joints and
tendons—was only really defined (and named
"proprioception") in the 1890s. And the
complex mechanisms and controls by which
15   our bodies are properly aligned and balanced in
space—these have only been defined in the
twentieth century, and still hold many mysteries.
Perhaps it will only be in this space age, with the
paradoxical license and hazards of gravity-free
20   life, that we will truly appreciate our inner ears,
our vestibules and all the other obscure receptors
and reflexes that govern our body orientation.
For normal man, in normal situations, they
simply do not exist.

1.   In line 1, the word "glory" most nearly means

   (A) acknowledge
   (B) praise
   (C) discover
   (D) become famous
   (E) take delight

2.   By saying that the mechanisms of
      proprioception "do not exist" (line 24) for most
      people, the author suggests that most people

   (A) have not discovered how they work
   (B) do not appreciate their function
   (C) have difficulty maintaining balance
   (D) are seldom aware of the location of their
       limbs
   (E) are not scientists

Passage 2

Line Now the word "knowledge" we use in two
distinct senses; we speak of a person as
"knowing" if he has knowledge but does not
apply it, and also if he applies his knowledge.
5   There will be a difference then between doing
wrong when one has knowledge, but does not
reflect on it, and doing so when one not only has
the knowledge but reflects on it. In the latter
case the wrongdoing seems strange but not in
10   the former.... For in a case where a person has
knowledge but does not apply it, we see that
"having" has a different meaning. In fact, in one
sense he has knowledge and in another sense he
does not have it, as, for example, in sleep or
15   madness or intoxication. Now this is the very
condition of people under the influence of
passion; for fits of anger and craving for sensual
pleasures and some such things do
unmistakenly produce a change in bodily
20   condition, and in some instances actually cause
madness.

3.   According to the passage, "wrongdoing seems
      strange" (line 8) when

   (A) the victim does not acknowedge the
       wrongdoing
   (B) the culprit does not think about his
       actions
   (C) the victim is capable of defending himself
   (D) the culprit reflects on his knowledge of
       right and wrong before committing the
       act
   (E) the culprit craves sensual pleasure

4.   An individual with the "condition" described
      in line 16 can be inferred to

   (A) apply the knowledge he has
   (B) lack knowledge of right and wrong
   (C) value reflection over action
   (D) be incapable of passion
   (E) both have knowledge and lack it

First passage: *The Man Who Mistook His Wife for a Hat*, Oliver Sacks. © 1987 Summit Books, Simon & Schuster. Second passage: *Nicomachean Ethics*, Aristotle. Public domain.

Critical Reading Practice 7

*The following passages discuss current
controversies regarding the origin of the human
species*, homo sapiens.

Passage 1

Line Researchers have been puzzling over modern
human origins for decades. Numerous
explanations have been put forward, but these
have tended to lean toward one or the other of
5   two competing theories.

One theory posits that modern humans
arose as early as 200,000 years ago in Africa,
then spread to the Near East, and then
colonized the rest of the Old World. This "Out-
10   of-Africa" theory claims that these early
modern Africans replaced all indigenous
populations of archaic humans, including the
Neanderthals, by about 30,000 years ago and
that all people living today are descended from
15   these Africans. Support for this theory comes
from the fact that fossils of modern humans
from Africa and the Near East are much older
than those found elsewhere. These fossils are
100,000 to 120,000 years old, and some may be
20   even older. This is long before the period 30,000
to 40,000 years ago when modern humans
began appearing in other regions. These early
modern Africans and Near Easterners could
therefore have served as source populations for
25   subsequent migrations of modern humans.

Numerous genetic studies of DNA from
living people also appear to support the "Out-
of-Africa" theory. These studies indicate a
relatively recent common ancestry for all the
30   far-flung peoples inhabiting the globe today.
They also consistently show present-day
Africans to be the most genetically divergent,
and therefore the most ancient, branch of
humanity. These findings point toward a recent
35   African origin for modern humans. These
studies have recently been enhanced by
analyses of ancient DNA from actual
Neanderthal remains. The scientists studying
this DNA have reported that the Neanderthal
40   DNA differs significantly from our own, which
they see as support for the Out-of-Africa theory.

The competing theory of modern human
origins, the "multiregional evolution" theory,
argues that present-day humans are descended
45   not from a new type of humanity that appeared
in Africa a mere 200,000 years ago, but from
much earlier African emigrants.

This theory posits that our ancestry goes
back to the hominids known as Homo erectus
50   or Homo ergaster. These were the first
hominids to spread out from Africa into
Eurasia, beginning 1 to 2 million years ago, and
they spawned the various archaic Homo
sapiens populations of the Old World. The
55   theory holds that these archaic Homo sapiens
groups, including the Neanderthals, all evolved
into modern humans within their own
geographic regions. It sees this as the primary
mechanism by which modern humans
60   appeared, although it does not rule out
the possibility of some migration between
regions.

As support for their view of localized,
regional evolution, multiregionalists claim that
65   in each region of the Old World, certain
distinctive traits can be identified in fossil
bones from some of the earliest archaic
humans to occupy the region. These traits then
continue to show up in modified forms in
70   subsequent human remains from the same
region, down to the present day.

Passage 2

We are a bright species. We have gone into
space and walked on the moon. Yet you would
never have guessed that if you traveled back to
75   between 100,000 and 40,000 years ago. At that
time our ancestors and Neanderthals coexisted.
Neanderthals were like us but physically
stronger, with large bones and teeth,
protruding brows and face, and hardly a chin.
80   Perhaps what we lacked in brawn we made up
for in brains. But for most of our history, our
species was not bright enough to act very
differently from the Neanderthals, let alone be
more successful than they were. Only around
85   40,000 to 32,000 years ago, in Western Asia and
Europe, did Neanderthal people disappear, to
be replaced by our species.

Why did we coexist with Neanderthals for
60,000 years—a far longer case of hominids

90　living side by side than any other in human history? And why did we eventually win out? Brains alone cannot provide the answer, as Neanderthals may in fact have had the larger ones. Perhaps they lacked the long vocal

95　chamber needed for speech. Equal certainty exists among those who study the base of their skulls that they did and that they did not. If they did lack one, then this could be the explanation, but maybe not, since even without

100　a voice box, gestures can communicate, as can be seen among the deaf. Indeed, hunters find advantages in using sign language (speech sounds would warn off potential prey), and not just while hunting but in everyday life.

105　Anthropologists find that hunter-gatherers use sophisticated sign languages to complement their speech. Sign language might even have other advantages—evidence even suggests that it is easier to learn than speech: deaf children

110　start to pick up signs earlier than hearing ones learn to speak. So "spoken speech" is not in all ways superior to "signed speech." It is not something that can explain our replacement of the Neanderthals.

115　　　The reason we—anatomically modern humans—won out lies, we suspect, not in being brighter or better able to speak but in our very physical frailty and our resulting need to exploit our minds. Neanderthals, stronger than us, did

120　not need to take this route. They could survive with their physical strength rather than tapping into the potential of their brains. An analogy is with countries: the richest ones, such as Switzerland, Finland, Singapore and Japan, are

125　not blessed with, but rather lack natural resources. Without them, they have been forced to use their brains to innovate, providing products and services ranging from mobile phones to diplomacy.

1. According to Passage 1, on which of the following issues do the "Out-of-Africa" theory and the "multiregional evolution" theory disagree?

  I. where modern humans first evolved
  II. whether modern humans descended from African ancestors
  III. whether Neanderthals evolved into modern humans

(A) I only
(B) II only
(C) I and II only
(D) I and III only
(E) I, II, and III

2. According to Passage 1, proponents of the "Out-of-Africa" theory believe that present-day Africans must be the "most ancient" (line 33) branch of humanity because

(A) their skeletal structure most resembles the most ancient relatives of humans
(B) their DNA is more diverse than that of any other human group
(C) they are the most successful hunters of all human groups
(D) their ancestors were Neanderthals
(E) they have settled in all regions of the world

3. Which of the following pieces of evidence supports the "multiregional evolution" theory over the "Out-of-Africa" theory?

(A) distinctive human traits that have remained within regional populations since the earliest fossil records
(B) genetic diversity among modern humans in a single region
(C) genetic dissimilarities between modern humans and Neanderthals
(D) the finding of modern human remains that date from 120,000 to 30,000 years ago
(E) evidence of the migration of modern humans from Africa

4. The main purpose of the second paragraph of Passage 2 is to

(A) make a suggestion
(B) examine some claims
(C) explain a situation
(D) present information objectively
(E) tell a story

5. In line 91, the phrase "win out" most nearly means

(A) become justified
(B) defeat their foes by force
(C) come to dominate
(D) become politically successful
(E) become more popular

6. The evidence in the sentence beginning on line 105 ("Anthropologists find . . . speech") is presented in order to

(A) refute the misconception that hunter-gatherers were not good communicators
(B) explain how modern humans replaced the Neanderthals
(C) support the claim that hunter-gatherers have larger brains than Neanderthals
(D) suggest that long vocal chambers may not provide an advantage to a particular species
(E) show why some humans prefer gestures to spoken language

7. In Passage 2, the "physical frailty" (line 118) is

(A) the reason our ancestors struggled to survive
(B) the result of a harsh physical environment
(C) an ironic advantage to modern humans
(D) something the Neanderthals exploited
(E) a trait that arose late in human history

8. In lines 128–129, "mobile phones" and "diplomacy" are mentioned as examples of

(A) innovations that are used worldwide
(B) different ways of communicating
(C) luxuries that are denied to the physically frail
(D) inventions that Neanderthals could never use
(E) products or services that require intellectual rather than natural resources

9. With which of the following statements about the "multiregional evolution" theory would the authors of Passage 2 most likely agree?

(A) It is one of many possible ways of describing the dominance of modern humans over the Neanderthals.
(B) It is false because it posits that Neanderthals evolved into modern humans.
(C) It is true because it explains the variety of modes in human communication.
(D) It is unlikely to be true because it does not account for the violence of human societies.
(E) It is a helpful theory for explaining the similarities among countries like Switzerland, Finland, and Japan.

Answer Key

Critical Reading Practice 1

1. **B** The mystery is the paradox...*that protons stick together* even though a law of physics says they should repel each other.

2. **D** In saying that *these gluons are responsible for the force that binds quarks within protons and neutrons*, the author means that the gluons bind the parts of protons and neutrons together. Since gluons are not people, they can't be (A) *guardians of* or (B) *guilty of* anything. This sentence is talking about what gluons *do*, not what they *represent*, so (C) *representative of* doesn't work. Choice (E) does not work because the sentence is discussing what *produces* the strong force, not what *reacts* to it, so (D) is the best choice.

3. **B** The phrase *according to the passage* suggests that there is clear literal evidence in the passage. The answer is found in the fourth paragraph (lines 47–51), where it says that *pions carry the nuclear force only over distances greater than half a fermi– the radius of a proton–yet the distance between bound protons is far less than that*. This means that pions can't be what hold protons together, because they aren't effective between protons.

4. **A** The fifth paragraph explains how *physicists have refined Yukawa's theory* in order to resolve the problem described in paragraph four, namely, experimental evidence that showed that the pion is not effective in the narrow space between bound nuclear particles.

5. **B** This question is essentially key question 3: *what is the structure of this passsage?* The passage begins by describing a problem: physicists do not really know what holds a nucleus together, and then proceeds to discuss their attempts to find out. The passage ends, however, without the solution to the puzzle: scientists still don't know. Thus, the best description of the structure of the passage is (B) *description of a problem followed by a history of attempts to solve it*.

Critical Reading Practice 2

1. **C** This question is based on key question 2: *what is the central idea?* The title must concisely capture the central idea of the passage. This passage is an argument, and its thesis is that it's impossible to repeat the art of the past because art is "a child of its age." It then goes on to explain how this pertains to the revival of ancient art forms called primitivism. Therefore, choice (C) best summarizes the main idea in a title.

2. **B** The passage says that a monkey can look at a book with a *thoughtful aspect* but really have no understanding of the book. Since the monkey does not understand the book, choices (A) and (D) are illogical. The sentence is saying that the monkey only *looks* thoughtful, so choice (B) is the only sensible one.

3. **E** The *fundamental truth* described in the second paragraph is that of a *revival of external forms*; that is, art forms that resemble those of the past can only occur when there is *a similarity of inner tendency in the whole moral and spiritual atmosphere*. The only example given that suggests that fact is (E).

4. **A** In these lines, the author is using a metaphor to describe how *our minds* and *souls*, by which he means our artistic and spiritual souls, are affected by the materialism of the age. Artistic inspiration is described as a *spark*, and materialism as a *nightmare* and a *vast gulf of darkness*. The soul *trembles* because it doubts that the light is *not a dream*, meaning that the light might be a dream and the darkness reality. Therefore the author suggests that materialism might still hold the artistic soul in its grip.

5. **D** The metaphor in the final paragraph makes it clear that materialism *holds the awakening soul still in its grip* (lines 40–41). This is not a nurturing grip, because the soul *trembles* (line 44) before the *nightmare of materialism* (line 38). Therefore, according to the author, materialism oppresses the artistic soul.

Critical Reading Practice 3

1. **A** The theory of spontaneous generation is described as one in which life arises from substances that do not contain the reproductive elements of that life-form.

2. **B** The important difference between the flask with the neck intact and the flask with the neck removed was the presence of microorganisms in the fermentable material. When the neck was removed, *microorganisms in the air promptly entered the fermentable material and proliferated*.

3. **C** The experiment, Pasteur claimed, *killed* the theory of spontaneous generation, so it dealt a *fatal* blow.

4. **A** The *prebiotic assembly* is said to occur over a *long period*. This must not be an example of *spontaneous generation*, that is, generation of life over a short period of time from nonliving material,

because the theory of spontaneous generation has been disproved.

5. **E** The first paragraph mentions that *warmth, moisture, sunlight and even starlight often were mentioned as factors that encouraged spontaneous generation of living organisms*, but the theory of spontaneous generation was then disproved. It is ironic, then, that water was found, in fact, to be a necessary precursor to life.

Critical Reading Practice 4

1. **A** The passage compares mechanistic explanations to teleological ones and explains why mechanistic ones are *more useful*. Choices (B), (C), and (D) describe tasks that go far beyond what this passage accomplishes, and choice (E) describes an idea that is only mentioned in the last paragraph.

2. **C** *Teleological* explanations are those that *describe causes and effects in terms of desires or purposes*. Saying that a bird sings because it *likes the sound* implies that the bird's action is caused by a desire.

3. **E** Socrates is said to *be far more likely to ask you about your vehicle's nature, or its desires, or its soul than about how the engine worked*. This underscores the author's belief that Socrates explained things in terms of their *purposes*.

4. **B** Socrates, the author tells us, would believe that the SUV possessed a soul, so the *possessed machine* is one with a living spirit and will.

5. **A** The fourth paragraph tells us that teleological explanations *are convenient*, and goes on to explain why people continue to use them.

6. **E** The *possessed machine* in lines 36–37 is the SUV that Socrates would believe has a soul. The *mindless machines* of lines 61–62 represent the conception of human beings that many would have if human behavior were explained "mechanistically," thereby removing (they would think) our free will and soul.

Critical Reading Practice 5

1. **E** This passage analyzes (examines closely) the phenomenon of group behavior, first in terms of birds flying together, then in terms of human beings acting as teams, and then in terms of human group identification. This passage is not focused on a "problem" because group behavior is often depicted as a positive thing, particularly in the first three paragraphs, so choice (A) is incorrect. Since the passage only discusses birds in the first couple of paragraphs, (B) must be incorrect.

Also, since no alternative to a situation or refutation of a theory is presented, (C) and (D) cannot be right.

2. **B** The authors begin with a question: *Where can freedom be found?* and a rhetorical answer: *Perhaps in a flock of estuary birds?* This leads us to believe that the author might use the example of birds flying as an example of freedom. However, the paragraph (and the passage as a whole) goes on to suggest that bird flight is not as *free* as it seems and often typifies group behavior.

3. **C** The example of the marching soldiers follows the examples of the estuary birds, the chorus line, the jazz band, and the basketball team. All of these examples reinforce the common theme of group behavior being an organized whole.

4. **C** The sentence says that *The reason you belong to one group rather than another may be no more than a preference for abstract artists, Paul Klee rather than Wassily Kandinsky*. This means that those who like the art of Klee might form a distinct group.

5. **A** The authors indicate the positive benefits of group behavior in the first three paragraphs, then its *darker side* in the last two paragraphs. This is an example of *ambivalence*, where the authors are not saying that group behavior is always good or always bad.

Critical Reading Practice 6

1. **E** The sentence says that we *glory in* our five senses, but that others are *unlauded* (line 6). In this context, *glory* means much the same as *take delight*.

2. **B** The previous sentence says that perhaps someday *we will truly appreciate our inner ears, our vestibules and all the other obscure receptors and reflexes that govern our body orientation* (lines 20–24) but that for most people the *do not exist*, thereby implying that most people do not appreciate them.

3. **D** The passage says that *In the latter case, the wrongdoing seems strange*, the latter case being the case in which *one not only has knowledge but reflects on it*. In other words, it is strange when one does wrong while reflecting on his knowledge that it is wrong.

4. **E** A person with the "condition" *in one sense ... has knowledge and in another sense ... does not have it* (lines 12–14).

Critical Reading Practice 7

1. **D** The Out-of-Africa theory claims that *modern humans arose as early as 200,000 years ago in Africa* (lines 6–7) but the multiregional evolution theory says that modern humans evolved *within their own geographic regions* (lines 57–58) in Eurasia as well as Africa. They differ, also, on the question of Neanderthals: the Out-of-Africa theory claims that modern humans *replaced all indigenous populations of archaic humans, including the Neanderthals* (lines 11–13), while the multiregional evolution theory claims that *Neanderthals ... evolved into modern humans* (lines 56–57). They agree, however, that the *ancestors* of modern humans came from Africa.

2. **B** The passage states that present-day Africans are *the most genetically divergent, and therefore most ancient, branch of humanity* (lines 32–34). Therefore, because their DNA is more diverse than that of any other human group, they are the most ancient branch of modern humans.

3. **A** The *support* that multiregionalists cite for their claims is that *distinctive traits can be identified in fossil bones from ... the region* which *continue to show up ... in subsequent human remains from the same region* (lines 66–71).

4. **B** Words and phrases like *perhaps*, *if*, and *maybe not* indicate that Passage 2 is exploring possibilities.

5. **C** The passage is exploring the question of how modern humans "won out" over the Neanderthals, in other words, how they came to thrive while the Neanderthals died out; how we *came to dominate* them.

6. **D** The sentence *Anthropologists find ... speech* (lines 105–107) is used to support the later claim that *"spoken speech" is not in all ways superior to "signed speech"* (lines 111–112), which would cast doubt on the advantages of the *long vocal chamber needed for speech* (lines 94–95).

7. **C** According to Passage 2, the *physical frailty* (line 118) of modern humans relative to Neanderthals created a need to exploit our creative brains, which led to our dominance over the Neanderthals.

8. **E** The *mobile phones* and *diplomacy* are examples of how countries *that lack natural resources* (lines 125–126) can still *use their brains to innovate* (line 127).

9. **B** The authors of Passage 2 clearly believe that modern humans came to dominate Neanderthals and are giving their explanation for this phenomenon. The multiregional evolution theory, however, claims that *Neanderthals ... evolved into modern humans* rather than being supplanted by them.

CHAPTER 6

SENTENCE COMPLETION SKILLS

1. What Are Sentence Completion Questions?

2. How to Attack Sentence Completion Questions

▌ WHAT ARE SENTENCE COMPLETION QUESTIONS?

Every PSAT contains 13 "sentence completion" questions to test your verbal inference skills. Verbal inference skills are the skills you use to figure out new words when you read or hear them in sentences. They include vocabulary skills, knowledge of word roots, and your ability to analyze sentences logically.

To understand what verbal inference skills are, consider the following sentence:

As part of our game, we ran twice around the cregiendo until we became so trepindant that we collapsed in a heap on the porch.

Is the word *cregiendo* a noun, a verb, or an adjective? How about *trepindant*? Since you've never heard these words before, only your verbal inference skills can help you to figure them out.

Cregiendo must be a noun because it's the *thing* we ran around, and *trepindant* must be an adjective, because it describes us after we ran around the *cregiendo*. With your verbal inference skills, you've probably figured out more than just the part of speech of *cregiendo* and *trepindant*.

A *cregiendo* is about as big as

(A) a spider
(B) a pillow
(C) a car
(D) a house
(E) a village

A *cregiendo* is something that kids can run around, but running around it twice makes you so tired that you'd collapse. Your common sense tells you that such a thing would be roughly as big as a house. A village is way too big to run around in a game, and the other things are much too small to exhaust you.

Can a *cregiendo* be *trepindant*?

Since we became *trepindant* after running around the *cregiendo*, the word *trepindant* describes human beings, and perhaps other animals that can run, rather than, say, rocks. It also seems to describe a *temporary state* rather than a permanent trait, since we weren't *trepindant* before we started running around. What would make us collapse in a heap? Exhaustion, of course. So *trepindant* probably means *exhausted*, which big objects like *cregiendos* could never be.

Exercise Set 1

Read the following sentence containing a nonsense word and answer the questions that follow. Answers are at the bottom of the page.

Car buyers, when given a choice of engines, will typically choose the most powerful and gas-guzzling option, refuting the popular belief that fellinance is the primary concern of consumers.

1. *Fellinance* is (A) a verb (B) a noun (C) an adjective (D) an adverb (E) a preposition (F) a pronoun.
2. Are all car engines *fellinant*?
3. Is fellinance more likely to be associated with a small sedan or a large pickup truck?
4. *Fellinance* most nearly means (A) longevity (B) continuity (C) propriety (D) efficiency (E) luxury

---

2   HOW TO ATTACK SENTENCE COMPLETION QUESTIONS

When answering sentence completion questions, always use your natural verbal inference skills first. Your common sense is far more powerful than any test-taking "trick."

To take advantage of your verbal inference skills, simply read the entire sentence, saying "blank" in place of the missing words, and just try to make sense of the sentence. Think about the relationships that are shown in the sentence. Then write your own word or phrase in each blank to complete the sentence in a way that makes sense to you. Don't worry about finding the "perfect" word, and don't worry if you repeat a word from elsewhere in the sentence. If a good word or phrase doesn't come, but you know the tone of the word, that is, if it's a *positive* or a *negative* word, just write + or − in the blank. Then scan the choices and look for the best match. Here is an example:

> Although these animals migrate, they are not ------; they remain loyal to their established ranges and seldom stray into new areas.

Don't worry about the choices yet; just read the sentence and think of your own word to complete the sentence. The sentence says that these animals *seldom stray*, so obviously they must not be *roamers* or something like that. Write your answer in the blank. Now check the choices.

(A) predators
(B) burrowers
(C) grazers
(D) scavengers
(E) wanderers

Wanderers should jump off the page. Of course, it's possible that these animals are also not *predators* or *burrowers* or *grazers* or *scavengers*, but that doesn't matter. Your job is to use the information in the sentence. The sentence doesn't provide any information about those traits.

Reread the Sentence

After you've made your choice, reread the sentence with your choice inserted. Make sure that the sentence makes sense as a logical whole. It's a simple step, but an easy one to overlook.

Focus on the Logic

Sentence completion questions are as much a test of logic as vocabulary. Your task is not to find the most "educated" way to complete the sentence, but rather to choose the *only logical* way to complete the sentence from among the five choices. Only one choice will complete the sentence logically. The other choices will be illogical, unsupported, or incomplete.

For instance, consider this sentence:

> What Mr. Harrison's writing lacked in clarity it made up for in ------, for it contained enough information for a clever craftsman to re-create his invention down to the most minute detail.

At first, it may seem as if there are many different ways to complete the sentence. There are many ways in which a piece of writing might make up for a lack of clarity: it might be clever, or funny, or useful, or thought provoking. But when you look at the sentence as a whole, there is only one logical way to complete the sentence. The second part of the sentence is key. It says that his writing contains *enough information for a clever craftsman to re-create his invention down to the most minute detail.* In other words, it provides a lot of *detail.* This must be what makes up for its lack of clarity! So while there are many "good" ways to complete the sentence, only a word like *meticulousness, comprehensiveness, completeness, detail,* etc., will make the sentence logically complete.

Find the Logical Structure of the Sentence

Every sentence in a sentence completion question has a clear logical structure that shows the relationships among the ideas in the sentence. This structure always includes one or more of the four basic logical relationships:

Logical contrast	*Although we waited over two hours for a table, it seemed like only a few minutes.* The word *although* indicates that the two ideas in the sentence contrast each other.
Logical support	*We loved staying at the cottage; the sounds of the ocean calmed us, and the sea air invigorated us.* The semicolon indicates that the two statements support each other.
Cause and effect	*We were irritated by the noise, so we moved to the next room.* The conjunction *so* indicates that the first statement explains the next.
Definition of a term	*Joel was a nihilist, someone who doesn't believe that any truth is absolute.* The phrase following the comma is an *appositive*, a noun phrase that defines or explains the noun that it follows.

Many sentences include more than one logical relationship. Look at all parts of each sentence to find all of them.

> The motion of the region's glaciers is both ------ and ------; they seem not to be moving at all, and yet they transform the landscape more profoundly than any other force of nature.

The phrase *both ------ and ------* at first seems to imply that the two missing words are similar. But reading the whole sentence gives a different picture. The semicolon separates two statements that support each other, and in fact the two statements have a parallel structure that helps you to complete the sentence. The word *yet* in the second statement shows a contrast. Therefore, the first missing word should mean something like *seemingly motionless*, and the second word should mean something like *having a profound effect*. Words like *imperceptible* and *dramatic* work nicely.

Notice the Structural Key Words

Structural key words are those words or phrases that show the logical relationship among ideas in the sentence. For instance, words like *because, therefore, thus, in order to,* and *consequently* are used to show cause and effect. As you read the sentences, underline any structural key words you see, and **think** about these key words first. They are essential to solving sentence completion questions.

Contrast	*but*	*however*	*in contrast*	*nevertheless*
	whereas	*although*	*instead of*	*rather*
	despite	*unusual*	*unexpected*	*surprising*
	abnormal	*anomalous*	*curious*	*illogical*
Support	*furthermore*	*likewise*	*moreover*	*also*
	besides	*additionally*	*similarly*	*like*
	for instance	*that is*	*for example*	
Cause and effect	*because*	*thus*	*consequently*	*therefore*
	so ... that	*in order to*	*if ... then*	*since*
Definition	*that is*	*which means*	*in other words*	

Notice Semicolons and Colons

Two punctuation marks can also be essential to solving sentence completion questions. Semicolons (;) and colons (:) are used to join complete statements that support each other. But these two punctuation marks can mean slightly different things. A semicolon often indicates that the second statement *extends* or *develops* the previous statement. A colon between two statements usually indicates that the second statement *explains* the previous one. Here are some examples:

> Newton inferred that the law of gravity was ------: even the gravitational pull of an ant on Earth will ------ a star millions of light-years away.
>
> (A) universal . . influence
> (B) inconsequential . . accelerate
> (C) intense . . support
> (D) minute . . affect
> (E) complete . . replace

The colon indicates that the second statement *explains* the first, in this case by giving an example. To understand this sentence, first try to understand the second statement and then ask: "What general idea does that example explain?" The second part says that *the gravitational pull of an ant will ------ a star millions of light-years away*. Well, a scientist like Isaac Newton wouldn't be so silly as to say that an ant's gravity could *support* or *replace* a star, so it must *influence, accelerate,* or *affect* it. If this is true, then even small gravitational effects must travel a very long way. This is the important idea in the sentence, so Newton's theory must have been that gravity is *universal*.

> The string arrangements by Rob Mathes are unobtrusive yet ------; the violins rise ------, but soon they reach deeply into the piece and transform it into a lyrically rich and moving experience.
>
> (A) carefree . . stiffly
> (B) reserved . . involuntarily
> (C) profound . . subtly
> (D) detached . . carefully
> (E) hesitant . . methodically

The semicolon indicates that the second statement develops the first, repeating the same general idea but with more detail. The repetition of an idea is reinforced with *parallelism*, the repetition of grammatical forms. The overall structure is like this: *These are A yet B; they do C but then D.* The parallelism indicates that A is similar to C and that B is similar to D. If the arrangements are *unobtrusive*, then they rise *subtly*, and if they *reach deeply into the piece and transform it*, they must be *profound*. The answer is (C).

When at a Loss, Choose Support

Sometimes a sentence will not contain an obvious logical clue such as a key word or semicolon. In these cases, the ideas in the sentence probably support each other. Pay close attention to the other specialized vocabulary in the sentence—the nouns, verbs, and modifiers—and think about what they imply.

> In need of a ------ from persecution, many young refugees wandered far from their homeland seeking ------ communities in which to settle.
>
> (A) nightmare . . just
> (B) haven . . tolerant
> (C) light . . magnanimous
> (D) pledge . . malevolent
> (E) sanctuary . . invidious

This sentence doesn't contain any of the logical key words or punctuation marks mentioned earlier. So what should you do? First, assume that all of the ideas in the sentence support each other to make one coherent point. Next, notice the specialized vocabulary words: *persecution* and *refugees. Persecution* is oppression, which no one enjoys. *Refugees* are people fleeing a bad situation such as war, disaster, or oppression. What do all refugees *need*? A safe place, so the answer is (B).

Exercise Set 2

Read each of the following sentences. Then circle the choice that describes the logical structure. Answers are at the bottom of the page.

5. The herd of lemmings always acted ------, thus ensuring that either they all survived or they all perished.

       support   contrast   cause and effect   definition

6. While the script for the movie skillfully captured the wit and charm of Oscar Wilde, the incompetent actor portraying him did not do justice to the ------ lines.

       support   contrast   cause and effect   definition

7. By ------ his announcement of the new promotions, Carl felt that he could maintain his employees' eagerness with the element of anticipation.

       support   contrast   cause and effect   definition

8. Deer in the wild often seem ------ to the concept of death; they are utterly unaware of any danger even when they notice their friends nearby dropping one by one.

       support   contrast   cause and effect   definition

9. Few of us appreciated our group leader's ------; we were too intelligent and had too much self-esteem to be persuaded by her constant use of insult and humiliation.

       support   contrast   cause and effect   definition

Simplify the Tough Questions

Don't panic if a sentence doesn't make sense right away. When this happens, try to simplify your task by using *process of elimination, tone,* **or** *paraphrasing.*

Work by Process of Elimination

Even if you understand only part of a tough "two-blank" sentence, use that understanding to rule out wrong choices. Just eliminate those choices that clearly don't make sense for that portion you *do* **understand.**

    Statistics are often ------ useful information, but this is an ------ impression, because they must, by definition, obscure data by reducing many values to a single number.

  (A) equated with . . erroneous   (B) mistaken for . . aesthetic   (C) superior to . . inaccurate
  (D) relegated to . . insidious   (E) substituted for . . interesting

This sentence may be tough to understand at the first reading, so completing the sentence yourself may be tough. In this situation, simply plug in the choices and eliminate those that don't create a logically coherent statement. If you just focus on the relationship between *statistics* and *information*, you can probably eliminate choices (C), (D), and (E). In the context of the whole sentence, choice (A) is the only one that makes logical sense.

If a sentence does contain two blanks, it is usually easier to complete the second blank first. Why? Because by the time you get to the second blank, you will have read more context clues. Of course, there will be occasional exceptions to this rule, but *usually* the second blank is easier to complete than the first.

Focus on Tone

If you can't find the right word or words to complete the sentence, try at least to determine the *tone* of the word, that is, whether it's *positive*, *negative*, or *neutral*. Then eliminate any choices that lack the correct tone.

> Without David's ------, the dispute between the parties may never have been resolved so tactfully.
>
> (A) conciliation   (B) antagonism   (C) embarrassment   (D) indelicacy   (E) ridicule

The right word might not come right to mind, but it should be pretty clear that whatever David used was a *good* thing, because it helped resolve the dispute *tactfully*, which means *with careful regard of everyone's feelings*. Therefore, you can eliminate any choices that have a negative or neutral tone. You don't have to know the meaning of every word in the choices. Just eliminate those that you know lack the correct tone. The answer, by the way, is (A).

Exercise Set 3

Write +, −, or = in each blank to indicate whether the word should be positive, negative, or neutral in tone. Then use these tone clues to determine and check the answer to each question. Answers are at the bottom of the page.

10. His inability to relate to the latest trends in art led him to fear that his critical faculties had ------ during his long hiatus.

    (A) diversified   (B) atrophied   (C) converted   (D) enhanced   (E) multiplied

11. To her chagrin, Ellen soon learned that she could not hide her ------; her friends at the party could see the signs of weariness on her face.

    (A) amusement   (B) incoherence   (C) gratefulness   (D) sorrow   (E) exhaustion

12. McLanham's ------ prose, particularly when compared to that of his more flamboyant ------, illustrates how artists of the same era can reflect startlingly different perspectives on the same reality.

    (A) stark . . contemporaries   (B) spartan . . enemies   (C) imprecise . . role models
    (D) flowery . . friends (E) well-crafted . . teachers

Paraphrase

You may also often find it helpful to paraphrase the sentence, that is, to restate it in your own words. This helps you to focus on the logic of the sentence as a whole, without getting stuck on any particular words or phrases. Just read the sentence completely. Then try to restate the idea in the simplest terms possible. When you read the sentence again, you will probably find it easier to complete, or at least to eliminate wrong choices.

Don't Be Afraid to Cut and Paste

Remember that you don't have to find the perfect word to fill each blank. You simply need to capture the right general idea. Often, you will find it easy to just use a word—or a form of it—from elsewhere in the sentence.

> Her account was so sterile that it made all of the other ------ seem ------ by contrast.

To complete the sentence, just reuse the words: *accounts* and *unsterile* sound a bit redundant, but they do the job!

Look for Parallelism

Parallelism can be an important part of the logical structure of a sentence. When you notice parallel structures, completing SAT sentences is simpler. Parallelism is the use of similar words or phrases when listing or comparing things in a sentence. It is discussed in more detail in Chapter 13, Lesson 3.

> Rather than being dull and arcane, her lecture on galaxy formation was ------ and ------.

This contains two phrases that are parallel: *dull and arcane* and ------ and ------. Parallelism suggests that the first missing word is an adjective contrasting *dull*, and the second is an adjective contrasting *arcane* (which means *obscure and hard to understand*). The missing words should contrast both the tone and meaning of the first two adjectives, in the same order. So a parallel way to complete the sentence is

> Rather than being dull and arcane, her lecture on galaxy formation was exciting and easy to understand.

Exercise Set 4

Complete the following sentences with your own words or phrases, using parallelism. Answers are at the bottom of the page.

13. The speakers ran the gamut from the eloquent to the bumbling; some were _____, while others spoke with_____.

14. I did not want to sit through another lecture that was rambling and mind-numbing; rather, I was hoping for one that was_____ and _____.

Notice the Modifiers

The modifiers—adjectives and adverbs—in SAT sentences are always chosen carefully. They play key roles in the logical scheme of the sentences. **If the main idea of a sentence isn't perfectly clear after the first reading, try focusing primarily on the adjectives and adverbs, and think about what they suggest.**

> The clean and regimented training center is ------ to those seeking the ------ once associated with boxing.
>
> (A) surprising . . austerity   (B) disappointing . . seediness   (C) convincing . . chaos
> (D) refreshing . . camaraderie   (E) inspiring . . ambition

The modifiers in this sentence are *clean* and *regimented*. These could be positive descriptions, so such a training center might *impress* people who seek *cleanliness and order*. But no choice really fits this reading. There is another important modifier that is easy to overlook: *once*. It suggests that people seek something that *is no longer* part of boxing (though it *once* was). Therefore, these people would be disappointed by its absence, and so they must have been seeking something that is the *opposite* of *clean and regimented*, like *seedy and undisciplined*. (It may seem strange, but some people like that kind of stuff!)

Use Your Common Sense about People and Things

Your common sense about people and things is one of your best tools on sentence completion questions. If an SAT sentence refers to a *scientist*, for instance, it's for a reason. What do scientists do or think that make

Answers: 13. The speakers ran the gamut from the eloquent to the bumbling; some were *articulate*, while others spoke with profound *ineptitude*. (You may have used different words, but be sure that the first word is *positive* in tone and corresponds roughly to *articulate* and the second word is negative and corresponds roughly to *ineptitude* in meaning.) 14. I did not want to sit through another lecture that was rambling and mind-numbing; rather, I was hoping for one that was *focused* and *engaging*. (You may have used different words, but be sure that both words are *positive* in tone and that the first corresponds roughly to *focused* and that the second word corresponds roughly to *engaging* in meaning.)

them different from nonscientists? Or how about *teachers*, or *politicians*, or *advocates*, or *critics*, etc.? SAT sentences won't always show people acting in typical ways, but they generally require you to understand how these folks *typically* act or think.

An inveterate procrastinator, Pat could always be counted on to ------ any assignment he is given.

The only real context clue we have here is the fact that Pat is a procrastinator. If you know what a procrastinator does, then you know how to complete the sentence. Procrastinators *postpone* things.

Practice Your Verbal Inference Skills

Read plenty of college-level books and articles to hone your verbal inference skills. If you challenge yourself in your reading, you will continually run across unfamiliar terms that you can try to decode from their context. Just like every other reading skill, verbal inference skills are best improved by actually using the skills in a meaningful context, such as trying to understand a Shakespeare sonnet or a philosophical text or a book on physics. When you run across a new word, don't look it up immediately. Instead, make an educated guess about the meaning before looking it up in a dictionary. This will reinforce your verbal inference skills. Of course, once you do look it up to check your guess, make a flashcard using the College Hill system described in Chapter 4, and practice it with the other words in your vocabulary stack.

How to Deal with Tough Sentences

Some sentences are hard because of tough vocabulary, but others are hard because of complex or ambiguous logical structure. **Don't panic when you come to a hard sentence. If you can't eliminate a couple of choices within a minute, move on. It's better to move on to easier questions than it is to get bogged down on a hard one. Circle any question that you skip in your test booklet so that you can come back to it if you have time at the end of the section.**

Notice the Negatives

Negative words such as *not, hardly, rarely*, and *lacking* can complicate a sentence. They are also easy to overlook. **Watch carefully for negative words.** They are important to the logical structure of the sentence. When you encounter a sentence with negatives, it may help to paraphrase the sentence more "positively."

Their approach was not unlike that of the Neo-Darwinians, whose lack of respect for quasi-scientific methods was far from unknown in the university community.

This sentence is simpler when it is phrased without so many negatives.

Their approach was like that of the Neo-Darwinians, whose support for the scientific method was well-known in the university community.

Exercise Set 5

Paraphrase the following sentence to minimize negatives. The answer is at the bottom of the page.

15. It is not uncommon to find people who refuse to deny that ghosts exist.

Be Careful with Ambiguous Sentences

Some sentences with missing parts are hard to understand because they are ambiguous; that is, they can be completed in more than one way. Usually, one of the ways of interpreting the sentence is positive and the other is negative. In these cases, you may have to consider both possible interpretations.

The recent trend of using ------ dialogue in films can be traced to directors who have ------ the natural half-sentences and interrupted thoughts that characterize genuine human speech.

(A) halting . . embraced   (B) formal . . assumed   (C) imperfect . . eschewed
(D) stilted . . adopted   (E) passionate . . endured

There are two ways to complete this sentence. Modern film directors might *like* or *dislike* the *natural half-sentences and interrupted thoughts that characterize genuine human speech.* If they like them, they would probably use them in their films. Choice (A) supports this reading. If they don't like them, they would prefer more *formal* dialogue. Choice (B) gives *formal* and (D) gives *stilted*, which convey the right idea. But if the directors use *formal* language, they wouldn't *assume* imperfect dialogue, so (B) doesn't work. Likewise, if the directors used *stilted* (formal) dialogue, they wouldn't *adopt* imperfect dialogue. So (A) is the correct response.

Exercise Set 6

Complete the following ambiguous sentences in two different ways. Answers are at the bottom of the page.

16. Despite the_____of the climb, the explorers were beginning to believe that the trek would soon become_____.

Despite the_____of the climb, the explorers were beginning to believe that the trek would soon become_____.

17. Far from being_____on the issue of gun control, Will has_____on the issue for many years.

Far from being_____on the issue of gun control, Will has_____on the issue for many years.

Watch for Abstract Nouns

Concrete nouns, which usually represent *people* and *objects*, are easier to understand than abstract nouns, which usually represent *quantities, qualities,* or *ideas.* **If you focus on the concrete nouns in a sentence more than the abstract ones, you can misread the sentence. Pay special attention to abstract nouns in sentences.**

> The dissent regarding the new restrictions on student parking was ------ those who wanted to be able to drive freely to school.
>
> (A) spearheaded by
> (B) surprising to
> (C) troublesome to
> (D) disputed by
> (E) disregarded by

This sentence is not about the *parking restrictions*, but rather about the *dissent.* This sentence is easy to misread if you don't focus on the word *dissent.* We tend to overlook it because it's abstract. If you wanted to drive freely to school, how would you feel about the *dissent* regarding parking restrictions? You'd probably be one of the people dissenting! You may even *initiate* the dissent, which is why (A) is the best choice.

Exercise Set 7

Circle the abstract nouns and underline the concrete nouns in the sentence below. Answers are at the bottom of the page.

18. The lack of interest among the voters ensured that the referendum about the new playground could sneak through, even though it contained some objectionable clauses.

Answers: 18. *The lack* (abstract noun) *of interest* (abstract noun) *among the voters* (concrete noun) *ensured that the referendum* (concrete noun) *about the new playground* (concrete noun) *could sneak through, even though it contained some objectionable clauses* (abstract noun).

Sentence Completion Practice 1

Each of the sentences below is missing one or two portions. Read each sentence. Then select the word or words that most logically complete the sentence, taking into account the meaning of the sentence as a whole.

Example:

Rather than accepting the theory unquestioningly, Deborah regarded it with ------.

(A) mirth
(B) sadness
(C) responsibility
(D) ignorance
(E) skepticism

Correct response: (E)

1. Although he clearly was obsessed with the ------ of moral integrity, he was also aware of its potential ------: self-righteousness, arrogance, and condescension.

(A) pursuit . . pitfalls
(B) likelihood . . dangers
(C) contemplation . . insights
(D) morality . . tenets
(E) sanctity . . inequities

2. Whereas Gerald was always the frivolous one, Bernard felt compelled to compensate for his brother's indiscretions by exercising profound moral ------.

(A) hysteria
(B) embarrassment
(C) prudence
(D) acceptance
(E) equivocation

3. The synthesized voices from today's computerized machines are a far cry from the ------ sounds of older machines; rather, they sound almost like real human speech.

(A) melancholy
(B) cordial
(C) fervid
(D) inflammatory
(E) mechanical

4. Even in communities that value ------, investment in technologically advanced industries can be an important source of ------.

(A) progress . . prestige
(B) liberty . . concern
(C) competition . . decay
(D) tradition . . income
(E) profits . . dismay

5. Some contend that the quatrains of Nostradamus ------ events that would not take place for centuries, including ------ like wars, conflagrations, and earthquakes.

(A) foreboded . . cataclysms
(B) mitigated . . marvels
(C) impersonated . . myths
(D) transcended . . auguries
(E) disrupted . . coincidences

6. Rather than ------ the attitude of the entire community from that of a few individuals, she was willing to concede that there were many conflicting opinions on the matter.

(A) distinguishing
(B) concealing
(C) protecting
(D) inferring
(E) expelling

7. Sadly, most people who say they want change in public schools will struggle to resist it, or at least ------ its effects on them.

(A) initiate
(B) distort
(C) palliate
(D) defend
(E) enhance

Sentence Completion Practice 2

Each of the sentences below is missing one or two portions. Read each sentence. Then select the word or words that most logically complete the sentence, taking into account the meaning of the sentence as a whole.

Example:

> Rather than accepting the theory unquestioningly, Deborah regarded it with ------.
>
> (A) mirth
> (B) sadness
> (C) responsibility
> (D) ignorance
> (E) skepticism

Correct response: (E)

1. Possessing seemingly boundless energy, DeVare fights for the causes she supports with a ------ that would leave others ------ at the end of the workday.

   (A) grace . . scandalized
   (B) commitment . . uncertain
   (C) loyalty . . contrite
   (D) vigor . . exhausted
   (E) sincerity . . disillusioned

2. The members of the committee saw Vance's reign as chairman becoming more and more ------; his decisions seemed based more on personal whim than on the opinion of his fellow members.

   (A) inclusive
   (B) abstract
   (C) irresistible
   (D) illusory
   (E) arbitrary

3. The boundary between Canada and the United States is more a political than a cultural ------; the people on both sides ------ a great deal in terms of artistic sensibilities.

   (A) demarcation . . share
   (B) partition . . estrange
   (C) event . . partake
   (D) affiliation . . admit
   (E) division . . conflict

4. Some criminal investigators believe that polygraphs reliably ------ deception by recording ------ reactions in a subject such as slight changes in breathing rate or perspiration elicited by a set of questions.

   (A) judge . . imaginative
   (B) detect . . physiological
   (C) predict . . imperceptible
   (D) subvert . . simulated
   (E) induce . . verifiable

5. The author intentionally combines the vernacular of the Bronx with pretentious academic jargon, creating a uniquely ------ style that makes her novel particularly difficult to translate into other languages.

   (A) mundane
   (B) taciturn
   (C) alliterative
   (D) idiosyncratic
   (E) orthodox

6. The fact that polar bears are tremendously strong indicates the degree of ------ they must have in their aggressive play, for they never hurt each other.

   (A) intensity
   (B) stamina
   (C) concentration
   (D) instinct
   (E) restraint

7. Long an advocate of deterrence, General Wallace had hoped that the ------ display of force would ------ the need for further military action.

   (A) formidable . . obviate
   (B) subtle . . require
   (C) impressive . . generate
   (D) unnecessary . . prevent
   (E) unbridled . . sustain

Sentence Completion Practice 3

Each of the sentences below is missing one or two portions. Read each sentence. Then select the word or words that most logically complete the sentence, taking into account the meaning of the sentence as a whole.

Example:

Rather than accepting the theory unquestioningly, Deborah regarded it with ------.

(A) mirth
(B) sadness
(C) responsibility
(D) ignorance
(E) skepticism

Correct response: (E)

1. During the day crabs move slowly and ------, but at night they roam ------ across sandy sea bottoms, climbing reefs or foraging for kelp.

(A) frantically . . wildly
(B) cautiously . . freely
(C) gradually . . sluggishly
(D) deliberately . . carefully
(E) rashly . . rapidly

2. Because the President was used to receiving the support of his advisors, he was ------ when he discovered that their views on the handling of the crisis were ------ with his own.

(A) stunned . . irreconcilable
(B) relieved . . inconsistent
(C) amused . . consonant
(D) oblivious . . compatible
(E) sorry . . commensurate

3. The building should be ------ not only for its long-recognized architectural merit but also for its ------ in the history of Black American theater.

(A) designed . . role
(B) commissioned . . usefulness
(C) preserved . . importance
(D) demolished . . future
(E) constructed . . place

4. The lecture on number theory and its applications might have been particularly trying for the nonspecialists in the audience had the professor not ------ it with humorous asides.

(A) exhorted
(B) leavened
(C) intercepted
(D) countermanded
(E) rebuffed

5. His ------ maintained that Mr. Frank was constantly at odds with the corporate officers; yet the truth was that his ideas were not at all ------ with the officers' reasonable goals.

(A) detractors . . in accord
(B) supporters . . at variance
(C) advocates . . harmonious
(D) disparagers . . incompatible
(E) apologists . . in conflict

6. In spite of the ------ of Larry's speech, most of the audience was ------ well before he had finished.

(A) conciseness . . cheering
(B) humor . . intrigued
(C) appropriateness . . enrapt
(D) brevity . . asleep
(E) cleverness . . reluctant

7. Although the government has frequently ------ some parental responsibilities, at heart it must still be parents, not agencies, who are ------ to care for children.

(A) obscured . . assumed
(B) precluded . . adjured
(C) exulted . . incompetent
(D) disavowed . . impelled
(E) usurped . . obligated

Sentence Completion Practice 4

Each of the sentences below is missing one or two portions. Read each sentence. Then select the word or words that most logically complete the sentence, taking into account the meaning of the sentence as a whole.

Example:

> Rather than accepting the theory unquestioningly, Deborah regarded it with ------.

(A) mirth
(B) sadness
(C) responsibility
(D) ignorance
(E) skepticism

Correct response: (E)

1. In genetic research, ------ mice are often essential because their ------ allows scientists to pose questions answerable only if all the mice in a group have similar hereditary traits.

   (A) sedated . . temperament
   (B) cloned . . unpredictability
   (C) adaptable . . vigor
   (D) inbred . . uniformity
   (E) adult . . familiarity

2. Historians generally ------ the film, not only for its excessive sentimentality and unrealistic dialogue, but because it did not ------ a true understanding of the problems of the era.

   (A) advocated . . exhibit
   (B) challenged . . hinder
   (C) panned . . demonstrate
   (D) exalted . . ascertain
   (E) censured . . eliminate

3. The fact that even the most traditional European languages have ------ such words as "email" seems to indicate that no language is impervious to foreign influences.

   (A) originated
   (B) prohibited
   (C) invalidated
   (D) recounted
   (E) incorporated

4. Although many have ------ the theoretical undergirdings of her research, her experimental protocols have always been beyond reproach.

   (A) espoused
   (B) disputed
   (C) presumed
   (D) interpreted
   (E) publicized

5. The humanists in the class emphasized the ------ of scientific discovery, asserting that although the world could have formulated calculus without Newton, it would never have produced the Hammerklavier Sonata without Beethoven.

   (A) monotony
   (B) triviality
   (C) symmetry
   (D) impersonality
   (E) intricacy

6. Although his manner was didactic and imperious, this fact was generally ------ and occasionally even ------ as qualities befitting a man of his stature.

   (A) encouraged . . dismissed
   (B) overlooked . . ignored
   (C) discussed . . denounced
   (D) criticized . . glorified
   (E) tolerated . . applauded

7. The novel's realistic depiction of social injustice in early nineteenth-century America was an unmistakable ------ of the new republic's ------ to its democratic ideals.

   (A) denunciation . . infidelity
   (B) disavowal . . reversion
   (C) trivialization . . devotion
   (D) revelation . . gratitude
   (E) commendation . . allegiance

Sentence Completion Practice 5

Each of the sentences below is missing one or two portions. Read each sentence. Then select the word or words that most logically complete the sentence, taking into account the meaning of the sentence as a whole.

Example:

Rather than accepting the theory unquestioningly, Deborah regarded it with ------.

(A) mirth
(B) sadness
(C) responsibility
(D) ignorance
(E) skepticism

Correct response: (E)

1. Most art critics regard her early style as pedestrian and conventional, utterly devoid of technical or artistic ------.

(A) lucidity
(B) analysis
(C) articulation
(D) mediocrity
(E) innovation

2. Historical buildings in many developing towns, rather than being razed, are now being ------.

(A) constructed
(B) renovated
(C) described
(D) condemned
(E) designed

3. Some linguists claim that French is characterized by brevity of expression and, therefore, may be the most ------ of all languages.

(A) beautiful
(B) vivid
(C) concise
(D) accessible
(E) concrete

4. The melée that punctuated the meeting between the rival factions was not entirely ------; the groups have long ------ each other on many important issues.

(A) surprising . . supported
(B) unusual . . copied
(C) explicit . . evaluated
(D) unanticipated . . opposed
(E) expected . . encountered

5. Having been devastated by the earthquake, the freeway was ------ to all but the most rugged of vehicles.

(A) destroyed
(B) impassable
(C) improper
(D) winding
(E) unnecessary

6. Those who assume that they can easily be ------ chefs in the classic tradition are almost as ------ as those who think they can write a novel if they simply sit down and type.

(A) amateur . . candid
(B) renowned . . skeptical
(C) superb . . timid
(D) clumsy . . pessimistic
(E) competent . . naive

7. Under certain conditions, the virus can mutate into ------ strain, transforming what was once simply ------ into a menacing poison.

(A) a new . . an epidemic
(B) a deficient . . a derivative
(C) an erratic . . a rudiment
(D) a virulent . . a nuisance
(E) an advanced . . a disease

Sentence Completion Practice 6

Each of the sentences below is missing one or two portions. Read each sentence. Then select the word or words that most logically complete the sentence, taking into account the meaning of the sentence as a whole.

Example:

Rather than accepting the theory unquestioningly, Deborah regarded it with ------.

(A) mirth
(B) sadness
(C) responsibility
(D) ignorance
(E) skepticism

Correct response: (E)

1. The country's confidence, formerly sustained by an ------ sense of power, was replaced by an equally exaggerated sense of ------ following the hasty evacuation of its troops from three foreign capitals.

   (A) inflated . . weakness
   (B) overwhelming . . inviolability
   (C) erratic . . hysteria
   (D) unquestioned . . omnipotence
   (E) arbitrary . . resolution

2. According to their detractors, the leaders of the Union for Progressive Politics do not truly ------ change, but simply rehash old and discredited theories of political philosophy.

   (A) admonish
   (B) censor
   (C) advocate
   (D) caricature
   (E) hinder

3. Dr. Cuthbert often ------ his former associates for not continuing to support him; apparently he harbored great animosity because of their ------ of him.

   (A) disparaged . . endorsement
   (B) excoriated . . abandonment
   (C) exonerated . . denunciation
   (D) extolled . . betrayal
   (E) venerated . . dismissal

4. Despite her gregariousness, Andrea seems to have been a woman who cherished her ------ highly.

   (A) colleagues
   (B) friendships
   (C) privacy
   (D) integrity
   (E) humility

5. It is extremely rare to see a politician ------ any opinion which is widely unpopular; it seems that, for them, public censure is more ------ even than death.

   (A) conform to . . desirable
   (B) tolerate . . exciting
   (C) reject . . feared
   (D) espouse . . painful
   (E) manipulate . . natural

6. The haiku, with its ------, its reduction of natural and everyday events to their mere essence, seems to depict economically the ------ of even the simplest human experience.

   (A) casualness . . destructiveness
   (B) optimism . . barrenness
   (C) capriciousness . . rigidity
   (D) digressiveness . . precariousness
   (E) conciseness . . poignancy

7. Despite the ------ literature debunking the theory of ESP, a critical and rational awareness of the subject continues to ------ most of the public.

   (A) vivid . . pervade
   (B) voluminous . . elude
   (C) provocative . . captivate
   (D) ambiguous . . perplex
   (E) incomprehensible . . escape

Answer Key

Sentence Completion Practice I

1. A The colon introduces examples. What are *self-righteousness*, *arrogance*, and *condescension* examples of? Certainly not something good, like *insights* or *tenets* (core beliefs). The *likelihood of perfection* doesn't have *dangers*, the *sanctity of perfection* doesn't have *inequities* (unequal treatments), but the *pursuit of perfection* can certainly have *pitfalls* (negative consequences) like those listed. *contemplation* = deep thought; *sanctity* = holiness

2. C *Whereas* indicates a contrast. *Frivolous* means lacking soberness or seriousness. The missing word has to indicate a quality that a serious person would have, like *prudence* (conservative wisdom). *hysteria* = irrational and excessive emotion; *equivocation* = failure to commit to a position

3. E *Today's computerized machines* make sounds that are *almost like real human speech*, so they must be *a far cry* from artificial-sounding speech, or *mechanical* speech. *melancholy* = depressed; *cordial* = friendly; *fervid* = passionate; *inflammatory* = tending to incite anger

4. D *Even in* indicates irony (a reversal of expectations). If *technologically advanced industries* bring something *important*, that important thing will likely not be *concern*, *decay*, or *dismay*. Since technological advances are far from traditional, it would be ironic that a *traditional* community would value *technology*. *prestige* = public esteem; *liberty* = freedom

5. A If the events *would not take place for centuries*, he must have *predicted* them. *Wars, conflagrations, and earthquakes* are types of *cataclysms* (events that cause widespread destruction). *foreboded* = predicted; *mitigated* = improved a situation; *transcended* = rose above; *auguries* = predictions

6. D If you aren't *willing to concede that there were many conflicting opinions*, then you must believe that everyone shares the same opinion. Therefore, you would not have to ask everyone's opinion, but could *infer* (make a generalization about) everyone's attitude from the attitude of just a few individuals. *distinguishing* = recognizing as distinct; *expelling* = throwing out

7. C If they *resist* it, then they want to prevent its effects on them, or at least *minimize* its effects on them. *initiate* = cause to begin; *distort* = twist; *palliate* = make less severe; *enhance* = make better

Sentence Completion Practice 2

1. D *Boundless energy* is the definition of *vigor*. This is the kind of thing that would cause someone to be *exhausted* at the end of the day. *grace* = elegance; *scandalized* = shamed publicly; *contrite* = filled with regret; *vigor* = great energy; *disillusioned* = with lowered esteem of another

2. E This sentence contains a definition. The missing word means *based more on personal whim than on the opinion of his fellow members*. *inclusive* = including; *abstract* = not concrete; *illusory* = based on or characteristic of illusion; *arbitrary* = based on whim or random power

3. A The semicolon indicates that the ideas in the two clauses support each other. The phrase *more ... than ...* indicates a contrast. The word *boundary* is the definition of the first missing word. *demarcation* = boundary; *estrange* = cause to grow apart; *partake* = participate; *affiliation* = close association

4. B *Such as* indicates support through example. *Breathing rate* and *perspiration* are examples of *physiological* reactions. (They aren't *imperceptible* because they're being recorded!) The word *by* indicates a cause-and-effect relationship. The recording of such reactions would not *induce* (cause) deception, but might just *detect* it. *imperceptible* = incapable of being detected; *subvert* = undermine; *simulated* = artificial; *induce* = cause; *verifiable* = capable of being proved true

5. D The sentence shows a cause and effect: something about the novel *makes it* (causes it to be) *difficult to translate*. The description makes it sound *quirky*, which would indeed make it hard to translate. *mundane* = ordinary; *taciturn* = not talkative; *alliterative* = using words that begin with the same sound; *idiosyncratic* = quirky; *orthodox* = adhering strictly to teachings

6. E This sentence shows a cause and effect. Some quality of the bears causes them not to hurt each other, even in *aggressive play*. Particularly since they are so strong, they would have to have a lot of *restraint*. *stamina* = endurance; *concentration* = focus; *instinct* = inborn ability; *restraint* = ability to hold back

7. A *Deterrence* is the belief that a strong offensive capability will *deter* (prevent) attack from one's enemies, that is, that a *formidable* (awesome) display of force would *obviate* (render unnecessary through foresight) the need for further military action. *subtle* = hard to detect; *unbridled* = lacking restraint

Sentence Completion Practice 3

1. **B**   The *but* indicates contrast. The first missing word must fit well with *slowly. frantically* = wildly; *sluggishly* = slowly; *rashly* = hastily

2. **A**   *Because* indicates cause and effect. The word *discover* indicates surprise. If the President *was used to receiving the support of his advisors*, then it would be surprising to discover that they didn't agree with him on something. *irreconcilable* = unable to be made to agree; *consonant* = in agreement with; *oblivious* = unaware; *compatible* = fitting well together; *commensurate* = in proportion to

3. **C**   *Not only . . . but also . . .* indicates a supportive relationship between the ideas. *commissioned* = paid for an artistic work to be created; *demolished* = destroyed

4. **B**   It *might have been . . . trying* (difficult to tolerate) *. . . had the professor not ------ it with humorous asides.* What do humorous asides do to make something easier to tolerate? They *lighten* it up. *exhorted* = urged strongly; *leavened* = lightened with humor; *intercepted* = caught in transit; *countermanded* = canceled; *rebuffed* = refused abruptly

5. **D**   It's not particularly good to be *constantly at odds with the corporate officers*, so this is something that *critics* would say of him. The word *yet* indicates a contrast. If the officers' goals were *reasonable*, then one would likely *not disagree* with them.   *detractors* = critics;   *accord* = agreement; *variance* = disagreement;   *advocates* = supporters; *harmonious* = in pleasant agreement; *disparagers* = critics; *incompatible* = difficult to reconcile; *apologists* = those who make supportive arguments

6. **D**   *In spite of* shows irony. It would certainly be ironic if the speech were short and yet still put people to sleep. *conciseness* = brevity; *enrapt* = enthraled; *brevity* = briefness

7. **E**   *Although* indicates contrast. The sentence makes it clear that although government has *overtaken* some parental responsibilities, still parents, not agencies, *should* care for children. *obscured* = made less clear; *precluded* = prevented; *adjured* = commanded solemnly; *exulted* = rejoiced; *disavowed* = renounced; *impelled* = urged to action; *usurped* = took over; *obligated* = morally compelled

Sentence Completion Practice 4

1. **D**   The sentence indicates that the fact that the mice all have similar hereditary traits is essential to the genetic research. Since hereditary traits are only passed on in families, such mice must be very closely related. *sedated* = put to sleep; *temperament* = disposition; *vigor* = energetic health; *inbred* = bred with family members; *uniformity* = lack of variation

2. **C**   If the film has *excessive sentimentality and unrealistic dialogue*, historians would probably not like it because they would appreciate historical realism. They would *criticize* the film. It must not have *shown* a *true understanding of the problems of the era. advocated* = spoke in favor of; *exhibit* = display;   *hinder* = impede;   *panned* = criticized harshly;   *exalted* = praised   highly;   *ascertain* = determined the truth of; *censured* = criticized

3. **E**   If this fact indicates *that no language is impervious to foreign influences*, it must reveal a strong influence from foreign sources. *Incorporating such words as "email"* would show that influence. *originated* = started;   *invalidated* = made worthless; *recounted* = retold;   *incorporated* = assumed into a whole

4. **B**   *Although* indicates contrast. Although her *protocols have always been beyond reproach*, many must have *questioned* the undergirdings of her research. *disputed* = called   into   question;   *presumed*   = assumed to be true;

5. **D**   To say that *the world could have formulated calculus without Newton* is to suggest that scientific discovery does not depend on the creativity of particular individuals. *monotony* = tedium;   *triviality* = ordinariness;   *impersonality* = detachment from personal qualities; *intricacy* = complicatedness

6. **E**   If being *didactic* (preachy) *and imperious* (overbearing) were thought as *befitting* (appropriate), they must have been *accepted.*

7. **A**   What is the relationship between a *depiction of social injustice* in a society and that society's *democratic ideals*? Such a depiction would certainly call those ideals into question, perhaps even *denounce* them. *denunciation* = harsh   criticism; *infidelity* = unfaithfulness; *disavowal* = swearing off; *reversion* = return   to   a   previous   state;   *devotion* = strong commitment;   *revelation* = revealing   experience; *commendation* = praise; *allegiance* = faithfulness

Sentence Completion Practice 5

1. **E** Something *pedestrian and conventional* is ordinary and uses methods that have been used many times before. Therefore it is not *new* or *interesting*. *lucidity* = clarity; *analysis* = examination of parts; *articulation* = expression; *mediocrity* = averageness; *innovation* = novelty, creativity

2. **B** To *raze* something is to destroy it completely. If a historical building is not *razed*, it is at least left alone or, even better, preserved or made new again. *renovated* = made new again

3. **C** *Brevity of expression* is *conciseness*. *vivid* = full of lively forms or colors; *concise* = to the point; *accessible* = easily understood; *concrete* = perceived through the senses

4. **D** A *melée* is a fight. If the groups were fighting, they probably have *disagreed with* each other. Therefore the melée was not *anticipated*.

5. **B** A highway that has *been devastated by the earthquake* would be *hard to travel through*. Although the highway was clearly damaged, in this context *destroyed* does not work because destruction is not a relative state. A highway cannot be *destroyed* to one vehicle but not to another, but it can be *impassable* to one vehicle but not another. *impassable* = unable to be traveled through

6. **E** Those who *think they can write a novel if they simply sit down and type* are unaware of how challenging such a task is. The sentence suggests that such people are *naive*. *amateur* = nonprofessional; *candid* = frank and honest; *renowned* = reputable, well known; *skeptical* = inclined to doubting; *superb* = exceptional; *timid* = shy; *naive* = lacking a sophisticated understanding

7. **D** If something is *transformed* into a *menacing poison*, it must not have been so bad previously. Likely it was only a little bit *troublesome*. *epidemic* = a broad outbreak; *derivative* = repetitive of previous works; *rudiment* = basic element; *virulent* = dangerous; *nuisance* = annoyance

Sentence Completion Practice 6

1. **A** A *hasty evacuation* of a country's troops would logically be accompanied by a feeling of *defeat* or *weakness*. This feeling, the sentence states, is just as *exaggerated* as the sense of power just

prior to the withdrawal. *inviolability* = invincibility; *erratic* = irregular; *hysteria* = irrational and exaggerated emotion; *omnipotence* = supreme power; *arbitrary* = based on whim and random power; *resolution* = determination

2. **C** If their *detractors* (critics) believe that they only *rehash old and discredited theories*, then they are suggesting that they do not really *speak out for* change. *admonish* = reprimand; *censor* = eliminate objectionable material; *advocate* = speak in favor of; *caricature* = exaggerate comically; *hinder* = get in the way of

3. **B** If his associates did not continue to support him, they must have *abandoned* him. If he harbored *animosity* for them, he must have *criticized* them. *disparaged* = criticized harshly; *endorsement* = show of support; *excoriated* = criticized harshly; *exonerated* = proved innocent; *denunciation* = condemnation; *extolled* = praised highly; *venerated* = honored

4. **C** *Despite* indicates contrast. *Gregariousness* is sociability. Its opposite is *solitude*, *reclusiveness*, or *privacy*.

5. **D** If *public censure* is like *death*, politicians must not like it. They must never *openly adopt* a widely unpopular opinion. *conform* = do what is expected; *espouse* = adopt publicly; *manipulate* = take control of

6. **E** The logical structure of the sentence suggests a definition. The first word must mean something like *reduction to its essence*, and the second word must mean something like *essence*. *barrenness* = starkness; *capriciousness* = whimsy, randomness; *digressiveness* = tendency to go off-topic; *precariousness* = danger; *conciseness* = brevity; *poignancy* = sharpness of feeling

7. **B** *Despite* indicates irony. If there is *literature debunking the theory of ESP*, it would be ironic if the public *failed to develop* a critical and rational awareness of the subject. If such literature were *plentiful*, the irony would be even more pronounced. *vivid* = full of vibrant imagery; *pervade* = fill completely; *voluminous* = plentiful; *elude* = escape capture or understanding; *provocative* = tending to elicit strong reactions; *captivate* = capture; *ambiguous* = unclear; *perplex* = confuse; *incomprehensible* = beyond understanding

CHAPTER 7

MATH REASONING SKILLS: WHAT THE PSAT MATH TEST IS *REALLY* TESTING

1. What Is the PSAT Math Test Really Testing?

2. The Eight Basic Reasoning Skills: MAPS-CATCH

1   WHAT IS THE PSAT MATH TEST REALLY TESTING?

The math portions of the PSAT test your math *reasoning skills* more than your math *knowledge*. What's the difference? Your math *knowledge* is your ability to recall and apply facts and procedures, like long division, adding fractions, solving equations, using the Pythagorean theorem, and so on. Tests of math knowledge usually aren't too tricky. Either you know the fact or procedure or you don't. Your math *reasoning skills*, on the other hand, are the skills you use to solve problems that you've never seen before. They include your ability to figure out what a question is asking, determine the relevant information, analyze the problem, find patterns in the problem, recall essential facts and procedures, simplify the problem, look at the problem from different angles, check your work, and so on. Tests of math reasoning also assess your math knowledge—so you do have to know how to add fractions and apply the Pythagorean theorem—but just knowing those facts and procedures isn't enough.

Here is an example of a hard PSAT math problem:

A,870,720

The seven-digit integer above is the product of six consecutive even integers. What is the value of *A*?

If you're like most high school math students, you haven't seen many problems like that, if any. You almost certainly haven't been taught any specific procedures for solving such problems. Some students complain that these questions are unfair, because they aren't testing what they learned in school, meaning regurgitation of standard memorized procedures. But the PSAT and SAT are testing something more important: your ability to think.

If you are a good thinker, you will first consider the important information in the problem and the goal of the problem. The goal is to find one digit in a big number. This number is the *product* of six numbers, which means that when you multiply six numbers together, you get the big number. The numbers you multiply are *even*, which means they are multiples of 2. They are also *consecutive*, so they follow in sequence, like 2, 4, 6, 8, 10, and 12. (But these can't be the

numbers, because their product doesn't look like the number you're given.) This knowledge is enough to start solving by *trial and error*, which is often a very good problem-solving strategy. You can try picking six consecutive even numbers and multiplying them on your calculator, and keep trying until you get a product that looks like the number you're given.

Sometimes trial and error is a great problem-solving method, and sometimes it's not. It's great when you can easily check your guess and make a better guess if it's wrong. In this case, though, you don't have a very good idea of how big the number is, except that it's between 1,870,720 and 9,870,720. So if your product is below that range, you know to guess bigger numbers, and if the product is above that range, you know to guess smaller numbers. Try it, and see if you get the answer.

But there's always an easier way on PSAT and SAT math problems. If you are really good at analyzing problems and finding patterns, you will almost *never* need to use your calculator on the PSAT or SAT. Here's how the really good thinkers solve this problem:

First, they notice a pattern in the six consecutive even numbers, and they recall a divisibility fact. They notice that any list of three consecutive even numbers contains a multiple of 3. (Try it and see. No matter what even number you start with, if you write out three consecutive even numbers, the list will always contain a multiple of 3.) Therefore, six consecutive even integers must contain *two* multiples of 3. When you multiply these numbers together, then, you are multiplying two multiples of 3, which must produce a multiple of 9. *So the seven-digit number must be a multiple of 9.* Then comes the divisibility fact: *the sum of the digits of any multiple of 9 is also a multiple of 9.* (Again, if this fact is unfamiliar to you, just try it out. Pick any multiple of 9 and add its digits. Notice that they always equal another multiple of 9. For instance, 18, 72, and 999 are all multiples of 9, and $1 + 8 = 9$, $7 + 2 = 9$, and $9 + 9 + 9 = 27$.) Therefore, $A + 8 + 7 + 0 + 7 + 2 + 0$, which simplifies to $A + 24$, must equal a multiple of 9. Since *A* is just a single digit, it shouldn't be hard to see (if you know your 9 multiplication table) that the only solution is $A = 3$, so that the sum of digits is 27.

2   THE EIGHT BASIC REASONING SKILLS: MAPS-CATCH

The eight basic reasoning skills can be summarized with a handy mnemonic: MAPS-CATCH.

M is for mapping, or determining the relevant information and goal of the problem.

A is for analyzing, or taking a problem apart and seeing how the parts relate.

P is for finding patterns, or noticing repeating terms or relationships.

S is for simplifying, or reducing the amount of information you must deal with in the problem.

C is for connecting to facts and procedures, or recalling the important knowledge from math class.

A is for considering alternatives, or approaching the problem from different angles.

T is for thinking logically, or using deduction to test theories and solve problems.

CH is for checking, or rereading the problem to make sure your solution is correct.

Reasoning Skill 1: Mapping

To "map" a problem simply means to represent the important information from the problem in a form that you can use. The important information includes the goal of the problem and the facts of and conditions on the problem. If you want to find out how to get from point A to point B, and you've never been to either place before, what would you do? You'd find a map that represents point A, point B, and all of the roads and obstacles between them. This is "mapping." If you try to get from A to B without a map, you're likely to get lost.

If a problem is simple, you can probably keep all of the relevant information in your head and still have room to think about it. If the problem is tougher, though, you should write the information on your scratch paper.

Use the Test for Scratchwork

PSAT and SAT math problems are written with plenty of space for scratchwork. Use it! You don't get points for neatness, so feel free to make marks all over your test booklet. (Be careful not to scribble so much over the problem that you can't read the original words, though.)

Underline Commonly Overlooked or Confused Terms

Even the brightest students get questions wrong simply because they have misread them. Below are the most frequently overlooked or confused terms on PSAT and SAT math questions. To avoid overlooking or confusing them, always underline these terms when you see them, and think about what they mean.

Perimeter is often confused with *area*. The perimeter of a figure is the distance around its edges. The area of a figure is the number of square units that fit inside it.

Circumference ($2\pi r$) is often confused with *circle area* (πr^2). This is simply a special instance of perimeter and area. It's easy to confuse these two formulas because they contain the same three symbols. To avoid confusing the circumference formula with the circle area formula, remember that area is always measured in *square* units, so its formula contains the "square." Also, remember that the circumference and circle area formulas are always given at the beginning of any PSAT or SAT math section.

Odd numbers are often confused with *negative numbers*. You may not believe it, but smart kids make this mistake all the time when they're not thinking carefully. It's easy to confuse the two terms because we use these words a lot outside of mathematics, and they are both "bad" words. Being an *odd* person is usually considered a *negative* thing. Don't assume you won't make this mistake. Underline the words *odd* and *negative* whenever you see them in problems. Odd numbers are integers that are not divisible by 2. Negative numbers are real numbers that are less than 0.

Even numbers are often confused with *positive numbers*, for much the same reason as *odd* and *negative* are often confused. Outside of math, being *even* is a *positive* thing. Again, don't assume you won't confuse these terms, and underline them when you see them.

Integers are often thought to be the same as *whole numbers*. In fact, the PSAT and SAT will never use the term *whole number*, so you only need to know what an *integer* is. An integer is a positive or negative whole number. Remember also that 0 is an integer. Many students mistakenly think that integers can't be 0 or negative.

Product is often confused with *sum*. Even excellent students often confuse these two. A product is the result of a *multiplication*, and a *sum* is the result of an *addition*. The product of 4 and 3 is 12, but the sum of 4 and 3 is 7.

Radius is often confused with *diameter*. To avoid this mistake, think of the roots of each word. (Yes, verbal skills help in math!) The word *radius* has the same root as *ray* and *radiate*. Visualize the sun's rays *radiating*:

Every ray starts at the center, where the sun is, right? And so does every radius. The word *diameter*, however, comes from the roots *dia*, meaning across, and *meter*, meaning measure. So it is the measure all the away *across* the circle, through the center.

Represent the Problem Situation

Once you've noticed all of the key terms in the problem, you must represent the problem situation as a whole. Don't assume that you can do every problem in your head or on your calculator. The basic tools for representing a problem are *diagrams*, *equations*, *graphs*, and *tables*. Of course, not every problem requires a table or a graph or an equation. You have to think about each problem individually and how best to represent its information.

Notice carefully any *restrictions* on the problem. For instance, do the unknowns have to be *integers* or *positive numbers* or *multiples of some number*? Are they measures of *angles* or *segments* or *areas* in a figure?

Notice carefully whether the unknowns must have only *one* value or can have *many* values. In other words, can an unknown take any value that you choose, or does it have only one particular value that you have to find? If the unknowns can have many possible values, then you may be able to find a possible solution just by guessing. If not, you may have to use a more direct procedure.

Understand the Goal

Have you ever given a brilliant answer on a test, only to find that you've answered the wrong question? This happens a lot on the PSAT and SAT math, because reasoning questions are trickier than knowledge questions. **Don't assume that, because a question looks similar to questions you've seen before, it is asking for the same thing**. Always pay special attention to what exactly the problem is asking you to find. Does the problem ask you to solve an equation? Find the value of an expression? Find an area?

> If four less than the square root of a number is 4, what is half the number?

Here it's easy to get absorbed in finding the mystery number and lose track that the question is ultimately asking for *half* that number. You might set up a beautiful equation ($\sqrt{x} - 4 = 4$), solve it flawlessly ($x = 64$), and even check your answer in the original equation. But if you choose an answer of 64 (instead of 32), you'd be wrong.

Notice whether the question is multiple choice. This can be very helpful information. Your goal on a multiple-choice question is simply to pick the right answer out of five possibilities. Perhaps it is easier to simply work by process of elimination. Perhaps with little work you can see that four of the choices *don't* work. This is the same as proving that one of them *does* work.

How are the choices expressed? As *fractions, decimals, radicals, algebraic expressions*? Again, this is potentially useful information. If the choices are all given as fractions, then you should be "thinking fractions" as you solve the problem, or if you really hate fractions, convert those fractions to decimals and then "think decimals."

If the answer choices are numbers, notice the range of their values. This is also potentially valuable information. If the numbers are far apart, for instance, it may be easiest to simply estimate a solution and choose the closest value. Also, if a question asks you to count things, and the largest answer choice is 10, then you may be able to simply list the items and count them by hand, because listing 10 things won't take very long. If the largest choice is 240, however, then it's probably not smart to try to list them. You'll need a different method.

Don't Use "Tricks"—Think

If you want a high PSAT or SAT math score, you have to learn to think, not to memorize mindless tricks. Many students mistakenly believe that they can simply memorize the "best way" to solve each "type" of question on the PSAT or SAT. A lot of SAT books and courses try to make you believe that they have the "secrets" to "cracking" the test. They don't.

Many of the "tricks" taught in SAT-prep courses or books are designed to show you how to avoid thinking, which is a bad habit on a reasoning test. These tricks are knee-jerk approaches of the form "when you see A, don't think about it and just do B." They avoid the crucial step of mapping. If you get caught up in this approach, you will never be able to solve the tough math problems on the PSAT and SAT. Smart students read every PSAT and SAT math problem carefully before deciding how to solve it. Many students worry that examining every problem carefully will waste too much time. In fact, careful mapping will save time, not waste it. It will help you to see the important relationships and restrictions on the problems that help you to simplify them.

Exercise Set I

Map each of the following problems before solving. Use the space for scratchwork, underline key words in the problem, write any helpful equations, and draw useful diagrams. Answers are at the end of the chapter.

<u>Do Your Scratchwork Here</u>

1. The product of five consecutive even integers is 0. What is the greatest possible value of any one of these integers?

2. Carlos begins with twice as much money as David. After Carlos gives $12 to David, Carlos still has $10 more than David. How much money did they have <u>combined</u> at the start?

    (A) $32
    (B) $66
    (C) $68
    (D) $92
    (E) $102

3. Corinne travels from home to work at an average speed of 50 miles per hour and returns home by the same route at 60 miles per hour. It takes her 10 more <u>minutes</u> to get to work than it takes her to get home. How many miles is it from Corinne's home to work?

    (A) 25
    (B) 35
    (C) 50
    (D) 75
    (E) 90

Reasoning Skill 2: Analyzing

To analyze a problem means to break it into smaller parts and examine the relationships among those parts. A PSAT question will give you *certain* pieces of information, but often you have to examine *other* pieces of information that are not explicitly mentioned in the question. For example:

> What is the maximum area of a right triangle with a hypotenuse of 10 inches?

As with any tough problem, your first job is to map it. Hopefully you remember what a right triangle is, what a hypotenuse is, and what the formula for the area of a triangle is. Then you can draw a nice diagram and write down the formula for the area of a triangle:

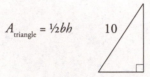

$$A_{\text{triangle}} = \frac{1}{2}bh \qquad 10$$

Good enough. But now you have a problem. To find the area of a triangle, you need to know its base and height. But all you know here is the *hypotenuse*, which isn't part of the formula. So you must make a connection between the parts. Aha! You can turn the hypotenuse into the base, just by rotating the triangle:

That shows you the base, but what about the height? Drawing it is easy, but how do you find its length? Actually, it can be many possible lengths. The problem suggests this. Notice that the problem asks for the *maximum* area. This implies that there are *many possible* areas, and your job is to find the greatest one. Since the base is fixed at 10, there must be different possible heights. So you must try to visualize the range of possibilities, remembering that the triangle must be a *right* triangle:

If you can visualize the possibilities, as in the diagram above, you should be able to see that *the*

height of the triangle is greatest when the lengths of the two legs are equal. This is very helpful. If the two legs are equal, then not only is the biggest possible triangle a right triangle, it is an *isosceles* triangle. If you know the *isosceles triangle theorem*, the problem is nearly solved. The isosceles triangle theorem says that if a triangle has two equal sides, then the two angles opposite those sides are equal too. The converse is also true: if two *angles* in a triangle are equal, then the *sides* opposite those angles are equal too. You must also know that the sum of the angles in a triangle is 180°. Applying these theorems to the diagram gives you lots of information:

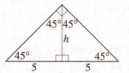

Since the big triangle is isosceles, the two base angles are equal. Since the three angles must have a sum of 180°, the base angles must each be 45°. Since the sum of the angles in the *smaller* triangles must also be 180°, then the smaller triangles must also be 45°-45°-90° triangles. The isosceles triangle theorem tells us that the legs of the smaller triangles must also be equal, so h must be 5! Therefore, the area of the biggest triangle is $\frac{1}{2}(10)(5) = 25$ square inches.

If You Can't Find What You Want Directly, Find What You Can!

In the problem we just solved, we had to find the measures of several angles and lengths before we could find the one we needed. You should expect to do that kind of work to solve tough problems. **If you can't find what you want right away, just look at the parts of the problem one at a time and find what you can**. Often, going step-by-step will eventually lead you to the answer you need.

Look for Simple Relationships

Once you see the parts of a problem, look for the simple relationships between them. Simple relationships usually lead to simple solutions. For example:

> If $2x + 5y = 19$, what is the value of $20x + 50y$?

There is no need to worry about "solving" for x and y. You need only see that $20x + 50y$ is 10 times $2x + 5y$.

So, by substitution, $20x + 50y$ must equal 10 times 19, or 190.

The figure below shows a square in which a smaller square is inscribed. The vertices of the smaller square are the midpoints of the sides of the larger square. If the area of the smaller square is 5, what is the area of the larger square?

When you are given the area of the square, the first relationship that probably comes to mind is the area formula: $A = s^2$. So you might try to find the length of the side of the small square and then try to find the length of a side of the larger square. But there is a much simpler relationship between the given information and the information you need to find. Draw the two lines shown below, and it becomes clear that the smaller square is half the area of the larger square. So the big square has an area of $5 \times 2 = 10$.

Exercise Set 2

Analyze each of the following problems carefully before solving. Think about the relationships among the parts. Answers are at the end of the chapter.

1. If $20,000 is divided among three people in the ratio of $2:3:5$, how much does each person get?

2.

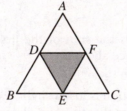

In the figure above, equilateral triangle *ABC* has an area of 20, and points *D*, *E*, and *F* are the midpoints of their respective sides. What is the area of the shaded region?

3. In the sophomore class at Hillside High School, the ratio of boys to girls is 2 to 3. The junior class contains as many boys as the sophomore class does, and the ratio of boys to girls in the junior class is 5 to 4. If there are 200 students in the sophomore class, how many students are there in the junior class?

Reasoning Skill 3: Finding Patterns

An important part of mathematical reasoning is looking for and using patterns. Good mathematical thinkers always look for repeating shapes, terms, and relationships. When they find them, they check to see if the repetition makes it easier to solve the problem.

> If $5x^2 + 7x + 12 = 4x^2 + 7x + 12$, what is the value of x?

This question is much simpler than it looks at first because of the repetition in the equation. If you subtract the repetitive terms from both sides of the equation, it reduces to $5x^2 = 4x^2$. Subtracting $4x^2$ from both sides then gives $x^2 = 0$, so $x = 0$.

Play Around to Find Relationships

Sometimes the repetition doesn't become clear until you start moving around the terms or shapes in a problem. **Play around with the parts of a problem until you find simple patterns or relationships**.

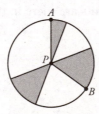

> If P is the center of the circle above, $AP = 3$, and $\angle APB$ has a measure of $120°$, what is the total area of the shaded regions?

This one is easier than it looks. Remember that if you can't find what you want, you should at least find what you can, and see if that gets you any closer to what you want. You can find the area of the circle with the formula $A = \pi r^2$. Since AP is the radius and $AP = 3$, the area of the circle is $\pi(3)^2 = 9\pi$. Now, play around with the pieces, as if they are part of a jigsaw puzzle. Do you notice how they all fit together inside $\angle APB$? Since $\angle APB$ is $120°$, which is one-third of $360°$, the shaded region is just one-third of the whole circle, or $9\pi/3 = 3\pi$.

Sequence Questions

Some PSAT and SAT questions specifically ask you to analyze a sequence of terms. In these problems, it is especially important to look for patterns.

> $1, 0, -1, 1, 0, -1, 1, 0, -1\ldots$

> If the sequence above continues according to the pattern shown, what will be the 200th term of the sequence?

The key here is to notice how the pattern repeats. It repeats every 3 terms. In 200 terms, then, the pattern repeats itself $200 \div 3 = 66$ times with a remainder of 2. Because of the repetition, the 200th term must be the same as the second term, which is 0.

> What is the *sum* of the first 200 terms in the sequence above?

This question is just a slight tweak of the previous one. Notice that the sum of each pattern is simply $1 + 0 + -1 = 0$. So the first 66 repetitions of this pattern have a sum of $66 \times 0 = 0$. The twist is the "remainder" of 2. The last two terms start at the beginning again: $\ldots 1, 0$. So the sum of all 200 terms is just $1 + 0 = 1$.

To solve problems involving sequences, write out the terms of the sequence until you notice the pattern. Then use your understanding of division with remainders to find what the question asks for.

> What is the units digit of 27^{40}?

The units digit is the "ones" digit, or final digit, of an integer. You might try to just calculate 27^{40} on your calculator and look at the last digit. This probably won't work, though, because the result is 58 digits long, and most calculators only show the first 12 digits or so. So how do you find the units digit? This doesn't look like a sequence problem, but it really is. You just have to look at it in a clever way. Think of 27^{40} as the fortieth term in the sequence 27^1, 27^2, 27^3, 27^4, and so on. Calculate the first 6 or so terms of this sequence, and notice the last digit of each one. These last digits follow a pattern: 7, 9, 3, 1, 7, 9, 3, 1, and so on, repeating every four terms. Every fourth term is 1, so the fortieth term is 1 also. Therefore, the units digit of 27^{40} is 1. We figured it out without even calculating 27^{40}. Cool, huh?

Exercise Set 3

Look for repeated terms or relationships in the following problems before solving them. Answers are at the end of the chapter.

1. If 5 less than 28% of x^2 is 10, what is 15 less than 28% of x^2?

2. If m is the sum of all multiples of 3 between 1 and 100 and n is the sum of all multiples of 3 between 5 and 95, what is $m - n$?

3. If $\dfrac{3}{y} + \dfrac{x}{2} = 10$, then $\dfrac{6}{y} + x =$

    (A) 5
    (B) 15
    (C) 20
    (D) 40
    (E) 60

4. Every term of a sequence, except the first, is 6 less than the square of the previous term. If the first term is 3, what is the fifth term of this sequence?

    (A) 3
    (B) 15
    (C) 19
    (D) 30
    (E) 43

Reasoning Skill 4: Simplifying

To simplify a problem means to reduce the amount of information you need to think about to solve the problem. Once you've mapped and analyzed a problem, you might be left with an overwhelming amount of information. When this happens, simplify. There are many ways to simplify a problem, including *beelining*, *substituting*, *combining*, and *canceling*.

Look for the Direct Route, or "Beeline"

Remember that mapping the problem means representing *where you are* and *where you want to be*. **The simplest way from A to B is often the "beeline"—the most direct route possible—from the given information to the information you want**. (This term comes from the assumption that bees always fly directly to their destinations.) Sometimes you can get so caught up in the standard procedures you learned in math class that you don't see the "beeline."

If $\dfrac{3a}{2b} = \dfrac{1}{4}$ and $\dfrac{b}{5c} = 3$,

what is the value of $\dfrac{a}{10c}$?

This seems like a tough problem because there are so many unknowns. A knee-jerk response might be to try to solve for *a*, *b*, and *c*. But the question doesn't ask for the values of *a*, *b*, and *c*, and there is a much more direct route to the answer you need. Notice that just multiplying the two given expressions gets you *almost* there:

$$\frac{3a}{2b} \times \frac{b}{5c} = \frac{3a}{10c}$$

Substitute: $\left(\dfrac{1}{4}\right)(3) = \dfrac{3a}{10c}$

Divide by 3: $\dfrac{1}{4} = \dfrac{a}{10c}$

Substitute to Simplify

One of the easiest ways to simplify a problem is to substitute a simple expression for a complicated one. One of the most useful theorems in math is also the simplest—the law of substitution, which simply says that if two things are equal, one can always be substituted for the other.

If $3x^2 + 5x + y = 8$, and $x \neq 0$,

what is the value of $\dfrac{16 - 2y}{3x^2 + 5x}$?

Both the equation and the fraction look complicated, but you can simplify by using the law of substitution, which says that if two things are equal, one can always be substituted for the other. Notice that $3x^2 + 5x$ appears in both the equation and the fraction. What does it equal? If you subtract *y* from both sides of the equation, you get $3x^2 + 5x = 8 - y$. If you substitute $8 - y$ for $3x^2 + 5x$ in the fraction, you get

$$\frac{16 - 2y}{8 - y} = \frac{2(8 - y)}{8 - y} = 2$$

Combine to Simplify

Another easy way to simplify a problem is to combine parts that can be easily combined. For instance, five problems ago, we showed how a tough geometry problem could be simplified by combining areas. You can also simplify by combining algebraic terms. For example, $3m - (2m - 1)$ can be simplified by combining like terms:

$$3m - (2m - 1) = 3m - 2m + 1 = m + 1$$

Cancel to Simplify

Many problems can be simplified with cancellation. For instance, fractions can be simplified by dividing common factors in the numerator and denominator:

$$\frac{4x^2 - 4}{x^2 + 3x + 2} = \frac{4(x - 1)(x + 1)}{(x + 1)(x + 2)} = \frac{4(x - 1)}{(x + 2)}$$

And equations can be simplified by subtracting common terms from both sides of the equation:

$$7x^2 + 3x + 8 = 7x^2 + 4x + 6 \text{ simplifies to } 2 = x$$

Exercise Set 4

Each of the following problems has a "hard" solution and an "easy" solution. Try to find the simplified solution. Answers are at the end of the chapter.

1. If $3y - 4z = 6$ and $2y + z = 10$, then $y - 5z =$

   (A) 12
   (B) 6
   (C) 4
   (D) 0
   (E) −4

2. If $y = 1 - x$ and $2y + x = 5$, what is the value of x?

   (A) −5
   (B) −4
   (C) −3
   (D) −1
   (E) 3

3. If $3 + m + n = n^2 + m^2$, what is the value of $\dfrac{(n^2 - n) + (m^2 - m)}{6}$?

4. If $\dfrac{2x^2 - 18}{x^2 + 2x - 3} = 9$, what is the value of $\dfrac{x - 3}{x - 1}$?

Reasoning Skill 5: Connecting to Knowledge

To solve many PSAT and SAT math problems, you have to recall facts and procedures you learned in school, but probably not as many as you think. You have to *think* before you use these facts and procedures, but you will have to use them. For the PSAT, you will only have to know facts and procedures from *pre-algebra, first-year algebra,* and *basic geometry.* For the SAT, you may also need to know a few of the basic facts and procedures from *second-year algebra.*

What You Need and What You Don't

The PSAT and SAT are not tests of your calculation skills. If you're doing a lot of calculations to solve a PSAT or SAT math problem, you're probably missing something important. You should never need to do complicated calculations to solve a PSAT or SAT math problem.

Know Where to Find the Formulas

One nice thing about the PSAT and SAT is that they give you most of the formulas you need. At the beginning of each math section you will see this *Reference Information:*

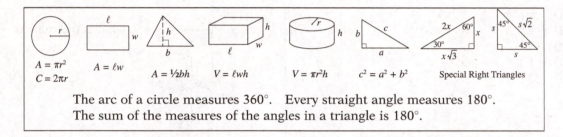

$$A = \pi r^2 \qquad A = \ell w \qquad A = \tfrac{1}{2}bh \qquad V = \ell wh \qquad V = \pi r^2 h \qquad c^2 = a^2 + b^2 \qquad \text{Special Right Triangles}$$
$$C = 2\pi r$$

The arc of a circle measures 360°.   Every straight angle measures 180°.
The sum of the measures of the angles in a triangle is 180°.

Know the Other Standard Facts and Procedures

To solve some PSAT math problems, you have to make quick connections to standard facts and procedures. The faster you can make these connections and see if they are helpful, the faster you will solve the problems. Some problems on the PSAT and SAT will be similar to problems you have done in math class.

Rate Problems

Problems involving speed or work are usually rate problems. To solve rate problems, you need to know the rate formula:

distance (or work) = rate × time

Often, you simply need to substitute the given information into the formula and solve for the missing part. For more practice with rate problems, see Lesson 4 in Chapter 10.

If a problem says *at this rate* . . . it implies that two rates are equal, which lets you set up a proportion. For practice with these kinds of problems, see Lesson 4 in Chapter 8 and Lesson 4 in Chapter 10.

Mean/Median/Mode Problems

Some problems will ask you to deal with *averages* (arithmetic means), *medians*, or *modes*. Here, the important thing is knowing how to find each one (and not mixing them up). **The *average (or arithmetic mean)* is the sum of the numbers divided by how many there are. The *median* is the middle number or the average of the two middle numbers when the numbers are listed in order. The *mode* is the number that appears most frequently in the set**. For more practice with these kinds of problems, see Lesson 2 in Chapter 10.

Right Triangle Problems

If a problem includes a right triangle, you should connect to two important facts: the Pythagorean theorem and the fact that angles in a triangle add up to 180°. If you know two sides of a right triangle, you can always find the third with the Pythagorean theorem (see Lesson 3 in Chapter 11). If you know one of the acute angles in a right triangle, you can always subtract its measure from 90° to find the other angle.

Parallel Lines Problems

Whenever you see parallel lines in a diagram, mark up the equal angles or supplementary angles. If you have trouble finding them, see Lesson 1 in Chapter 11. **You should be able to look at a diagram with parallel lines and tell quickly which angles are equal and which are supplementary.**

Exercise Set 5

Each of the following problems draws on a standard formula, theorem, or procedure from math class. Answers are at the end of the chapter.

1. If x is the average (arithmetic mean) of k and 10, and y is the average (arithmetic mean) of k and 4, what is the average of x and y, in terms of k?

(A) $\dfrac{k+14}{4}$

(B) $\dfrac{k+14}{2}$

(C) $\dfrac{k+7}{2}$

(D) $7k$

(E) $14k$

2. If, on average, x cars pass a certain point on a highway in y hours, then, at this rate, how many cars should be expected to pass the same point in z hours?

(A) xyz

(B) $\dfrac{xy}{z}$

(C) $\dfrac{z}{xy}$

(D) $\dfrac{xz}{y}$

(E) $\dfrac{x}{yz}$

3.

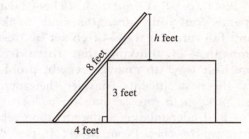

Note: Figure not drawn to scale.

A straight 8-foot board is resting on a rectangular box that is 3 feet high, as shown in the diagram above. Both the box and the board are resting on a horizontal surface and one end of the board rests on the ground 4 feet from the edge of the box. If h represents the height, in feet, of the other end of the board from the top of the box, what is h?

Reasoning Skill 6: Finding Alternatives

There are usually several good ways of approaching an PSAT or SAT question. **The "best way" depends on your strengths and weaknesses. Don't fall into the trap—often set by "test-prep" companies—of thinking that there is always "one best way" to answer certain problems**. In fact, the best students consider their options on each problem before settling on a "best way" to solve it. Understanding different approaches also helps you to check your work. If two different approaches give you the same answer, you are probably right!

Testing the Choices

One way to approach some multiple-choice questions is to simply test the choices. It only works on certain questions, but it can sometimes be simpler than solving the question directly.

> Which of the following represents all of the solutions of the equation $5x - 9 = x^2 - 9$?
>
> (A) $\{0, 1.8, 5\}$
> (B) $\{1.8, 3, 5\}$
> (C) $\{5\}$
> (D) $\{0, 5\}$
> (E) $\{-3, 3\}$

Here you can just "test" each choice by plugging its values into the equation and working by process of elimination. Test 0 first, because it's easiest: $5(0) - 9 = (0)^2 - 9$ is true, so 0 works. That's helpful, because now you can eliminate choices (B), (C), and (E), which don't have 0. Since both of the remaining choices, (A) and (D), also contain 5, you don't need to test 5 to know that it works. Just test 1.8 now: $5(1.8) - 9 = (1.8)^2 - 9$, which simplifies to $0 = -5.76$, which obviously isn't true, so 1.8 is not a solution. Therefore, by process of elimination, the answer is (D).

Another approach is to solve algebraically:

$$5x - 9 = x^2 - 9$$

Add 9: $\qquad 5x = x^2$
Divide by x: $\qquad 5 = x$

Looks good, right? Nope. We made a subtle error. The last step involved dividing by x, which is not allowed if x is 0! Check that possibility. Plug $x = 0$ into the original equation. It works: $5(0) - 9 = (0)^2 - 9$. You won't miss the extra solution if you avoid dividing by 0.

$$5x - 9 = x^2 - 9$$

Add 9 and subtract $5x$: $\qquad 0 = x^2 - 5x$
Factor: $\qquad 0 = x(x - 5)$
Use the 0 product property: $\qquad x = 0$ or 5

When solving a multiple-choice question by testing the choices, it's usually best to start with choice (C), because the answers are usually given in numerical order. That way, if it doesn't work, you might still be able to tell whether it's too big or too small and eliminate two more choices, leaving you with only two choices remaining. If there is no pattern to the choices, start with the number that's easiest to test.

Plugging In

Some multiple-choice questions can be simplified by plugging in values for unknowns in the problem. This is sometimes a handy strategy in problems where the *answer choices* contain unknowns or where the value of an unknown in the problem doesn't affect the answer.

When you solve by plugging in, be careful and be logical. You have to work by process of elimination. The basic idea is that exactly one of the five choices is correct, so once you've eliminated four choices, you're done. First check that the values you plug in satisfy any given equations or other restrictions given in the problem. Then write down the values you are plugging in for each unknown. Next, solve the problem *numerically* and write down the solution. Finally, plug in the values to *every* choice and eliminate those that don't give the right answer. If more than one choice gives the right answer, plug in again with different numbers until four choices are eliminated.

If $3m = mn + 1$, what is the value of m in terms of n?

(A) $n + 1$

(B) $n - 2$

(C) $\dfrac{1}{3 - n}$

(D) $\dfrac{1}{2 + n}$

(E) $\dfrac{2}{3 + n}$

Since the answer choices contain unknowns, you can plug in values for m and n to simplify. Plug in a simple number for m to start, like 1. Write down $m = 1$ on your paper. This gives $3(1) = 1n + 1$. The only way this will work is if

$n = 2$. Write this down, too, and check that the equation works. Now the question asks "what is the value of m?" Obviously it's 1, so write that down and circle it. Now plug in $n = 2$ to all of the choices and see what you get: (A) 3 (B) 0 (C) 1 (D) 1/4 (E) 2/5. Only (C) gives the right answer, so you're done! You could also have solved algebraically:

$$3m = mn + 1$$

Subtract mn: $3m - mn = 1$

Factor: $m(3 - n) = 1$

Divide by $(3 - n)$: $m = \dfrac{1}{3 - n}$

Exercise Set 6

Find two different methods for solving each of the following problems, and make sure both methods give the same answer. Answers are at the end of the chapter.

1. Three squares have sides with lengths a, b, and c, respectively. If b is 20% greater than a, and c is 25% greater than b, what percent greater is the area of the largest square than the area of the smallest square?

    (A) 20%
    (B) 50%
    (C) 75%
    (D) 125%
    (E) 225%

2. Jim and Ellen together weigh 290 pounds. Ellen and Ria together weigh 230 pounds. All three together weigh 400 pounds. What is Ellen's weight?

    (A) 110 lbs
    (B) 120 lbs
    (C) 130 lbs
    (D) 140 lbs
    (E) 170 lbs

3. If $m = 2x - 5$ and $n = x + 7$, which of the following expresses x in terms of m and n?

    (A) $\dfrac{m - n + 2}{2}$

    (B) $m - n + 2$

    (C) $\dfrac{m - n + 12}{2}$

    (D) $m - n + 12$

    (E) $2(m - n + 12)$

Reasoning Skill 7: Thinking Logically

Thinking logically doesn't mean just doing what makes sense. It means _drawing inescapable conclusions_, or making statements that follow necessarily from previous statements. One logical system that you learned in math class is the system for solving equations. This system helps us turn the statement "$x + 3 = 7$" and the statement "if $a = b$, then $a - 3 = b - 3$" into the logical conclusion "$x = 4$."

There are lots of other helpful mathematical facts that can help you to solve problems logically, like _odd + odd = even_ and _the sum of the angles in a triangle is always 180°_. Using these facts to draw logical conclusions is an essential element of problem solving.

Deduction and Process of Elimination

If $(b)(b - 1)(b - 2)$ is negative, which of the following must also be negative?

(A) b
(B) $b - 1$
(C) $b - 2$
(D) $b^2 - 1$
(E) $2 - b$

A problem like this can be solved with either of two logical methods: deduction from the laws of arithmetic or the process of elimination. To solve deductively, you must know your laws of arithmetic. The problem says that the product of three numbers is negative. One law of arithmetic states that a product can only be negative if an odd number of the factors is negative. In other words, this product can only be negative if one or three of the factors are negative. Let's say that just one of the numbers is negative. Which one could it be? It can't be just any of them. Look closely: each factor is 1 less than the previous one, so if only one is negative, it must be the least one, which is $b - 2$. Notice that this is the expression in choice (C). The only other possibility is that all three terms are negative, in which case $b - 2$ is still negative. Therefore you have proved deductively that $b - 2$ must be negative.

To solve it by the process of elimination, first find a value of b that "works" with the given information. $b = -1$ works, because $(-1)(-1 - 1)(-1 - 2) = (-1)(-2)(-3) = -6$, which is negative. But if b can equal -1, then we can eliminate choices (D) and (E) because (D) would equal 0 and (E) would equal 3, which aren't negative. Now you might notice that (C) has the lowest value of the remaining choices, so it's most likely to be negative. Next notice that b could equal 1.5 because $(1.5)(1.5 - 1)(1.5 - 2) = (1.5)(.5)(-.5) = -.375$, and this option shows that (A) and (B) don't have to be negative, so the answer is (C).

Test Your Formulas and Theorems

Good math students don't just memorize formulas and theorems; they test them logically to make sure they work. This is especially important on the PSAT and SAT, because many of the formulas and theorems you use to solve PSAT and SAT problems are not the standard formulas and theorems you use in math class. For example:

For a certain fence, vertical posts must be placed 6 feet apart with supports in between, as shown below. How many vertical posts are needed for a fence 120 feet in length?

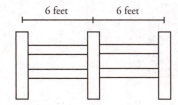

It seems like you can solve this one with a simple formula. Dividing 120 feet by 6 feet gives you 20 posts, right? If you trusted this formula, you'd be wrong. A good student would test it. How can you test it without filling the page with fence posts? Test the formula on a simpler version of the problem. How many posts do you need for a 12-foot fence? The answer is 12 feet divided by 6 feet gives 2 posts. But the figure above tells us that the answer should really be 3! What gives? Think about it. Dividing 12 by 6 only gives the number of _spaces_ between the posts. But there is always one more post than spaces, So we must add 1 after doing the division. Logically testing the formula helped us to modify it so that it works. So a 120-foot fence will require $(120 \div 6) + 1 = 21$ vertical posts.

Guessing and Checking

Most people don't think of guessing and checking as a logical method. They think it's kind of cheating. They mistakenly think that mathematical thinking is just memorizing standardized procedures for solving particular problems. Hogwash! **Guessing and checking is the essence of good mathematical reasoning**. In fact, much of what professional mathematicians do is guessing and checking. It's just that their guesses and checks are educated. Don't hesitate to guess and check to solve problems, as long as you're logical with your guesses and careful with your checking!

> A bin in a sporting goods store contains a total of 20 basketballs and soccer balls. If there are 8 more basketballs than soccer balls in the bin, how many soccer balls are in the bin?

There are no choices given here, but don't worry: you can make an educated guess. Your first thought might be that there are $20 - 8 = 12$ soccer balls. But a quick check shows that this doesn't make sense, because if there are 12 soccer balls, there must be only 8 basketballs

(for a total of 20), but the problem says that there are 8 more basketballs than soccer balls. So your guess was too big. Your next guess might be to subtract 8 from your last guess: $12 - 8 = 4$. Does that work? No—too small, because if there are 4 soccer balls, there must be 16 basketballs to make a total of 20, and there would be 12 more basketballs than soccer balls, not 8. So increase your guess a bit, to 6. Does this work? Yup: if there are 6 soccer balls, then there must be $20 - 6 = 14$ basketballs, and 14 is 8 greater than 6!

Algebra provides a good shortcut. Let x be the number of soccer balls. Then $x+8$ represents the number of basketballs, and the total number of balls is

$$(x) + (x + 8) = 20$$

Simplify:	$2x + 8 = 20$
Subtract 8:	$2x = 12$
Divide by 2:	$x = 6$

Exercise Set 7

Solve the following problems by deduction, process of elimination, or guessing and checking. Answers are at the end of the chapter.

1.   If $a > b$ and $b(b - a) > 0$, which of the following must be true?

   I. $b < 0$
   II. $a - b < 0$
   III. $a < 0$

(A) I only
(B) II only
(C) I and II only
(D) I and III only
(E) I, II, and III

2.   If a, b, and c are positive integers greater than 1, $ab = 15$ and $bc = 21$, what is the value of $a + b + c$?

3.   In the expression

$$k = (2n + 3)(n + 2)$$

   n is an integer and k is an odd integer. Which of the following must be even?

(A) n
(B) $2n + 1$
(C) $n(n + 1)$
(D) n^2
(E) $n^2 + 2$

Reasoning Skill 8: Checking

Checking is an important part of logical thinking. Good thinkers want to know whether their strategies really work. Many students worry that they won't have enough time to check their work on the PSAT and SAT. **You should work quickly, but you should always take the time to check your answers on the tougher questions as well as on questions where you're prone to making careless errors**. PSAT and SAT questions can be tricky, and there are plenty of subtle traps for students who aren't thinking carefully. So practice checking your work with a variety of methods.

Always Check Your Algebra

Checking your work on an algebra problem is straightforward—just plug your answer back in and make sure it works in the given equation or word problem. Always plug back into the *original* equation or word problem; otherwise, you are failing to check important steps. In other words, if you set up an equation to solve a word problem; don't simply plug your answer back into that equation, because it might be wrong! Instead, reread the word problem to make sure your answer makes sense.

Rereading Is Easy

You should reread every PSAT and SAT math problem one last time before filling in your answer—not just algebra problems. As we discussed in the beginning of the chapter, one of the most common mistakes that students make on the PSAT and SAT is misreading the question. Rereading is easy, and it may save you some costly mistakes. Make sure you have considered all the special terms in and restrictions on the problem, and answered the question it asked.

Use All of the Information—*Usually*

Another simple way to check your work on a PSAT or SAT math problem is to check that you've used all of the information in the problem. The folks who write these tests *usually* phrase the questions so that they contain all of the information you need and no more. So if your solution leaves out a piece of information from the problem, you may very well have made a mistake. Every once in while, a PSAT or SAT math problem will contain a piece of unnecessary information. But this is rare. If you have to leave out a piece of information, make sure that you can explain why.

Answer Key

Exercise Set 1

1. 8 If the product of a set of integers is 0, then one of the numbers must be 0. To maximize the value of any one of them, let 0 be the smallest of the integers. If they are *consecutive even* integers, they must be 0, 2, 4, 6, and 8. If your answer was 4, then you overlooked the fact that the numbers are *even*.

2. E Let c be the number of dollars Carlos had to start and d be the number of dollars David had to start. The question asks for the value of $c+d$. If Carlos begins with twice as much money as David, then $c = 2d$. After Carlos gives \$12 to David, he has $c - \$12$, and David has $d + \$12$. If Carlos still has \$10 more than David, then $c - 12 = (d + 12) + 10$

$$
\begin{aligned}
\text{Simplify:} && c - 12 &= d + 22 \\
\text{Add 12:} && c &= d + 34 \\
\text{Substitute } c = 2d: && 2d &= d + 34 \\
\text{Subtract } d: && d &= 34 \\
\text{Plug back in:} && c &= 2(34) = 68 \\
\text{So} && c + d &= 34 + 68 = 102
\end{aligned}
$$

3. C To map this problem, you need to know the rate formula *distance = speed × time*. The goal is to find the number of miles from Corinne's home to work. Let's call that value d. If she travels from home to work at an average speed of 50 miles per hour, then it must take her $d/50$ hours, or $60 \times d/50 = 6d/5$ minutes. If she returns home at 60 miles per hour, it must take her $d/60$ hours, or $60 \times d/60 = d$ minutes. If it takes her 10 more minutes to get to work than it takes her to get home, then

$$
\frac{6d}{5} - d = 10
$$

$$
\begin{aligned}
\text{Simplify:} && \frac{d}{5} &= 10 \\
\text{Multiply by 5:} && d &= 50
\end{aligned}
$$

Exercise Set 2

1. \$4,000, \$6,000, and \$10,000 If the total is divided in the ratio of $2:3:5$, then it is divided into $2 + 3 + 5 = 10$ parts. The individual parts, then, are $2/10$, $3/10$, and $5/10$ of the total. Multiplying these fractions by \$20,000 gives parts of \$4,000, \$6,000, and \$10,000.

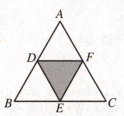

2. 5 Your first thought might be to use the formula for the area of a triangle: *area = (base × height)/2*. But this would involve finding the base and height of the triangle, which are not given and would be hard to find. What *are* you given? The area of the big triangle. Analyze the diagram to see the relationship among the parts. The four smaller triangles are all equal in size, so the shaded region is just 1/4 of the big triangle. Its area, then, is $20/4 = 5$.

3. 144 If the ratio of boys to girls in the sophomore class is 2 to 3, then 2/5 are boys and 3/5 are girls. If the class has 200 students, then $(2/5)(200) = 80$ are boys and $(3/5)(200) = 120$ are girls. If the junior class has as many boys as the sophomore class, then it has 80 boys also. If the ratio of boys to girls in the junior class is 5 to 4, then there must be $5n$ boys and $4n$ girls. Since $5n = 80$, n must be 16. Therefore there are 80 boys and $4(16) = 64$ girls, for a total of 144 students in the junior class.

Exercise Set 3

1. 0 If you notice the repetition, the problem is easy. Just notice that the expression you are asked to find is 10 less than the expression you are given.

$$5 \text{ less than } 28\% \text{ of } x^2 \text{ is } 10$$

$$\text{Translate:} \qquad .28(x^2) - 5 = 10$$

$$\text{Subtract 10:} \qquad .28(x^2) - 15 = 0$$

So 15 less than 28% of x^2 is 0.

---

2. 198

$$m = 3 + 6 + 9 + \cdots + 93 + 96 + 99$$
$$n = 6 + 9 + \cdots + 93$$

When you subtract n from m, notice that all the terms cancel except $3 + 96 + 99 = 198$.

---

3. C Notice that the expression you are asked to evaluate is just twice the expression you are given.

$$\frac{6}{y} + x = 2\left(\frac{3}{y} + \frac{x}{2}\right) = 2(10) = 20$$

---

4. A If every term is 6 less than the square of the previous term, then the second term must be $(3)^2 - 6 = 9 - 6 = 3$. The third term, then, is also $(3)^2 - 6 = 3$, and so on. Every term, then, must be 3, including the fifth.

Exercise Set 4

1. E Don't worry about solving the system for y and z. That's far more work than necessary. Just notice that the expression you are asked to find is the difference of the expressions you are given. So subtract the equations:

$$\begin{array}{r} 3y - 4z = 6 \\ -(2y + z = 10) \\ \hline y - 5z = -4 \end{array}$$

---

2. C Notice that you don't need to find the value of y. Substitute $y = 1 - x$ into $2y + x = 5$ to get

$$2(1 - x) + x = 5$$

$$\text{Distribute:} \qquad 2 - 2x + x = 5$$

$$\text{Simplify} \qquad 2 - x = 5$$

$$\text{Subtract 2:} \qquad -x = 3$$

$$\text{Multiply by } -1: \qquad x = -3$$

3. 1/2 or 0.5 Finding solutions for m and n is pretty tricky here. The key is to just "create" the expression the question asks for by using the laws of equality and substitution:

$$3 + m + n = n^2 + m^2$$

$$\text{Subtract } n \text{ and } m: \qquad 3 = (n^2 - n) + (m^2 - m)$$

$$\text{Substitute:} \qquad \frac{(n^2 - n) + (m^2 - m)}{6} = \frac{3}{6} = \frac{1}{2}$$

---

4. 9/2 or 4.5 Solving this equation for x is needlessly complicated. Instead, simplify the expression until it starts to look like the expression you are looking for.

$$\frac{2x^2 - 18}{x^2 + 2x - 3} = 9$$

$$\text{Factor:} \qquad \frac{2(x + 3)(x - 3)}{(x + 3)(x - 1)} = 9$$

$$\text{Cancel common factors:} \qquad \frac{2(x - 3)}{(x - 1)} = 9$$

$$\text{Divide by 2:} \qquad \frac{(x - 3)}{(x - 1)} = \frac{9}{2}$$

Exercise Set 5

1. C The key formula here is the average formula: *average = sum ÷ number of things*. So if x is the average of k and 10, then $x = (k + 10)/2$. And if y is the average of k and 4, then $y = (k + 4)/2$. The average of x and y, then, is

$$\frac{\frac{k+10}{2} + \frac{k+4}{2}}{2} = \frac{k+10}{4} + \frac{k+4}{4} = \frac{2k+14}{4} = \frac{k+7}{2}$$

---

2. D The key formula is the rate formula, which in this case is *number of cars = rate × time*. Another useful form of this formula is *rate = number of cars/time*. Since x is the number of cars and y is the time in hours, the rate is x/y cars per hour. Using the first formula, then, the number of cars that would pass in z hours is

$$(x/y \text{ cars per hour})(z \text{ hours}) = \frac{xz}{y} \text{ cars.}$$

An alternative to this algebraic approach is to plug in values for x, y, and z. This eliminates the unknowns from the problem, but it forces you to do more calculation. Say, for instance, that $x = 10$ cars pass every $y = 2$ hours. In $z = 4$ hours, then, it should be clear that 20 cars should pass by, because twice as much time has passed. When you plug these values into the choices, (D) is the only choice that gives an answer of 20.

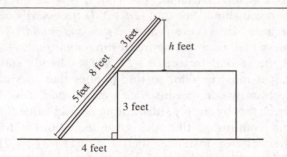

3. **1.8** The key formula here is the Pythagorean theorem: $c^2 = a^2 + b^2$. A key theorem is the similarity theorem: in similar triangles, corresponding sides are proportional. Notice that the figure has two right triangles, and they are similar. The hypotenuse of the bottom triangle is 5 because $3^2 + 4^2 = 5^2$. Therefore, the hypotenuse of the top triangle is $8 - 5 = 3$. Since the two triangles are similar, the corresponding sides are proportional:

$$\frac{3}{5} = \frac{h}{3}$$

Cross-multiply: $5h = 9$

Divide by 5: $h = 1.8$

Exercise Set 6

1. **D** Method 1: Plug in numbers. Let a be 100. If b is 20% greater than a, then $b = 120$. If c is 25% greater than b, then $c = 150$. The area of the largest square, then, is $(150)^2 = 22,500$, and the area of the smallest square is $(100)^2 = 10,000$. The percent difference is $(22,500 - 10,000)/10,000 = 1.25 = 125\%$ (D).

Method 2: Use algebra. $b = 1.2a$ and $c = (1.25)(1.2a) = 1.5a$. So the area of the smallest square is a^2, and the area of the largest square is $(1.5a)^2 = 2.25a^2$. Since $2.25a^2 - a^2 = 1.25a^2$, the area of the bigger square is 125% larger.

2. **B** Method 1: Test the choices, starting with (C). If Ellen weighs 130 pounds, then Jim weighs $290 - 130 = 160$ pounds, and Ria weighs $230 - 130 = 100$ pounds. All together, their weight would be $130 + 160 + 100 = 390$ pounds. Close, but too small. This means that our guess for Ellen's weight is too *big* (because increasing Ellen's weight decreases *both* Jim's and Ria's weight by the same amount, for a net *decrease*.) This lets us eliminate choices (C), (D), and (E). Since our guess wasn't far off, it makes sense to test choice (B) next. If Ellen weighs 120 pounds, then Jim weighs $290 - 120 = 170$ pounds, and Ria weighs $230 - 120 = 110$ pounds. In total, they weigh $120 + 170 + 110 = 400$ pounds. Bingo! The answer is (B).

Method 2: Use algebra. Let e = Ellen's weight, j = Jim's weight, and r = Ria's weight. Translate the problem into equations:

$$e + j = 290$$
$$e + r = 230$$
$$e + j + r = 400$$

Add first two equations: $2e + j + r = 520$

Subtract third equation: $-(e + j + r = 400)$

$$e = 120$$

3. **D** Method 1: The problem asks you to solve for x in terms of m and n. Notice that every choice contains the expression $m - n$.

By substitution: $m - n = (2x - 5) - (x + 7)$

Simplify: $m - n = x - 12$

Add 12: $m - n + 12 = x$

So the answer is (D).

Method 2: Just plug in simple values for the unknowns. If $x = 1$, then $m = (2)(1) - 5 = -3$, and $n = (1) + 7 = 8$. Since the problem asks for x, write down its value, 1, and circle it. Then plug in $m = -3$ and $n = 8$ to every choice, and simplify:

(A) -4.5
(B) -9
(C) 0.5
(D) 1
(E) 2

So the answer is (D).

Exercise Set 7

1. A Start by picking simple values for a and b that satisfy the conditions. If $a > b$, then you might start with $a = 2$ and $b = 1$. This doesn't work, though, because $b(b - a) = 1(1 - 2) = -1$, which is not > 0. To change the sign, you might pick a negative value for b. So try $a = 2$ and $b = -1$. This satisfies both inequalities. This example clearly rules out statement II, because $a - b = 2 - (-1) = 3$, which is not < 0. This means that we can also eliminate any choice that contains statement II in it, so (B), (C), and (E) are eliminated. This example also rules out statement III, because if a can be 2, it doesn't have to be less than 0. This lets us eliminate choice (D), so (A) must be the right answer by process of elimination.

---

2. 15 If a and b must be positive integers greater than 1, and $ab = 15$, then they could only be 3 and 5. (The answers $a = 15$ and $b = 1$ don't work; the numbers must both be *greater* than 1.) Let's guess that $a = 3$ and $b = 5$. Does this work? Check with the other equation: if $bc = 21$, then $5c = 21$, and $c = 4.2$. But that can't be, because the problem says that c must be an integer. So make a better guess: $a = 5$ and $b = 3$. If this is true, then $3c = 21$ and $c = 7$. This must be the solution, because all of the given information is satisfied: the equations both work, and the numbers are integers greater than 1. Therefore $a + b + c = 5 + 3 + 7 = 15$.

---

3. C Here, it pays to know your "parity rules," that is, the rules about odds and evens. For instance, you should know that $odd \times odd = odd$ and $odd + odd = even$, and so on. You are told that k is an odd integer and that it is the product of two other integers: $(2n + 3)$ and $(n + 2)$. How can you multiply two integers together to get an odd number? The only way is if both numbers in the product are odd. Look at the first factor: $(2n + 3)$. If n is an integer, then you should see that $(2n + 3)$ is necessarily odd, because $2n$ is even and $even + odd = odd$. This doesn't tell us anything interesting about n. So look at the second factor: $(n + 2)$. We've already stated that it must be odd, so this implies that n is also necessarily odd, because $odd + even = odd$. You can check this by simply substituting an odd value for n and confirming that the given equation is true. If $n = 1$, for instance, then $k = [2(1) + 3](1 + 2) = (5)(3) = 15$, which is indeed odd. Now, substituting $n = 1$ into the choices gives

(A) 1
(B) 3
(C) 2
(D) 1
(E) 3

Since (C) is the only even choice, the answer must be (C).

CHAPTER 8

ESSENTIAL PRE-ALGEBRA SKILLS

1. Numbers and Operations

2. Laws of Arithmetic

3. Fractions

4. Ratios and Proportions

5. Percents

6. Negatives

7. Divisibility

Lesson 1: Numbers and Operations

Number Sets

The only two number sets that will be mentioned on the PSAT are integers and real numbers. An *integer* is a positive or negative whole number, like … $-3, -2, -1, 0, 1, 2, 3$ … A *real number* is any number that you can imagine on the number line, including integers. Real numbers include decimals, negatives, fractions, and roots.

Every number on the PSAT is a *real number*. But do not assume it is an *integer* unless you are told that it is. If you are told that $x > 3$, don't assume x is just 4 or 5 or 6 … It might be 3.125 or the like.

Operations

The PSAT only deals with the basic operations: *addition*, *subtraction*, *multiplication*, *division*, *powers*, and *roots*. **Don't worry about operations like *logarithms*, *sine*, *cosine*, or *tangent*.**

Two operations are never allowed: dividing by 0 and taking the square root of a negative number, because they don't yield real numbers. Often, a PSAT problem will include a restriction to prevent such things, as in $y = 1/x$, where $x \neq 0$. **Don't let those restrictions like $x \neq 0$ distract you—they're only there so that you don't have to think about numbers that aren't real.**

A sum is the result of an addition, and a product is the result of a multiplication. Don't confuse the two! For instance, the *sum* of 2 and 3 is 5, but the *product* of 2 and 3 is 6.

Inverse Operations

Every operation is paired with an inverse: *addition/subtraction*, *multiplication/division*, *powers/roots*. Inverse operations are operations that "undo" each other. In other words, if you do an operation, then do its inverse, you're back where you started!

Dividing by 6 is the inverse of multiplying by 6 because $x \times 6 \div 6 = x$.

Taking a square root is almost the inverse of squaring, but not quite! For instance, $\sqrt{5^2} = 5$, but does $\sqrt{(-3)^2} = -3$?

You must use inverse operations to "isolate" a variable when solving simple equations.

$$3x - 7 = 38$$

Get rid of the operation -7
by adding 7 to both sides: $\qquad 3x = 45$

Get rid of the operation $\times 3$ by
dividing both sides by 3: $\qquad x = 15$

Alternative Ways of Expressing Operations

Any operation can be expressed in terms of its inverse to simplify the problem. For instance, dividing by any number is equivalent to multiplying by its reciprocal, so $13 \div 1/5$ is the same as 13×5, which is easier to do in your head. Similarly, subtracting a number is the same as adding its opposite, so $5 - (-0.5)$ is equivalent to $5 + 0.5$, which is easier to do in your head. Also, taking the nth root of a number is equivalent to raising the number to the $1/n$ power, so $\sqrt{8}$ is equivalent to $8^{1/2}$. You should be able to go back and forth between these equivalent expressions, so you can use the one that is simplest to deal with for the given problem.

The <u>Real</u> Order of Operations

The real order of operations has a GERM in it: PG-ER-MD-AS. These are the steps you should use when evaluating an expression:

1. PG: Evaluate what is in parentheses or within the two other *grouping symbols*: fraction bars and radicals.
2. ER: Evaluate any *exponentials* and *roots*, from left to right.
3. MD: Evaluate any *multiplication* and *division*, from left to right.
4. AS: Evaluate any *addition* and *subtraction*, from left to right.

Worksheet 1: Numbers and Operations

1. What is the least integer greater than -7.5?

2. Four consecutive odd integers have a sum of 64. What is the least of these numbers?

3. The result of an addition is called a _____

4. The result of a subtraction is called a _____

5. The result of a multiplication is called a _____

What is the alternative way to express each of the following operations?

    6. $-(4)$ 7. $\div(6)$ 8. $\times\dfrac{4}{7}$ 9. $\div\dfrac{8}{3}$

Simplify without a calculator:

    10. $5 - 8 \div 4 \times 6 - (1+3)^2 =$ _____   11. $\sqrt{(136 - (\sqrt{16} + \sqrt{36})^2)} =$ _____

---

12. Which of the following can be expressed as the product of two consecutive odd integers?

    (A) 12
    (B) 15
    (C) 20
    (D) 21
    (E) 24

---

13. If $\sqrt{m} + 4 = 10$, what is the value of m?

    (A) 6
    (B) 14
    (C) 36
    (D) 44
    (E) 90

---

14. For what integer value of y is $2y + 7 < 13$ and $4y + 2 > 6$?

    (A) 1
    (B) 2
    (C) 3
    (D) 4
    (E) 5

---

15. If one splunk is equivalent to 5 genks and one gromp is equivalent to 3 genks, then how many genks are equivalent to 3 splunks and 4 gromps?

---

16. If $\dfrac{x}{3}, \dfrac{x}{6}$, and $\dfrac{x}{7}$ each represent fully reduced fractions, then which of the following could be the value of x?

    I. 4
    II. 5
    III. 8

    (A) I only
    (B) II only
    (C) I and II
    (D) II and III
    (E) I, II, and III

17. If, $(k - (1 - (1 - 4))) - (3 - (2 - (1 - 2))) = -2$, then $k =$

(A) 1
(B) 2
(C) 3
(D) 4
(E) 5

18. When 6 is added to three times a number, the result is 33. What is twice the number?

(A) 4.5
(B) 9
(C) 13
(D) 18
(E) 26

Lesson 2: Laws of Arithmetic

When evaluating expressions, you don't always have to follow the order of operations strictly. Sometimes you can play around with the expression first. You can commute (with addition or multiplication), associate (with addition or multiplication), or distribute (multiplication or division over addition or subtraction). Know your options!

When simplifying an expression, consider whether the laws of arithmetic help to make it easier.

$57(71) + 57(29)$ is much easier to simplify if, rather than using the order of operations, you use the distributive law and think of it as $57(71 + 29) = 51(100) = 5,100$

The Commutative and Associative Laws

Whenever you add or multiply terms, the order of the terms doesn't matter, so pick a convenient **arrangement** or **commutation**. To *commute* means to *move around*. (Just think about what commuters do!)

$$1 + 2 + 3 + 4 + 5 + 6 + 7 + 8 + 9 =$$
$$1 + 9 + 2 + 8 + 3 + 7 + 4 + 6 + 5$$

Notice that the second arrangement is more convenient than the first.

Whenever you add or multiply, the grouping of the terms doesn't matter, so pick a convenient **grouping** or **association**. To *associate* means to *group together*. (Just think about what an association is!)

$$(32 \times 4) \times (25 \times 10) \times (10 \times 2)$$
$$= 32 \times (4 \times 25) \times (10 \times 10) \times 2$$

Notice that the second grouping is more convenient than the first.

Whenever you subtract or divide, the grouping of the terms *does* matter. Subtraction and division are neither commutative nor associative.

$$15 - 7 - 2 \neq 7 - 15 - 2$$

You can't commute the numbers in a difference until you convert it to addition:

$$15 + -7 + -2 = -7 + 15 + -2$$

$$24 \div 3 \div 2 \neq 3 \div 2 \div 24$$

You can't commute the numbers in a quotient until you convert it to multiplication:

$$24 \times \frac{1}{3} \times \frac{1}{2} = \frac{1}{3} \times \frac{1}{2} \times 24$$

The Distributive Law

Although the order of operations says to perform operations in parentheses first, the *distributive law* gives you another option in certain situations. When multiplying or dividing a group sum or difference, you may perform the multiplication or division first, as long as you "distribute":

$$a(b + c) = ab + ac$$

$$\frac{(b + c)}{a} = \frac{b}{a} + \frac{c}{a}$$

Distribution is never something that you *have to* do. Think of distribution as a tool, rather than a requirement. Use it when it simplifies your task. For instance, $13(832 + 168)$ is actually much easier to do if you don't distribute: $13(832 + 168) = 13(1,000) = 13,000$. Notice how annoying it would be if you distributed.

Use the distributive law "backwards" whenever you factor polynomials, add fractions, or combine "like" terms:

$$9x^2 - 12x = 3x(3x - 4)$$
$$\frac{3}{b} + \frac{a}{b} = \frac{3 + a}{b} \qquad 5\sqrt{7} - 2\sqrt{7} = 3\sqrt{7}$$

Follow the rules when you distribute. Avoid these common mistakes:

$(3 + 4)^2$ is not $3^2 + 4^2$
(Tempting, isn't it? Check it and see!)
$3(4 \times 5)$ is not equal to $3(4) \times 3(5)$

Worksheet 2: Laws of Arithmetic

Do the following calculations mentally by using the appropriate laws of arithmetic. (No calculator!)

1. $37 + 54 + 26 + 63 + 46 + 74 =$ _____

2. $(5 \times 2x)(3x \times 4) =$ _____

3. $12(300) + 12(700) =$ _____

4. $3(x + 5)^2 =$ _____

Rewrite the expression $4b^3 + 16b^2$ according to the following laws:

5. distributive law: 6. commutative law of addition: 7. commutative law of multiplication:

_____   _____   _____

If x and y are not zero:

8. What is the relationship between $\dfrac{y}{x}$ and $\dfrac{x}{y}$?

9. What is the relationship between xy and yx?

10. What is the relationship between $x - y$ and $y - x$?

11. The sum of two positive integers is 10, and their difference is 6. What is the quotient when the larger number is divided by the smaller number?

(A) 4
(B) 6
(C) 10
(D) 16
(E) 20

12. Which of the following is equivalent to $4x(3x \times 2) - 10x^2$?

(A) $22x^2 + 8x$
(B) $2x^2 + 8x$
(C) $22x^2 - 8x$
(D) $14x^2$
(E) $8x + 5$

13. For all real numbers b, $2 - (3 - (4 - b) - 1) =$

(A) $-b - 6$
(B) $b + 2$
(C) $b - 6$
(D) $b + 5$
(E) $4 - b$

14. Jaymie bought 3 sodas from the store. She gave the cashier a $10 bill and received $7.30 in change. How much change would she receive if she bought 5 sodas with a $10 bill?

(A) $2.70
(B) $3.60
(C) $4.50
(D) $5.50
(E) $6.40

15. When Joyelle organizes her dolls into groups of 5, she has 3 left over. When she divides them into groups of 6, she has 4 left over. If she has fewer than 50 dolls, how many would be left over if she divided them into groups of four?

(A) 0   (B) 1   (C) 2   (D) 3   (E) 4

16. If $(m - n) + 4 = 3 - (-3 - n)$, then what is the value of n in terms of m?

(A) $m + 2$

(B) $2m + 4$

(C) $\dfrac{m - 2}{2}$

(D) $\dfrac{m + 2}{2}$

(E) $\dfrac{m + 4}{2}$

Lesson 3: Fractions

Adding and Subtracting Fractions

Just as 2 apples + 3 apples = 5 apples, so 2 sevenths + 3 sevenths = 5 sevenths! **So to add or subtract fractions, you must first write them so that they have the same denominator. If the denominators are not equal, make them equal by multiplying "top and bottom" by the same number until the denominators are the same. Then simply combine the numerators.**

$$\frac{5}{18} + \frac{4}{9} = \frac{5}{18} + \frac{4 \times 2}{9 \times 2} = \frac{5}{18} + \frac{8}{18} = \frac{13}{18}$$

One simple method for adding fractions is the "zip-zap-zup" method: simply multiply the "top and bottom" of each fraction by the denominator of the *other* fraction. This method is easy to do in your head, and it guarantees a common denominator. You may have to simplify the fractions as a last step.

$$\frac{x}{3} + \frac{2}{5} = \frac{5x \quad 6}{\cancel{x} \times \cancel{2}} = \frac{5x}{15} + \frac{6}{15} = \frac{5x + 6}{15}$$

$$\frac{5}{6} + \frac{7}{8} = \frac{40 \quad 42}{\cancel{5} \times \cancel{7}} = \frac{40}{48} + \frac{42}{48} = \frac{82}{48} = \frac{41}{24}$$

Multiplying and Dividing Fractions

To multiply fractions, don't worry about getting common denominators. Just multiply straight across.

$$\frac{3}{4} \times \frac{7}{11} = \frac{3 \times 7}{4 \times 11} = \frac{21}{44}$$

$$\frac{y}{4} \times \frac{3}{x} = \frac{y \times 3}{4 \times x} = \frac{3y}{4x}$$

To multiply a fraction and a nonfraction, multiply just the numerator by the nonfraction.

$$\frac{4}{7} \times 5 = \frac{4 \times 5}{7} = \frac{20}{7}$$

$$5y \times \frac{3x}{5} = \frac{5y \times 3x}{5} = \frac{15xy}{5} = 3xy$$

Don't confuse multiplying fractions with cross-multiplying a proportion. (We will discuss that in the next lesson.) Just think of a simple multiplication like 1/2 (times) 1/2 to see why "multiplying straight across" makes sense.

To divide by a fraction, just multiply by its reciprocal, just as we did in Lesson 1.

$$\frac{\frac{2}{5}}{\frac{7}{3}} = \frac{2}{5} \times \frac{3}{7} = \frac{6}{35}$$

$$\frac{3m}{7} \div \frac{5}{2m} = \frac{3m}{7} \times \frac{2m}{5} = \frac{6m^2}{35}$$

Simplifying Fractions

If a fraction contains other fractions, or if the numerator and denominator have a common factor, it should be simplified. **Simplify fractions by dividing common factors or multiplying common denominators on top and bottom.**

$$\frac{4x + 2}{2} = \frac{\cancel{2}(2x + 1)}{\cancel{2}} = 2x + 1$$

$$\frac{\frac{2}{5} + \frac{2}{3}}{\frac{1}{4}} = \frac{60 \times \left(\frac{2}{5} + \frac{2}{3}\right)}{60 \times \left(\frac{1}{4}\right)} = \frac{24 + 40}{15} = \frac{64}{15}$$

When simplifying fractions, don't "cancel" terms that are not common *factors*. Remember that a *factor* is part of a *product*. Only cancel terms that are part of multiplications in both the numerator and denominator.

Wrong: $\dfrac{x^2 \cancel{-1}}{x \cancel{-1}} = \dfrac{x^2}{x} = x$

Right: $\dfrac{x^2 - 1}{x - 1} = \dfrac{(x + 1)\cancel{(x - 1)}}{\cancel{(x - 1)}} = x + 1$

Worksheet 3: Fractions

Simplify the following expressions:

1. $\dfrac{2}{3}+\dfrac{3}{5}=$ _____

2. $\dfrac{3}{8}\times\dfrac{12}{9}=$ _____

3. $\dfrac{\frac{5}{7}}{\frac{8}{14}}=$ _____

4. $\dfrac{5}{3x}+\dfrac{7}{9}=$ _____

5. $\dfrac{3n-6}{6n-6}=$ _____

6. $\dfrac{1}{4}+\dfrac{2}{7}+\dfrac{1}{2}=$ _____

7. How do you convert a fraction to a decimal?

8. If a bowl of fruit contains 8 apples and 12 oranges, what fraction of the fruit is apples?

9. One out of every three cars produced at a factory is red. If 200 non-red cars are produced on a given day, how many total cars were produced?

10. Which of the following is greatest?

   (A) $\dfrac{3}{4}\div\dfrac{5}{8}$ (B) $\dfrac{3}{4}-\dfrac{5}{8}$

   (C) $\dfrac{3}{4}+\dfrac{5}{8}$ (D) $\dfrac{3}{4}\times\dfrac{5}{8}$

   (E) $1-\left(\dfrac{3}{4}\times\dfrac{5}{8}\right)$

11. During a football game, a team scored one-seventh of its points in the first quarter, one-third of its points in the second quarter, and twelve points in the third quarter. If the team scored a total of 42 points, how many points did the team score in the fourth quarter?

   (A) 6 (B) 8 (C) 10 (D) 12 (E) 14

12.

   If $3+\dfrac{1}{y}=4+\dfrac{1}{4}$, what is the value of y?

13. If, $\dfrac{a}{b}=\dfrac{5}{4}$, what is the value of $\dfrac{4a}{3b}$?

14. Three-sevenths of the eggs in Martha's basket are broken, and three-quarters of the intact eggs are brown. What fraction of Martha's eggs are intact nonbrown eggs?

   (A) $\dfrac{1}{7}$ (B) $\dfrac{3}{7}$ (C) $\dfrac{4}{9}$ (D) $\dfrac{3}{5}$ (E) $\dfrac{5}{6}$

15. If $\dfrac{a+b}{ab}=2$, what is the value of a in terms of b?

   (A) $\dfrac{2b}{b-1}$ (B) $\dfrac{2b-1}{b+3}$

   (C) $\dfrac{2b-1}{b}$ (D) $\dfrac{2b+1}{b-1}$

   (E) $\dfrac{b}{2b-1}$

Lesson 4:
Ratios and Proportions

Ratios

Many simple ratios are just like fractions. For instance, the ratio of 5 to 7 is $5:7$ or $\frac{5}{7}$.

In a "ratio of parts," the sum of the parts represents the whole. Think of each part as a fraction of the whole.

> If something is divided into parts in a ratio of $3:4:5$, then the whole is $3+4+5=12$, so you think of the ratio as
>
> $$\frac{3}{12}:\frac{4}{12}:\frac{5}{12}=\frac{1}{4}:\frac{1}{3}:\frac{5}{12},$$
>
> which shows each part as a fraction of the whole.

Rates are ratios, too. In a rate, the word *per* means *divided by*

> miles per gallon means number of miles: number of gallons

Proportions

A proportion is a statement that two fractions are equal, such as $\frac{3}{5}=\frac{9}{15}$

The law of **cross-multiplication**: If two fractions are equal, then their **cross-products** are always equal.

> If $\frac{3}{7}=\frac{9}{21}$, then $3\times21=7\times9$
>
> If $\frac{x}{3}=\frac{y}{4}$, then $4x=3y$

If two fractions are equal, terms may be cross-swapped without changing the equality.

> If $\frac{3}{7}=\frac{9}{21}$, then $\frac{21}{7}=\frac{9}{3}$
>
> If $\frac{x}{3}=\frac{y}{4}$, then $\frac{4}{3}=\frac{y}{x}$

The phrase *at this rate* indicates that two rates are the same, so you can set up a proportion.

> A bird can fly 420 miles in one day. At this rate, how many miles can the bird fly in 14 hours?

> The rate, in miles per hour, is the same in both situations, so

$$\frac{420 \text{ miles}}{24 \text{ hours}} = \frac{x \text{ miles}}{14 \text{ hours}}$$

Cross-multiply: $420\times14=24x$

Divide by 24: $x=245$ miles

When setting up a proportion, you will find it helpful to make sure that the units "match up." For instance, in the example above, the "miles" go in the numerators and the "hours" go in the denominators.

Similarity

Two triangles are *similar* (have the same shape) if their corresponding angles all have the same measure. **If two triangles are similar, then their corresponding sides are proportional.**

 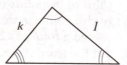

In the figure above,

$$\frac{m}{k}=\frac{n}{l} \text{ or } \frac{m}{n}=\frac{k}{l}$$

Just as with proportions involving units, proportions of corresponding sides in similar figures should "match up." For instance, notice how corresponding sides match up in the proportions above.

Worksheet 4: Ratios and Proportions

1. A speed is a ratio of _____ to _____ .   2. An annual salary is a ratio of _____ to _____ .

3. Define a proportion:

4. If the winners of a tournament split a $14,000 prize in a ratio of $4:2:1$, what is the value of each portion?

5. A butcher, working at a constant rate, can trim 5 steaks every 2 minutes. At this rate how many minutes will it take to trim 40 steaks?

6. A cable car, moving at a constant rate, is able to travel 4 miles in 20 minutes. At this rate how many miles will it travel in 4 hours?

7. Write three equations that are equivalent to $\frac{a}{4} = \frac{6}{b}$.

8. On a map, $\frac{1}{2}$ inch represents 2 miles. If a stretch of highway measures 24 miles, what is its length, in inches, on the map?

(A) 3.5
(B) 4.0
(C) 5.0
(D) 5.5
(E) 6.0

9. There are 80 people in a theater. The ratio of men to women in the theater is 5 to 3. How many men are in the theater?

(A) 25
(B) 30
(C) 35
(D) 45
(E) 50

10. A recipe for stuffed shells for 6 people requires 3 containers of cheese. At this rate, how many containers of cheese would need to be purchased to make enough stuffed shells for a group of 42 people?

11. In the figure below, $AB \parallel DE$. What is the value of x?

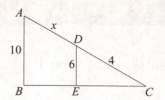

Note: Figure not drawn to scale.

12. The price of pancake mix is d dollars for 12 ounces, and 4 ounces make b batches of pancakes. In terms of b and d, what is the cost, in dollars, of the mix required to make 6 batches of pancakes?

(A) $\dfrac{4d}{b}$

(B) $\dfrac{2d}{b}$

(C) $\dfrac{2b}{d}$

(D) $\dfrac{d}{2b}$

(E) $4bd$

13. To make a certain green paint, yellow and blue paints are mixed in the ratio of 2 : 3. To make a certain purple paint, blue and red paints are mixed in a ratio of 7 : 3. If equal amounts of the green and purple paints are mixed, what fraction of the mixture will be blue paint?

(A) $\dfrac{7}{20}$

(B) $\dfrac{1}{2}$

(C) $\dfrac{13}{20}$

(D) $\dfrac{3}{4}$

(E) $\dfrac{17}{20}$

Lesson 5: Percents

Translating Percent Problems

Many percent problems practically solve themselves, as long as you know the translation key. **Use the following key to turn basic percent problems into simple equations:**

percent	means	÷ 100
is	means	=
of	means	×
what	means	x, y, n, etc.

What number is 5 percent of 36?

Translate the question: What number is 5 percent of 36?

$$x = \frac{5}{100} \times 36 \qquad \text{so } x = 1.8$$

If the problem is worded in a tricky way, you can use "is over of equals the percent" to set up the problem. In other words, the quantity next to the word "is" goes over the quantity next to the word "of" to equal the percent.

What percent is 24 of 18?

This can be translated as: what percent of 18 is 24? or can be set up correctly with "is over of equals the percent:"

$$\frac{24}{18} = \frac{x}{100}$$

To convert a percent to a decimal, just move the decimal point two places to the left. This is equivalent to dividing by 100, which is what percent means!

5% is .05   125% is 1.25
35.7% is .357   100% is 1

Finding Percent Change

To find a percent increase or percent decrease, just use this simple formula:

Percent change

$$= \frac{\text{final amount} - \text{starting amount}}{\text{starting amount}} \times 100\%$$

What percent greater than 25 is 30? The starting amount is 25, because it's the amount we're comparing 30 to. Using the formula:

$$\text{Percent change} = \frac{30 - 25}{25} \times 100\%$$

$$= \frac{5}{25} \times 100\% = .20 \times 100\% = 20\%$$

Changing Quantities by Percents

You can always change a quantity by x percent by just multiplying it by $1 + x/100$, which is the "final" percentage. Remember that the starting amount is always 100%.

For instance, if you want to reduce a number by 15%, your final percentage is $100\% - 15\% = 85\%$. So, just multiply by 0.85. If you want to increase a number by 20%, your final percentage is $100\% + 20\% = 120\%$, so just multiply by 1.20!

What is the final cost of a $22.60 lunch bill after a 15% tip has been added?

Adding 15% to the bill means paying 115% of the bill, so simply multiply by 1.15:

$22.60 (times) 1.15 = $25.99

Here's a cool and (occasionally) useful fact about percents: $a\%$ of b always equals $b\%$ of a! If you translate, it's easy to see why:

$$a\% \ b = \frac{a}{100} \times b = \frac{ab}{100}$$

$$b\% \ of \ a = \frac{b}{100} \times a = \frac{ab}{100}$$

What is 36 percent of 25?

36% of 25 = 25% of 36 = 1/4 of 36 = 9

Worksheet 5: Percents

1. Complete the translation key:

Word(s) in problem	Mathematical translation
what, what number, how much	
of	
	=
percent	

2. Write the formula for percent change: Percent change =

3. To increase a quantity by 40%, multiply it by _____

4. To decrease a quantity by 16%, multiply it by _____

Translate the following word problems and solve them:

5. 12 is what percent of 38?   Translation: _____   Solution: _____

6. 34 is 20% of what number?   Translation: _____   Solution: _____

7. What is 60% of 80?   Translation: _____   Solution: _____

8. What number is 25% greater than 80?_____

9. A factory produced 400 new vehicles in the first week of 2005. Because of a worker strike, its production decreased by 40% from the first week to the second week. How many vehicles did the factory produce in the second week?

12. If 4 liters of a 20% salt solution are mixed with 6 liters of a 30% salt solution, what is the percent concentration of salt in the final mixture? (Ignore the percent sign when entering the answer. For instance, grid 50% as 50.)

10. Patricia bought shares of TWRP corporation in the beginning of 2004. The value of her shares increased by 25% in the first quarter, decreased by 20% in the second quarter, decreased by 10% in the third quarter, and increased by 20% in the fourth quarter. By what percent did the value of her shares increase for the whole year?

(A) 6%
(B) 8%
(C) 12%
(D) 15%
(E) 18%

11. 50% of 40% of x is equal to 20% of 70% of y. What is the value of x in terms of y?

(A) $0.4y$
(B) $0.5y$
(C) $0.6y$
(D) $0.7y$
(E) $0.8y$

13. If the height of a triangle is increased by 40% and the base is increased by 20%, by what percent is the area of the triangle increased?

(A) 20%
(B) 66%
(C) 68%
(D) 74%
(E) It cannot be determined from the given information

14. If $x + 4y$ is equal to 150% of $3y$, what is the value of $\dfrac{x}{y}$?

(A) 0.25
(B) 0.50
(C) 1.00
(D) 1.50
(E) 2.00

Lesson 6: Negatives

Visualize the Number Line

Visualize the number line when comparing, adding, or subtracting numbers. *Greater than* always means to the right on the number line, and *less than* means to the left on the number line. A negative number is <u>greater</u> than another if it is <u>closer to 0</u>.

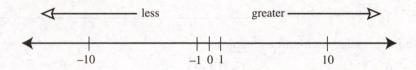

Which is greater, or −2/5 or −7/5?

Visualize the number line. Although 2/5 is less than, 7/5, on the negative side this relationship is "flipped." Thus −2/5 is closer to 0 than −7/5 is, so −2/5 is greater.

Adding and Subtracting with Negatives

To add, visualize the number line. To add a positive, jump to the right. To add a negative, jump to the left.

To add $-5 + -12$, start at −5 and move 12 spaces to the left (negative), to land on − 17. (Or you could start at − 12 and jump 5 spaces to the left!)

To subtract, you can change the subtraction to addition by changing the sign of the second number.

To subtract $-5 - (-12)$, change it to addition by changing the sign: $-5 + 12 = 12 - 5 = 7$.

To subtract, you can also "swap" the numbers and change the sign of the result, because $a - b$ is the opposite of $b - a$.

$$4 - 18 = -(18 - 4) = -14$$

Remember these helpful facts about subtracting:

- $a - b$ is <u>positive</u> if a is greater than b, and <u>negative</u> if b is greater than a (regardless of the signs).
- $a - b$ is always the <u>opposite</u> of $b - a$.

Products, Quotients, and Powers of Negatives

Any product, quotient, or power is <u>negative</u> if it has an <u>odd</u> number of negatives, and <u>positive</u> if it has an <u>even</u> number of negatives.

$- 12 \times 5 \times 7$ is negative: it has an odd number (1) of negatives.

$\dfrac{(-4x)(-3x)}{(-2x)(-6x^3)}$ is positive: it has an even, number (4) of negatives.

$(-3)^{12}(5)^7(-2)^5$ is negative: it has an odd number $(12 + 5 = 17)$ of negatives.

Inequalities and Negatives

Any inequality must be "flipped" whenever you multiply or divide both sides by a negative.

Solve $-3x > 6y - 3$ for x.

We must divide both sides by − 3 to get the x alone, but this means that the inequality "flips" because we changed the sign (just as 1 is less than 2 but −1 is greater than −2). So $x < -2y + 1$.

Worksheet 6: Negatives

Write the correct inequality ($<$ or $>$) in each space.

1. $-\dfrac{4}{5}$ _____ $\dfrac{2}{5}$
2. -31 _____ -18
3. $-\dfrac{3}{8}$ _____ $-\dfrac{5}{7}$
4. $\dfrac{6}{5}$ _____ $\dfrac{4}{5}$

5. How could the expression $-y$ represent a positive number? _____

6. An inequality must be "flipped" whenever _____

Simplify the following expressions without a calculator.

7. If $a \neq 4$, then $\dfrac{4a - 16}{16 - 4a} =$ _____

8. $\dfrac{(-3)^3(-1)^4(2)^6}{(-2)^5(1)^5(3)^3} =$ _____

9. $-20x^2 - (-5x^2) =$ _____

10. $-30x^2 - (-4x)^2 =$ _____

Solve the following inequalities for x:

11. $-5x + 12 > -38$

12. $-2x - 8 \leq 10$

13. For all real numbers x, $-x^2 - (-x^2) + (-x^3) =$

(A) $x^3 - 2x^2$
(B) $x^3 - x^2$
(C) x^3
(D) $-x^3$
(E) $-x^3 - 2x^2$

14. If $a = -b$ and $a \neq 0$, then which of the following must be true?

    I. $a^2b^3 < 0$
    II. $(a + b)^2 = 0$
    III. $\dfrac{a}{b} > 0$

(A) II only
(B) I and II only
(C) II and III only
(D) I and III only
(E) I, II, and III

15. If $x^3yz^4 < 0$ and $y > 0$, which of the following expressions must be negative?

(A) xz^2
(B) x^2z
(C) yz^2
(D) xyz
(E) y^2z

16. If $-1 < x < 0$, which of the following statements must be true?

(A) $x < x^2 < x^3$
(B) $x < x^3 < x^2$
(C) $x^3 < x^2 < x$
(D) $x^3 < x < x^2$
(E) $x^2 < x < x^3$

17. If x represents any negative number, which of the following must be positive?

(A) $2x$
(B) x^3
(C) $x - 4$
(D) $4 - x$
(E) $x + 3$

18. If the set of integers from -40 to n, inclusive, is added together, the sum is 83. How many members are in the set?

Lesson 7: Divisibility

Divisibility

There are five different ways of saying that one integer *a* is a multiple of another integer *b*. Understand each phrasing.

- *a* is divisible by *b*.
- *a* is a multiple of *b*.
- *b* is a factor of *a*.
- When *a* is divided by *b*, the remainder is 0.
- *a/b* is an integer.

    42 is a multiple of 7, so

- 42 is divisible by 7.
- 42 is a multiple of 7.
- 7 is a factor of 42.
- When 42 is divided by 7, the remainder is 0.
- 42/7 is an integer (6).

To see if integer *a* is divisible by integer *b*, divide *a* by *b* on your calculator and see whether the result is an integer. Or use one of these "quick checks":

- If an integer is a multiple of 3, its digits add up to a multiple of 3.

    345 is a multiple of 3 because $3 + 4 + 5 = 12$, which is a multiple of 3.

- If an integer is a multiple of 5, it ends in 0 or 5.
- If an integer is a multiple of 6, it ends in an even digit and its digits add up to a multiple of 3.
- If an integer is a multiple of 9, its digits add up to a multiple of 9.
- If an integer is a multiple of 10, it ends in 0.

    882 is a multiple of 9 because

- $882 \div 9 = 98$ (which is an integer)
- Its digit sum is a multiple of 9: $8 + 8 + 2 = 18$ and $1 + 8 = 9$

Remainders

A remainder is a whole number "left over" when one whole number is divided by another whole number a whole number of times. To understand remainders, think of dividing *a* by *b* as giving out *a* balloons to *b*

children at a party. If every child gets the same number of balloons, then the remainder is the number of balloons that "remain" because they can't be divided. If you try to divide 34 balloons among 4 kids, each kid can get 8 balloons, but then you will have 2 balloons left over. This is your remainder.

To find a remainder with a calculator, divide the two whole numbers on your calculator; then multiply the "decimal part" of the result by the divisor.

What is the remainder when 34 is divided by 5?

$34 \div 5 = 6.8$ and $0.8 \times 5 = 4$

Remainders can be very useful in solving PSAT "pattern" problems.

What is the 50th term in this sequence? 7, 9, 3, 1, 7, 9, 3, 1 . . .

The pattern repeats every four terms. The remainder when 50 is divided by 4 is 2, so the 50th term is the same as the 2nd term, which is 9.

Primes, Evens, and Odds

A *prime* number is any integer greater than 1 that is divisible only by 1 and itself (like 3, 5, 7, 11, 13, 17 . . .).

An *even* number is any multiple of 2. It can always be expressed as $2n$, where *n* is some integer. For example, $28 = 2(14)$.

An *odd* number is any integer that is not a multiple of 2. Any odd number can be expressed as $2n + 1$, where *n* is some integer. For example, $37 = 2(18) + 1$.

Be careful not to confuse *odd* with *negative* (and *even* with *positive*). Students commonly do this because *odd* and *negative* are "bad" words and *even* and *positive* are "good" words. To avoid this mistake, pay special attention to the words *odd, even, negative,* and *positive* by underlining them when you see them in problems.

Worksheet 7: Divisibility

1. What is a prime number?

2. What is a remainder?

3. What can you do to avoid confusing *odd* with *negative* or *even* with *positive*?

4. When a whole number is divided by 6, what are the possible remainders?

5. What is the 66th term of this sequence? 5, 3, 1, 7, 5, 3, 1, 7, . . .

6. What is the remainder when 804 is divided by 5?

7. When an odd number is divided by 2, the remainder is always

8. How many multiples of 4 between 1 and 100, inclusive, are also multiples of 3?

9. If a divided by b leaves a remainder of r, then a must be _____ greater than a multiple of _____.

10. An odd number is _____ and can always be expressed as _____.

11. How do you find a remainder with your calculator?

12. When an integer, w, is divided by 4, the remainder is 3. What is the remainder when $w+2$ is divided by 4?

13.   1, 2, 4, 6, 8, 1, 2, 4, 6, 8, ...
If the sequence above follows the pattern shown, what is the 94th term in the sequence?

(A) 1
(B) 2
(C) 4
(D) 6
(E) 8

14. Over the holidays, Jacques used 6 pieces of tape, each 3 inches long, to wrap each of his gifts. He started with a 200-foot roll of tape and wrapped g gifts. If no tape was wasted, which of the following represents the number of feet of tape that was left over after he was done wrapping gifts?
(1 foot = 12 inches)

(A) $200 - 18g$
(B) $200 - 6g$
(C) $200 - 1.5g$
(D) $200 - g$
(E) $200 - 0.5g$

15. If $\dfrac{x}{5}$ and $\dfrac{x}{9}$ are both positive integers, which of the following must also be an integer?

(A) $\dfrac{x}{40}$

(B) $\dfrac{x}{25}$

(C) $\dfrac{x}{18}$

(D) $\dfrac{x}{15}$

(E) $\dfrac{x}{10}$

16. a and b are positive integers. If a is divided by b, the quotient is 6 with a remainder of 3. Which of the following expresses a in terms of b?

(A) $6b - 3$
(B) $6b + 3$
(C) $3b - 6$
(D) $\dfrac{b}{6} + 3$
(E) $3b + 6$

17. If a is a positive integer and is divisible by 4 and b is a positive integer and is divisible by 7, which of the following must be divisible by 28?

      I. $4b + 7a$
     II. ab
    III. $4(b + 7)$

(A) I only
(B) II only
(C) I and II only
(D) II and III only
(E) I, II, and III

Detailed Answer Key:
Essential Pre-Algebra Skills

Worksheet 1

1. -7 (Remember: least means farthest to the left on the number line.)

2. 13 ($13 + 15 + 17 + 19 = 64$. Just divide 64 by 4 to get the "middle" of the set $= 16$.)

3. sum

4. difference

5. product

6. $+(-4)$

7. $\times (1/6)$

8. $\div (7/4)$

9. $\times (3/8)$

10. $-\mathbf{23}$
$$5 - 8 \div 4 \times 6 - (1 + 3)^2$$

Simplify in parentheses:	$5 - 8 \div 4 \times 6 - (4)^2$
Exponents:	$5 - 8 \div 4 \times 6 - (16)$
Divide:	$5 - 2 \times 6 - (16)$
Multiply:	$5 - 12 - (16)$
Subtract:	-23

11. $\mathbf{6}$
$$\sqrt{136 - \left(\sqrt{16} + \sqrt{35}\right)^2} = \sqrt{136 - (4 + 6)^2}.$$
$$= \sqrt{(136 - (10)^2)} = 6$$

12. **B** $\quad 15 = 3 \times 5$

13. **C** $\qquad\qquad \sqrt{m} + 4 = 10$

Subtract 4:	$\sqrt{m} = 6$
Square both sides:	$m = 36$

14. **B** $\qquad\qquad 2y + 7 < 13$

Subtract 7:	$2y < 6$
Divide by 2:	$y < 3$
	$4y + 2 > 6$
Subtract 2:	$4y > 4$
Divide by 4:	$y > 1$

Therefore y must be 2 since this is the only integer greater than one but less than three.

15. **27** Set up proportions to solve this problem:

$$\frac{1 \text{ splunk}}{5 \text{ genks}} = \frac{3 \text{ splunk}}{x \text{ genks}}$$

Cross-multiply: $\quad x = 15$

$$\frac{1 \text{ gromp}}{5 \text{ genks}} = \frac{3 \text{ gromps}}{y \text{ genks}}$$

Cross-multiply: $\quad y = 12$ genks

3 splunk + 4 gromps $= 15$ genks $+ 12$ genks
$= 27$ genks

16. **B** I does not work because 4/6 can be reduced to 2/3. II works because 5/3, 5/6, and 5/7 are fully reduced. III does not work because 8/6 can be reduced to 4/3.

17. **B**
$$(k - (1 - (1 - 4))) - (3 - (2 - (1 - 2))) = -2$$
$$(k - (1 - (-3))) - (3 - (2 - (-1))) = -2$$
$$(k - 4) - (3 - 3) = -2$$
$$(k - 4) - 0 = -2$$
Add 4: $\qquad\qquad\qquad\qquad\qquad k = 2$

18. **D** $\qquad\qquad\qquad 3x + 6 = 33$

Subtract 6:	$3x = 27$
Divide by 3:	$x = 9$
Multiply by 2:	$2x = 18$

Worksheet 2

1. 300 Reorder to get pairs with sums of 100: $(37 + 63) + (54 + 46) + (26 + 74)$

2. $120x^2$ You cannot FOIL here even though it looks like you can because the terms in the parentheses are separated by a $\times$ and not a $+$ or $-$. Instead, reorder them:

$$(5)(4)(2x)(3x) = 20(6x^2) = 120x^2$$

3. 12,000 Use the distributive law: $12(300 + 700)$.

4. $3x^2 + 30x + 75$ $3(x+5)^2$

     FOIL: $3(x^2 + 5x + 5x + 25)$

     Combine terms: $3(x^2 + 10x + 25)$

     Distribute: $3x^2 + 30x + 75$

5. $4b^2(b+4)$

6. $16b^2 + 4b^3$

7. $b^2 \times 16 + b^3 \times 4$

8. They are reciprocals. Their product is 1.

9. They are the same.

10. They are opposites. Their sum is 0.

11. **A** $x + y = 10$

                      $x - y = 6$

     Add straight down: $2x = 16$

     Divide by 2: $x = 8$

     Solve for y: $8 + y = 10$

     Subtract 8: $y = 2$

     Divide x by y: $8 \div 2 = 4$

12. **D** $4x(3x \times 2) - 10x^2$

     Simplify in parentheses: $4x(6x) - 10x^2$

     Simplify: $24x^2 - 10x^2$

     Combine terms: $14x^2$

13. **E** $2 - (3 - (4 - b) - 1) =$

             $2 - (3 - 4 + b - 1) =$

                $2 - (b - 2) =$

                $2 - b + 2 =$

                   $4 - b$

14. **D**   If she received \$7.30 in change from a \$10 bill, she spent $10 - \$7.30 = \$2.70$ on 3 sodas.

                         $3s = \$2.70$

     Divide by 3: $s = \$0.90$

     If she buys 5 sodas: $5s = 5(\$0.90) = \$4.50$

     If she pays with a \$10 bill: $\$10 - \$4.50 = \$5.50$

15. **A**   If she divides the dolls into piles of 6, there are 4 left over. This means that the number of dolls is 4 more than a multiple of 6. 10, 16, 22, 28, 34, 40, 46 are the possibilities.

    If she divides them into groups of 5, she has 3 left over. This means that the number of dolls is 3 more than a multiple of 5. It therefore must be an integer ending in 3 or 8. Among the possibilities,

only 28 remains. If she divided 28 dolls into piles of 4, there would be 7 piles with none left over.

16. **C** $(m - n) + 4 = (3 - (-3 - n))$

     Distribute: $m - n + 4 = 3 + 3 + n$

     Add n: $m + 4 = 6 + 2n$

     Subtract 6: $m - 2 = 2n$

     Divide by 2: $\dfrac{m-2}{2} = n$

Worksheet 3

1. $\dfrac{19}{15}$ Zip-zap-zup! $\dfrac{2}{3} + \dfrac{3}{5} = \dfrac{10 \quad 9}{3 \times 5} = \dfrac{10}{15} + \dfrac{9}{15} = \dfrac{19}{15}$

2. $\dfrac{1}{2}$ $\dfrac{3}{8} \times \dfrac{12}{9} = \dfrac{36}{72} = \dfrac{1}{2}$

3. $\dfrac{5}{4}$ $\dfrac{5}{7} \times \dfrac{14}{8} = \dfrac{70}{56} = \dfrac{5}{4}$

4. $\dfrac{15 + 7x}{9x}$ Zip-zap-zup!

   $\dfrac{5}{3x} + \dfrac{7}{9} = \dfrac{45 \quad 21x}{3x \times 9} = \dfrac{45}{27x} + \dfrac{21x}{27x} = \dfrac{45 + 21x}{27x} = \dfrac{15 + 7x}{9x}$

5. $\dfrac{n-2}{2n-2}$ Factor: $\dfrac{3(n-2)}{3(2n-2)} = \dfrac{n-2}{2n-2}$

6. $\dfrac{29}{28}$ $\dfrac{7}{28} \times \dfrac{8}{28} + \dfrac{14}{28} = \dfrac{29}{28}$

7. Just divide the numerator by the denominator by hand or on a calculator.

8. $\dfrac{2}{5}$ $\dfrac{8 \text{ apples}}{20 \text{ pieces of fruit}} = \dfrac{8}{20} = \dfrac{2}{5}$

9. 300   If one out of every three cars is red, then two out of every three cars is not red. Set up a ratio:

$$\dfrac{2}{3} = \dfrac{200}{x}$$

     Cross-multiply: $2x = 600$

     Divide by 2: $x = 300$

10. **C**

(A) $\dfrac{3}{4} \div \dfrac{5}{8} = \dfrac{3}{4} \times \dfrac{8}{5} = \dfrac{24}{20} = \dfrac{6}{5}$

(B) $\dfrac{3}{4} - \dfrac{5}{8} = \dfrac{6}{8} - \dfrac{5}{8} = \dfrac{1}{8}$

(C) $\dfrac{3}{4} + \dfrac{5}{8} = \dfrac{6}{8} + \dfrac{5}{8} = \dfrac{11}{8}$

(D) $\dfrac{3}{4} \times \dfrac{5}{8} = \dfrac{15}{32}$

(E) $1 - \left(\dfrac{3}{4} \times \dfrac{5}{8}\right) = 1 - \dfrac{15}{32} = \dfrac{17}{32}$

11. **C** 1st quarter: (1/7) of $42 = 6$ points; 2nd quarter: (1/3) of $42 = 14$ points; 3rd quarter $= 12$ points. This leaves a total of $42 - 14 - 12 - 6 = 10$ points in the 4th.

12. 4/5 or 0.8 $3 + \dfrac{1}{y} = 4 + \dfrac{1}{4}$

Subtract 3: $\dfrac{1}{y} = \dfrac{5}{4}$

Cross-multiply: $5y = 4$

Divide by 5: $y = \dfrac{4}{5}$

13. 5/3 or 1.66 or 1.67

If $\dfrac{a}{b} = \dfrac{5}{4}$, then $\dfrac{4a}{3b} = \dfrac{4}{3}\left(\dfrac{5}{4}\right) = \dfrac{20}{12} = \dfrac{5}{3}$

14. **A** If 3/7 are broken, then 4/7 are intact. If 3/4 of the intact eggs are brown, then 1/4 of the intact eggs are not brown. To find the fraction of eggs that are intact and nonbrown, multiply the two fractions:

$$\dfrac{4}{7} \times \dfrac{1}{4} = \dfrac{1}{7}$$

15. **E** $\dfrac{a+b}{ab} = 2$

Multiply by ab: $a + b = 2ab$

Subtract a: $b = 2ab - a$

Factor out a: $b = a(2b - 1)$

Divide by $2b - 1$: $\dfrac{b}{2b-1} = a$

Worksheet 4

1. distance to time

2. money to time

3. A proportion is a statement that two fractions or ratios are equal to each other.

4. $8,000, $4,000, and $2,000. The sum of the parts is $4 + 2 + 1 = 7$, so the parts are 4/7, 2/7, and 1/7 of the whole.

5. 16 $\dfrac{5 \text{ steaks}}{2 \text{ minutes}} = \dfrac{40 \text{ steaks}}{x}$

Cross-multiply: $5x = 80$

Divide by 5: $x = 16$

6. 48   There are 240 minutes in 4 hours.

$$\dfrac{4 \text{ miles}}{20 \text{ minutes}} = \dfrac{x}{240 \text{ minutes}}$$

Cross-multiply: $960 = 20x$

Divide by 20: $48 = x$

7. a) $ab = 24$ b) $\dfrac{a}{6} = \dfrac{4}{b}$ c) $\dfrac{6}{a} = \dfrac{b}{4}$

8. **E**   Set up a ratio: $\dfrac{1/2}{2} = \dfrac{x}{24}$

Cross-multiply: $12 = 2x$

Divide by 2: $6 = x$

9. **E** 5:3 is a part to part ratio, with a sum of 8. Therefore 5/8 of the people are men and 3/8 are women. 5/8 of 80 is 50.

10. 21 $\dfrac{6 \text{ people}}{3 \text{ containers}} = \dfrac{42 \text{ people}}{x}$

Cross-multiply: $6x = 126$

Divide by 6: $x = 21$

11. $\dfrac{8}{3}$ The triangles are similar. $\dfrac{6}{10} = \dfrac{4}{4+x}$

Cross-multiply: $6(4 + x) = 40$

Distribute: $24 + 6x = 40$

Subtract 24: $6x = 16$

Divide by 6: $x = \dfrac{16}{6} = \dfrac{8}{3}$

12. **B** First find the cost *per ounce*:

$$\dfrac{d \text{ dollars}}{12 \text{ ounces}} = \dfrac{d/12 \text{ dollars}}{1 \text{ ounce}}$$

Next, find out how much one batch costs:

$$\dfrac{4 \text{ ounces}}{b \text{ batches}} = \dfrac{4/b \text{ ounces}}{1 \text{ batch}} \times \dfrac{d/12 \text{ dollars}}{1 \text{ ounce}}$$

$$= \dfrac{4d \text{ dollars}}{12b \text{ batches}}$$

Finally, find the cost of 6 batches:

$$\dfrac{4d \text{ dollars}}{12b \text{ batches}} \times 6 \text{ batches} = \dfrac{24d}{12b} = \dfrac{2d}{b}$$

Alternatively, pick a number for d and b. Let's say the price is $d = \$10$ dollars for 12 ounces and that 4 ounces makes $b = 2$ batches. This means that each batch requires 2 ounces and that there are $6 \times 2 = 12$ ounces in 6 batches. 12 ounces cost $10. Plug 10 in for d and 2 in for b and pick the answer choice that equals 10.

$$(B) \qquad 2d/b = 2(10)/2 = 20/2 = 10$$

13. **C** Let's say you mix 10 gallons of each paint. In 10 gallons of green paint there are 4 gallons $(2/5 \times 10 = 4)$ of yellow and 6 gallons $(3/5 \times 10 = 6)$ of blue paint. In 10 gallons of purple paint there are 7 gallons $(7/10 \times 10 = 7)$ of blue paint and 3 gallons $(3/10 \times 10 = 3)$ of red paint. Therefore in 20 gallons of a mixture, there are 13 gallons of blue paint, or $13/20$.

Worksheet 5

1. x, y, or any unknown; $\times$; is; $\div 100$

2. $\dfrac{\text{final amount} - \text{starting amount}}{\text{starting amount}} \times 100$

3. 1.40

4. 0.84

5. $12 = \dfrac{x}{100} \times 38 \qquad x = 31.58\%$

6. $34 = \dfrac{20}{100}x \qquad x = 170$

7. $x = \dfrac{60}{100} \times 80 \qquad x = 48$

8. 100 $x = 1.25\,(80) \qquad x = 100$

9. 240 $400 \times 0.60 = 240$

10. **B**   Starting price: x
   After 1st quarter: $1.25x$
   After 2nd quarter: $0.80(1.25x)$
   After 3rd quarter: $0.90[0.80(1.25x)]$
   After 4th quarter: $1.20[0.90[0.80(1.25x)]]$
   Simplify: $1.08x$

11. **D** $(0.50)(0.40)(x) = (0.20)(0.70)(y)$
   Simplify: $d0.20x = 0.14y$
   Divide by 0.20 $x = 0.70y$

12. **26** The total amount of salt is $(0.20)(4) + (0.30)(6) = 0.8 + 1.8 = 2.6$ liters. The total amount of solution is 10 liters, and $2.6/10 = 26\%$.

13. **C** First find the area of the original triangle:
$$A = 1/2 bh$$
   Find the new area: $= 1/2(1.20)(b)(1.40)(h)$
   Simplify: $= 1/2(1.68)bh = 1.68A$

14. **B**
   $$x + 4y = 1.5(3y)$$
   Simplify: $x + 4y = 4.5y$
   Subtract $4y$: $x = 0.5y$
   $$\dfrac{x}{y} = \dfrac{0.5y}{y} = 0.5$$

Worksheet 6

1. $<$ 2. $<$ 3. $>$ 4. $>$

5. If y is negative.

6. You multiply or divide by a negative on both sides.

7. -1 $\dfrac{4a - 16}{16 - 4a} = \dfrac{-4(4 - a)}{4(4 - a)} = -1$

8. 2 $\dfrac{(-3)^3(-1)^4(2)^6}{(3)^3(1)^5(-2)^5} = \dfrac{(-27)(1)(64)}{(27)(1)(-32)}$
   $$= (-1)(1)(-2) = 2$$

9. $-15x^2$
   $$-20x^2 - (-5x^2) =$$
   Convert to addition: $-20x^2 + 5x^2 = -15x^2$

10. $-46x^2$ $-30x^2 - (-4x)^2 =$
   Simplify: $-30x^2 - 16x^2 = -46x^2$

11. $x < 10$ $-5x + 12 > -38$
   Subtract 12: $-5x > -50$
   Divide by -5: $x < 10$

12. $x \geq -9$
   $$-2x - 8 \leq 10$$
   Add 8: $-2x \leq 18$
   Divide by -2: $x \geq -9$

13. **D** $-x^2 - (-x^2) + (-x^3)$
   Distribute: $-x^2 + x^2 - x^3 = -x^3$

14. **A**   If $a = -1$ and $b = 1$, then statement I is false. If $a = -b$, then $a + b = -b + b = 0$, and $0^2 = 0$, so statement II is true. If $a = -b$, then $a/b = -b/b = -1$, so statement III is false.

15. **A**   You are told that $x^3 y z^4$ is negative and that y is positive. z^4 must be positive because any non-zero number raised to an even exponent must be ≥ 0. (z cannot be 0 because the product of $x^3 y z^4$ is not 0.) Because yz^4 is positive ($+ \times + = +$), x^3 must be negative in order for $x^3 y z^4$ to be negative. This means that x must be negative. Answer choice A is correct because x is negative and z^2 is positive.

16. **B**   Plug in a sample value, like -0.5, for x: $x = -0.5$, $x^2 = 0.25$, $x^3 = -0.125$. Therefore $x < x^3 < x^2$.

17. **D**   Plug in a sample value, like -1, for x:

(A) $2(-1) = -2$
(B) $(-1)^3 = -1$
(C) $-1 - 4 = -5$
(D) $4 - (-1) = 5$
(E) $-1 + 3 = 2$.

This sample value eliminated answers A, B, and C. Plug in another sample value, like -4, for x:

(D) $4 - (-4) = 8$
(E) $-4 + 3 = -1$

Therefore, the correct answer is (D).

18. **83**   When the integers from -40 to $+40$ are added together, the sum is zero: $-40 + -39 + -38 + \ldots + 38 + 39 + 40 = 0$. Add the next two integers, 41 and 42, to that sum and you get 83. The number of integers from -40 to 42, inclusive, is $42 - (-40) + 1 = 83$.

Worksheet 7

1. Any integer greater than 1 that is divisible only by 1 and itself.

2. The whole number "left over" when one whole number is divided by another whole number a whole number of times.

3. Underline and think about those words when you see them in problems.

4. 0, 1, 2, 3, 4, and 5

5. **3**   The pattern is 4 terms long, and 66 divided by 4 has a remainder of 2, so the 66th term is the same as the 2nd term.

6. 4

7. 1

8. **8**   The least common multiple of 3 and 4 is 12 and $100 \div 12 = 8\ 1/3$, which means that there are 8 multiples of 12 between 1 and 100.

9. a must be r greater than a multiple of b.

10. Any integer that is not divisible by 2. It can be expressed as $2n + 1$ where n is an integer.

11. Divide the two integers, then multiply the decimal part of the result by the divisor (the number you divided by).

12. **I**   Plug in a number for w that gives a remainder of 3 when it is divided by 4. Let's say $w = 15$. 15 divided by $4 = 3$ remainder 3. $w + 2 = 15 + 2 = 17$. 17 divided by $4 = 4$ remainder 1.

13. **D**   The sequence that repeats is 5 terms long. 94 divided by 5 leaves a remainder of 4, so the 94th term must be the same as the 4th term, which is 6.

14. **C**   First figure out how much tape he uses per package. Each package uses 6 pieces 3 inches long for a total of $6 \times 3 = 18$ inches $= 1.5$ feet. If he wraps g gifts, he will use up a total of $1.5g$ feet of tape. To find out how much is left over, subtract that from 200: $200 - 1.5g$.

15. **D**   If $x/5$ and $x/9$ are both positive integers, then x must be a common multiple of 5 and 9. The least common multiple of 5 and 9 is 45. If you substitute 45 for x, the only choice that yields an integer is (D): $x/15$.

16. **B**   When a is divided by b, the answer is 6 with remainder 3. This means that b goes into a 6 times with 3 left over; this means that a is 3 more than $6b$: $a = 6b + 3$.

17. **E**   Pick values for a and b. Let's say $a = 8$ and $b = 14$.

I. $4b + 7a = 4(14) + 7(8) = 56 + 56 = 112$
$112 \div 28 = 4$. No matter what numbers you pick, both $4b$ and $7a$ will be divisible by 28, and two multiples of 28 added together, must equal a multiple of 28.

II. $ab = 8 \times 14 = 112$ $112 \div 28 = 4$
When a multiple of 7 and a multiple of 4 are multiplied together, the product will be divisible by 28. Therefore statement II is true.

III. Since b is a multiple of 7, $b + 7$ must also be a multiple of 7. When any multiple of 7 is multiplied by 4, the result must be a multiple of 28. Therefore statement III is true.

CHAPTER 9

ESSENTIAL ALGEBRA I SKILLS

1. Solving Equations

2. Systems

3. Working with Exponents

4. Working with Roots

5. Factoring

6. Inequalities, Absolute Values, and Plugging In

7. Word Problems

Lesson 1: Solving Equations

Equations as Balanced Scales

Algebra is really common sense once you start thinking of every equation as a balanced scale. The terms on either side of the equal sign must be "balanced," just like the weights on a scale. Imagine that you are the keeper of a scale, and you must keep it balanced. What would you do if someone took weights from one side of the scale? You'd remove an equal weight from the other side, of course. This is a law of equality: anything you do to one side of the equation, you must do to the other to maintain the balance.

If $12x - 8 = 28$, what is the value of $3x - 2$?

Don't worry about solving for x, because that's not what the question is asking for. Notice that the expression you are given, $12x - 8$, is 4 times the expression you are looking for, $3x - 2$. So to turn the given expression into the one you want, divide by 4. Of course, you must do the same to the other side to keep the balance:

$$\frac{12x - 8}{4} = \frac{28}{4} \longrightarrow 3x - 2 = 7$$

Solving as Unwrapping

Solving simple algebraic equations is basically the same thing as unwrapping a present. (And it's just as fun, too, right?) Wrapping a present involves a sequence of steps: (1) Put the gift in the box. (2) Close the box. (3) Wrap the paper around the box. (4) Put the bow on. Here's the important part: unwrapping the present just means inverting those steps and reversing their order: (1) Take off the bow. (2) Unwrap the paper. (3) Open the box. (4) Take out the gift.

Solve for x: $5x^2 - 9 = 31$.

The problem is that x is not alone on the left side; it is "wrapped up" like a gift. How is it wrapped?

Think of the order of operations for turning x into $5x^2 - 9$:

1. Square it x^2
2. Multiply by 5 $5x^2$
3. Subtract 9 $5x^2 - 9$

So to "unwrap it," you reverse and invert the steps:

1. Add 9 $(5x^2 - 9) + 9 = 5x^2$

2. Divide by 5 $\dfrac{5x^2}{5} = x^2$

3. Find the square roots (both of them)!
   $\pm\sqrt{x^2} = \pm|x|$

If you perform these steps to both sides, $5x^2 - 9 = 31$ transforms into $x = \pm\sqrt{8}$.

Watch Your Steps

To solve that last equation, we had to perform three *operations*. Many equations, as you probably know, require more steps to solve. **It is very important that you keep track of your steps so that you can check your work if you need to.** In other words, the equation we just solved should really look like this on your scratch paper:

$$5x^2 - 9 = 31$$

Step 1: $\dfrac{+9 \quad +9}{}$

Step 2: $\dfrac{\dfrac{5x^2}{5} = \dfrac{40}{5}}{}$

Step 3: $\begin{aligned} x^2 &= 8 \\ x &= \pm\sqrt{8} \end{aligned}$

Check by Plugging Back In

Always check your answer by plugging it back into the original equation to see if it works. Remember that solving an equation means simply finding the value of each unknown that makes the equation true.

Are $\pm\sqrt{8}$ solutions to $5x^2 - 9 = 31$? Plug them in:

$$5\left(\pm\sqrt{8}\right)^2 - 9 = 5(8) - 9 = 40 - 9 = 31 \text{ (Yes!)}$$

Worksheet 1: Solving Equations

1. Explain the laws of equality.

_____

_____

_____

_____

_____

Show your steps and check your work in solving the following equations.

2. $5x - 12 = 10x + 3$

3. $\dfrac{4y^2}{6} = 2y^2$

4. $(5 - x)^2 = 9$

5. $\dfrac{3 - x}{4} = \dfrac{x + 2}{10}$

Solve the following equations for the given expression.

6. If $24x + 12y = 20$, then $4x + 2y =$

7. If $\dfrac{3}{5}y + \dfrac{2}{3}x = \dfrac{1}{4}$, then $12y + \dfrac{40}{3}x =$

8. If $4x - 8 = 24$,
then $4x + 8 =$

9. What number decreased by 8 equals 5 times that number?

(A) -3
(B) -2
(C) 0
(D) 2
(E) 3

10.
$$(x + 7)^2 = (x - 4)^2$$

The equation above is true for which of the following values of x?

(A) -1.5 only
(B) -0.5 only
(C) 4 and -7
(D) 4 and 7
(E) 2.5 only

11. If $\dfrac{a}{a + 4} = \dfrac{6}{7}$, then $a =$

12. If $40 - \sqrt{x} = 15$, which of the following gives all the possible values of x?

(A) 5 only
(B) 5 and -5
(C) 25 only
(D) 25 and -25
(E) 625 only

13. If $m = 3(n + 2) + p$, what is n in terms of m and p?

(A) $\dfrac{m + p}{2} - 3$
(B) $\dfrac{m + p}{2} + 3$
(C) $\dfrac{m - p}{3} - 2$
(D) $\dfrac{m - p}{3} + 2$
(E) $\dfrac{m + p}{3} - 2$

Lesson 2: Systems

Systems

A system is simply a set of equations that are true at the same time, such:

$$\begin{cases} 3x - 2y = 12 \\ x + 3y = 15 \end{cases}$$

Although many values for x and y "satisfy" the first equation, like $(4, 0)$ and $(2, -3)$ (plug them in and check!), there is only one solution that works in both equations: $(6, 3)$. (Plug this into both equations and check!)

The Law of Substitution

The law of substitution simply says that if two things are equal, you can always substitute one for the other.

$$\begin{cases} 3x + y^2 = 7 \\ y = x + 1 \end{cases}$$

The easiest way to solve is to use the second equation (which is already "solved" for y) to substitute into the first, so that you eliminate one of the unknowns. Since $y = x + 1$, you can replace the y in the first equation with $x + 1$ and get

$$3x + (x + 1)^2 = 7$$

FOIL the squared binomial: $3x + x^2 + 2x + 1 = 7$

Combine like terms: $x^2 + 5x + 1 = 7$

Subtract 7: $x^2 + 5x - 6 = 0$

Factor the left side: $(x + 6)(x - 1) = 0$

Apply the "0 product property": $x = -6$ or $x = 1$

Plug back into second equation: $y = (-6) + 1 = -5$

or $y = (1) + 1 = 2.$

Solutions: $(-6, -5)$ and $(1, 2)$ (Check!)

Combining Equations

If the two equations in the system are alike enough, you can sometimes solve more easily by combining equations. The idea is simple: if you add or subtract the corresponding sides of two true equations together, the result should also be a true equation, because we are adding equal things to both sides. This strategy can be simpler than substitution:

$$\begin{cases} 2x - 5y = 7 \\ 3x + 5y = 23 \end{cases}$$

Adding the corresponding sides will eliminate the y's from the system: $5x = 30$
Divide by 5: $x = 6$
Plug back in and solve for y:

$$2(6) - 5y = 7$$

Simplify: $12 - 5y = 7$

Subtract 12: $-5y = -5$

Divide by -5: $y = 1$

Special Kinds of "Solving"

Sometimes a question gives a system, but rather than asking you to solve for each unknown, it simply asks you to evaluate another expression. **Look carefully at what the question asks you to evaluate, and see whether there is a simple way of combining the equations (adding, subtracting, multiplying, dividing) to find the expression.**

If $3x - 6y = 10$ and $4x + 2y = 2$, what is the value of $7x - 4y$?

Don't solve for x and y. Just notice that $7x - 4y$ equals $(3x - 6y) + (4x + 2y) = 10 + 2 = 12.$

"Letter-Heavy" Systems

An equation with more than one unknown, or a system with more unknowns than equations, can be said to be "letter heavy." Simple equations and systems usually have unique solutions, but these letter-heavy equations and systems usually have more than one solution. Therefore you can often easily find solutions simply by plugging in values.

If $2m + 5n = 10$ and $m \neq 0$, what is the value of $\dfrac{4m}{10 - 5n}$?

You can "guess and check" a solution to the equation pretty easily. Notice that $m = -5$, $n = 4$ works. If you plug these values into the expression that you're evaluating, you'll see it simplifies to 2.

Worksheet 2: Systems

1. What is a system?

2. What are two algebraic methods for solving systems?

3. How can you check the solution of a system?

Solve the following systems by substitution.

4. $5x + 7y = 31$
   $y = x + 1$

5. $4y - 3x = 26$
   $x = y - 7$

6. $4n - 3m = 6$
   $m = \dfrac{3}{2}n$

Solve the following systems by combination, and check your solution.

7. $2a - 3b = 10$
   $4a + 3b = 14$

8. $-5x + 7y = 16$
   $5x + 7y = 12$

9. $3m - 5n = 12$
   $4m + 5n = 9$

10. If $5x + 3y = 33$ and $y = 2x$, then $x =$

14. If $\dfrac{x}{3y} = \dfrac{5}{9}$ and $\dfrac{6y}{5z} = \dfrac{2}{7}$, then $\dfrac{x}{z} =$

(A) $\dfrac{18}{63}$

(B) $\dfrac{25}{63}$

(C) $\dfrac{31}{63}$

(D) $\dfrac{50}{63}$

(E) $\dfrac{71}{63}$

11. The sum of two numbers is 8 and their difference is 12. What is their product?

(A) -20
(B) -16
(C) -8
(D) 8
(E) 20

15. The cost of a large box of popcorn and two large sodas is $12.50. The cost of two large boxes of popcorn and one large soda is $14.50. What is the cost of one large box of popcorn?

12. If $3a + 6b = 12$ and $4a - 7b = 16$, what is the value of $7a - b$?

(A) 18
(B) 22
(C) 26
(D) 28
(E) 32

13. If $3a + 4b - 6c = 18$, and a, b, and c are all positive, what is the value of $\dfrac{3 + c}{3a + 4b}$?

Lesson 3: Working with Exponents

What Are Exponentials?

An exponential is simply any term with these three parts:

$$\underset{\text{Base}}{\underset{\displaystyle 4}{\underbrace{}}}\overset{\text{Coefficient}}{x}\overset{\overset{\text{Exponent}}{3}}{}$$

If a term seems not to have a coefficient or exponent, the coefficient or exponent is always assumed to be 1.

$2x$ means $2x^1$ y^3 means $1y^3$

Expand to Understand

Good students memorize the rules for working with exponentials, but great students understand where the rules come from. They come from applying simple arithmetic to their "expanded" forms.

What is $(x^5)^2$ in simplest terms? Do you *add* exponents to get x^7? *Multiply* to get x^{10}? *Power* to get x^{25}?

The answer is clear when you expand the exponential. Just remember that *raising to the nth power* means *multiplying by itself n times*. So $(x^5)^2 = (x^5)(x^5) = (x \cdot x \cdot x \cdot x \cdot x)(x \cdot x \cdot x \cdot x \cdot x) = x^{10}$. Doing this helps you to see and understand the rule of "multiplying the powers."

Adding and Subtracting Exponentials

When adding or subtracting exponentials, you can only combine like terms, that is, terms with the same base and same exponent. When adding or subtracting like exponentials, remember to leave the bases and exponents alone.

$5x^3 + 6x^3 + 4x^2 = (5x^3 + 6x^3) + 4x^2 = x^3(5 + 6) + 4x^2 = 11x^3 + 4x^2$

Notice that combining like terms always involves the law of distribution (Chapter 8, Lesson 2).

Multiplying and Dividing Exponentials

You can simplify a product or quotient of exponentials when the bases are the same or the exponents are the same.

If the bases are the same, add the exponents (when multiplying) or subtract the exponents (when dividing) and leave the bases alone.

$$(5m^5)(12m^2) = (5)(m)(m)(m)(m)(m)(12)(m)(m)$$
$$= (5)(12)(m)(m)(m)(m)(m)(m)(m)$$
$$= 60m^7$$

$$\frac{6p^7}{3p^4} = \frac{6(p)(p)(p)(\cancel{p})(\cancel{p})(\cancel{p})(\cancel{p})}{3(\cancel{p})(\cancel{p})(\cancel{p})(\cancel{p})}$$
$$= 2p^3$$

If the exponents are the same, multiply (or divide) the bases and leave the exponents alone.

$$(3m^4)(7n^4) = (3)(m)(m)(m)(m)(7)(n)(n)(n)(n)$$
$$= (3)(7)(mn)(mn)(mn)(mn)$$
$$= 21(mn)^4$$

$$\frac{5(12)^5}{(3)^5} = \frac{5(12)(12)(12)(12)(12)}{(3)(3)(3)(3)(3)}$$
$$= 5\left(\frac{12}{3}\right)\left(\frac{12}{3}\right)\left(\frac{12}{3}\right)\left(\frac{12}{3}\right)\left(\frac{12}{3}\right)$$
$$= 5(4)^5$$

Raising Exponentials to Powers

When raising an exponential to a power, multiply the exponents, but don't forget to raise the coefficient to the power and leave the base alone.

$$(3y^4)^3 = (3y^4)(3y^4)(3y^4)$$
$$= (3y \cdot y \cdot y \cdot y)(3y \cdot y \cdot y \cdot y)(3y \cdot y \cdot y \cdot y)$$
$$= (3)(3)(3)(y \cdot y \cdot y \cdot y)(y \cdot y \cdot y \cdot y)(y \cdot y \cdot y \cdot y)$$
$$= 27y^{12}$$

Worksheet 3: Working with Exponents

1. The three parts of an exponential are the _____, _____, and _____.

2. When multiplying two exponentials *with the same base*, you should _____ the coefficients, _____ the bases, and _____ the exponents.

3. When dividing two exponentials *with the same exponent*, you should _____ the coefficients, _____ the bases, and _____ the exponents.

4. When multiplying two exponentials *with the same exponent*, you should _____ the coefficients, _____ the bases, and _____ the exponents.

5. When dividing two exponentials *with the same base*, you should _____ the coefficients, _____ the bases, and _____ the exponents.

6. To raise an exponential to a power, you should _____ the coefficient, _____ the base, and _____ the exponents.

Simplify, if possible.

7. $a^2b + 4a^2b =$

8. $4x^3 + 5x^4 - 3x^3 =$

9. $(5)^{3x}(4)^{3x} =$

10. $8(24)^4 \div 2(24)^3 =$

11. $(a^4 + b^3)^2 =$

12. $[5w^3(5)^2]^2 =$

13. If $4^{3x} = 64$, then $x =$

14. If $(x^3)(x^b) = x^{12}$, and $(x^3)^c = x^{15}$, what is the value of $b \times c$?

(A) 14
(B) 16
(C) 24
(D) 45
(E) 48

15. If $3^{3x} = 9^{2x-1}$, what is the value of x?

(A) -2
(B) -1
(C) 0
(D) 1
(E) 2

16. For all real numbers, x, $\dfrac{(3^x)(3^x)}{(3^x)(3)} =$

(A) 3
(B) 3^x
(C) 3^{x+1}
(D) 3^{x-1}
(E) 3^{2x-1}

17. For all values of r, which of the following is equivalent to $4^r + 4^r$?

(A) 4^{2r}
(B) 4^{r+2}
(C) 2^{2r}
(D) 2^{2r+1}
(E) 2^{4r}

18. The value of t is given by the formula $t = \dfrac{x^3 y^2 z^2}{w^3}$. For a particular set of values of $w, x, y,$ and z, the value of t is 48. If x is then doubled, y is tripled, z is divided by 2, and w is tripled, what is the value of t?

Lesson 4: Working with Roots

What Are Roots?

The Latin word *radix* means *root* (remember that *radishes* grow underground), so the word *radical* means *the root of a number* (or *a person who seeks to change a system "from the roots up"*). What does the root of a plant have to do with the root of a number?

Think of a square with an area of 9 square units sitting on the ground:

The bottom of the square is "rooted" to the ground, and it has a length of 3. So we say that 3 is the *square root* of 9!

The square root of a number is what you must square to get the number.

All positive numbers have two square roots. For instance, the square roots of 9 are both 3 and -3.

The radical symbol, $\sqrt{}$, however, means only the nonnegative square root. So although the square root of 9 equals either 3 or -3, $\sqrt{9}$ equals only 3.

The number inside a radical is called a radicand.

If x^2 is equal to 9 or 16, what is the least possible value of x^3?

Since x is the square root of 9 or 16, it could be -3, 3, -4, or 4. Therefore x^3 could be -27, 27, -64, or 64. The least of these, of course, is -64.

Remember that $\sqrt{x^2}$ does not always equal x. It does, however, always equal $|x|$.

Simplify $\sqrt{\left(\dfrac{3x+1}{y}\right)^2}$

Don't worry about squaring first. Just remember the rule above. It simplifies to $\left|\dfrac{3x+1}{y}\right|$.

Working with Roots

Memorize the first nine perfect squares: 4, 9, 16, 25, 36, 49, 64, 81, 100. This will make working with roots easier.

To simplify a square root expression, factor any perfect squares from the radicand and simplify.

Simplify $3\sqrt{27}$

Factor out perfect squares from the radicand.

$$3\sqrt{27} = 3\sqrt{9 \times 3} = 3\sqrt{9} \times \sqrt{3} = 3 \times 3 \times \sqrt{3} = 9\sqrt{3}$$

Simplify $\sqrt{m^2 + 10m + 25}$

Factor out perfect squares from the radicand.

$$\sqrt{m^2 + 10m + 25} = \sqrt{(m+5)^2} = |m+5|$$

When adding or subtracting roots, treat them like exponentials: only combine *like* terms—those with the same radicand.

Simplify $3\sqrt{7} + 5\sqrt{2} + 13\sqrt{7}$

Combine like terms.

$$3\sqrt{7} + 5\sqrt{2} + 13\sqrt{7} = (3\sqrt{7} + 13\sqrt{7}) + 5\sqrt{2}$$
$$= 16\sqrt{7} + 5\sqrt{2}$$

When multiplying or dividing roots, multiply or divide the coefficients and radicands separately.

Simplify $\dfrac{8\sqrt{6}}{2\sqrt{2}}$

Just follow the rule above.

$$\frac{8\sqrt{6}}{2\sqrt{2}} = \frac{8}{2}\sqrt{\frac{6}{2}} = 4\sqrt{3}$$

Simplify $5\sqrt{3x} \times 2\sqrt{5x^2}$

Just follow the rule above.

$$5\sqrt{3x} \times 2\sqrt{5x^2} = (5 \times 2)\sqrt{3x \times 5x^2} = 10\sqrt{15x^3}$$

You can also use the commutative and associative laws when simplifying expressions with radicals.

Simplify $\left(2\sqrt{5}\right)^3$

Just expand and re-group

$$\left(2\sqrt{5}\right)^3 = 2\sqrt{5} \times 2\sqrt{5} \times 2\sqrt{5}$$
$$= (2 \times 2 \times 2)(\sqrt{5} \times \sqrt{5}) \times \sqrt{5}$$
$$= 8 \times 5 \times \sqrt{5} = 40\sqrt{5}$$

Worksheet 4:
Working with Roots

1. List the first 10 perfect square integers greater than 1. _____

2. When are two radicals "like" terms?

3. An exponential is a perfect square only if its coefficient is _____ and its exponent is _____.

Simplify the following expressions, if possible.

4. $6\sqrt{5} - 3\sqrt{5} =$

5. $8\sqrt{3} + 4\sqrt{2} - 5\sqrt{3} =$

6. $\sqrt{32} + \sqrt{8} =$

7. $(x\sqrt{7})(x\sqrt{7}) =$

8. $\sqrt{8} + \sqrt{27} =$

9. $(\sqrt{3})(\sqrt{12}) =$

10. $\sqrt{81x^2} =$

11. $\sqrt{x^4 y^3 z^5} =$

12. $((5\sqrt{x})(4\sqrt{x})) - 10x =$

13. If $\frac{1}{4}x < \sqrt{x} < x$, what is one possible value of x?

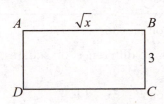

14.

$$A \quad \overset{\sqrt{x}}{} \quad B$$

In the figure above, what is the length of diagonal AC of rectangle $ABCD$?

(A) $9 + x$
(B) $3 + \sqrt{x}$
(C) $9 - x$
(D) $\sqrt{9 + x}$
(E) $9 + \sqrt{x}$

15. If $x^2 - 4 = 21$ and $y^2 + 7 = 43$, what is the smallest possible value of $x - y$?

(A) -11
(B) -10
(C) 0
(D) 10
(E) 11

16. The area of circle A is 16 times the area of circle B. What is the ratio of the circumference of circle A to the circumference of circle B?

(A) 2:1
(B) $2\sqrt{2}$:1
(C) 4:1
(D) $4\sqrt{2}$:1
(E) 8:1

17. If $x^2 = 16$, $y^2 = 4$, and $(x + 4)(y - 2) \neq 0$, then $x^3 + y^5 =$

(A) -96
(B) -32
(C) 32
(D) 64
(E) 96

18. If a and b are both positive and $\frac{4\sqrt{a} + 2\sqrt{b}}{6} = 7\sqrt{b}$, what is the value of a in terms of b?

(A) $10\sqrt{b}$
(B) $40\sqrt{b}$
(C) $10b$
(D) $100b$
(E) $500b$

Lesson 5: Factoring

Factoring

To *factor* means to write as a product. All of the terms in a product are called *factors* of the product.

> There are many ways to factor 12: 12×1, 6×2, 3×4, or $2 \times 2 \times 3$.
> Therefore, 1, 2, 3, 4, 6, and 12 are the factors of 12.

Know how to factor a number into prime factors, and how to use those factors to find the greatest common factors and least common multiples.

> Two bells, A and B, ring simultaneously. Then bell A rings once every 168 seconds, and bell B rings every 360 seconds. What is the minimum number of seconds between simultaneous rings?

This question is asking for the least common multiple of 168 and 360. The prime factorization of 168 is $2 \times 2 \times 2 \times 3 \times 7$ and the prime factorization of 360 is $2 \times 2 \times 2 \times 3 \times 3 \times 5$. A common multiple must have all of the factors that each of these numbers has, and the smallest of these is $2 \times 2 \times 2 \times 3 \times 3 \times 5 \times 7 = 2{,}520$. So they ring together every 2,520 seconds.

Know how to multiply polynomials by the law of distribution (and FOILing), and use these to check your factoring of polynomials.

> The law of FOIL:
>
> $\overset{F\quad L}{a + b)(c + d)}$
> $\underset{O}{\quad I \quad}$
>
> $= (a)(c + d) + (b)(c + d)$ (distribution)
> $= ac \;+ ad \quad\; + bc \quad\; + bd$ (distribution)
> First + Outside + Inside + Last

> Factor $3x^2 - 18x$.
> Common factor is $3x : 3x^2 - 18x = 3x(x - 6)$ (check by distributing)

> Factor $z^2 + 5z - 6$.
> $z^2 + 5z - 6 = (z - 1)(z + 6)$ (check by FOILing)

Factoring Formulas

To factor polynomials, it often helps to know some common factoring formulas:

> Difference of squares: $x^2 - b^2 = (x + b)(x - b)$
> Perfect square
> trinomials: $x^2 + 2xb + b^2 = (x + b)(x + b)$
> $x^2 - 2xb + b^2 = (x - b)(x - b)$
> Simple
> trinomials: $x^2 + (a + b)x + ab = (x + a)(x + b)$

> Factor $x^2 - 36$

This is a "difference of squares," so $x^2 - 36 = (x - 6)(x + 6)$.

> Factor $x^2 - 5x - 14$

This is a simple trinomial. Look for two numbers that have a sum of -5 and a product of -14. With a little guessing and checking, you'll see that -7 and 2 work. So $x^2 - 5x - 14 = (x - 7)(x + 2)$.

The Zero Product Property

Factoring is a great tool for solving equations if it's used with the **zero product property**, which says that if the product of a set of numbers is 0, then at least one of the numbers in the set must be 0.

> Solve $x^2 - 5x - 14 = 0$
> Factor: $(x - 7)(x + 2) = 0$. Since their product is 0, either $x - 7 = 0$ or $x + 2 = 0$, so $x = 7$ or 2.

The *only* product property is the *zero* product property. Don't assume that any factor always equals the product.

> $(x - 1)(x + 2) = 1$ does not imply that $x - 1 = 1$. This would mean that $x = 2$, which clearly doesn't work!

Worksheet 5: Factoring

1. What does it mean to factor a number or expression?

2. Write the four basic factoring formulas for quadratics.

3. What is the zero product property?

4. Write the prime factorization of 180.

5. Find the least common multiple of $36ab^2$ and $48a^2b$.

Factor and check by FOILing:

6. $x^2 + 6x + 8$ _____

7. $12x^2 + 7x - 10$ _____

8. $1 - 25a^2$ _____

FOIL:

9. $(3 + \sqrt{b})(3 - \sqrt{b})$ _____

10. $\left(\dfrac{y}{2} + \dfrac{1}{4}\right)\left(\dfrac{y}{4} + \dfrac{1}{3}\right)$ _____

11. $(4x + 3\sqrt{5})^2$ _____

12. If for all real values of x,
$(x + b)(x + 4) = x^2 + 8x + 4b$,
then $b =$

13. If $(a + b)^2 = 64$ and $a^2 + b^2 = 40$, what is the value of $4ab$?

(A) 12
(B) 24
(C) 36
(D) 48
(E) 50

14. If $r = 2s$ and $s \neq 4$, then $\dfrac{r^2 - 64}{(r - 8)^2} =$

(A) 1

(B) $\dfrac{s + 4}{s - 4}$

(C) $\dfrac{2s + 4}{2s - 4}$

(D) $\dfrac{s + 2}{s}$

(E) $\dfrac{s^2 - 32}{s + 8}$

15. If $a > 0$ and $16x^2 + bx + 9 = (4x + a)^2$ for all values of x, what is the value of b?

(A) 3
(B) 8
(C) 16
(D) 24
(E) 72

16. If $(x - 2)(x + 4) = (x - 4)(x + 7)$, then $x =$

(A) 14
(B) 17
(C) 20
(D) 24
(E) 27

17. If $g^2 - h^2 = 40$ and $g + h = 10$, what is the value of $g - h$?

Lesson 6: Inequalities, Absolute Values, and Plugging In

Inequalities as Unbalanced Scales

Inequalities are just unbalanced scales. Nearly all of the laws of equality pertain to inequalities, with one exception. **When solving inequalities, keep the direction of the inequality (remember that "the alligator < always eats the bigger number") unless you divide or multiply by a negative, in which case you "switch" the inequality.**

Solve $x^2 > 6x$ for x.

You might be tempted to divide both sides by x and get $x > 6$, but this incorrectly assumes that x is positive. If x is positive, then $x > 6$; but if x is negative, then $x < 6$. (Switch the inequality when you divide by a negative!) But of course any negative number is less than 6, so the solution is either $x > 6$ or $x < 0$. (Plug in numbers to verify.)

Absolute Values as Distances

The absolute value of x, written as $|x|$, means the distance from x to 0 on the number line. Since distances are never negative, neither are absolute values. For instance, since -4 is four units away from 0, we say $|-4| = 4$.

The distance between numbers is found from their difference. For instance, the distance between 5 and -2 on the number line is $5 - (-2) = 7$. But differences can be negative, and distances can't! That's where absolute values come in. **Mathematically, the distance between a and b is $|a - b|$.**

Graph the solution of $|x + 2| \geq 3$.

You can think about this in two ways. First, think about distances. $|x + 2|$ is the same as $|x - (-2)|$, which is the distance between x and -2. So if this distance must be greater than or equal to 3, you can just visualize those numbers that are at least 3 units away from -2:

Or you can do it more "algebraically" if you prefer. The only numbers that have an absolute value greater than or equal to 3 are numbers greater than or equal to 3 or less than or equal to -3, right? Therefore, saying $|x + 2| \geq 3$ is the same as saying $x + 2 \geq 3$ or $x + 2 \leq -3$. Subtracting 2 from both sides of both inequalities gives $x \geq 1$ or $x \leq -5$, which confirms the answer by the other method.

Plugging In

After solving any equation or inequality, plug in your solution to confirm that it works. Plugging in values can also help you to simplify multiple-choice problems that ask you to find an expression with variables rather than a numerical solution. If a multiple-choice question has choices containing unknowns, you can often simplify the problem by just plugging in values for the unknowns. But *think* first. Plugging in is not always the simplest method.

If $y = r - 6$ and $z = r + 5$, which of the following expresses r in terms of y and z?

(A) $y + z - 1$

(B) $y + z$

(C) $y + z + 1$

(D) $\dfrac{y + z - 1}{2}$

(E) $\dfrac{y + z + 1}{2}$

If you pick r to be 6 (It can be whatever you want, so pick an easy number!) then y is $6 - 6 = 0$ and z is $6 + 5 = 11$. The question is asking for an expression for r, so look for 6 among the choices. Plugging in your values gives (A) 10, (B) 11, (C) 12, (D) 5, and (E) 6. Always evaluate all of the choices, because you must work by process of elimination. Only (E) gives 6, so it must be the right answer!

Worksheet 6:
Inequalities, Absolute Values,
and Plugging In

Express each of the following statements as equations or inequalities using absolute values:

1. The distance from x to 4 is greater than 6. _____

2. The distance from w to 7 is equal to the distance from v to -4. _____

3. The distance from x to y is no more than three times the distance from x to z. _____

Graph the solution to each of the following inequalities on the given number line. Check your answer by testing points.

4. $|x - 2| > 5$

$\longleftrightarrow$

5. $w^2 \leq 9$

$\longleftrightarrow$

6. $x + 4 < x - 2$

$\longleftrightarrow$

7. $-5y > 20$

$\longleftrightarrow$

8. $12y \leq 3y^3$

$\longleftrightarrow$

9. $6 - x^2 < 2$

$\longleftrightarrow$

10. Which of the following is equivalent to the statement $|x - 6| < 4$?

   (A) $x < 10$
   (B) $2 < x < 10$
   (C) $x < -2$ or $x > 10$
   (D) $-2 < x$
   (E) $-10 < x < 2$

11. If $6 - 3y < 18$, then all of the following are possible values of y EXCEPT

   (A) -4
   (B) -3
   (C) -2
   (D) -1
   (E) 0

12. If $2|x + 5| = 10$ and $4|3 - y| = 16$, then $x + y$ could equal each of the following EXCEPT

   (A) -11
   (B) -3
   (C) -1
   (D) 3
   (E) 7

13. If $w = 4x + 2$ and $z = 7x - 6$, which of the following expresses x in terms of w and z?

   (A) $\dfrac{w + z - 4}{11}$
   (B) $\dfrac{w + z + 4}{11}$
   (C) $w + z + \dfrac{4}{3}$
   (D) $\dfrac{w + z - 4}{3}$
   (E) $\dfrac{w + z + 4}{3}$

14. If x, y, and z are distinct positive integers greater than 1 and if $xy = 27$ and $yz = 33$, then which of the following must be true?

   (A) $z > x > y$
   (B) $y > z > x$
   (C) $y > x > z$
   (D) $x > z > y$
   (E) $z > y > x$

15. How many integer pairs (x, y) satisfy the statements $0 < x + y < 50$ and $\dfrac{x}{y} = 8$?

Lesson 7: Word Problems

A Word about Word Problems

Don't be afraid of word problems. They are no harder than any other kind of PSAT problems, as long as you know how to translate them. Even long word problems are often very simple. Sometimes they are wordy because they have lots of information to help you simplify the problem!

Algebraic Word Problems

Word problems are written problems that can be translated into algebraic equations or systems. Use the basic reasoning skills, MAPS-CATCH, to solve them.

MAP the problem: Read the entire problem carefully and think about the situation before you decide how to start. Try to "see" the whole problem situation in your mind. Understand what every quantity means. Note carefully what the question is asking you to find.

ANALYZE the problem: Look at the parts of the problem, especially the unknowns. Give each unknown a convenient name, like x, n, or some other letter.

Find the **PATTERNS** in the problem: Think carefully about the relationships among the quantities. Write an equation or inequality from each important statement in the problem. *Remember*: if you have one unknown, one equation will do, but if you have two unknowns, you need two equations. The following translation key can help you to set up the equation.

percent	means	$\div 100$
of	means	*times*
what	means	x
is	means	$=$
per	means	$\div$
y less than x	means	$x - y$
decreased by	means	$-$
is at least	means	$\geq$
is no greater than	means	$\leq$

SIMPLIFY the problem: Don't introduce any more unknowns than are necessary.

CONNECT to your algebra skills: Solve the equation or the inequality with the laws we discussed in earlier lessons.

Consider **ALTERNATIVES**: Remember that you often have choices in solving equations or systems: consider your options and choose wisely.

THINK LOGICALLY: Sometimes you can guess and check a solution without doing all the algebra!

CHECK your answer: Read the problem again to check that your solution "works" in the problem. Remember that the solution to the equation is not necessarily the answer to the question! Read the problem carefully to make sure that you've found exactly what it's asking for.

> Ellen is twice as old as Julia. Five years ago, Ellen was three times as old as Julia. How old is Julia now? (Try this one before checking the explanation below.)

Let's say this is a grid-in question, so we can't just test the choices. Guessing and checking might work, but algebra might be more reliable. First think about the unknowns. The one we really care about is Julia's current age, so let's call that J. Ellen's current age is also unknown, so let's call that E. Now interpret the statements: *Ellen is twice as old as Julia* is easy to translate: $E = 2J$. But two unknowns require two equations, so interpret the next statement: *Five years ago, Ellen was three times as old as Julia*. Be careful: five years ago, Ellen was $E - 5$ years old, and Julia was $J - 5$. So the statement translates into $E - 5 = 3(J - 5)$. Now it's a system, and you know what to do:

	$E - 5$	$= 3(J - 5)$
Distribute:	$E - 5$	$= 3J - 15$
Add 5:	E	$= 3J - 10$
Substitute with $E = 2J$:	$2J$	$= 3J - 10$
Subtract $2J$:	0	$= J - 10$
Add 10:	10	$= J$

Now reread the problem and make sure the answer makes sense. If Julia is 10, Ellen must be 20 because she's twice as old. Five years ago, then they were 5 and 15, and 15 is three times 5! It works!

Worksheet 7: Word Problems

For each of the following statements, specify and name the unknowns and translate the statement into an equation.

1. Julia has an IQ that is four more than twice Dave's IQ.

2. After $\frac{1}{4}$ of the guests left a cocktail party, 3 more than $\frac{2}{3}$ of the guests remained.

3. In a bowl, there are 7 more than three times as many blue M&Ms as yellow M&Ms.

4. After Eric gave Matilda 5 apples, he had four more than twice as many as Matilda originally had.

Solve the following word problems.

5. If the average of a and b is twice the average of m and n, what is b in terms of a, m, and n?

6. Dumbbell A weighs 15 pounds more than dumbbell B, and dumbbell B weighs 25 pounds more than dumbbell C. If dumbbell A and dumbbell C together weigh 100 pounds, what is the weight of dumbbell B?

7. When the positive number p is multiplied by 6, the result is the same as when $2p$ is subtracted from the square of p. What is the value of p?

8. Two years ago, Jennie was twice as old as her sister is now. If Jennie is 10 years older than her sister, how old is Jennie now?

(A) 14
(B) 16
(C) 18
(D) 20
(E) 22

9. Over the past four seasons, the Vikings football team has won three times as many games as it has lost. If, in that time span, the team played a total of 64 games, and no games ended in a tie, how many games did the Vikings win?

(A) 40
(B) 42
(C) 44
(D) 46
(E) 48

10. Each month, a car salesperson is paid $2,800 plus 5% commission on her sales for the month. If she made $6,000 in January, what was the value of her sales for that month?

(A) $6,400
(B) $10,000
(C) $32,000
(D) $64,000
(E) $80,000

11. Nortown High School has 3,000 students enrolled, and 40% of the students take the bus to school each day. Of the students who do not take the bus to school, 30% live close enough to walk. The rest of the students drive themselves to school each day. How many more students drive to school each day than take the bus?

(A) 30
(B) 60
(C) 140
(D) 600
(E) 720

12. During a holiday sale, one CD costs c dollars. Each additional CD purchased at the same time costs d dollars less than the first one. Which of the following represents the cost, in dollars, of x CDs bought during this sale, if x is an integer greater than 1?

(A) $cx + dx$
(B) $c + (x - 1)(c - d)$
(C) $c + x(c - d)$
(D) cx
(E) $cx - x(c - d)$

Detailed Answer Key: Essential Algebra I Skills

Worksheet 1

1. The laws of equality say that whatever you do to one side of an equation you must do to the other side, to maintain the balance.

2. **−3**

$$5x - 12 = 10x + 3$$

Add 12: $5x = 10x + 15$
Subtract $10x$: $-5x = 15$
Divide by -5: $x = -3$

3. **0**

$$\frac{4y^2}{6} = 2y^2$$

Multiply by 6: $4y^2 = 12y^2$
Divide by 4: $y^2 = 3^2$
Subtract y^2: $0 = 2y^2$
Divide by 2: $0 = y^2$
Take square root: $0 = y$

4. **2 or 8**

$$(5 - x)^2 = 9$$

Take square root: $5 - x = \pm 3$
            $5 - x = 3$ or $5 - x = -3$
Subtract 5: $-x = -2$ or $-x = -8$
Divide by -1: $x = 2$ or $x = 8$

5. **11/7**

$$\frac{3 - x}{4} = \frac{x + 2}{10}$$

Cross-multiply: $10(3 - x) = 4(x + 2)$
Distribute: $30 - 10x = 4x + 8$
Add $10x$: $30 = 14x + 8$
Subtract 8: $22 = 14x$
Divide by 14: $22/14 = x = 11/7$

6. **10/3**   Divide both sides of the equation by 6 to get $4x + 2y = 20/6 = 10/3$.

7. **5**   Multiply both sides of the equation by 20 to get $12y + \frac{40}{3}x = 5$.

8. **40**

$$4x - 8 = 24$$

Add 8: $4x = 32$
Add 8: $4x + 8 = 40$

9. **B**

$$x - 8 = 5x$$

Subtract x: $-8 = 4x$
Divide by 4: $-2 = x$

10. **A**

FOIL both sides: $(x^2 + 14x + 49) = (x^2 - 8x + 16)$
Subtract x^2: $14x + 49 = -8x + 16$
Add $8x$: $22x + 49 = 16$
Subtract 49: $22x = -33$
Divide by 22: $x = -1.5$

11. **24**

$$\frac{a}{a + 4} = \frac{6}{7}$$

Cross-multiply: $7a = 6(a + 4)$
Distribute: $7a = 6a + 24$
Subtract $6a$: $a = 24$

12. **E**

$$40 - \sqrt{x} = 15$$

Subtract 40: $-\sqrt{x} = -25$
Divide by -1: $\sqrt{x} = 25$
Square both sides: $x = 625$

13. **C**
$$m = 3(n + 2) + p$$
Distribute: $m = 3n + 6 + p$
Subtract $(6 + p)$ $m - 6 - p = 3n$
Divide by 3:

$$\frac{m - 6 - p}{3} = \frac{m - p}{3} - \frac{6}{3} = \frac{m - p}{3} - 2$$

Worksheet 2

1. Any set of equations that are true at the same time.

2. Substitution and combination.

3. Plug the solutions back into the equations and check that both equations are true.

4.
$$5x + 7y = 31$$
Substitute $x + 1$ for y: $5x + 7(x + 1) = 31$
Distribute: $5x + 7x + 7 = 31$
Subtract 7: $12x = 24$
Divide by 12: $x = 2$
Substitute for x: $5(2) + 7y = 31$
Subtract 10: $7y = 21$
Divide by 7: $y = 3$

5.
$$4y - 3x = 26$$
Substitute $y - 7$ for x $4y - 3(y - 7) = 26$
Distribute: $4y - 3y + 21 = 26$
Subtract 21: $y = 5$
Substitute for y: $4(5) - 3x = 26$
Subtract 20: $-3x = 6$
Divide by -3: $x = -2$

6.
$$4n - 3m = 6$$
Substitute $1.5n$ for m: $\quad 4n - 3(1.5n) = 6$
Simplify: $\qquad\qquad\qquad 4n - 4.5n = 6$
Combine like terms: $\qquad\qquad -0.5n = 6$
Divide by -0.5: $\qquad\qquad\qquad n = -12$
Substitute for n, in
original equation:
$$4(-12) - 3m = 6$$
Add 45: $\qquad\qquad\qquad\qquad -3m = 54$
Divide by -3: $\qquad\qquad\qquad\quad m = -18$

7.
$$2a - 3b = 10$$
Add equations: $\quad\dfrac{4a + 3b = 14}{6a = 24}$
Divide by 6: $\qquad\qquad\qquad\qquad a = 4$
Substitute for a, solve for b: $\quad 4(4) + 3b = 14$
Subtract 16: $\qquad\qquad\qquad\qquad 3b = -2$
Divide by 3: $\qquad\qquad\qquad\qquad\quad b = -\dfrac{2}{3}$

8.
$$-5x + 7y = 16$$
Add equations: $\quad\dfrac{5x + 7y = 12}{14y = 28}$
Divide by 14: $\qquad\qquad\qquad\quad y = 2$
Substitute for y: $\quad 5x + 7(2) = 12$
Subtract 14: $\qquad\qquad\qquad\quad 5x = -2$
Divide by 5: $\qquad\qquad\qquad\qquad x = -\dfrac{2}{5}$

9.
$$3m - 5n = 12$$
Add equations: $\quad\dfrac{4m + 5n = 9}{7m = 21}$
Divide by 7: $\qquad\qquad\qquad\quad m = 3$
Substitute for m: $\quad 4(3) + 5n = 9$
Subtract 12: $\qquad\qquad\qquad\quad 5n = -3$
Divide by 5: $\qquad\qquad\qquad\qquad n = -\dfrac{3}{5}$

10. 3
$$5x + 3y = 33$$
Substitute $2x$ for y: $\quad 5x + 3(2x) = 33$
Distribute: $\qquad\qquad\qquad 5x + 6x = 33$
Combine like terms: $\qquad\quad 11x = 33$
Divide by 11: $\qquad\qquad\qquad\quad x = 3$

11. A
$$x + y = 8$$
Add equations: $\quad\dfrac{x - y = 12}{2x = 20}$
Divide by 2: $\qquad\qquad\qquad x = 10$
Substitute for x: $\quad 10 + y = 8$
Subtract 10: $\qquad\qquad\qquad y = -2$
Find product xy: $\quad xy = (10)(-2) = -20$

12. D
$$3a + 6b = 12$$
Add equations: $\quad\dfrac{4a - 7b = 16}{7a - b = 28}$

13. $\dfrac{1}{6}$
$$3a + 4b - 6c = 18$$
Add $6c$: $\qquad\quad 3a + 4b = 18 + 6c$

To simplify, $\dfrac{3 + c}{3a + 4b}$ substitute $18 + 6c$ for $3a + 4b$.

$$\dfrac{3 + c}{3a + 4b} = \dfrac{3 + c}{18 + 6c} = \dfrac{3 + c}{6(3 + c)} = \dfrac{1}{6}$$

14. B   Multiply the two fractions:

$$\dfrac{x}{3y} \times \dfrac{6y}{5z} = \dfrac{6xy}{15yz} = \dfrac{2x}{5z}$$

Substitute $\dfrac{5}{9}$ for $\dfrac{x}{3y}$ and $\dfrac{2}{7}$ for $\dfrac{6y}{5z}$

$$\dfrac{5}{9} \times \dfrac{2}{7} = \dfrac{10}{63} = \dfrac{2x}{5z}$$

Multiply both sides by 5/2: $\quad \left(\dfrac{5}{2}\right)\dfrac{10}{63} = \dfrac{2x}{5z}\left(\dfrac{5}{2}\right)$

Simplify: $\qquad\qquad\qquad \dfrac{50}{126} = \dfrac{x}{z} = \dfrac{25}{63}$

15. 5.50

Translate first
statement: $\qquad\qquad\qquad 2P + 1S = 14.50$
Subtract $2P$: $\qquad\qquad\qquad 1S = 14.50 - 2P$
Translate second
statement: $\qquad\qquad\qquad 1P + 2S = 12.50$
Substitute for S: $\quad 1P + 2(14.5 - 2P) = 12.50$
Distribute: $\qquad\qquad 1P + 29 - 4P = 12.50$
Combine like terms: $\quad -3P + 29 = 12.50$
Subtract 29: $\qquad\qquad\qquad -3P = -16.50$
Divide by -3: $\qquad\qquad\qquad P = 5.50$

Worksheet 3

1. Coefficient, base, and exponent
2. *Multiply* the coefficients, *keep* the bases, and *add* the exponents.
3. *Divide* the coefficients, *divide* the bases, and *keep* the exponents.
4. *Multiply* the coefficients, *multiply* the bases, and *keep* the exponents.
5. *Divide* the coefficients, *keep* the bases, and *subtract* the exponents.
6. *Raise* the coefficient (to the power), *keep* the base, and *multiply* the exponents.
7. $a^2b + 4a^2b = 5a^2b$

8. $4x^3 - 3x^3 + 5x^4 = x^3 + 5x^4$

9. $(5)^{3x}(4)^{3x} = 20^{3x}$

10. $\dfrac{8(24)^4}{2(24)^3} = 4(24)^1 = 96$

11. $(a^4 + b^3)^2 = (a^4 + b^3)(a^4 + b^3)$

$$a^8 + a^4b^3 + a^4b^3 + b^6$$

Combine like terms: $a^8 + 2a^4b^3 + b^6$

12.
Simplify: $[5w^3(5)^2]^2$
Simplify: $[5w^3(25)]^2$
Simplify: $(125w^3)^2$
            $15625w^6$

13. **I** $4^{3x} = 64$
Rewrite with common base: $4^{3x} = 4^3$
Set exponentials equal: $3x = 3$
Divide by 3: $x = 1$

14. **D**
                                    $x^3x^b = x^{12}$
Divide by x^3: $x^b = x^9$
Set exponentials equal: $b = 9$
                                  $(x^3)^c = x^{15}$
Simplify: $x^{3c} = x^{15}$
Equate exponents: $3c = 15$
Divide by 3: $c = 5$
                          $b \times c = 9 \times 5 = 45$

15. **E** $3^{3x} = 9^{2x-1}$
Rewrite in base 3: $3^{3x} = (3^2)^{2x-1}$
Simplify: $3^{3x} = 3^{4x-2}$
Equate exponents: $3x = 4x - 2$
Subtract $4x$: $-x = -2$
Divide by -1: $x = 2$

16. **D**
                          $\dfrac{(3^x)(3^x)}{(3^x)(3)} =$
Simplify: $\dfrac{3^{x+x}}{3^{x+1}} = \dfrac{3^{2x}}{3^{x+1}} = 3^{2x-(x+1)} = 3^{x-1}$

This problem could also be solved by first canceling the common factor, 3^x.

$\dfrac{(3^x)(3^x)}{(3^x)(3)} = \dfrac{(3^x)}{(3^1)} = 3^{x-1}$

17. **D** $4^r = (2^2)^r = 2^{2r}$.
$$2^{2r} + 2^{2r} = 2(2^{2r}) = 2^1(2^{2r}) = 2^{2r+1}$$

18. **32**   Since x is raised to the third power, if x is
doubled, t is multiplied by 8 ($2 \times 2 \times 2$). Since y
is squared, if y is tripled, then t is multiplied by
9 (3×3). Since z is squared, if z is halved, then

t is multiplied by 1/4 ($1/2 \times 1/2$). Since w is
raised to the third power, if w is tripled, t is
divided by 27 ($3 \times 3 \times 3$). The total effect on t is
the product of $48 \times 8 \times 9 \times 1/4 \div 27 = 32$

Worksheet 4

1. 4, 9, 16, 25, 36, 49, 64, 81, 100, 121

2. They are "like" if their radicands (what's inside
the radical) are the same.

3. An exponential is a perfect square only if its coefficient is a *perfect square* and its exponent is *even*.

4. $6\sqrt{5} - 3\sqrt{5} = 3\sqrt{5}$

5. $8\sqrt{3} - 5\sqrt{3} + 4\sqrt{2} = 3\sqrt{3} + 4\sqrt{2}$

6. $\sqrt{32} + \sqrt{8} = 4\sqrt{2} + 2\sqrt{2} = 6\sqrt{2}$

7. $(x\sqrt{7})(x\sqrt{7}) = 7x^2$

8. $\sqrt{8} + \sqrt{27} = 2\sqrt{2} + 3\sqrt{3}$

9. $(\sqrt{3})(\sqrt{12}) = \sqrt{36} = 6$

10. $\sqrt{81x^2} = 9x$

11. $\sqrt{x^4y^3z^5} = x^2yz^2\sqrt{yz}$

12. $((5\sqrt{x})(4\sqrt{x})) - 10x = 20x - 10x = 10x$

13. **I $< x < 16$** $\sqrt{x} < x$ for all values of $x > 1$

$$\sqrt{x} > \frac{1}{4}x \text{ for } 0 < x < 16$$

14. **D**   The length of the diagonal can be found by
using the Pythagorean theorem. $(\sqrt{x})^2 + 3^2 = d^2$
    Simplify: $x + 9 = d^2$
    Take the square root: $\sqrt{9+x} = d$

15. **A** $x^2 - 4 = 21$
    Add 4: $x^2 = 25$
    Take the square root: $x = 5$ or -5
                                    $y^2 + 7 = 43$
    Subtract 7: $y^2 = 36$
    Take the square root: $y = 6$ or -6

To get the smallest possible difference, take the
largest y and subtract it from the smallest x:
$-5 - 6 = -11$.

16. **C**   The ratio of areas $\pi r_a^2 : \pi r_b^2 = 16:1$.
                    Therefore, $r_a^2 : r_b^2 = 16:1$
    Take the square root: $r_a : r_b = 4:1$

The ratio of the circumferences of two circles is
equal to the ratio of the radii of those two
circles. For this problem, that ratio is 4:1.

17. **C**   If $x^2 = 16$, then x can be 4 or -4.
If $y^2 = 4$, then y can be 2 or -2.

Since $(x+4)(y-2) \neq 0$, we know that x cannot
be -4 and y cannot be 2. This means that $x = 4$
and $y = -2$.
                                          $x^3 + y^5 =$
Substitute for x and y: $(4)^3 + (-2)^5 =$
Simplify: $64 + -32 = 32$

18. D

$$\frac{4\sqrt{a} + 2\sqrt{b}}{6} = 7\sqrt{b}$$

Multiply by 6: $\quad 4\sqrt{a} + 2\sqrt{b} = 42\sqrt{b}$
Subtract $2\sqrt{b}$: $\qquad\quad 4\sqrt{a} = 40\sqrt{b}$
Divide by 4: $\qquad\qquad \sqrt{a} = 10\sqrt{b}$
Square both sides: $\qquad\quad a = 100b$

Worksheet 5

1. To write it as a product (result of multiplication).
2.

$$x^2 - b^2 = (x + b)(x - b)$$
$$x^2 + 2xb + b^2 = (x + b)(x + b)$$
$$x^2 - 2xb + b^2 = (x - b)(x - b)$$
$$x^2 + (a + b)x + ab = (x + a)(x + b)$$

3. If the product of a set of numbers is 0, then at least one of the numbers must be 0.

4. $180 = (2)(2)(3)(3)(5)$

5. $36ab^2 = (2)(2)(3)(3)(a)(b)(b)$ and $48a^2b = (2)(2)(2)(2)(3)(a)(a)(b)$, so the least common multiple is $(2)(2)(2)(2)(3)(3)(a)(a)(b)(b) = 144a^2b^2$

6. $x^2 + 6x + 8 = (x + 2)(x + 4)$

7. $12x^2 + 7x - 10 = (4x + 5)(3x - 2)$

8. $1 - 25a^2 = (1 - 5a)(1 + 5a)$

9. $(3 + \sqrt{b})(3 - \sqrt{b}) = 9 - 3\sqrt{b} + 3\sqrt{b} - b = 9 - b$

10. $\left(\dfrac{y}{2} + \dfrac{1}{4}\right)\left(\dfrac{y}{4} + \dfrac{1}{3}\right) = \dfrac{y^2}{8} + \dfrac{y}{6} + \dfrac{y}{16} + \dfrac{1}{12}$

Find common denominator: $\dfrac{6y^2}{48} + \dfrac{8y}{48} + \dfrac{3y}{48} + \dfrac{4}{48}$

Combine like terms: $\dfrac{6y^2 + 11y + 4}{48}$

11. $(4x + 3\sqrt{5})(4x + 3\sqrt{5}) = 16x^2 + 24x\sqrt{5} + 45$

12. 4

$$(x + b)(x + 4) = x^2 + 8x + 4b$$

FOIL: $\quad x^2 + 4x + bx + 4b = x^2 + 8x + 4b$
Subtract x^2: $\qquad 4x + bx + 4b = 8x + 4b$
Subtract $4b$: $\qquad\quad 4x + bx = 8x$
Factor out x: $\qquad\quad x(4 + b) = 8x$
Divide by x: $\qquad\qquad 4 + b = 8$
Subtract 4: $\qquad\qquad\quad b = 4$

13. D

$$(a + b)^2 = 64$$

FOIL: $\quad a^2 + 2ab + b^2 = 64$
$\qquad\qquad\qquad a^2 + b^2 = 40$
Substitute 40: $\qquad 2ab + 40 = 64$
Subtract 40: $\qquad\qquad 2ab = 24$
Multiply by 2: $\qquad\qquad 4ab = 48$

14. B

$$\frac{r^2 - 64}{(r - 8)^2}$$

Factor: $\qquad\qquad\qquad\dfrac{(r - 8)(r + 8)}{(r - 8)(r - 8)}$

Cancel common factors: $\dfrac{(r + 8)}{(r - 8)}$

Substitute for r: $\qquad\dfrac{(2s + 8)}{(2s - 8)} = \dfrac{2(s + 4)}{2(s - 4)}$

$$= \frac{s + 4}{s - 4}$$

15. D

$$16x^2 + bx + 9 = (4x + a)^2$$

FOIL: $\qquad 16x^2 + bx + 9 = 16x^2 + 8ax + a^2$
Subtract $16x^2$ $\qquad\qquad bx + 9 = 8ax + a^2$

This must be true for all values fo x, such as 0. If $x = 0$, then the equation becomes $9 = a^2$. Take the square root and $a = 3$.

Substitute for a: $\quad bx = 8(3)x = 24x$
Divide by x: $\qquad\qquad b = 24$

16. C

$$(x - 2)(x + 4) = (x - 4)(x + 7)$$

FOIL: $\quad x^2 - 2x + 4x - 8 = x^2 + 7x - 4x - 28$
Combine like terms: $x^2 + 2x - 8 = x^2 + 3x - 28$
Subtract x^2: $\qquad\qquad 2x - 8 = 3x - 28$
Add 28: $\qquad\qquad\quad 2x + 20 = 3x$
Subtract $2x$: $\qquad\qquad\quad 20 = x$

17. 4

$$g^2 - h^2 = (g - h)(g + h)$$

Substitute: $\qquad 40 = (g - h)(10)$
Divide by 10: $\qquad 4 = (g - h)$

Worksheet 6

1. $|x - 4| > 6$
2. $|w - 7| = |v + 4|$
3. $|x - y| \le 3|x - z|$
4.

$$|x - 2| > 5$$

Translate without absolute value:

$$x - 2 > 5 \quad \text{or} \quad x - 2 < -5$$
Add 2: $\qquad\quad x > 7 \quad \text{or} \quad x < -3$

5.

$$w^2 \le 9$$

Take square root: $\qquad |w| \le 3$
Translate without absolute value:

$$w \le 3 \quad \text{or} \quad w \ge -3$$

6.
$$x + 4 < x - 2$$
Subtract x: $4 < -2$

This is impossible! There is no solution.

7.
$$-5y > 20$$
Divide by -5: $y < -4$

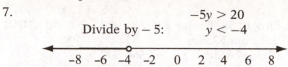

8.
$$12y \le 3y^3$$
Divide by 3: $4y \le y^3$
Subtract y^3: $4y - y^3 \le 0$
Factor out y: $y(4 - y^2) \le 0$
Factor binomial: $y(2 - y)(2 + y) \le 0$

Notice that the expression on the left equals 0 when y equals 0, 2 or -2. It is negative when y is between -2 and 0 or when y is greater than 2. Therefore the solution is $-2 \le y \le 0$ or $y \ge 2$.

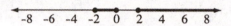

9.
$$6 - x^2 < 2$$
Subtract 6: $-x^2 < -4$
Divide by -1: $x^2 > 4$
Take square root: $|x| > 2$
Translate without absolute value:

$$x > 2 \quad \text{or} \quad x < -2$$

10. **B**
$$|x - 6| < 4$$
Translate without absolute value: $-4 < x - 6 < 4$
Add 6: $2 < x < 10$

11. **A**
$$6 - 3y < 18$$
Subtract 6: $-3y < 12$
Divide by -3: $y > -4$

12. **D**
$$2|x + 5| = 10$$
Divide by 2: $|x + 5| = 5$
Translate without absolute value $x + 5 = 5$ or $x + 5 = -5$
Subtract 5: $x = 0$ or $x = -10$
$$4|3 - y| = 16$$
Divide by 4: $|3 - y| = 4$
Translate without absolute value: $3 - y = 4$ or $3 - y = -4$
Subtract 3: $-y = 1$ or $-y = -7$
Divide by -1: $y = -1$ or $y = 7$

(A) $x = -10, y = -1$ $-10 + -1 = -11$
(B) $x = -10, y = 7$ $-10 + 7 = -3$
(C) $x = 0, y = -1$ $0 + -1 = -1$
(D) cannot be done
(E) $x = 0, y = 7$ $0 + 7 = 7$

13. **B**   One way to solve this is to plug in a simple value for x, like 4. Then $w = 4(4) + 2 = 18$ and $z = 7(4) - 6 = 22$. The question asks for an expression that equals x, so look for 4 in the choices when you plug in $w = 18$ and $z = 22$. The only choice that gives you 4 is (B).

14. **A**   If $xy = 27$ and both x and y are integers, then y must be either 1, 3, 9, or 27. If $yz = 33$, however, then y must be a factor of 33, so it must be 3. Therefore $x = 27/3 = 9$, and $z = 33/3 = 11$, so $y < x < z$.

15. **5**

From the given information: $x/y = 8$
Multiply by y: $x = 8y$
$$0 < x + y < 50$$
Substitute for x: $0 < 8y + y < 50$
Combine like terms: $0 < 9y < 50$
Divide by 9: $0 < y < 5\frac{5}{9}$

Since y must be an integer, y can be 1, 2, 3, 4, or 5.

Worksheet 7

1. j = Julia's IQ, d = Dave's IQ $j = 4 + 2d$
2. g = total number of guests $g - \frac{1}{4}g = \frac{2}{3}g + 3$
3. b = blue, y = yellow $b = 3y + 7$
4. e = the number of apples Eric had originally m = the number of apples Matilda had originally $e - 5 = 2m + 4$

5. $b = 2m + 2n - a$
$$\frac{a + b}{2} = 2\left(\frac{m + n}{2}\right)$$

Simplify: $\dfrac{a + b}{2} = m + n$
Multiply by 2: $a + b = 2(m + n)$
Distribute: $a + b = 2m + 2n$
Subtract a: $b = 2m + 2n - a$

6. **55**   Dumbbells A and C together weigh 100 pounds.
$$A + C = 100$$

Dumbbell A weighs 15 more pounds than B.
$$A = B + 15$$

Dumbbell B weighs 25 more pounds than C

$$B = C + 25$$

Substitute $C + 25$ for B: $A = (C + 25) + 15$
Simplify: $A = C + 40$
                                 $A + C = 100$
Substitute $C + 40$
  for A: $(C + 40) + C = 100$
Simplify: $2C + 40 = 100$
Subtract 40: $2C = 60$
Divide by 2: $C = 30$
Solve for B: $B = C + 25 = 30$
                                 $+25 = 55$

7. **8**   Write an equation: $6p = p^2 - 2p$
            Add $2p$: $8p = p^2$
            Divide by p: $8 = p$

8. **C** $J =$ Jennie's current age $S =$ sister's current age If Jennie is 10 years older than her sister, then

$$J = 10 + S$$
Subtract 10: $J - 10 = S$

If two years ago Jennie was twice as old as her sister is now, then

$$J - 2 = 2S$$
Substitute $J - 10$ for S: $J - 2 = 2(J - 10)$
Distribute: $J - 2 = 2J - 20$
Add 20: $J + 18 = 2J$
Subtract J: $18 = J$

9. **E**
$W =$ number of wins
$L =$ number of losses

$$W = 3L$$
$$W + L = 64$$
Substitute $3L$ for W: $3L + L = 64$
Combine like terms: $4L = 64$
Divide by 4: $L = 16$
Substitute 16 for L: $W + 16 = 64$
Subtract 16: $W = 48$

10. **D** $E =$ monthly earnings for salesperson in dollars
   $S =$ monthly sales for salesperson in dollars

$$E = \$2,800 + .05S$$
Plug in \$6,000 for E: $\$6,000 = \$2,800 + .05S$
Subtract \$2,800: $\$3,200 = .05S$
Divide by .05: $\$64,000 = S$

11. **B**   First find out how many students take the bus each day. 40% of 3,000: $3,000(0.40) = 1,200$ students take the bus each day.

Second, find out how many students do *not* take the bus.

$$3,000 - 1,200 = 1,800.$$

Of the students who do not, 30% walk, so $1,800(0.30) = 540$ students walk.

Of the students who do not, $1,800 - 540 = 1,260$ drive.

Therefore, $1,260 - 1,200 = 60$ more students drive than take the bus.

12. **B**   This problem can be solved by making a chart. If you bought 1 CD ($x = 1$), the price would be c dollars. If you bought 2 CDs ($x = 2$), the price would be c for the first CD and $(c - d)$ for the second CD or $c + (c - d)$. If you bought 3 CDs, ($x = 3$), the price would be c dollars for the first CD and $(c - d)$ for the second and third CDs. The total price of 3 CDs would thus be $c + 2(c - d)$. The sale price $(c - d)$ is always multiplied by one less than the total number of CDs purchased, which is why the correct answer is $c + (x - 1)(c - d)$.

#CDs bought (x)	price
1	c
2	$c + (c - d)$
3	$c + 2(c - d)$
4	$c + 3(c - d)$
x	$c + (x - 1)(c - d)$

CHAPTER 10

SPECIAL MATH PROBLEMS

Lesson 1: New Symbol or Term Problems

New Symbol or Term Problems

Don't be intimidated by PSAT questions with strange symbols or new terms that you haven't seen before. You're not supposed to have seen the symbol or term before. The PSAT folks just made it up for that problem! Just read the definition of the new symbol or term carefully, and use it to "translate" the expressions with the new symbol or term.

> Let the "kernel" of a number be defined as the square of its greatest prime factor. For instance, the kernel of 18 is 9, because the greatest prime factor of 18 is 3 (prime factorization: $18 = 2 \times 3 \times 3$), and 3^2 equals 9.

What is the kernel of 39?

> Don't worry about the fact that you haven't heard of a "kernel" before. Just read the definition carefully. By the definition, the kernel of 39 is the square of its greatest prime factor. So just find the greatest prime factor and square it. First, factor 39 into 3×13, so it's greatest prime factor is 13, and $13^2 = 169$.

What is the greatest integer less than 20 that has a kernel of 4?

> This requires a bit more thinking. If a number has a kernel of 4, then 4 must be the square of its greatest prime factor, so its greatest prime factor must be 2. The only numbers that have a greatest prime factor of 2 are the powers of 2. The greatest power of 2 that is less than 20 is $2^4 = 16$.

For all real numbers a and b, let the expression $a \mathbin{¿} b$ be defined by the equation $a \mathbin{¿} b = 10a + b$.

What is $5 \mathbin{¿} 10$?

Just substitute 5 for a and 10 for b in the given equation: $5 \mathbin{¿} 10 = 10(5) + 10 = 60$.

If $2.5 \mathbin{¿} x = 50$, what is the value of x?

Just translate the left side of the equation:

$$2.5 \mathbin{¿} x = 10(2.5) + x = 50$$

Then solve for x:
$$25 + x = 50$$
$$x = 25$$

What is $1.5 \mathbin{¿} (1.5 \mathbin{¿} 1.5)$?

According to the order of operations, evaluate what is in parentheses first:

	$1.5 \mathbin{¿} (1.5 \mathbin{¿} 1.5)$
Substitute:	$1.5 \mathbin{¿} (10(1.5) + 1.5)$
Simplify:	$1.5 \mathbin{¿} (16.5)$
Substitute again:	$10(1.5) + 16.5$
Simplify:	$15 + 16.5 = 31.5$

Worksheet 1: New Symbol or Term Problems

Use the definitions below to translate and simplify the expressions in questions 1–6.

For any real number w, let Σw be defined as the least integer greater than or equal to twice the value of w.

1. $\Sigma 5.5 \quad = \quad$ _____

2. $\Sigma 4.3 \quad = \quad$ _____

3. $\Sigma - 3.6 \quad = \quad$ _____

Both b and c represent positive integers. Let $b * c$ be defined by the equation $b * c = b^2 \sqrt{c}$.

4. $5 * 4 \quad = \quad$ _____

5. $\sqrt{x} * x^2 \quad = \quad$ _____

6. $(x + 2) * 9 \quad = \quad$ _____

7. For any integer a and any nonzero number b, let $a \ \cancel{c} \ b$ be defined by the equation
$$a \ \cancel{c} \ b = \frac{ab}{b^{a-1}}.$$
If $3 \ \cancel{c} \ x = \dfrac{1}{2}$, what is the value of x?

9. Let $x \ \S \ y$ be defined for all integers x and y by $x \ \S \ y = \dfrac{xy}{x - y}$. What is the value of $(6 \ \S \ 4) \ \S \ 3$?

(A) 3
(B) 4
(C) 6
(D) 9
(E) 12

8. For all integers n, let $\underline{n}$ be defined as follows:
$$\underline{n}\begin{cases} n^2 & \text{if } n \text{ is odd} \\ n^3 & \text{if } n \text{ is even} \end{cases}$$
What is the value of $\underline{2} + \underline{3}$?

10. For all positive integers n and k, let $n \ \square \ k$ be defined as $n \ \square \ k = k\sqrt{n} + n\sqrt{k}$. If $(4 \ \square \ 9) + w = 36$, what is the value of w?

(A) 4
(B) 6
(C) 8
(D) 10
(E) 12

11. For any positive integer x, let $<x>$ be defined as the product of the digits of x. For instance, $<216> = 2 \times 1 \times 6 = 12$. What is the value of $\ll 472 \gg$?

12. For all nonnegative real numbers b, let Δb be defined by the equation $\Delta b = \dfrac{\sqrt{b}}{3}$. For what value of b does $\Delta b = 4$?

(A) 6
(B) 12
(C) 24
(D) 36
(E) 144

Lesson 2: Mean/Median/Mode Problems

Average (Arithmetic Mean) Problems

Every PSAT will include at least one question about averages. The test will often phrase these questions in a tricky way, so the best way to prepare for them is to really understand the concept of average and how to use the formula creatively.

You probably know how to find an average: add up the numbers in the set, and divide by how many numbers you have. For instance, the average of 3, 7, and 8 is $(3 + 7 + 8)/3 = 6$. You can describe this procedure with the "average formula":

$$\text{average} = \frac{\text{sum}}{\text{how many numbers}}$$

Since this is an algebraic equation, you can manipulate it just like any other equation, and get two more formulas:

$$\text{sum} = \text{average} \times \text{how many numbers}$$

$$\text{how many numbers} = \frac{\text{sum}}{\text{average}}$$

All three of these formulas can be summarized in one handy little "pyramid":

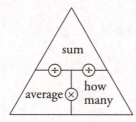

This is a great tool for setting up tough problems. To find any one of the three quantities, next find the other two, and then perform the operation between them. For instance, if the problem says "The average (arithmetic mean) of five numbers is 30," just write 30 in the "average" place and 5 in the "how many" place. Notice that there is a multiplication sign between them, so multiply $30 \times 5 = 150$ to find the third quantity: their sum.

Medians

The median of a set is the number that splits the set into two equal parts. Just think of the median of a highway: it splits the highway exactly in half.

The median of a set of numbers, then, is the middle number when they are listed in increasing order. For instance, the median of $\{-3, 7, 65\}$ is 7, because the set has as many numbers that are bigger than 7 as less than 7. If the set contains an even number of numbers, like $\{2, 4, 7, 9\}$, then the set doesn't have one "middle" number, so the median is the average of the two middle numbers. (Thus the median of $\{2, 4, 7, 9\}$ is $(4 + 7)/2 = 5.5$.)

When you take standardized tests like the PSAT, your score report often gives your score as a percentile, which shows the percentage of students whose scores were lower than yours. If your percentile score is 50%, this means that you scored at the median of all the scores: just as many (50%) of the students scored below your score as above your score.

Don't forget to arrange the numbers in order before looking for the median!

The median and the average are not always the same, but in special cases they are. For instance, the median of $\{-3, 7, 65\}$ is 7, but the average is $(-3 + 7 + 65)/3 = 23$. Clearly, the median and average are different. **However, if a set of numbers is evenly spaced, its average (arithmetic mean) equals its median.**

Consider any set of numbers that is evenly spaced, like 4, 9, 14, 19, and 24:

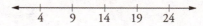

The average is always somewhere in the middle of the numbers, but if they are evenly spaced, the average is *exactly* in the middle. It's easy to check: $(4 + 9 + 14 + 19 + 24)/5 = 14$, which is the median!

Modes

Occasionally the PSAT may ask you about the mode of a set of numbers. **A mode is the number that appears the most frequently in a set.** (Just remember: MOde = MOst.) It's easy to see that not every set of numbers has a mode. For instance, the mode of $\{-3, 4, 4, 1, 12\}$ is 4, but $\{4, 9, 14, 19, 24\}$ doesn't have a mode.

Worksheet 2: Mean/Median/ Mode Problems

1. Draw the "average pyramid."

2. Explain how to use the average pyramid to solve a problem involving averages.

3. Define a median.

4. Define a mode.

5. In what situations is the mean of a set of numbers the same as its median?

6. The average (arithmetic mean) of 3 numbers is 20. If one of the numbers is 16, what is the average of the remaining two numbers?

7. The average (arithmetic mean) of 6 different positive integers is 30. What is the greatest possible value of one of those numbers?

8. The median of 4, 7, 3, 2, 10, and x is 5. What is the value of x?

9. The average (arithmetic mean) of two numbers is 10. If the larger of the two numbers is four more than the other number, what is the value of the smaller number?

(A) 6
(B) 8
(C) 10
(D) 12
(E) 14

10. During a particular television program, 60 percent of the commercials are 30 seconds long, 25 percent of the commercials are 20 seconds long, and 15 percent of the commercials are 40 seconds long. What is the average (arithmetic mean) number of seconds per commercial?

(A) 26
(B) 27
(C) 28
(D) 29
(E) 30

11. If a 60% acid solution is mixed with a 40% acid solution, which of the following could be the acid concentration of the resulting mixture?

    I. 40%
   II. 50%
  III. 55%

(A) I only
(B) II only
(C) I and III only
(D) II and III only
(E) I, II, and III

12.

RESULTS OF MIDTERM

Midterm Score	Number of Students
75	6
80	7
85	9
90	11
91 or more	12

The table above shows the distribution of the scores of 45 students on a midterm test. Based on the information in the table, which of the following must be true?

    I. Fewer than half the students scored above 85.
   II. The average (arithmetic mean) score is less than the median score.
  III. The mode of the scores is 90.

(A) I only
(B) II only
(C) I and II only
(D) I and III only
(E) I, II, and III

Lesson 3:
Numerical Reasoning Problems

Arithmetic Reasoning

The most common problems on the PSAT are numerical reasoning problems. These questions ask you to think about what happens to numbers when you perform basic operations on them. **To do well on these questions, you just need to know the common numerical and arithmetic rules and think logically**.

> If $a + b$ is negative, which of the following CANNOT be negative?
>
> (A) ab
> (B) ab^2
> (C) a^2b
> (D) a^2b^2
> (E) $a - b$

Start by thinking about what *might* be true about a and b and what *must* be true about a and b. First think of possible values for a and b. The values -2 and 1 work, because $a + b = -2 + 1 = -1$. Notice that this proves that (A), (B), and (E) are incorrect because they can be negative: (A) $ab = (-2)(1) = -2$, (B) $ab^2 = (-2)(1)^2 = -2$, and (E) $a - b = (-2) - (1) = -3$. But (C) $a^2b = (-2)^2 (1) = 4$ is positive, so does that mean the answer is (C)? Not so fast! Your job is not to find which one can be positive, but rather which cannot be negative. Notice that (C) can be negative if a and b are, say, 1 and -2 (notice that $a + b$ is still negative, so those values work): (C) $a^2b = (1)^2(-2) = -2$. Therefore, by process of elimination, the answer is (D).

This question is much easier if you remember a simple fact: if x is a real number, then x^2 is never negative. If you don't know this already, play around with possible values of x until you see why this is true. Then look at choice (D) a^2b^2. a^2 can't be negative, and neither can b^2, so a^2b^2 can't be negative.

> If $m < n < p < r$, $mnpr = 0$, and $m + n + p + r = 0$, then which of the following must be true?
>
>   I. If m and n are negative, then $p = 0$.
> II. $np = 0$
> III. $m + r = 0$
>
> (A) I only   (B) II only
> (C) I and II only   (D) I and III only
> (E) I, II, and III

The first statement, $m < n < p < r$, tells you that the alphabetical order is also the numerical order of the numbers. The second statement, $mnpr = 0$, tells you that one of the numbers must be 0. (This is the "zero product property.") The third statement, $m + n + p + r = 0$, tells you that you must have at least one positive and one negative, and all the numbers must cancel out. This means that m can't be 0, because then none of the numbers would be negative, and r can't be 0, because then none of the numbers would be positive. Thus, either n or p is 0. This means that both I and II are necessarily true, so you can eliminate choices (A), (B), and (D). The example $m = -3$, $n = 0$, $p = 1$, $r = 2$ shows that statement III is not necessarily true, so the answer is (C).

Digit Problems

You may see a question on the PSAT like the one below, where letters represent digits. **Remember that digits can only take the values 0, 1, 2, 3, 4, 5, 6, 7, 8, and 9. Also remember that you may have to consider "carried" digits when looking at a sum or product**. Lastly, you may find it best to work from left to right rather than right to left.

$$
\begin{array}{r}
1BA \\
+\,8B \\
\hline
211
\end{array}
$$

> If A and B represent distinct digits in this addition problem, what is the value of $A - B$?
>
> (A) -9
> (B) -7
> (C) 2
> (D) 7
> (E) 9

Look at the left (hundreds) column first. Since the sum has a 2 in the hundreds place, there must be a carry of 1 from the tens place. Therefore, $B + 8 +$ (carry from ones column, if any) $= 11$. This means $B = 2$ or 3. Trying each one shows that only $B = 2$ and $A = 9$ works, giving $129 + 82 = 211$. Therefore, $A - B = 9 - 2 = 7$, so the answer is (D).

Worksheet 3: Numerical Reasoning Problems

1. If neither a nor b is 0, what is the relationship between $a \div b$ and $b \div a$?

2. What is the relationship between $a - b$ and $b - a$?

Complete the following "parity rules."

3. odd $\times$ even $=$ _____

4. even $\times$ even $=$ _____

5. odd $\times$ odd $=$ _____

6. even $+$ even $=$ _____

7. odd $+$ even $=$ _____

8. odd $+$ odd $=$ _____

Complete the following "sign rules."

9. If n is odd, $(-1)^n =$ _____.

10. If n is even, $(-1)^n =$ _____.

11. If $x + y = 0$ and $x \neq 0$, then $\dfrac{x}{y} =$ _____.

12. Dividing by x is the same as multiplying by _____.

13. Subtracting $(x + 1)$ is the same as adding _____.

14.

$$3AB$$
$$+2BA$$
$$\overline{B99}$$

If A and B represent distinct digits in the correctly worked addition problem above, what is the value of A?

15. Set X consists of the numbers between 1 and 200 that are divisible by 6. Set Y consists of the numbers between 1 and 200 that are divisible by 8. How many numbers are in both set X and set Y?

(A) 6
(B) 8
(C) 10
(D) 12
(E) 14

16. If x is an odd integer, y and z are whole numbers, and $x(y+z)+x$ is odd, which of the following must be true?

(A) z is even.
(B) z is odd.
(C) y and z are either both odd or both even.
(D) If y is odd, then z is even.
(E) If y is even, then z is odd.

17. How many integers between 15 and 40, inclusive, are the product of two different prime numbers?

18. If x and y are both even integers, which of the following must be true?

  I. $2x+3y$ is even
  II. $x+y$ is divisible by 4
  III. $(x-y)^3 > 0$

(A) I only
(B) I and II only
(C) I and III only
(D) II and III only
(E) I, II, and III

19.

$$x+y+z = 10$$
$$a+b+z = 20$$

What is the average (arithmetic mean) of a and b if the average (arithmetic mean) of x and y is 3?

(A) 2
(B) 4
(C) 8
(D) 12
(E) 16

Lesson 4: Rate Problems

What Are Rates?

The word *rate* comes from the same Latin root as the word ratio. Thus, all rates are ratios. The most common type of rate is speed, which is a ratio with respect to time, as in miles per hour or words per minute, but some rates don't involve time at all, as in miles per gallon. **Rate units always have per in their names: miles *per* gallon, meters *per* second, etc**. *Per*, remember, means *divided by*, and is like the colon (:) or fraction bar (/) in a ratio.

The Rate Pyramid

The name of any rate is equivalent to its formula. For instance, speed in miles per hour

can be translated as $\text{speed} = \dfrac{\text{number of miles}}{\text{number of hours}}$

or $\text{speed} = \dfrac{\text{distance}}{\text{time}}$

Since this formula is similar to the average formula, you can make a rate pyramid. This can be a great tool for solving rate problems. If a problem gives you two of the quantities, just put them in their places in the pyramid, and do the operation between them to find the missing quantity.

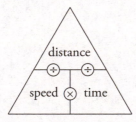

How long will it take a car to travel 20 miles at 60 miles per hour?

Simply fill the quantities into the pyramid: 20 miles goes in the distance spot, and 60 miles an hour goes in the speed spot. Now what? Just do the division like the diagram says: 20 miles ÷ 60 miles per hour = 1/3 hour.

Watch Your Units

Whenever you work with formulas, you can check your work by paying attention to units. For instance, the problem above asks *how long*, so the calculation has to produce a time unit. Check the units in the calculation:

$$\frac{\text{miles}}{(\text{miles/hours})} = \cancel{\text{miles}} \times \frac{\text{hours}}{\cancel{\text{miles}}} = \text{hour}$$

Two-Part Rate Problems

Rate problems are tougher when they involve two parts. When a problem involves, say, two people working together at different rates and times, or a two-part trip, you have to analyze the problem more carefully.

Toni bicycles to work at a rate of 20 miles per hour and then takes the bus home <u>along the same route</u> at a rate of 40 miles per hour. What is her average speed for the entire trip?

At first glance, it might seem that you can just average the two rates: $(20 + 40)/2 = 30$ miles per hour, since she is traveling the same distance at each of the two speeds. But this won't work, because she isn't spending the same time at each speed, and that is what's important. But if that's true, you might notice that she spends twice as much time going 20 miles per hour as 40 miles per hour (since it's half as fast), so instead of taking the average of 20 and 40, you can take the average of two 20s and a 40: $(20 + 20 + 40)/3 = 26.67$ miles per hour. Simple! But if that doesn't make sense to you, think of it this way: Imagine, for simplicity's sake, that her trip to work is 40 miles. (It doesn't matter what number you pick, and 40 is an easy number to work with here.) Now the average speed is simply the total distance divided by the total time (like the pyramid says). The total distance, there and back, is 80 miles. The total time is in two parts. Getting to work takes her 40 miles ÷ 20 miles per hour = 2 hours. Getting home takes her 40 miles ÷ 40 miles per hour = 1 hour. So the total time of the trip is 3 hours. The average speed, then, must be 80 miles ÷ 3 hours = 26.67 miles per hour!

Worksheet 4: Rate Problems

For each of the following rates, write the formula of the rate and the corresponding "rate pyramid."

1. A falling object's rate of descent is meters per second.

2. Interest rate is percent per year.

3. Billable hours is hours per week.

Find the missing quantity, including the units, in each of these rate situations.

4. A car is traveling at 40 miles per hour for 6 hours.

5. A rock falls 80 meters in 4 seconds.

6. A bank account earns 12% interest in 3 years.

7. A painter who paints 120 square feet per hour paints a room that is 18 feet by 20 feet.

8. A bus leaves New Haven, Connecticut, for Boston at noon, going at an average speed of 35 miles per hour. A bus leaves Boston at the same time headed for New Haven at an average speed of 25 miles per hour. If Boston is 120 miles from New Haven, at what time would the buses pass each other?

    (A) 1:30 p.m.
    (B) 1:45 p.m.
    (C) 2:00 p.m.
    (D) 2:15 p.m.
    (E) 2:30 p.m.

9. What is the average speed, in meters per second, of a bicycle that travels 480 meters in 2 minutes? (1 minute = 60 seconds)

    (A) 3
    (B) 4
    (C) 24
    (D) 48
    (E) 240

10. Rodrigo is able to type a 1,200-word document in 15 minutes. If he instead typed at an average rate that was 25% faster, how many fewer minutes would it take him to type the same document?

    (A) 2.5
    (B) 3.0
    (C) 3.5
    (D) 4.0
    (E) 4.5

11. How many hours would it take a train that is traveling at $(x - 4)$ miles per hour to travel a distance of $x^2 + 3x - 28$ miles, if $x > 4$?

    (A) $\dfrac{1}{x - 7}$

    (B) $x + 7$

    (C) $x - 8$

    (D) $x + 2$

    (E) $\dfrac{1}{x - 8}$

12. Bill is able to rake his backyard in 5 hours. His wife Barbara is able to rake the yard in only 3 hours. When they work together, their combined rate is the sum of their rates working separately. How many hours would it take them to rake the yard if they worked together?

13. Ramesh drove to work in the morning at an average speed of 50 miles per hour. He returned home along the same route at an average speed of 40 miles per hour. If Ramesh spent a total of 90 minutes commuting to and from work, how many miles did he drive to work in the morning?

    (A) 20
    (B) 30
    (C) 33⅓
    (D) 36
    (E) 40

Lesson 5: Counting Problems

The Fundamental Counting Principle

Some PSAT questions ask you to count things. Sometimes, it's easy enough to just write out the things in a list and count them by hand. Other times, though, there will be too many, and it will help to use the fundamental counting principle.

To use the fundamental counting principle, think of the things you're counting as being created from a sequence of choices. The fundamental counting principle says that the number of ways an event can happen is equal to the product of the choices that must be made to "create" the event.

> How many ways can five people be arranged in a line?

You might consider calling the five people A, B, C, D, and E and listing the number of arrangements. After a while, though, you'll see that this is going to take a lot of time, because there are a lot of possibilities. (Not to mention, it's really easy to miss some of them.) Instead, think of "building" the line with a sequence of choices: first pick the first person, then pick the second person, etc. There are five choices to make, so we'll have to multiply five numbers. Obviously, there are 5 people to choose from for the first person in line. Once you do this, though, there are only 4 people left for the second spot, then 3 for the second spot, etc. By the fundamental counting principle, then, the num-ber of possible arrangements is $5 \times 4 \times 3 \times 2 \times 1 = 120$.

> How many odd integers greater than 500 and less than 1,000 have an even digit in the tens place?

This seems a lot harder than it is. Again, think of "building" the numbers in question. All integers between 500 and 1,000 have three digits so building the number involves choosing three digits; thus we must multiply three numbers together. If the number is between 500 and 1,000, there are only five choices for the first digit: 5, 6, 7, 8, or 9. If the tens digit must be even, we have five choices again: 2, 4, 6, 8, or 0. If the whole number is odd, then we have five choices for the last digit as well: 1, 3, 5, 7, or 9. Therefore, the total number of such integers is $5 \times 5 \times 5 = 125$.

Using Venn Diagrams to Keep Track of Sets

Some counting problems involve "overlapping sets," that is, sets that contain elements that also belong in other sets. In these situations, Venn diagrams are very helpful for keeping track of things.

> A class of 29 students sponsored two field trips: one to a zoo and one to a museum. Every student attended at least one of the field trips, and 10 students attended both. If twice as many students went to the zoo as went to the museum, how many students went to the zoo?

Set up a Venn diagram of the situation: We represent the two sets—those who went to the museum and those who went to the zoo—as two overlapping circles, because some students went to both. Notice that there are three regions to consider. We know that 10 students are in the overlapping region, but we don't know how many are in the other two regions,

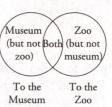

so let's use algebra. Let's say that x students are in the first region, representing those who went to the museum but not the zoo. This means that $x + 10$ students must have gone to the museum all together. Since twice as many students went to the zoo, the total number in the zoo circle must be $2(x + 10) = 2x + 20$. Since 10 of these are already accounted for in the overlapping region, there must be $2x + 20 - 10 = 2x + 10$ in the third region. So now the diagram should look like:

The total number of students is 29, so

$$(x) + (10) + (2x + 10) = 29$$

Simplify: $3x + 20 = 29$

Solve: $x = 3$

So the number of students who went to the zoo is $2(3) + 20 = 26$.

Worksheet 5: Counting Problems

1. What is the fundamental counting principle?

2. If the first and last letter of a three-letter code must be vowels, and letters can be repeated, how many different codes are possible?

3. A parking attendant must park five cars in the five remaining spots in the parking lot. How many different arrangements of cars are possible?

4. If that same parking attendant is not allowed to park the largest car in the middle spot, how many arrangements are possible?

5. At Streams Private School, 40 students play soccer, 30 students play softball, 50 students play field hockey, and 20 students play exactly two sports. If no students play all three sports and every student plays at least one sport, how many students attend the school?

6. A deli offers three different types of bread, four different types of meat, and three different types of cheese. How many different sandwiches are possible if each sandwich has one type of bread, one type of meat, and one type of cheese?

(A) 10
(B) 24
(C) 36
(D) 48
(E) 64

7. A stickball team has five players. How many different lineups are possible if the captain must bat first?

(A) 10
(B) 24
(C) 25
(D) 64
(E) 120

8. From a group of seven students, five are to be selected and arranged randomly at the front of the room. How many different such arrangements are possible?

(A) 35
(B) 120
(C) 840
(D) 2,520
(E) 5,040

9. Every person in a room is wearing either a jacket, a sweater, or both. The ratio of jacket wearers to non-jacket wearers is 2:1. The ratio of sweater wearers to non-sweater wearers is 5:4. If four people are wearing both a jacket and a sweater, how many people are in the room?

10. In the state championship tennis tournament, each player plays two matches against every other player in the bracket. If there are eight players in the bracket, how many total matches are to be played?

11.

A, C, G, H, I, J, M, W, X, Z

A four-letter code is to be created using only the letters listed above. Each letter can be used only once, the first letter must be a vowel, and the third letter must be after M in the alphabet. How many different codes are possible?

(A) 20
(B) 55
(C) 242
(D) 336
(E) 445

Lesson 6: Probability Problems

Probability

A probability is a number between 0 and 1 that represents the likelihood of an event. An event with a probability of 0 is impossible, and an event with a probability of 1 is certain. Most probabilities, of course, are somewhere in between 0 and 1. For instance, the probability of rolling a 5 on a fair die is 1/6. It's best to think of a probability as a part-to-whole ratio. There are six possible outcomes when you roll a die (the whole), but only one of them is 5 (the part). Thus, the probability of rolling a 5 is 1/6.

What is the probability of rolling a sum of 5 on two dice?

Here is a table showing all the possible sums on a roll of two dice:

		Die 1					
		1	2	3	4	5	6
	1	2	3	4	5	6	7
	2	3	4	5	6	7	8
Die 2	3	4	5	6	7	8	9
	4	5	6	7	8	9	10
	5	6	7	8	9	10	11
	6	7	8	9	10	11	12

There are four ways of getting a sum of 5 out of a possible 36, so the probability is 4/36 or 1/9.

Geometrical Probability

A PSAT question may ask you to find the probability that something hits a certain region, like a dart hitting a dartboard. In these situations, the probability is just the ratio of the particular area to the entire area.

A landing target for skydivers consists of two concentric circles. The smaller circle has a radius of 3 meters, and the larger one has a radius of 6 meters. If a skydiver hits the target, what is the probability that she hits the smaller circle?

It might help to sketch the target:

If she hits the target, then she hits an area that is $\pi(6)^2 = 36\pi$ square meters in area. The smaller circle, though, is only $\pi(3)^2 = 9\pi$ square meters in area, so the probability that she lands within the smaller region should be just $9\pi/36\pi = 1/4$.

Worksheet 6: Probability Problems

1. The probability of an impossible event is _____.

2. The probability of an event that is certain is _____.

3. If a bowl contains 4 apples, 5 oranges, and 6 bananas, what is the probability of randomly choosing

   an apple? _____

   an orange? _____

   a banana? _____

4. A jar contains 8 apples and 7 oranges. What is the probability of drawing an apple?

   If three more apples are added, what is the probability of drawing an apple?

5. A jar contains 36 white and black marbles. If the probability of selecting a white marble at random is 4/9, how many white marbles must be added so that the probability of randomly selecting a white marble becomes 1/2?

6. A box contains only red, white, and blue poker chips. The probability of randomly choosing a red chip is 3/4. If there are 3 times as many blue chips as white chips, what is the least possible number of chips in the box?

7. A jar contains 8 blue marbles, 10 orange marbles, and 12 brown marbles. How many blue marbles must be added so that the probability of randomly choosing a blue marble is $\frac{1}{3}$?

    (A) 3
    (B) 4
    (C) 5
    (D) 6
    (E) 7

8. In a certain game, when two six-sided dice with faces numbered 1 through 6 are rolled and a sum larger than 8 comes up, the roller gets a point. What is the probability that a roller will get a point on her first attempt?

    (A) $\dfrac{7}{36}$

    (B) $\dfrac{5}{18}$

    (C) $\dfrac{11}{36}$

    (D) $\dfrac{15}{36}$

    (E) $\dfrac{7}{12}$

9.

    Set X: {4, 5, 10, 11, 13}
    Set Y: {1, 3, 9, 14, 17}

    If one number is to be selected at random from each of set X and set Y shown above, what is the probability that both numbers selected will be prime?

    (A) $\dfrac{6}{25}$

    (B) $\dfrac{9}{25}$

    (C) $\dfrac{2}{5}$

    (D) $\dfrac{11}{25}$

    (E) $\dfrac{3}{5}$

10. In the town of Saskatoon, the probability of a snowfall greater than 1 inch on a given night in the month of January is $\frac{3}{4}$. Independently, the probability that someone will need a tow truck on the highway on a given night in the month of January is $\frac{1}{6}$. What is the probability that, on any given night, there will be a snowfall greater than 1 inch *and* someone will need a tow truck?

11. When FixyFridge repair company sends out a crew to fix a refrigerator, the company sends a three-person team to do the job. Each team consists of one of the three company partners, one experienced employee, and one trainee. Two of the three company partners are males, five of the nine experienced employees are males, and one of the four trainees is a male. What is the probability that a randomly chosen team will consist of all females?

    (A) $\dfrac{7}{108}$

    (B) $\dfrac{1}{9}$

    (C) $\dfrac{15}{108}$

    (D) $\dfrac{17}{54}$

    (E) $\dfrac{37}{108}$

Lesson 7: Sequences

Kinds of Sequences

A *sequence* is simply a list of numbers, each of which is called a *term*. The PSAT may ask you to identify and use a pattern in a sequence of numbers. For instance, "How many odd numbers are in the first 100 terms of the sequence 1, 2, 3, 1, 2, 3, …?"

An *arithmetic sequence* is a sequence in which each term is formed by adding a constant number to the previous term (e.g., **1, 5, 9, 13, 17**…). The difference between any two consecutive terms is always the same.

A *geometric sequence* is a sequence in which each term is formed by multiplying the previous term by a constant (e.g., 2, 4, 8, 16, 32, 64,…). The ratio or quotient between any two consecutive terms is always the same.

What a Sequence Problem Will Ask For

Most sequence problems give the first few terms of the sequence, or the rule for generating them, and ask you to:

- **Find a specific term.** For instance, "What is the value of the 214th term of the sequence 1, 2, 3, 1, 2, 3,…?"

- **Analyze a subset of the sequence.** For instance, "How many odd numbers are in the first 100 terms of the sequence 1, 2, 3, 1, 2, 3,… or" "What is the sum of the first 36 terms of the sequence 1, 2, 3, 1, 2, 3,…?"

Three Steps to Solving a Sequence Problem

Step 1: **Write out the first 5–8 terms of the sequence following the rules.** Usually 5–8 terms is plenty.

Step 2: **Identify the pattern and how often it repeats.** Perhaps "bracketing" the pattern will help it stand out.

Step 3: **Use this pattern and whole-number division (Chapter 8, Lesson 7) to solve the problem.**

Some Sequence Practice

$$-1, 2, -2, \ldots$$

The first three terms of a sequence are given above. Each subsequent term is found by dividing the preceding term by the term before that, for example, the third term $2 \div -1 = -2$. What is the value of the 218th term in the sequence?

Begin by writing out the first 5–8 terms. The third term of the sequence is $2 \div -1 = -2$. The fourth term is $-2 \div 2 = -1$. The fifth term is $-1 \div -2 = \frac{1}{2}$. The sixth term is $\frac{1}{2} \div -1 = -\frac{1}{2}$. The seventh term is $-\frac{1}{2} \div \frac{1}{2} = -1$. The eighth term is $-1 \div -\frac{1}{2} = 2$.

$$\{-1, 2, -2, -1, \tfrac{1}{2}, -\tfrac{1}{2}\}, \{-1, 2, \ldots$$

You should notice that the terms are beginning to repeat by now. This pattern repeats every 6 digits, as shown within the brackets above. If we were to write out the first 218 terms (which we won't!), this pattern would repeat $218 \div 6 = 36$ times with a remainder of 2, which means that the 218th term is the same as the 2nd term of the sequence, which is 2.

$$-1, 1, 0, -1, 1, 0, -1, 1, 0\ldots$$

If the pattern above repeats indefinitely as shown, what is the sum of the first 43 terms?

The question has written out the first nine terms for you, so your first job is to identify the pattern.

$$-1, 1, 0, -1, 1, 0, -1$$

The pattern repeats every 3 digits, and the sum of each repetition is $-1 + 1 + 0 = 0$.

The pattern occurs $43 \div 3 = 14\frac{1}{3}$ times, or 14 with remainder 1.

The 14 full repetitions have a sum of $14(0) = 0$. Since the 43rd term is -1, the sum is $0 + -1 = -1$.

Worksheet 7: Sequences

1. If the pattern of a sequence repeats every 4 terms, how do you determine the 113th term of the sequence?

2. If the pattern of a sequence repeats every 5 terms, how do you find the sum of the first 20 terms of the sequence?

3. If a pattern repeats every 3 terms, how do you determine how many of the first 23 terms are negative?

4. The first term in a sequence is 2, and each subsequent term is 5 more than half the preceding term. What is the value of the fifth term?

5. The word EAGLE is written 100 times in a row on a piece of paper. How many of the first 121 letters are vowels?

6. The fourth term of a sequence is x. If each term in the sequence except the first is found by subtracting 4 from the previous term and dividing that difference by 3, what is the first term of the sequence in terms of x?

7.   The first term in a sequence is 500. Every subsequent term is 10 less than $\frac{1}{2}$ the immediately preceding term. What is the fourth term in the sequence?

(A) 35.50
(B) 45.00
(C) 58.75
(D) 62.00
(E) 73.25

8.   The first term in a sequence is -3, and each subsequent term is 5 more than the immediately preceding term. What is the value of the 103rd term?

(A) 497
(B) 502
(C) 507
(D) 510
(E) 512

9.

4, 3, 1, 5, 4, 3, 1, 5, . . .

In the sequence above, the digits continue according to the pattern shown. How many of the first 119 terms are odd?

10.

$-2, 1, -2 \ldots$

After the second term in the sequence above, each subsequent term is the product of the preceding two terms. For example, the third term is $-2 \times 1 = -2$. How many of the first 92 terms in this sequence are negative?

(A) 58
(B) 59
(C) 60
(D) 61
(E) 62

11. A 50-digit number is created by writing all the positive integers in succession beginning with 1. What is the 34th digit of the number?

12. What is the units digit of 4^{27}?

(A) 2
(B) 3
(C) 4
(D) 5
(E) 6

Lesson 8: Data Analysis

Tables, Charts, and Graphs

A table is a set of data arranged in rows and columns. **When given a table, chart or graph, first read the labels carefully to understand what the table, chart or graph values represent**. Some PSAT questions may ask you to complete the data in a table or to solve for variables in a table. You might be asked to cross-reference information in two or more tables. Be sure you know how the two tables are related.

Household Electric Equipment

	Thompson Family	Shields Family
Computers	2	3
Televisions	x	4
Stereos	2	2

Televisions

	Plasma	LCD
Thompson	y	4
Shields	1	3

If the Thompsons own as many pieces of electronic equipment as the Shields, how many plasma televisions does the Thompson family own?

The Shields own $3 + 4 + 2 = 9$ pieces of equipment.

Therefore $9 = 2 + 2 + x$
Subtract 4: $5 = x$

Using the "televisions" table, use the fact that the Thompsons have 5 TVs.

$$y + 4 = 5$$
Subtract 4: $y = 1$ plasma TV

In a pie chart, a sector that contains x% of the total data has a central angle of $\left(\frac{x}{100}\right)(360°)$.

THE FAVORITE COLOR OF
4,000 KINDERGARTEN STUDENTS

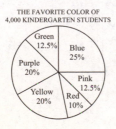

In the pie chart at the bottom left, what is the angle measure of the sector represented by the color purple?

Purple accounts for 20% of the circle, or 20% of 360°. $(0.2)(360°) = 72°$.

With bar graphs, as with the others, read the labels carefully to understand what the data represent.

Be prepared to answer questions that ask about percent change from one bar to the next.

According to the bar graph below, between what two consecutive years was there the greatest percent change in the number of home births?

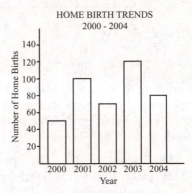

Remember the "percent change" formula:

percent change =

$$\frac{(\text{final amount}) - (\text{original amount})}{(\text{original amount})} \times 100$$

The percent change between 2000 and 2001 is $\frac{(100) - (50)}{(50)} \times 100\% = 100\%$

Be prepared to answer questions that relate one or two bars to the rest of the bars in the graph

According to the bar graph above, what fraction of the home births that occurred between 2000 and 2004 took place in 2001 and 2002?

There was a total of $50 + 100 + 70 + 120 + 80 = 420$ home births. The graph shows that $100 + 70 = 170$ occurred in 2001 and 2002. Therefore $170/420$ or $17/42$ of the home births took place in 2001 and 2002.

Worksheet 8: Data Analysis Problems

Questions 1 and 2 refer to the graph below:

MONTHLY TICKET SALES
AT ZOGWITH ZOO

1. According to the graph above, Zogwith Zoo experienced its largest increase in park attendance between which two consecutive months?

   (A) March and April   (B) April and May
   (C) May and June   (D) June and July
   (E) July and August

2. The number of visitors in the month of June was what percent greater than the number of visitors in the month of March?

   (A) 45%   (B) 100%
   (C) 200%   (D) 300%
   (E) 400%

3.

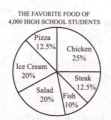

THE FAVORITE FOOD OF
4,000 HIGH SCHOOL STUDENTS

The pie chart above shows the results of a survey that asked 4,000 high school students to name their favorite food. How many more students said chicken was their favorite food than said salad was their favorite food?

4.

	Revenue per unit	Cost per unit
Troggets	a	$4
Lodards	b	$3
Plackets	$6	c

Cost Revenue Analysis

The table above shows the per unit revenue and cost of three products. If profit equals revenue minus cost, how much profit is made from the production and sale of two of each item?

   (A) $2a + 2b - 2c - 2$ (B) $2c - 2b - 2a - 2$
   (C) $a + b - c - 1$ (D) $b + 2a + c - 7$
   (E) $2b + 2c - 2y + 2$

Questions 5 and 6 refer to the graph below:

5.

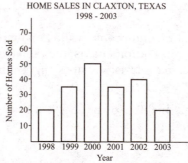

HOME SALES IN CLAXTON, TEXAS
1998 - 2003

According to the graph above, the largest percent change in number of home sales occurred between which two years?

   (A) 1998 and 1999   (B) 1999 and 2000
   (C) 2000 and 2001   (D) 2001 and 2002
   (E) 2002 and 2003

6.

What percentage of total home sales during this six year period occurred in 2002 and 2003?

Detailed Answer Key: Special Math Problems

Worksheet 1

1. $\Sigma 5.5 = 11 \quad 2(5.5) = 11$

2. $\Sigma 4.3 = 9 \quad 2(4.3) = 8.6$, and 9 is smallest integer greater than or equal to 8.6.

3. $\Sigma -3.6 = -7 \quad 2(-3.6) = -7.2$, and -7 is smallest integer greater than or equal to -7.2.

4. $5 * 4 = 5^2 \sqrt{4} = 25(2) = 50$

5. $\sqrt{x} * x^2 = (\sqrt{x})^2 \sqrt{(x^2)} = x \cdot x = x^2$

6. $(x + 2) * 9 = (x + 2)^2 \sqrt{9} = (x^2 + 4x + 4)(3)$
   $= 3x^2 + 12x + 12$

7. $3 \notcent x = \dfrac{3x}{x^{3-1}} = \dfrac{1}{2}$

   Cross-multiply: $6x = x^2$
   Divide by x: $6 = x$

8. **289**   Because 2 is even, $\underline{2} = 2^3 = 8$ and because 3 is odd, $\underline{3} = 3^2 = 9$

   Therefore $\underline{2} + \underline{3} = 8 + 9 = 17$

   Because 17 is odd, $\underline{17} = 17^2 = 289$

9. **B**   Begin by finding the value of 6 § 4, which equals:

   $$\frac{6(4)}{6-4} = \frac{24}{2} = 12$$

   Next substitute 12 for (6 § 4) and solve for 12 § 3.

   $$\frac{12(3)}{12-3} = \frac{36}{9} = 4$$

10. **B**   Begin by simplifying 4 ¤ 9:

    $4 ¤ 9 = 9\sqrt{4} + 4\sqrt{9} = 9(2) + 4(3) = 18 + 12 = 30$

    Now solve for w: $30 + w = 36$
    Subtract 30: $w = 6$

11. **30**   First find the value of $<472>$:

    $$<472> = 4 \times 7 \times 2 = 56$$

    Next find the value of $<56>$:

    $$<56> = 5 \times 6 = 30$$

12. **E**

    $$\Delta b = \frac{\sqrt{b}}{3} = 4$$

    Multiply by 3: $\sqrt{b} = 12$

    Square both sides: $b = 144$

Worksheet 2

1. It should look like this:

2. When two of the three values are given in a problem, write them in the pyramid and perform the operation between them. The result is the other value in the pyramid.

3. A median is the "middle" number when the numbers are listed in order. If there is an even number of numbers in the set, it is the average of the two middle numbers.

4. The number that appears the most frequently in a set.

5. When the numbers are evenly spaced, the mean is always equal to the median. This is true more generally if the numbers are distributed "symmetrically" about the mean, as in $\{-10, -7, 0, 7, 10\}$.

6. If the average of three numbers is 20, then their sum must be $3(20) = 60$. If one of the numbers is 16, the sum of the remaining two numbers must be $60 - 16 = 44$. Therefore, the average of the remaining two must be $44/2 = 22$.

7. If the average of 6 different positive integers is 30, then their sum must be $6(30) = 180$. It is important to note that they must be *different* integers. If you want one of the integers to be as *large* as possible, you must make the others as *small*

as possible. You know that $a + b + c + d + e + f = 180$.

Plug in numbers: $1 + 2 + 3 + 4 + 5 + f = 180$

Combine terms: $15 + f = 180$

Subtract 15: $f = 165$

8. **6** Put the "known" numbers in order: 2, 3, 4, 7, 10.

The median of the set of numbers is 5; therefore x must be larger than 4 because the median is the "middle" number and if x is smaller than 4, the median would also be smaller than 4. When a group of numbers contains an even number of members, the median is the average of the middle two numbers. The numbers 4 and 7 cannot be the middle numbers of this set because that would produce a median of 5.5. Therefore, x must come after 4.

So $\dfrac{x + 4}{2} = 5$

Multiply by 2: $x + 4 = 10$

Subtract 4: $x = 6$

9. **B**

$\dfrac{a + b}{2} = 10$

Multiply by 2: $a + b = 20$

If a is 4 more than b: $a = 4 + b$

Substitute for a: $(4 + b) + b = 20$

Combine terms: $4 + 2b = 20$

Subtract 4: $2b = 16$

Divide by 2: $b = 8$

10. **D** Find a weighted average. Imagine there were 100 commercials. There would be 60 30-second commercials, 25 20-second commercials, and 15 40-second commercials.

$$\frac{60(30) + 25(20) + 15(40)}{100} = \frac{1,800 + 500 + 600}{100}$$

$$= 29$$

11. **D** When a 60% and a 40% solution are combined, the concentration must be anywhere between 40% and 60%, depending on how much of each was added.

12. **B** To answer this question, first find out how many total grades there were by adding up the column on the right: $6 + 7 + 9 + 11 + 12 = 45$ students.

I. To decide if statement I is correct, find out how many students scored higher than 85. $(11 + 12 = 22)$ 23 out of 45 students is actually *more* than one-half. So statement I is incorrect.

II. To decide if statement II is correct, find the mean and median for the data. The median can be calculated for sure, but the mean cannot. From the last row of data we know that 12 students scored 91 or higher, but we don't know their exact scores. It could be that 12 students scored 92, but it could also be that 12 students scored 95. We cannot find the average without knowing more about the grades received. We can calculate the *smallest* possible mean, however, by imagining that all 12 of the students in the last row scored 91. The mean would thus be:

$$\frac{6(75) + 7(80) + 9(85) + 11(90) + 12(91)}{45}$$

$$= 85.71$$

We can also calculate the *largest* possible mean by imagining that all 12 students scored 100. This mean would be 88.11.

To find the median, put the data in order from least to greatest and find the middle value. Here it doesn't matter what the values in the last row are because they are cancelled out in the location of the median. There are 45 students, so the median should be the 23rd out of the 45.

The median of this set is 90. The mean ranges from 85.71 to 88.11, So the mean *must* be smaller than the median. So statement II is correct.

III. To decide whether statement III is correct, find out which score occurs the most often. There are 11 students who scored 90. It's likely that 90 is the mode, but it's *possible* that 91 or higher could be the mode if all 12 of the students indicated in the last row received the same score. Therefore statement III is incorrect.

Worksheet 3

1. They are reciprocals, so their product is 1.

2. They are opposites, so their sum is 0.

3. odd × even = even

4. even × even = even

5. odd × odd = odd

6. even + even = even

7. odd + even = odd

8. odd + odd = even

9. If n is odd, $(-1)^n = -1$.

10. If n is even, $(-1)^n = 1$.

11. If $x + y = 0$ and $x \neq 0$, then $x/y = -1$.

12. Dividing by x is the same as multiplying by $1/x$.

13. Subtracting $(x+1)$ is the same as adding $-x - 1$.

14. **4** Begin by looking at the far-right column. $A + B = 9$. The middle column tells us the same information, and the far-left column tells us that $3 + 2 = B$.
Therefore $B = 5$ and $A = 9 - 5 = 4$.

15. **B** The numbers that are in *both* sets are the "common multiples" of 6 and 8, which are 24, 48, 72, 96, 120, 144, 168, and 192. These are the multiples of 24. There are 8 of them.

16. **C** To solve this problem, recall that even + even = even, even + odd = odd, and odd + odd = even.

Replace x with an odd number such as 1.

You are told that $x(y + z) + x$ is odd.
Substitute 1 for x: $1(y + z) + 1$ is odd
Distribute: $y + z + 1$ is odd

If $y + z + 1$ is odd, then $(y + z)$ must be even because even plus odd equals odd.

(A) This is not *always* true because if z is odd *and* y is odd, the statement works.
(B) This is not *always* true because if z is even *and* y is even, the statement works.
(C) This is always true. y and z must both be odd or both be even.
(D) This is not always true because y and z can both be odd.
(E) This is not always true because both y and z can be even.

17. **9** The prime numbers less than 30 are 2, 3, 5, 7, 11, 13, 17, 19, 23, and 27. Listed below are all the products between 15 and 40 that can be found by multiplying two of the listed primes together.

$2 \times 11 = 22$; $2 \times 13 = 26$; $2 \times 17 = 34$; $2 \times 19 = 38$
$3 \times 5 = 15$, $3 \times 7 = 21$, $3 \times 11 = 33$, $3 \times 13 = 39$
$5 \times 7 = 35$

18. **A** odd × odd = odd, odd × even = even,
even × even = even, odd + odd = even
odd + even = even, even + even = even

I. $2x + 3y$:
Because both 2 and x are even numbers, $2x$ must be even because an even times an even is even. Because 3 is odd and y is even, $3y$ must be even because an odd times an even is even. Therefore $2x + 3y$ is even because an even plus an even is always even.

II. $x + y$ is divisible by 4.
While it is true that an even plus an even is even, it is not true that this even will necessarily be a multiple of 4. If x is 2 and y is 4, $x + y = 6$, which is not divisible by 4.

III. $(x - y)^3$ is positive. This is not true because it does not say x and y must be different, so their difference could be zero if $x = y$ and zero cubed is not positive.
Therefore only statement I is correct.

19. **C** The average value of x and y is 3, and $\dfrac{x + y}{2} = 3$.

Multiply by 2:	$x + y = 6$
	$x + y + z = 10$
Substitute for $(x + y)$:	$6 + z = 10$
Subtract 6:	$z = 4$
	$a + b + z = 20$
Substitute for z:	$a + b + 4 = 20$
Subtract 4:	$a + b = 16$
Divide by 2:	$\dfrac{a + b}{2} = \dfrac{16}{2} = 8$

Worksheet 4

1. rate of descent = meters ÷ seconds:

2. interest rate = percent ÷ years:

3. billable hours = hours ÷ weeks:

4. 40 miles per hour × 6 hours = 240 miles

5. 80 meters ÷ 4 seconds = 20 meters per second

6. 12% interest ÷ 3 years = 4% interest per year

7. 360 square feet ÷ 120 square ft per hour = 3 hours

8. **C**   Set up an equation for each bus that shows its distance from New Haven (NH).

New Haven bus:	distance from NH = $35t$
Boston bus:	distance from NH = $120 - 25t$
Set them equal:	$35t = 120 - 25t$
Add $25t$:	$60t = 120$
Divide by 60:	$t = 2$ hours

Therefore the buses would pass each other at $12 + 2 = 2$ pm.

9. **B**   480 meters ÷ 120 seconds = 4 meters per second

10. **B**   1,200 words ÷ 15 minutes = 80 words per minute. 25% of 80 is 20 words per minute. His new rate would be $80 + 20 = 100$ wpm. 1,200 words ÷ 100 wpm = 12 minutes. It would take 3 fewer minutes. $(15 - 12)$

11. **B**   distance = rate × time

$$(x^2 + 3x - 28) = (x - 4)(\text{time})$$
Factor left side: $(x + 7)(x - 4) = (x - 4)(\text{time})$
Divide by $(x - 4)$: $(x + 7) = \text{time}$

12. **15/8**   Bill can rake 1/5 of the yard in an hour, and his wife Barbara can rake 1/3 of the yard in one hour. If they work together, their combined rate is $1/5 + 1/3 = 8/15$ of the yard in one hour:

	1 yard = rate × time
	1 yard = $8/15$ × time
Divide by 8/15	15/8 hours = time

13. **C**   Set up $d = rt$ equations for heading to work and returning from work:

To work:	$d = 50(t)$
From work:	$d = 40(1.5 - t)$

You can use d for both because it says "along the same route." You cannot use the same t for both because it does not say he spent the same amount of time going each direction. Since he spent a total of 1.5 hours driving, if he spent t hours going to work, then he spent $1.5 - t$ hours going home. Set the equations equal to solve:

	$50t = 40(1.5 - t)$
Distribute:	$50t = 60 - 40t$
Add $40t$:	$90t = 60$
Divide by 90:	$t = 2/3$ hour
Solve for d:	$d = 50(2/3) = 33\frac{1}{3}$

Worksheet 5

1. The number of ways an event can happen is equal to the product of the choices that must be made to "create" the event.

2. Using the fundamental counting principle (FCP), there are 5 choices for the first letter, 26 choices for the second letter, and 5 choices for the final letter. So there are $5 \times 26 \times 5 = 650$ choices altogether.

3. Use the FCP: In the first spot, the attendant can choose from five cars. Once this spot is filled, he has four cars to choose from. For the next spot he has three cars to choose from. For the fourth spot he has two cars to choose from, and for the final spot he has only one car to choose. There are $5 \times 4 \times 3 \times 2 \times 1 = 120$ possible arrangements of cars.

4. If there is a "restricted" spot, fill that spot first. The largest car cannot be in the middle, so there are only *four* choices for the middle spot. Going back to the first spot, there are now only four choices because a car has already been parked. For the second spot there are now only three choices. For the fourth spot there are only two choices, and for the final spot only one. There

are $4 \times 3 \times 4 \times 2 \times 1 = 96$ possible arrangements of cars.

5. Set up a Venn diagram to solve this problem.

   We know that 20 students play *two* sports. It does not matter which two sports they play; we can choose that when making our Venn diagram. Just be sure that exactly 20 people play two sports. Let's say 20 people play soccer and softball. This means 0 people play soccer and field hockey, and 0 people play field hockey and softball, and 0 people play all 3. Since 40 students play soccer and 20 play soccer *and* softball, $40 - 20 = 20$ play *just* soccer. $30 - 20 = 10$ play just softball, and 50 play just field hockey:

   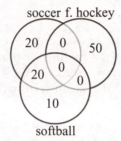

   There are $20 + 20 + 10 + 50 = 100$ students.

6. **C**   Use the FCP. There are $3 \times 4 \times 3 = 36$ possible sandwiches.

7. **B**   There is only one choice (the captain) for the first spot. The second spot has four choices, the third has three choices, the fourth has two choices, and the final spot just one. There are $1 \times 4 \times 3 \times 2 \times 1 = 24$ possible lineups.

8. **D**   There are seven choices for the first spot, six choices for the second spot, five choices for the third spot, four choices for the second spot, and three choices for the final spot. There are a total of $7 \times 6 \times 5 \times 4 \times 3 = 2{,}520$ possible arrangements.

9. **18** Set up a Venn diagram:

   Since the ratio of sweater wearers to non-sweater wearers is 5:4, you can set up the equation:

   $$s + 4 = \frac{5}{4}(j)$$

   Since the ratio of jacket wearers to non-jacket

wearers is 2:1, $j + 4 = 2(s)$.

$$j + 4 = 2s$$

Subtract 4: $j = 2s - 4$

Substitute $2s - 4$ for j: $s + 4 = \frac{5}{4}(2s - 4)$

Distribute: $s + 4 = 2.5s - 5$
Subtract s: $4 = 1.5s - 5$
Add 5: $9 = 1.5s$
Divide by 1.5: $6 = s$

Plug back in to solve for j:

$$j = 2(6) - 4 = 12 - 4 = 8$$

Therefore, there are a total of $8 + 4 + 6 = 18$ people.

10. **56**   Find out how many matches there would be if they play each other once:

    Player A has seven matches: AB, AC, AD, AE, AF, AG, and AH. Player B has 6 matches we have not yet counted (AB should not be counted again): BC, BD, BE, BF, BG, and BH. Player C has five uncounted matches: CD, CE, CF, CG, and CH. Player D has four uncounted matches: DE, DF, DG, and DH. Player E has three uncounted matches: EF, EG, and EH. Player F has two uncounted matches: FG and FH. Player G has one match not yet counted: GH.

    There are a total of $1 + 2 + 3 + 4 + 5 + 6 + 7 = 28$ matches. They play each player twice, which means there are $28 \times 2 = 56$ matches.

11. **D**   There are two vowels in the list. The first letter must be a vowel, so there are *two* choices, A and I. The third letter must come from the second half of the alphabet (N through Z) so there are three choices, W, X, and Z. The second letter has $10 - 2 = 8$ choices (since two have already been placed), and the final letter has seven choices. There are $2 \times 8 \times 3 \times 7 = 336$ possible codes.

Worksheet 6

1. 0

2. 1

3. $\frac{4}{15}$; $\frac{5}{15} = \frac{1}{3}$; $\frac{6}{15} = \frac{2}{5}$

4. $\frac{8}{15}$; $\frac{11}{18}$

5. If the probability of selecting a white marble is 4/9 and there are 36 marbles total, then there are $(4/9) \times 36 = 16$ white marbles and $36 - 16 = 20$ black marbles. If you add 4 white marbles, there will be 20 of each type and a 1/2 probability of selecting a white marble.

6. If there are x white chips, and there are 3 times as many blue chips as white chips, then there are $3x$ blue chips. If 3/4 of the chips are red, then 1/4 of the chips are not red. If there are $4x$ non-red chips that represent 1/4 of the total number of chips, there must be $3(4x) = 12x$ red chips. There are a total of $12x + 4x = 16x$ chips. The least possible number of chips can be found by calculating the total number of chips if there is only one white chip $(x = 1)$. This number would be $16x = 16(1) = 16$ chips.

7. **A**   To start, there are $8 + 10 + 12 = 30$ total marbles, and x blue marbles are added. After adding x blue marbles, there are $8 + x$ blue marbles. After adding x blue marbles, there are $30 + x$ total marbles. Set up a proportion to show that the number of blue marbles after the addition of x marbles is $\frac{1}{3}$ of the new total.

$$\frac{8 + x}{30 + x} = \frac{1}{3}$$

Cross-multiply:	$3(8 + x) = 30 + x$
Distribute:	$24 + 3x = 30 + x$
Subtract 24:	$3x = 6 + x$
Subtract x:	$2x = 6$
Divide by 2:	$x = 3$

8. **B**   To solve this problem you must determine how many different rolls will provide a sum larger than 8:

	1	2	3	4	5	6	<–Die 1
1	2	3	4	5	6	7	
2	3	4	5	6	7	8	
Die 2– > 3	4	5	6	7	8	9	
4	5	6	7	8	9	10	
5	6	7	8	9	10	11	
6	7	8	9	10	11	12	

There are 36 possible outcomes, and 10 of them are larger than 8. $10/36 = 5/18$.

9. **A**   First find the probability of selecting a prime number from set X. There are 3 primes: 5, 11, and 13 out of 5 numbers. The probability is 3/5. Next find the probability of selecting a prime number from set Y. There are 2 primes: 2 and 17, out of 5 numbers. The probability is 2/5. The probability of *both* being prime is $3/5 \times 2/5 = 6/25$

10. $\frac{1}{8}$ Mathematically, we can just multiply the two probabilities, as long as they are undependent, to get the *joint* probability: $(\frac{3}{4} \times \frac{1}{6} = \frac{3}{24} = \frac{1}{8})$

11. **B**   First find out how many different teams are possible. There are 3 possible partners to choose from, 9 experienced employees, and 4 trainees. The fundamental counting principle (FCP) tells us there are $3 \times 9 \times 4 = 108$ different

possible teams. There is 1 female partner, 4 experienced female employees, and 3 female trainees. The FCP tells us there are $1 \times 4 \times 3 = 12$ possible combinations of all-female teams. Therefore $\frac{12}{108} = \frac{1}{9}$ of the possible teams are all female.

This problem can also be solved by finding the probability of each event and then multiplying. The probability of choosing a female partner is $\frac{1}{3}$. The probability of choosing a female experienced employee is $\frac{4}{9}$, and the probability of choosing a female trainee is $\frac{3}{4}$. The probability of choosing all three of those things is $\frac{1}{3} \times \frac{4}{9} \times \frac{3}{4} = \frac{1}{9}$.

Worksheet 7

1. If the sequence repeats every 4 terms, you can find the 113th term by finding the remainder when 113 is divided by 4. Since $113 \div 4$ equals 28 with remainder 1, the 113th term will be the same as the first term.

2. Begin by finding the sum of the repeating pattern. Next, determine how many times the pattern occurs in the first 20 terms: $20 \div 5 = 4$ times. Then multiply the sum of the pattern by 4 to obtain the sum.

3. Count the number of negative terms in each repetition of the pattern. Then find how many times the pattern repeats in the first 23 terms. Since $23 \div 3 = 7$ remainder 2, the pattern repeats 7 times and is 2 terms into the 8th repetition. Multiply the number of negative terms per repetition by 7, and if the 1st or 2nd term of the sequence is negative, add it to the total.

4. The first term is 2. The second term is $\frac{1}{2}(2) + 5 = 6$. The third term is $\frac{1}{2}(6) + 5 = 8$. The fourth term is $\frac{1}{2}(8) + 5 = 9$. The fifth term is $\frac{1}{2}(9) + 5 = 9.5$.

5. The pattern repeats every 5 terms, and each repetition contains 3 vowels. Since $121 \div 5 = 24$ remainder 1, the first 121 letters contain $24 \times 3 = 72$ vowels plus the 1 vowel in the first letter of the word EAGLE, for a total of $72 + 1 = 73$.

6. Work backward to solve. x was found by subtracting 4 from the third term and dividing by 3. Therefore, multiply x by 3 and add 4 to get the third term: $3x + 4$. Repeat to find the second term: $3(3x + 4) + 4 = 9x + 12 + 4 = 9x + 16$. Repeat to find the first term: $3(9x + 16) + 4 = 27x + 48 + 4 = 27x + 52$.

7. **B**   The first term is 500, after which each term is 10 less than $\frac{1}{2}$ the previous term. The second term is $\frac{1}{2}(500) - 10 = 240$. The third

term is $\frac{1}{2}(240) - 10 = 110$. The fourth term is $\frac{1}{2}(110) - 10 = 45$.

8. **C**   In this arithmetic sequence you must add 5 to each term. To get from the 1st to the 103rd term you will add 5 a total of 102 times. The value of the 103rd term is thus $-3 + (102)(5) = 507$.

9. **89**   The sequence contains a repeating 4-term pattern: 4315. To find out how many times the pattern repeats in the first 119 terms, divide 119 by 4: $119 \div 4 = 29\frac{3}{4}$. By the 119th term, the pattern has repeated 29 full times and is $\frac{3}{4}$ of the way through the 30th repetition. Each repetition of the pattern contains 3 odd digits, so in the 29 full repetitions there are $29 \times 3 = 87$ odd digits. In the first $\frac{3}{4}$ of the pattern there are 2 odd digits, therefore there are $87 + 2 = 89$ odd digits in the first 119 terms.

10. **D**   In this problem, only the signs of the terms matter. The first term is negative, and the second is positive. The third term is $(-)(+) = -$. The fourth term is $(+)(-) = -$. The fifth term is $(-)(-) = +$. The sixth term is $(-)(+) = -$. The first six terms of the sequence are $-, +, -, -, +, -$. The three-term pattern $-, +, -$ repeats indefinitely. In the first 92 terms, the pattern repeats $92 \div 3 = 30\frac{2}{3}$ times. Each full repetition contains 2 negative numbers, so in 30 full repetitions there are $30 \times 2 = 60$ negative numbers. The 91st term is negative, and the 92nd term is positive. Therefore there are $60 + 1 = 61$ negative numbers.

11. **2**   You can solve this problem by writing it out: 1234567891011121314151617181920212
   The numbers 1–9 require 9 digits
   The numbers 10–19 require 20 digits (29 total).
   The number 20 is two more digits (31 total).
   The number 21 is two more digits (33 total).
   The 2 of 22 is the 34th digit.

12. **C** $4^1 = 4$; $4^2 = 16$; $4^3 = 64$; $4^4 = 256$; $4^5 = 1,024$; $4^6 = 4,096$
   The units digit repeat in the pattern 4, 6, 4, 6, … Every odd term ends in 4; every even term ends in 6. Since 27 is an odd number, 4^{27} will have a units digit of 4.

Worksheet 8

1. **C**

From March to April:	$30 - 15 = 15,000$
From April to May:	$30 - 30 = 0$
From May to June:	$60 - 30 = 30,000$
From June to July:	$65 - 60 = 5,000$
From July to August:	$69 - 65 = 4,000$

2. **D**   The number of visitors in June: 60,000
The number of visitors in March: 15,000

60,000 is what percent greater than 15,000?

$$\frac{(60,000) - (15,000)}{(15,000)} \times 100\% = 300\%$$

3. **200**   25% of the 4,000 students said that chicken was their favorite food. 25% of $4,000 = (0.25) \times 4,000 = 1,000$.
20% of the 4,000 students said that salad was their favorite food. 20% of $4,000 = (0.20) \times 4,000 = 800$.
   Therefore, $1,000 - 800 = 200$ more students preferred chicken.

4. **A**   The revenue generated from 2 troggets, 2 lodards, and 2 plackets is $2a$, $2b$, and $2(6)$, respectively. The total revenue is therefore $2a + 2b + 12$.
   The cost of producing 2 troggets, 2 lodards, and 2 plackets is $2(\$4)$, $2(\$3)$, and $2(c)$, respectively. The total cost is therefore $8 + 6 + 2c = 14 + 2c$
   Therefore the total profit can be found by subtracting the total cost from the total revenue:

$$(2a + 2b + 12) - (14 + 2c) =$$

Distribute: $2a + 2b + 12 - 14 - 2c =$

Combine terms: $2a + 2b - 2 - 2c =$

5. **A**   Find the percent change between each year:

1998–1999: $\dfrac{(35) - (20)}{(20)} \times 100\% = 75\%$

1999–2000: $\dfrac{(50) - (35)}{(35)} \times 100\% = 43\%$

2000–2001: $\dfrac{(35) - (50)}{(50)} \times 100\% = -43\%$

2001–2002: $\dfrac{(40) - (35)}{(35)} \times 100\% = 14\%$

2002–2003: $\dfrac{(20) - (40)}{(40)} \times 100\% = -50\%$

6. **30**   Total number of homes sold between 1998 and 2003 can be found by adding up the number of homes sold during each year:

$$20 + 35 + 50 + 35 + 40 + 20 = 200 \text{ homes sold}$$

The number of homes sold in 2002 and 2003 is $40 + 20 = 60$.
   Therefore the percentage of homes sold after that time period is $\dfrac{60}{200} \times 100\% = 30\%$.

CHAPTER 11

ESSENTIAL GEOMETRY SKILLS

1. Lines and Angles

2. Triangles

3. The Pythagorean Theorem

4. Coordinate Geometry

5. Areas and Perimeters

6. Similar Figures

7. Volumes and 3-D Geometry

8. Circles

Lesson 1: Lines and Angles

When Two Lines Cross

Whenever two lines cross, forming an "X", the angles "across" from each other are always *equal*, and the angles "adjacent" to each other are always *supplementary*, that is, they have a sum of 180°.

Don't be fooled by diagrams that look like vertical angles but aren't. Vertical angles are formed by two and only two crossed lines.

vertical   not vertical

When a Line Crosses Parallel Lines

Imagine taking two crossed lines, making a "copy" of them, and sliding the copy down one of the lines so that together they look like this:

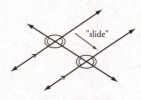

"slide"

This produces a pair of parallel lines crossed by a third line. When two parallel lines are crossed by a third line:

- **All of the *acute* (less than 90°) angles are equal.**
- **All of the *obtuse* (greater than 90°) angles are equal.**
- **Any obtuse angle + any acute angle = 180°.**

To show that two lines are parallel in a diagram, use the arrow marks " > " like those in the figure above. To show that two angles are equal, use the arc marks ")" like those in the figure above.

Don't be fooled by diagrams that only look like they have two parallel lines crossed by another line. **Don't *assume* that two lines are parallel just because they look parallel**. You must be *given* or *deduce* that they are parallel.

If two parallel lines are intersected by a third line, you can look for these special "letters" to find the relationships among the angles:

- **Angles that make Z's are equal:**

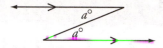

- **Angles that make C's or U's are *supplementary*, that is, they have a sum of 180°.**

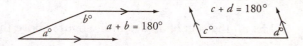

- **Angles that make F's are equal:**

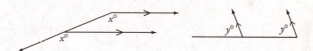

Worksheet 1: Lines and Angles

For questions 1–4, if two parallel lines are intersected by a third line then

1. Angles that make Z's are _____ .

2. Angles that make C's are _____ .

3. Angles that make F's are _____ .

4. Angles that make U's are_____ .

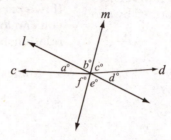

Questions 5 and 6 refer to the figure above in which lines l and m are intersected by rays c and d.

5. List all the pairs of congruent angles in the figure above.

6. List all the sets of angles in the figure above that have a sum of 180°.

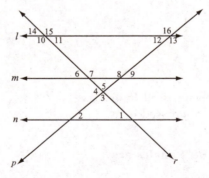

For questions 7–10, if lines l, m, and n are parallel in the figure above, then state whether each pair of angles is *supplementary* (having a sum of 180°), *equal*, or *neither*.

7. ∠9 and ∠12 _____

8. ∠3 and ∠5 _____

9. ∠7 and ∠11 _____

10. ∠8 and ∠14 _____

11.

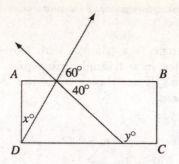

Note: Figure not drawn to scale.

In rectangle *ABCD* above, what is the value of $x + y$?

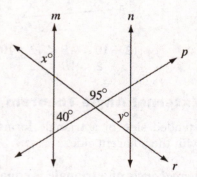

12.

In the figure above, $m \parallel n$. What is the value of $x + y$?

(A) 55
(B) 80
(C) 110
(D) 120
(E) 150

13.

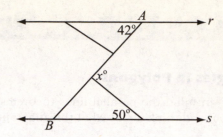

Note: Figure not drawn to scale.

If $r \parallel s$ and line *AB* passes through lines *r* and *s*, what is the value of *x*?

(A) 42
(B) 50
(C) 88
(D) 92
(E) 98

Lesson 2: Triangles

Angles in Polygons

Keep in mind the parallel lines theorems from last lesson, and think about what this diagram shows:

We drew line l so that it is parallel to the opposite side of the triangle. Do you see the two Z's? The angles marked with a are equal, and so are the angles marked with c. We also know that angles that make up a straight line have a sum of 180°, so $a + b + c = 180°$. The angles inside the triangle are also a, b, and c.

The sum of the angles in a triangle is always 180°.

Every polygon with n sides can be divided into $n-2$ triangles that share their vertices (corners) with the polygon:

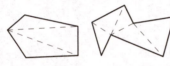

5 sides, 3 triangles   7 sides, 5 triangles

The sum of the angles in any polygon with n sides is $180(n-2)°$.

Angle-Side Relationships in Triangles

A triangle is like an alligator mouth with a stick in it: The wider the mouth, the bigger the stick, right?

Therefore, the largest angle of a triangle is always across from the largest side, and vice versa. Likewise, the smallest angle is always across from the smallest side.

In the figure below, 72 > 70, so $a > b$.

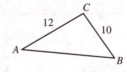

An isosceles triangle is a triangle with two equal sides. **If two sides in a triangle are equal, then the angles across from those sides are equal, too. And vice versa.**

The Triangle Inequality

Look closely at the figure below. The shortest path from point A to point B is the line segment connecting them. Therefore, unless point C is "on the way" from A to B, that is, unless it's on $\overline{AB}$, then the distance from A to B through C must be longer than the direct route. In other words:

- **The sum of any two sides of a triangle is always greater than the third side.**

- **This means that the length of any side of a triangle must be between the sum and the difference of the other two sides.**

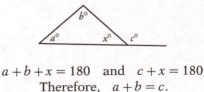

$$12 - 10 < AB < 12 + 10$$
$$2 < AB < 22$$

The External Angle Theorem

The extended side of a triangle forms an *external angle* with the adjacent side.

The *external angle* of a triangle is equal to the sum of the two "remote interior" angles. Notice that this follows from our angle theorems:

$$a + b + x = 180 \quad \text{and} \quad c + x = 180$$
$$\text{Therefore,} \quad a + b = c.$$

Worksheet 2: Triangles

1. The sum of the measures of the angles in a quadrilateral is _____ .

2. In $\triangle ABC$, if the measure of $\angle A$ is 55° and the measure of $\angle B$ is 52°, which side is longest? _____ .

3. The angles in an equilateral triangle must have a measure of _____ .

4. Can an isosceles triangle include angles of 45° and 70°? Why or why not?

5. Draw a diagram to illustrate the external angle theorem.

6. If a triangle has sides of length 12 and 8, then the third side must be less than _____ but greater than _____ .

7. Is it possible for a triangle to have sides of length 4, 6, and 11? Why or why not?

8.

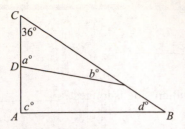

Note: Figure not drawn to scale.

In the figure above, what is the value of $a + b + c + d$?

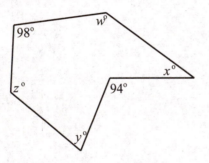

9.

In the figure above, what is the average value (arithmetic mean) of w, x, y, and z?

(A) 86
(B) 87
(C) 88
(D) 89
(E) 90

10.

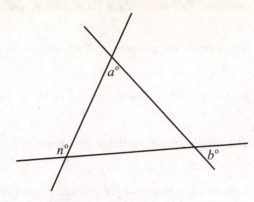

Note: Figure not drawn to scale.

In the figure above, what is the value of n in terms of a and b?

(A) $a - b$
(B) $90 - a + b$
(C) $a + b$
(D) $180 - a + b$
(E) $90 - a - b$

11. The three sides of a triangle have lengths of 8, 12, and m. Which of the following could be the area of the triangle?

      I. 28
     II. 48
    III. 54

(A) I only
(B) II only
(C) I and II only
(D) II and III only
(E) I, II, and III

Lesson 3: The Pythagorean Theorem

The Pythagorean Theorem

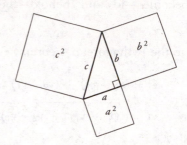

The Pythagorean theorem says that in any right triangle, the sum of the squares of the two shorter sides is equal to the square of the longest side, or

$$a^2 + b^2 = c^2$$

Remember that the Pythagorean theorem *only* applies to right triangles.

If you know two sides of any right triangle, the Pythagorean theorem can always be used to find the third side.

What is x?

Pythagorean theorem:	$9^2 + x^2 = 15^2$
Simplify:	$81 + x^2 = 225$
Subtract 81:	$x^2 = 144$
Take the square root:	$x = 12$

You can also use the *modified Pythagorean theorem* to find whether a triangle is acute or obtuse:

If $(side_1)^2 + (side_2)^2 < (longest\ side)^2$, the triangle is obtuse. (If the stick gets bigger, the alligator's mouth gets wider!)

If $(side_1)^2 + (side_2)^2 > (longest\ side)^2$, the triangle is acute. (If the stick gets smaller, the alligator's mouth gets smaller!)

Special Right Triangles

Certain special right triangles show up frequently on the PSAT. If you see that a triangle fits one of these patterns, it may save you the trouble of using the Pythagorean theorem. But be careful: you must know two of the three "parts" of the triangle in order to assume the third part.

3-4-5 triangles: More accurately, these can be called $3x$-$4x$-$5x$ triangles, because the multiples of 3-4-5 also make right triangles. Notice that the sides satisfy the Pythagorean theorem.

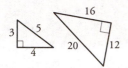

5-12-13 triangles: Likewise, these can be called $5x$-$12x$-$13x$ triangles, because the multiples of 5-12-13 also make right triangles. Notice that the sides satisfy the Pythagorean theorem.

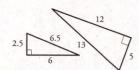

45°-45°-90° triangles: These triangles can be thought of as squares cut on the diagonal. This shows why the angles and sides are related the way they are. Notice that the sides satisfy the Pythagorean theorem.

30°-60°-90° triangles: These triangles can be thought of as equilateral triangles cut in half. This shows why the angles and sides are related the way they are. Notice that the sides satisfy the Pythagorean theorem.

The Distance Formula

Some PSAT problems ask you to find the distance between two points (x_1, y_1) and (x_2, y_2). Look carefully at this diagram and notice that you can find the distance with the Pythagorean theorem. Just think of the distance between the points as the hypotenuse of a right triangle, and the Pythagorean theorem becomes—lo and behold—the distance formula!

According to the Pythagorean theorem,

$$d^2 = (x_2 - x_1)^2 + (y_2 - y_1)^2$$

so $\quad d = \sqrt{(x_2 - x_1)^2 + (y_2 - y_1)^2}$

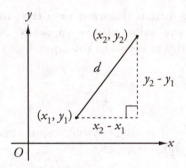

Worksheet 3: The Pythagorean Theorem

1. Draw an example of each of the four "special" right triangles.

Use the modified Pythagorean theorem and the triangle inequality to determine whether a triangle with the given side lengths is *acute, obtuse* or *right*, or *impossible*.

2. 4, 5, 8

3. 4, 4, 14

4. 5, 7, 10

5. 3.5, 5.5, 7.5

6. 4, 14, 14

7. 2, 4, 6

8. Angie leaves her office building and drives 3 miles east, then 4 miles south, then 8 miles west, then 8 miles south. At this point, how many miles is Angie from her office building?

9.

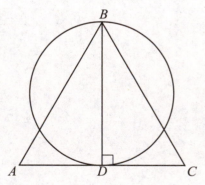

In the figure above, triangle *ABC* is equilateral and *BD* is the diameter of the circle. If the area of the circle is 48π, what is the perimeter of the triangle?

(A) $12\sqrt{3}$
(B) $16 + 4\sqrt{3}$
(C) 24
(D) 36
(E) 48

10. The area of a right triangle is 14 square feet. If the length of each leg, in feet, is a positive integer, what is the <u>least</u> possible length, in feet, of the hypotenuse?

(A) 6
(B) $\sqrt{65}$
(C) 10
(D) $\sqrt{200}$
(E) $\sqrt{785}$

11.

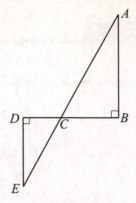

Note: Figure not drawn to scale.

In the figure above, $AB = 8$, $DE = 4$, and $DB = 5$. What is AE?

Lesson 4: Coordinate Geometry

Plotting Points

Some PSAT questions may ask you to work with points on the x-y plane (also known as the coordinate plane or the René Cartesian plane after the mathematician and philosopher René Descartes). **When plotting points, remember these four basic facts to avoid the common mistakes:**

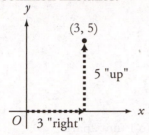

- **The coordinates of a point are always given alphabetically: x-coordinate first and then the y-coordinate.**

- **The x-axis is always horizontal, and the y-axis is always vertical.**

- **On the x-axis, the positive direction is to the right of the origin [where the x- and y-axes meet, point $(0, 0)$].**

- **On the y-axis, the positive direction is up from the origin (where the x- and y-axes meet, point $(0, 0)$).**

Working with Slopes

Every line has a slope, which is the distance you move up or down as you move one unit to the right along the line. Imagine walking between any two points on the line. As you move, you go a certain distance "up or down." This distance is called the *rise*. You also go a certain distance "left or right." This distance is called the *run*.

- **The *slope* is simply the *rise* divided by the *run*.**

$$\text{Slope} = \frac{\text{rise}}{\text{run}} = \frac{y_2 - y_1}{x_2 - x_1}$$

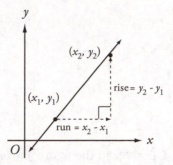

- **You should be able to tell at a glance whether a line has a positive, negative, or zero slope. If the line goes up as it goes to the right, it has a *positive* slope. If it goes down as it goes to the right, it has a *negative* slope. If it's horizontal, it has a *zero* slope.**

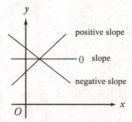

- **If two lines are *parallel*, they must have the *same slope*.**

Finding Midpoints

The *midpoint* of a line segment is the point that divides the segment into two equal parts.

Think of the midpoint as the average of the two endpoints.

$$\text{Midpoint} = \left(\frac{x_1 + x_2}{2}, \frac{y_1 + y_2}{2} \right)$$

Worksheet 4: Coordinate Geometry

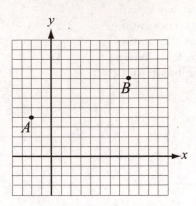

Questions 1–7 refer to the figure above. Horizontal and vertical lines are 1 unit apart.

1. What are the coordinates of point A?

2. What are the coordinates of the midpoint of $\overline{AB}$?

3. What is the slope of $\overline{AB}$?

4. What is the distance from point A to point B?

5. If point A is the midpoint of $\overline{BC}$, what are the coordinates of point C?

6. If point D has the coordinates (8, 4), what is the area of $\triangle ABD$?

7. If line segment $\overline{AB}$ were reflected over the x-axis, what would be the new coordinates for points A and B?

8. The point (5, 12) is on a circle with its center at the origin. Which of the following points is located on the interior of the circle?

    I. (4, 11)
   II. (10, 9)
  III. (−11, −6)

(A) I only
(B) I and II only
(C) I and III only
(D) II and III only
(E) I, II, and III

10.

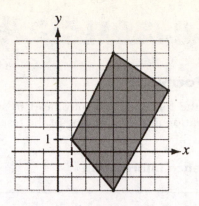

What is the area, in square units, of the shaded region in the figure above?

(A) 16.5
(B) 22.0
(C) 34.5
(D) 38.5
(E) 44.0

9. Line m is a horizontal line that passes through the point (2, 6), and line n is a vertical line that passes through the point (4, 5). What is the x-coordinate of the midpoint of the line segment connecting the point of intersection of lines m and n and the point located at (8, 12)?

11. In the xy-coordinate plane, line m passes through the point (4, 6) and is perpendicular to the line $4x + y = 7$. At what point does line m intersect the y-axis?

(A) (0, 4)
(B) (0, 7)
(C) (0, 2)
(D) (0, 5)
(E) (0, 8)

Lesson 5: Areas and Perimeters

The Formulas

All of the formulas you may need to solve a PSAT area or perimeter problem are given in the Reference Information at the beginning of the test, as shown below.

Reference Information

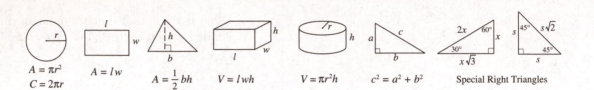

$A = \pi r^2$
$C = 2\pi r$

$A = l w$

$A = \frac{1}{2} bh$

$V = l w h$

$V = \pi r^2 h$

$c^2 = a^2 + b^2$

Special Right Triangles

The arc of a circle measures 360°.
Every straight angle measures 180°.
The sum of the measures of the angles in a triangle is 180°.

Don't confuse the area formula for a circle (πr^2) with the circumference formula ($2\pi r$). Just remember that areas are measured in square units, so the area formula is the one with the radius squared.

Make sure you can find the height of an obtuse triangle when the height is "outside" the triangle: **The height always starts from the vertex opposite the base and must be perpendicular to the line containing the base.**

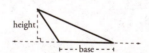

Remember that any side of the triangle can be the base; rotate the triangle if you need to.

Using Diagrams

If a geometry problem doesn't include a figure, draw one! If it does include a diagram, mark it up with any information you find!
If a figure is drawn to scale, you can use the diagram to estimate the lengths of segments or the lengths of angles. You can assume that any figure is drawn to scale, unless it is labeled *"Note: Figure not drawn to scale,"* which means that the figure is drawn inaccurately or in only one of many different possible ways. If the figure is not drawn to scale, it often helps to redraw the figure—if it's drawn inaccurately, redraw it accurately, and see whether anything

important changes. If it can be drawn in different ways, redraw it so that it is as different as possible from the original, but maintaining all of the given information.

Strange Shapes

Don't panic when you see a strange-looking shape on a PSAT. **Just notice how the shape relates to simple shapes.**

In the figure below, the shaded region is constructed of only horizontal or perpendicular sides. That is, all angles are right angles. What is the perimeter of the shaded region?

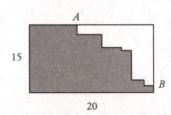

Compare the shaded region with the rectangle, and don't confuse perimeter with area! Even though the area of the shaded region is clearly less that the area of the rectangle, their perimeters must be the same! How do we know? Consider the two different paths from A to B. Notice that all the horizontal segments of the "jagged" path add up in length to the horizontal part of the "simple" path along the rectangle. The same is true of the vertical parts. So the perimeter is $15 + 20 + 15 + 20 = 70$.

If the circle with center C has an area of 16π, what is the area of the shaded region?

Piece together the strange shape from simple shapes. Notice that the shaded region is simply a quarter of the circle minus the triangle. If the area of the circle is 16π, then a quarter of the circle has an area of 4π. Since $\pi r^2 = 16\pi$, the radius must be 4. Therefore, the base and height of the triangle are both 4, and the area of the triangle is $(4 \times 4)/2 = 8$. Thus, the area of the shaded region is $4\pi - 8$.

Worksheet 5: Areas and Perimeters

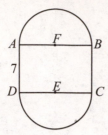

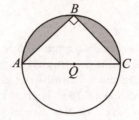

Questions 1 and 2 refer to the figure above, in which *E* and *F* are the centers of two semicircles.

1. If the area of rectangle *ABCD* is 56, what is the perimeter of the figure?

2. If the area of rectangle *ABCD* is 56, what is the area of the entire figure?

Questions 3 and 4 refer to the figure above, in which *Q* is the center of a circle.

3. If the area of isosceles right triangle *ABC* is 18, what is the perimeter of triangle *ABC*?

4. If the area of isosceles right triangle *ABC* is 18, what is the area of the shaded region?

5.

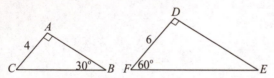

Note: Figure not drawn to scale.

In the figure above, how much greater is the perimeter of triangle *DEF* than the perimeter of triangle *ABC*?

(A) $6 + 2\sqrt{3}$
(B) $5 + 2\sqrt{2}$
(C) 8
(D) $8 + 4\sqrt{3}$
(E) $2 + 6\sqrt{3}$

6.

Note: Figure not drawn to scale.

The figure above consists of two concentric circles. If the shaded circle has a circumference of 10π and the larger circle has a circumference of 36π, what is the area of the <u>unshaded</u> region?

(A) 7π
(B) 121π
(C) 299π
(D) 319π
(E) 324π

7.

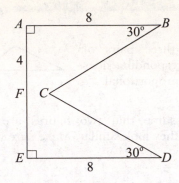

In the figure above, if *F* is the midpoint of side *AE*, what is the area of ΔBCD?

(A) $16\sqrt{2}$
(B) 24
(C) $16\sqrt{3}$
(D) 36
(E) $32\sqrt{3}$

8.

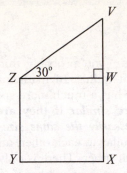

In the figure above, *WXYZ* is a square and *VW* = 4. What is the area of the square?

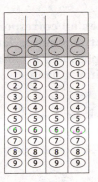

Lesson 6: Similar Figures

Similar Figures

When you think of *similar*, you probably think of "almost the same, but not quite." In mathematics, however, the word *similar* has a much more specific meaning. **Two figures are *similar* if they are *the same shape, but not necessarily the same size.*** For instance, all circles are similar to each other, and all squares are similar to each other. There is only one "shape" for a circle and only one "shape" for a square. But there are many different shapes that a rectangle may have, so two rectangles aren't necessarily similar.

If two shapes are similar, then all corresponding angles are equal and all corresponding lengths are proportional. Use proportions to find the lengths of unknown sides in similar figures.

What is x in the figure below?

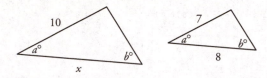

The two triangles are similar because all of their corresponding angles are equal. (Even though only two angles are given as equal, we know that the other pair are equal also, because the angles in a triangle must add up to 180°.) So we can set up a proportion of corresponding sides:

$$\frac{10}{7} = \frac{x}{8}$$

Cross-multiply: $7x = 80$

Divide by 7: $x = 80/7 \approx 11.43$

Two triangles are similar if any of the following is true:

- Two pairs of corresponding angles are equal. (If two pairs are equal, the third pair must be equal, too.)
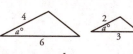

- Two pairs of corresponding sides are proportional, and the angles between them are equal.
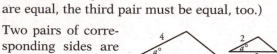

- All three pairs of corresponding sides are proportional.
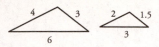

Don't assume that two figures are similar just because they look similar. Make sure you can prove it!

Ratios of Areas

Consider two squares: one with a side length of 2 and the other with a side length of 3. Clearly, their sides are in the ratio of 2:3. What about their areas? That's easy: their areas are $2^2 = 4$ and $3^2 = 9$, so the areas are in a ratio of $4:9$. This demonstrates a fact that is true of all similar figures:

If corresponding lengths of two similar figures have a ratio of $a:b$, then the areas of the two figures have a ratio of $a^2:b^2$.

A garden that is 30 feet long has an area of 600 square feet. A blueprint of the garden that is drawn to scale depicts the garden as being 3 inches long. What is the area of the blueprint drawing of the garden?

It is tempting to want to say 60 square inches because $30:600 = 3:60$. But be careful: the ratio of areas is the square of the ratio of lengths! You can draw a diagram, assuming the garden to be a rectangle. (The shape of the garden doesn't matter: it's convenient to draw the garden as a rectangle, but it doesn't have to be.) Or you can simply set up the proportion using the theorem above:

$$\frac{x}{600} = \frac{3^2}{30^2} = \frac{9}{900}$$

Cross-multiply: $900x = 5400$

Divide by 900: $x = 6$

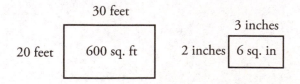

Worksheet 6: Similar Figures

1. If two figures are similar, then their corresponding sides are _____ and their corresponding angles are _____ .

2. What are the three sets of conditions, any one of which is sufficient to show that two triangles are similar?

    a.

    b.

    c.

3. The hypotenuses of two similar right triangles are 6 inches and 8 inches long, respectively. If the area of the smaller triangle is 20 square inches, what is the area of the larger one?

4. The ratio of the areas of two similar rectangles is $9:1$. If the perimeter of the larger rectangle is 30, what is the perimeter of the smaller rectangle?

    (A) 10
    (B) 15
    (C) 20
    (D) 45
    (E) 190

5.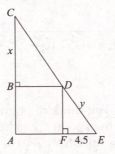

    Note: Figure not drawn to scale.

    If the area of square $ABDF$ in the figure above is 36 and CDE is a line segment, what is the value of $x + y$?

6. In an 8 inch by 12 inch rectangular photograph, the image of a building is 5 inches high. If the photograph is magnified until its perimeter is 720 inches, what is the height, in inches, of the image of the building in the larger photograph?

    (A) 50
    (B) 60
    (C) 90
    (D) 110
    (E) 130

7.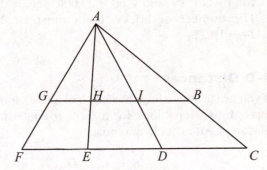

    Note: Figure not drawn to scale.

    In the figure above, $\overline{GB}$ is parallel to $\overline{FC}$, $AG = 6$, $GF = 6$, and $GH = 2HI = 4IB$. If $FC = 14$, what is the value of GH?

    (A) 1
    (B) 2
    (C) 4
    (D) 6
    (E) 7

Lesson 7: Volumes and 3-D Geometry

Volume

The PSAT math section may include a question or two about volumes. Remember two things:

- The volume of a container is nothing more than the number of "unit cubes" it can hold.

- The only volume formulas you will need are given to you in the "Reference Information" on every math section.

How many rectangular bricks measuring 2 inches by 3 inches by 4 inches must be stacked together (without mortar or any other material) to create a solid rectangular box that measures 15 inches by 30 inches by 60 inches?

Don't be too concerned with how the bricks could be stacked to make the box; there are many possible arrangements, but the arrangement doesn't affect the answer. All you need to know is that it can be done. If so, just looking at the volumes is enough: if you use n bricks, then the box must have a volume that is n times larger than the volume of one brick. Each brick has a volume of $2 \times 3 \times 4 = 24$ cubic inches. The box has a volume of $15 \times 30 \times 60 = 27{,}000$ square inches. The number of bricks, then, must be $27{,}000/24 = 1{,}125$.

3-D Distances

If you are trying to find the length of a line segment in three dimensions, look for a right triangle that has that segment as its hypotenuse.

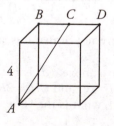

The figure above shows a cube with edges of length 4. If point C is the midpoint of edge BD, what is the length of $\overline{AC}$?

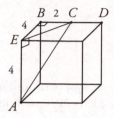

Draw segment $\overline{CE}$ to see that $\overline{AC}$ is the hypotenuse of right triangle $\triangle AEC$. Leg $\overline{AE}$ has a length of 4, and leg $\overline{EC}$ is the hypotenuse of right triangle $\triangle EBC$, with legs of length 2 and 4. Therefore,

$$EC = \sqrt{2^2 + 4^2} = \sqrt{4 + 16} = \sqrt{20}, \text{ and}$$

so $AC = \sqrt{(\sqrt{20})^2 + 4^2} = \sqrt{20 + 16} = \sqrt{36} = 6.$

One possible shortcut for finding lengths in three dimensions is the three-dimensional distance formula:

$$d = \sqrt{(x_2 - x_1)^2 + (y_2 - y_1)^2 + (z_2 - z_1)^2}$$

In the question above, if you think of point A as being the origin $(0, 0, 0)$, then point C can be considered as $(4, 4, 2)$. The distance from A to C, then, is

$$\sqrt{(4-0)^2 + (4-0)^2 + (2-0)^2} = \sqrt{16 + 16 + 4}$$
$$= \sqrt{36} = 6.$$

Worksheet 7: Volumes and 3-D Geometry

1. What is the definition of volume?

2. Write the formula for the volume of a rectangular box.

3. Write the 3-D distance formula.

4. Write the formula for the volume of a cylinder.

5. If the base of a cylinder has a circumference of 20π inches and a height that is equal to the side length of a cube that has a volume of 125 cubic inches, what is the volume of the cylinder?

6.

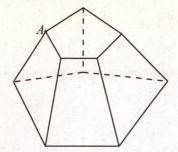

The three-dimensional solid above has two parallel pentagonal bases and 15 edges. If line segments are drawn to connect vertex A with each of the other vertices in the solid, what fraction of these segments lie on an edge of the figure?

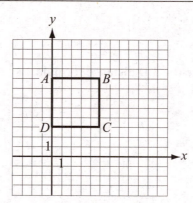

7. A water removal company charges a service fee of $200 per pool emptied and an additional $1.00 per cubic foot of water drained. How much would it cost to hire the company to drain four rectangular pools that are each 50 feet long, 20 feet wide, and uniformly 8 feet deep?

(A) $28,400
(B) $30,500
(C) $32,000
(D) $32,800
(E) $36,000

8.

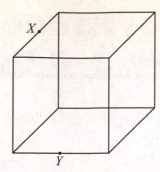

In the figure above, points X and Y are both midpoints of their respective edges, and the volume of the cube is 64. What is the distance from X to Y?

(A) 4
(B) $\sqrt{19}$
(C) 5
(D) $\sqrt{24}$
(B) 6

9.

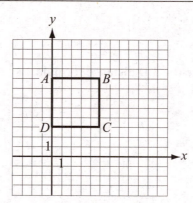

If square ABCD in the figure above is rotated 360° about the y-axis, what is the volume of the solid that is generated?

(A) 125
(B) 64π
(C) 216
(D) 125π
(E) 164π

Lesson 8: Circles

Circle Basics

Okay, we all know a circle when we see one, but it often helps to know the mathematical definition of a circle.

A circle is all of the points in a plane that are a certain distance, *r*, from the center.

The *radius* is the distance from the center to any point on the circle.

Radius means *ray* in Latin; a radius comes from the center of the circle like *a ray of light from the sun.*

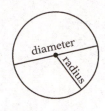

The *diameter* is twice the radius: *d = 2r*.

Dia- means *through* in Latin, so the diameter is a segment that goes *all the way through* the circle.

The Circumference and Area of a Circle

It's easy to confuse the circumference formula with the area formula, because both formulas contain the same symbols arranged differently: circumference $= 2\pi r$ and area $= \pi r^2$. There are two simple ways to avoid that mistake:

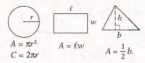

Reference Information

$A = \pi r^2$
$C = 2\pi r$ $A = \ell w$ $A = \frac{1}{2} b.$

The arc of a circle measures 360°.

Remember that the formulas for circumference and area are given in the reference information at the beginning of every math section:

Remember that area is always measured in square units, so the area formula is the one with the "square": area $= \pi r^2$.

Tangents

A *tangent* to a circle is a line that touches (or *intersects*) the circle in only one point.

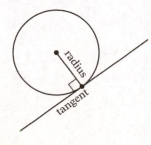

A tangent line is always perpendicular to the radius drawn to the point of tangency. Just think of a bicycle tire (the circle) on the road (the tangent): notice that the center of the wheel must be "directly above" where the tire touches the road, so the radius and tangent must be perpendicular.

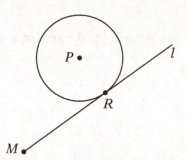

In the diagram above, point *M* is 7 units away from the center of the circle, *P*. If line *l* is tangent to the circle and *MR = 5*, what is the area of the circle?

First, connect the dots. Draw *MP* and *PR* to make a triangle.

Since *PR* is a radius and *MR* is a tangent, they are perpendicular.

Since you know two sides of a right triangle, you can use the Pythagorean theorem to find the third side:

$$5^2 + (PR)^2 = 7^2$$

Simplify: $25 + (PR)^2 = 49$

Subtract 25: $(PR)^2 = 24$

$(PR)^2$ is the radius squared. Since the area of the circle is πr^2, it is 24π.

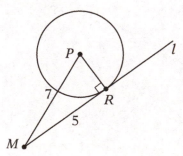

Worksheet 8: Circles

1. What is the formula for the circumference of a circle?

2. What is the formula for the area of a circle?

3. What is a tangent line?

4. What is the relationship between a tangent to a circle and the radius to the point of tangency?

5. In the figure to the right, $\overline{BC}$ is tangent to circle A. If $BC = 4$ and $BD = 2$, what is the area of circle A?

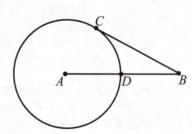

6. What is the area, in square inches, of a circle with a circumference of 36π inches?

(A) 12π
(B) 16π
(C) 81π
(D) 216π
(E) 324π

---

7. Points A and B both lie on circle O. A line containing point A and point B passes through the center of the circle. If the distance from point A to point B is 13 inches, and the distance from point B to point C, another point on the circle, is 5 inches, what is the area, in square inches, of right triangle ABC?

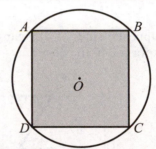

8.

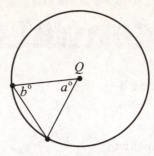

Note: Figure not drawn to scale.

In the figure above, point Q is the center of the circle. If $b = 50$, what is the value of a?

(A) 50
(B) 60
(C) 70
(D) 80
(E) 90

9.

In the figure above, all four vertices of square $ABCD$ lie on the circle O. If $DB = 12\sqrt{2}$, what is the area of the unshaded region?

(A) $36\pi - 81$
(B) $64\pi - 144$
(C) $72\pi - 144$
(D) $108\pi - 81$
(E) $144\pi - 144$

Detailed Answer Key: Essential Geometry Skills

Worksheet I

1. equal

2. supplementary

3. equal

4. supplementary

5. *b* and *e* are congruent; *f* and *c* are congruent.

6. $b + c + d = 180°$; $a + f + e = 180°$;
   $b + a + f = 180°$; $c + d + e = 180°$.

7. equal

8. equal

9. supplementary

10. neither

11. **170** Opposite sides of a rectangle are parallel, so look for a *Z* in the diagram.

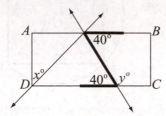

There are 180° in a triangle: $40 + y = 180$
    Subtract 40: $y = 140$

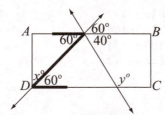

Each angle of a rectangle is 90°; therefore $60 + x = 90$.

    Subtract 60: $x = 30$
    Therefore, $x + y =$ $30 + 140 = 170$

12. **C** Because angles that form a linear pair add up to 180°, you can determine the angles in the central intersection (or "*x*"). Because there are 180° in a triangle, you can fill in the 55°.

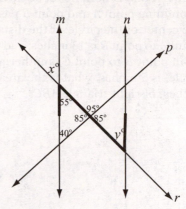

Because vertical angles are equal, $x = 55$. Because lines *m* and *n* are parallel, we know that *y* also equals 55. Therefore $x + y = 55 + 55 = 110$.

13. **D** Because line *r* is parallel to line *s*, the Z-angles (or alternate interior angles) are equal, so they are both 42°:

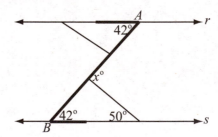

Because there are 180° in a triangle, you can determine that the third angle of the bottom triangle equals 88°:

$42 + 50 + w = 180$
Combine like terms: $92 + w = 180$
        Subtract 92: $w = 88$
Adjacent angles add up to 180°: $x + 88 = 180$
        Subtract 88: $x = 92$

Worksheet 2

1. $360°$

2. Draw a diagram. If the measure of $\angle A$ is $55°$ and the measure of $\angle B$ is $52°$, then the measure of $\angle C$ must be $73°$, because the angles must have a sum of $180°$. Since $\angle C$ is the largest angle, the side opposite it, $\overline{AC}$, must be the longest side.

3. $60°$. Since all the sides are equal, all the angles are, also.

4. No, because an isosceles triangle must have two equal angles, and the sum of all three must be $180°$. Since $45 + 45 + 70 \neq 180$, and $45 + 70 + 70 \neq 180$, the triangle is impossible.

5. Your diagram should look something like this:

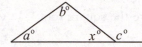

6. Less than $12 + 8 = 20$; greater than $12 - 8 = 4$.

7. No. The sum of the two shorter sides of a triangle is always greater than the third side, but $4+6$ is not greater than 11. So the triangle is impossible.

8. **288**   There are $180°$ in a triangle. Therefore,

$$36 + a + b = 180$$
Subtract 36: $$a + b = 144$$
$$36 + c + d = 180$$
Subtract 36: $$c + d = 144$$
$$a + b + c + d =$$
Substitute: $$144 + 144 = 288$$

9. **D**   The figure in the diagram has 6 sides. So the sum of the angles must be $(6 - 2)180° = 4(180°) = 720°$.

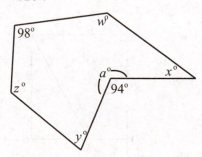

There are $360°$ in a circle: $a + 94 = 360$
Subtract 94: $a = 266$

There are $720°$ in a hexagon (6 sides), so:

$$y + a + z + 98 + w + x = 720$$
Substitute for a: $y + 266 + z + 98 + w + x = 720$
Combine like terms: $y + 364 + z + w + x = 720$
Subtract 364: $y + z + w + x = 356$

Divide by 4: $\dfrac{y + z + w + x}{4} = 89$

10. **C**   There are $180°$ in a triangle, so

$$a + b + (180 - n) = 180$$
Subtract 180: $$a + b - n = 0$$
Add n: $$a + b = n$$

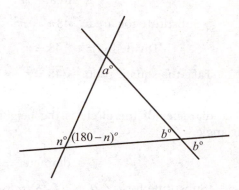

11. **C**   Consider the side of length 8 to be the base and "attach" the side of length 12. Notice that the triangle has the greatest possible height when the two sides form a right angle. Therefore, the greatest possible area of such a triangle is $\frac{1}{2}(12)(8) = 48$, and the minimum possible area is 0. Statements I and II are possible.

Worksheet 3

1. Your diagrams should include one each of a $3x$-$4x$-$5x$ triangle, a $5x$-$12x$-$13x$ triangle, a $30°$-$60°$-$90°$ triangle, and a $45°$-$45°$-$90°$ triangle.

2. Obtuse: $4^2 + 5^2 = 41 < 8^2 = 64$

3. Impossible: $4 + 4$ is not greater than 14

4. Obtuse: $5^2 + 7^2 = 74 < 10^2 = 100$

5. Obtuse: $3.5^2 + 5.5^2 = 42.5 < 7.5^2 = 56.25$

6. Acute: $4^2 + 14^2 = 212 > 14^2 = 196$

7. Impossible: $2 + 4$ is not greater than 6.

8. **13** Draw a diagram like this:

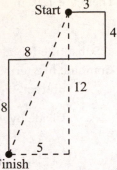

The distance from the starting point to the finishing point is the hypotenuse of a right triangle with legs of 5 and 12. Therefore the distance can be found with the Pythagorean theorem: $5^2 + 12^2 = 25 + 144 = 169 = c^2$. So $c = 13$. Notice this is a 5-12-13 triangle!

9. **E** If the area of the circle is 48π, you can find the radius of the circle using

$$\text{Area} = \pi r^2$$

Substitute for area: $\quad 48\pi = \pi r^2$

Divide by π: $\quad 48 = r^2$

Take the square root: $\quad \sqrt{48} = r = 4\sqrt{3}$

The diameter of the circle is the height of the triangle.

$$\text{diameter} = 2r$$

Substitute for r: $\quad 2r = 2(4\sqrt{3}) = 8\sqrt{3}$

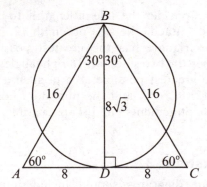

Any equilateral triangle can be split into two 30°-60°-90° triangles. The perimeter $= 8 + 8 + 16 + 16 = 48$

10. **B**
$$\text{Area} = \frac{1}{2}(\text{base})(\text{height})$$

Substitute: $\quad 14 = \frac{1}{2}(\text{base})(\text{height})$

Multiply by 2: $\quad 28 = (\text{base})(\text{height})$

The base and the height are both integers. Find all the "factor pairs" of 28: 1×28, 2×14, and 4×7.

Plug each pair into the Pythagorean theorem to find the least possible length of the hypotenuse.

$$a^2 + b^2 = c^2$$
$$1^2 + 28^2 = c^2$$

Simplify: $\quad 1 + 784 = c^2$

Combine like terms: $\quad 785 = c^2$

Take the square root: $\quad \sqrt{785} = c$

$$a^2 + b^2 = c^2$$
$$2^2 + 14^2 = c^2$$

Simplify: $\quad 4 + 196 = c^2$

Combine like terms: $\quad 200 = c^2$

Take the square root: $\quad \sqrt{200} = c$

$$a^2 + b^2 = c^2$$
$$4^2 + 7^2 = c^2$$

Simplify: $\quad 16 + 49 = c^2$

Combine like terms: $\quad 65 = c^2$

Take the square root: $\quad \sqrt{65} = c$

$\sqrt{65}$ is the shortest possible hypotenuse.

11. **13** Mark the diagram with the given information. The dotted lines show that AE is the hypotenuse of a right triangle with legs of length 5 and 12. So to find it, just use the Pythagorean theorem

$$5^2 + 12^2 = (AE)^2$$

Simplify: $\quad 25 + 144 = (AE)^2$

Combine like terms: $\quad 169 = (AE)^2$

Take the square root: $\quad 13 = AE$

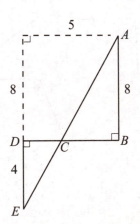

Worksheet 4

1. $(-2, 4)$

2. $(3, 6)$

3.
$$\text{Slope} = \frac{8 - 4}{8 - (-2)} = \frac{8 - 4}{8 + 2} = \frac{4}{10} = \frac{2}{5}$$

4.
$$\text{Distance} = \sqrt{(8 - 4)^2 + (8 - (-2)^2} = \sqrt{4^2 + 10^2}$$
$$= \sqrt{116}$$

5. To get from B to A, you must go down 4 and over 10. If A is the midpoint of BC, then to get from A to C, you must also go down 4 and over 10. Thus the coordinates of point C would be $(-12, 0)$.

6. Area $= \frac{1}{2}(\text{base})(\text{height}) = \frac{1}{2}(10)(4) = 20$

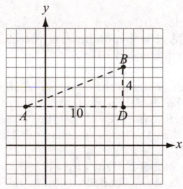

7. The reflected points would be A: $(-2, -4)$ and B: $(8, -8)$.

8. **C** You can solve this by using the distance formula.

Find the length of the radius: $5^2 + 12^2 = r^2 = 13^2$
        Take the square root: $r = 13$

Any segment longer than 13 is outside the circle. Use the distance formula to find the distance of each of the points listed in the three statements from the origin $(0, 0)$.

I.
$(4,11)$ $\sqrt{(4 - 0)^2 + (11 - 0)^2} = \sqrt{4^2 + 11^2}$
$$= \sqrt{137}$$

II.
$(10,9)$ $\sqrt{(10 - 0)^2 + (9 - 0)^2} = \sqrt{10^2 + 9^2}$
$$= \sqrt{181}$$

III.
$(-11, -6)$ $\sqrt{(-11 - 0)^2 + (-6 - 0)^2}$
$$= \sqrt{(-11)^2 + (-6)^2} = \sqrt{157}$$

The values in I and III are less than 13, so these points are inside the circle.

This can also be solved by drawing a graph and plotting the points.

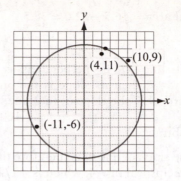

9. **6** The lines intersect at $(4, 6)$.

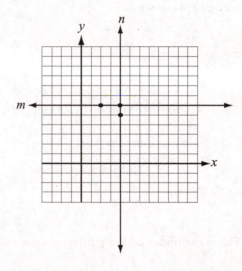

The midpoint between $(4, 6)$ and $(8, 12)$ is

$$\left(\frac{(8 + 4)}{2}, \frac{(12 + 6)}{2}\right) = \left(\frac{12}{2}, \frac{18}{2}\right) = (6, 9)$$

10. **D** One way to find the area is to split the figure into two triangles:

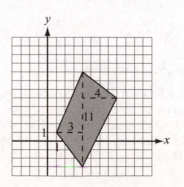

Area of the left triangle $= \frac{1}{2}(11)(3) = 16.5$

Area of the right triangle $= \frac{1}{2}(11)(4) = 22.0$

Total area $= 16.5 + 22.0 = 38.5$

11. **D** If line m is perpendicular to the line $4x + y = 7$, then its slope is the opposite of the reciprocal of the slope of that line.

$$4x + y = 7$$

Subtract $4x$: $y = -4x + 7$

The slope of line m is therefore the opposite of the reciprocal of -4, which is $+1/4$.

The question wants to know the value of the y-intercept. Use $y = mx + b$ form (b is the y-intercept) to solve.

$$y = mx + b$$

Substitute for m: $y = \frac{1}{4}x + b$

Substitute for y and x: $6 = \frac{1}{4}(4) + b$

Subtract 1: $5 = b$

The coordinates of the y-intercept are (0, 5).

Worksheet 5

1. If the area of the rectangle is 56 and $AD = 7$, then AB must equal 8 because   area $= lw$.

Substitute: $56 = 7(w)$

Divide by 7: $8 = w$

Therefore the perimeter is $7 + 8 + 8 + 7 = 30$.

2. If $AB = 8$, then the radius of semicircle F is 4. The area of the semicircle $= \frac{1}{2}(\pi r^2) = \frac{1}{2}(\pi(4)^2) = \frac{1}{2}(16\pi) = 8\pi$. Semicircle E has the same area. So the total area of the figure is $56 + 8\pi + 8\pi = 56 + 16\pi$.

3. The area of triangle $ABC = \frac{1}{2}$(base)(height).

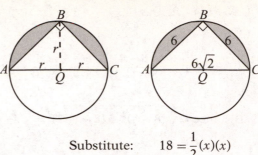

Substitute: $18 = \frac{1}{2}(x)(x)$

Simplify: $18 = \frac{1}{2}x^2$

Divide by $\frac{1}{2}$: $36 = x^2$

Take square root: $6 = x$

Triangle ABC is an isosceles 45°-45°-90° right triangle. The hypotenuse is therefore $6\sqrt{2}$, and the perimeter is $12 + 6\sqrt{2}$.

4. If the diameter of the circle is $6\sqrt{2}$, then the radius must be $3\sqrt{2}$. To find the area of the shaded region, find the area of half the circle and subtract from that the area of triangle ABC. $A = \pi r^2 = \pi(3\sqrt{2})^2 = 18\pi$.

The area of half the circle is $\frac{1}{2}(18\pi) = 9\pi$, and so the area of the shaded region is $9\pi - 18$.

5. **A**   They are both 30°-60°-90° triangles. Therefore, the sides are proportional to those in the 30°-60°-90° triangle in the reference information: $x - x\sqrt{3} - 2x$. The perimeter of triangle ABC is $4+8 +4\sqrt{3} = 12 + 4\sqrt{3}$. The perimeter of triangle DEF is $6 + 12 + 6\sqrt{3} = 18 + 6\sqrt{3}$. The difference between them is $(18 + 6\sqrt{3}) - (12 + 4\sqrt{3}) = 6 + 2\sqrt{3}$.

6. **C**   Find the radius of each circle. $C = 2\pi r$. Substitute circumference of smaller circle:

$$10\pi = 2\pi r$$

Divide by 2π. $5 = r$

$$C = 2\pi r$$

Substitute circumference of larger circle:

$$36\pi = 2\pi r$$

Divide by 2π. $18 = r$

To find the unshaded area, find the area of the bigger circle and subtract the area of the smaller circle.

Smaller circle: $A = \pi r^2$

Substitute: $A = \pi(5)^2 = 25\pi$

Larger circle: $A = \pi r^2$

Substitute: $A = \pi(18)^2 = 324\pi$

Unshaded area $= 324\pi - 25\pi = 299\pi$

7. **C**   If you draw in the dotted line from B to D, it creates a right angle and you can fill in two $60°$ angles. Since there are $180°$ in a triangle, triangle BCD must be equilateral.

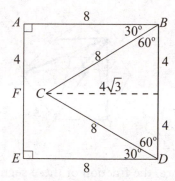

F is the midpoint of AE, which is 4. Therefore $AE = 8$ because $2(4) = 8$. The dotted line connecting points B and D has a length equal to AE, which is 8.

If you draw in the height of triangle BCD, you split it into two $30°$-$60°$-$90°$ triangles. Therefore, the sides are proportional to those in the $30°$-$60°$-$90°$ triangle in the reference information: $x - x\sqrt{3} - 2x$. From this you can determine that the height of triangle BCD is $4\sqrt{3}$.

Area of triangle $BCD = \frac{1}{2}(8)(4\sqrt{3}) = 16\sqrt{3}$

8. **48**   Triangle ZWV is a $30°$-$60°$-$90°$ triangle. Therefore, the sides are proportional to those in the $30°$-$60°$-$90°$ triangle in the reference information: $x - x\sqrt{3} - 2x$.

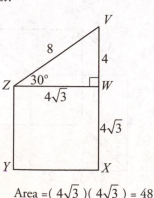

Area $= (4\sqrt{3})(4\sqrt{3}) = 48$

Worksheet 6

1. If two figures are similar, then their corresponding sides are *proportional* and their corresponding angles are *equal (or congruent)*.

2. a. Two pairs of corresponding angles are equal.
   b. Two pairs of corresponding sides are proportional, and the included angles are equal.
   c. All three pairs of corresponding sides are proportional.

3. The ratio of the sides is $6:8$ or $3:4$. The ratio of the areas is the square of the ratio of sides, which is $9:16$. If x is the area of the larger triangle, then $20/x = 9/16$. Solving for x gives $x = 35\frac{5}{9}$.

4. **A**   If the ratio of the areas is $9:1$, then the ratio of the corresponding lengths is the square root: $\sqrt{9}: \sqrt{1}$, or $3:1$. If the perimeter of the larger rectangle is 30, then the perimeter of the smaller one is $1/3$ the size, or 10.

5. **15.5**   If the area of the square is 36, then the length of its sides must be 6. Triangles DFE and CBD are similar, and the ratio of their sides is $6:4.5$, or $4:3$.

To solve for x, set up a ratio:

$$\frac{6}{4.5} = \frac{x}{6}$$

Cross-multiply: $36 = 4.5x$

Divide by 4.5: $8 = x$

Use the Pythagorean theorem to determine the hypotenuse of triangle BCD.

$$6^2 + 8^2 = CD^2$$

Simplify: $100 = CD^2$

Take the square root: $10 = CD$

To solve for y, set up a ratio:

$$\frac{10}{y} = \frac{6}{4.5}$$

Cross-multiply: $6y = 45$

Divide by 6: $y = 7.5$

$$x + y = 8 + 7.5 = 15.5$$

6. **C**   The original perimeter of the photo is $8 + 8 + 12 + 12 = 40$. If it is magnified to 18 times its original size ($40 \times 18 = 720$), then the image of the building will be magnified by 18 times also: $5 \times 18 = 90$.

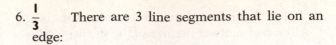

7. **C**   Since the lines are parallel, ΔABG is similar to ΔACF, and the ratio of the side lengths is

$$AF: AG = 12:6 = 2:1.$$

This is equal to the ratio of FC to GB

$$\frac{FC}{GB} = \frac{2}{1}$$

Substitute for FC: $\dfrac{14}{GB} = \dfrac{2}{1}$

Cross-multiply: $14 = 2(GB)$

Divide by 2: $7 = GB$

Because $GH = 2HI = 4IB$, if $IB = x$, then $GH = 4x$ and $HI = 2x$. $GB = GH + HI + IB$

Substitute: $7 = 4x + 2x + x = 7x$

Divide by 7: $1 = x$

Therefore the length of GH is $4(x) = 4(1) = 4$.

Worksheet 7

1. The volume of a solid is the number of unit cubes that fit inside of it.
2. $V = lwh$
3. $$d = \sqrt{(x_2 - x_1)^2 + (y_2 - y_1)^2 + (z_2 - z_1)^2}$$

4. $V = \pi r^2 h$

5. If the base of the cylinder has a circumference of 20π, its radius can be found using: $C = 2\pi r$

    Substitute: $20\pi = 2\pi r$
    Divide by: $2\pi \quad 10 = r$

    If the volume of a cube is 125, its side length can be found using: $V = s^3$

    Substitute: $125 = s^3$
    Take cube root: $5 = s$

                        $V = \pi r^2 h$

    Substitute: $V = \pi(10)^2(5)$
    Simplify: $V = 500\pi$

6. $\dfrac{1}{3}$ There are 3 line segments that lie on an edge:

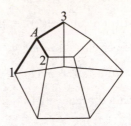

There are 6 line segments that do not lie on an edge:

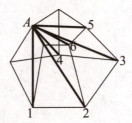

Therefore, the fraction of these segments that lie on an edge is $\dfrac{3}{9}$, or $\dfrac{1}{3}$.

7. **D**   Begin by determining the cost of emptying one pool. The price of emptying a pool, P, is a function of x, the volume of the pool in cubic feet: $P = \$200 + \$1.00(x)$.

    A pool that is $8 \times 50 \times 20$ can hold 8,000 cubic feet of water. The cost of emptying that pool is

$$\$200 + \$1.00(8,000) = \$8,200$$

The cost of emptying four such pools would be $4 \times \$8,200 = \$32,800$

8. **D**   Volume of cube $= 64 = s^3$

    Take cube root: $4 = s$

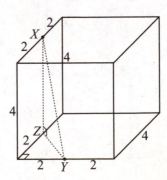

To find the distance from X to Y, you must first find the distance from Y to Z. $\quad 2^2 + 2^2 = (ZY)^2$

Simplify: $\qquad\qquad\qquad\qquad 8 = (ZY)^2$

Take square root: $\qquad\qquad\quad \sqrt{8} = ZY$

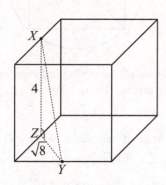

Now you can find the distance from X to Y:

$$(\sqrt{8})^2 + 4^2 = (XY)^2$$

Simplify: $\qquad\qquad 24 = (XY)^2$

Take square root: $\quad \sqrt{24} = XY$

9. **D** If square $ABCD$ is rotated about the y-axis, it creates a cylinder. The radius of the cylinder is 5, and the height of the cylinder is 5.

$$V = \pi r^2 h$$

Substitute: $\quad V = \pi(5)^2(5)$

Simplify: $\quad V = 125\pi$

Worksheet 8

1. circumference $= 2\pi r$

2. area $= \pi r^2$

3. A tangent line is a line that intersects a circle in only one point.

4. Any tangent to a circle is perpendicular to the radius drawn to the point of tangency.

5. BC is perpendicular to radius AC. The value of r can be found using the Pythagorean theorem:

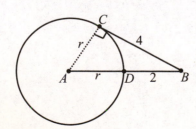

$$r^2 + 4^2 = (r + 2)^2$$

$$r^2 + 16 = r^2 + 4r + 4$$

Subtract r^2: $\qquad 16 = 4r + 4$

Subtract 4: $\qquad\quad 12 = 4r$

Divide by 4: $\qquad\;\; 3 = r$

The area of the circle $= \pi(3)^2$.

Simplify: $\quad A = 9\pi$

6. **E** $\qquad\qquad\qquad\qquad C = 2\pi r$

Substitute: $\quad 36\pi = 2\pi r$

Divide by 2π: $\quad 18 = r$

$$A = \pi r^2$$

Substitute: $\quad A = \pi(18)^2$

Simplify: $\quad A = 324\pi$

7. **30** Draw a diagram that represents the given information:

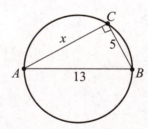

Use the Pythagorean theorem to solve for x in right triangle ACB.

$$5^2 + x^2 = 13^2$$

Simplify: $\quad 25 + x^2 = 169$

Subtract 25: $\qquad x^2 = 144$

Take square root: $\qquad x = 12$

$$A = \frac{1}{2}bh$$

Substitute: $\qquad A = \frac{1}{2}(5)(12)$

Simplify: $\qquad A = 30$

8. **D**   In the diagram below, $QX = QY$ because they are both radii of the circle.

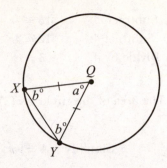

Because the two sides are equal, triangle QXY is isosceles and the two angles opposite those sides are equal to each other.

There are 180° in a triangle, so $b + b + a = 180$

Substitute: $50 + 50 + a = 180$

Subtract 100: $a = 80$

9. **C**   If the diameter of the circle is $12\sqrt{2}$, then the radius is $6\sqrt{2}$ and the side length of the square is 12, because every square can be split into two 45°-45°-90° triangles.

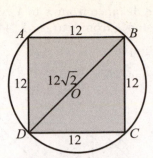

To find the area of the unshaded region, first find the area of the circle. Then subtract the area of the square.

Area of the circle $= \pi(6\sqrt{2})^2$

Simplify: $A = 72\pi$

Area of the square $= (12)^2 = 144$

The unshaded area $= 72\pi - 144$.

CHAPTER 12

ATTACKING THE PSAT WRITING QUESTIONS

1. Don't Sweat the Small Stuff

2. How to Attack Identifying Sentence Errors Questions

3. How to Attack the Tougher Questions

4. How to Attack Improving Sentences Questions

5. How to Attack Improving Paragraphs Questions

▌ DON'T SWEAT THE SMALL STUFF

Most of us have been scolded by an English teacher to "never end a sentence with a preposition," "never start a sentence with *and, but,* or *because,*" "never use *I* or *you* in a formal essay," or "never split an infinitive." If you have heard enough of these, you may think that grammar involves little more than memorizing scores of arbitrary and nonsensical rules. In fact, the "rules" stated above are more pet peeves than solid rules of English grammar, and so they are not tested on the PSAT Writing test.

The PSAT Writing section tests your knowledge of only about a dozen rules of grammar, all of which will be discussed in detail in Chapter 13. These are sound rules of effective and clear writing, and not nit-picky pet peeves. The rules discussed below, on the other hand, may bother some of your English teachers, but they shouldn't bother you when you take the PSAT, because they *won't* be included.

Don't worry about *who* vs. *whom*

The PSAT Writing test will almost certainly not include questions involving the choice between *who* and *whom*. These pronouns differ in *case,* a topic discussed in Chapter 13, Lesson 6. You should know how to correct certain mistakes involving pronoun case, such as correcting *just between you and I* to read *just between you and me.* The distinction between *who* and *whom,* however, is not as clear as the distinction between *I* and *me.* For instance, *me* is always used in situations that call for an **object** to a verb, as in *The man approached me.* Similarly, *whom* is usually preferred in situations that call for an object, but **not always**. For instance, a sentence like *For whom are you voting?* is often excessively formal, even for published prose. Therefore, it is often acceptable to write *Who are you voting for?* even though the pronoun is acting as an object to the verb.

In fact, English pronouns have been evolving away from such "case markers" for centuries. For instance, where English used to have the subjective *thou* and the objective *thee,* it now has just one word to play both roles: *you.* Quite likely, English is evolving away from *whom* in the same way.

Don't worry about split infinitives

Split infinitives will not appear on the PSAT Writing, so you won't have to spot or correct them. An infinitive is a *to* phrase, like *to drop,* that

represents the basic form of a verb (see Chapter 13, Lesson 3). An infinitive is "split" when an adverb is wedged in the middle, as in *The news caused the stock price **to suddenly drop**.* In this case, you should "unsplit" the infinitive: *The news caused the stock price **to drop suddenly**.* The "rule" against splitting an infinitive, however, is not universal, because some ideas can't be expressed concisely without splitting infinitives. For instance, any "unsplitting" of the infinitive in the sentence *The company plans **to more than double** its revenue next year* will make the sentence wordier or more awkward. Try it and see!

Don't worry about ending a sentence with a preposition

One of the most popular pet peeves among English teachers is the preposition at the end of a sentence, as in *Who are you going with?* **The PSAT will not include prepositions at the ends of sentences, so you won't need to spot or correct them.** You should know, however, that the "rule" against them is really just a suggestion and that clear expression sometimes requires ending sentences with prepositions. We already noted one example above: the sentence *Who are you voting for?* sounds needlessly formal when we try to avoid ending it with a preposition. Winston Churchill once said, after someone had chastised him about this rule, *"That is the type of arrant pedantry up with which I will not put!"* The best way to understand the "rule" is as a suggestion: avoid ending sentences with a preposition unless you have no better option.

Don't worry about starting a sentence with *and, but,* or *because*

Another thing that upsets some English teachers is starting a sentence with *and, but,* or *because.* **Because such "rules" are frequently broken by very good writers, you shouldn't worry about them on the PSAT.**

Next to the groundless notion that it is incorrect to end an English sentence with a preposition, perhaps the most widespread of many false beliefs about the use of our language is the equally groundless notion that it is incorrect to begin one with "but" or "and." As in the case of the superstition about the prepositional ending, no textbook supports it, but apparently about half of our teachers of English go out of their way to handicap their pupils by inculcating it. One cannot help wondering whether those who teach such monstrous doctrine ever read any English themselves.

> —Charles Allen Lloyd,
> *We Who Speak English, and
> Our Ignorance of Our Mother Tongue* (1938)

Many eminent writers have flouted this "rule."

Because of the war the situation in hospitals is, of course, serious.

> —E. B. White, "A Weekend with the Angels,"
> in *The Second Tree from the Corner* (1954)

If we view the paragraph as a discursive development of a proposition, we can predict that the topic sentence of the paragraph in question will generate a development based on objectives. And this is exactly what we do find.

> —W. Ross Winterowd,
> *Rhetoric: A Synthesis* (1968)

But it must not be assumed that intelligent thinking can play no part in the formation of the goal and of ethical judgments.

> —Albert Einstein, "Science and Religion"
> (1939) in *Ideas and Opinions* (1954)

Don't worry about fixing sentences on the PSAT that begin with *and, but*, or *because*. However, **always** fix clauses following a semicolon (;) or colon (:) that begin with *and, but*, or *because*. A clause that follows a semicolon or colon must usually be an *independent clause* (see Chapter 13, Lesson 15) that supports the previous independent clause. Therefore, starting such a clause with *and* is redundant, because the semicolon or colon already performs the job of a conjunction. Starting such a clause with *but* is illogical, because the semicolon or colon indicates a **supportive** relationship between the clauses, not a contrasting one. Starting such a clause with *because* is ungrammatical, because such a clause is **dependent** rather than **independent**.

Don't worry about starting sentences with adverbs like *hopefully* or *clearly*

Some English teachers claim that every adverb must modify a particular verb, adjective, or adverb in the sentence, so a sentence like *Obviously, the muddy windshield obscured her vision* is wrong, because the adjective *obviously* doesn't properly modify the verb *obscured*. (How can something *obscure obviously*?) These teachers are wrong. The word *obviously* in this sentence is a **sentence modifier**. It conveys the speaker's attitude toward the statement

the sentence makes, rather than modifying a particular word in the sentence. The word *obviously* here simply means *I consider the following fact to be obvious*. But I think you'd agree it says so in a much more concise and elegant way.

Here is a partial list of some common sentence modifiers:

accordingly	*admittedly*	*arguably*	*consequently*
clearly	*curiously*	*fortunately*	*hopefully*
ironically	*paradoxically*	*regrettably*	*sadly*
strangely	*theoretically*		

Don't worry about possessive antecedents

The 2002 PSAT Writing contained the following question:

> Toni Morrison's genius enables <u>her to create</u>
>   A
>
> novels <u>that arise from</u> <u>and express</u> the injustice
>   B   C
>
> African Americans <u>have endured</u>. <u>No error</u>
>   D   E

The ETS gave an original answer of E, no error. But some teachers argued that the answer should be A, because *her* refers to the possessive *Toni Morrison's*. Possessives such as *Toni Morrison's* are adjectives, not nouns, and some English teachers were taught that pronouns cannot refer to nouns that have been "possessified" into adjectives. The ETS responded, appropriately, that to correct such an "error" would make the sentence sound very awkward—the word *her* would have to be replaced by *Toni Morrison*, which is clearly redundant. To avoid needless wrangling, however, the ETS threw out the question. Although no reputable textbook contains such a rule against possessive antecedents—the antecedent is the word the pronoun refers to—you can be sure the ETS will try to avoid such "mistakes" on future PSATs.

You won't need to worry about the "problem" of possessive antecedents on the PSAT. However, you do need to be sure that definite pronouns such as *it, he, she*, or *they* refer to clear and unambiguous antecedents.

Don't worry about *that* vs. *which*

Some writers make themselves nuts trying to figure out whether to use *that* or *which* when they write. Thankfully, you won't need to worry about this on the PSAT Writing test.

However, if you want to know how best to choose between *that* and *which* when you write, here's the rule: *which* is best in **nonrestrictive** clauses, and *that* is best in **restrictive** clauses. A restrictive clause gives essential information about the noun that precedes it, as in *The books* that are on that table *are for sale*. A nonrestrictive clause, on the other hand, gives incidental or nonessential information about the noun that precedes it, as in *The books*, which have been discounted, *are all bestsellers*. Still too complicated? Here's a simpler rule: which almost always follows a comma. If there's no comma, *that* probably works better. Another simple rule: *what* usually works better than *that which*.

Not good: *Second Federal is the only bank in town which does not finance mortgages.*
Better: *Second Federal is the only bank in town that does not finance mortgages.*

The clause following *town* is **restrictive**. If it were omitted, the meaning of the sentence would change completely.

Not good: *The corporation approved of the commercial which lasted all of 20 seconds.*
Better: *The corporation approved of the commercial, which lasted all of 20 seconds.*

The clause following *commercial* is **nonrestrictive** and so should be separated from the main part of the sentence with a comma. Even if this clause were omitted, the sentence would still make sense.

Not good: *We pursue most fervently that which we cannot have.*
Better: *We pursue most fervently what we cannot have.*

The two adjacent pronouns in the original sentence serve as the objects of the two clauses, but since they refer to the same thing, we replace them with a single pronoun.

Don't worry too much about *bad/badly* and *good/well*

On the PSAT Writing test, you will sometimes be expected to spot and fix problems with modifiers, such as an adjective being used where an adverb is needed. **Don't worry too much about the *bad/badly* or *good/well* issue, though**.

Some folks think that you should never say *I feel good*, that you should say *I feel well* instead, because *well* is an adverb modifying the verb *feel*. Likewise, they think you shouldn't say *This tastes bad*, but rather *This tastes badly* because *badly* is an adverb modifying the verb *taste*. Such an analysis is completely wrong. Both *I feel good* and *I feel well* are good, grammatical sentences. In the first sentence, *feel* is a linking verb joining *I* to its adjective *good*. Likewise, in the second sentence, *feel* is a linking verb joining *I* to its adjective *well*. In this sentence, *well* is **not** an adverb (as in *she plays very well*), but an adjective meaning *healthy* (as in *they were sick, but now they are well*). The sentence *This tastes badly*, on the other hand, is illogical. The sentence is describing the *bad taste* of something, not the *bad manner in which something tastes*. The correct phrasing is *This tastes bad*.

Don't worry about disappearing *thats*

On some PSAT Writing questions, you might notice a "disappearing" *that* as in *I like the sweater you gave me* rather than *I like the sweater **that** you gave me*. You should know that either sentence is fine. The sentence *I like the sweater you gave me* uses **standard ellipsis**. *Ellipsis* **is the omission of one or more words from a sentence because they are understood implicitly**. Since no one would ever be confused about what *I like the sweater you gave me* means, there's no need for the *that*.

2 HOW TO ATTACK IDENTIFYING SENTENCE ERRORS QUESTIONS

Every PSAT will include about 14 Identifying Sentence Errors questions, each of which consists of a sentence with four underlined parts. Your job is to determine whether the sentence contains an error in grammar or usage. If it does, choose the underlined portion that contains the error. If it does not, choose E, for "no error."

You don't need to correct the error, just locate it.

Any error in these sentences must be correctable by replacing *only* the selected underlined portion. Every other part of the sentence must remain the same.

> The team <u>diligently</u> practiced and
>   A
> <u>prepared</u> several trick plays, but
>   B
> <u>were</u> never given the opportunity to
> C
> use <u>them</u>. <u>No error</u>
>   D   E

You might prefer to say the team *practiced diligently* rather than that the team *diligently practiced*. But choosing A would be incorrect, because this "correction" would involve moving a word rather than merely replacing it. (Remember, every other part of the sentence must remain unchanged, so that kind of moving around isn't allowed.) In fact, either phrasing is fine: the adverb can come before or after the verb. The sentence does contain a blatant grammatical error, though. The subject of the verb *were*, which is plural, is the noun *team*, which is singular. (At least it is in standard *American* English. In standard British English, however, collective words like *team* are considered plural, so be careful, Brits—this is an American test!) So choice C is the correct response, because the correct verb form is *was*.

Listen for the clunker

To attack "Identifying Sentence Errors" questions, first read the entire sentence *normally*, and listen for any part of the sentence that sounds bad. **Don't analyze the sentence too much the first time through—ignore the underlines and just read normally.** If something sounds wrong, it probably is.

The more well-written English prose you have read, the more you can trust your "ear" to tell you what part of the sentence is wrong. As the questions get more difficult, however, your ear may become less reliable.

Make sure it's a real mistake

If an underlined part of the sentence sounds wrong, try to identify the error. Make sure that it's a *legitimate grammatical mistake*. Just because you can say something differently doesn't mean that the original phrasing is wrong.

> <u>Had the speeches been</u> any longer,
>   A
> the assembly <u>would have needed to be</u>
>   B
> extended <u>into</u> the next class <u>period</u>.
>   C   D
> <u>No error</u>
>   E

The first phrase, *Had the speeches been*, may sound strange to your ear. You may prefer to say *If the speeches had been*. However, both phrases are acceptable. The original phrase doesn't violate any rule of grammar. Similarly, instead of *would have needed to be*, you might prefer to say *would have had to be*. But this is merely a matter of preference. The original phrasing is fine too. The correct response to this question is E, no error. All of the grammar or usage errors that you are expected to spot and correct are detailed in Chapter 13.

3   HOW TO ATTACK THE TOUGHER QUESTIONS

Process of Elimination

What if your ear doesn't catch a mistake? In this case, the sentence might be correct, or it might contain a subtle error. **When this happens, eliminate the underlined portions that are clearly okay.** If you can get it down to just two choices, it's probably better to guess than to leave it blank.

The Systematic Approach

If you're not sure whether an underlined portion contains an error or not, take a systematic approach. To use this approach, though, you must be familiar with the 15 grammatical issues discussed in Chapter 13. Identify the parts of speech in the suspicious portion, and check the following issues systematically.

Check any verbs

- Does the verb agree with its subject in person and number? (See Chapter 13, Lessons 1 and 2.)
- Is the verb in the right tense? (See Chapter 13, Lesson 9.)
- Does the verb require the subjunctive mood? If so, is it in standard form? (See Chapter 13, Lesson 14.)
- Are any past participles in the incorrect form? (See Chapter 13, Lesson 13.)

Check any pronouns

- Does the pronoun require an antecedent, and if so, is the antecedent clear? (See Chapter 13, Lesson 5.)
- Does the pronoun agree in number and person with its antecedent? (See Chapter 13, Lesson 5.)
- Is the pronoun in the proper case, that is, subjective (*I, he, she, we, they*), objective (*me, him, her, us, them*), or possessive (*my, your, his, her, our, their*)? (See Chapter 13, Lesson 6.)

Check any prepositions

- Is the preposition part of an idiomatic phrase, and if so, is it in the standard form? (See Chapter 13, Lesson 10.)

Check any modifiers

- Is every modifier near the word it modifies, or is it misplaced or dangling? (See Chapter 13, Lessons 6 and 7.)
- Is every modifier in the correct form? (See Chapter 13, Lesson 12.)
- Is every modifier logical? (See Chapter 13, Lesson 12.)

Check any comparisons

- Are the things being compared the same *kind* of thing? (See Chapter 13, Lesson 4.)
- Are any of the *two vs. many* errors being made? (See Chapter 13, Lesson 4.)
- Are any of the *countable vs. uncountable* errors being made? (See Chapter 13, Lesson 4.)
- Are the things being compared in parallel form? (See Chapter 13, Lesson 3.)

Check any lists

- Are the items in the list in parallel form? (See Chapter 13, Lesson 3.)

Check any odd-sounding words

- Is an illogical or redundant word being used? (See Chapter 13, Lesson 11.)

Don't fear perfection

Like any other answer choice, E, no error, should occur about one-fifth of the time in the answer key. (If it didn't, the test would contain a bias that the "test-tricks" folks would jump all over.) **Therefore, don't be afraid to choose E, no error, when the sentence seems to have no clear problems.**

Exercise Set 1

The following sentences may contain errors in grammar, usage, diction (choice of words), or idiom. Some of the sentences are correct. No sentence contains more than one error.

If the sentence contains an error, it is underlined and lettered. The parts that are not underlined are correct.

If there is an error, select the part that must be changed to correct the sentence.

If there is no error, choose (E).

EXAMPLE:

By the time <u>they reached</u> the halfway point
         A

<u>in the race</u>, most <u>of the runners</u>
   B   C

<u>hadn't hardly</u> begun to hit their stride.
     D

<u>No error</u>
  E

Ⓐ Ⓑ Ⓒ ● Ⓔ

---

1. The abundance <u>of</u> recent <u>business failures</u>
          A   B
<u>have intimidated</u> many <u>prospective</u>
    C   D
entrepreneurs. <u>No error</u>
             E

2. When scientists <u>theorize</u> about the traits that
            A
all humans have come to share, they must
be keenly aware <u>of the fact</u> that these traits
           B
<u>are evolving</u> over <u>thousands of generations</u>
    C   D
<u>No error</u>
  E

3. The entire industry has steadfastly
maintained <u>their</u> position <u>that</u> tobacco
        A   B
<u>is not addictive</u> and that smoking
    C
is an <u>inalienable right</u> of consumers.
           D
<u>No error</u>
  E

4. <u>In bestowing</u> the award, the critics'
    A
guild praised the head writer, <u>saying that</u>
                       B
her writing for the television series
continued to be consistently more
<u>intelligent and provocative</u> than
         C
<u>anything on the air.</u> <u>No error</u>
    D   E

5. The <u>challenge</u> of Everest, its conquerors
      A
claim, is far more the <u>lack of oxygen</u> at its
               B
rarefied heights <u>than even</u> the <u>precarious ice</u>
            C   D
falls or precipitous ascents. <u>No error</u>
                    E

6. Those who talk more <u>respectful</u>
               A
to <u>their employers</u> are <u>more likely</u> to have
   B   C
their <u>grievances</u> addressed. <u>No error</u>
    D   E

4 | HOW TO ATTACK IMPROVING SENTENCES QUESTIONS

The PSAT Writing will include about 20 Improving Sentences questions, each of which consists of a sentence with only *one* underlined portion. This portion may contain one or more errors in grammar, wordiness, or awkwardness, or it may contain no error. If the portion contains an error, your job is to choose the best correction among the choices. If it is correct, choose (A), which leaves the sentence as it is.

Identify the mistake

Improving Sentences questions, unlike the Identifying Sentence Errors questions, require you to *fix* mistakes rather than merely *find* them. Therefore, it is more important on these questions that you find any errors and think about how to correct them before looking at the choices.

If the sentence contains an error, having a correction in mind will make it easier to choose the best answer. Your correction may not match the correct answer perfectly, but it will probably be close.

❑ The underlined portion may have more than one mistake, so don't stop when you've corrected one. **Check to see if there is another mistake!**

Eliminate the clunkers, but be careful!

To attack Improving Sentences questions, first read the sentence naturally and let your ear tell you if anything sounds wrong. **If the underlined portion contains an obvious error discussed in Chapter 13, immediately eliminate choice (A) as well as any choices that repeat the same error.**

Remember:
- Make sure the error is a legitimate grammar or usage error, and not just a matter of personal preference.
- There is often more than one way to fix a mistake, so be flexible.

The coaches weren't very interested in winning games during <u>spring training, they considered it</u> as an opportunity to experiment with different permutations of players.

(A) spring   training,   they   considered   it
(B) spring training; but they considered it
(C) spring training, but
(D) spring training as they were in using it
(E) spring training they were in using it

You might notice that the original sentence is a "run-on." It joins two related independent clauses with only a comma. Usually, run-ons can be fixed by replacing the comma with a semicolon, colon, or conjunction. (If these rules don't sound familiar, read Chapter 13, Lesson 15.) So you might go through the choices and eliminate those that also don't contain a semicolon, colon, or conjunction, leaving you with (B) and (C). But these don't work. Choice (B) incorrectly combines the semicolon and the conjunction, and choice (C) is illogical. Choice (D) is the correct answer because it is the only one that logically completes the *as* comparison.

Check the sentence again

Before moving on, reread the sentence with any necessary correction to check your answer. Make sure the "corrected" sentence doesn't have any problems.

The shorter the better

If you have developed an ear for well-written English prose, then if a sentence sounds okay, it probably is, and you should be inclined to choose (A). But some writing problems are tricky. For instance, some needlessly wordy phrases sound okay at first. To catch subtle problems with wordiness, read any choices that are *shorter* than the original. If a choice says the same thing in fewer words, it's probably better. **Unlike Identifying Sentence Errors questions, Improving Sentences questions often include problems with wordiness.**

> Several reviewers suggested that the article was not only frequently inaccurate, <u>but additionally it was needlessly obtuse and, ultimately, it was insubstantial</u>.

(A) but additionally it was needlessly obtuse and, ultimately, it was insubstantial
(B) but it was also needlessly obtuse and it was ultimately also insubstantial
(C) but they also commented on the needless obtuseness and also the ultimate insubstantiality
(D) although it was also needlessly obtuse and ultimately insubstantial
(E) but also needlessly obtuse and ultimately insubstantial

This sentence doesn't contain an obvious grammatical mistake, but it is wordy and awkward. Don't pick (A) immediately just because no mistake jumps out. Notice that (B), (D), and (E) are more concise than the original. The most concise is (E), which is the correct answer.

Check for danglers

Improving Sentences questions often test your ability to correct **dangling modifiers** (Chapter 13, Lessons 7 and 8), so make sure you know how to handle them. Just remember a simple rule: **any modifying phrase must be as close as possible to the word it modifies.**

> <u>Chosen from the best players from around the county</u>, the coaches found the recruits to be extraordinarily easy to work with.

(A) Chosen from the best players from around the county
(B) Being chosen from the best players from throughout the county
(C) Having chosen the best players from around the county
(D) Being the best players from throughout the entire county
(E) The best players having been chosen by them from throughout the county

The underlined phrase is a modifying phrase (more specifically, a participial phrase). The word it modifies is the subject of the participle *chosen*. Who was chosen? The *recruits*, not the *coaches*. Since *coaches* is closer to the modifying phrase than *recruits* is, the phrase **dangles** for a while (see Chapter 18, Lessons 7 and 8). Notice that choice (C) changes the participial phrase so that it modifies *coaches*, the noun that follows. The coaches *have chosen the best players*.

Watch out for "extra" problems

Remember that the sentence may have more than one problem. **Always reread the sentence with your choice to make sure there are no "extra" problems.**

> The entire editorial staff wrote <u>diligent for completing</u> the article in time for the midnight deadline.

(A) diligent for completing
(B) diligent in order to complete
(C) diligently for completing
(D) diligent to complete
(E) diligently to complete

The most obvious problem is that *diligent*, an adjective, should be *diligently*, an adverb, because it modifies the verb *wrote*. But don't jump right to choice (C), because the sentence also contains an error in **idiom**. To show purpose, the infinitive *to complete* should be use instead of *for completing*. The best answer is (E).

Exercise Set 2

Each of the sentences below contains one underlined portion. The portion may contain one or more errors in grammar, usage, construction, precision, diction (choice of words), or idiom. Some of the sentences are correct.

Consider the meaning of the original sentence, and choose the answer that best expresses that meaning. If the original sentence is best, choose (A), because it repeats the original phrasing. Choose the phrasing that creates the clearest, most precise, and most effective sentence.

EXAMPLE:

The children <u>couldn't hardly believe their eyes</u>.

(A) couldn't hardly believe their eyes
(B) would not hardly believe their eyes
(C) could hardly believe their eyes
(D) couldn't nearly believe their eyes
(E) could hardly believe his or her eyes

1. <u>Being highly efficient and with plentiful fuel, physicists consider nuclear fusion to represent</u> a profoundly promising source of energy.

   (A) Being highly efficient and with plentiful fuel, physicists consider nuclear fusion to represent
   (B) Being so efficient and its sources so plentiful, physicists consider nuclear fusion to be
   (C) Because nuclear fusion is so efficient and its fuel so plentiful, physicists consider it to be
   (D) Being an efficient and plentiful energy source, nuclear fusion is what physicists considered as being
   (E) For an energy source that physicists consider as efficient and plentiful, nuclear fusion is

2. Committed to improving student achievement, <u>the use of standardized tests in the elementary grades by the administration has increased dramatically</u>.

   (A) the use of standardized tests in the elementary grades by the administration has increased dramatically
   (B) standardized tests have been used by the administration increasingly in the elementary grades
   (C) the administration has used standardized tests increasingly in the elementary grades
   (D) the use of standardized tests by the administration has increased dramatically in the elementary grades
   (E) the administration have used more standardized tests in the elementary grades

3. More and more athletes are turning to yoga as a means of <u>increasing flexibility, refining balance, to control their energy, and they can use it to enhance their awareness of their bodies</u>.

   (A) increasing flexibility, refining balance, to control their energy, and they can use it to enhance their awareness of their bodies.
   (B) increasing their flexibility, refining their balance, controlling their energy, and enhancing their body awareness.
   (C) increasing one's flexibility, balance, energy, and body awareness.
   (D) to increase flexibility, to refine balance, to control energy, and the enhancement of the awareness of one's body.
   (E) increasing the flexibility and the balance and controlling the energy and the awareness of the body.

4. Many of the rights granted by the Constitution were not regarded by the founding fathers <u>as self-evident at all</u>, but rather the subject of often vicious debate.

   (A) as self-evident at all, but rather
   (B) so much as self-evident at all as they were more
   (C) so self-evidently as they were
   (D) as self-evident as
   (E) as being self-evident, but nevertheless were

5   HOW TO ATTACK IMPROVING PARAGRAPHS QUESTIONS

The last part of the PSAT Writing contains Improving Paragraphs questions. In this section, you are given a draft of a short essay that needs revision. You are then asked questions regarding how to improve the diction, logic, and grammar of the passage.

Improving Paragraphs questions are not like Critical Reading questions, except in one regard: some of the questions may require you to think about the overall purpose of the essay. You don't need to read the passage as carefully as you would a Critical Reading passage, but it's a good idea to read it quickly to get the basic gist.

Isolated Sentences

Some "Improving Paragraphs" questions ask you to improve a single sentence in the passage. These are like "Improving Sentences" questions, except that often choice (A) might *not* leave the sentence as is. In other words, there may not be a "no error" choice.

> Which of the following is the best way to revise sentence seven (reproduced below)? <u>If the students would of known</u> in advance about the shortage, they could have prevented the crisis.
>
> (A) If the students would have known
> (B) It being that the students might have known
> (C) If the students had known
> (D) Being known by the students
> (E) If it had been that the students knew

The verb phrase *would of known* uses improper diction for the subjunctive mood. Choice (C) corrects the problem.

Sentences in Context

Some Improving Paragraphs questions ask you to revise particular sentences in terms of the context of the passage. These questions usually begin with the phrase *In context* . . .

To answer these questions, read the preceding sentences and think about how to link the new sentence logically with those preceding sentences. These questions often focus on **transitions**, or logical guideposts for a reader. Transition words include *therefore, yet, nonetheless, although, furthermore*, and so on.

> In context, which of the following is the best version of sentence 12 (reproduced below)? <u>The racers were shivering</u> as the race began.
>
> (A) (as it is now)
> (B) Nevertheless, the racers were shivering
> (C) Furthermore, the racers were shivering
> (D) Therefore, the racers were shivering
> (E) All the while, the racers were shivering

Since the question begins with the phrase *In context*, the correct answer depends on what immediately precedes sentence 12. If the previous sentence were something like *The race organizers had arranged for large, powerful heaters to be placed all around the starting line*, then (B) would provide the most logical transition, because the sentence describes something unexpected. If, however, the previous sentence were *The temperature had plummeted 20° in the hours before the race was to start*, then (D) would make more sense because it shows a cause and effect.

Adding, Arranging, or Removing Sentences

Some "Improving Paragraphs" questions ask you how adding, rearranging, or removing sentences might improve the unity or logic of the paragraph.

- Which of the following sentences contributes the least to the cohesiveness of the third paragraph?

- Which of the following is the most logical order for the sentences in the second paragraph?

- Which of the following would be the most suitable sentence to insert after sentence 5?

These questions require you to consider how the sentences fit together in a paragraph. A paragraph may require an extra sentence or phrase to clarify an idea. Also, any sentence that doesn't pertain to the main idea of the paragraph should be removed. A paragraph may also be more logical if the sentences are rearranged.

Consider your attack options

When you reach the "Improving Paragraphs" section, you may simply want to read the passage quickly and answer the questions in the order they are given—a classic, straightforward approach. Getting the gist of the passage helps most students to answer the questions more efficiently, and it doesn't take too long. **However, you may prefer to first answer the "Isolated Sentences" questions—before even reading the passage—because they don't require you to understand the passage as a whole.** For some students, this approach helps to give them a sense of control over the questions and helps them to get through the questions more efficiently.

Exercise Set 3

> Below is a draft of an essay that needs improvement. Some sentences may contain grammatical errors, and the paragraphs may need to be altered to improve their logic, clarity, and cohesiveness. Read the passage and answer the questions that follow.

(1) *John D. Rockefeller, Jr. was born in 1854 as the only son of America's richest man and first billionaire.* (2) *Intensely shy as a child and young man, he came out of his shell at Brown University, where he was elected president of the junior class and senior manager of the football team.* (3) *After graduating from Brown, John had the opportunity to follow his father into the oil business and add to the family fortune.* (4) *He soon discovered that wealth, rather than being something to hoard, was "an instrumentality of constructive social living."* (5) *Because of the hard-nosed business practices of John's father, John D. Rockefeller, Sr., the name Rockefeller had become synonymous with greed and trade-busting.* (6) *The younger John decided that he could make this better.*

(7) *Perhaps no American has ever done more in the area of philanthropy than John D. Rockefeller, Jr.* (8) *He created charitable foundations like the Rockefeller Foundation, the Rockefeller Institute, and the General Education Board.* (9) *He sponsored the construction of Rockefeller Center in New York City, financed the reconstruction of Colonial Williamsburg, which stands to this day as an invaluable historical treasure, and donated the land in New York City for the United Nations complex.*

(10) *The scope of Rockefeller's conservation efforts, also, was profound.* (11) *He donated thousands of acres of land to national parks like Acadia, Shenandoah, the Great Smoky Mountains, and the Grand Tetons.* (12) *He also financed the construction of museums in Yellowstone, the Grand Canyon and Mesa Verde.*

(13) *John D. Rockefeller, Jr., is considered the father of philanthropy in the United States never before or since has any one person made such an impact on public institutions.* (14) *Although always willing to support a good cause, Rockefeller never sought accolades for himself.* (15) *He was offered dozens of honorary degrees from prestigious universities, and declined all but one, from his alma mater.*

1. In context, which of the following is the best revision of the underlined portion of sentence 4 (reproduced below)?

   He soon discovered that wealth, rather than being something to hoard, was "an instrumentality of constructive social living."

   (A) However, he soon discovered
   (B) Furthermore, he soon discovered
   (C) He would only have soon discovered
   (D) Therefore, he soon discovered
   (E) When he soon discovered

2. Where is the most logical place to insert the following sentence?

   John's discovery of philanthropy could hardly have come at a better time for the Rockefellers.

   (A) After sentence 1
   (B) After sentence 3
   (C) After sentence 4
   (D) Before sentence 7, to begin the second paragraph
   (E) After sentence 8

3. Which of the following revisions of sentence 6 (reproduced below) best improves its clarity in the context of the first paragraph?

   The younger John decided that he could make this better.

   (A) The younger John, the son of John D. Rockefeller, Sr., decided that he could make this better.
   (B) The younger John decided that he could restore the prestige of his family name.
   (C) The younger John, who was affectionately called "Johnny D," decided that he could make this better.
   (D) This was something that the younger John himself thought he could improve greatly.
   (E) But this was something that young John knew he could do something about the problem of his family honor.

Answer Key

Exercise Set 1

1. **C** The subject is *abundance*, which is singular, so the verb should be *has intimidated*. (Chapter 13, Lesson 1)

2. **C** The phrase *over thousands of generations* indicates that the evolution occurred over an extended time in the past. Therefore, the verb should be in the present perfect form: *have evolved*. (Chapter 13, Lesson 9)

3. **A** *Their* is a plural pronoun, but it refers to *industry*, which is singular, so the pronoun should be *its*. (Chapter 13, Lesson 5)

4. **D** Since the sentence indicates that the show *continued to be*, it must have been still on the air. Since it could not be better written than itself, choice D should be replaced by *anything else on the air*. (Chapter 13, Lesson 9)

5. **E** The sentence is correct.

6. **A** The word *respectful* is modifying the verb *talk*, so it should be in the form of an adverb: *respectfully*. (Chapter 13, Lesson 12)

Exercise Set 2

1. **C** The original sentence is awkward and contains a dangling participle. *Being* is the participle, but its subject does not follow the participial phrase. Furthermore, the logic of the sentence is unclear. Choice C shows the essential cause-and-effect relationship. (Chapter 13, Lesson 7)

2. **C** The original sentence contains a dangling participle. *Committed* is the participle, and the phrase should be followed by its subject. *Who is committed?* Certainly not *the use of standardized tests*, but rather *the administration*. Notice that

choice E is incorrect because the verb *have* does not agree with its subject *administration*. (Chapter 13, Lessons 1 and 7)

3. **B** The original sentence violates the law of parallelism. In a list, all items should have the same grammatical form. Choice C is parallel and concise, but it changes the meaning of the sentence from the original and uses the pronoun *one's* inappropriately. (Chapter 13, Lesson 3)

4. **A** The original sentence is best.

Exercise Set 3

1. **A** Sentence 3 indicates that John could have added to the family fortune. Sentence 4 indicates that he did not, but rather used the money for philanthropic purposes. This contrast of ideas should be accompanied by a contrasting transition, as provided by the word *however*.

2. **C** Sentence 4 introduces John's *discovery of philanthropy*, and sentence 5 explains why it *could hardly have come at a better time*, so this sentence belongs most logically between sentence 4 and sentence 5.

3. **B** The original sentence is unclear because the pronoun *this* lacks a clear antecedent. A reader could probably figure out that it refers to the problem with the Rockefeller reputation, discussed in the previous sentence, but sentence 5 does not actually contain the words *the problem with the Rockefeller reputation*, so the reference is unclear. Choice B is the only sentence that clarifies that reference.

CHAPTER 13

ESSENTIAL PSAT GRAMMAR SKILLS

1. Subject-Verb Disagreement

2. Trimming Sentences

3. Parallelism

4. Comparison Errors

5. Pronoun Agreement

6. Pronoun Case

7. Dangling and Misplaced Participles

8. Other Misplaced Modifiers

9. Tricky Tenses

10. Idiom Errors

11. Diction Errors

12. Other Problems with Modifiers

13. Irregular Verbs

14. The Subjunctive Mood

15. Coordinating Ideas

Lesson 1: Subject-Verb Disagreement

One of the most common grammatical mistakes tested on the PSAT Writing is subject-verb disagreement.

> The children is playing in the park.

Here, the verb *is* does not agree in number with its subject *children*. *Children* is plural, but *is* is singular. Clearly, the verb should be changed to *are*. You can catch the mistake easily in the sentence above, because the verb immediately follows the subject. PSAT Writing questions, however, won't be quite this easy. They will include sentences in which the agreement between subject and verb is harder to determine, because the verb won't immediately follow the subject. **You should be able to pick out the subject and verb of each clause in a sentence, and determine whether or not they agree.** It helps to know the tricky ways that sentences can hide subject-verb disagreement.

Inverted Sentences

In most clauses, the subject comes *before* the verb. Sometimes, however, a clause is **inverted**—its subject comes *after* the verb. Sentences that start with *There is* or *There are*, for instance, are inverted. **To check subject-verb agreement in these sentences, it helps to "uninvert" them.**

> There is many flies in the barn.

This sentence is inverted. The verb *is* comes before its subject *flies*. The word *There* serves as a **dummy subject**, holding the place for the real subject, *flies*. Since *there* can be either plural or singular, you can't tell that the sentence has a problem after reading just the first two words. To see the problem more clearly, "uninvert" the sentence.

> Many flies is in the barn.

The sentence is now right side up. The verb *is* immediately follows the subject *flies*, and you have eliminated the dummy subject. Now the mistake is even more obvious. The verb should be *are*.

Intervening Words

Sometimes a subject and verb are separated by a bunch of other words. You need to be able to ignore the intervening words and focus just on the subject and verb.

> The columnist, like so many other experts, were convinced that the new program would fail.

If you read this sentence quickly, it may not sound wrong because the verb *were convinced*, which is plural, immediately follows the noun *experts*, which is also plural. But *experts* is not the subject of the verb. It is part of a modifying phrase between commas. This kind of modifying phrase is called an **interrupter. Every good sentence must remain "grammatical" even when its interrupters are removed.** In other words, an interrupter can never contain the main subject and verb of the sentence.

> The columnist were convinced that the new program would fail.

Now that the interrupter has been removed, the mistake is obvious. The verb should be *was convinced*.

Tricky Subjects

Sometimes it's hard to tell whether a subject is singular or plural. Here are some helpful rules.

The word *and* combines two nouns into a plural subject, as in *Jane and Bob are sick*. **Any nouns within interrupters, however, are not included in the subject, as in *Jane, as well as Bob, is sick.***

The words *neither* and *either* are singular when they stand alone as subjects.

> Neither *is* very expensive. Either *is* sufficient.

They are also singular when they are part of a *neither of* or *either of* phrase.

> Neither of the boys *is* ready to take the test.

However, the phrases *neither A nor B* **and** *either A or B* **have the same number as the noun in** *B.*

Either Ben or his brothers *have taken* the car.

The second noun, the *B*, in the *Either A or B* phrase is the plural *his brothers*, so the subject as a whole is regarded as plural.

People often confuse the numbers of the following words, so here's a list to keep them straight.

Singular	Plural	Correct sentence
phenomenon	*phenomena*	*Phenomena* like that *are* surprisingly common.
medium	*media*	The *media have ignored* this story completely.
datum	*data*	The *data* on my computer *have been* corrupted.
criterion	*criteria*	Such a *criterion has* yet to be met.

Exercise Set 1

Next to each noun or noun phrase, write "S" if it is singular and "P" if it is plural.

1. *Neither rain nor snow*   _____
2. *A crowd of rowdy fans*   _____
3. *Media*   _____
4. *Criterion*   _____
5. *One or two*   _____
6. *Everything*   _____
7. *Either of the candidates*   _____
8. *Phenomena*   _____

Circle the subject in each sentence, and choose the correct verb.

9. *The flock of geese (was/were) startled by the shotgun blast.*
10. *The data on my computer (was/were) completely erased when the power failed.*
11. *Neither of the twins (is/are) allergic to penicillin.*
12. *Much of what I hear in those lectures (go/goes) in one ear and out the other.*
13. *Amy, along with Jamie and Jen, (is/are) applying to Mount Holyoke.*
14. *Amid the lilies and wildflowers (were/was) one solitary rose.*
15. *Either David or his brothers (is/are) in charge of bringing the drinks.*
16. *There (is/are) hardly even a speck of dirt left on the carpet.*
17. *"Stop right there!" (shout/shouts) the Bailey brothers, who are standing in front of me.*
18. *There (were/was) at least a hundred people in the room.*
19. *There (is/are), in my opinion, far too many smokers in this restaurant.*
20. *Over that hill (is/are) thousands of bison.*
21. *Never before (have/has) there been such voices heard on the public airwaves.*

Label each verb in the following sentences with a "V" and each subject with an "S." If any verbs are incorrect, cross them out and write the correct form in the blank.

22. *Every player on both the Falcons and the Rockets were at the party after the game.*   _____
23. *There has been a theater and a toy store in the mall ever since it opened.*   _____
24. *Either Eric or his brother is hosting the party this year.*   _____
25. *The proceeds from the sale of every auctioned item goes to charity.*   _____
26. *There is more than three years remaining on her contract.*   _____
27. *Neither of the girls were frightened by the wild animals that scurried incessantly past their tent.*   _____
28. *The technology behind high-definition television, DVDs, and CDs have transformed nearly every aspect of the home entertainment industry.*   _____
29. *Every player on both teams were concerned about the goalie's injury.*   _____
30. *The company's sponsorship of charitable foundations and mentorship programs have garnered many commendations from philanthropic organizations.*   _____
31. *Neither the children nor their parents utters a word when Mrs. Denny tells her stories.*   _____
32. *How important is your strength training and your diet to your daily regimen?*   _____

Lesson 2: Trimming Sentences

As we just discussed, spotting subject-verb problems is easier when you ignore the "nonessential" parts of a sentence. At College Hill Coaching, we call this process "trimming," and we teach it as an essential writing tool. It does more than just help you to spot subject-verb disagreement. Trimming isolates the most important part of each sentence, the subject-predicate "core," so that you can check whether your writing is clear and effective.

How to trim a sentence

Let's examine a sentence and see how trimming helps you to improve it.

> My chief concern with this budget, which I have not voiced until today, are the drastic cuts in school funds.

Step 1:   Cross out all nonessential prepositional phrases.

A **preposition** is a word like *to, from, of, for, by, in, before, with, beyond,* or *up* that shows relative position or direction. Think of prepositions as words that can be used to complete either of the following sentences.

> The squirrel ran _____ the tree.
> Democracy is government _____ the people.

A **prepositional phrase** is a phrase that starts with a preposition and includes the noun or noun phrase that follows.

> from sea to shining sea
> in the beginning
> with hat in hand

> My chief concern ~~with this budget~~, which I have not voiced ~~until today~~, are the drastic cuts ~~in school funds~~.

Step 2: Cross out all interrupting phrases.

An **interrupting phrase** is a modifying phrase, usually separated from the main sentence by commas, that interrupts the flow of the sentence. In this case, the interrupter is the phrase between the commas.

> My chief concern ~~with this budget, which I have not voiced until today~~, are the drastic cuts ~~in school funds~~.

Step 3:   Cross out any other nonessential modifiers and modifying phrases.

Modifiers are **adjectives** and **adverbs**, as well as modifying phrases like **participial phrases** (see Lesson 5). Most modifiers are not essential to the basic meaning of a sentence, but some are, such as *smart* in the sentence *Martha is smart.* In this case, *smart* is the **predicate adjective** and is therefore essential to the sentence. In our sentence, the nonessential modifiers are *chief* and *drastic.*

> My ~~chief~~ concern ~~with this budget, which I have not voiced until today~~, are the ~~drastic~~ cuts ~~in school funds~~.

What remains is the essential "core" of the sentence: *My concern are the cuts.* The most obvious problem here is the subject-verb disagreement—*concern* is singular, but *are* is plural. To make it more grammatical, you may want to simply change the verb: *My concern is the cuts.* But this isn't a great sentence either. The *concern* is singular, but the *cuts* are plural, so equating them seems illogical. Furthermore, the verb *is* is very weak and doesn't convey much meaning. Trimming the sentence shows us that the core of the sentence is weak. It should be reworded with a stronger verb.

> Although I have not said so until today, I object to the drastic cuts in school funds that are proposed in this budget.

Who kicked whom?

Trimming helps you to strengthen your sentences. When writing an important sentence in an essay, play the "who kicked whom?" game. That is, trim the sentence, look at the subject-verb-object (*Who kicked whom?*) core, and check that it conveys a clear and forceful idea.

Original: The lack of economic programs and no big country being ready to join it symbolized the problems the League of Nations had in getting established.

Trimmed: The lack and no country being ready to join it symbolized the problems.   X

Yikes! That does *not* convey a clear and forceful idea. Revise it using a stronger subject-verb-object.

Revised: The League of Nations never established itself because it lacked viable economic programs and the support of the larger countries.   ✓

Exercise Set 2

Trim each sentence below, and correct any verb problems.

1. *The team of advisors, arriving ahead of schedule, were met at the airport by the Assistant Prime Minister.*

2. *The flock of birds that darted over the lake were suddenly an opalescent silver.*

3. *Carmen, along with her three sisters, are unlikely to be swayed by arguments supporting David's position.*

4. *Juggling the demands of both school and my social agenda often seem too much to bear.*

5. *Others on the committee, like the chairman Amanda Sanders, is concerned about the lack of attention given to school safety.*

6. *One in every three Americans agree strongly with the statement: "Anyone who would run for political office is not worth voting for."*

7. *The fact that humans have committed so many atrocities have forced some historians to adopt a cynical perspective on human nature.*

Trim each sentence. Then revise it to make it clearer and more forceful, changing the subject and verb, if necessary.

8. *Nearly inevitably, advancements, or those being popularly regarded as such, have to do with modifications, not overhaul.*

   Trimmed: _____

   Revised: _____

9. *The development of the new country's governmental system was affected in a negative regard by the lack of cohesiveness of the revolutionary army.*

   Trimmed: _____

   Revised: _____

Lesson 3: Parallelism

Whenever a sentence contains a list or comparison, the items in that list or comparison should be *parallel*; that is, they should have the same grammatical form. This rule is called the *law of parallelism*.

> Gina hated to take charge, draw attention to herself and she hated seeming like a know-it-all. **X**

This sentence lists three things that Gina hated, but those things have different forms. The phrases to *take charge, draw attention, and she hated seeming like a know-it-all* are not parallel. The sentence sounds much better if the three items are phrased as **gerunds**.

> Gina hated *taking* charge, *drawing* attention to herself, and *seeming* like a know-it-all. **✓**

The italicized words all have the same form, so the sentence reads more smoothly.

Comparisons should be parallel also.

> Believe it or not, I like to read more than I like going to parties.   **X**

This sentence compares two things: *to read* and *going to parties*. The first phrase is an **infinitive**, but the second contains a **gerund**. The sentence reads more smoothly if the items have the same form.

> Believe it or not, I like to *read* more than I like *to go to* parties. **✓**

> Believe it or not, I like *reading* more than I like *going* to parties. **✓**

Infinitives and gerunds

As the previous examples show, using the law of parallelism often involves choosing between **infinitives** and **gerunds**. Infinitives are phrases like *to run, to see*, and *to think*. Although they are the basic forms of verbs, they usually serve as nouns when they are used in sentences. Gerunds are words like *running, seeing*, and *thinking* when they are used as nouns. To understand how infinitives and gerunds work, consider the following sentences.

> *I like pizza.   I like to swim.   I like swimming.*

These sentences all have the same basic structure. In the first sentence, *pizza* is a noun serving as the object of the verb *like*. In the next two sentences, *pizza* is replaced by *to swim* (an infinitive) and *swimming* (a gerund). In other words, these words play the same grammatical role as *pizza* did in the first sentence, so they must also be nouns. Often, gerunds and infinitives are interchangeable. For instance, the second and third sentences above seem to say the same thing. If you swim all the time and enjoy it, then both sentences convey that idea. But what if you are unable to swim, but enjoy watching swim meets? In this case, you can say *I like swimming* but not *I like to swim*.

Although infinitives and gerunds are often interchangeable, here are some simple rules to help you to choose between them in certain situations.

The gerund is usually better for indicating a general class of activity, while the infinitive is often better for indicating a specific activity in which someone actively participates.

Good: *Kayaking* is a healthful sport, but can sometimes be dangerous.

Good: Curtis and Dan want *to kayak* this afternoon.

The **infinitive** indicates **purpose** more strongly than does the gerund.

> Maia went to the store *to buy* groceries.

Notice that replacing the infinitive with the gerund *buying* would make the sentence illogical. Maia had a *purpose* in going to the store, and this purpose is conveyed by an infinitive and not by a gerund.

Comparison idioms

The English language contains many **comparison idioms**. These are the common ways of phrasing comparisons.

A is like B	A more than B	prefer A to B
neither A nor B	either A or B	both A and B
the more A, the less B	the better A, the better B	not only A but also B
not A but B	less A than B	more A than B

When you use any of these idioms, make sure of two things: that you phrase the idiom correctly and that the A and B parts of the comparison are parallel. If you ever struggle with parallelism in your writing, you should practice underlining the A's and B's when you use comparison idioms, and you should make sure that they have the same form.

> We should be concerned *more*
> <u>*about saving the planet* than</u>
>   A
> <u>*about making higher profits.*</u>
>   B

Exercise Set 3

In each of the sentences below, circle the words or phrases that are parallel. Then write the *form* of those words or phrases (adjectives, prepositional phrases, gerunds, infinitives, nouns, etc.) in the blank.

1. *You can register for the test by mail, by phone, or on the Web.*   _____

2. *Having good study practices is even more important than working hard.*   _____

3. *The more you get to know her, the more you will like her.*   _____

4. *The produce is not only exceptionally fresh, but also reasonably priced.*   _____

5. *The show is less a concert than it is a three-hour nightmare.*   _____

Complete each of the sentences below with the appropriate word or phrase–infinitive or gerund–using the given verb.

6. *(Exercise)* _____ *is essential, but so is (eat)* _____ *intelligently.*

7. *The purpose of this trip is (show)* _____ *you what life was like in the eighteenth century.*

8. *I have always loved (dance)* _____ *although my condition has always prevented me from doing it myself.*

9. *Is it better (study)* _____ *a little each night, or a lot the night before?*

10. *The director called a meeting (discuss)* _____ *the coordination of the marketing phase.*

Correct any infinitive/gerund problems in the sentences below.

11. *The defendant was unwilling to give up his right of having his lawyer present at all questioning.*

12. *I would not dream to try out for the team until I have learned to throw a football.*

13. *Within the next three weeks, we plan having all of the work on the roof completed.*

Fix the parallelism errors in the following sentences.

14. *I like working with Miss Bennett because she is very supportive and has a lot of knowledge.*

_____

15. *I can't decide whether I should give Maria the tickets or Caitlyn.*

_____

Lesson 4: Comparison Errors

On the PSAT Writing, always pay close attention to **comparisons** in sentences. We have just discussed the fact that a comparison must have the correct idiomatic phrasing and parallel structure, but comparisons can have other problems as well.

Illogical comparisons

Any items being compared in a sentence must be logically comparable; that is, they must be in the same general category. For instance, comparing *apples* to *apples* is much more logical than comparing *apples* to *the increase in the price of apples due to an unforeseen climatological disaster*.

> Her chances of passing that test aren't much better than the lottery.   X

The comparison here is illogical: *chances* are not in the same category as *lottery*, so the comparison doesn't make sense. The sentence should compare *chances* to *chances*.

> Her chances of getting an A aren't much better *than her chances of winning* the lottery.   ✓

Nothing can be different from itself. Any sentence that suggests otherwise should be revised.

> Elisa has sung in more concerts than any singer in her school.   X

This sentence suggests that Elisa is a singer who goes to school. So *any singer in her school* includes Elisa herself. Of course, she could not have sung in more concerts than herself, so the comparison is illogical.

> Elisa has sung in more concerts than any *other* singer in her school.   ✓

Countability: fewer/less, number/ amount, and many/much

When should you use *less* and when should you use *fewer*? **Use *fewer* (or *number* or *many*) only when comparing countable things like *cars*, *dollars* and *popsicles*. Use *less* (or *amount* or *much*) when comparing uncountable or continuous quantities like *traffic*, *money*, and *food*.**

> There have been a lot less fans at the games ever since ticket prices were increased.   X

Since fans can be counted and don't come in fractional parts, using *less* is incorrect. Use *fewer* instead.

> There have been a lot *fewer* fans at the games ever since ticket prices were increased   ✓

Remember that the same rule applies to the choice between *number* and *amount* or between *many* and *much*.

> The team owners showed concern about the increasing *number* (not *amount*) of rowdy fans.

The situation is trickier when the quantity is both **countable** *and* **continous**. For instance, units like *miles* and *pounds* and *gallons* are countable, but they can also come in fractional parts, such as *1.23 miles*. **The PSAT Writing avoids such tricky cases**. When confronted with this issue in your own writing, however, consider whether you want to emphasize the countability of the quantity (in which case you should use *fewer, number,* or *many*) or the continuity of the quantity (in which case you should use *less, amount,* or *much*).

Two or more: *more/most, between/ among,* and *-er/-est*

When should you use *more* and when should you use *most*? The rule is simple. **Use *more* (or *between* or an *-er* adjective) whenever you are comparing exactly two things. Use *most* (or *among* or an *-est* adjective) when comparing more than two things.**

> The two superpowers seemed to be in a constant battle to see who was the strongest.   X

Since there are only two superpowers, the superlative *strongest* is incorrect.

> The two superpowers seemed to be in a constant battle to see who was the *stronger*.   ✓

Remember that the same rule applies to the choice between *more* and *most* or between *many* and *much*.

> Of the dozens of students in the club, Deborah was the more popular.   X

Since there are more than two students, the comparative *more* is incorrect.)

> Of the dozens of students in the club, Deborah was the *most* popular.   ✓

Number shift
Items being compared or equated should, if possible, be either both plural or both singular.

> They were both hoping to be a winner. X
>
> They were both hoping to be *winners*. ✓

The sailors' main point of reference was the two lighthouse beacons. X

The sailors' main *points of reference were* the two lighthouse beacons. ✓

Exercise Set 4

In each sentence below, underline any items that are being compared or equated. If the comparison is illogical or contains some other error, correct the sentence.

1. *The critics' guild praised the show, saying that it was consistently more intelligent and provocative than anything on the air.*

2. *Team unity and commitment to practice were regarded by the players as the key to their success.*

3. *Mathematics lessons in Japanese classrooms, unlike American classrooms, are often focused on solving a single complex problem rather than many simple problems.*

4. *The electric-combustion engines of the new hybrid cars burn much more cleanly and efficiently than conventional cars.*

5. *To the critics of the time, the surrealists were regarded as being as inscrutable, if not more so, than the dadaists.*

6. *I prefer a lot of modern poetry to Shakespeare.*

7. *Her suitcase would not close because she had packed too much of her towels into it.*

8. *The year-end bonus was equally divided between Parker, Herriot, and me.*

9. *Many students wanted to be a lifeguard at the club.*

10. *The toughest thing about her class is you have to do tons of homework every night.*

Lesson 5: Pronoun Agreement

A **pronoun** is a word such as *it*, *he*, *she*, *what*, or *that* that substitutes for a noun. Some pronouns—like *it*, *you*, *she*, and *I*—are **definite** because they refer to a specific thing. Other pronouns—like *anyone*, *neither*, and *those*—are **indefinite** because they do *not* refer to a specific thing.

Every definite pronoun must have a clear antecedent with which it agrees in number and kind. In other words, every definite pronoun must "point" unambiguously to a noun, called the *antecedent*, in the sentence. If the antecedent is singular, the pronoun must be singular also. If the antecedent is personal, the pronoun must be personal also.

> Roger told Mike that he was going to start the next game.   X

This sentence contains the definite pronoun *he*. Whom does it refer to, Roger or Mike? The sentence could make sense either way, so the pronoun is **ambiguous**. You must revise the sentence to eliminate the ambiguity.

> Roger told Mike that Mike would start the game.   ✓

> The policy of the bank is to maintain the confidentiality of their clients.   X

This sentence contains the definite pronoun *their*, which is plural. What does it refer to? It must refer to *bank*, because the clients are the bank's clients. But *bank* is singular, so the pronoun does not agree with its antecedent.

> The policy of the bank is to maintain the confidentiality of its clients.   ✓

> David was the one that first spotted the error.   X

This sentence uses an impersonal pronoun, *that*, to refer to a person, *David*. This is a disagreement in **kind**.

> David was the one *who* first spotted the error.   ✓

An interrogative pronoun like *what, where, when, why, who*, or *how* must agree in kind with its antecedent. Use *what* only to refer to a thing, *where* to refer to a place, *when* to refer to a time, *why* to refer to a reason, *who* to refer to a person, and *how* to refer to an explanation.

> A filibuster is where senators extend a debate in order to delay a vote.   X

Even if you don't already know what a filibuster is, the sentence makes clear that it isn't a *place*, but rather an event or action. Therefore, you shouldn't refer to it as a *where*.

> A filibuster is *when* senators extend a debate in order to delay a vote.   ✓

Or more specifically

> A filibuster is *a procedure by which* senators extend a debate in order to delay a vote.   ✓

A pronoun in a modifying phrase usually takes the closest preceding noun as its antecedent.

> The actors will design their own sets, who are participating in the workshop.   X

The modifying phrase *who are participating in the workshop* modifies *actors*, not *sets*. Move it over.

> The actors *who are participating in the workshop* will design their own sets.   ✓

Pronoun consistency

Be consistent with any pronouns that refer to the same noun.

> Even when one is dieting, you should always try to get enough vitamins.   X

Make up your mind about who you're talking to!

> Even when *you are* dieting, *you* should always try to get enough vitamins.   ✓

Exercise Set 5

Circle all pronouns, and make any necessary corrections.

1. *There are many times in a game where a player can lose focus.*

2. *If a student wants to memorize the meaning of a word, you should begin by understanding the concept it represents.*

3. *Caroline passed the phone to Julia, but she couldn't bring herself to speak.*

4. *Not wanting to be the one that slowed the team down, David dropped out of the race.*

5. *Brown University is committed to assisting their students by providing him or her with any necessary financial aid.*

6. *The media ignored the reports because it didn't consider them newsworthy.*

7. *No one that has been through the first week of boot camp ever believes that they will make it through the entire six weeks.*

8. *Although you shouldn't read carelessly, one doesn't need to read slowly, either.*

9. *Neither Glen nor Don thought that their team would lose the championship.*

10. *Students sometimes aren't ready to handle the extra work when his or her courses become more demanding.*

11. *The anthology is filled with stories where love goes unrequited.*

12. *Everyone is expected to do their share.*

13. *The museum received so many donations that they actually had to return over a million dollars to the benefactors.*

14. *The judges usually give the trophy to the skater that makes the fewest mistakes.*

15. *I like movies where the bad guy gets punished in the end.*

16. *Each swimmer will have a lane to themselves.*

17. *Who was the player that hit the home run?*

Lesson 6: Pronoun Case

The case of a pronoun indicates its role within the sentence. English uses four common cases. **Subjective** pronouns like *I, you, he, she, we, they,* and *who* are usually subjects of verbs. **Objective** pronouns like *me, you, him, her, them,* and *whom* are usually objects of verbs or prepositions. **Possessive** pronouns like *my, mine, her, hers, their, their,* and *whose* indicate attribution or ownership. **Reflexive** pronouns like *myself, yourself, himself, herself,* and *themselves* usually show that the object of a verb is the same as the subject.

Subjective pronouns

If a pronoun is the subject of a verb or is equated with the subject of a verb, it must take the subjective case. Choosing the proper case can be tricky when the sentence contains a **compound subject**, an **implied verb**, or a **predicate nominative.**

A compound subject is a subject involving *and*.

> Jenna and me were the only two at the meeting. **X**

The subject of this sentence is *Jenna and me*, a compound subject. But *me* is in the objective case, not the subjective case. To catch such errors easily, "isolate" the pronoun in the subject. You would never say *Me was at the meeting*.

> Jenna and *I* were the only two at the meeting. ✓

Sometimes a pronoun is the subject of an implied verb, and so must take the subjective case.

> My brother is taller than me. **X**

You can say this in conversation, but not in formal writing, because the sentence suggests an implied verb. It is really saying that *My brother is taller than I am*. The verb *am* is omitted because it is understood by the reader even if it is not stated. The pronoun, however, should still take the subjective case.

> My brother is taller than *I*. ✓

A pronoun may also be equated with the subject in a predicate nominative. Such pronouns must take the subjective case.

> The winner of the prize was her. **X**

The subject of the sentence is *winner*, and the verb is *was*. But this verb is a **linking verb**, which links the subject to a noun or adjective, rather than conveying an action. Since this linking verb equates the subject and the pronoun, the pronoun should take the subjective case.

> The winner of the prize was *she*. ✓

Objective pronouns

If a pronoun is the object of a verb or preposition, it must take the objective case.

> My father raised my brother and I all by himself. **X**

This sentence contains a very common mistake. The object of the verb *raised* is the compound object *my brother and I*. But *I* is in the subjective case, not the objective case. As we discussed above, you can catch such errors easily by "isolating" the pronoun. You would never say *My father raised I*.

> My father raised my brother and *me* all by himself. ✓

> This should be a great opportunity for you and she. **X**

The verb of this sentence is *should be*, the subject is *this*, and the object is *a great opportunity*. So it seems as if the pronouns *you* and *her* are neither subjects nor objects. But in fact they are objects of *for*, which is a preposition. **All objects of prepositions must take the objective case.**

> This should be a great opportunity for you and *her*. ✓

Possessive pronouns

Don't confuse the objective and possessive cases within an object. Analyze the object logically to determine which pronoun to use.

> Mrs. Brown enjoyed him taking such an interest in literature. **X**

What is the object of the verb *enjoyed*? In other words, *what* did Mrs. Brown enjoy? Since the pronoun *him* is in the objective case, the sentence suggests that Mrs. Brown enjoyed *him*. But that isn't what the sentence really means. Mrs. Brown actually enjoyed the *interest* he took in literature. To avoid this confusion, put the pronoun in the possessive case.

> Mrs. Brown seemed to enjoy *his* taking such an interest in literature. ✓

Reflexive pronouns

Only use reflexive pronouns to show that the object of a verb is the same as its subject or to emphasize a noun or pronoun. For instance, when you use the reflexive pronoun *myself* in a sentence like *I pinched myself to make sure I wasn't dreaming*, you are indicating that you *did* the pinching and you also *received* the pinching. Also, when you use the reflexive pronoun *himself* in a sentence like *She was standing next to Usher himself*, you are emphasizing *Usher*.

My opponent did not prepare his case as diligently as myself.   ✗

Since this sentence does not indicate that the person who performed an action also received it, and since the pronoun *myself* is not used to emphasize an adjacent noun, the pronoun should not take the reflexive case.

My opponent did not prepare his case as diligently as *I did*.   ✓

Exercise Set 6

Circle the correct pronoun in each sentence.

1. *The climb was much easier for them than it was for Jeff and (I/me/myself).*

2. *The other contestants did not seem as confident as (he/him/himself).*

3. *(Us/we) detectives are always careful to follow every lead.*

4. *Every student should make (his or her/their) own study plan.*

5. *They never seem to listen to the opinions of (us/we) students.*

6. *Jim gave control of the project to Fiona and (me/myself/I).*

7. *The university presented the honor to David and (he/him).*

8. *Justine and (me/I) have always been closest friends.*

9. *There is no point in (our/us) delaying the tests any longer.*

10. *It seems quite clear that you and (I/me) will have to work together to solve this problem.*

11. *It might be hard for (him and me/he and I) to agree.*

12. *(We/Us) and the other members debated the issue for over two hours.*

13. *The owners of the club offered my wife and (me/I) a free bottle of wine with dinner.*

14. *No other runner on the team could outrun (myself/me).*

15. *The teachers were getting tired of (him/his) constantly falling asleep in class.*

16. *The ballpark always held a special attraction for Dave and (I/me).*

Lesson 7: Dangling and Misplaced Participles

A participle is a verb form that serves as part of a verb phrase or as an adjective. There are two kinds of participles. **Present participles** are words like *colliding*, *writing*, and *fighting* whenever they are used in verb phrases like *was fighting* or as adjectives as in *the fighting fish*. They look exactly like **gerunds**, which we discussed in Lesson 3, but they are used differently. Gerunds are used as nouns, but present participles are used as verb parts or adjectives. **Past participles** are words like *collided*, *written*, and *fought*. They often end in *-ed* or *-en*, but not always. They are used in verb phrases like *had written* or as adjectives as in *the written language*.

A participial phrase is a modifying phrase that includes a participle but not its subject. It is usually separated from the main part of the sentence by one or more commas.

> *Eating ravenously*, the vultures remained on the carcass until it was picked clean.

> The runners, *exhausted from the final sprint*, stumbled through the finish line.

Notice that, in each of these sentences, the participial phrase does not contain the subject of the participle. The subject of *eating* in the first participial phrase is *vultures*, and the subject of *exhausted* in the second participial phrase is *runners*. Although the subject of the participle does not appear in a participial phrase, it must appear elsewhere in the sentence. If it does not, the participle is said to dangle.

Every participial phrase must be near the subject of the participle. If it is not, then the phrase is unclear.

> After having studied all night, the professor postponed the test until Friday. **X**

The participial phrase in this sentence is *having studied all night*. What is the subject of this participle? In other words, *who* studied all night? Certainly *the professor* didn't study, but the sentence doesn't indicate who did, so the participle **dangles**. One way to fix a dangling participle is to insert its subject next to the participial phrase.

> After having studied all night, I learned that the professor had postponed the test until Friday. ✓

You can also fix the dangling participle by incorporating the subject into the phrase, so that the phrase becomes a dependent clause.

> After *I had studied* all night, the professor postponed the test until Friday. ✓

> Bob found his watch walking to the bathroom. **X**

The participial phrase in this sentence is *walking to the bathroom*. Who or what was *walking*? The sentence makes it seem as if the *watch* were walking, but that's absurd. You can fix the problem by just moving the phrase or by turning it into a dependent clause.

> Walking to the bathroom, Bob found his watch. ✓

> Bob found his watch as he was walking to the bathroom. ✓

> It was difficult for William to hear the announcements waiting for the train. **X**

Were the *announcements* waiting for the train? Of course not.

> While waiting for the train, William found it difficult to hear the announcements. ✓

> William found it difficult to hear the announcements while he was waiting for the train. ✓

Exercise Set 7

Circle the participle in each sentence. Then circle its subject and draw an arrow between them. Rewrite the sentence to fix any problems with the participle.

1. *Looking at your essay, it seems to me that you need to use more specific examples.*

   _____

2. *Turning the corner, the stadium came into my view.*

   _____

3. *Although exhausted after the night's work, Martha's creative instincts compelled her to keep writing.*

   _____

4. *Without waiting for an answer, David's eagerness got the better of him and he rushed out the door.*

   _____

5. *Thinking her friends were right behind her, it was frightening for Alison to discover that they were gone.*

   _____

6. *Although angered by the irrationality of his opponent, Senator Sanchez's plan was to address each point calmly.*

   _____

7. *Watching from the bridge, the fireworks bloomed spectacularly over the water.*

   _____

8. *Exhausted from the day's climbing, the looming storm forced the hikers to pitch an early camp.*

   _____

9. *Having studied for hours, it was very disappointing that I did so poorly on the exam.*

   _____

10. *Without being aware of it, termites can infest your home if you don't take the proper precautions.*

    _____

11. *Before getting the job at the bank, no one thought I could hold such a responsible position.*

    _____

12. *Lacking any real sailing skills, David's concern was mainly with keeping the ship afloat.*

    _____

Lesson 8: Other Misplaced Modifiers

Many kinds of modifying phrases other than participial phrases can dangle or be misplaced. Such phrases must obey the same rule than governs participial phrases—the law of proximity. **Every modifying phrase should be as close as possible to the word it modifies.**

Misplaced prepositional phrases

Prepositional phrases, as we discussed in Lesson 2, are phrases that begin with a preposition and include the object of the preposition. **Prepositional phrases can be *adjectival*, meaning they modify nouns, or *adverbial*, meaning they modify verbs, adjectives, or adverbs.**

> The dog *in the car* was barking.
>
> David walked *into the pole*.

In the first sentence, the prepositional phrase *in the car* answers the question *which dog?* Since *dog* is a noun, this prepositional phrase is adjectival. In the second sentence, the prepositional phrase *into the pole* answers the question *where did he walk?* Since *walk* is a verb, the prepositional phrase is adverbial.

> In an emergency, I am amazed at how calm Juanita can be.   X

This sentence suggests that I am only *amazed* in an emergency. What it really means, however, is that Juanita *is calm* in an emergency. To clarify, move the prepositional phrase *in an emergency* closer to the verb it modifies.

> I am amazed at how calm Juanita can be in an emergency.   ✓

Misplaced appositives

An appositive is a noun phrase that explains an adjacent noun. An appositive is often set off by a comma or commas.

> Franklin, *the only one of us who owned a car*, agreed to drive us all to the game.
>
> A splendid example of Synthetic Cubism, Picasso painted *Three Musicians* in the summer of 1924.   X

The phrase *a splendid example of Synthetic Cubism* is an appositive, and so it must be adjacent to the noun it explains. But *Picasso* is not an example of Synthetic Cubism, the painting is.

> A splendid example of Synthetic Cubism, *Three Musicians* was painted by Picasso in the summer of 1924.   ✓
>
> Picasso painted *Three Musicians*, a splendid example of Synthetic Cubism, in the summer of 1924.   ✓

Misplaced infinitives

As we discussed in Lesson 3, infinitives are often used as nouns. **However, they are also sometimes used as modifiers, and so can be misplaced.**

> We have many more math problems *to do*.
> We are working *to earn* money for the trip.

In the first sentence, the infinitive *to do* modifies the noun *problems*. In the second sentence, the infinitive *to earn* modifies the verb *are working*.

> To get our attention, we saw Mr. Genovese take out a giant boa constrictor.   X

The infinitive *to get* logically modifies the verb *take*. But it is incorrectly placed closer to a different verb, *saw*.

> To get our attention, Mr. Genovese took out a giant boa constrictor.   ✓
>
> We saw Mr. Genovese take out a giant boa constrictor to get our attention.   ✓

Exercise Set 8

In each of the following sentences, underline and label all participial phrases (PART), prepositional phrases (PREP), appositives (APP), and infinitive phrases (INF). Rewrite any sentence to fix any misplaced modifiers.

1. *Without so much as a blink, the gleaming sword was unsheathed by the warrior.*

   _____

2. *To maintain good health, physicians suggest that both vigorous exercise and good eating habits are required.*

   _____

3. *We found my lost earring walking through the parking lot.*

   _____

4. *Having run for over four hours, the finish line was still ten miles ahead of her.*

   _____

5. *Even with a sprained ankle, the coach forced Adam back into the game.*

   _____

6. *To find a good restaurant, there are many good online guides to help you.*

   _____

7. *In search of a good calculator, not a single store in the mall could help me.*

   _____

8. *A dutiful wife and mother, we were surprised to hear Carol complaining about domestic life.*

   _____

9. *To get a good jump out of the starting blocks, most sprinters say that good body positioning is essential.*

   _____

10. *Among the most sought-after collectibles on the market, we found the antique toys at a garage sale.*

   _____

Lesson 9: Tricky Tenses

The tense of a verb must logically indicate place and extent in time.

> Since the early twentieth century, the United States was the world's wealthiest nation.   ✗

The phrase *since the early twentieth century* indicates a condition that has lasted from the distant past to the present. However, the verb in this sentence, *was*, is in the simple past tense. To indicate a condition that extends from the past to the present, you must use the present perfect tense.

> Since the early twentieth century, the United States *has been* the world's wealthiest nation.   ✓

Fortunately, most of us can spot and correct most tense problems, so we won't discuss every English verb tense in detail. We will discuss just the trickiest situations.

The perfect tenses

The perfect tenses in English use the helping verb *to have* together with a past participle, as in *has eaten, have begun*, and *will have swum*. Perfect tense verbs usually indicate that some event or condition is **completed** before some other point in time. The word *perfect* in this case means *completed*, not *flawless*. Perfect tenses are **relative tenses**; that is, they show a relationship to *another* time reference in the sentence.

The past perfect tense, which uses the helping verb *had*, indicates that an event was completed *before* another point in the past. You can think of it as the "before the past" tense.

> By the time we arrived at the reception, Glen *had already given* the toast.

This sentence contains two verbs: *arrived* and *had given*. The first is in the simple past tense, and the second is in the past perfect tense. This suggests that the second event mentioned, the giving of the toast, was completed before the first event mentioned, the arrival at the reception. It may help to visualize the events on a timeline.

When a sentence contains two past tense verbs, check whether one event was completed before the other. If so, the earlier event should be in the past *perfect* tense.

> We ate the entire pie by the time Ellen realized it was missing.   ✗

This sentence contains two verbs in the past tense: *ate* and *realized*. The sentence suggests, however, that the eating of the pie was completed before Ellen realized it was missing. Therefore you need the past perfect tense to indicate the proper sequence.

> We *had eaten* the entire pie by the time Ellen realized it was missing.   ✓

The present perfect tense, which uses the helping verb *has* or *have*, indicates that an event or condition either extends from the past to the present or *possibly* extends from the past to the present or beyond. You can think of it as the "past plus present or future" tense.

> She *has been* very nice to me.

> We *have taken* only two tests this semester.

The first sentence contains the present perfect verb *has been*. This indicates that something was true in both the past *and* the present—she *was* nice to me and she *still is* nice to me. The present perfect tense here combines past and present. In the second sentence, the present perfect verb *have taken* indicates that we took the tests in the past, but *also* that we might take more in the future.

If a single event or condition starts and finishes in the past, it is best described with the **past tense**. If an event or condition extends from the past to the present, it is best described with the **present perfect tense**.

> In the short time since her sixteenth birthday, she became a best-selling artist.   ✗

The phrase *since her sixteenth birthday* suggests a condition that is still true in the present. Therefore, the present perfect tense works better than the past tense.

> In the short time since her sixteenth birthday, she *has become* a best-selling artist.   ✓

The future perfect tense indicates an event or condition that will have been completed before some time in the future.

> By Friday, *we will have completed* the entire project.

The verb *will have completed* suggests that the project will be complete before some future point in time–*Friday*.

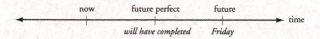

Present participles can be perfect also. A participle must be in the perfect form, using the helping verb *having*, whenever it indicates an action or condition completed before the event or condition expressed in the main part of the sentence.

> Walking all night, we were desperate to find rest at dawn.   X

The sentence indicates that the *walking* occurred at night, but the main idea of the sentence, that *we were desperate*, happened at dawn. Therefore, the walking was completed *by dawn, and should be expressed with the present perfect participle.*

> *Having walked* all night, we were desperate to find rest at dawn.   ✓

Verbs expressing ideas or works of art

A verb indicating a theory, artistic work, or a non-historic fact indicates the time and extent of the work or idea, *not* the time or extent of the person who created it.

> The ancient Greek philosopher Zeno believed that all motion was an illusion.   X

This sentence contains two verbs, *believed* and *was*. Since Zeno isn't around to believe things anymore, the first verb must be in the past tense. But Zeno's theory is still available to us. We can still wonder whether motion *is* an illusion or *is not* an illusion. Therefore, the second verb should be in the present tense.

> The ancient Greek philosopher Zeno believed that all motion *is* an illusion.   ✓

> In *Macbeth*, Shakespeare portrayed the madness that accompanies the pursuit of power.   X

Although Shakespeare wrote *Macbeth* centuries ago and is long dead, the play is still available to us, so you should use the present tense to indicate its life today.

> In *Macbeth*, Shakespeare *portrays* the madness that accompanies the pursuit of power.   ✓

Exercise Set 9

Circle the correct verb.

1. Glen (came/has come) to work exhausted this morning because he (stayed/had stayed) up all last night.

2. Already, and without (spending/having spent) so much as an hour on research, Dale (wrote/has written) the first draft of her essay.

3. (Developing/Having developed) the first compressed-air automobile, he (hoped/had hoped) to reveal it to the world at the exposition.

Fix any tense problems in the following sentences.

4. Right after school, we had gone to Mario's for a pizza and a few Cokes.

5. Finding no evidence against the accused, the detective had to release him.

6. When I got home, I wrote an essay about the baseball game that I saw that afternoon.

7. By the time the committee had adjourned, it voted on all four key proposals.

8. In the evening, we ate a nice meal with the same group of people we skied with that afternoon.

9. By the time I am done with finals, I will write four major papers.

10. It surprised us to learn that Venus was almost the same size as Earth.

11. Over the last three years, real estate values increased by over 20 percent.

12. Buyers often worry too much about finding a good motgage rate and will forget to scrutinize the terms of the contract.

13. By the time we arrived at the tent where the reception would be held, the caterers set up all the chairs.

Lesson 10: Idiom Errors

Idioms are standard phrases in a language. English has two kinds of idioms. One kind of idiom is a phrase that means something different from what it actually says, such as *carry through, across the board, come on strong, get your feet wet, bang for the buck, all ears, pull your leg*, and *eat crow*. The second kind of idiom is simply a "standard" way of phrasing something. For instance, English idiom requires us to say *in order to see* rather than *in order for seeing* or some other phrasing. For native English speakers, most idioms are so ingrained in our minds that we hardly notice them. When learning a new language, however, idioms are the hardest part of a language to learn.

> The house was on fire, so the firemen put it out.

This sentence contains two idioms: *on fire* and *put it out*. Neither of these makes sense *literally*. The house wasn't really *on* a fire, and the firemen didn't put the fire *out* of the house. However, these idioms are necessary to a good sentence because more literal language sounds too formal.

> The house was aflame, so the firemen extinguished the blaze.

When we speak so literally, our language sounds unnatural.

Watch your prepositions

The PSAT Writing occasionally includes a sentence with an idiom error. The sentence will use an idiom, but with the wrong preposition. As we discussed in Lesson 2, prepositions are words like *to, from, of, for, by, in, before, with, beyond*, and *up* that show relative position or direction. Certain idioms require a specific preposition. For instance, English idiom requires us to say *arguing with* a person, but *arguing against* an idea.

When a preposition is underlined in a PSAT Writing sentence, consider whether it is part of an idiomatic phrase, and if so, whether it is the correct preposition for that idiom.

> We were no longer satisfied at the level of service we were receiving.   **X**

This sentence contains two idioms: *satisfied with* and *level of service*. Are the prepositions correct? The *of* in *level of service* is correct, but the *at* in *satisfied at* is not. The correct idiom is *satisfied with*.

> We were no longer satisfied *with* the level of service we were receiving.   ✓

ESP: eliminate superfluous prepositions

Casual English speakers often use extra prepositions to make their language sound less formal. These prepositions are usually redundant and therefore unnecessary. **In formal writing, you should eliminate any unnecessary prepositions.** Notice that in phrases like the following, the preposition is unnecessary and therefore "nonstandard."

> The pole did not extend ~~out~~ far enough.

> Ever since I was injured, it hurts to climb ~~up~~ the stairs.

> Although clearly angry, the students were not yet ready to fight ~~against~~ the ruling.

> We were unsuccessful in our attempt to extract ~~out~~ the chemical from the venom.

> The illness can make one dizzy and prone to falling ~~down~~.

> If you don't hurry, you'll miss ~~out on~~ all the fun!

> There were plenty of volunteers to help ~~out~~ with the race.

> Before we prepare the steaks, we should fry ~~up~~ some peppers.

> Her speed and strength helped her to dominate ~~over~~ her opponents.

Exercise Set 10

Choose the correct preposition or phrase (if any) to complete each of the following sentences. If no word or phrase is required, circle —.

1. *I prefer spaghetti (to/over/more than/—) linguine.*

2. *We all agreed (on/with/about/—) the decision to go skiing rather than hiking.*

3. *The defendant would not agree (to/on/with/about) the plea bargain.*

4. *We found dozens of old photographs hidden (in/—) between the pages.*

5. *Good study habits are necessary (to/for/in/—) academic success.*

6. *The new house color is not very different (from/than/to/—) the old one.*

7. *His girlfriend was angry (with/at/—) him for not calling sooner.*

8. *They were both angry (about/at/with) the boys' behavior.*

9. *We will make sure that your contract complies (with/to/—) the laws of your state.*

Consider the idiom in each sentence, and fill in the correct preposition, if one is required.

10. *The interview provided insight _____ what great directors think about.*

11. *We were very angry _____ him for ignoring our phone calls.*

12. *We all agreed _____ the color scheme for the wedding.*

13. *Her tests include questions that seem very different _____ those that we see in the homework.*

14. *My mother preferred my singing _____ my practicing guitar.*

15. *When she arrived on campus, she felt truly independent _____ her parents for the first time.*

16. *We were very angry _____ the exorbitant price of gasoline at the corner gas station.*

17. *It was hard not to agree _____ her offer of a free movie ticket.*

18. *I arrived at the meeting too late to raise my objection _____ the proposal.*

19. *If we don't act soon, we may miss _____ the opportunity to lock in the lowest rates.*

Lesson 11: Diction Errors

Some PSAT Writing sentences contain errors in diction, or "wrong word" errors. Typically, such errors involve using a word that *sounds* like the correct word, but is in fact wrong, for instance saying *we interviewed perspective candidates* instead of *we interviewed prospective candidates*. *Perspective* means *point of view*, but *prospective* means *potential*.

Common diction errors

accept/except
accept (v) agree to take <*accept* an offer>

except (prep) excluding <everyone went *except* him>

adapt/adopt/ adept
adapt (v) make suitable for a particular purpose (from *apt*, which means *suitable*)

adopt (v) choose as one's own <*adopt* a child>

adept (adj) highly skilled <an *adept* soccer player>

affect/effect
affect (v) influence <it *affected* me deeply>

effect (n) result or consequence <it had a good *effect*>

allude/elude/ illusion
allude to (v) make an indirect reference to

elude (v) escape from capture <the suspect *eluded* us>

allusion (n) indirect reference *illusion* (n) deception or misconception

ambivalent/ ambiguous
ambivalent (adj) having conflicting feelings <I feel *ambivalent* about going to the party>

ambiguous (adj) unclear or having more than one interpretation <the message was *ambiguous*>

compliment/ complement
compliment (v) to make a praising personal comment <I *complimented* her on her performance>

complement (v) to make complete <the jacket *complemented* the outfit nicely>

cite/site/sight
cite (v) mention as a source of information <*cite* an article> or *commend publicly* <*cite* her heroism>

site (n) a place where something occurs

sight (v) see at a specific location <*sight* a new galaxy>

council/ counsel
council (n) a consultative committee <the executive *council*> *councilor* (n) member of a committee

counsel (v) to give advice <he *counseled* me on how to act> *counselor* (n) advisor

discrete/ discreet
discrete (adj) distinct <another *discrete* item>

discreet (adj) prudently modest <please conduct yourself *discreetly*>

elicit/illicit
elicit (v) cause to come forth <the joke *elicited* laughter>

illicit (adj) illegal <*illicit* behavior>

eminent/ imminent
eminent (adj) prominently distinguished <an *eminent* historian>

imminent (adj) about to occur <*imminent* doom>

phase/faze
phase (n) stage in a process <third *phase* of the project> *phase out* (v) eliminate in stages

faze (v) disturb someone's composure <I was a bit *fazed* by the interruption>

flaunt/flout
flaunt (v) show something off <*flaunt* your talents>

flout (v) show contempt for <*flout* the rules>

gambit/gamut
gambit (n) careful strategy or opening move

gamut (n) complete range <run the *gamut*>

imply/infer

imply (v)   suggest or hint at <she *implied* that she was bored by staring upward>

infer (v)   conclude from evidence <I *infer* from your yawn that you are bored>

its/it's, their/they're, whose/who's, your/you're

Apostrophes can show possession (as in *David's bike*) or indicate missing letters in a contraction (as in *can't* as a contraction of *cannot*). In each of the word pairs listed here, the words with apostrophes are **contractions**, and those without apostrophes are **possessives**.

it's = it is or *it has they're = they are you're = you are who's = who is*

morale/moral

morale (mor-AL)   (n)   shared enthusiasm for and dedication to a goal <the team's *morale* was very high>

moral (MOR-al)   (n)   lesson or principle about good behavior <the story had a good *moral*>

precede/ proceed/ proceeds

precede (v)   come before (*pre-* before) <the ceremony *preceded* the game>

proceed (v)   go on, usually after a pause (*pro-* forward) <it was hard to *proceed* after the interruption>

proceeds (n)   funds received from a charity drive <*proceeds* from the raffle>

principal/ principle

principal (n)   head of a school <*principal* Skinner> or the initial investment in an account

principle (n)   guiding rule <the company is guided by sound business *principles*>

reticent/ reluctant

reticent (adj)   reserved or reluctant to talk

reluctant (adj)   resistant by disposition or mood (The phrase *reticent to speak* is redundant.)

Exercise Set 11

Correct any diction errors in the following sentences.

1. *Although most of the manuscripts were signed by their authors, some were written unanimously.*   _____

2. *It was hard for the comic to illicit even the slightest laugh from the crowd.*   _____

3. *We needed to adopt the old engine to fit the new go-cart.*   _____

4. *The imminent congresswoman was reelected easily.*   _____

5. *She thought she should be discrete about her previous relationship with the defendant.*   _____

6. *The counsel will decide how to finance the new city park.*   _____

7. *Rather than cooperating with the rest of the team, Richard always tries to flaunt the rules.*   _____

8. *His knowledge of sports runs the gambit from table tennis to arena football.*   _____

9. *The jury should not imply guilt from the defendant's refusal to answer these questions.*   _____

10. *We are amazed at how adapt a juggler Carl was.*   _____

11. *Rather than eliminate the department all at once, they decided to faze it out gradually.*   _____

12. *Barking dogs can often signal eminent danger.*   _____

13. *After our vacation, we decided to precede with the plan.*   _____

14. *I was trying to infer that I didn't enjoy the movie.*   _____

15. *I always felt reticent to talk in class.*   _____

16. *Deanne's concentration was not even phased by the fire alarm.*   _____

17. *The police officer was sighted for her efforts in the hostage rescue.*   _____

18. *Even the most trivial news seems to effect the stock price immediately.*   _____

19. *David felt ambiguous about testifying against his partner.*   _____

20. *The moral of the troops was at an all-time low during the Christmas season.*   _____

21. *That scarf really compliments your outfit.*   _____

22. *I tried to stay awake for the lecture, but I was so disinterested that I dozed off before the professor was finished.*   _____

23. *The article mentioned the low voter turnout in order to infer that the senator may not have been elected by a true majority.*   _____

24. *Although the police initially had many solid leads, the suspect alluded them for several months.*   _____

25. *It may be years before we understand how pollution from the new power plant might effect the regional environment.*   _____

26. *The new online store's musical offerings run the gambit from arias to zydeco.*   _____

27. *Heather was the principle author of the study that was recently published in a prominent scientific magazine.*   _____

28. *All of the invited guests accept Anthony arrived promptly.*   _____

29. *For nearly the entire semester, I felt so inhabited that I never so much as razed my hand in class.*   _____

30. *Try as they might, the hikers could not find the anecdote to the snake venom.*   _____

31. *The acid solution was so potent that we had to delude it with water before we could use it safely.*   _____

32. *The symbols on the cave walls are ambivalent; scientists have been debating their meaning for decades.*   _____

33. *Despite a minor setback with the caterers, the Breedens managed to give an eloquent party.*   _____

34. *As someone committed to fairness in education, she could not accept the iniquity of the admissions policy.*   _____

Lesson 12: Other Problems with Modifiers

We have already discussed dangling and misplaced modifiers, but modifiers can be misused in other ways as well. **Make sure that you know the proper form that modifiers should take and that you know how to eliminate redundant modifiers.**

Using adjectives for adverbs

Don't use an adjective to do the job of an adverb. Adjectives like *green*, *generous*, and *gargantuan* modify nouns. Adverbs like *gently*, *globally*, and *grossly* modify verbs, adjectives, or other adverbs.

> I was impressed by how cogent his argument was presented. **X**

The modifer *cogent* is intended to answer the question *how* was it *presented?* Therefore it modifies a verb and so should take the adverbial form *cogently*.

> I was impressed by how *cogently* his argument was presented. **✓**

Some modifiers can be used as either adjectives or adverbs. For instance, *fast* and *well* can be used either way. In the phrase *the fast car*, the word *fast* is used as an adjective modifying the noun *car*. But in the clause *he ran fast*, it is an adverb modifying the verb *ran*. In the clause *I haven't been well lately*, the word *well* is an adjective meaning *healthy* modifying the pronoun *I*. But in the clause *she sings very well*, it is an adverb modifying the verb *sings*.

> I couldn't write fast enough to finish the essay on time.

> I feel pretty good.

Although some people might tell you these sentences are incorrect, they are actually both fine. In the first sentence, the word *fast* is an adverb meaning *quickly* modifying the verb *write*. In the second sentence, the word *good* is an adjective modifying the pronoun *I* and joined to it by a linking verb *feel*. It is also fine to say *I feel well*, but only because *well* in this case is also an adjective meaning *healthy*.

Comparative adjectives and adverbs

Use the proper form when using comparative modifiers. **Comparative adjectives** come in one of two forms. For instance, *fast* becomes the comparative *faster* by adding *-er*, but *adorable* becomes the comparative *more adorable* by adding *more*. (*Adorabler* just doesn't sound

right, does it?) **Comparative adverbs** almost always include *more*, as in *more rapidly*, but some irregular adverbs can take *-er*, as in *she runs faster than her brother*.

> The briefcase feels more light than it did this morning. **X**

The phrase *more light* is in the incorrect comparative form.

> The briefcase feels *lighter* than it did this morning. **✓**

> Please try to hold the baby gentler next time. **X**

The word *gentler* is a comparative adjective, not a comparative adverb. Most comparative adverbs use *more*.

> Please try to hold the baby *more gently* next time. **✓**

Some modifiers should never take the comparative form because they are absolute modifiers. For instance, one thing cannot logically be *more unique* than another thing, because *unique* means *one of a kind*, which indicates an absolute quality. Nothing can be *somewhat* unique; it either *is* unique or *isn't* unique.

> The loss was made more inevitable by the injury to our starting pitcher. **X**

The concept of inevitability doesn't come in degrees. Either something is *inevitable*, or it's not. There is no in-between, so the phrase *more inevitable* is illogical.

> The loss was made *inevitable* by the injury to our starting pitcher. **✓**

Redundancy

The PSAT Writing will occasionally test your ability to eliminate **redundancy**. A **redundancy** is an unnecessary repetition of an idea. **To check whether a word or phrase is redundant, reread the sentence without that word or phrase. If the meaning of the sentence remains unchanged, the word or phrase is redundant.**

> With only seconds remaining to go in the game, Michael sped quickly down the court. **X**

Since *remaining* means roughly the same as *to go*, we don't need to say both. Also, to *speed* means to *move quickly*, so *sped quickly* is redundant. Eliminate the redundancies.

> With only seconds remaining in the game, Michael sped down the court. **✓**

Exercise Set 12

1. Cross out any redundant words or phrases in the paragraph below. (*Hint*: There are at least 10 redundancies.)

> *When we refer back to past history, we can see that whenever a new innovation is introduced for the first time, people rarely accept the whole entire concept, at least not right away. If and when something threatens the ways of the past, people don't easily accept this new concept. Although not everyone necessarily needs to maintain the status quo, consistency and predictability make people feel comfortable. Even when technology comes up with a way to do things better, people often continue on with their older, less efficient ways. For instance, it's not uncommon for people to use e-mail while at the same time continuing to correspond through "snail mail." If they would quickly pause for a moment, they would see that they can communicate more effectively through the Internet—and save some trees!*

Correct any modifier problems in the sentences below.

2. *The latest political commercials make their points stronger than previous ones.*

3. *My shirt smelled quite foully after rugby practice.*

4. *We never usually get to go to such elegant restaurants.*

5. *Although both of my parents are level-headed, my father is the most patient.*

6. *The third graders weren't hardly interested in going to the museum after school.*

7. *I can sing in front of a crowd easier than I can give a speech.*

8. *In many areas of the country, wind energy can be converted to electricity even more efficient than can fossil energy.*

9. *I felt surprisingly good after Saturday's ten-mile run.*

10. *The microscopic size of the fracture made it more impossible to detect, even with special instruments.*

11. *These measures won't barely address the state's deficit.*

12. *The teacher never told us about the test until the day before.*

13. *Students never usually bother to examine the veracity of the "facts" they are supposed to memorize in history class.*

Lesson 13: Irregular Verbs

Don't confuse past tense verbs with past participles. The perfect tenses and past participial phrases require the **past participle** of the verb, not the **past tense** form of the verb. For some verbs, both forms look the same. But for many **irregular verbs**, these forms are different. You should know the **irregular past participle** forms of common verbs. Perhaps you should put these on flashcards.

Common irregulars

Infinitive	Past tense	Past participle
to arise	arose	arisen
to awake	awoke	awoken
to beat	beat	beaten
to begin	began	begun
to blow	blew	blown
to break	broke	broken
to burst	burst	burst
to cast	cast	cast
to come	came	come
to creep	crept	crept
to do	did	done
to draw	drew	drawn
to drink	drank	drunk
to drive	drove	driven
to forsake	forsook	forsaken
to get	got	got, gotten
to go	went	gone
to hurt	hurt	hurt
to kneel	kneeled, knelt	knelt
to know	knew	known
to lay (to put or place)	laid	laid
to lie (to recline)	lay	lain
to ride	rode	ridden
to run	ran	run
to shrink	shrank, shrunk	shrunk, shrunken
to sink	sank	sunk
to speak	spoke	spoken
to spring	sprang	sprung
to take	took	taken
to tear	tore	torn
to write	wrote	written

Exercise Set 13

Complete the following sentences with the correct form of the verb:

1. We might have _____ (to ride) the bus as far as Los Angeles if we had had enough money.

2. Those issues have not yet _____ (to arise) in this discussion.

3. In the last two years, the Patriots have _____ (to beat) the Jets four times.

4. Peter told me that I should not have _____ (to drink) the water.

5. We should have _____ (to go) to the mall.

6. I could not have _____ (to get) such good grades this quarter if I had not changed my study habits.

7. The Donnellys have _____ (to run) their corner store for over 20 years.

8. Before last night, they had not even _____ (to speak) about the incident.

9. I can't believe you put my wool sweater in the dryer and _____ (to shrink) it.

10. His batting average has really _____ (to sink) ever since his injury.

11. I wish that she had not _____ (to speak) for so long.

12. It seems as if the flowers have _____ (to spring) out of the ground overnight.

13. We should have _____ (to take) that shortcut to work.

Circle the past participle(s) or past-tense verbs in each sentence, and make any necessary corrections.

14. Elisha could never have went to the state finals if I had not convinced her to join the team in the first place.

15. In retrospect, it seems I might have took too much time on the essay portion of the test.

16. While we played video games, Danny lay on the couch all afternoon.

17. Most people find it amazing to consider that, millions of years ago, life sprung from a primordial swamp.

18. Carl would have tore his uniform if he had not stopped his slide at the last second.

19. The generals forsook their own troops to surrender and save their own lives.

20. When the temperature sunk below zero, the pipes bursted like water balloons.

21. The assets of the company were froze as soon as it declared bankruptcy.

22. .When the cook rung the bell for dinner, the whole camp raced up the hill.

23. George needed his friends more than ever, but they had forsook him.

24. We sung just about every song we knew; then we went to bed.

25. The senator could have spoke a lot longer, but she yielded the floor to her colleague.

Lesson 14: The Subjunctive Mood

The **mood** of a verb indicates the *factuality* or *urgency* of an action or condition. Every verb in English takes one of three moods. Verbs in the **indicative mood** indicate something real or factual, as in *you are going*. Verbs in the **subjunctive mood** indicate something hypothetical, conditional, wishful, suggestive, or counter to fact, as in *I wish you were going*. Verbs in the **imperative mood** indicate a direct command, as in *go!*

The only mood that students occasionally struggle with is the subjunctive mood. The PSAT Writing might contain a question or two involving verbs in the subjunctive mood, but they are not very common. You should recognize the common situations in which the subjunctive mood must be used, and know how to change the form of the verb accordingly.

A verb that is in the subjunctive mood is usually accompanied by auxiliaries like *would, should, might,* **and** *may.* **When the verb** *to be* **is in the subjunctive mood, it usually takes the form** *were* **or** *be.* Verbs in the subjunctive mood indicate something **hypothetical, conditional, wishful, suggestive,** or **counter to fact**.

He *would feel* better if only he would eat.
If I *were* faster, I could play wide receiver.
(hypothetical)

I wish that he *would not act* so superior.
I wish I *were* 2 inches taller.
(wishful)

She said that we *should practice* harder.
He asks that we *be* there at six o'clock sharp.
(suggestive)

I truly doubt that she *would ever say* such a thing.
I think she *might be* in over her head.
(doubtful)

We thought that she *might win* the election, but she lost by a lot.
He plays as though he *were* not even injured.
(counter to fact)

Don't overdo it

In English, the subjunctive is a **mood**, not a **tense**. This means that the rules for altering verbs are not as strict as they are with a tense. Sometimes, a sentence gives enough clues about the "subjunctivity" of a verb so that auxiliaries are not necessary. Other times, the subjunctive form just sounds too archaic. **Don't use subjunctive forms if they make the sentence sound awkward or archaic.**

If that *be* so, we may see dramatic changes in the market. ✗

The sentence indicates a condition, and the verb *be* is, strictly speaking, in subjunctive form. But today this form is considered to be archaic. It is now standard English to keep the verb in the indicative mood, even though the situation is subjunctive.

If that *is* so, we may see dramatic changes in the market. ✓

Watch your *if*s

One common mistake is using improper idiom in the subjunctive mood. **The past subjunctive construction** *if…had* **is often mistakenly phrased as** *if…would have.*

If he would have arrived a minute sooner, he would not have missed her. ✗

The first verb is subjunctive, but it is not proper idiom to use the auxiliary *would* here.

If he *had* arrived a minute sooner, he would not have missed her. ✓

Exercise Set 14

Circle the correct verb form in each of the following sentences

1. If our wide receiver (was/were) a little faster, he would be more open in the secondary.

2. As a matter of fact, Theo (was/would have been) only six years old when the Civil War began.

3. Denny would be more successful if only he (promoted/would promote) himself.

4. The brochure suggested that we (are/be) at the camp first thing in the morning.

5. I wish that my horse (were/was) not so lethargic this morning.

6. If the goalie (would have/had) lifted his glove even slightly, the puck would have gotten through.

7. He acted as though the concert hall (was/were) filled with screaming fans.

8. I wish that summer camp (was/were) two weeks longer.

9. If the class (would have/had) voted against it, we would not have been given the chance to visit the museum.

Circle the verb(s) in each sentence. If the verb mood is incorrect, fix it.

10. We were very doubtful that Jonna will get the part since she was sick during her audition.

11. If I was in Paris, I'd probably spend most of my time in cafés.

12. If I would have known that the food was so good here, I would have come sooner.

13. The coach demanded that we were in bed by 11 o'clock.

14. Yvonne spoke as if she was a medieval serf complaining about her master.

15. Gina wished that she would have chosen the red dress instead of the pink one.

16. The professor spoke to us as if he was a member of the British Parliament.

17. I would have wanted to have seen the countryside, but I was sick in bed for the entire vacation.

18. Had I found his wallet, I would have returned it to him immediately.

19. If only the doctor would have told me to cut back on eating red meat, I would have complied.

Lesson 15: Coordinating Ideas

If a sentence contains more than one idea, those ideas must coordinate logically with one other. The main idea must be conveyed with an **independent clause**, but related ideas may be conveyed with **independent clauses, subordinate clauses,** or **modifying phrases**.

> In addition to being a best-selling author, Frances Brown is a native New Yorker, and she has written a new book; this new book is likely to cause quite a stir. ✗

This sentence contains many ideas, but they are poorly coordinated. It contains three independent clauses: *Frances Brown is a native New Yorker, she has written a new book,* and *this new book is likely to cause quite a stir.* Which of these conveys the main idea? The first idea seems trivial compared with the other two. The second and the third are intriguing, but are so closely related that they perhaps belong in the same clause. A good revision would likely combine the last two ideas into the main clause of the sentence, and relegate the other to a modifying phrase with the other less-important idea that she is *a best-selling author.*

> Frances Brown, a native New Yorker and a best-selling author, has written a new book that is likely to cause quite a stir. ✓

Run-on sentences

A run-on sentence is not just a sentence that seems too long. It is a sentence that joins two independent clauses—that is, clauses that could be sentences by themselves—with only a comma between them. This error is also called a **comma splice.** Sometimes two independent clauses are so closely related that they belong in the same sentence, but to join them you must use a **colon** (:), a **semicolon** (;), or a **conjunction** like *but, or, yet, for, and, nor,* or *so.* (You can remember all of those coordinating conjunctions with the mnemonic BOYFANS.)

> I took several science courses last year, my favorite was neuroscience. ✗

This sentence contains two independent clauses that are joined only by a comma, so the sentence is a run-on. There are many ways to correct this problem. How you fix it depends on what you want to emphasize. For instance, if you want to emphasize the first idea, you should relegate the second idea to a **modifying phrase.**

> I took several science courses last year, my favorite being neuroscience. ✓

Now the sentence clearly emphasizes the first idea, that *I took several science courses,* and de-emphasizes the second idea by reducing it to the modifying phrase *my favorite being neuroscience.* However, you may want to emphasize the *second* idea by relegating the first idea to a modifying phrase.

> Of the several science courses I took last year, my favorite was neuroscience. ✓

Now the sentence clearly emphasizes the second idea, that *my favorite (course) was neuroscience.* A third way to coordinate these ideas is to emphasize the contrast between the *several* courses and the single course, *neuroscience,* by simply joining the original clauses with the conjunction *but.*

> I took several science courses last year, but my favorite was neuroscience. ✓

Using colons and semicolons

The **colon** (:) and the **semicolon** (;) can be used to combine two closely related independent clauses into a single sentence. The colon has a slightly more specific meaning than the semicolon: it usually introduces an **example** or **explanation.** Remember two important rules when using a colon or semicolon to splice clauses: **make sure that the clauses are independent and do not begin with a conjunction, and make sure that the clauses have a strong supporting relationship.**

> The test was unbelievably difficult; and hardly anyone finished it on time. ✗

This sentence uses a semicolon, but the second clause begins with the conjunction *and.* This is redundant. You may use a semicolon *or* a conjunction to join two clauses, but not both. You can fix the mistake by simply removing the conjunction.

> The test was unbelievably difficult; hardly anyone finished it on time. ✓

You can also combine the two ideas into a single clause since they are so closely related.

> The test was so difficult that hardly anyone finished it on time. ✓

> The meeting went well, and everyone was impressed by my presentation. ✗

This sentence does not contain a blatant grammatical error. However, it is a bit disjointed and ambiguous. How are the *meeting* and the *presentation* related? Did the meeting go well *because* of the successful presentation, or for another reason? If the good presentation **explains** why the meeting went well, the colon works nicely.

> The meeting went well: everyone was impressed by my presentation. ✓

The ride was harrowing, several times the car nearly skidded off the mountain. X

This sentence is a run-on. It uses only a comma to join two independent clauses. Since the second clause seems to explain the first, that is, it tells *why* the ride was so harrowing, a colon works well.

> The ride was harrowing: several times the car nearly skidded off the mountain. ✓

Exercise Set 15

Write a single sentence that logically and concisely coordinates the given clauses.

1. *Helen Schaffer's latest movie has received widespread critical acclaim. She directed the movie. It is third movie that she has directed. She is the daughter of famous screenwriter George Schaffer. Her latest movie is a comedy entitled* The Return.

2. *Scientists have made an important discovery. The scientists who made the discovery are from universities and research institutions from all over the world. The discovery concerns a region of the brain called the prefrontal cortex. The scientists have discovered that this region governs impulse control in humans. Studying this region of the brain can help scientists learn more about criminal behavior.*

Make any necessary corrections to the following sentences so that the clauses coordinate logically and concisely.

3. *Electric cars may not be as environmentally sound as they seem, but the electricity they use actually comes from fossil fuels; that electricity is produced in power plants that often burn coal or other fossil fuels.*

4. *Regular exercise is good for your muscles and heart, but it is good for your brain too by keeping it well oxygenated and helping it to work more efficiently, which is surprising.*

5. *More Americans than ever are obese; this can be explained by the fact that processed, high-calorie food is easily available, but our ancestors used to have to work hard to get their food, not just go to a store.*

6. *We are motivated by our principles; our principles change all the time, though: our experiences and our priorities evolve as we grow.*

7. *There were two important factors contributing to the victory; one thing is that the team never gave up, and they could have when they were down three games in the playoffs, but another is that they had a lot of fans rooting for them.*

Answer Key

Exercise Set 1

1. *S*
2. *S*
3. *P*
4. *S*
5. *P*
6. *S*
7. *S*
8. *P*
9. *was* (the subject is *flock*)
10. *were* (the subject is *data*)
11. *is* (the subject is *neither*)
12. *goes* (the subject is *much*)
13. *is* (the subject is *Amy*)
14. *was* (the subject is *rose*)
15. *are* (the subject is *brothers*)
16. *is* (the subject is *speck*)
17. *shout* (the subject is *Bailey brothers*)
18. *were* (the subject is *people*)
19. *are* (the subject is *smokers*)
20. *are* (the subject is *thousands*)
21. *have* (the subject is *voices*)
22. s: *player*, v: were (change to *was*)
23. S-*a theater and a toy store;* V-*has been* (change to *have been*)
24. S-*either Eric or his brother,* V-*is* (no change)
25. S-*proceeds,* V-*goes* (change to *go*)
26. S-*years,* V-*is* (change to *are*)
27. S-*neither,* V-*were* (change to *was*)
28. S-*technology,* V-*have transformed* (change to *has transformed*)
29. S-*player,* V-*were* (change to *was*)
30. S-*sponsorship,* V-*have garnered* (change to *has garnered*)
31. S-*Neither the children nor their parents,* V-*utters* (change to *utter*); S-*Mrs. Denny,* V-*tells* (no change)
32. S-*your strength training and your diet,* V-*is* (change to *are*)

Exercise Set 2

1. *The team were* (change to *was*) *met.*
2. *The flock were* (change to *was*) *silver.*
3. *Carmen are* (change to *is*) *unlikely to be swayed.*
4. *Juggling the demands seem* (change to *seems*) *too much to bear.*
5. *Others is* (change to *are*) *concerned.*
6. *One agree* (change to *agrees*) *with the statement:* "Anyone who would run for political office is not worth voting for."
7. *The fact have forced* (change to *has forced*) *some historians to adopt a cynical perspective.*
8. Trimmed: *Advancements have to do with modification.*
   The verb *(have to do with)* is weak, vague, and inactive, and the subject *(advancements)* and object *(modification)* are abstract and vague. To improve the sentence, think about the *intended* meaning of the sentence, and use stronger and less abstract terms. Here's a good revision: *Typically, societies progress by making small modifications to their institutions, not by overhauling them completely.*
9. Trimmed: *The development was affected.*
   The verb *(was affected)* is weak, passive, and vague. Here's a good revision: *The incohesiveness of the revolutionary army hindered the development of the new government.*

Exercise Set 3

1. *by mail; by phone; on the web* prepositional phrases
2. *having; working* gerunds
3. *you get to know her; you will like her* independent clauses
4. *exceptionally fresh; reasonably priced* adverb-adjective phrases
5. *concert; three-hour nightmare* nouns
6. <u>*Exercising*</u> *is essential, but so is* <u>*eating*</u> *intelligently.* The sentence discusses general activities, so gerunds are more appropriate.
7. *The purpose of this trip is* <u>*to show*</u> *you what life was like in the eighteenth century.* The infinitive shows purpose more effectively than does the gerund.

8. *I have always loved* dancing *although my condition has always prevented me from doing it myself.* Since the speaker cannot dance, the infinitive is inappropriate.

9. *Is it better* to study *a little each night, or a lot the night before?* The infinitive shows a clearer link between the action and a particular subject.

10. *The director called a meeting* to discuss *the coordination of the marketing phase.* The infinitive shows purpose more effectively than does the gerund.

11. *The defendant was unwilling to give up his right* to have *his lawyer present at all questioning.*

12. *I would not dream* of trying *out for the team until I have learned to throw a football.*

13. *Within the next three weeks, we plan* to have *all of the work on the roof completed.*

14. *I like working with Miss Bennett because she is very supportive and* knowledgeable.

15. *I can't decide whether I should give* the tickets to Maria or to Caitlyn.

Exercise Set 4

1. This is an illogical comparison. The sentence compares *the show* to *anything on the air*, which includes the show itself. Logically, *the show* can only be better than *anything* else *on the air*.

2. This contains a number shift. The sentence equates *team unity and commitment*, which is plural, with *the key*, which is singular. The word *key* should be replaced with *keys*.

3. This is an illogical comparison. The sentence compares *mathematics lessons* to *American classrooms*. Instead, it should compare *the lessons in Japanese classrooms* to *the lessons in American classrooms*.

4. This is an illogical comparison. The sentence compares *electric-combustion engines* to *conventional cars*. Instead, it should compare *electric-combustion engines* to *the engines in conventional cars*.

5. This comparison is logical but not grammatically correct. The sentence should make sense even when the interrupter *if not more so* is removed. The comparison should read *the surrealists were regarded as being as inscrutable as the Dadaists, if not more so*.

6. This is an illogical comparison. It should read *I prefer a lot of modern poetry to* the poetry of Shakespeare.

7. This contains a *many/more* error. It should read *Her suitcase would not close because she had packed too* many *of her towels into it.*

8. *The year-end bonus was equally divided* among *Parker, Herriot, and me.*

9. *Many students wanted to be* lifeguards *at the club.*

10. *The toughest thing about her class is* having *to do tons of homework every night.*

Exercise Set 5

1. pronouns: *there, where.* There are many times in a game when *a player can lose focus.*

2. pronouns: *you, it.* If a student wants to memorize the meaning of a word, he or she *should begin by understanding the concept it represents.*

3. pronouns: *she, herself.* Caroline passed the phone to Julia, but Julia *couldn't bring herself to speak.*

4. pronouns: *one, that.* Not wanting to be the one who *slowed the team down, David dropped out of the race.*

5. pronouns: *their, him, her.* Brown University is committed to assisting its *students by providing* them *with any necessary financial aid.*

6. pronouns: *it, them.* The media ignored the reports because they *didn't considered* those reports *newsworthy.*

7. pronouns: *no one, that, that, they, it.* No one who *has been through the first week of boot camp ever believes that* he or she *will make it through the entire six weeks.*

8. pronouns: *you, one.* Although you shouldn't read carelessly, you don't *need to read slowly, either.*

9. pronouns: *neither, that, their.* Neither Glen nor Don thought that his *team would lose the championship.*

10. pronouns: *his, her.* Students sometimes aren't ready to handle the extra work when their *courses become more demanding.*

11. pronoun: *where.* The anthology is filled with stories in which *love goes unrequited.*

12. pronouns: *everyone, their.* Everyone is expected to do his or her *share.*

13. pronoun: *they.* The museum received so many donations that it *actually had to return over a million dollars to the benefactors.*

14. pronoun: *that.* They usually give the trophy to the skater who *makes the fewest mistakes.*

15. pronouns: *I, where.* I like movies in which *the bad guy gets punished in the end.*

16. pronoun: *themselves. Each swimmer will have a lane to <u>herself (or himself)</u>.*

17. pronouns: *who, that. Who was the player <u>who</u> hit the home run?*

Exercise Set 6

1. *The climb was much easier for them than it was for Jeff and <u>me</u>.*

2. *The other contestants did not seem as confident as <u>he</u> (was).*

3. *<u>We</u> detectives are always careful to follow every lead.*

4. *Every student should make <u>his or her</u> own study plan.*

5. *They never seem to listen to the opinions of <u>us</u> students as they should.*

6. *Jim gave control of the project to Fiona and <u>me</u>.*

7. *The university presented the honor to David and <u>him</u>.*

8. *Justine and <u>I</u> have always been closest friends.*

9. *There is no point in <u>our</u> delaying the tests any longer.*

10. *It seems quite clear that you and <u>I</u> will have to work together to solve this problem.*

11. *It might be hard for <u>him and me</u> to agree.*

12. *<u>We</u> and the other members debated the issue for over two hours.*

13. *The owners of the club offered my wife and <u>me</u> a free bottle of wine with dinner.*

14. *No other runner on the team could outrun <u>me</u>.*

15. *The teachers were growing tired of <u>his</u> constantly falling asleep in class.*

16. *The ballpark always held a special attraction for Dave and <u>me</u>.*

Exercise Set 7

Each sentence below represents only one possible revision. There may be other correct answers.

1. The participle *looking* is not close to its subject. *As I look at your essay, it seems to me that you need to use more specific examples.*

2. The participle *turning* dangles. *As I turned the corner, the stadium came into view.*

3. The participle *exhausted* dangles. *Although Martha was exhausted after the night's work, her creative instincts compelled her to keep writing.*

4. The participle *waiting* dangles. *David's eagerness got the better of him, and without waiting for an answer, he rushed out the door.*

5. The participle *thinking* is not close to its subject. *Thinking her friends were right behind her, Alison was frightened to discover that they were gone.*

6. The participle *angered* dangles. *Although angered by the irrationality of her opponent, Senator Sanchez planned to address each point calmly.*

7. The participle *watching* dangles. *As we watched from the bridge, the fireworks bloomed spectacularly over the water.*

8. The participle *exhausted* is not close to its subject. *The looming storm forced the hikers, exhausted from the day's climbing, to pitch an early camp.*

9. The participle *having* is not close to its subject. *Having studied for hours, I was very disappointed to have done so poorly on the exam.*

10. The participle *being* dangles. *Without your being aware of it, termites can infest your home if you don't take the proper precautions.*

11. The participle *getting* is not close to its subject. *Before I got the job at the bank, no one thought I could hold such a responsible position.*

12. The participle *lacking* dangles. *Lacking any real sailing skills, David was mainly concerned with keeping the ship afloat.*

Exercise Set 8

Each of these answers provides only one possible correction. On some sentences, other corrections are possible.

1. *<u>Without so much as a blink</u> (PREP), the gleaming sword was unsheathed <u>by the warrior</u> (PREP).*

    Correction: *Without so much as a blink, the warrior unsheathed the gleaming sword.*

2. *<u>To maintain good health</u> (INF), physicians suggest that both vigorous exercise and good eating habits are required.*

    Correction: *Physicians suggest that both vigorous exercise and good eating habits are required to maintain good health.*

3. *We found my lost earring <u>walking through the parking lot</u> (PART containing a PREP).*

    Correction: *Walking through the parking lot, we found my lost earring.*

4. *<u>Having run for over four hours</u> (PART containing a PREP), the finish line was still ten miles ahead <u>of her</u> (PREP).*

Correction: *Although she had run for over four hours, the finish line was still ten miles ahead of her.*

5. *Even <u>with a sprained ankle</u> (PREP), the coach forced Adam back <u>into the game</u> (PREP).*

   Correction: *Even though Adam had a sprained ankle, the coach forced him back into the game.*

6. *<u>To find a good restaurant</u> (INF), there are many good online guides <u>to help you</u> (INF).*

   Correction: *There are many good online guides to help you find a good restaurant.*

7. *<u>In search of a good calculator</u> (PREP), not a single store clerk <u>in the mall</u> (PREP) could help me.*

   Correction: *Not a single store clerk in the mall could help me find a good calculator.*

8. *<u>A dutiful wife and mother</u> (APP), we were surprised to hear Carol complaining <u>about domestic life</u> (PREP).*

   Correction: *We were surprised to hear Carol, a dutiful wife and mother, complaining about domestic life.*

9. *<u>To get a good jump</u> (INF) <u>out of the starting blocks</u> (PREP), most sprinters say that good body positioning is essential.*

   Correction: *Most sprinters say that good body positioning is required for getting a good jump out of the starting blocks.*

10. *<u>Among the most sought-after collectibles</u> (PREP) <u>on the market</u> (PREP), we found the antique toys <u>at a garage sale</u> (PREP).*

    Correction: *We found the antique toys, which are among the most sought-after collectibles on the market, at a garage sale.*

Exercise Set 9

1. *came; had stayed*
2. *having spent; has written*
3. *having developed; hoped*
4. *Right after school, we <u>went</u> to Mario's for a pizza and a few Cokes. Since there is only one even being discussed, ther is no need for the past perfect tense.*
5. *<u>Having found</u> no evidence against the accused, the detective had to release him. The search for evidence was completed before the* release.
6. *When I got home, I wrote an essay on the baseball game that I <u>had seen</u> that afternoon. The* seeing *was completed before the* writing.

7. *By the time the committee <u>adjourned</u>, it <u>had voted</u> on all four key proposals. The* voting *was completed before the* adjournment.
8. *In the evening, we ate a nice meal with the same group of people we <u>had skied</u> with that afternoon. The* skiing *was completed before the* eating.
9. *By the time I am done with finals, <u>I will have written</u> four major papers. The* writing *will be completed before the finals.*
10. *It surprised us to learn that Venus <u>is</u> almost the same size as Earth. This fact is true even now.*
11. *Over the last several years, real estate values <u>have increased</u> by over 20 percent. The* increase *occurred from the past to the present.*
12. *Buyers often worry too much about finding a good mortgage rate and <u>forget</u> to scrutinize the terms of the contract. Tense consistency requires the present tense.*
13. *By the time we arrived at the tent where the reception would be held, the caterers <u>had set</u> up all the chairs. The* setting up *was completed before we arrived.*

Exercise Set 10

1. *I prefer spaghetti <u>to</u> linguine.*
2. *We all agreed <u>on</u> the decision to go skiing rather than hiking. (You* agree on *mutual decisions or plans.)*
3. *The defendant would not agree <u>to</u> the plea bargain. (You* agree to *offers.)*
4. *We found dozens of old photographs hidden (none needed) between the pages.*
5. *Good study habits are necessary <u>to (or sometimes for)</u> academic success.*
6. *The new house color is not very different <u>from</u> the old one. (Only use* than *with* **comparatives** *like* bigger; different *is not a comparative.)*
7. *His girlfriend was angry <u>with</u> him for not calling sooner. (You get* angry with *people.)*
8. *They were both angry <u>about</u> the boys' behavior. (You get* angry about *situations.)*
9. *We will make sure that your contract complies <u>with</u> the laws of your state.*
10. *The interview provided insight <u>into</u> what great directors think about.*
11. *We were very angry <u>with</u> him for ignoring our phone calls.*
12. *We all agreed <u>on</u> the color scheme for the wedding.*
13. *Her tests include questions that seem very different <u>from</u> those that we see in the homework.*

14. *My mother preferred my singing <u>to</u> my practicing guitar.*

15. *When she arrived on campus, she felt truly independent <u>of</u> her parents for the first time.*

16. *We were very angry <u>about</u> the exorbitant price of gasoline at the corner gas station.*

17. *It was hard not to agree <u>to</u> her offer of a free movie ticket.*

18. *I arrived at the meeting too late to raise my objection <u>to</u> the proposal.*

19. *If we don't act soon, we may miss (no preposition required) the opportunity to lock in the lowest rates.*

Exercise Set 11

1. *Although most of the manuscripts were signed by their authors, some were written <u>anonymously</u>.*

2. *It was hard for the comic to <u>elicit</u> even the slightest laugh from the crowd.*

3. *We needed to <u>adapt</u> the old engine to fit the new go-cart.*

4. *The <u>eminent</u> congresswoman was reelected easily.*

5. *She thought it wise to be <u>discreet</u> about her previous relationship with the defendant.*

6. *The <u>council</u> will decide how to finance the new city park.*

7. *Rather than cooperating with the rest of the team, Richard is always trying to <u>flout</u> the rules.*

8. *His knowledge of sports runs the <u>gamut</u> from table tennis to arena football.*

9. *The jury should not <u>infer</u> guilt from the defendant's refusal to answer these questions.*

10. *We are amazed at how <u>adept</u> a juggler Carl was.*

11. *Rather than eliminate the department all at once, they decided to <u>phase</u> it out gradually.*

12. *Dogs barking can often signal <u>imminent</u> danger.*

13. *After our vacation, we decided to <u>proceed</u> with the plan.*

14. *I was trying to <u>imply</u> that I should be considered for the new position.*

15. *I always felt <u>reluctant</u> to talk in class.*

16. *Deanne's concentration was not even <u>fazed</u> by the fire alarm.*

17. *The police officer was <u>cited</u> for her efforts in the hostage rescue.*

18. *Even the most trivial news seems to <u>affect</u> the stock price immediately.*

19. *David felt <u>ambivalent</u> about testifying against his partner.*

20. *The <u>morale</u> of the troops was at an all-time low during the Christmas season.*

21. *That scarf really <u>complements</u> your outfit.*

22. *I tried to stay awake for the lecture, but I was so <u>uninterested</u>. . . (Disinterested means impartial.)*

23. *The article mentioned the low voter turnout in order to <u>imply</u> . . .*

24. *Although the police initially had many solid leads, the suspect <u>eluded</u> them for several months.*

25. *It may be years before we understand how pollution from the new power plant might <u>affect</u> the regional environment.*

26. *The new online store's musical offerings run the <u>gamut</u> from arias to zydeco.*

27. *Heather was the <u>principal</u> author of the study . . .*

28. *All of the invited guests <u>except</u> Anthony arrived promptly.*

29. *For nearly the entire semester, I felt so <u>inhibited</u> that I never so much as <u>raised</u> my hand in class.*

30. *Try as they might, the hikers could not find the <u>antidote</u> . . .*

31. *The acid solution was so potent that we had to <u>dilute</u> it with water before we could use it safely.*

32. *The symbols on the cave walls are <u>ambiguous</u>; scientists have been debating their meaning for decades.*

33. *Despite the setbacks with the caterers, the Breedens managed to give a splendidly <u>elegant</u> party. (Eloquent means well-spoken.)*

34. *As someone committed to fairness in education, she could not accept the inequity . . . (Iniquity is sin.)*

Exercise Set 12

1. *When we refer ~~back~~ to ~~past~~ history, we can see that whenever ~~a new~~ an innovation is introduced ~~for the first time~~, people don't easily accept the ~~whole~~ entire concept, at least not right away. ~~If and~~ when something threatens the ways of the past, people don't part easily with their old ways. Although not everyone ~~necessarily~~ needs to maintain the status quo, consistency and predictability make people feel comfortable. Even when technology comes up with a way to do things better, people often continue ~~on~~ with their older, less efficient ways. For instance, it's not uncommon for people to use e-mail while ~~at the same time~~ continuing to correspond via "snail mail." If they would ~~quickly~~ pause for a moment, they would see that*

they can communicate more effectively through the Internet—and save some trees!

2. *The latest political commercials make their points* <u>more strongly</u> *than previous ones.* (Use an adverb, not an adjective.)

3. *My shirt smelled quite* <u>foul</u> *after rugby practice.* (The modifier is an adjective describing the noun *shirt.* The verb *smelled* acts as a linking verb.)

4. *We* <u>rarely</u> *get to go to such elegant restaurants.* (The use of *never* is illogical since going to restaurants occasionally happens.)

5. *Although both of my parents are level-headed, my father is the* <u>more</u> *patient.* (Use *more* when comparing two things.)

6. *The third graders* <u>were hardly</u> *interested in going to the museum after school.* (The phrase *weren't hardly* is a double negative.)

7. *I can sing in front of a crowd* <u>more easily</u> *than I can give a speech.* (Use an adverb, not an adjective.)

8. *In many areas of the country, wind energy can be converted to electricity even* <u>more efficiently</u> *than fossil energy.* (Use an adverb, not an adjective.)

9. *I felt surprisingly* <u>good</u> *after Saturday's ten-mile run.* (This is fine. You don't have to say *I felt well* unless you mean that you are simply not sick.)

10. *The microscopic size of the fracture made it* <u>impossible</u> *to detect, even with special instruments.* (*Impossible* is an absolute adjective.)

11. *These measures* <u>won't</u> *address the state's deficit.* (The phrase *won't barely* is a double negative.)

12. *The teacher* <u>didn't tell</u> *us about the test until the day before.* (The use of *never* is illogical since it eventually happened.)

13. *Students* <u>rarely</u> *bother to examine the veracity of the "facts" they are supposed to memorize in history class.* (*Never usually* is illogical.)

Exercise Set 13

1. *We might have* <u>ridden</u> *the bus...*

2. *Those issues have not yet* <u>arisen</u> *in this discussion.*

3. *In the last two years the Patriots have* <u>beaten</u>...

4. *Peter told me that I should not have* <u>drunk</u> *the water.*

5. *We should have* <u>gone</u> *to the mall.*

6. *I could not have* <u>gotten</u> *such good grades...*

7. *The Donnellys have* <u>run</u> *their corner store...*

8. *Before last night, they had not even* <u>spoken</u> *about...*

9. *I can't believe you put my wool sweater in the dryer and* <u>shrank</u> *it.*

10. *His batting average has really* <u>sunk</u> *ever since his injury.*

11. *I wish she had not* <u>spoken</u> *for so long.*

12. *It seems as if the flowers have* <u>sprung</u> *out of...*

13. *We should have* <u>taken</u> *that shortcut to work.*

14. *Elisha could never have* <u>gone</u> *to the state finals...*

15. *In retrospect, it seems I might have* <u>taken</u> *too much...*

16. *While we played video games, Danny lay on the couch all afternoon.* (The sentence is correct. *Lay* is the past tense of *to lie.*)

17. *Most people find it amazing that, millions of years ago, life* <u>sprang</u> *from a primordial swamp.*

18. *Carl would have* <u>torn</u> *his uniform if he had not stopped his slide at the last second.*

19. *The generals forsook their own troops to surrender and save their own lives.* (The sentence is correct. *Forsook* is the past tense of *to forsake.*)

20. *When the temperature* <u>sank</u> *below zero, the pipes* <u>burst</u> *like water balloons.*

21. *The assets of the company were* <u>frozen</u> *as soon as it declared bankruptcy.*

22. *When the cook* <u>rang</u> *the bell for dinner, the whole camp raced up the hill.*

23. *George needed his friends more than ever, but they had* <u>forsaken</u> *him.*

24. *We* <u>sang</u> *just about every song we knew...*

25. *The senator could have* <u>spoken</u> *a lot longer...*

Exercise Set 14

1. *If our wide receiver* <u>were</u> *a little faster...* (The verb indicates a conditional situation.)

2. *As a matter of fact, Theo* <u>was</u> *only six years old when the Civil War began.* (The sentence inidcates a fact, so the subjunctive mood is inappropriate.)

3. *Denny would be more successful if only he* <u>would promote</u> *himself.* (The verb indicates a situation that is counter to fact.)

4. *The brochure suggested that we* <u>be</u> *at the camp first thing in the morning.* (The verb indicates an indirect command.)

5. *I wish that my horse* <u>were</u> *not so lethargic this morning.* (The verb indicates a wishful situation.)

6. *If the goalie had lifted his glove even slightly, the puck would have gotten through.* (This is proper subjunctive idiom.)

7. *He acted as though the concert hall were filled with screaming fans.* (The verb indicates a situation that is counter to fact.)

8. *I wish that summer camp were two weeks longer.* (The verb indicates a situation that is counter to fact.)

9. *If the class had voted against it, we would not have been given the chance to visit the museum.* (This is proper subjunctive idiom.)

10. *We were very doubtful that Jonna would get the part since she was sick during her audition.* (This verb expresses a doubtful situation.)

11. *If I were in Paris, I'd probably spend most of my time in cafés.* (This verb expresses a conditional situation.)

12. *If I had known that the food was so good here, I would have come sooner.* (This is proper subjunctive idiom.)

13. *The coach demanded that we be in bed by eleven o'clock.* (This verb expresses a suggestion.)

14. *Yvonne spoke as if she were a medieval serf complaining about her master.* (This verb expresses a situation that is counter to fact.)

15. *Gina wished that she had chosen the red dress instead of the pink one.* (This is proper subjunctive idiom.)

16. *The professor spoke to us as if he were a member of the British Parliament.* (This verb expresses a situation that is counter to fact.)

17. *I wanted to see the countryside, but I was sick in bed for the entire vacation.* (This verb expresses a fact, so the subjunctive mood is incorrect.)

18. *Had I found his wallet, I would have returned it to him immediately.* (The sentence is correct.)

19. *If only the doctor had told me to cut back on eating red meat, I would have complied.* (This is proper subjunctive idiom.)

Exercise Set 15

Each sentence below represents one of many possible correct answers.

1. *Director Helen Schaffer, daughter of famous screenwriter George Schaffer, has received widespread critical acclaim for her third movie, a comedy entitled* The Return.

2. *An international team of scientists believes that studying a region of the human brain called the prefrontal cortex, which they have found to govern impulse control, will help them to learn more about criminal behavior.*

3. *Although electric cars may seem environmentally sound, the electricity they use actually comes from power plants that often burn coal or other fossil fuels.*

4. *Regular exercise is good not only for your muscles and heart, but for your brain as well; it helps your brain work more efficiently by keeping it well oxygenated.*

5. *More Americans than ever are obese because, unlike our ancestors who had to work hard to get their food, we can easily go to the store and buy processed, high-calorie food.*

6. *Although we are motivated by our principles, these principles change all the time because our experiences cause our priorities to evolve.*

7. *The team won for two important reasons: the players never gave up, even when they were down three games in the playoffs, and they had a lot of fans rooting for them.*

CHAPTER 14

THREE PRACTICE PSATs WITH DETAILED ANSWER KEYS

PRACTICE PSAT 1

ANSWER SHEET

Last Name: _____   First Name: _____

Date: _____   Testing Location: _____

Administering the Test

- **Remove this answer sheet** from the book and use it to record your answers to this test.
- This test will require **2 hours and 10 minutes** to complete. Take this test in one sitting.
- Use a stopwatch to time yourself on each section. The time limit for each section is written clearly at the beginning of each section. The first four sections are 25 minutes long, and the last section is 30 minutes long.
- Each response must **completely fill the oval. Erase all stray marks completely**, or they may be interpreted as responses.
- **You must stop ALL work on a section when time is called.**
- If you finish a section before the time has elapsed, check your work on that section. **You may NOT move on to the next section until time is called.**
- Do not waste time on questions that seem too difficult for you.
- Use the test book for scratchwork, but you will only receive credit for answers that are marked on the answer sheets.

Scoring the Test

- Your scaled score, which will be determined from a conversion table, is based on your raw score for each section.
- You will receive one point toward your raw score for every correct answer.
- You will receive no points toward your raw score for an omitted question.
- For each wrong answer on a multiple-choice question, your raw score will be reduced by 1/4 point. For each wrong answer on a numerical "grid-in" question (Section 4, questions 29–38), your raw score will receive no deduction.

SECTION 1 — Critical Reading — 25 minutes

1. Ⓐ Ⓑ Ⓒ Ⓓ Ⓔ   9. Ⓐ Ⓑ Ⓒ Ⓓ Ⓔ   17. Ⓐ Ⓑ Ⓒ Ⓓ Ⓔ
2. Ⓐ Ⓑ Ⓒ Ⓓ Ⓔ   10. Ⓐ Ⓑ Ⓒ Ⓓ Ⓔ   18. Ⓐ Ⓑ Ⓒ Ⓓ Ⓔ
3. Ⓐ Ⓑ Ⓒ Ⓓ Ⓔ   11. Ⓐ Ⓑ Ⓒ Ⓓ Ⓔ   19. Ⓐ Ⓑ Ⓒ Ⓓ Ⓔ
4. Ⓐ Ⓑ Ⓒ Ⓓ Ⓔ   12. Ⓐ Ⓑ Ⓒ Ⓓ Ⓔ   20. Ⓐ Ⓑ Ⓒ Ⓓ Ⓔ
5. Ⓐ Ⓑ Ⓒ Ⓓ Ⓔ   13. Ⓐ Ⓑ Ⓒ Ⓓ Ⓔ   21. Ⓐ Ⓑ Ⓒ Ⓓ Ⓔ
6. Ⓐ Ⓑ Ⓒ Ⓓ Ⓔ   14. Ⓐ Ⓑ Ⓒ Ⓓ Ⓔ   22. Ⓐ Ⓑ Ⓒ Ⓓ Ⓔ
7. Ⓐ Ⓑ Ⓒ Ⓓ Ⓔ   15. Ⓐ Ⓑ Ⓒ Ⓓ Ⓔ   23. Ⓐ Ⓑ Ⓒ Ⓓ Ⓔ
8. Ⓐ Ⓑ Ⓒ Ⓓ Ⓔ   16. Ⓐ Ⓑ Ⓒ Ⓓ Ⓔ   24. Ⓐ Ⓑ Ⓒ Ⓓ Ⓔ

Time: 25 minutes   Start: _____   Stop: _____

SECTION 2 — Math — 25 minutes

1. Ⓐ Ⓑ Ⓒ Ⓓ Ⓔ   9. Ⓐ Ⓑ Ⓒ Ⓓ Ⓔ   17. Ⓐ Ⓑ Ⓒ Ⓓ Ⓔ
2. Ⓐ Ⓑ Ⓒ Ⓓ Ⓔ   10. Ⓐ Ⓑ Ⓒ Ⓓ Ⓔ   18. Ⓐ Ⓑ Ⓒ Ⓓ Ⓔ
3. Ⓐ Ⓑ Ⓒ Ⓓ Ⓔ   11. Ⓐ Ⓑ Ⓒ Ⓓ Ⓔ   19. Ⓐ Ⓑ Ⓒ Ⓓ Ⓔ
4. Ⓐ Ⓑ Ⓒ Ⓓ Ⓔ   12. Ⓐ Ⓑ Ⓒ Ⓓ Ⓔ   20. Ⓐ Ⓑ Ⓒ Ⓓ Ⓔ
5. Ⓐ Ⓑ Ⓒ Ⓓ Ⓔ   13. Ⓐ Ⓑ Ⓒ Ⓓ Ⓔ
6. Ⓐ Ⓑ Ⓒ Ⓓ Ⓔ   14. Ⓐ Ⓑ Ⓒ Ⓓ Ⓔ
7. Ⓐ Ⓑ Ⓒ Ⓓ Ⓔ   15. Ⓐ Ⓑ Ⓒ Ⓓ Ⓔ
8. Ⓐ Ⓑ Ⓒ Ⓓ Ⓔ   16. Ⓐ Ⓑ Ⓒ Ⓓ Ⓔ

Time: 25 minutes   Start: _____   Stop: _____

SECTION 3 — Critical Reading — 25 minutes

25. Ⓐ Ⓑ Ⓒ Ⓓ Ⓔ   33. Ⓐ Ⓑ Ⓒ Ⓓ Ⓔ   41. Ⓐ Ⓑ Ⓒ Ⓓ Ⓔ
26. Ⓐ Ⓑ Ⓒ Ⓓ Ⓔ   34. Ⓐ Ⓑ Ⓒ Ⓓ Ⓔ   42. Ⓐ Ⓑ Ⓒ Ⓓ Ⓔ
27. Ⓐ Ⓑ Ⓒ Ⓓ Ⓔ   35. Ⓐ Ⓑ Ⓒ Ⓓ Ⓔ   43. Ⓐ Ⓑ Ⓒ Ⓓ Ⓔ
28. Ⓐ Ⓑ Ⓒ Ⓓ Ⓔ   36. Ⓐ Ⓑ Ⓒ Ⓓ Ⓔ   44. Ⓐ Ⓑ Ⓒ Ⓓ Ⓔ
29. Ⓐ Ⓑ Ⓒ Ⓓ Ⓔ   37. Ⓐ Ⓑ Ⓒ Ⓓ Ⓔ   45. Ⓐ Ⓑ Ⓒ Ⓓ Ⓔ
30. Ⓐ Ⓑ Ⓒ Ⓓ Ⓔ   38. Ⓐ Ⓑ Ⓒ Ⓓ Ⓔ   46. Ⓐ Ⓑ Ⓒ Ⓓ Ⓔ
31. Ⓐ Ⓑ Ⓒ Ⓓ Ⓔ   39. Ⓐ Ⓑ Ⓒ Ⓓ Ⓔ   47. Ⓐ Ⓑ Ⓒ Ⓓ Ⓔ
32. Ⓐ Ⓑ Ⓒ Ⓓ Ⓔ   40. Ⓐ Ⓑ Ⓒ Ⓓ Ⓔ   48. Ⓐ Ⓑ Ⓒ Ⓓ Ⓔ

Time: 25 minutes   Start: _____   Stop: _____

SECTION

4

Math

25 minutes

21. Ⓐ Ⓑ Ⓒ Ⓓ Ⓔ   25. Ⓐ Ⓑ Ⓒ Ⓓ Ⓔ
22. Ⓐ Ⓑ Ⓒ Ⓓ Ⓔ   26. Ⓐ Ⓑ Ⓒ Ⓓ Ⓔ
23. Ⓐ Ⓑ Ⓒ Ⓓ Ⓔ   27. Ⓐ Ⓑ Ⓒ Ⓓ Ⓔ
24. Ⓐ Ⓑ Ⓒ Ⓓ Ⓔ   28. Ⓐ Ⓑ Ⓒ Ⓓ Ⓔ

Time: 25 minutes

Start: _____

Stop: _____

29. 30. 31. 32. 33.

34. 35. 36. 37. 38.

SECTION

5

Writing
Skills

30 minutes

1. Ⓐ Ⓑ Ⓒ Ⓓ Ⓔ   14. Ⓐ Ⓑ Ⓒ Ⓓ Ⓔ   27. Ⓐ Ⓑ Ⓒ Ⓓ Ⓔ
2. Ⓐ Ⓑ Ⓒ Ⓓ Ⓔ   15. Ⓐ Ⓑ Ⓒ Ⓓ Ⓔ   28. Ⓐ Ⓑ Ⓒ Ⓓ Ⓔ
3. Ⓐ Ⓑ Ⓒ Ⓓ Ⓔ   16. Ⓐ Ⓑ Ⓒ Ⓓ Ⓔ   29. Ⓐ Ⓑ Ⓒ Ⓓ Ⓔ
4. Ⓐ Ⓑ Ⓒ Ⓓ Ⓔ   17. Ⓐ Ⓑ Ⓒ Ⓓ Ⓔ   30. Ⓐ Ⓑ Ⓒ Ⓓ Ⓔ
5. Ⓐ Ⓑ Ⓒ Ⓓ Ⓔ   18. Ⓐ Ⓑ Ⓒ Ⓓ Ⓔ   31. Ⓐ Ⓑ Ⓒ Ⓓ Ⓔ
6. Ⓐ Ⓑ Ⓒ Ⓓ Ⓔ   19. Ⓐ Ⓑ Ⓒ Ⓓ Ⓔ   32. Ⓐ Ⓑ Ⓒ Ⓓ Ⓔ
7. Ⓐ Ⓑ Ⓒ Ⓓ Ⓔ   20. Ⓐ Ⓑ Ⓒ Ⓓ Ⓔ   33. Ⓐ Ⓑ Ⓒ Ⓓ Ⓔ
8. Ⓐ Ⓑ Ⓒ Ⓓ Ⓔ   21. Ⓐ Ⓑ Ⓒ Ⓓ Ⓔ   34. Ⓐ Ⓑ Ⓒ Ⓓ Ⓔ
9. Ⓐ Ⓑ Ⓒ Ⓓ Ⓔ   22. Ⓐ Ⓑ Ⓒ Ⓓ Ⓔ   35. Ⓐ Ⓑ Ⓒ Ⓓ Ⓔ
10. Ⓐ Ⓑ Ⓒ Ⓓ Ⓔ   23. Ⓐ Ⓑ Ⓒ Ⓓ Ⓔ   36. Ⓐ Ⓑ Ⓒ Ⓓ Ⓔ
11. Ⓐ Ⓑ Ⓒ Ⓓ Ⓔ   24. Ⓐ Ⓑ Ⓒ Ⓓ Ⓔ   37. Ⓐ Ⓑ Ⓒ Ⓓ Ⓔ
12. Ⓐ Ⓑ Ⓒ Ⓓ Ⓔ   25. Ⓐ Ⓑ Ⓒ Ⓓ Ⓔ   38. Ⓐ Ⓑ Ⓒ Ⓓ Ⓔ
13. Ⓐ Ⓑ Ⓒ Ⓓ Ⓔ   26. Ⓐ Ⓑ Ⓒ Ⓓ Ⓔ   39. Ⓐ Ⓑ Ⓒ Ⓓ Ⓔ

Time: 30 minutes

Start: _____

Stop: _____

Section I

Time—25 minutes
24 Questions (1–24)

Each of the sentences below is missing one or two portions. Read each sentence. Then select the choice that most logically completes the sentence, taking into account the meaning of the sentence as a whole.

Example:

Rather than accepting the theory unquestioningly, Deborah regarded it with ------.

(A) mirth
(B) sadness
(C) responsibility
(D) ignorance
(E) skepticism

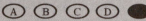

---

1. The seemingly offhand remark was in fact part of a ------ effort by the director to make the actors feel that their jobs were at risk.

   (A) celebrated
   (B) calculated
   (C) required
   (D) reflexive
   (E) conventional

2. In true ------, two different animal species develop a mutually ------ relationship in the same habitat.

   (A) parasitism..helpful
   (B) cooperation..itemized
   (C) mortality..precarious
   (D) antagonism..resourceful
   (E) symbiosis..beneficial

3. Danitra knew at an early age that dancing was her ------; it was what she was meant to do, and she pursued it with single-minded commitment.

   (A) embodiment
   (B) acquisition
   (C) vocation
   (D) corollary
   (E) acceptance

4. Although history has shown that the value of our liberty is timeless, our appreciation of such national ------ seems all too often ------.

   (A) benevolence..solid
   (B) virtues..fleeting
   (C) concepts..permanent
   (D) anachronisms..transitory
   (E) diversions..ephemeral

5. Jill Ker Conway's autobiography explores the ------ of childhood, the unexpected changes that occur in a young life.

   (A) vicissitudes
   (B) veneers
   (C) evanescence
   (D) vulnerabilities
   (E) attachments

6. Many scientists believe that an ancient supernova may have ------ human evolution by bombarding the Earth with cosmic rays that altered the global climate, thereby ------ our ancestors to climb down from the trees and walk upright.

   (A) hastened..pursuing
   (B) resolved..forcing
   (C) terminated..daring
   (D) spurred..impelling
   (E) propelled..defying

GO ON TO THE NEXT PAGE ▶▶▶

7. When the Senator decided to ------ his
    political party and affiliate himself with the
    opposition, he was understandably treated as
    ------ by those former colleagues whom he
    had left behind.

    (A) repudiate..a curator
    (B) abandon..a recluse
    (C) ascertain..a champion
    (D) complement..an expatriate
    (E) forsake..an apostate

8. Despite the many attempts at ------, the
    dictator could not be assuaged, and the
    bellicose nature of his public announcements
    made it clear that conflict could not be ------.

    (A) diplomacy..disclosed
    (B) conciliation..averted
    (C) tact..denigrated
    (D) belligerence..forestalled
    (E) jingoism..circumvented

The passages below are followed by questions
based on their content and the relationship
between the passages. Answer each question
based on what is stated or implied in the
passages.

**Questions 9–12 are based on the
following passages.**

Passage 1

Line   I have given in to the practice, adopted long
        ago by many of my colleagues, known as the
        "beginning-of-the-year review," even though
        it abrades the very fiber of my being. It is,
5   fundamentally, an admission of failure.
        Imagine the manager of a professional baseball
        team spending the first few weeks of spring
        training reviewing the names of the positions or
        in what direction to run the bases. Yet the
10   students coming to us from the best high
        schools in America need to be reminded of the
        most fundamental academic tasks and tools—
        forming hypotheses, adding fractions,
        constructing a clear sentence. I can't say with
15   great certainty what is happening in our high
        schools, but I can say that glittering grades do
        not always indicate glittering minds. There
        seems to be no grounding, no sense of the

fundamental reasoning skills and concepts of
20   academia. I often wonder if our high schools
        shouldn't be spending more time making sure
        their ladders are on secure footing before
        sending so many students scrambling up.

Passage 2

        In every choreographed educational crisis,
25   the "back to basics" line always kicks up its
        heels the highest. The thinking is seemingly
        irrefutable: our children won't succeed without
        a solid foundation in basic skills. They can't do
        calculus before they learn long division. They
30   can't write a good college essay before they
        learn the five-paragraph model. They can't read
        Shakespeare before learning the phonetic code.
        The model is the pyramid: we must build a solid
        foundation if our children are ever to reach
35   the pinnacle of education, where the most
        profound questions of our era are examined.
        But we are losing too many students in building
        the pyramid. It is worth the risk to take them to
        the top of the pyramid, unfinished as it may be,
40   so that they might see the glorious expanse of
        knowledge before them, yet to be reached. If we
        don't take the time to show them that expanse,
        they will likely never learn that their hard labor
        has any real purpose. We are too worried about
45   failure, about not getting the right answers, that
        our questions and our tasks have lost almost all
        of their meaning.

9. Passage 1 is written from the perspective of

    (A) a politician
    (B) a college professor
    (C) a high school teacher
    (D) a high school student
    (E) a parent

10. In Passage 2, the "top of the pyramid"
    (line 39) represents the point at which students

    (A) have mastered all of the basic skills
    (B) have been accepted into college
    (C) have acquired a degree
    (D) can glimpse the most challenging
        academic problems
    (E) can outperform other students on
        standardized tests

GO ON TO THE NEXT PAGE ▶▶▶

11. The two authors differ in their perspectives
     on fundamental academic skills in that the
     author of Passage 1 believes that

     (A) they should not be taught, while the
         author of Passage 2 believes that they form
         the foundation of a good education
     (B) they should be taught in high school, while
         the author of Passage 2 believes that they
         should be taught in college
     (C) they are underemphasized in high school,
         while the author of Passage 2 believes that
         they are overemphasized
     (D) they can be mastered by all students, while
         the author of Passage 2 believes that they
         are beyond the ability of some students
     (E) they are inimical to higher education,
         while the author of Passage 2 believes that
         they should be the focus of a college
         education

12. Which of the following devices is used
     by BOTH authors?

     (A) statistics
     (B) vignette
     (C) hyperbole
     (D) personification
     (E) metaphor

The questions below are to be answered on the
basis of what is stated or implied in the
passage below or the introductory material
that precedes the passage.

**Questions 13–24 are based on the
following passages.**

*The following passages examine the work of F. Scott
Fitzgerald, the American twentieth-century novelist.*

Passage 1

Line   Regarding most of the criticism and much
         of Fitzgerald's work, I am once again struck by
         the urge to respond to Fitzgerald's writing.
         Sometimes—often—that response is only an
5   exclamation of delight. Other times it is a need
         to try to write out a response in one's own
         words. This is no time, at the end of a brief
         introduction, to be starting an essay on
         Fitzgerald. What follows are some jottings

10   occasioned by this encounter with Fitzgerald
         and his critics.
             First, modern criticism (certainly not of
         Fitzgerald alone) is often too refined. The big
         things having been said, young critics tend
15   to make too much of small things. Color
         symbolism, the guest list in *The Great Gatsby*,
         and the "gat" in "Gatsby" are examples of what
         one hopes will not dominate criticism of
         Fitzgerald's work in the future.
20   Second, there is joy in Fitzgerald's work that
         should not be passed over in dwelling upon
         profundities, complexities, and tragic
         implications. Edmund Wilson described it early
         as a "quality exceedingly rare among even the
25   young American writers of the day; he is almost
         the only one among them who has any real
         light-hearted gaiety." Recognizing that quality
         and acknowledging its worth may draw
         attention to the variety to be found in a writer
30   who is commonly charged with having too
         narrow a range. It also adds to the dimensions
         of *The Great Gatsby* and *Tender Is the Night*,
         those novels that do most to maintain
         Fitzgerald's reputation as a serious writer.
35   For it is not only theme and technique that
         distinguish these novels, but the flashes of
         brilliance, comic as well as tragic, that
         illuminate individual scenes.
             Third, Fitzgerald's style, as has been said
40   over and over, is his great strength. Here
         scholarship has done a great service to
         Fitzgerald. One's awareness of his style is
         enhanced by examining the manuscripts
         through which the finished phrases and
45   paragraphs came into existence. One feels
         better about one's own strikeovers, and
         pencillings, and second and third thoughts.
         One learns.
             Fourth, in the presence of so much
50   Fitzgerald scholarship, it is easy to become
         both solemn and heavy about Fitzgerald, man
         and work. Perhaps there should be some
         licensing procedure that would prevent bad
         writers, pretentious and heavy scholars, from
55   dealing with Fitzgerald. Lacking that, a reader
         can be grateful that, despite some notable
         exceptions, students as well as professional
         critics seem attracted to Fitzgerald out of a
         common respect for his prose style and the
60   storyteller's art. Like Fitzgerald's work, much of
         Fitzgerald criticism is distinguished by
         extraordinary felicity of expression.

GO ON TO THE NEXT PAGE ▶▶▶

Finally, Fitzgerald will probably continue to claim the interest of both the general reader
65 and the scholar-critic. The mysteries of his genius, like the mysteries of his style, remain to be pondered. As our own perspectives change, his various works will be seen in different lights. The final test of Fitzgerald, as of all writers,
70 is that others want to read his works and to share the pleasures they receive.

Passage 2

After a brief revival, the novels of Scott Fitzgerald seem destined again for obscurity, labeled this time, by their most recent critics, as
75 darkly pessimistic studies of America's spiritual and ideological failures. *The Great Gatsby*, we are now told, is not simply a chronicle of the Jazz age but rather a dramatization of the betrayal of the naïve American dream in a
80 corrupt society.

From the start, Fitzgerald's personal dreams of romance contained the seeds of their own destruction. In his earliest works, his optimistic sense of the value of experience is
85 overshadowed by a personal intuition of tragedy; his capacity for naïve wonder is chastened by satiric and ironic insights which make surrender to the romantic impulse incomplete. Though able to idealize the
90 sensuous excitement of an exclusive party or a lovely face, Fitzgerald could not ignore the speciosity inherent in the romantic stimuli of his social world—in the unhurried gracious poise that money can buy.
95   At the same time that Fitzgerald perceived the melancholy nature of romantic illusion, his attitude towards the rich crystallized. The thirst for money is a crucial motive in *Gatsby* as in Fitzgerald's other novels, and yet none of his
100 major characters are materialists, for money is never their final goal. The rich are too accustomed to money to covet it. It is simply the badge of their "superiority" and the justification of their consuming snobberies.
105   Inevitably then, Fitzgerald saw his romantic dream threaded by a double irony. Those who possess the necessary means lack the will, motive, or capacity to pursue a dream. Those with the heightened sensitivity to the promises
110 of life have it because they are the disinherited, forever barred from the white palace where "the king's daughter, the golden girl" awaits "safe and proud above the struggles of the poor."

13. The first paragraph of Passage 1 reveals that the author of Passage 1

(A) has recently been introduced to Fitzgerald's novels
(B) has met F. Scott Fitzgerald personally
(C) has been critical of many of Fitzgerald's earlier works
(D) is writing an introduction to a book of literary criticism
(E) is a novelist

14. As it is used in line 13, "refined" most nearly means

(A) processed
(B) formal
(C) concerned with minor details
(D) challenging
(E) pure

15. The author of Passage 1 mentions Edmund Wilson in line 23 as an example of one who

(A) has deeply explored the tragic implications of Fitzgerald's novels
(B) has written novels that were inspired by Fitzgerald's work
(C) has criticized certain themes in Fitzgerald's novels
(D) recognizes a quality in Fitzgerald's works that others may overlook
(E) focuses excessively on irrelevant aspects of Fitzgerald's style

16. In line 30, the phrase "charged with" most nearly means

(A) emboldened by
(B) weakened by
(C) given the responsibility of
(D) electrified by
(E) accused of

GO ON TO THE NEXT PAGE ▸▸▸

17. The sentence "One learns" (line 48) is intended primarily to convey the idea that

(A) Fitzgerald's editors often destroyed his best work
(B) college English classes should study more of Fitzgerald's lesser-known novels
(C) scholars should revisit Fitzgerald's novels many times
(D) most professors of literature enjoy Fitzgerald's prose
(E) literary craft includes a good deal of reworking

18. The purpose of the fifth paragraph (lines 49–62) of Passage 1 is primarily to express the author's concern about

(A) the unrestricted access to Fitzgerald's personal archives
(B) the tone and quality of some criticism about Fitzgerald
(C) insufficient seriousness in criticism about Fitzgerald
(D) the excessive quantity of criticism about Fitzgerald
(E) the difference in quality between the work of students and the work of professional scholars

19. In saying that "Fitzgerald's personal dreams of romance contained the seeds of their own destruction" (lines 81–83), the author of Passage 2 means that

(A) Fitzgerald's works have always lacked popular appeal
(B) Fitzgerald's life was cut tragically short
(C) Fitzgerald's novels contain elements of tragedy
(D) Fitzgerald was never satisfied with the quality of his own work
(E) Fitzgerald's romantic scenes were unrealistic

20. The "white palace" (line 111) represents

(A) the distinctive status of writers
(B) moral superiority
(C) literary perfection
(D) a life of privilege
(E) power acquired by force

21. How would the author of Passage 1 likely respond to the statement made in Passage 2 that "the novels of Scott Fitzgerald seem destined again for obscurity" (lines 72–73)?

(A) He would reluctantly agree because he believes that readers are finding it increasingly difficult to understand Fitzgerald's themes.
(B) He would strongly agree, because he believes that Fitzgerald's works are fatally flawed.
(C) He would reluctantly disagree because he believes that they will continue to be a popular, but not a critical, success.
(D) He would strongly disagree because he believes that Fitzgerald's work will continue to have strong appeal.
(E) He would suggest that the statement is irrelevant because the popularity of Fitzgerald's novels is not important.

22. How does the "joy" (line 20) mentioned in Passage 1 differ from the "wonder" (line 86) mentioned in Passage 2?

(A) The "joy" is regarded as something that makes Fitzgerald's work distinctive, while the "wonder" is regarded as being compromised.
(B) The "joy" is regarded as insincere, while the "wonder" is regarded as too blatant.
(C) The "joy" is regarded as a flaw in Fitzgerald's work, while the "wonder" is regarded as a positive feature of his work.
(D) The "joy" is regarded as something unique in American literature, while the "wonder" is regarded as being common to most novels of the twentieth century.
(E) The "joy" is regarded as a feature of Fitzgerald's life, while the "wonder" is regarded as a feature of Fitzgerald's work, but not his life.

GO ON TO THE NEXT PAGE ▶▶▶

23. Which statement would most likely be supported by the authors of both passages?

(A) Some critics of Fitzgerald's work have focused on the tragic implications of his novels.

(B) Fitzgerald's works are even more popular today than they were in his time.

(C) The characters in *The Great Gatsby* are materialists.

(D) Fitzgerald's works are far more optimistic than many believe.

(E) Scholarship on Fitzgerald's works should focus more on their style than on their themes.

24. How would the author of Passage 1 likely respond to the analysis of Fitzgerald's work presented in lines 81–94?

(A) He would disagree with its claim that Fitzgerald had a "capacity for naïve wonder."

(B) He would agree with its focus on irony.

(C) He would regard it as an unnecessary focus on the tragic aspects of Fitzgerald's works.

(D) He would regard it as insufficiently critical of Fitzgerald's choice of theme.

(E) He would suggest that it ignores important details about Fitzgerald's personal life that would explain the themes in his works.

STOP

You may check your work, on this section only, until time is called.

Section 2

Time—25 minutes

20 Questions

Directions for Multiple-Choice Questions

In this section, solve each problem, using any available space on the page for scratchwork. Then decide which is the best of the choices given and fill in the corresponding oval on the answer sheet.

- You may use a calculator on any problem. All numbers used are real numbers.
- Figures are drawn as accurately as possible EXCEPT when it is stated that the figure is not drawn to scale.
- All figures lie in a plane unless otherwise indicated.

Reference Information

$A = \pi r^2$
$C = 2\pi r$
$A = \ell w$
$A = \frac{1}{2}bh$
$V = \ell wh$
$V = \pi r^2 h$
$c^2 = a^2 + b^2$
Special Right Triangles

The arc of a circle measures 360°.
Every straight angle measures 180°.
The sum of the measures of the angles in a triangle is 180°.

---

1. The area of a rectangle with a height of 4 cm and a base of 6 cm is how many times greater than the area of a triangle with a height of 4 cm and a base of 4 cm?

(A) 1
(B) 1.5
(C) 2
(D) 2.5
(E) 3

2. If $x = 2y + 2$, how much greater is $6x$ than $12y$?

(A) 2
(B) 6
(C) 8
(D) 12
(E) 24

3. How many integers between 10 and 40 are divisible by both 2 and 6?

(A) Two
(B) Three
(C) Four
(D) Five
(E) Six

4. If it is now 4:30 p.m., what time will it be exactly 100 hours from now?

(A) 4:30 p.m.
(B) 8:30 p.m.
(C) 12:30 a.m.
(D) 2:30 a.m.
(E) 4:30 a.m.

5. Carrie, Denise, and Emily sold a total of 48 candy bars. If Emily sold four times as many candy bars as Denise did, and Denise sold three times as many candy bars as Carrie did, how many candy bars did Denise sell?

(A) 3
(B) 6
(C) 9
(D) 12
(E) 15

GO ON TO THE NEXT PAGE ▶▶▶

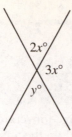

Note: Figure not drawn to scale.

6. In the figure above, what is the value of y?

    (A) 72
    (B) 60
    (C) 48
    (D) 36
    (E) 40

7. Let the function $f(x)$ be defined by the equation $f(x) = 2x - x^2$. Which of the following has a positive value?

    (A) $f(0.5)$
    (B) $f(0)$
    (C) $f(-0.5)$
    (D) $f(-1.5)$
    (E) $f(-2.5)$

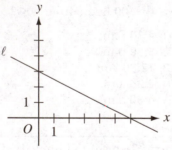

8. What is the equation of line ℓ in the figure above?

    (A) $y = -2x + 3$

    (B) $y = -\frac{1}{2}x + 3$

    (C) $y = -\frac{1}{2}x + 6$

    (D) $y = \frac{1}{2}x + 3$

    (E) $y = 2x + 6$

9. In a certain homeroom, the number of girls is 6 less than twice the number of boys. If the class contains b boys, which of the following would express the total number of students present in the class if 2 girls were absent?

    (A) $2b - 8$
    (B) $2b - 4$
    (C) $3b - 8$
    (D) $3b - 6$
    (E) $3b - 4$

10. If $(x + 5)^2 = 0$, what is the value of $(x - 1)(x + 1)$?

    (A) -26
    (B) -24
    (C) 0
    (D) 24
    (E) 26

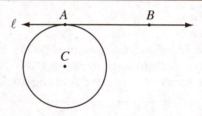

Note: Figure not drawn to scale.

11. In the figure above, the circle with center at C has a circumference of 6π. If line ℓ is tangent to the circle and $AB = 4$, what is the distance from B to C?

    (A) 4.8
    (B) 5.0
    (C) 6.2
    (D) 7.0
    (E) 7.2

12. A set consists of five consecutive integers. The sum of these integers is -10. What is the greatest possible product that can be obtained by multiplying three different integers from this set?

    (A) -24
    (B) -6
    (C) 0
    (D) 6
    (E) 24

GO ON TO THE NEXT PAGE ▶▶▶

13. The first day of a 30-day month is a Monday. Which of the following is closest to the probability that a day picked at random from this month will be a Wednesday?

(A) 0.03
(B) 0.07
(C) 0.10
(D) 0.13
(E) 0.17

14. If $|x| > 2$, which of the following statements must be true?

I. $x > 0$
II. $x^2 > 2$
III. $x^3 > 2$

(A) II only
(B) I and II only
(C) I and III only
(D) II and III only
(E) I, II, and III

15. A jar contains only red, white, and blue marbles. If the number of red marbles is $\frac{5}{6}$ the number of white marbles, and the number of red marbles is $\frac{6}{7}$ the number of blue marbles, what is the least possible number of marbles in the jar?

(A) 18
(B) 72
(C) 101
(D) 113
(E) 123

$$8, a, b, 27$$

16. In the sequence above, each term, except the first, is equal to the previous term times a constant. What is the value of $\frac{b}{a}$?

(A) 1.125
(B) 1.50
(C) 3.375
(D) 4.75
(E) 6.33

17. The graph of which of the following points is below the graph of the line $y = \frac{2}{3}x + 1$?

(A) $(-1, 1)$
(B) $(1, 1)$
(C) $(1, 2)$
(D) $(3, 3)$
(E) $(4, 4)$

18. If $3^{n-1} = 27^{-1}$, then $n =$

(A) -3
(B) -2
(C) -1
(D) 1
(E) 2

19. If $x + \frac{1}{x} = y$, where $x \neq 0$, which of the following expresses $x^2 + \frac{1}{x^2}$ in terms of y?

(A) $y^2 + 2$
(B) $y^2 + 1$
(C) y^2
(D) $y^2 - 1$
(E) $y^2 - 2$

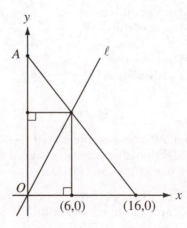

Note: Figure not drawn to scale.

20. If line ℓ in the figure above has a slope of 2, what are the coordinates of point A?

(A) $(0, 7.2)$
(B) $(0, 13.2)$
(C) $(0, 14.4)$
(D) $(0, 18.4)$
(E) $(0, 19.2)$

STOP

You may check your work, on this section only, until time is called.

Section 3

Time—25 minutes
24 Questions (25–48)

Each of the sentences below is missing one or two portions. Read each sentence. Then select the choice that most logically completes the sentence, taking into account the meaning of the sentence as a whole.

Example:

Rather than accepting the theory unquestioningly, Deborah regarded it with ------.

(A) mirth
(B) sadness
(C) responsibility
(D) ignorance
(E) skepticism

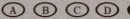

---

25. Unlike most farmers, who regarded rain as a great benefit, Harold often regarded it as ------.

(A) an abundance
(B) a hardship
(C) a scheme
(D) a response
(E) a distortion

26. Pablo Picasso is considered ------ of artistic perfectionism because he would destroy any of his works that he considered ------.

(A) an enemy . . poor
(B) an example . . beautiful
(C) a paragon . . mediocre
(D) a proponent . . aesthetic
(E) an advocate . . monetary

27. Joseph often picked fights with anyone who challenged his ideas, until his friends made it clear that such ------ was unacceptable.

(A) belligerence
(B) diligence
(C) fortitude
(D) restraint
(E) eloquence

28. The store employees tried to ------ the angry shoppers with offers of discounted merchandise and free gift wrapping.

(A) exculpate
(B) impede
(C) mollify
(D) pilfer
(E) abridge

29. Some European governments are concerned that severe immigration restrictions, while rendering nations less ------ to foreign terrorists, would also ------ the influx of creative ideas from abroad.

(A) pervious . . stem
(B) impregnable . . halt
(C) durable . . promote
(D) penetrable . . hasten
(E) potent . . restrict

GO ON TO THE NEXT PAGE ▶▶▶

Each passage below is followed by one or two questions based on its content. Answer each question based on what is stated or implied in the passage that precedes it.

Questions 30–31 are based on the following passage.

Line   Historical evidence takes many forms, including oral traditions and archaeology as well as written texts. Study of the very distant past necessarily relies primarily on oral
5   traditions and archaeology; these two kinds of evidence offer different perspectives on the past and answer different historical questions. Oral tradition is the means by which knowledge— both fact and myth—was passed on until it was
10   written down. Archaeology, in contrast, is the scientific study of the material remains of past human life and activities: fossil relics, artifacts, and monuments. Archaeology supplies physical evidence of material culture, while oral sources
15   provide insight into the nonmaterial world of ideas, values and beliefs. Archaeological investigation may present evidence from millions of years before the present or from the most recent historical past. Oral traditions,
20   some of which are ultimately written down, are more ephemeral, extending across a single lifetime or as far back as the past 10,000 years or so of remembered human experience.

30.   The primary purpose of this passage is to

(A) promote the study of archaeology
(B) describe different oral traditions
(C) discuss a few important historical discoveries
(D) compare two means of gathering information
(E) suggest an improvement to the study of archaeology

31.   The passage indicates that the "nonmaterial world of ideas, values and beliefs" (lines 15–16) is

(A) a subject that only archaeologists can study
(B) not sufficiently emphasized in historical texts
(C) an unreliable source of historical evidence
(D) evidence of material culture
(E) the substance of oral tradition

Questions 32–33 are based on the following passage.

Line   After having—with agony and despair— lived through the irrational tidal waves of the last big war, the world of planners settled down to a rose-colored rational optimism: "To give
5   education, food and health care would suffice to bring peace and stability to this world; satisfying the 'basic needs' for information and acceptable material living conditions would guarantee mutual understanding and
10   democratic tolerance within and between nations." This belief has been badly shaken by now; we are beginning to see that man is not rational enough to make the expected use of the improvements achieved in the last 30 years,
15   that unrest, prejudice, ideological distortion, and violence do not come from the poor (who might have most reason for such reactions), but to a considerable extent from the well-cared-for and well-educated classes in many nations—by
20   no means always the most underdeveloped ones—of the world. We discover that reality does not conform to our rational prescriptions, and we are forced to ponder whether our present level of rationality is at all adequate for
25   dealing with the problems of our world.

32.   This passage most directly criticizes

(A) poverty
(B) war
(C) dishonesty
(D) irrationality
(E) technology

33.   The parenthetical comment in lines 16–17 indicates that the poor

(A) are ignored by the more affluent classes
(B) should be granted more political power
(C) are more justified than the wealthy in acting rebelliously
(D) should be the focus of postwar planning
(E) have talents that are underappreciated in modern societies

First paragraph: *In the Balance: Themes in Global History*, Candice L. Goucher, Charles A. Le Guin, Linda A. Walton, ©1998 McGraw-Hill, p xxxi
Second paragraph: *Culture and Industrialization: An Asian Dilemma*, Rolf E. Vente, Peter S.J. Chen, ©1980 McGraw-Hill, p 52

GO ON TO THE NEXT PAGE ▸▸▸

Questions 34–40 are based on the following passage.

The following is an excerpt from a story written by a twentieth-century Yugoslav writer.

Line   I like to get up early and go down to sit on my bench by the bank of the river just at the crack of dawn, before even the sparrows are awake and before the traffic has begun to make
5   its daily assault on my nerves. The men with hoses have just set out to clean the pavements, everything is quiet and happy, just as it must have looked a million years ago. The river gurgles along, clean and gay, rejoicing at its
10   brief moment of rest before the beginning of another exhausting day. I'm no hermit or misanthrope. Just every now and again I get fed up with everything, and I mean *everything*, and I feel the need to be alone, completely alone. But
15   not for long, for in fact without that "everything," I can't get along either. People and things simply get me down; maybe because both are human products, and there's something of that exhausted human core that
20   remains in them too. And so I start to want to change. The fashionable word for it is recreation. We used to have our own word for it. Maybe it doesn't convey everything that the foreign one does, but in any case none of that is
25   so very important as long as a man does have a rest and get his strength back regularly. That's the thing that we haven't managed to pull out of our dusty old dictionaries. Anyway, I go off down to the river to get my strength back. And
30   that's really what happens; I come to life again. I may have come to our appointment with a heavy, care-worn head, or I may have been thinking all the way about what I might do to avoid this or that; still when I arrive, my body
35   seems to become light and my mind keen; and the river's quiet friendly voice restores the joy and hope that had fled before trivial everyday anxieties and become hidden away in the darkest gloom. I've seldom met anyone who has
40   answered my question with anything other than that threadbare "very well," and a "very well" so bloodless and feeble that you feel wretched yourself and don't want to ask again. That plague of very well has spread so far, that
45   whenever I feel there's so much of it mounting up inside me that it's starting to choke me, I go off to have a chat with the river. Only then am I capable of looking inside myself, bathed, refreshed, cleansed (not of sin, I didn't want to
50   imply that). And I feel then just how much I've

forgotten myself, lost myself somewhere along the way, mislaid an illusion or two, and altogether subordinated myself to external obsessions and barren desires.
55   I try to prove to myself, starting always right at the beginning, that that's life as well, that everyday toil and moil, that perpetual bustle and panicky attention to the implacable dictates of the hands of a clock, that "hello,
60   how's it going, be seeing you, in a hurry" tossed off in passing … somehow I manage to put together the *pro et contra*, get back my balance, and make use of that skill a man has for always finding a way of compromising with himself.
65   But it's really only putting off the main issue. Putting off and putting off, a constant flight from open conflict, cowardice.
    That much-praised business of working has become an end in itself, work for work's sake, a
70   sort of undefined elemental need to shake out some "surplus life," to exploit one's own self. It's lost its original meaning long since its primeval, ennobling, creative function; it shouldn't really be called *work* any longer, we ought to find
75   another word for it.
    Fortunately, this mood passes. The wood right over on the other side that comes down to the water's edge doesn't let me sink too far down this particular slough. Like green
80   lightning, it flashes before me and disperses these black thoughts like so much dust.
    When the city starts waking up behind me, I know that the alloted time of my appointment with the river has expired. It ceases to be mine
85   and only mine, and becomes an ordinary, broad, flat river; tugs harnessed in steel cables crawl and struggle upstream towards some destination and fishing boats float aimlessly about; if there is a wind, a yacht or two can be
90   seen. Pensioners come crawling out to their favorite bench, children set up a hubbub in a nearby school-yard, waiters in the restaurant built right over the water begin to discreetly clink crockery and cutlery. The day begins.
95   I go off without looking back. The market I pass through is brimming with life, peasants and housewives on all sides. Slowly I make my way home. Invariably I meet some acquaintance on the way. From the distance, I
100   can see him smiling. If he has the time, he'll stop to shake hands, but usually we don't shake hands, he just flicks "Hello, how are you?" at me as he passes, and smiles, and I smile and say

GO ON TO THE NEXT PAGE ▶▶▶

105 "Very well, thanks and what about you?" and he says something in reply, and I suddenly get the desire to run after him and catch him up and look at him closely, really eyeball to eyeball, to see if he's still smiling as cheerfully as he was when he was that far away, and I stand still for a 110 moment in indecision and look around. He's long way off, too far for it to be worthwhile chasing after him, you can never catch up with anyone anyway.

So I just keep going in the same direction, 115 smiling to myself. Today I've been down to the river.

34. The first paragraph indicates that, to the narrator, the river is primarily a source of

(A) food
(B) reminiscence
(C) information
(D) anxiety
(E) rejuvenation

35. The sentence in lines 14–16 ("But not for ... I can't get along either) indicates that the narrator

(A) has been receiving professional therapy
(B) is not well understood by his peers
(C) is often frustrated by his inability to get away from people
(D) needs those aspects of his life that occasionally oppress him
(E) has been coming to the river for many years

36. Which of the following is the closest to "the thing that we haven't managed to pull out of our dusty old dictionaries" (lines 27–28)?

(A) emotion
(B) weakness
(C) restoration
(D) verbalization
(E) assault

37. In line 66, the word "flight" most nearly means

(A) obligation
(B) fleeing
(C) jumping
(D) floor
(E) swarm

38. In the third paragraph (lines 68–75) the narrator suggests that long ago, unlike now, work was

(A) more challenging
(B) not necessary for survival
(C) a social experience
(D) a creative endeavor
(E) performed in nature

39. The "pensioners" (line 90) are mentioned as examples of people who

(A) do not appreciate the beauty of the river
(B) speak in a perfunctory manner
(C) are obsessed with work
(D) have a balanced perspective on life
(E) have disrupted the narrator's solitude

40. The conflict in this passage is primarily between

(A) solitude and sociability
(B) the past and the future
(C) life and death
(D) desire and virtue
(E) wealth and poverty

Questions 41–48 are based on the following passage.

The following is an excerpt from an article about Immanuel Kant, an eighteenth-century British philosopher.

According to Kant, his reading of David Hume awakened him from his dogmatic
Line slumber and set him on the road to becoming the "critical philosopher," whose position can
5   be seen as a synthesis of the Leibniz-Wolffian rationalism and the Humean skepticism. Kant termed his basic insight into the nature of knowledge "the Copernican revolution in philosophy."
10   Instead of assuming that our ideas, to be true, must conform to an external reality independent of our knowing, Kant proposed that objective reality is known only insofar as it conforms to the essential structure of the
15   knowing mind. He maintained that objects of experience—phenomena—may be known, but that things lying beyond the realm of possible experience—noumena, or things-in-themselves—are unknowable, although their
20   existence is a necessary presupposition. Phenomena that can be perceived in the pure forms of sensibility, space, and time must, if they are to be understood, possess the characteristics that constitute our categories of
25   understanding. Those categories, which include causality and substance, are the source of the structure of phenomenal experience.
     The scientist, therefore, may be sure only that the natural events observed are knowable
30   in terms of the categories. Our field of knowledge, thus emancipated from Humean skepticism, is nevertheless limited to the world of phenomena. All theoretical attempts to know things-in-themselves are bound to fail. This
35   inevitable failure is the theme of the portion of the *Critique of Pure Reason* entitled the "Transcendental Dialectic." Here Kant shows that the three great problems of metaphysics—God, freedom, and immortality—are insoluble
40   by speculative thought. Their existence can be neither affirmed nor denied on theoretical grounds, nor can they be scientifically demonstrated, but Kant shows the necessity of a belief in their existence in his moral
45   philosophy.
     Kant's ethics centers in his categorical imperative (or moral law)—"Act as if the maxim from which you act were to become through your will a universal law." This law has

50   its source in the autonomy of a rational being, and it is the formula for an absolutely good will. However, since we are all members of two worlds, the sensible and the intelligible, we do not act infallibly in accordance with this law
55   but, on the contrary, almost always act according to inclination. Thus what is objectively necessary, i.e., to will in conformity to the law, is subjectively contingent; and for this reason the moral law confronts us as an
60   "ought."
     In the *Critique of Practical Reason* Kant went on to state that morality requires the belief in the existence of God, freedom, and immortality, because without their existence
65   there can be no morality. In the *Critique of Judgment* Kant applied his critical method to aesthetic and teleological judgments. The chief purpose of this work was to find a bridge between the sensible and the intelligible worlds,
70   which are sharply distinguished in his theoretical and practical philosophy. This bridge is found in the concepts of beauty and purposiveness that suggest at least the possibility of an ultimate union of the two
75   realms.

41. The passage suggests that Kant found David Hume's philosophy to be

(A) logically unfounded
(B) inspirational
(C) open-minded
(D) morally repugnant
(E) charmingly naïve

42. The author uses the term "dogmatic slumber" (line 2) to suggest that

(A) Hume wrote very dull prose.
(B) Kant was a controversial political figure.
(C) Kant was more intellectually rigid before reading Hume.
(D) Kant found Hume's writing to be humorous.
(E) Hume wrote many more books than Kant did.

43. According to the passage, the major theme of the "Transcendental Dialectic" is that

(A) one cannot know things-in-themselves
(B) ethical behavior is unique to humans
(C) the existence of God can be proved
(D) people should be optimistic
(E) philosophers must take a more scientific approach

44. According to the passage, Kant's *Critique of Pure Reason* suggests that free will is

(A) an illusion
(B) gained only through struggle
(C) a requirement of ethical behavior
(D) knowable as a thing-in-itself
(E) an attribute of all living things

45. One who behaves strictly according to Kant's "categorical imperative" (lines 46–47) necessarily believes that any valid moral law should

(A) apply to all human beings
(B) be determined by religious dictate
(C) be submitted to scientific testing
(D) derive from a democratic process
(E) change according to the situation

46. The author implies that we "do not infallibly act in accordance with this law" (lines 53–54) because we

(A) are innately selfish
(B) cannot escape the subjectivity of human experience
(C) are concerned more with beauty than morality
(D) do not understand the history of the law
(E) do not have completely free will

47. The "bridge" in line 68 is a bridge between

(A) skeptical philosophy and optimism
(B) ethics and aesthetics
(C) the past and the future
(D) the philosopher and the common person
(E) things that can be perceived and things that can be understood

48. The primary purpose of the final paragraph is to

(A) address an objection to Kant's philosophy
(B) illustrate Kant's impact on later philosophers
(C) explain the origin of Kant's beliefs
(D) describe further works of Kant
(E) qualify a claim made in the previous paragraph

"Kant, Immanuel," *Columbia Encyclopedia, Sixth Edition*, New York: Columbia University Press, ©2001-2004

You may check your work, on this section only, until time is called.

Section 4

Time—25 minutes
18 Questions (21–38)

Directions for Multiple-Choice Questions

In this section, solve each problem, using any available space on the page for scratchwork. Then decide which is the best of the choices given and fill in the corresponding oval on the answer sheet.

- You may use a calculator on any problem. All numbers used are real numbers.
- Figures are drawn as accurately as possible EXCEPT when it is stated that the figure is not drawn to scale.
- All figures lie in a plane unless otherwise indicated.

Reference Information

$A = \pi r^2$
$C = 2\pi r$

$A = \ell w$

$A = \frac{1}{2}bh$

$V = \ell wh$

$V = \pi r^2 h$

$c^2 = a^2 + b^2$

Special Right Triangles

The arc of a circle measures 360°.
Every straight angle measures 180°.
The sum of the measures of the angles in a triangle is 180°.

---

21. If a square has a perimeter of 20 centimeters, what is one-half its area, in square centimeters?

(A) 10
(B) 12.5
(C) 20
(D) 25
(E) 50

---

22. Which of the following numbers is equal to one-third of its square?

(A) $\frac{1}{9}$

(B) $\frac{1}{3}$

(C) 3

(D) 6

(E) 9

---

23. Checkers are stacked into four piles such that each pile has k more checkers than the previous pile. If the first pile contains 3 checkers, and there are 30 checkers in total in the four piles, what is the value of k?

(A) 2
(B) 3
(C) 4
(D) 5
(E) 6

---

24. What number is equal to $\frac{3}{5}$ of itself plus 240?

(A) 144
(B) 280
(C) 360
(D) 400
(E) 600

GO ON TO THE NEXT PAGE ▶▶▶

Total Sales of Different Book Genres
(in thousands)

25. The pie graph above shows the book sales for a publishing company in a single year. If x represents the measure, in degrees, of the central angle of the sector representing the sales of nonfiction books, what is the value of x?

(A) 120
(B) 125
(C) 135
(D) 145
(E) 150

26. Set S consists of 10 consecutive even integers that have an average (arithmetic mean) of 23. Which of the following must be true?

   I. The median of set S is 23.
   II. No two integers in set S have a difference greater than 10.
   III. There are no multiples of 5 in set S.

(A) I only
(B) II only
(C) I and II only
(D) I and III only
(E) I, II, and III

27. If $2^n = \dfrac{2}{2^k}$, what is the value of $n + k$?

(A) -2
(B) -1
(C) 0
(D) 1
(E) 2

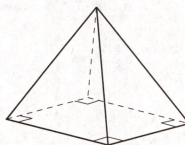

28. The pyramid in the figure above has a square base and four congruent triangular faces. If the area of the base is 144 square inches and the height of the pyramid is 8 inches, what is the area of one of the triangular faces, in square inches?

(A) 42
(B) 48
(C) 60
(D) 96
(E) 120

Directions for Student-Produced Response Questions

Each of the questions in this section requires you to solve the problem and enter your answer in a grid, as shown below.

- If your answer is 2/3 or .666..., you must enter **the most accurate value the grid can accommodate**, but you may do this in one of four ways:

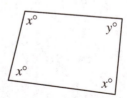

- In the example above, gridding a response of 0.67 or 0.66 is **incorrect** because it is less accurate than those above.
- The scoring machine cannot read what is written in the top row of boxes. You **MUST** fill in the numerical grid accurately to get credit for answering any question correctly. You should write your answer in the top row of boxes only to aid your gridding.
- Do **not** grid in a mixed fraction like $3\frac{1}{2}$ as $\boxed{3}\,\boxed{1}\,\boxed{/}\,\boxed{2}$ because it will be interpreted as $\frac{31}{2}$. Instead, convert it to an improper fraction like $7/2$ or a decimal like 3.5 before gridding.
- None of the answers will be negative, because there is no negative sign in the grid.
- Some of the questions may have more than one correct answer. You must grid only one of the correct answers.
- You may use a calculator on any of these problems.
- All numbers in these problems are real numbers.
- Figures are drawn as accurately as possible EXCEPT when it is stated that the figure is not drawn to scale.
- All figures lie in a plane unless otherwise indicated.

---

29. What is the result when $\frac{1}{4}$ of 80 is divided by $\frac{1}{3}$ of 90?

---

30. For all real numbers x and y, let $x \,ø\, y$ be defined by the equation $x \,ø\, y = (x+y)(x-y)$. What is the value of $5 \,ø\, 3$?

Note: Figure not drawn to scale.

31. In the figure above, if $x = 89$, what is the value of y?

32. If the maximum value in the range of the function $y = f(x)$ is 6, what is the maximum value in the range of the function $y = 3f(x - 1)$?

$$m = 4A3$$
$$n = 7B9$$

33. Suppose m and n are 3-digit integers, as shown, where A and B represent digits. If m is divisible by 3 and n is divisible by 9, what is the <u>greatest</u> possible value of $m + n$?

34. If $2^{m+1} = 8^4$, what is the value of m?

$$m, n, 9, 5$$

35. If the product of the four numbers above is 0 and the median of these four numbers is 3.5, what is the average (arithmetic mean) of these four numbers?

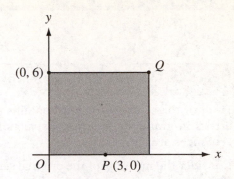

Note: Figure not drawn to scale.

36. In the figure above, if the shaded rectangle has an area of 90 square units, what is the slope of line PQ (not shown)?

37. A water pump, working at a constant rate, fills $\frac{2}{7}$ of a tank in $1\frac{1}{3}$ hours. What fraction of the tank will be filled, at this rate, after 3 hours?

38. A box contains only red, blue, and yellow crayons. The ratio of red crayons to blue crayons is 2:3, and the ratio of blue crayons to yellow crayons is 2:1. If there is a whole number of each color of crayon in the box, what is the probability that a crayon chosen randomly from the box is blue?

You may check your work, on this section only, until time is called.

Section 5

Time—30 minutes
39 Questions (1–39)

Directions for "Improving Sentences" Questions

Each of the sentences below contains one underlined portion. The portion may contain one or more errors in grammar, usage, construction, precision, diction (choice of words), or idiom. Some of the sentences are correct.

Consider the meaning of the original sentence, and choose the answer that best expresses that meaning. If the original sentence is best, choose (A), because it repeats the original phrasing. Choose the phrasing that creates the clearest, most precise, and most effective sentence.

EXAMPLE:

The children <u>couldn't hardly believe their eyes</u>.

(A) couldn't hardly believe their eyes
(B) would not hardly believe their eyes
(C) could hardly believe their eyes
(D) couldn't nearly believe their eyes
(E) could hardly believe his or her eyes

---

1. When used intelligently, <u>you can use mnemonics to help you to memorize cumbersome facts</u>.

   (A) you can use mnemonics to help you to memorize cumbersome facts
   (B) cumbersome facts can be memorized with the use of mnemonics
   (C) mnemonics can help you to memorize cumbersome facts
   (D) you can memorize cumbersome facts more easily with mnemonics
   (E) cumbersome facts are more easily memorized by using mnemonics

2. The annual conference, traditionally used as a forum for presenting new research, <u>instead this year dedicated to</u> resolving theoretical disputes.

   (A) instead this year dedicated to
   (B) was instead this year dedicated to
   (C) being dedicated this year instead to
   (D) was instead dedicated for this year
   (E) instead was dedicated toward this year

3. Jenna went to have her arm examined by the doctor, <u>which was the time when she was told by him</u> that she would not be able to play soccer for at least six weeks.

   (A) which was the time when she was told by him
   (B) which was when she was told by him
   (C) that then told her
   (D) at which time she was told
   (E) who told her

4. The effects of a flu <u>epidemic, possibly being exacerbated by social conditions because of the fact that</u> the virus spreads quickly when people live in close quarters.

   (A) epidemic, possibly being exacerbated by social conditions because of the fact that
   (B) epidemic are possibly exacerbated by social conditions due to the fact of
   (C) epidemic can be exacerbated by social conditions, because
   (D) epidemic, possibly being exacerbated by social conditions because
   (E) epidemic can be exacerbated by social conditions due the fact of

GO ON TO THE NEXT PAGE ▶▶▶

5. One aspect of the play that receives universal acclaim is <u>it analyzes a meaningful social issue with insight while at the same time humor</u>.

    (A) it analyzes a meaningful social issue with insight while at the same time humor
    (B) it uses humor and insight to analyze a meaningful social issue
    (C) it providing a humorous and insightful analysis of a meaningful social issue
    (D) its insightful yet humorous analysis of a meaningful social issue
    (E) its analysis of a meaningful social issue, which is both insightful and humorous

6. Carl Sagan's engaging presentation of scientific concepts inspired many <u>people who had never before been interested in science</u>.

    (A) people who had never before been interested in science
    (B) people and they had never been interested in science before
    (C) people; previously they had not been interested in science
    (D) people, never having been interested in science before
    (E) people of whom they had not previously been interested in science

7. <u>Campaigning for over ten consecutive months</u>, the Senator was glad to finally be home with her family.

    (A) Campaigning for over ten consecutive months
    (B) While campaigning for over ten consecutive months
    (C) Over ten consecutive months in which she was campaigning
    (D) Being over ten consecutive months of her campaigning
    (E) Having campaigned for over ten consecutive months

8. The film is not so much a suspense thriller as <u>being a realistic depiction of</u> modern suburbia.

    (A) being a realistic depiction of
    (B) it is like a realistic depiction of
    (C) a realistic depiction of
    (D) depicting realistically
    (E) realistic in its depiction of

9. The voyage was not as harrowing as the captain later made it <u>seem; in fact, the trade winds were even stronger than they were predicted to be</u>.

    (A) seem; in fact, the trade winds were even stronger than they were predicted to be
    (B) seem; nevertheless the trade winds were in fact stronger than predicted
    (C) seem so the trade winds were even stronger than the prediction of them
    (D) seem, the trade winds were even stronger than they were predicted to be
    (E) seem; the trade winds being even stronger than they were predicted to be

10. Although Jermaine had never played handball before, he moved around the court as <u>if playing</u> all his life.

    (A) if playing
    (B) having played
    (C) if from playing
    (D) if he would have been playing
    (E) if he had been playing

11. Many factors influence the price of crude oil, including advancements in technology, patterns in the weather, and <u>how the global political climate changes</u>.

    (A) how the global political climate changes
    (B) the changing nature of how the political climate is
    (C) changes in the global political climate
    (D) how the political climate is changing globally
    (E) what the changes are in the global political climate

GO ON TO THE NEXT PAGE ▸▸▸

12. Four of the five symphonies performed in the music <u>festival showcased instruments from the colonial era, particularly that of the *Mississippi Pastoral*</u>.

   (A) festival showcased instruments from the colonial era, particularly that of the *Mississippi Pastoral*

   (B) festival, particularly the *Mississippi Pastoral*, showcased instruments from the colonial era

   (C) festival showcased instruments from the colonial era, which included especially the *Mississippi Pastoral*

   (D) festival, particularly the *Mississippi Pastoral*, showcasing instruments from the colonial era

   (E) festival, particularly the *Mississippi Pastoral*, as a showcase of instruments from the colonial era

13. The pasta now known as spaghetti originated in China <u>and many though think it came from</u> Italy.

   (A) and many though think it came from

   (B) and not, as many people think, in

   (C) but not, as many people think, from

   (D) not where people think it came from

   (E) but many people think it is

14. The course requires that students work a great deal in the laboratory and <u>which includes weekly seminars in which they discuss their findings</u>.

   (A) which includes weekly seminars in which they discuss their findings

   (B) discussions of their findings in weekly seminars as well

   (C) discuss their findings in weekly seminars

   (D) discussing their findings in weekly seminars

   (E) to discuss their findings in weekly seminars

15. Having a stronger will than most preschoolers, <u>Brice's stubbornness often caused her to alienate her classmates</u>.

   (A) Brice's stubbornness often caused her to alienate her classmates

   (B) Brice's classmates were often alienated by her being stubborn

   (C) Brice being stubborn often alienated her classmates

   (D) Brice often alienated her classmates by being stubborn

   (E) and so Brice alienated her classmates because of her stubbornness

16. The entire legal team had to spend nearly two days revising the contracts <u>to conform with the new changes in</u> the federal industrial regulations.

   (A) to conform with the new changes in

   (B) for them conforming to the new changes in

   (C) in their conformance toward the new changes of

   (D) to get them to conform for the new changes of

   (E) in conforming to the new changes about

17. Those students who convince themselves that they have the talent to become professional <u>athletes, often neglecting</u> their studies because they feel they will never need to use them.

   (A) athletes, often neglecting

   (B) athletes in often neglecting

   (C) athletes often neglect

   (D) athletes, and so often neglect

   (E) athletes would nevertheless often neglect

18. Seat belts were extremely unpopular when they were first introduced by Ford Motors, but <u>for those who used them they saved hundreds of lives</u>.

(A) for those who used them they saved hundreds of lives
(B) they saved the lives of hundreds of those who used them
(C) the ones that used them had hundreds of their lives saved by them
(D) hundreds of the ones who used them had their lives saved by them
(E) hundreds of lives were saved of those who were the ones using them

19. The demand for American goods and services increases as the value of the dollar decreases and <u>because of the lowering of trade barriers</u>.

(A) because of the lowering of trade barriers
(B) in the lowering of trade barriers
(C) lower trade barriers
(D) for lower trade barriers
(E) as trade barriers are lowered

20. The professional hockey strike has most acutely affected the officials, most <u>of them depend</u> on the seasonal work for their livelihood.

(A) of them depend
(B) of them have been depending
(C) which depend
(D) of whom depend
(E) depend

Directions for "Identifying Sentence Error" Questions

The following sentences may contain errors in grammar, usage, diction (choice of words), or idiom. Some of the sentences are correct. No sentence contains more than one error.

If the sentence contains an error, it is underlined and lettered. The parts that are not underlined are correct.

If there is an error, select the part that must be changed to correct the sentence.

If there is no error, choose (E).

EXAMPLE:

By the time <u>they reached</u> the halfway point
                  A
<u>in the race</u>, most <u>of the runners</u> <u>hadn't hardly</u>
     B   C   D
begun to hit their stride. <u>No error</u>
                               E

---

21. Thomas Jefferson <u>invented</u> the dumbwaiter
                           A
in 1795, <u>and they have been</u> used <u>ever since</u>
              B   C
as a valuable <u>labor-saving</u> device. <u>No error</u>
                  D   E

22. The sudden rush of investors <u>to withdraw</u>
                                        A
their money <u>from their accounts</u> <u>caused</u>
                  B   C
many banks <u>to have closed</u> their doors for
                  D
several weeks. <u>No error</u>
                   E

23. Charles Evans Hughes <u>was</u> not only
                                A
an <u>exemplary</u> Chief Justice of the Supreme
        B
Court <u>and also was</u> a governor of New York
          C
and the Republican <u>candidate for president</u>
                            D
in 1916. <u>No error</u>
             E

GO ON TO THE NEXT PAGE ▶▶▶

24. The dramatic geometric design
    of the arboretum, which was a stark
         A   B
    departure from the naturalism of
    C
    traditional English gardens, attest to
                                    D
    Colcott's love of order and beauty. No error
                                          E

25. Although the delay in the deployment of
                        A
    troops was a tactful blunder, it did not
                    B   C
    diminish the effectiveness of the general's
                     D
    overall strategy. No error
                      E

26. The conference delegates were astonished
                               A
    not only by the sheer number of protestors,
                            B
    but also by the smooth coordination of the
    C   D
    many simultaneous demonstrations.

    No error
    E

27. The professors usually never cancel classes,
                    A
    even when there is a snowstorm, because
         B
    they believe that knowledge is too important

    to compromise for anything but the most
    C   D
    dire circumstances. No error
                        E

28. Helene found it hard to believe that a
                    A
    student as diligent as her could ever be
                        B
    singled out as an example of laziness.
    C   D
    No error
    E

29. Because it is abundant and burns clean,
            A   B
    hydrogen is likely to become the preferred
                        C
    energy source of the future. No error
                    D   E

30. Although it is approximately 5 percent
    more likely that a child will be born male
                     A   B
    than female, the higher mortality rate of
                                C
    males ensures that the number of adult men
    and women will be about the same at
                         D
    reproductive age. No error
                      E

31. Only in the last several years has the
            A   B
    economic ministers of the neighboring

    countries

    come to realize that punitive tariffs
    C
    have hurt the overall economy of the region.
    D
    No error
    E

32. Although it was first used

    by news organizations to transmit
            A   B
    photographs for publication in the 1920s,

    fax machines did not come into widepread
    C   D
    use until nearly 60 years later. No error
                                    E

33. Since the itinerary allotted very little time
                         A
    for unexpected delays, our tour guide

    insisted that we be at least 30 minutes early
             B   C
    for any scheduled train departure. No error
    D   E

34. There is at least two oxygen tanks for each
    A   B
    climber at the base camp, although rarely
                              C
    does anyone need more than one. No error
    D   E

GO ON TO THE NEXT PAGE ▶▶▶

Questions 35–39 pertain to the following passage.

Line *(1) Although many people consider science and art to be very different fields of endeavor, they came together in many surprising ways during the Renaissance, which dawned in 15th-century Europe. (2) One way was through the detailed mechanical and anatomical drawings by brilliant artists like Leonardo da Vinci. (3) According to modern painter David Hockney, science and art came together in yet another remarkable way around 1425. (4) Even a casual analysis of portraits of this era reveals a sudden and dramatic increase in realism, which Hockney thinks is best explained through science.*

(5) Whereas previous portraits were characterized by awkwardness, artificiality and formalism, the new portraits by artists like Jan van Eyck and Robert Campin showed natural, almost photorealistic expressions. (6) Hockney suggests that the best explanation for the reason about why such a dramatic shift in realism occurred is because of the use of optical devices, which caused them to become more realistic. (7) Hockney believes that some artists of this era, most notably van Eyck, used concave lenses for projecting full-color images of his subjects on a flat screen. (8) You can see how such a device might work if you take a concave makeup mirror on a sunny morning and angle it to reflect the outside landscape onto your bathroom wall. (9) The image is upside-down, but this was no problem; artists could simply trace the image, then invert the canvas and paint.

(10) Hockney's theory is still very controversial in the scientific and artistic communities. (11) Many scientists argue that the science of optics was not nearly well-developed enough in the 15th century to support the development of the sophisticated instruments

that Hockney suggests. (12) Many art historians also prefer to believe that van Eyck's realism was achieved through his skilled artistic eye, and not some optical aid.

35. To improve clarity, which of the following changes should be made to sentence 1?

(A) *they* should be changed to *these fields*
(B) *which* should be changed to *of which*
(C) *came* should be changed to *will have come*
(D) *Although* should be changed to *Because*
(E) *consider* should be changed to *consider that*

36. Where is the best place to insert the sentence below?
Another way is through the use of linear perspective, as seen in the architectural drawings of Michelangelo, Brunelleschi, and Rembrandt.

(A) between sentences 1 and 2
(B) between sentences 2 and 3
(C) between sentences 3 and 4
(D) before sentence 5, to begin the second paragraph
(E) between sentences 5 and 6

37. Which of the following is the best version of the underlined portion of sentence 6 (reproduced below)?
Hockney suggests that the best explanation for the reason about why such a dramatic shift in realism occurred is because of the artists' use of optical devices, which caused them to become more realistic.

(A) (as it is now)
(B) it was because of optical devices why the paintings of the artists became so much more realistic
(C) because of optical devices was why these artists' pictures got more realistic
(D) these artists used optical devices to produce dramatically more realistic paintings
(E) the reason why these paintings had a dramatic increase in realism is because of the artists' using optical devices

38. Which of the following is the best version of the underlined portion of sentence 7 (reproduced below)?

Hockney believes that some artists of this era, most notably van Eyck, <u>used concave lenses for projecting full-color images of his subjects on a flat screen</u>.

(A) used concave lenses for the purpose of projecting full-color images of his subjects onto flat screens

(B) used concave lenses to project his image in full color on flat screens

(C) would have used concave lenses for projecting full-color images of their subjects to a flat screen

(D) using concave lenses to project full-color images of his subject onto a flat screen

(E) used concave lenses to project full-color images of their subjects onto flat screens

39. Which of the following sentences would best conclude the passage on a hopeful note while maintaining the unity of the final paragraph?

(A) Arguments like this do not really help artists to become better artists, so it is best to leave such matters to the scientists that really care about them.

(B) The optical instruments that Hockney suggests Renaissance artists used wouldn't be as difficult to make as many people think.

(C) In the nineteenth century, many artistic movements, like Impressionism, blossomed as a reaction against photo-realism.

(D) Perhaps future artists will use even better optical tools to create paintings that are almost indistinguishable from photographs.

(E) Although this controversy continues, it has inspired scientists and artists alike to revisit the art of the Renaissance, and perhaps to appreciate anew the mind of another age.

ANSWER KEY

Section 1 Critical Reading	Section 3 Critical Reading	Section 2 Math	Section 4 Math	Section 5 Writing
				☐ 1. C
☐ 1. B	☐ 25. B	☐ 1. E	☐ 21. B	☐ 2. B
☐ 2. E	☐ 26. C	☐ 2. D	☐ 22. C	☐ 3. E
☐ 3. C	☐ 27. A	☐ 3. D	☐ 23. B	☐ 4. C
☐ 4. B	☐ 28. C	☐ 4. B	☐ 24. E	☐ 5. D
☐ 5. A	☐ 29. A	☐ 5. C	☐ 25. E	☐ 6. A
☐ 6. D	☐ 30. D	☐ 6. A	☐ 26. A	☐ 7. E
☐ 7. E	☐ 31. E	☐ 7. A	☐ 27. D	☐ 8. C
☐ 8. B	☐ 32. D	☐ 8. B	☐ 28. C	☐ 9. A
☐ 9. B	☐ 33. C	☐ 9. C		☐ 10. E
☐ 10. D	☐ 34. E	☐ 10. D	# Right (A):	☐ 11. C
☐ 11. C	☐ 35. D	☐ 11. B		☐ 12. B
☐ 12. E	☐ 36. C	☐ 12. C	————	☐ 13. B
☐ 13. D	☐ 37. B	☐ 13. D	# Wrong (B):	☐ 14. C
☐ 14. C	☐ 38. D	☐ 14. A		☐ 15. D
☐ 15. D	☐ 39. E	☐ 15. C	————	☐ 16. A
☐ 16. E	☐ 40. A	☐ 16. B	# (A) $-\frac{1}{4}$ (B):	☐ 17. C
☐ 17. E	☐ 41. B	☐ 17. B		☐ 18. B
☐ 18. B	☐ 42. C	☐ 18. B	————	☐ 19. E
☐ 19. C	☐ 43. A	☐ 19. E		☐ 20. D
☐ 20. D	☐ 44. C	☐ 20. E	☐ 29. 2/3 or .666 or .667	☐ 21. B
☐ 21. D	☐ 45. A		☐ 30. 16	☐ 22. D
☐ 22. A	☐ 46. B		☐ 31. 93	☐ 23. C
☐ 23. A	☐ 47. E		☐ 32. 18	☐ 24. D
☐ 24. C	☐ 48. D		☐ 33. 1212	☐ 25. B
			☐ 34. 11	☐ 26. E
			☐ 35. 4	☐ 27. A
			☐ 36. 1/2 or .5	☐ 28. B
			☐ 37. 9/14 or .642 or .643	☐ 29. B
			☐ 38. 6/13 or .461 or .462	☐ 30. E
				☐ 31. B
				☐ 32. C
				☐ 33. E
				☐ 34. A
				☐ 35. A
				☐ 36. B
				☐ 37. D
				☐ 38. E
				☐ 39. E

# Right (A):	# Right (A):	# Right (A):	# Right (A):	# Right (A):
————	————	————	————	————
# Wrong (B):	# Wrong (B):	# Wrong (B):		# Wrong (B):
————	————	————		————
# (A) $-\frac{1}{4}$(B):	# (A) $-\frac{1}{4}$(B):	# (A) $-\frac{1}{4}$(B):		# (A) $-\frac{1}{4}$(B):
————	————	————		————

SCORE CONVERSION TABLE

How to score your test

Use the answer key on the previous page to determine your raw score on each section. Your raw score on any section is equal to the number of correct answers on that section minus 1/4 of the number of wrong answers, with the exception of the mathematical "grid-in" section, on which wrong answers are not deducted from your score. Remember to add the raw scores from Sections 1 and 3 to get your Critical Reading raw score, and to add the raw scores from Sections 2 and 4 to get your Math raw score. Write the three raw scores here:

Raw Critical Reading score (Section 1 + Section 3): _____

Raw Math score (Section 2 + Section 4): _____

Raw Writing score (Section 5): _____

Use the table below to convert these to scaled scores.

Scaled scores: Critical Reading: _____   Math: _____   Writing: _____

Raw Score	Critical Reading Scaled Score	Math Scaled Score	Writing Scaled Score	Raw Score	Critical Reading Scaled Score	Math Scaled Score	Writing Scaled Score
48	80			20	49	52	54
47	80			19	48	51	52
46	78			18	47	50	51
45	76			17	46	48	50
44	74			16	45	47	49
43	72			15	44	46	48
42	71			14	43	45	46
41	69			13	42	44	45
40	68			12	41	43	44
39	67		80	11	40	42	43
38	66	80	80	10	39	41	41
37	64	77	78	9	38	40	40
36	63	74	77	8	37	39	39
35	62	72	76	7	36	38	37
34	62	70	74	6	34	36	36
33	61	68	73	5	33	35	35
32	60	66	71	4	32	34	33
31	59	65	69	3	30	32	32
30	58	64	68	2	29	30	31
29	57	62	66	1	27	29	30
28	56	61	65	0	25	26	29
27	55	60	63	−1	22	23	28
26	54	59	62	−2	20	20	27
25	54	58	60	−3	20	20	25
24	54	57	59	−4	20	20	24
23	52	55	57	−5	20	20	22
22	51	54	56	−6	20	20	21
21	50	53	55	−7 or less	20	20	20

Detailed Answer Key

Section 1

1. B If the remark was only *seemingly offhand*, then it must have actually been *deliberate*. *celebrated* = famous; *calculated* = planned for deliberate effect; *reflexive* = automatic; *conventional* = conforming to custom

2. E The term *symbiosis* refers to a situation in which different species act in a mutually beneficial way to one another. *parasitism* = relationship in which one organism harms another by taking advantage of it; *precarious* = dangerous; *antagonism* = hostility; *beneficial* = helpful

3. C A career to which one feels called is a *vocation*, which derives from the Latin *vocare*, to call. *embodiment* = a representation in bodily form; *acquisition* = something acquired; *corollary* = a logical deduction

4. B The word *although* indicates a contrast between the fact that the value of liberty is *timeless* and the fact that our appreciation of it is not. The first word, logically, should be a synonym of *value* and the second a synonym of *temporary*. *benevolence* = kindness; *fleeting* = short-lived; *anachronisms* = things that are out of place in time; *transitory* = temporary; *diversions* = entertainments; *ephemeral* = short-lived

5. A This sentence contains a reiteration or definition. The missing word means *unexpected changes*. *vicissitudes* = unexpected changes; *veneers* = superficial pretenses or outward shows; *evanescence* = quality of being able to vanish quickly

6. D The words *by* and *thereby* indicate logical cause-and-effect relationships within the sentence. Use your common sense to complete the sentence in a logical way. What would one expect a change in global climate to do to our ancestors in trees, and what would one expect to happen to human evolution as a result of this? A change in climate would produce a change in food availability, encouraging our ancestors to climb out of the trees and to evolve. *hasten* = to cause to occur more quickly; *resolve* = solve a problem; *spur* = encourage; *impel* = force; *propel* = to push forward

7. E If a Senator chose to *affiliate himself with the opposition*, he would have *abandoned* his own party, which would likely have treated him as a *traitor*. *repudiate* = to reject the validity of; *curator* = director of a museum; *recluse* = hermit; *ascertain* = determine the truth of; *complement* = something that, when added to something else, forms a whole; *expatriate* = one who lives in a country other than his or her native land; *forsake* = abandon; *apostate* = one who abandons one's party or faith

8. B If a dictator could not be *assuaged* (pacified), and issued *bellicose* (war-mongering) announcements, then it would seem almost impossible to avoid conflict. *diplomacy* = attempts at peaceful conciliation; *disclosed* = revealed; *conciliation* = appeasement; *averted* = prevented; *tact* = the ability to appreciate the delicacy of a situation and act appropriately; *denigrated* = defamed, disparaged; *belligerence* = antagonism, pugnaciousness; *forestalled* = delayed; *jingoism* = excessive and aggressive nationalism; *circumvented* = overcame through clever maneuvering

9. B The author states that *students [come] to us from the best high schools in America* (lines 10–11). This suggests that the author is a college professor.

10. D The top of the pyramid (as opposed to the rest of the pyramid) is described as the place *where the most profound questions of our era are examined* (lines 35–36).

11. C The author of Passage 1 states that *there seems to be no grounding* (lines 17–18) in the fundamental academic skills for college students, but suggests, through the ladder metaphor, that there should be. The author of Passage 2, however, claims that *we are losing too many students in building the pyramid* (of fundamental skills) (lines 37–38).

12. E The author of Passage 1 uses the ladder as a metaphor for academic learning, and the author of Passage 2 uses the pyramid as a metaphor.

13. D The author of Passage 1 states that he is writing *at the end of a brief introduction* (lines 7–8) and that he is *regarding most of the criticism and much of Fitzgerald's work* (lines 1–2). Therefore, he suggests that he is writing an introduction to a book of criticism.

14. C   The author explains that in saying that *modern criticism… is… too refined* (lines 12–13), he means that *critics tend to make too much of small things* (lines 14–15).

15. D   The author states that *there is joy in Fitzgerald's work that should not be passed over* (lines 20–21) and that Edmund Wilson, in particular, recognized this quality in Fitzgerald's work.

16. E   In saying that *a writer… is commonly charged with having too narrow a range* (lines 29–31), he is saying that the writer is accused of dealing only with a short list of themes.

17. E   The author suggests that examining Fitzgerald's original manuscripts, which contain *strikeovers, and pencillings, and second and third thoughts* (lines 46–47), can help a writer to appreciate that good writing involves a good deal of reworking.

18. B   The fifth paragraph of Passage 1 expresses a concern that some Fitzgerald scholarship is *solemn and heavy* (line 51), after expressing in a previous paragraph that Fitzgerald's work is filled with *joy* (line 20). He also suggests that *there should be some licensing procedure that would prevent bad writers… from dealing with Fitzgerald* (lines 52–55). He is therefore showing a concern about the quality and tone of Fitzgerald scholarship.

19. C   The following sentence goes on to explain that, in his earliest works, Fitzgerald's *optimistic sense of the value of experience is overshadowed by a personal intuition of tragedy* (lines 83–86). In other words, Fitzgerald's novels contain tragic elements.

20. D   This final paragraph contrasts *those who possess the necessary means* (line 107), that is, the wealthy, with *the disinherited* (line 110), that is, the poor. When the author states that *the disinherited [are] forever barred from the white palace* (lines 110–111), he means that they do not have access to the wealth and privilege of the affluent.

21. D   The author of Passage 1 would strongly disagree because he states, in lines 63–64, that *Fitzgerald will probably continue to claim the interest of both the general reader and the scholar-critic.*

22. A   The *joy* mentioned in line 20 of Passage 1 is described as a feature of Fitzgerald's work that *should not be passed over* (line 21) and as something that is *exceedingly rare* (line 24) and has *worth* (line 28), but the *wonder* described in line 86 of Passage 2 is a feature of Fitzgerald's work that, the author of Passage 2 claims, is *chastened by satiric and ironic insights* (line 87). In other words, the author of Passage 1 considers this quality to be a unique and worthy feature of Fitzgerald's work, while the author of Passage 2 considers it to be compromised by intimations of tragedy.

23. A   The author of Passage 1 suggests that some criticism dwells *upon profundities, complexities, and tragic implications* (lines 21–23) in Fitzgerald's work. The author of Passage 2 states that Fitzgerald's works have been *labeled… by their most recent critics, as darkly pessimistic studies* (lines 74–75).

24. C   The author of Passage 1 states in the third paragraph, as well as in the fifth, that critics dwell excessively on *profundities, complexities, and tragic implications* (lines 22–23) in Fitzgerald's works, and that too much scholarship on Fitzgerald has become *solemn and heavy* (line 51). He emphasizes Fitzgerald's *extraordinary felicity of expression* (line 62) and suggests that good criticism of Fitzgerald should be likewise felicitous, not heavy and tragic.

Section 2

1. E   The area of a rectangle is given by the formula $A = bh$, and the area of a triangle is given by the formula $A = \frac{1}{2}bh$. So the rectangle has an area of $(4)(6) = 24$, and the triangle has an area of $\frac{1}{2}(4)(4) = 8$. So the area of the rectangle is 3 times the area of the triangle.
(Chapter 11 Lesson 5: Areas and Perimeters)

2. D

The algebraic method:	$x = 2y + 2$
Multiply by 6:	$6x = 12y + 12$

This equation states that $6x$ is 12 more than $12y$. (Don't forget to *distribute* the multiplication on the right-hand side!)
Although the algebraic method is the simplest, and should be easy to understand, you can also solve this by simply choosing values for x and y that work in the original equation. For instance, if $x = 2y + 2$, then x could be 4 and y could be 1, because $4 = 2(1) + 2$. The question *how much greater is 6x than 12y* now becomes *how much greater is 6(4) than 12(1)* or *how much greater is 24 than 12?* The answer is clearly $24 - 12 = 12$.
(Chapter 9 Lesson 1: Solving Equations)
(Chapter 9 Lesson 2: Systems)
(Chapter 8 Lesson 2: The Laws of Arithmetic)

3. **D**   First, notice that any number that is divisible by 6 must necessarily be divisible by 2 also, since $6 = (3)(2)$. Therefore, the question is simply asking: how many multiples of 6 are there between 10 and 40? The answer choices quickly tell you that the answer can be no more than 6, so it's easy enough to list them: 12, 18, 24, 30, 36.
(Chapter 8 Lesson 7: Divisibility)

4. **B**   First notice that 100 hours is a little bit more than 4 days, because 100 hours $\times$ (1 day/24 hours) $= 4\ 1/6$ days, or 4 days and 4 hours. Since 4 days later it will be 4:30 p.m. again, in 4 days and 4 hours it will be 8:30 p.m.
(Chapter 7 Reasoning Skill 3: Finding Patterns)

5. **C**   To use the algebraic method, start by defining d as the number of candy bars that Denise sold (since this is what the question is asking for). If Emily sold four times as many candy bars as Denise, then Emily sold $4d$ candy bars. If Denise sold 3 times as many as Carrie, then Carrie sold $\frac{1}{3}d$ candy bars. Since they sold 48 altogether,

$$d + 4d + \tfrac{1}{3}d = 48$$

Simplify: $(16/3)d = 48$

Multiply by 3/16: $d = 9$

Alternatively, you can simply "test" the answer choices and work by process of elimination. Remember that if you "work backward" like this, you should always start with the middle value, which is almost always at (C). You would simply check whether, if Denise sold 9 candy bars, the total would come out to 48. It does, because Emily would have sold $(4)(9) = 36$, and Carrie would have sold $\frac{1}{3}(9) = 3$, and $9 + 36 + 3 = 48$.
(Chapter 9 Lesson 7: Word Problems)

6. **A**   Remember that a straight angle has a measure of 180°. Therefore

$$2x + 3x = 180$$

Simplify: $5x = 180$

Divide by 5: $x = 36$

Since the $y°$ angle is "vertical" with the $2x°$ angle, the two must be congruent, so $y = 2x = 2(36) = 72$.
(Chapter 11 Lesson 1: Lines and Angles)

7. **A**   The brute force method is to simply evaluate $2x - x^2$ for each of the "input" values until you get a positive result. It's a bit easier, though, to simply factor the expression and pay attention to the signs of the factors. First, factor the function expression: $f(x) = 2x - x^2 = x(2 - x)$. Now check the signs:

	x	$(2 - x)$	$x(2 - x)$
(A) $x = 0.5$	$+$	$+$	$+$
(B) $x = 0$	0	$+$	0
(C) $x = -0.5$	$-$	$+$	$-$
(D) $x = -1.5$	$-$	$+$	$-$
(E) $x = -2.5$	$-$	$+$	$-$

(Chapter 9 Lesson 5: Factoring)
(Chapter 10 Lesson 1: New Symbol or Term Problems)

8. **B**   You might start by noticing that the line contains the points (0, 3) and (6, 0). Remember that the slope of the line is simply the "rise" between two points divided by the "run" between those same two points. If you walk from (0, 3) to (6, 0), your "run" would be $6 - 0 = 6$, and your "rise" would be $0 - 3 = -3$. Therefore the slope of this line is $-3/6 = -1/2$. Now look at the choices. Notice that all of the equations are in the form $y = mx + b$, and in this form m stands for the slope, and b stands for the y-intercept. Since the y-intercept is clearly 3, the correct equation is (B).
Alternatively, you can just "plug in" the points (0, 3) and (6, 0) to the equations, and eliminate any equations that aren't true for both points. For instance:

	Plug in (0, 3)		Plug in (6, 0)	
(A)	$3 = -2(0) + 3$	(Yes)	$0 = -2(6) + 3$	(No)
(B)	$3 = -1/2(0) + 3$	(Yes)	$0 = -1/2(6) + 3$	(Yes)
(C)	$3 = -1/2(0) + 6$	(No)	$0 = -1/2(6) + 6$	(No)
(D)	$3 = 1/2(0) + 3$	(Yes)	$0 = 1/2(6) + 3$	(No)
(E)	$3 = 2(0) + 6$	(No)	$0 = 2(6) + 6$	(No)

(Chapter 11 Lesson 4: Coordinate Geometry)

9. **C**   You can use simple algebra or plug in a value for b, whichever is easier. If g is the total number of girls in the class, and "the number of girls is 6 less than twice the number of boys," then $g = 2b - 6$. The total number of students in the class, therefore, is $b + g = b + (2b - 6) = 3b - 6$. But if 2 girls are absent, the number of students present is $3b - 6 - 2 = 3b - 8$.
Alternatively, you could just pick a simple value for b, like 10. If the number of girls is 6 less than twice the number of boys, then there are $20 - 6 = 14$ girls, for a total of $10 + 14 = 24$ students. If 2 are absent, there must be 22 present. Notice that choice (C) is the only one that gives a value of 22 when you plug in 10 for b.
(Chapter 9 Lesson 7: Word Problems)

10. **D**

$$(x + 5)^2 = 0$$

Take the square root: $(x + 5) = 0$

Subtract 5: $x = -5$

Therefore $(x-1)(x+1)=(-5-1)(-5+1)=(-6)(-4)=24$
(Chapter 10 Lesson 3: Numerical Reasoning Problems)

---

11. **B**   Be sure to mark up the diagram with the information you are given and the information you can deduce:

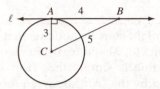

Remember that the formula for the circumference of a circle is $c=2\pi r$. Since the circumference of the circle is 6π,

$$6\pi=2\pi r$$

Divide by 2π: $3=r$

Also, recall that any tangent to a circle is perpendicular to the radius that touches the point of tangency. Therefore, ΔABC is a right triangle with legs of 3 and 4. To find BC, the hypotenuse, you might notice that this is the common 3-4-5 triangle, or you can simply use the Pythagorean theorem:

$$3^2+4^2=(BC)^2$$
Simplify: $25=(BC)^2$
Take the square root: $5=BC$

(Chapter 11 Lesson 8: Circles)
(Chapter 11 Lesson 3: The Pythagorean Theorem)

---

12. **C**   Since the integers are consecutive and their sum is -10, you might be able to find them simply by guessing and checking. Or if you prefer, you can find them algebraically. Just call the least of the integers x. Then, the statement that the five consecutive integers have a sum of -10 becomes

$$x+(x+1)+(x+2)+(x+3)+(x+4)=-10$$
Simplify: $5x+10=-10$
Subtract 10: $5x=-20$
Divide by 5: $x=-4$

Therefore the five numbers are $-4,-3,-2,-1$, and 0. Now you are to find the greatest possible *product* of *three* of these numbers. All the numbers are negative except 0. The product of any three negatives is always negative, but the product of any number and 0 is always 0. Therefore, the greatest product you can get by multiplying three of these numbers is 0.
(Chapter 10 Lesson 3: Numerical Reasoning Problems)

---

13. **D**   Just focus on the Wednesdays. Since the first of the month is a Monday, the first Wednesday

must be the 3rd. Since Wednesdays happen to occur every 7 days, the other Wednesdays are on the 10th, 17th, and 24th. (There is no 31st because there are only 30 days.) Therefore 4 of the 30 days are Wednesdays, so the probability is $4/30=.1333...$
(Chapter 10 Lesson 3: Numerical Reasoning Problems)
(Chapter 7 Reasoning Skill 3: Finding Patterns)

---

14. **A**   Remember that $|x|$ means the distance from x to 0 on the number line. So if $|x|>2$, then either $x>2$ or $x<-2$. (Think about it.) So two simple *possible* values of x are 3 and -3. If x can be -3, then statements I and III are not necessarily true since $-3>0$ is not true and $(-3)^3>2$ is not true. If you eliminate every answer choice that contains statement I or statement III, you are left only with (A). Statement II must be true because if you square both sides of $|x|>2$, you get $x^2>4$, and if x^2 is greater than 4, it must certainly also be greater than 2.
(Chapter 9 Lesson 6: Inequalities, Absolute Values, and Plugging In)

---

15. **C**   Since marbles only come in whole numbers, if the number of red marbles is 5/6 the number of white marbles, then the number of red marbles must be a multiple of 5. (Just think of the ways it could happen: 5 red and 6 white, 10 red and 12 white, etc.) Likewise, if the number of red marbles is 6/7 the number of blue marbles, then the number of red marbles must also be a multiple of 6. Since the smallest multiple of 5 and 6 is 30, this is the least possible number of red marbles. Since the number of red marbles is 5/6 the number of white marbles,

$$30=(5/6)w$$
Multiply by 6/5: $36=w$

Since the number of red marbles is 6/7 the number of blue marbles,

$$30=(6/7)b$$
Multiply by 7/6: $35=b$

So the least possible total number of marbles is $30+36+35=101$.
(Chapter 8 Lesson 3: Fractions)
(Chapter 8 Lesson 4: Ratios and Proportions)

---

16. **B**   A sequence in which each term is equal to the previous term times a constant (a fixed number) is called a *geometric* sequence. The number you must multiply each time is the common ratio, b/a, which is also equal to $a/8$ and $27/b$. You might simply test the answer choices, starting with (C), to see how the sequence works out. For instance, testing (C) 3.375 means multiplying the first term,

8, by 3.375 to get the next term, and so on. This gives you

$$8, 27, 91.125, 307.55$$

but this doesn't work, because the *fourth* term should be 27. Therefore, 3.375 is too big, and so we can eliminate (C), (D), and (E). Next, try choice (B). Multiplying by 1.5 each time works perfectly:

$$8, 12, 18, 27$$

So the answer is (B).
(Chapter 7 Reasoning Skill 3: Finding Patterns)

---

17. **B**   You should be able to sketch a quick graph of this line using one of two methods. The first way is to use the fact that, when a linear equation is in the form $y = mx + b$, the slope is m and the y-intercept is b. So the slope of this line is 2/3 and its y-intercept is 1. First plot a point at the y-intercept. Then move up 2 and right 3 and plot a second point. Then connect the points:

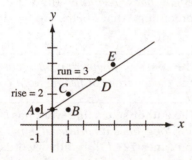

The other simple method is to choose easy values for x, like 0 and 3, and plug these into the equation to get the corresponding values of y. Just as in the previous method, this will give you the points (0, 1) and (3, 3). Now simply plot the points in the choices and notice that only choice (B) (1, 1) is below the line.
(Chapter 11 Lesson 4: Coordinate Geometry)

---

18. **B**   First you must notice that 27 is a power of 3: $3^3 = 27$. Use this to make a substitution: $3^{n-1} = 27^{-1}$

Substitute 3^3 for 27:	$3^{n-1} = (3^3)^{-1}$
Simplify:	$3^{n-1} = 3^{-3}$
Equate the powers:	$n - 1 = -3$
Add 1:	$n = -2$

(Chapter 9 Lesson 3: Working with Exponents)

---

19. **E**   You can do this algebraically or by plugging in. Here, perhaps plugging in is easier. Notice that if you plug in $x = 1$, you get $y = 1 + 1/1 = 2$. Now, the question asks for the value of $x^2 + 1/x^2$ in terms

of y. Since we assumed that $x = 1$,

$$x^2 + 1/x^2 = (1)^2 + 1/(1)^2 = 2$$

Therefore, we want to know which choice has a value of 2 when we plug in $y = 2$. Evaluate each choice:

(A) $y^2 + 2 =$	$(2)^2 + 2 =$	6
(B) $y^2 + 1 =$	$(2)^2 + 1 =$	5
(C) $y^2 =$	$(2)^2 =$	4
(D) $y^2 - 1 =$	$(2)^2 - 1 =$	3
(E) $y^2 - 2 =$	$(2)^2 - 2 =$	2

Clearly, only choice (E) gives the value we want: 2. You can also solve this problem algebraically:

	$(x + 1/x) = y$
Square both sides:	$(x + 1/x)(x + 1/x) = y^2$
FOIL:	$x^2 + x/x + x/x + 1/x^2 = y^2$
Simplify:	$x^2 + 1 + 1 + 1/x^2 = y^2$
Simplify:	$x^2 + 2 + 1/x^2 = y^2$
Subtract 2:	$x^2 + 1/x^2 = y^2 - 2$

(Chapter 9 Lesson 6: Inequalities, Absolute Values, and Plugging In)
(Chapter 9 Lesson 1: Solving Equations)

---

20. **E**   Be sure to mark up the diagram with any given information and any information you can deduce:

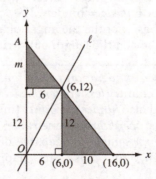

First, since the slope of the line is 2 and the line passes through (0, 0), it must also pass through (6, 12). (Remember *slope = rise/run* = 12/6 = 2.) So, label the top right corner of the rectangle (6, 12). Next, notice that the two shaded right triangles must be similar, because all of their corresponding angles are congruent by the parallel lines theorem. Therefore all of the corresponding sides are proportional:

$$\frac{m}{6} = \frac{12}{10}$$

Multiply by 6: $m = 7.2$

Therefore, the y-coordinate of point A is $12 + 7.2 = 19.2$

(Chapter 11 Lesson 1: Lines and Angles)
(Chapter 11 Lesson 4: Coordinate Geometry)
(Chapter 11 Lesson 6: Similar Figures)

Section 3

25. B If Harold is *unlike* other farmers, then he thinks of rain as something contrasting a *benefit*. *hardship* = a trying situation

26. C A *perfectionist* is one who cannot accept flaws in his or her work. Therefore, the tendency to destroy works that are less than perfect would be a hallmark of perfectionism. *paragon* = prime example; *mediocre* = of average quality; *proponent* = supporter, advocate; *aesthetic* = relating to a sense of the beautiful; *advocate* = one who speaks out for a cause; *monetary* = pertaining to money

27. A Clearly, Joseph has the tendency to *pick fights*. *belligerence* = eagerness to fight; *diligence* = persistent application to one's work; *fortitude* = strength; *restraint* = ability to control one's urges; *eloquence* = ability to speak fluently and persuasively

28. C *Discounted merchandise and free gift wrapping* are things that are likely to appeal to shoppers. If the shoppers were *angry*, such offers seem to be attempts to *appease* their anger. *exculpate* = free from blame; *impede* = hinder the progress of; *mollify* = appease, soothe the anger of; *pilfer* = steal; *abridge* = to shorten the length of a written work

29. A *Severe immigration restrictions* would logically render a country *less vulnerable* to *foreign terrorists*, but would also *hinder* the *influx* (inward flow) of creative ideas. *pervious* = penetrable; *stem* = stop the flow of; *impregnable* = incapable of being penetrated; *hasten* = to cause to happen sooner; *potent* = strong

30. D This passage compares and contrasts *two kinds of evidence* (lines 5–6) in history: *oral traditions and archaeology* (lines 4–5).

31. E The *nonmaterial world of ideas, values and beliefs* (lines 15–16) is said to be provided by *oral sources* (line 14). This *nonmaterial world*, according to the passage, is worthy of study but only ascertainable through oral traditions.

32. D The overall purpose of the passage is to criticize irrationality. The first sentence characterizes the *irrational tidal waves of the last big war* (lines 2–3) as causing *agony and despair*. It then goes on to bemoan the fact that *man is not rational enough*

(lines 12–13) to take advantage of ␠
ments and that reality *does not c␠
rational prescriptions* (line 22).

33. C The parenthetical comment ␠
poor *might have most reason for suc␠
unrest and violence*). In other words␠
the most justified in acting rebelliously␠

34. E The author states *I go off down␠
get my strength back* (lines 28–29). In oth␠
river rejuvenates him.

35. D The author states that *without␠
thing," I can't get along either*. The "*ever␠
he is referring to is the *traffic* (line 4), w␠
gets on his nerves, and the *people and ␠
16–17*) that he encounters every day␠
words, he needs these things, but ␠
needs to get away from them also.

36. C The *thing that we haven't mana␠
out of our dusty old dictionaries* (lines 27␠
recreation (line 22) or the *rest [that helps␠
one's] strength back regularly* (line 26),␠
words, something that helps to rest␠
strength.

37. B The *constant flight from open con␠
66–67*) is the *escape from* or *fleeing from* co␠

38. D The author states that work has *lo␠
inal meaning long since its primeval, ennob␠
tive function* (lines 72–73). In other words␠
work was meant as a creative endeavor, ␠
lost its meaning as such.

39. E This paragraph describes how the␠
appointment with the river has expired (lin␠
because the city is *waking up* (line 82) be␠
The *pensioners* (line 90) are mentioned as ␠
of those people and things that are intrud␠
solitude at the river.

40. A The passage as a whole describe␠
flict that the narrator feels between *his␠
people and things* (lines 16–17) and the te␠
these things to occasionally *get [him] d␠
17*), whereupon he seeks solitude and rej␠
at the river. Therefore, the main conflict i␠
solitude and sociability.

41. B The first line of the passage s␠
*according to Kant, his reading of David Hu␠
ened him from his dogmatic slumber and ␠

3. D   First, notice that any number that is divisible by 6 must necessarily be divisible by 2 also, since $6 = (3)(2)$. Therefore, the question is simply asking: how many multiples of 6 are there between 10 and 40? The answer choices quickly tell you that the answer can be no more than 6, so it's easy enough to list them: 12, 18, 24, 30, 36.
(Chapter 8 Lesson 7: Divisibility)

4. B   First notice that 100 hours is a little bit more than 4 days, because 100 hours $\times$ (1 day/24 hours) = 4 1/6 days, or 4 days and 4 hours. Since 4 days later it will be 4:30 p.m. again, in 4 days and 4 hours it will be 8:30 p.m.
(Chapter 7 Reasoning Skill 3: Finding Patterns)

5. C   To use the algebraic method, start by defining d as the number of candy bars that Denise sold (since this is what the question is asking for). If Emily sold four times as many candy bars as Denise, then Emily sold $4d$ candy bars. If Denise sold 3 times as many as Carrie, then Carrie sold $\frac{1}{3}d$ candy bars. Since they sold 48 altogether,

$$d + 4d + \tfrac{1}{3}d = 48$$

Simplify: $$(16/3)d = 48$$

Multiply by 3/16: $$d = 9$$

Alternatively, you can simply "test" the answer choices and work by process of elimination. Remember that if you "work backward" like this, you should always start with the middle value, which is almost always at (C). You would simply check whether, if Denise sold 9 candy bars, the total would come out to 48. It does, because Emily would have sold $(4)(9) = 36$, and Carrie would have sold $\frac{1}{3}(9) = 3$, and $9 + 36 + 3 = 48$.
(Chapter 9 Lesson 7: Word Problems)

6. A   Remember that a straight angle has a measure of 180°. Therefore

$$2x + 3x = 180$$

Simplify: $$5x = 180$$

Divide by 5: $$x = 36$$

Since the $y°$ angle is "vertical" with the $2x°$ angle, the two must be congruent, so $y = 2x = 2(36) = 72$.
(Chapter 11 Lesson 1: Lines and Angles)

7. A   The brute force method is to simply evaluate $2x - x^2$ for each of the "input" values until you get a positive result. It's a bit easier, though, to simply factor the expression and pay attention to the signs of the factors. First, factor the function expression: $f(x) = 2x - x^2 = x(2 - x)$. Now check the signs:

	x	$(2 - x)$	$x(2 - x)$
(A) $x = 0.5$	+	+	+
(B) $x = 0$	0	+	0
(C) $x = -0.5$	−	+	−
(D) $x = -1.5$	−	+	−
(E) $x = -2.5$	−	+	−

(Chapter 9 Lesson 5: Factoring)
(Chapter 10 Lesson 1: New Symbol or Term Problems)

8. B   You might start by noticing that the line contains the points (0, 3) and (6, 0). Remember that the slope of the line is simply the "rise" between two points divided by the "run" between those same two points. If you walk from (0, 3) to (6, 0), your "run" would be $6 - 0 = 6$, and your "rise" would be $0 - 3 = -3$. Therefore the slope of this line is $-3/6 = -1/2$. Now look at the choices. Notice that all of the equations are in the form $y = mx + b$, and in this form m stands for the slope, and b stands for the y-intercept. Since the y-intercept is clearly 3, the correct equation is (B).
Alternatively, you can just "plug in" the points (0, 3) and (6, 0) to the equations, and eliminate any equations that aren't true for both points. For instance:

	Plug in (0, 3)		Plug in (6, 0)	
(A)	$3 = -2(0) + 3$	(Yes)	$0 = -2(6) + 3$	(No)
(B)	$3 = -1/2(0) + 3$	(Yes)	$0 = -1/2(6) + 3$	(Yes)
(C)	$3 = -1/2(0) + 6$	(No)	$0 = -1/2(6) + 6$	(No)
(D)	$3 = 1/2(0) + 3$	(Yes)	$0 = 1/2(6) + 3$	(No)
(E)	$3 = 2(0) + 6$	(No)	$0 = 2(6) + 6$	(No)

(Chapter 11 Lesson 4: Coordinate Geometry)

9. C   You can use simple algebra or plug in a value for b, whichever is easier. If g is the total number of girls in the class, and "the number of girls is 6 less than twice the number of boys," then $g = 2b - 6$. The total number of students in the class, therefore, is $b + g = b + (2b - 6) = 3b - 6$. But if 2 girls are absent, the number of students present is $3b - 6 - 2 = 3b - 8$.
Alternatively, you could just pick a simple value for b, like 10. If the number of girls is 6 less than twice the number of boys, then there are $20 - 6 = 14$ girls, for a total of $10 + 14 = 24$ students. If 2 are absent, there must be 22 present. Notice that choice (C) is the only one that gives a value of 22 when you plug in 10 for b.
(Chapter 9 Lesson 7: Word Problems)

10. D

$$(x + 5)^2 = 0$$

Take the square root: $$(x + 5) = 0$$

Subtract 5: $$x = -5$$

Therefore $(x-1)(x+1) = (-5 \quad -1)(-5+1) =$ $(-6)(-4) = 24$
(Chapter 10 Lesson 3: Numerical Reasoning Problems)

---

11. **B**   Be sure to mark up the diagram with the information you are given and the information you can deduce:

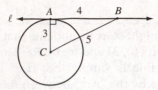

Remember that the formula for the circumference of a circle is $c = 2\pi r$. Since the circumference of the circle is 6π,
$$6\pi = 2\pi r$$
Divide by 2π: $3 = r$
Also, recall that any tangent to a circle is perpendicular to the radius that touches the point of tangency. Therefore, $\triangle ABC$ is a right triangle with legs of 3 and 4. To find BC, the hypotenuse, you might notice that this is the common 3-4-5 triangle, or you can simply use the Pythagorean theorem:
$$3^2 + 4^2 = (BC)^2$$
Simplify: $25 = (BC)^2$
Take the square root: $5 = BC$
(Chapter 11 Lesson 8: Circles)
(Chapter 11 Lesson 3: The Pythagorean Theorem)

---

12. **C**   Since the integers are consecutive and their sum is -10, you might be able to find them simply by guessing and checking. Or if you prefer, you can find them algebraically. Just call the least of the integers x. Then, the statement that the five consecutive integers have a sum of -10 becomes

$$x + (x+1) + (x+2) + (x+3) + (x+4) = -10$$
Simplify: $5x + 10 = -10$
Subtract 10: $5x = -20$
Divide by 5: $x = -4$

Therefore the five numbers are $-4, -3, -2, -1$, and 0. Now you are to find the greatest possible *product* of *three* of these numbers. All the numbers are negative except 0. The product of any three negatives is always negative, but the product of any number and 0 is always 0. Therefore, the greatest product you can get by multiplying three of these numbers is 0.
(Chapter 10 Lesson 3: Numerical Reasoning Problems)

---

13. **D**   Just focus on the Wednesdays. Since the first of the month is a Monday, the first Wednesday

must be the 3rd. Since Wednesdays happen to occur every 7 days, the other Wednesdays are on the 10th, 17th, and 24th. (There is no 31st because there are only 30 days.) Therefore 4 of the 30 days are Wednesdays, so the probability is $4/30 = .1333\ldots$
(Chapter 10 Lesson 3: Numerical Reasoning Problems)
(Chapter 7 Reasoning Skill 3: Finding Patterns)

---

14. **A**   Remember that $|x|$ means the distance from x to 0 on the number line. So if $|x| > 2$, then either $x > 2$ or $x < -2$. (Think about it.) So two simple *possible* values of x are 3 and -3. If x can be -3, then statements I and III are not necessarily true since $-3 > 0$ is not true and $(-3)^3 > 2$ is not true. If you eliminate every answer choice that contains statement I or statement III, you are left only with (A). Statement II must be true because if you square both sides of $|x| > 2$, you get $x^2 > 4$, and if x^2 is greater than 4, it must certainly also be greater than 2.
(Chapter 9 Lesson 6: Inequalities, Absolute Values, and Plugging In)

---

15. **C**   Since marbles only come in whole numbers, if the number of red marbles is 5/6 the number of white marbles, then the number of red marbles must be a multiple of 5. (Just think of the ways it could happen: 5 red and 6 white, 10 red and 12 white, etc.) Likewise, if the number of red marbles is 6/7 the number of blue marbles, then the number of red marbles must also be a multiple of 6. Since the smallest multiple of 5 and 6 is 30, this is the least possible number of red marbles. Since the number of red marbles is 5/6 the number of white marbles,
$$30 = (5/6)w$$
Multiply by 6/5: $36 = w$
Since the number of red marbles is 6/7 the number of blue marbles,
$$30 = (6/7)b$$
Multiply by 7/6: $35 = b$
So the least possible total number of marbles is $30 + 36 + 35 = 101$.
(Chapter 8 Lesson 3: Fractions)
(Chapter 8 Lesson 4: Ratios and Proportions)

---

16. **B**   A sequence in which each term is equal to the previous term times a constant (a fixed number) is called a *geometric* sequence. The number you must multiply each time is the common ratio, b/a, which is also equal to $a/8$ and $27/b$. You might simply test the answer choices, starting with (C), to see how the sequence works out. For instance, testing (C) 3.375 means multiplying the first term,

8, by 3.375 to get the next term, and so on. This gives you

$$8, 27, 91.125, 307.55$$

but this doesn't work, because the *fourth* term should be 27. Therefore, 3.375 is too big, and so we can eliminate (C), (D), and (E). Next, try choice (B). Multiplying by 1.5 each time works perfectly:

$$8, 12, 18, 27$$

So the answer is (B).
(Chapter 7 Reasoning Skill 3: Finding Patterns)

---

17. **B**   You should be able to sketch a quick graph of this line using one of two methods. The first way is to use the fact that, when a linear equation is in the form $y = mx + b$, the slope is m and the y-intercept is b. So the slope of this line is 2/3 and its y-intercept is 1. First plot a point at the y-intercept. Then move up 2 and right 3 and plot a second point. Then connect the points:

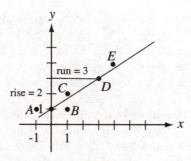

The other simple method is to choose easy values for x, like 0 and 3, and plug these into the equation to get the corresponding values of y. Just as in the previous method, this will give you the points (0, 1) and (3, 3). Now simply plot the points in the choices and notice that only choice (B) (1, 1) is below the line.
(Chapter 11 Lesson 4: Coordinate Geometry)

---

18. **B**   First you must notice that 27 is a power of 3: $3^3 = 27$. Use this to make a substitution: $3^{n-1} = 27^{-1}$

Substitute 3^3 for 27:	$3^{n-1} = (3^3)^{-1}$
Simplify:	$3^{n-1} = 3^{-3}$
Equate the powers:	$n - 1 = -3$
Add 1:	$n = -2$

(Chapter 9 Lesson 3: Working with Exponents)

---

19. **E**   You can do this algebraically or by plugging in. Here, perhaps plugging in is easier. Notice that if you plug in $x = 1$, you get $y = 1 + 1/1 = 2$. Now, the question asks for the value of $x^2 + 1/x^2$ in terms

of y. Since we assumed that $x = 1$,

$$x^2 + 1/x^2 = (1)^2 + 1/(1)^2 = 2$$

Therefore, we want to know which choice has a value of 2 when we plug in $y = 2$. Evaluate each choice:

(A) $y^2 + 2 =$	$(2)^2 + 2 =$	6
(B) $y^2 + 1 =$	$(2)^2 + 1 =$	5
(C) $y^2 \ \ \ \ =$	$(2)^2 \ \ \ \ =$	4
(D) $y^2 - 1 =$	$(2)^2 - 1 =$	3
(E) $y^2 - 2 =$	$(2)^2 - 2 =$	2

Clearly, only choice (E) gives the value we want: 2. You can also solve this problem algebraically:

	$(x + 1/x) = y$
Square both sides:	$(x + 1/x)(x + 1/x) = y^2$
FOIL:	$x^2 + x/x + x/x + 1/x^2 = y^2$
Simplify:	$x^2 + 1 + 1 + 1/x^2 = y^2$
Simplify:	$x^2 + 2 + 1/x^2 = y^2$
Subtract 2:	$x^2 + 1/x^2 = y^2 - 2$

(Chapter 9 Lesson 6: Inequalities, Absolute Values, and Plugging In)
(Chapter 9 Lesson 1: Solving Equations)

---

20. **E**   Be sure to mark up the diagram with any given information and any information you can deduce:

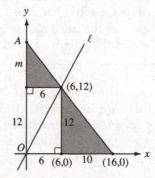

First, since the slope of the line is 2 and the line passes through (0, 0), it must also pass through (6, 12). (Remember *slope = rise/run* = 12/6 = 2.) So, label the top right corner of the rectangle (6, 12). Next, notice that the two shaded right triangles must be similar, because all of their corresponding angles are congruent by the parallel lines theorem. Therefore all of the corresponding sides are proportional:

$$\frac{m}{6} = \frac{12}{10}$$

Multiply by 6: $m = 7.2$

Therefore, the y-coordinate of point A is $12 + 7.2 = 19.2$

(Chapter 11 Lesson 1: Lines and Angles)
(Chapter 11 Lesson 4: Coordinate Geometry)
(Chapter 11 Lesson 6: Similar Figures)

Section 3

25. B If Harold is *unlike* other farmers, then he thinks of rain as something contrasting a *benefit*. *hardship* = a trying situation

26. C A *perfectionist* is one who cannot accept flaws in his or her work. Therefore, the tendency to destroy works that are less than perfect would be a hallmark of perfectionism. *paragon* = prime example; *mediocre* = of average quality; *proponent* = supporter, advocate; *aesthetic* = relating to a sense of the beautiful; *advocate* = one who speaks out for a cause; *monetary* = pertaining to money

27. A Clearly, Joseph has the tendency to *pick fights*. *belligerence* = eagerness to fight; *diligence* = persistent application to one's work; *fortitude* = strength; *restraint* = ability to control one's urges; *eloquence* = ability to speak fluently and persuasively

28. C *Discounted merchandise and free gift wrapping* are things that are likely to appeal to shoppers. If the shoppers were *angry*, such offers seem to be attempts to *appease* their anger. *exculpate* = free from blame; *impede* = hinder the progress of; *mollify* = appease, soothe the anger of; *pilfer* = steal; *abridge* = to shorten the length of a written work

29. A *Severe immigration restrictions* would logically render a country *less vulnerable to foreign terrorists*, but would also *hinder* the *influx* (inward flow) of creative ideas. *pervious* = penetrable; *stem* = stop the flow of; *impregnable* = incapable of being penetrated; *hasten* = to cause to happen sooner; *potent* = strong

30. D This passage compares and contrasts *two kinds of evidence* (lines 5–6) in history: *oral traditions and archaeology* (lines 4–5).

31. E The *nonmaterial world of ideas, values and beliefs* (lines 15–16) is said to be provided by *oral sources* (line 14). This *nonmaterial world*, according to the passage, is worthy of study but only ascertainable through oral traditions.

32. D The overall purpose of the passage is to criticize irrationality. The first sentence characterizes the *irrational tidal waves of the last big war* (lines 2–3) as causing *agony and despair*. It then goes on to bemoan the fact that *man is not rational enough* (lines 12–13) to take advantage of recent advancements and that reality *does not conform to our rational prescriptions* (line 22).

33. C The parenthetical comment states that the poor *might have most reason for such reactions* (as unrest and violence). In other words, the poor are the most justified in acting rebelliously.

34. E The author states *I go off down to the river to get my strength back* (lines 28–29). In other words, the river rejuvenates him.

35. D The author states that *without that "everything," I can't get along either*. The *"everything"* that he is referring to is the *traffic* (line 4), which he says gets on his nerves, and the *people and things* (lines 16–17) that he encounters every day. In other words, he needs these things, but occasionally needs to get away from them also.

36. C The *thing that we haven't managed to pull out of our dusty old dictionaries* (lines 27–28) is the *recreation* (line 22) or the *rest [that helps one to get one's] strength back regularly* (line 26), in other words, something that helps to restore one's strength.

37. B The *constant flight from open conflict* (lines 66–67) is the *escape from* or *fleeing from* conflict.

38. D The author states that work has *lost its original meaning long since its primeval, ennobling, creative function* (lines 72–73). In other words, long ago work was meant as a creative endeavor, and it has lost its meaning as such.

39. E This paragraph describes how the author's *appointment with the river has expired* (lines 83–84) because the city is *waking up* (line 82) behind him. The *pensioners* (line 90) are mentioned as examples of those people and things that are intruding on his solitude at the river.

40. A The passage as a whole describes the conflict that the narrator feels between his need for *people and things* (lines 16–17) and the tendency of these things to occasionally *get [him] down* (line 17), whereupon he seeks solitude and rejuvenation at the river. Therefore, the main conflict is between solitude and sociability.

41. B The first line of the passage states that *according to Kant, his reading of David Hume awakened him from his dogmatic slumber and set him on*

the road to becoming the "critical philosopher" (lines 1–4). In other words, Hume's writings inspired Kant in his philosophical thinking.

---

42. C   The term *dogmatic* means very rigid and preachy in one's views. By saying that he was *awakened… from his dogmatic slumber* (lines 2–3), the author is stating that Kant was far more rigid in his thinking before reading the work of David Hume.

---

43. A   The passage states that the *theme* (line 35) of the "Transcendental Dialectic" is *this inevitable failure* (lines 35) of *all theoretical attempts to know things-in-themselves* (lines 33–34).

---

44. C   According to the passage, in *Critique of Pure Reason*, Kant *shows the necessity of a belief in [the existence of God, freedom, and immortality] in his moral philosophy* (lines 43–45). In other words, Kant's moral system required the belief in free will.

---

45. A   According to the passage, Kant's *categorical imperative* (lines 46–47) is to *"Act as if the maxim from which you act were to become through your will a universal law"* (lines 47–49). In other words, act as if the principles behind your acts were the principles that everyone used; that is, they applied to all human beings.

---

46. B   The author states that, according to Kant, we *do not act infallibly in accordance with [the categorical imperative]* (lines 53–54) because we *almost always act according to inclination* (lines 55–56); that is, we do what our subjective needs and desires compel us to do. Another way of saying this is that our acts are necessarily *subjectively contingent* (line 58), that is, we can only act according to our "subjective" needs and desires, so we cannot do infallibly what is *objectively necessary* (line 57).

---

47. E   The *bridge* (line 73) is one *between the sensible and the intelligible worlds* (line 69), so it is a bridge between what can be sensed and what can be understood.

---

48. D   The final paragraph describes what Kant *went on to state* in *Critique of Practical Reason*. It then summarizes another later work of Kant, the *Critique of Judgment*.

Section 4

21. B   A square with perimeter of 20 centimeters must have sides of length $20 \div 4 = 5$ centimeters.

Since the area for a square is given by the formula $A = s^2$, the area of the square is $5^2 = 25$ square centimeters, and one-half of 25 is 12.5.
(Chapter 11 Lesson 5: Areas and Perimeters)

---

22. C   You can solve this one algebraically or by simply testing the choices. To solve algebraically, translate into an equation. If the number is equal to $1/3$ of its square,

	$x = (1/3)x^2$
Multiply by 3:	$3x = x^2$
Subtract $3x$:	$0 = x^2 - 3x$
Factor:	$0 = x(x - 3)$
Use the 0 product property:	$x = 0 \text{ or } x = 3$

Since 0 is not among the choices, the answer must be (C) 3.
Alternatively, you can simply test the choices, taking one-third of the square of each number until you get a result that equals the original number. Of course, that works with 3 because $3 = (1/3)(3^2)$.
(Chapter 9 Lesson 1: Solving Equations)

---

23. B   This one is probably most easily solved algebraically. Since each pile has k more checkers than the previous pile and the first pile has 3 checkers, the piles have 3, $3 + k$, $3 + 2k$, and $3 + 3k$ checkers, respectively. Since the total number of checkers is 30,

	$3 + (3 + k) + (3 + 2k) + (3 + 3k) = 30$
Simplify:	$12 + 6k = 30$
Subtract 12:	$6k = 18$
Divide by 6:	$k = 3$

(Chapter 9 Lesson 7: Word Problems)

---

24. E   If a number is equal to $3/5$ of itself plus 240,

	$x = (3/5)x + 240$
Subtract $(3/5)x$:	$(2/5)x = 240$
Multiply by $5/2$:	$x = 600$

(Chapter 9 Lesson 1: Solving Equations)
(Chapter 9 Lesson 7: Word Problems)

---

25. E   The total number of books sold (in thousands) is $500 + 325 + 375 = 1,200$. Since 500 nonfiction books have been sold, and x corresponds to the central angle of the sector representing nonfiction books, you can set up a proportion:

$$\frac{Part}{Whole} = \frac{500}{1,200} = \frac{x}{360}$$

Cross-multiply: $180,000 = 1,200x$
Divide by 1,200: $150 = x$

(Chapter 8 Lesson 4: Ratios and Proportions)

---

26. **A** It's helpful to know that if a set of numbers is evenly spaced, its median always equals its average (arithmetic mean). Since 10 consecutive even integers are certainly evenly spaced, statement I must be true. [This eliminates choice (B).] To check statements II and III, you should take a closer look at set *S*. You can find the 10 numbers fairly easily by using what we just deduced, namely, that 23 must be the median, and so it splits the set in half. Therefore set *S* must consist of the five even integers just before 23 and the five even integers just after 23:

14, 16, 18, 20, 22, 24, 26, 28, 30, and 32

Clearly the difference between 32 and 14 is greater than 10, so statement II is not true. Also, set *S* contains two multiples of 5: 20 and 30. Therefore, statement III is not true, and the answer is (A).
(Chapter 10 Lesson 2: Mean/Median/Mode Problems)

---

27. **D**

$$2^n = \frac{2}{2^k}$$

Multiply by 2^k: $(2^n)(2^k) = 2$
Simplify: $2^{n+k} = 2^1$
Equate exponents: $n + k = 1$

(Chapter 9 Lesson 3: Working with Exponents)

---

28. **C** Since the area of the square base is 144, the length of one side of the square must be $\sqrt{144} = 12$. This is also the base of one of the triangular faces. Let's call the height of this triangular face *h*. Notice that *h* is also the hypotenuse of a right triangle with legs of 6 and 8. (One leg is the height of the pyramid, which we know is 8, and the other leg is half the length of the side of the square.)

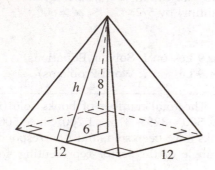

Next, notice that this right triangle is simply a multiple of a 3-4-5 triangle, so its sides have length 6-8-10. Alternatively, you can use the Pythagorean theorem to find *h*:

$$6^2 + 8^2 = h^2$$

Simplify: $36 + 64 = h^2$
Simplify: $100 = h^2$
Take the square root: $10 = h$

Thus the triangular face has a base of 12 and a height of 10, so its area is $(1/2)(12)(10) = 60$ square inches.
(Chapter 11 Lesson 3: The Pythagorean Theorem)
(Chapter 11 Lesson 5: Areas and Perimeters)
(Chapter 11 Lesson 7: Volumes and 3-D Geometry)

---

29. **2/3 or .666 or .667**
1/4 of 80 is $(1/4)(80) = 20$ and 1/3 of 90 is $(1/3)(90) = 30$. $20 \div 30 = 2/3$ or $.666\ldots$
(Chapter 8 Lesson 1: Numbers and Operations)

---

30. **16**
Using the definition, $5 \oslash 3 = (5+3)(5-3) = (8)(2) = 16$.
(Chapter 7 Reasoning Skill 1: Finding Patterns)

---

31. **93** Recall that the sum of the angles in a quadrilateral is always 360°, because a diagonal divides the quadrilateral into two triangles with 180° each. Therefore

$$x + x + x + y = 360$$

Substitute: $89 + 89 + 89 + y = 360$
Simplify: $267 + y = 360$
Subtract 267: $y = 93$

(Chapter 11 Lesson 2: Triangles)

---

32. **18** We know that, for some value of x, $f(x) = 6$, and this is the largest possible output of the function. Let's say that the value of x for which this is true is 1, so that $f(1) = 6$. Now we are asked to find the greatest possible value of $3f(x - 1)$. Notice that if we substitute $x = 2$, we get $3f(2 - 1) = 3f(1) = 3(6) = 18$. Since the value of $f(x)$ can be no greater than 6, this must be the greatest possible value of $3f(x - 1)$.
(Chapter 10 Lesson 1: New Symbol or Term Problems)

---

33. **1,212** It is convenient to know that if a number is divisible by 3, the sum of its digits will also be a multiple of 3. Likewise, if a number is divisible by 9, the sum of its digits will also be a multiple of 9. (Don't generalize this to any other factors, though; this is only true for numbers divisible by 3 or 9. For instance, the sum of the digits of a multiple of 5, like 25, is NOT necessarily a multiple of 5.) Therefore, we know that $4 + A + 3 = 7 + A$ is a

multiple of 3. The largest A could be, then, is 8, because $7 + 8 = 15$ is a multiple of 3. Also, $7 + B + 9 = 16 + B$ is a multiple of 9, so the largest B could be is 2, since $16 + 2 = 18$ is a multiple of 9. (Remember that A and B represent single digits.) Therefore, the greatest that $m + n$ could be is $483 + 729 = 1,212$.
(Chapter 8 Lesson 7: Divisibility)

---

34. 11

$$2^{m+1} = 8^4$$

Write 8 as a power of 2: $2^{m+1} = (2^3)^4$
Simplify: $2^{m+1} = 2^{12}$
Equate the exponents: $m + 1 = 12$
Subtract 1: $m = 11$

(Chapter 9 Lesson 3: Working with Exponents)

---

35. 4 If the product of four numbers is 0, then one of the numbers must be 0. If the median of the numbers is 3.5, then two of the numbers must be greater than 3.5, and two of the numbers must be less than 3.5. So, in increasing order, the numbers are 0, n, 5, 9. Since the median is the average of the two middle numbers,

$$(n + 5)/2 = 3.5$$

Multiply by 2: $n + 5 = 7$
Subtract 5: $n = 2$

So the average (arithmetic mean) of the four numbers is $(0 + 2 + 5 + 9)/4 = 16/4 = 4$.
(Chapter 10 Lesson 2: Mean/Median/Mode Problems)

---

36. 1/2 or .5 Notice first that the height of the rectangle is 6. The area of a rectangle is given by the formula $A = bh$, so if the area of the rectangle is 90, then

$$90 = 6b$$

Divide by 6: $15 = b$

So the base is 15. Write this into the diagram. The distance from O to P is 3, so the other part of the base is $15 - 3 = 12$. The slope of line PQ is the "rise" divided by the "run," which is $6/12 = 1/2$. Also, you can use the slope formula $slope = (y_2 - y_1)/(x_2 - x_1)$ with the two points on the line (3, 0) and (15, 6): $(6 - 0)/(15 - 3) = 6/12 = 1/2$.

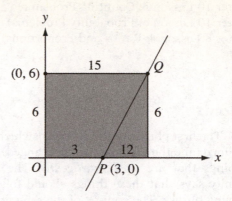

(Chapter 11 Lesson 6: Similar Figures)

---

37. 9/14 or .642 or .643 The phrase *at this rate* indicates that you can set up a proportion of equivalent rates:

$$\frac{\frac{2}{7}\,\text{tank}}{1\frac{1}{3}\,\text{hours}} = \frac{x\,\text{tank}}{3\,\text{hours}}$$

Simplify mixed number: $\dfrac{\frac{2}{7}\,\text{tank}}{\frac{4}{3}\,\text{hours}} = \dfrac{x\,\text{tank}}{3\,\text{hours}}$

Cross-multiply: $(3)\left(\dfrac{2}{7}\right) = \left(\dfrac{4}{3}\right)x$

Simplify: $\dfrac{6}{7} = \dfrac{4x}{3}$
Multiply by 21: $18 = 28x$
Divide by 28: $18/28 = x$
Simplify: $9/14 = x$

(Chapter 10 Lesson 4: Rate Problems)

---

38. 6/13 or .461 or .462 Since there is a whole number of crayons in the box, saying that the ratio of red crayons to blue crayons is 2:3 implies that the number of red crayons is a multiple of 2 and the number of blue crayons is a multiple of 3. Likewise, saying that the ratio of blue crayons to yellow crayons is 2:1 implies that the number of blue crayons is a multiple of 2 and the number of yellow crayons is a multiple of 1. So, the number of blue crayons must be a multiple of both 2 and 3. The smallest such number is 6, so let's assume that there are 6 blue crayons in the box. Since r:6 = 2:3, there must be 4 red crayons in the box, and since 6:y = 2:1, there must be 3 yellow crayons in the box. Therefore, there are $6 + 4 + 3 = 13$ crayons in the box, and since 6 of them are blue, the probability of choosing a blue

at random is 6/13.
(Chapter 10 Lesson 5: Counting Problems)
(Chapter 10 Lesson 6: Probability Problems)
(Chapter 8 Lesson 4: Ratios and Proportions)

Section 5

1. C   The first phrase of the sentence, which is not underlined (and therefore cannot be changed), modifies things that are *used intelligently*. The law of proximity says that these things should follow the modifying phrase. The context of the sentence indicates that these things are *mnemonics* (not *you* or *facts*), and so (C) is the best choice.
(Chapter 13 Lesson 8: Other Misplaced Modifiers)

2. B   The original sentence contains no verb. The core of the sentence should state that *the annual conference … was dedicated to … resolving disputes*. Choices (B), (D), and (E) make this correction, but since choices (D) and (E) contain errors in idiom—*dedicated for* and *dedicated toward* instead of *dedicated to*—the best choice is (B).
(Chapter 13 Lesson 2: Trimming Sentences)
(Chapter 13 Lesson 10: Idiom Errors)

3. E   The original sentence is unnecessarily wordy and suggests that *the doctor* was *a time*, which is illogical. Choice (E) uses 70% fewer words to say everything that the original phrase is trying to say, and so is much better.
(Chapter 13 Lesson 12: Other Problems with Modifiers)

4. C   The original "sentence" is not a complete thought, because it lacks a verb. It is also needlessly wordy: why say *because of the fact that* when *because* will do? Choice (C) is the most concise, yet expresses a clear and complete thought.
(Chapter 13 Lesson 12: Other with Modifiers Problems)
(Chapter 13 Lesson 15: Coordinating Ideas)

5. D   This sentence has the structure *A is B*, where *A* is *one aspect of the play*. Therefore, *B* must be a phrase that is logically and grammatically equivalent to *one aspect of the play*. As it stands, *B* is an independent clause, but should be a noun phrase, because *A* is a noun phrase. Choices (D) and (E) are noun phrases, but choice (E) suggests that the *social issue*, rather than the *play*, is *humorous*. Therefore, the best choice is (D).
(Chapter 13 Lesson 15: Coordinating Ideas)

6. A   The original phrasing is clear, complete, logical, and concise.

7. E   The Senator has completed campaigning, since she is now *home with her family*. Therefore, the present participle *campaigning* is incorrect and should instead be the present perfect participle: *having campaigned*.
(Chapter 13 Lesson 9: Tricky Tenses)

8. C   This sentence contains the parallel phrasing *not so much A as B*, and so *A* and *B* must have the same grammatical structure. Since *A* is the common noun phrase *a suspense thriller*, *B* should also be a common noun phrase, as in choice (C).
(Chapter 13 Lesson 3: Parallelism)

9. A   The original phrasing is clear, complete, logical, and concise.

10. E   Since the sentence suggests that Jermaine was playing at that time, and as if he had played over an extended time in the past, the tense should be the past perfect progressive: *had been playing*.
(Chapter 13 Lesson 9: Tricky Tenses)

11. C   This sentence lists the factors that influence the price of crude oil, and so the items in this list should follow the law of parallelism. The first two items in the list have the form *"something in something"*: *advancements in technology* and *patterns in the weather*, so the third item should have the same form: *changes in the global political climate*. Also, choice (C) is the most concise of the choices.
(Chapter 13 Lesson 3: Parallelism)

12. B   The *Mississippi Pastoral*, since it is italicized, must be the title of something. The context of the sentence makes it clear that it must be one of the *symphonies* performed in the festival. This modifying phrase is so far from the word it modifies, however, that its meaning is unclear. Choice (B) moves this phrase closer to the word it modifies, and so is the best choice.
(Chapter 13 Lesson 8: Other Misplaced Modifiers)

13. B   The sentence shows a contrast between a fact and a misconception. All of the choices indicate this contrast in some way, but only choice (B) uses the correct idiom: it *originated in* China and so did not *originate in* Italy.
(Chapter 13 Lesson 5: Pronoun Agreement)

14. C   The sentence indicates that the students do two things, so these should have parallel phrasing.

The course requires that *students work* and that *students discuss*.
(Chapter 13 Lesson 3: Parallelism)

15. **D** The opening phrase is a participial phrase that modifies *Brice*, and not *Brice's stubbornness*, so the original phrase dangles. Choices (C) and (D) correct the dangling problem, but (D) is the only one that is phrased logically.
(Chapter 13 Lesson 7: Dangling and Misplaced Participles)

16. **A** The original phrasing is clear, complete, logical, and concise.

17. **C** The original "sentence" does not convey a complete thought because it does not contain a verb. Choice (C) corrects this problem most concisely.
(Chapter 13 Lesson 2: Trimming Sentences)

18. **B** The original phrasing is unidiomatic. The seat belts do not save lives *for* people, but save the lives *of* people. Choice (B) is the most concise yet idiomatic choice.
(Chapter 13 Lesson 10: Idiom Errors)

19. **E** The original phrasing is not parallel. If the demand increases *as the value of the dollar increases*, then it also increases *as trade barriers are lowered*.
(Chapter 13 Lesson 3: Parallelism)

20. **D** As it is originally phrased, the sentence is a run-on, because two independent clauses are joined with only a comma. By changing this phrasing to that in choice (D), the second clause becomes dependent, and this fixes the problem. Choice (C) also creates a dependent clause, but it is illogical—officials are people, not things.
(Chapter 13 Lesson 15: Coordinating Ideas)

21. **B** Since the *dumbwaiter* is only one thing, choice (B) should be changed to *which has been*.
(Chapter 13 Lesson 5: Pronoun Agreement)

22. **D** Since the closing happened after the rush of investors, the use of the perfect infinitive *to have closed* is illogical. It should be changed to *to close*.
(Chapter 13 Lesson 9: Tricky Tenses)

23. **C** This sentence suggests the parallel phrasing *not only A but also B*. This requires changing choice (C) to *but also*.
(Chapter 13 Lesson 3: Parallelism)

24. **D** The subject of the sentence is *geometric design*, which is singular. Therefore the verb should be *attests to*.
(Chapter 13 Lesson 1: Subject-Verb Disagreement)

25. **B** The word *tactful* means *sensitive to the needs of others in delicate social situations*, and so is illogical in this context. The correct word here is *tactical*, which means *pertaining to tactics*.
(Chapter 13 Lesson 11: Diction Errors)

26. **E** This sentence is correct.

27. **A** The phrase *usually never* is logically contradictory. More logical phrasings that convey the right idea are *hardly ever* or *almost never*.
(Chapter 13 Lesson 12: Other Problems with Modifiers)

28. **B** The correct phrasing is *as she (is)* because the pronoun is the subject of an implied verb
(Chapter 18 Lesson 6: Pronoun Case)

29. **B** The word should be *cleanly*, because it is an adverb modifying the verb *burns*.
(Chapter 13 Lesson 12: Other Problems with Modifiers)

30. **E** The sentence is correct.

31. **B** The subject of the verb is *ministers*, which is plural. The correct verb conjugation, then, is *have*.
(Chapter 13 Lesson 1: Subject-Verb Disagreement)

32. **C** This phrase is the antecedent of the pronoun *it*, which is singular. Therefore it should be *the fax machine*.
(Chapter 13 Lesson 5: Pronoun Agreement)

33. **E** The sentence is correct.

34. **A** The subject of the verb is *two oxygen tanks*, which is plural. The correct phrasing, then, is *there are*.
(Chapter 13 Lesson 1: Subject-Verb Disagreement)

35. **A** The pronoun *they* has an ambiguous antecedent: it could refer to *many people* or *different fields*. Therefore, rephrasing it to *these fields* clarifies the sentence.
(Chapter 13 Lesson 5: Pronoun Agreement)

36. **B** This sentence should be placed between sentence 2 and sentence 3, because sentence 2 describes *one way*, and the inserted sentence follows logically

with *another way*. The inserted sentence must also precede sentence 3, because the inserted sentence provides only background information to the central idea of the passage, which is introduced in sentence 3.
(Chapter 13 Lesson 15: Coordinating Ideas)

---

37. **D**   The original phrasing is awkward and wordy. Choice (D) is far more concise, and is the clearest of the alternatives because it uses the active voice, a strong subject, and a concrete subject.
(Chapter 13 Lesson 15: Coordinating Ideas)

---

38. **E**   The original phrasing contains two errors in idiom: *used for projecting* and *projecting on*. The correct idioms are *used to project* and *project onto*. Also, since the sentence discusses many artists and many images, there must have been many *screens*.
(Chapter 13 Lesson 10: Idiom Errors)

(Chapter 13 Lesson 12: Other Problems with Modifiers)

---

39. **E**   Choice (A) undermines the purpose of the essay by suggesting that its topic is irrelevant, and so is a very poor ending. Choice (B) does not provide a concluding thought, but rather an incidental comment that is only tangentially related to the rest of the essay. Choice (C) likewise introduces a thought begging to be developed, rather than a conclusive and *hopeful* note as the question requires. Choice (D) seems to provide a conclusive thought with an air of hope, but it is not appropriate to the final paragraph, which discusses the *controversy* behind Hockney's theory. Choice (E) fits logically into such a discussion and also provides a hopeful concluding thought.
(Chapter 13 Lesson 15: Coordinating Ideas)

PRACTICE PSAT 2

ANSWER SHEET

Last Name: _____   First Name: _____

Date: _____   Testing Location: _____

Administering the Test

- **Remove this answer sheet** from the book and use it to record your answers to this test.
- This test will require **2 hours and 10 minutes** to complete. Take this test in one sitting.
- Use a stopwatch to time yourself on each section. The time limit for each section is written clearly at the beginning of each section. The first four sections are 25 minutes long, and the last section is 30 minutes long.
- Each response must **completely fill the oval. Erase all stray marks completely**, or they may be interpreted as responses.
- **You must stop ALL work on a section when time is called.**
- If you finish a section before the time has elapsed, check your work on that section. **You may NOT move on to the next section until time is called.**
- Do not waste time on questions that seem too difficult for you.
- Use the test book for scratchwork, but you will only receive credit for answers that are marked on the answer sheets.

Scoring the Test

- Your scaled score, which will be determined from a conversion table, is based on your raw score for each section.
- You will receive one point toward your raw score for every correct answer.
- You will receive no points toward your raw score for an omitted question.
- For each wrong answer on a multiple-choice question, your raw score will be reduced by 1/4 point. For each wrong answer on a numerical "grid-in" question (Section 4, questions 29–38), your raw score will receive no deduction.

SECTION 1 — Critical Reading — 25 minutes

Time: 25 minutes

Start: _____

Stop: _____

1. Ⓐ Ⓑ Ⓒ Ⓓ Ⓔ   9. Ⓐ Ⓑ Ⓒ Ⓓ Ⓔ   17. Ⓐ Ⓑ Ⓒ Ⓓ Ⓔ
2. Ⓐ Ⓑ Ⓒ Ⓓ Ⓔ   10. Ⓐ Ⓑ Ⓒ Ⓓ Ⓔ   18. Ⓐ Ⓑ Ⓒ Ⓓ Ⓔ
3. Ⓐ Ⓑ Ⓒ Ⓓ Ⓔ   11. Ⓐ Ⓑ Ⓒ Ⓓ Ⓔ   19. Ⓐ Ⓑ Ⓒ Ⓓ Ⓔ
4. Ⓐ Ⓑ Ⓒ Ⓓ Ⓔ   12. Ⓐ Ⓑ Ⓒ Ⓓ Ⓔ   20. Ⓐ Ⓑ Ⓒ Ⓓ Ⓔ
5. Ⓐ Ⓑ Ⓒ Ⓓ Ⓔ   13. Ⓐ Ⓑ Ⓒ Ⓓ Ⓔ   21. Ⓐ Ⓑ Ⓒ Ⓓ Ⓔ
6. Ⓐ Ⓑ Ⓒ Ⓓ Ⓔ   14. Ⓐ Ⓑ Ⓒ Ⓓ Ⓔ   22. Ⓐ Ⓑ Ⓒ Ⓓ Ⓔ
7. Ⓐ Ⓑ Ⓒ Ⓓ Ⓔ   15. Ⓐ Ⓑ Ⓒ Ⓓ Ⓔ   23. Ⓐ Ⓑ Ⓒ Ⓓ Ⓔ
8. Ⓐ Ⓑ Ⓒ Ⓓ Ⓔ   16. Ⓐ Ⓑ Ⓒ Ⓓ Ⓔ   24. Ⓐ Ⓑ Ⓒ Ⓓ Ⓔ

SECTION 2 — Math — 25 minutes

Time: 25 minutes

Start: _____

Stop: _____

1. Ⓐ Ⓑ Ⓒ Ⓓ Ⓔ   9. Ⓐ Ⓑ Ⓒ Ⓓ Ⓔ   17. Ⓐ Ⓑ Ⓒ Ⓓ Ⓔ
2. Ⓐ Ⓑ Ⓒ Ⓓ Ⓔ   10. Ⓐ Ⓑ Ⓒ Ⓓ Ⓔ   18. Ⓐ Ⓑ Ⓒ Ⓓ Ⓔ
3. Ⓐ Ⓑ Ⓒ Ⓓ Ⓔ   11. Ⓐ Ⓑ Ⓒ Ⓓ Ⓔ   19. Ⓐ Ⓑ Ⓒ Ⓓ Ⓔ
4. Ⓐ Ⓑ Ⓒ Ⓓ Ⓔ   12. Ⓐ Ⓑ Ⓒ Ⓓ Ⓔ   20. Ⓐ Ⓑ Ⓒ Ⓓ Ⓔ
5. Ⓐ Ⓑ Ⓒ Ⓓ Ⓔ   13. Ⓐ Ⓑ Ⓒ Ⓓ Ⓔ
6. Ⓐ Ⓑ Ⓒ Ⓓ Ⓔ   14. Ⓐ Ⓑ Ⓒ Ⓓ Ⓔ
7. Ⓐ Ⓑ Ⓒ Ⓓ Ⓔ   15. Ⓐ Ⓑ Ⓒ Ⓓ Ⓔ
8. Ⓐ Ⓑ Ⓒ Ⓓ Ⓔ   16. Ⓐ Ⓑ Ⓒ Ⓓ Ⓔ

SECTION 3
Critical Reading
25 minutes

25. Ⓐ Ⓑ Ⓒ Ⓓ Ⓔ
26. Ⓐ Ⓑ Ⓒ Ⓓ Ⓔ
27. Ⓐ Ⓑ Ⓒ Ⓓ Ⓔ
28. Ⓐ Ⓑ Ⓒ Ⓓ Ⓔ
29. Ⓐ Ⓑ Ⓒ Ⓓ Ⓔ
30. Ⓐ Ⓑ Ⓒ Ⓓ Ⓔ
31. Ⓐ Ⓑ Ⓒ Ⓓ Ⓔ
32. Ⓐ Ⓑ Ⓒ Ⓓ Ⓔ

33. Ⓐ Ⓑ Ⓒ Ⓓ Ⓔ
34. Ⓐ Ⓑ Ⓒ Ⓓ Ⓔ
35. Ⓐ Ⓑ Ⓒ Ⓓ Ⓔ
36. Ⓐ Ⓑ Ⓒ Ⓓ Ⓔ
37. Ⓐ Ⓑ Ⓒ Ⓓ Ⓔ
38. Ⓐ Ⓑ Ⓒ Ⓓ Ⓔ
39. Ⓐ Ⓑ Ⓒ Ⓓ Ⓔ
40. Ⓐ Ⓑ Ⓒ Ⓓ Ⓔ

41. Ⓐ Ⓑ Ⓒ Ⓓ Ⓔ
42. Ⓐ Ⓑ Ⓒ Ⓓ Ⓔ
43. Ⓐ Ⓑ Ⓒ Ⓓ Ⓔ
44. Ⓐ Ⓑ Ⓒ Ⓓ Ⓔ
45. Ⓐ Ⓑ Ⓒ Ⓓ Ⓔ
46. Ⓐ Ⓑ Ⓒ Ⓓ Ⓔ
47. Ⓐ Ⓑ Ⓒ Ⓓ Ⓔ
48. Ⓐ Ⓑ Ⓒ Ⓓ Ⓔ

Time: 25 minutes

Start: _____

Stop: _____

SECTION 4
Math
25 minutes

21. Ⓐ Ⓑ Ⓒ Ⓓ Ⓔ
22. Ⓐ Ⓑ Ⓒ Ⓓ Ⓔ
23. Ⓐ Ⓑ Ⓒ Ⓓ Ⓔ
24. Ⓐ Ⓑ Ⓒ Ⓓ Ⓔ

25. Ⓐ Ⓑ Ⓒ Ⓓ Ⓔ
26. Ⓐ Ⓑ Ⓒ Ⓓ Ⓔ
27. Ⓐ Ⓑ Ⓒ Ⓓ Ⓔ
28. Ⓐ Ⓑ Ⓒ Ⓓ Ⓔ

Time: 25 minutes

Start: _____

Stop: _____

29. 30. 31.  32.  33.

34. 35. 36.  37. 38.

SECTION 5
Writing Skills
30 minutes

1. Ⓐ Ⓑ Ⓒ Ⓓ Ⓔ
2. Ⓐ Ⓑ Ⓒ Ⓓ Ⓔ
3. Ⓐ Ⓑ Ⓒ Ⓓ Ⓔ
4. Ⓐ Ⓑ Ⓒ Ⓓ Ⓔ
5. Ⓐ Ⓑ Ⓒ Ⓓ Ⓔ
6. Ⓐ Ⓑ Ⓒ Ⓓ Ⓔ
7. Ⓐ Ⓑ Ⓒ Ⓓ Ⓔ
8. Ⓐ Ⓑ Ⓒ Ⓓ Ⓔ
9. Ⓐ Ⓑ Ⓒ Ⓓ Ⓔ
10. Ⓐ Ⓑ Ⓒ Ⓓ Ⓔ
11. Ⓐ Ⓑ Ⓒ Ⓓ Ⓔ
12. Ⓐ Ⓑ Ⓒ Ⓓ Ⓔ
13. Ⓐ Ⓑ Ⓒ Ⓓ Ⓔ

14. Ⓐ Ⓑ Ⓒ Ⓓ Ⓔ
15. Ⓐ Ⓑ Ⓒ Ⓓ Ⓔ
16. Ⓐ Ⓑ Ⓒ Ⓓ Ⓔ
17. Ⓐ Ⓑ Ⓒ Ⓓ Ⓔ
18. Ⓐ Ⓑ Ⓒ Ⓓ Ⓔ
19. Ⓐ Ⓑ Ⓒ Ⓓ Ⓔ
20. Ⓐ Ⓑ Ⓒ Ⓓ Ⓔ
21. Ⓐ Ⓑ Ⓒ Ⓓ Ⓔ
22. Ⓐ Ⓑ Ⓒ Ⓓ Ⓔ
23. Ⓐ Ⓑ Ⓒ Ⓓ Ⓔ
24. Ⓐ Ⓑ Ⓒ Ⓓ Ⓔ
25. Ⓐ Ⓑ Ⓒ Ⓓ Ⓔ
26. Ⓐ Ⓑ Ⓒ Ⓓ Ⓔ

27. Ⓐ Ⓑ Ⓒ Ⓓ Ⓔ
28. Ⓐ Ⓑ Ⓒ Ⓓ Ⓔ
29. Ⓐ Ⓑ Ⓒ Ⓓ Ⓔ
30. Ⓐ Ⓑ Ⓒ Ⓓ Ⓔ
31. Ⓐ Ⓑ Ⓒ Ⓓ Ⓔ
32. Ⓐ Ⓑ Ⓒ Ⓓ Ⓔ
33. Ⓐ Ⓑ Ⓒ Ⓓ Ⓔ
34. Ⓐ Ⓑ Ⓒ Ⓓ Ⓔ
35. Ⓐ Ⓑ Ⓒ Ⓓ Ⓔ
36. Ⓐ Ⓑ Ⓒ Ⓓ Ⓔ
37. Ⓐ Ⓑ Ⓒ Ⓓ Ⓔ
38. Ⓐ Ⓑ Ⓒ Ⓓ Ⓔ
39. Ⓐ Ⓑ Ⓒ Ⓓ Ⓔ

Time: 30 minutes

Start: _____

Stop: _____

Section 1

Time—25 minutes
24 Questions (1–24)

Each of the sentences below is missing one or two portions. Read each sentence. Then select the choice that most logically completes the sentence, taking into account the meaning of the sentence as a whole.

Example:

Rather than accepting the theory unquestioningly, Deborah regarded it with - - - - - -.

   (A) mirth
   (B) sadness
   (C) responsibility
   (D) ignorance
   (E) skepticism

Ⓐ Ⓑ Ⓒ Ⓓ ●

---

1. The lawyer was - - - - - - in her cross-examination; her aggressive questioning continued for what seemed like days.

   (A) unrelenting
   (B) sympathetic
   (C) casual
   (D) reflective
   (E) stagnant

2. A disaster was - - - - - - by the quick-thinking helmsman, who steered the ship away from the rocks that had - - - - - - emerged from the ocean.

   (A) predicted . . permanently
   (B) forestalled . . reluctantly
   (C) averted . . suddenly
   (D) dispelled . . passively
   (E) avoided . . serenely

3. The - - - - - - decline in the price of the stock caught many investors unprepared; they had expected its value to remain - - - - - - for many months, if not years.

   (A) sudden . . volatile
   (B) gradual . . low
   (C) improvised . . uniform
   (D) cumbersome . . liquid
   (E) precipitous . . stable

4. Unlike our previous manager, who often made sudden decisions without thinking carefully about them, the new one is far more - - - - - - and deliberate.

   (A) capricious
   (B) pensive
   (C) remorseful
   (D) intolerant
   (E) inexorable

5. When spending long periods of time among the tribal peoples whose cultures they are studying, - - - - - - should be careful not to introduce harmful germs or disruptive technologies into those societies.

   (A) herpetologists
   (B) oncologists
   (C) ornithologists
   (D) agronomists
   (E) anthropologists

GO ON TO THE NEXT PAGE ▶▶▶

6. Alicia's -------- performance in the company play astonished those who were familiar with her ------- demeanor at work.

(A) fearless..intrepid
(B) emotional..stolid
(C) inspiring..meticulous
(D) stable..attentive
(E) amusing..flippant

7. In an industry in which truthfulness is too often an impediment to success, many salespeople have had to become masters of -------- in order to advance their careers.

(A) prevarication
(B) timidity
(C) certitude
(D) perseverance
(E) consumption

8. Gina considered her thousands of hours of volunteer work to be selfish rather than -------; she simply enjoyed working with people and did not consider herself a paragon of -------.

(A) altruistic..magnanimity
(B) egotistical..placidity
(C) generous..diversity
(D) reassuring..distortion
(E) desperate..obsession

The passages below are followed by questions based on their content and the relationship between the passages. Answer each question based on what is stated or implied in the passages.

Questions 9–12 are based on the following passages.

Passage 1

Line   Reasoning is a vital human activity. For
        unlike some animals able to function
        instinctively, we need knowledge in order to
        survive. At the very least, knowledge facilitates
5   the pursuit of happiness. Some knowledge can
        be gained directly. In this way we know, for
        example, that an object in front of us looks

orange and tastes sweet. But we cannot know
that it is edible and nutritious, or that it
10   contains vitamin C, which prevents scurvy,
without a process of reasoning. Similarly, we
do not need reasons to believe that every
triangle has three angles. But we cannot know
that the angles of a triangle add up to 180°
15   without evidence or proof. The vast bulk of
human knowledge is based on reasoning.
Indeed, our knowledge can be described as a
pyramid, in which what is directly evident
provides the foundation on which all other
20   beliefs are based.

Passage 2

        All people ever want from us in an argument
is agreement, and they do not care how they get
it. Believing this leads to a very suspicious,
critical, investigative attitude which is the first
25   requirement of successful argumentation.
Believe nothing. The less we believe, the less
likely we are to believe something false. When
arguing we always assume our opposers are
both sharp-minded and low-minded, so we
30   never underrate their ability. Since many
argument maneuvers are not made *consciously*,
the simple fact that people are sincere does not
mean we can trust their arguments (though we
might be able to trust them). They might think
35   their arguments are correct when they may be
full of errors. And, some people who believe in a
position also believe that anything furthering
the position is acceptable. This is the attitude
that "the end justifies the means." But while they
40   are already convinced, we are not. We want the
straight goods, while they want to sell us a bill
of goods.

9. Passage 1 suggests that knowledge can be "gained directly" (line 5–6) through

(A) instruction
(B) instinctive reactions
(C) reading
(D) reasoning
(E) the physical senses

First paragraph: *An Introduction to Logic*, ©1985 by Prentice-Hall, Inc. Reproduced courtesy of the author, Professor Wayne A. Davis.
Second paragraph: *How to Win an Argument*, Michael A. Gilbert. © 1965 McGraw Hill, New York, p. 12. Reproduced courtesy of the author, Michael A. Gilbert.

GO ON TO THE NEXT PAGE ▸▸▸

10. The author of Passage 2 suggests that we should have which of the following attitudes toward argumentation?

(A) delight
(B) skepticism
(C) avoidance
(D) humor
(E) trust

11. The sentence beginning on line 30 ["Since many argument . . . to trust them"] assumes that many of those who make arguments

(A) are not fully aware of their reasoning
(B) are not sincere about their positions
(C) are too trusting of others
(D) rely on manipulative strategies of argumentation
(E) do not have any formal training in logical analysis

12. The two passages differ in their perspectives on belief in that Passage 1 regards it as

(A) a necessary prerequisite of scientific reasoning, while Passage 2 regards it to be exclusively in the domain of religious thought
(B) something that can be gained directly, while Passage 2 regards it as something unattainable
(C) the ultimate goal of reasoning, while Passage 2 claims it can be antithetical to good argumentation
(D) the result of an instinctual process, while Passage 2 regards it as the result of a conscious process
(E) something that people are trying to avoid, while Passage 2 regards it as something that everyone seeks

The questions below are to be answered on the basis of what is stated or implied in the passages below or the introductory material that precedes the passages.

Questions 13–24 are based on the following passages.

The following passages discuss the moral and social value of capital punishment.

Passage 1

Line   Reverence for human life is part of the moral foundation of a just society. The only justification for causing death is to prevent the deaths of others. Thus, individuals have the
5   right to use deadly force to save their own lives from criminal aggressors, and countries have the right to wage war to prevent their own destruction. Likewise, a community can and should use capital punishment to protect the
10   lives of its members. Saint Thomas Aquinas wrote: "The slaying of an evildoer is lawful inasmuch as it is directed to the welfare of the whole community."
    When judiciously applied as a punishment
15   for the willful killing of innocents, the death penalty serves to deter those who would murder and to protect society from those who have murdered. By reserving the ultimate penalty of death for those who wantonly kill, we are
20   clearly proclaiming our special reverence for life. It is society's ultimate means of self-defense.
    The death of a criminal can certainly be justified if it prevents the future deaths of
25   innocent victims. Since death is the greatest punishment a society can impose, it stands to reason that it is the most powerful way to deter those who would commit a crime.
    Economist Isaac Ehrlich compared the
30   murder rate in the United States with the rate of executions between 1933 and 1967. His conclusion: "The trade-off between the execution of an offender and the lives of potential victims it might have saved was of the
35   order of magnitude of 1 for 8." In other words, each use of the death penalty seems to have deterred the killing of eight potential victims. Homicides decreased by almost 36 percent immediately following a well-publicized

GO ON TO THE NEXT PAGE ▶▶▶

40 execution, according to the research of
sociologist David Phillips.

The absence of a death threat encourages
crime. In 1950, when 82 criminals were
executed, there were 7,020 homicides. In 1980,
45 after a decade of virtual abandonment of the
death penalty, there were 22,958 homicides, a
300 percent increase. As society became more
concerned with the life of the criminal, lives of
innocent victims became cheaper.

50 Another value of the death penalty is one
that has been unfairly disparaged in the
softhearted modern era; punishment for the
sake of doing justice. Some attack this notion
by labelling it retribution, and argue that our
55 system should seek only deterrence and
rehabilitation. Deterrence is important, but it is
a practical and utilitarian consideration rather
than a moral and just one. Rehabilitation is a
worthy ideal, but justice demands more.
60 Without punishment for the sake of
punishment, the age-old notion of justice
falters.

One clear way we show our respect for life is
to decree that those who unjustly take a life
65 should forfeit their own. The crime of murder is
so horrendous, so irrevocable, that it demands
a commensurate punishment. Those who
blithely dismiss retribution as barbaric are the
ones who in fact demean the value of human
70 life. As philosopher Ernest van den Haag says:
"Life becomes cheaper as we become kinder to
those who wantonly take it."

Passage 2

Reverence for human life is part of the moral
foundation of a just society. That is why no one
75 can justly kill another; just as it is wrong for an
individual to do so, it is wrong for the state to
do so.

There is simply no convincing evidence that
executions deter potential murders. In the
80 reams of studies on the issue, only one serious
work, that of economist Isaac Ehrlich, showed
a correlation, and his analysis was soundly
refuted by investigations into his procedures.
The most thorough research is that of Professor
85 J. Thorsten Sellin of the University of
Pennsylvania, who compared the murder rate
in similar communities that have and do not
have the death penalty. His conclusions:
"Capital executions have no demonstrable
90 effect on homicide rates. Police are killed as
frequently in death penalty states as in

abolitionist states . . . abolition or restoration of
the death penalty has no demonstrable effect on
the rate of subsequent homicides."
95 There is no logical reason to believe that
capital punishment will deter murder any more
effectively than a life prison term will. Murder
is an irrational act, often a crime of passion.
Those who kill tend not to balance the possible
100 penalties against their desires.

The fact that capital punishment violates
our ideal of rehabilitation is even more
apparent, for the death penalty is absolute and
irrevocable. It could permit the greatest
105 injustice of all, the murder of an innocent
person. Human beings are fallible, which is one
reason they should not have power of life and
death over each other. The number of murder
convictions that have been discovered to be in
110 error is a powerful argument against the death
penalty.

Fundamentally, the argument boils down to
the just role of the state. As part of the social
contract, people surrender some of their
115 natural rights to the state. But the state has no
right to take an individual's life, just as no
individual has that right over another. Most
murders are committed for reasons of
vengeance. We should not legitimize
120 murderous vengeance by making it part of our
system of justice.

13. The first paragraph of Passage 1 suggests that
individuals, communities, and countries

(A) must categorically denounce violence
(B) are using outdated theories of morality
(C) each have different priorities
(D) all have similar rights of self-protection
(E) do not adequately punish criminals

14. Passage 1 mentions Saint Thomas Aquinas as
one who

(A) denounces war
(B) values the rights of individuals over those
of society
(C) supports the death penalty
(D) was a former criminal
(E) shares a common misconception

GO ON TO THE NEXT PAGE ▶▶▶

15. According to Passage 1, a society can proclaim its "special reverence for life" (lines 20–21) by

(A) abstaining from declarations of war
(B) protecting those who are accused of crimes from physical retribution
(C) severely punishing those who kill others
(D) providing for the needs of the poor
(E) protecting children from abusive adults

16. Which of the following, if true, would most directly refute the argument made in the fifth paragraph (lines 43–47)?

(A) Most Americans favor the death penalty.
(B) Executions have always been highly publicized events.
(C) In 1950, the electric chair was more widely used than lethal injection.
(D) Most criminals come from low-income families.
(E) Far fewer murder weapons were available and the population was much lower in 1950 than in 1980.

17. Which of the following best characterizes Ernest van den Haag's attitude toward those who commit homicide, as it is presented in Passage 1?

(A) utilitarian and practical
(B) harsh and uncompromising
(C) sympathetic
(D) scientifically analytical
(E) indifferent

18. The author of Passage 2 mentions "reams" (line 80) in order to emphasize

(A) the dramatic effect of capital punishment in deterring crime
(B) the amount of legislation pertaining to capital punishment
(C) the many cases in which an innocent person has been executed for a crime
(D) the quantity of research that demonstrates no relationship between executions and future murder rates
(E) the extent to which the public disapproves of capital punishment

19. It can be inferred that "abolitionist states" (line 92) are those that

(A) have eliminated the death penalty
(B) have more severe penalties for those who kill police officers than for those who kill nonofficers
(C) use capital punishment intermittently
(D) use executions solely to deter future crimes
(E) do not have coherent laws regarding the punishment of those who commit homicide

20. In saying that "the death penalty is absolute" (line 103), the author of Passage 2 indicates that execution is

(A) endorsed by legislative bodies
(B) supported by a majority of the population
(C) a deterrent for potential criminals
(D) an act that cannot be reversed
(E) foreign to most systems of morality

21. Which of the following topics does the author of Passage 2 discuss in both the first paragraph and the final paragraph?

(A) revenge
(B) the social contract
(C) a just society
(D) rehabilitation
(E) motives for killing

22. Which of the following best characterizes the attitudes of the two passages toward the work of Isaac Ehrlich?

(A) Both passages praise it, but also indicate minor flaws.
(B) Passage 1 cites it uncritically, but Passage 2 dismisses it.
(C) Both passages use it to support their theses.
(D) Passage 1 criticizes it on moral grounds, while Passage 2 criticizes it on scientific grounds.
(E) Passage 1 praises it highly, but Passage 2 abstains from evaluating it.

23. Which of the following best summarizes the position of each passage on the death penalty?

(A) Both passages claim that it is ineffective.
(B) Passage 1 claims that it is a moral duty, while Passage 2 claims that it is a practical necessity.
(C) Passage 1 claims that it should be used only as a deterrent, while Passage 2 claims that it can be used for strictly punitive purposes.
(D) Passage 1 claims that it is necessary to a just society, while Passage 2 claims that is antithetical to a just society.
(E) Passage 1 claims that it demeans life, while Passage 2 claims that it honors life.

24. Those who "attack this notion" (line 53) are most likely to include which of the following?

(A) Saint Thomas Aquinas
(B) The author of Passage 1
(C) David Phillips
(D) The author of Passage 2
(E) Isaac Ehrlich

STOP

You may check your work, on this section only, until time is called.

Section 2

Time—25 minutes

20 Questions (1–24)

Directions for Multiple-Choice Questions

In this section, solve each problem, using any available space on the page for scratchwork. Then decide which is the best of the choices given and fill in the corresponding oval on the answer sheet.

- You may use a calculator on any problem. All numbers used are real numbers.
- Figures are drawn as accurately as possible EXCEPT when it is stated that the figure is not drawn to scale.
- All figures lie in a plane unless otherwise indicated.

Reference Information

$A = \pi r^2$ $A = \ell w$ $A = \frac{1}{2}bh$ $V = \ell wh$ $V = \pi r^2 h$ $c^2 = a^2 + b^2$ Special Right Triangles

$C = 2\pi r$

The arc of a circle measures 360°.

Every straight angle measures 180°.

The sum of the measures of the angles in a triangle is 180°.

---

1. Which of the following integers, when doubled, produces a number that is 2 greater than a multiple of 6?

(A) 5
(B) 6
(C) 7
(D) 8
(E) 9

2. What is the circumference, in inches, of a circle with an area of 16π square inches?

(A) 2π
(B) 4π
(C) 8π
(D) 16π
(E) 32π

3. If 4.5 zots are equivalent to 1 zat, how many zats are equivalent to 36 zots?

(A) 8
(B) 9
(C) 12
(D) 16
(E) 81

$$1, 2, 1, 2, 1, 2 \ldots$$

4. If the sequence above continues as shown, what is the sum of the first 20 terms?

(A) 20
(B) 30
(C) 40
(D) 45
(E) 60

GO ON TO THE NEXT PAGE ▶▶▶

5. Tom's weight is 20 pounds less than twice Carl's weight. If together Tom and Carl weigh 340 pounds, how much does Tom weigh?

(A) 120 pounds
(B) 160 pounds
(C) 180 pounds
(D) 200 pounds
(E) 220 pounds

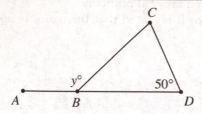

Note: Figure not drawn to scale.

6. In the figure above, if $BC = BD$, what is the value of y?

(A) 100
(B) 120
(C) 125
(D) 130
(E) 140

7. For all integers n, if $*n$ is defined by the equation

$$*n = \begin{cases} \dfrac{n}{3} & \text{if } n \text{ is divisible by 3} \\ 3n & \text{if } n \text{ is not divisible by 3} \end{cases}$$

which of the following is equivalent to $*10$?

(A) $*3$
(B) $*9$
(C) $*20$
(D) $*30$
(E) $*90$

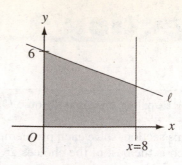

Note: Figure not drawn to scale.

8. In the figure above, if line ℓ has a slope of $-1/2$, what is the area of the shaded region, in square units?

(A) 28
(B) 32
(C) 36
(D) 40
(E) 42

9. If each box of pencils contains x pencils, and if 10 boxes of pencils cost d dollars, how many dollars should it cost to buy $50x$ pencils?

(A) $\dfrac{d}{5x}$

(B) $\dfrac{x}{5d}$

(C) $\dfrac{5}{dx}$

(D) $5d$

(E) $5dx$

10. Beth had planned to run an average of 6 miles per hour in a race. She had a very good race and actually ran at an average speed of 7 miles per hour, finishing 10 minutes sooner than she would have if she had averaged 6 miles per hour. How long was the race?

(A) 6 miles
(B) 7 miles
(C) 18 miles
(D) 60 miles
(E) 70 miles

GO ON TO THE NEXT PAGE ▶▶▶

11. On a certain map that is drawn to scale, 1.5 centimeters is equivalent to 2 miles. If two cities are 35 miles apart, how many centimeters apart should they be on this map?

   (A) 24.75
   (B) 26.00
   (C) 26.25
   (D) 45.00
   (E) 46.33

12. Jose needs a $\frac{5}{8}$-meter length of copper pipe to complete a project. Which of the following lengths of pipe can be cut to the required length with the least length of pipe left over?

   (A) $\frac{9}{16}$ meter
   (B) $\frac{3}{5}$ meter
   (C) $\frac{3}{4}$ meter
   (D) $\frac{4}{5}$ meter
   (E) $\frac{5}{6}$ meter

13. If $\frac{1}{2}a = 2b = 4c = 24$, what is the value of $a + b + c$?

   (A) 24
   (B) 40
   (C) 42
   (D) 64
   (E) 66

14. If $x^2 > 6$, which of the following statements must be true?

   I. $|x| > 3$
   II. $(x - 2)(x + 2) > 2$
   III. $x + 1,000 > 0$

   (A) II only
   (B) I and II only
   (C) I and III only
   (D) II and III only
   (E) I, II, and III

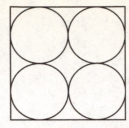

15. Each of the four circles in the figure above is tangent to two sides of the square and also tangent to two of the other circles. If each circle has a circumference of 4π inches, what is the area, in square inches, of the square?

   (A) 4
   (B) 16
   (C) 24
   (D) 32
   (E) 64

$$abc + df + g$$

16. If the expression above is an odd number, then at most how many of the integers a, b, c, d, f, and g could be even?

   (A) Two
   (B) Three
   (C) Four
   (D) Five
   (E) Six

17. The average (arithmetic mean) of six integers is 32. If the numbers are all different, and if none is less than 10, what is the greatest possible value of any of these integers?

   (A) 127
   (B) 132
   (C) 137
   (D) 142
   (E) 147

GO ON TO THE NEXT PAGE ▶▶▶

18. If $\left(\frac{1}{4}\right)^n = 2^{-3}$, then $n =$

(A) $-\frac{3}{2}$

(B) $-\frac{2}{3}$

(C) $\frac{2}{3}$

(D) $\frac{3}{2}$

(E) 3

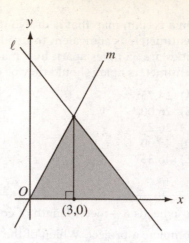

Note: Figure not drawn to scale.

20. If line m in the figure above has a slope of 2 and the shaded triangle has an area of 24 square units, what is the slope of line ℓ?

(A) -6

(B) $-\frac{6}{5}$

(C) $-\frac{5}{6}$

(D) $-\frac{2}{3}$

(E) $-\frac{1}{3}$

19. How many integers from 100 to 1,000 contain NO repeated digits? (Numbers like 252 and 991 are considered to have repeated digits.)

(A) 632
(B) 648
(C) 720
(D) 810
(E) 900

STOP

You may check your work, on this section only, until time is called.

Section 3

Time—25 minutes
24 Questions (25–48)

Each of the sentences below is missing one or two portions. Read each sentence. Then select the choice that most logically completes the sentence, taking into account the meaning of the sentence as a whole.

Example:

Rather than accepting the theory unquestioningly, Deborah regarded it with ------.

(A) mirth
(B) sadness
(C) responsibility
(D) ignorance
(E) skepticism

25. Since the publisher had only allotted 250 pages to the book, the author's 400-page manuscript had to be drastically ------.

(A) enhanced
(B) pursued
(C) accelerated
(D) abridged
(E) conducted

26. The critics agreed that the first film was ------ and artistically daring; but that its sequel, in direct contrast, was bland and ------.

(A) enchanting..conventional
(B) dull..innovative
(C) humorous..unique
(D) tedious..pedestrian
(E) trite.. foreign

27. For an inveterate gambler, even ------ rewards reinforce the obsession, disproving the assumption that payoffs must be consistent to support an addiction.

(A) luxurious
(B) steadfast
(C) sporadic
(D) placid
(E) continual

28. Those who denied a ------ between exercise and ------ were suprised by the finding that those who walked at least 10 miles per week lived an average of 7 years longer than those who were sedentary.

(A) causation..exhaustion
(B) relationship..diet
(C) dispute..fulfillment
(D) mediation..prosperity
(E) correlation..longevity

29. Even to physicists who study it for decades, subatomic physics is ------; to laypeople, then, it is downright ------.

(A) forthcoming..responsive
(B) daunting..fallow
(C) cryptic..routine
(D) challenging..inscrutable
(E) fatuous..singular

GO ON TO THE NEXT PAGE ▶▶▶

Each passage below is followed by one or two questions based on its content. Answer each question based on what is stated or implied in the passage that precedes it.

Questions 30–31 are based on the following passage.

Line   *Media* is a term that describes a variety of
people, structures, technologies, and
relationships. Traditional definitions of media
focus on messages that originate from some
5   institutional source, travel through some
channel, and reach a large, anonymous
audience. Although these basic components of
media are present today, their nature has
changed with the advent of new electronic
10   forms of communication. The current media
environment does not always fit this
description. Although previously constrained
by cost, individuals can now offer messages
inexpensively via the internet. Audiences for
15   media messages are sometimes small and on
occasion make themselves known to the
producers of the messages.

30.   The passage suggests that, unlike traditional
media, many new forms of media

(A) originate from institutions
(B) are anonymous
(C) focus exclusively on selling products or
services
(D) are difficult to understand
(E) are more accessible to users

31.   The tone of this passage is best described as

(A) pleading
(B) humorous
(C) objective
(D) skeptical
(E) indignant

Questions 32–33 are based on the following passage

Line   When mathematicians speak frankly about
their discipline, they tend to circle around a
fundamental question: are the ideas of
mathematicians discovered or invented?

5   Mathematicians speak of proofs as "elegant" or
"beautiful," praising work for its aesthetic
nature. Dr. Mina Rees, a logician, wrote,
"Mathematics is both inductive and deductive,
needing, like poetry, persons who are creative
10   and have a sense of the beautiful for its surest
progress." But, even so, most mathematicians
say that when they do their work they are
making discoveries—the great ideas of
mathematics exist independently of them. They
15   stumble upon these ideas, awkwardly, perhaps,
but eventually finding truths of nature.
        Dr. John Conway, for one, cannot imagine
he is doing anything but discovering results
that exist without him and that he did not
20   create. Why? "Because they couldn't be
otherwise than what they are," he said. "Two
and two might be five and pigs might fly. But in
the world I come from, two and two are four
and pigs don't fly."

32.   The quotation in lines 8–11 ("Mathematics is
both … its surest progress") makes the point
that

(A) mathematicians are often very good
writers
(B) aesthetic sense is an asset to mathematical
thought
(C) many mathematical claims cannot be
proved
(D) mathematical truths are discovered, not
invented
(E) poets have made many contributions to
mathematical progress

33.   The quotation in lines 21–24 ("Two and
two … don't fly") is intended to refute the idea
that

(A) mathematical discoveries do not require
intuition
(B) mathematical proofs are beautiful
(C) mathematicians do not require formal
education to make profound discoveries
(D) logic is never violated in mathematics
(E) mathematical truths are open to
interpretation

First paragraph: *Persuasion in the Media Age*, Timothy
    A. Borchers. ©2002 McGraw-Hill, p. 82
Second paragraph: "*Scientists at Work*," Science Times. ©2000
    McGraw-Hill, p. 99

GO ON TO THE NEXT PAGE ▸▸▸

**Questions 34–40 are based on
the following passage.**

*The following is an excerpt from a book about
American journalism that was written in 1939.*

Line   It is singular that newspapers, seldom
bashful about their virtues, have made so little
to-do about their achievements in crusading. As
champions of reforms, as defenders of
5   individuals, as protagonists of their
communities, they have exercised influences
quite as important as the transmission of
information and the expression of opinion.
    Yet this has been written only in
10   fragmentary form. Historians of daily journals,
biographers of newspaper publishers and
editors, and occasionally an instructor in a
school of journalism, have dealt with it in
particular, sometimes in its larger aspects, but
15   not sweepingly. A treatment at once minute and
comprehensive, indeed, is impossible within
the scope of a single volume, such is the wealth
of material available. What is presented here
must attempt a representative selection.
20   More than once a newspaper, at the
conclusion of a successful campaign, has
preened itself or has paid tribute to a fellow. Yet
by and large our most articulate institution,
sometimes almost as vainglorious as politics,
25   has been surprisingly reticent about one of its
primary responsibilities. It has nevertheless
recognized crusading as a natural function and
as a responsibility, and has discharged it for the
most part admirably, sometimes at severe
30   sacrifice. That there has been default in certain
areas none can deny, but the account balances
heavily to the credit of the press and to the
benefit of the public.
    Here lies the best argument for newspaper
35   freedom not only from governmental
interference but from the coercion of a
capitalist economy. The history of our press
since colonial days is shot through with the
struggle for unrestricted capital activity and the
40   right to crusade. Every crusade implies, to be
sure, the expression of opinion or of an attitude,
but it involves more than that. It means also a
willingness to fight if need be. It means,
according to my dictionary, "to contend
45   zealously against any evil, or on behalf of any
reform."
    To contend zealously must mean surely to
struggle with ardent devotion. The zeal which
fires a crusading editor may bring him to the

50   boiling point of fanaticism, and has done it time
and again. None who has undertaken a
campaign in the certainty that it would entail
loss of circulation and advertising, perhaps
permanently, was not a fanatic, just on the
55   sunny side of lunacy. Skeptics who deny that
campaigns are ever undertaken for other than
sordid motives may disabuse their minds by
examining the record. If newspapers have faced
actual losses in the discharge of their duties as
60   public servants, then they have an
unmistakable claim to the guarantee of the
First Amendment.

34.   The author's attitude toward newspapers is
best described as

    (A) laudatory
    (B) objectively analytical
    (C) exasperated
    (D) jocular
    (E) harshly critical

35.   In the first paragraph, the author indicates
surprise at the fact that newspapers

    (A) are still profitable
    (B) are not more widely read
    (C) transmit so little information that is
worthy of notice
    (D) do not exercise more influence in their
communities
    (E) have not acknowledged one of their
virtues

36.   The "wealth of material" (lines 17–18) is
information about

    (A) the means by which reporters get their
information
    (B) the corporate structure of certain
newspapers
    (C) the reading practices of Americans
    (D) the ability of newspapers to effect change
in their communities
    (E) the relationship between newspapers and
other media

Newspaper Crusaders: A Neglected Story, Silas Bent. ©1939
McGraw-Hill pp. 3–4. *Printed with permission of Ayer Company
Publishers.*

GO ON TO THE NEXT PAGE ▶▶▶

37. As it is used in line 28, "discharged" most
     nearly means

     (A) electrified
     (B) dismissed
     (C) accomplished
     (D) emitted
     (E) refused

38. The "skeptics" (line 55) believe that
     newspapers

     (A) are becoming less popular
     (B) are fundamentally self-serving
     (C) are fanatical about political causes
     (D) do not take advantage of the First
         Amendment
     (E) should be replaced by other forms of
         media

39. As it is used in line 49, "fires" most nearly
     means

     (A) destroys
     (B) dismisses
     (C) initiates
     (D) stimulates
     (E) interrogates

40. The final paragraph suggests that crusading
     poses a potential danger to newspapers by

     (A) causing a loss of revenue
     (B) increasing competition with other
         newspapers
     (C) encouraging reporters to abandon
         journalistic principles
     (D) restricting the freedom of journalists
     (E) spurring good journalists to quit their jobs

**Questions 41–48 are based on the
following passage.**

*The following passage discusses some of the work
of Henri Matisse, an influential twentieth-
century French artist.*

Line   Henri Matisse wrote in a 1948 letter:
          *I have always tried to hide my own efforts and
        wished my work to have the lightness and
        joyousness of a springtime which never lets
5   anyone know the labors it has cost. So I am*
*afraid the young, seeing in my work only the
apparent facility and negligence in the drawing,
will use this as an excuse for dispensing with
certain efforts I believe necessary.*

10   Matisse's *The Flowing Hair*, made of cut and
       pasted paper, appears so unlabored that one
       might misunderstand all that is behind and
       went before it. Few would guess that a work as
       lively and energetic as *The Flowing Hair* was
15   executed by a man eighty-three years old.
       Moreover, *The Flowing Hair* is just one work in
       an entire cut paper series of joyous, colorful
       pieces suggesting dance and music.
          The Flowing Hair shows no three-
20   dimensional modeling of the forms or shadows.
       The female form is depicted as an intense blue
       shape of flowing curves, a graceful rhythmic
       arabesque. The whole figure—arms, legs, torso,
       even the hair—seems to be in motion. The
25   footless legs have strength, and the arms have
       almost become wings. One feels that at any
       moment the figure might dance off the paper.
          How did Matisse, as an old man, come to
       create such vital works? One answer is his
30   development of a new art form: cut paper, or as
       it is called in French, *Papier collé, Papier
       découpé*, or *découpage*. Partly crippled by illness
       and repeated surgery in 1941, Matisse came to
       rely on the less strenuous medium of cut paper,
35   rather than oil painting, as his major art form.
       He could work in the new art form lying down
       in his bed or from his chair. He had studio
       assistants paint expanses of paper in brilliant
       hues of gouache, an opaque watercolor paint,
40   to his requirements. The old master then cut
       shapes directly out of the paper without any
       preparatory drawings. He felt he was drawing
       with scissors. He loved the directness of the
       process of cutting. After the shapes were cut,
45   Matisse instructed his assistants to pin the
       pieces onto his studio wall. The many tiny
       pinholes in the paper show that Matisse had his
       helpers adjust the arrangement of the cutouts
       numerous times until the most expressive
50   spatial relationship had been achieved.
          Out of the painted, cut, and pasted papers
       arose a self-sufficient medium of great pictorial
       strength. Cutting paper with scissors gave him
       a very strong feeling for line and enabled him to
55   develop forms of great simplicity and economy.
       Yet Matisse did not use his scissors to declare
       war on drawing and painting. Rather, his

GO ON TO THE NEXT PAGE ▸▸▸

scissors were an extension of pencil, charcoal
stick, and paintbrush. "My découpages," he
60 stated, "do not break away from my former
pictures. It is only that I have achieved more
completely and abstractly a form reduced to the
essential, and have retained the object, no
longer in the complexity of its space, but as the
65 symbol which is both sufficient and necessary
to make the object exist in its own right, as well
as for the composition in which I have
conceived it."

    Old and crippled, Matisse could have rested
70 on the laurels of his past accomplishments. But
not Matisse. He truly enjoyed the challenge, the
directness, the intimacy of his new approach to
collage. He relished the opportunity to select,
place, and reposition the cut paper shapes. His
75 habit of hard work in the studio was so deeply
rooted and his creative vitality was so strong
that he let nothing, not even bad health,
interrupt his art. In the end, Matisse came to
esteem his cut paper works as the high point of
80 his creative career.

41. The central purpose of this passage is to

(A) contrast the artistic works of Henri
      Matisse with those of his contemporaries
(B) enumerate the merits of *The Flowing Hair*
(C) analyze a controversy regarding the life of
      Henri Matisse
(D) describe the development of a new art
      form
(E) examine several artistic movements of the
      early twentieth century

42. The quotation in lines 2–9 suggests that
Matisse was concerned about people thinking
that his work

(A) was created in an inferior medium
(B) required less effort than it actually did
(C) evoked dark themes
(D) was not valuable
(E) too closely imitated the work of other
      artists

43. The author mentions that Matisse was "eighty-
three years old" (line 15) primarily in order to

(A) emphasize the influence Matisse had on
      the art world in general
(B) indicate that Matisse had begun his
      artistic career late in life
(C) refute the misconception that Matisse
      died young
(D) contrast Matisse's artistic style with that of
      the younger generation of artists
(E) contrast the litheness of Matisse's work
      with his physical condition

44. In line 38, the word "brilliant" most nearly
means

(A) intelligent
(B) flimsy
(C) celebrated
(D) shining
(E) intimidating

45. The quotation from Matisse in lines 59–68
emphasizes which of the following qualities of
découpage?

(A) pictorial simplicity
(B) changeability
(C) vividness
(D) three-dimensionality
(E) transparency

46. The "intimacy" mentioned in line 72
characterizes the relationship between
Matisse and

(A) his critics
(B) his fellow artists
(C) his medium
(D) his philosophy
(E) his assistants

Responding to Art: Form, Content, and Context, Robert Bersson.
©2004 McGraw-Hill, p. 32

GO ON TO THE NEXT PAGE ▶▶▶

47. The passage indicates that the medium of cut paper provided Matisse with all of the following EXCEPT

   (A) ease of use
   (B) the ability to manipulate forms
   (C) pictorial strength
   (D) the feeling of depth
   (E) vitality

48. The final paragraph characterizes Matisse primarily as

   (A) weak and ineffective
   (B) popular and outgoing
   (C) enthusiastic and diligent
   (D) sober and intellectual
   (E) critical and irascible

STOP

You may check your work, on this section only, until time is called.

Section 4

Time—25 minutes
18 Questions (21–38)

Directions for Multiple-Choice Questions

In this section, solve each problem, using any available space on the page for scratchwork. Then decide which is the best of the choices given and fill in the corresponding oval on the answer sheet.

- You may use a calculator on any problem. All numbers used are real numbers.
- Figures are drawn as accurately as possible EXCEPT when it is stated that the figure is not drawn to scale.
- All figures lie in a plane unless otherwise indicated.

Reference Information

$A = \pi r^2$ $A = \ell w$ $A = \frac{1}{2}bh$ $V = \ell wh$ $V = \pi r^2 h$ $c^2 = a^2 + b^2$ Special Right Triangles

$C = 2\pi r$

The arc of a circle measures 360°.
Every straight angle measures 180°.
The sum of the measures of the angles in a triangle is 180°.

---

21. If $\dfrac{18}{15} = \dfrac{x}{5}$, then $x =$

(A) $\dfrac{6}{5}$

(B) 3

(C) $\dfrac{75}{18}$

(D) 6

(E) 54

---

22. What is the height of a triangle with a base of 6 inches and an area of 24 square inches?

(A) 12 inches
(B) 8 inches
(C) 6 inches
(D) 4 inches
(E) 2 inches

Copies of *Artist's World* Magazine Sold

| 2002 | |
| 2003 | |

= 20,000 copies

23. According to the chart above, how many more copies of *Artist's World* were sold in 2003 than in 2002?

(A) 2,500
(B) 5,000
(C) 25,000
(D) 50,000
(E) 250,000

24. What number is 24 less than 3 times itself?

   (A) 12
   (B) 24
   (C) 36
   (D) 48
   (E) 72

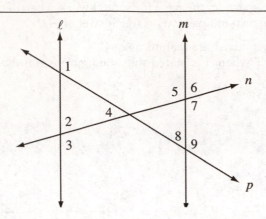

25. In the figure above, line ℓ is parallel to line m. Which of the following pairs of angles must have equal measures?

   I. 1 and 9
   II. 2 and 8
   III. 5 and 7

   (A) I only
   (B) II only
   (C) III only
   (D) I and II only
   (E) I and III only

26. The average (arithmetic mean) of 0, a, and b is $2a$. What is the value of b in terms of a?

   (A) a
   (B) $2a$
   (C) $3a$
   (D) $4a$
   (E) $5a$

27. If a, b, and c are integers greater than 1, and if $ab = 21$ and $bc = 39$, which of the following must be true?

   (A) $a < b < c$
   (B) $a < c < b$
   (C) $b < a < c$
   (D) $b < c < a$
   (E) $c < a < b$

28. David, Charlene, and Rudy earned a total of $22.00 yesterday. If Charlene earned three times as much as David did, and Rudy earned $2.50 less than Charlene did, then how much money did Rudy earn?

   (A) $3.50
   (B) $5.50
   (C) $8.00
   (D) $10.50
   (E) $11.00

GO ON TO THE NEXT PAGE ▶▶▶

Directions for Student-Produced Response Questions

Each of the questions in this section requires you to solve the problem and enter your answer in a grid, as shown below.

- If your answer is 2/3 or .666..., you must enter **the most accurate value the grid can accommodate**, but you may do this in one of four ways:

Start in first column	Start in second column	Grid as a truncated decimal	Grid as a rounded decimal

Grid result here

- In the example above, gridding a response of 0.67 or 0.66 is **incorrect** because it is less accurate than those above.
- The scoring machine cannot read what is written in the top row of boxes. You **MUST** fill in the numerical grid accurately to get credit for answering any question correctly. You should write your answer in the top row of boxes only to aid your gridding.
- Do **not** grid in a mixed fraction like $3\frac{1}{2}$ as $\boxed{3\ 1\ /\ 2}$ because it will be interpreted as $\frac{31}{2}$. Instead, convert it to an improper fraction like $7/2$ or a decimal like 3.5 before gridding.
- None of the answers will be negative, because there is no negative sign in the grid.
- Some of the questions may have more than one correct answer. You must grid only one of the correct answers.
- You may use a calculator on any of these problems.
- All numbers in these problems are real numbers.
- Figures are drawn as accurately as possible EXCEPT when it is stated that the figure is not drawn to scale.
- All figures lie in a plane unless otherwise indicated.

---

29. The ratio of 2.5 to 16 is the same as the ratio of .25 to what number?

30. For all real numbers x and y, let $x \Delta y$ be defined by the equation
$x \Delta y = (xy) - (x + y)$. What is the value of $12 \Delta 6$?

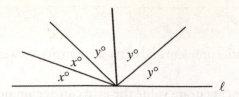

Note: Figure not drawn to scale.

31. In the figure above, if $x = 24$, what is the value of y?

32. One deck of cards consists of six cards numbered 1 through 6, and a second deck consists of six cards numbered 7 through 12. If one card is chosen at random from each deck, and the numbers on these cards are multiplied, what is the probability that this product is an even number?

33. When an integer m is divided by 5, the remainder is 3. When m is divided by 7, the remainder is 1. If m is greater than 40 but less than 80, what is one possible value of m?

34. If $(2x^2 + 5x + 3)(3x + 1) = ax^3 + bx^2 + cx + d$ for all values of x, what is the value of c?

35. In a sequence of numbers, each term except the first is 4 less than 4 times the previous term. If the fourth term in this sequence is 12, what is the first term?

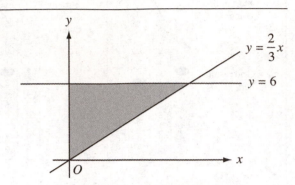

Note: Figure not drawn to scale.

36. In the figure above, the shaded triangle is bounded by the y-axis, the line $y = 6$, and the line $y = \frac{2}{3}x$. What is the area, in square units, of the shaded triangle?

37. The value of $\dfrac{2x + 10}{5} + \dfrac{3x - 2}{5}$ is how much greater than the value of x?

38. If $9\left(\dfrac{1}{3}\right)^n = (3^m)$, what is the value of $m + n$?

STOP

You may check your work, on this section only, until time is called.

Section 5

Time—30 minutes

39 Questions (1–39)

Directions for "Improving Sentences" Questions

Each of the sentences below contains one underlined portion. The portion may contain one or more errors in grammar, usage, construction, precision, diction (choice of words), or idiom. Some of the sentences are correct.

Consider the meaning of the original sentence, and choose the answer that best expresses that meaning. If the original sentence is best, choose (A), because it repeats the original phrasing. Choose the phrasing that creates the clearest, most precise, and most effective sentence.

EXAMPLE:

The children <u>couldn't hardly believe their eyes</u>.

   (A) couldn't hardly believe their eyes
   (B) would not hardly believe their eyes
   (C) could hardly believe their eyes
   (D) couldn't nearly believe their eyes
   (E) could hardly believe his or her eyes

---

1. As a young boy, <u>was when Francis discovered that he could spend his life</u> exploring the ocean he loved so much.

   (A) was when Francis discovered that he could spend his life
   (B) that was when Francis discovered that he could spend his life
   (C) Francis discovered then that his life could be spent
   (D) Francis discovered that he could spend his life
   (E) Francis discovered the spending of his life

2. Paleontologists disputed the authenticity of the <u>discovery, it was believed rather that</u> it was an elaborate hoax.

   (A) discovery, it was believed rather that
   (B) discovery; they believed that
   (C) discovery; but instead they believed that
   (D) discovery in believing that
   (E) discovery, it being believed that

3. Although the race was only five minutes long, James got out of the pool feeling as if <u>swimming</u> across the English Channel.

   (A) swimming
   (B) having swam
   (C) he had swum
   (D) he were swimming
   (E) in swimming

4. People often sign life insurance contracts even before <u>the provisions and contingencies of their policies are known by them</u>.

   (A) the provisions and contingencies of their policies are known by them
   (B) the provisions and contingencies of their policies being known by them
   (C) the provisions of their policies are known by them, or the contingencies
   (D) they know the provisions and contingencies of their policies
   (E) they know neither the provisions nor the contingencies of their policies

GO ON TO THE NEXT PAGE ♦♦♦

5. A major hurdle to educational reform is
    <u>parents expect the school experience to be</u>
    the same as it was decades ago.

    (A) parents expect the school experience
         to be
    (B) parents that are expecting the school
         experience being
    (C) parents are expecting that the school
         experience be
    (D) that parents expect the school experience
         being
    (E) that parents expect the school experience
         to be

6. Perelman was an essayist and travel writer
    <u>and many generations of humorists were
    inspired by him, such as Woody Allen.</u>

    (A) and many generations of humorists were
         inspired by him, such as Woody Allen
    (B) who inspired many generations of
         humorists such as Woody Allen
    (C) that inspired many generations, such as
         Woody Allen, of humorists
    (D) by whom many generation of humorists,
         like Woody Allen, were inspired
    (E) of whom many generations of humorists,
         such as Woody Allen, were inspired

7. <u>The fact is every human language shares a
    basic underlying structure, this a discovery of
    Noam Chomsky.</u>

    (A) The fact is every human language shares
         a basic underlying structure, this a
         discovery of Noam Chomsky.
    (B) Noam Chomsky having discovered that
         every human language shares a basic
         underlying structure.
    (C) Every human language shares a basic
         underlying structure and this Noam
         Chomsky discovered.
    (D) The fact of every human language
         sharing a basic underlying structure was
         discovered by Noam Chomsky.
    (E) Noam Chomsky discovered that every
         human language shares a basic
         underlying structure.

8. We would not be such an obese nation if <u>we
    had to hunt and gather our food as our
    ancestors did</u>.

    (A) we had to hunt and gather our food as
         our ancestors did
    (B) hunting and gathering of our food was
         required of us as our ancestors
    (C) we had to hunt and gather our food as
         our ancestors were doing
    (D) our hunting and gathering of food was as
         required of us as our ancestors
    (E) we had to be hunting and gathering our
         food like our ancestors

9. When your body is more erect, <u>one's mind
    is more alert</u>.

    (A) one's mind is more alert
    (B) your mind is more alert
    (C) your mind's alertness is greater
    (D) the alertness of one's mind increases
    (E) the mind is alerter

10. The reason the tent fell over was <u>that we did
    not anchor the center pole</u>.

    (A) that we did not anchor the center pole
    (B) because we did not anchor the center
         pole
    (C) we did not anchor the center pole
    (D) for our not anchoring the center pole
    (E) because of our not anchoring the center
         pole

11. Unable to meet all of its costs with such
    meager revenue, <u>bankruptcy could not be
    avoided by the small company</u>.

    (A) bankruptcy could not be avoided by the
         small company
    (B) the small company's bankruptcy could not
         be avoided
    (C) the small company could not avoid
         bankruptcy
    (D) it was not possible for the small company
         to avoid bankruptcy
    (E) the bankruptcy of the small company
         could not be avoided

GO ON TO THE NEXT PAGE ♦♦♦

12. The medium of watercolor requires precise brushwork, <u>careful timing and planning must be meticulous</u>.

    (A) careful timing and planning must be meticulous
    (B) the timing careful, and the planning meticulous
    (C) care in the timing, and meticulous planning
    (D) careful timing, and meticulous planning
    (E) care in the timing, and meticulousness in the planning

13. Many visitors were impressed by the monument's sheer <u>size, but for others it was</u> its solemn gravity.

    (A) size, but for others it was
    (B) size; but others thought it was
    (C) size, others were impressed by
    (D) size and not, like for others,
    (E) size; others by

14. Finding the mountain pass treacherous, <u>the safest thing, the expedition leader decided, was to stay in camp another night</u>.

    (A) the safest thing, the expedition leader decided, was to stay in camp another night
    (B) the expedition leader decided that it would be safest to stay in camp another night
    (C) staying in camp another night was the safest thing, the expedition leader decided
    (D) the expedition leader, deciding that the safest thing to do was to stay in camp another night
    (E) it was safest to stay in camp another night, the expedition leader decided

15. Most educators believe <u>peers teach students more values than their</u> school curricula.

    (A) peers teach students more values than their
    (B) it's more their peers that teach students values than their
    (C) that students learn more about values from their peers than from their
    (D) values are taught more by their peers than from a student's
    (E) that students learn more from their peers about values than their

16. The scientists decided to shut down the robot <u>to conserve its energy while they worked to fix</u> its processor.

    (A) to conserve its energy while they worked to fix
    (B) for conserving its energy while they worked on fixing
    (C) to conserve its energy and working to fix
    (D) in conserving its energy and in order to work on fixing
    (E) with regards to conserving its energy as they were working to fix

17. Those critics who deny that films ever do justice to literary <u>masterpieces, often failing</u> to recognize the unique limitations of each art form.

    (A) masterpieces, often failing
    (B) masterpieces in often failing
    (C) masterpieces often fail
    (D) masterpieces, and so often fail
    (E) masterpieces would nevertheless often fail

18. The professor asserted that, although ancient hominids were likely very intelligent, there is little hard evidence <u>of its being true</u>.

    (A) of its being true
    (B) of its truth
    (C) that it is the truth
    (D) of support to the claim
    (E) supporting this claim

19. I sometimes prefer <u>making a selection based on the advice of a friend over</u> my own analysis.

   (A) making a selection based on the advice of a friend over
   (B) to base a selection on the advice of a friend rather than on
   (C) basing a selection on the advice of a friend more than
   (D) making a selection based rather on the advice of a friend instead of
   (E) to make a selection based on what a friend says rather than

20. Marcus, who threw a remarkable pass to Reggie for a touchdown, <u>could not have completed the play if Doug had not made a stunning block</u>.

   (A) could not have completed the play if Doug had not made a stunning block
   (B) would not complete the play if Doug did not make a stunning block
   (C) if it was not Doug's stunning block, then could not have completed the play
   (D) didn't complete the play if not for Doug's stunning block
   (E) would not have completed the play but Doug made a stunning block

---

Directions for "Identifying Sentence Error" Questions

The following sentences may contain errors in grammar, usage, diction (word choice), or idiom. Some of the sentences are correct. No sentence contains more than one error.

If the sentence contains an error, it is underlined and lettered. The parts that are not underlined are correct.

If there is an error, select the part that must be changed to correct the sentence.

If there is no error, choose (E).

EXAMPLE:

By the time <u>they reached</u> the halfway point
                    A
<u>in the race</u>, most <u>of the runners</u> <u>hadn't hardly</u>
      B   C   D
begun to hit their stride. <u>No error</u>
                                     E

---

21. <u>In the basket</u> <u>was</u> several savory treats <u>that</u>
          A   B   C
     Helene knew her friends <u>would enjoy</u>.
                                    D
     <u>No error</u>
         E

22. Our girl scout troop <u>has already raised</u> twice
                                  A
     <u>as much</u> money <u>for the children's hospital</u>
         B   C
     this year as <u>last year</u>. <u>No error</u>
                       D   E

23. Since she was <u>committed to</u> becoming a great
                         A
     stage <u>performer</u>, Noelle <u>studied</u> not only voice
              B   C
     and acting, <u>and</u> dancing and stage combat as
                     D
     well. <u>No error</u>
               E

24. <u>Never seeing</u> a giraffe before, even
           A
     <u>in a picture book</u>, Dina <u>was astonished</u> to
             B   C
     come face to face with <u>one</u> at the city zoo.
                                 D
     <u>No error</u>
         E

25. <u>Having injured herself</u> in an unfortunate stage
              A
     accident during the opening act, the lead

     actress could no longer <u>precede</u> in her role,
                                   B
     and <u>had to be</u> replaced
             C
     by her understudy. <u>No error</u>
                              D   E

26. Ricardo, <u>like</u> so many other freshmen
                  A
     on the varsity team, <u>were intimidated</u> by both
            B   C
     the size and the <u>aggressiveness</u> of his
                            D
     teammates. <u>No error</u>
                      E

27. <u>Having spent</u> enormous sums on
           A
     infrastructure, many new companies

     <u>must operate</u> successfully for many years
           B
     <u>before</u> they <u>can recover</u> their initial
         C   D
     investments.

     <u>No error</u>
         E

28. As a former lead researcher

     <u>at a major observatory</u>, <u>our professor</u> is able
              A   B
     <u>to provide</u> many <u>insights</u> on the most current
         C   D
     astronomical research. <u>No error</u>
                                  E

29. We were surprised at how <u>close</u> the two sisters
                                   A
     resembled <u>each other</u>, even though they <u>were</u>
                    B   C
     actually fraternal,

     <u>rather than identical</u>, twins. <u>No error</u>
             D   E

GO ON TO THE NEXT PAGE ▶▶▶

30. The <u>inspiring</u> movies of Frank Capra, unlike
        A
    many modern directors, <u>capture</u> the most
            B   C
    hopeful <u>aspects</u> of American life. <u>No error</u>
          D   E

31. Such tragedies <u>as</u> the tsunami of December
                A
    2004 <u>show</u> the extent <u>to which</u> nature can
         B   C
    devastate <u>vast areas</u> in a very brief time.
            D
    <u>No error</u>
      E

32. Although they often roam in packs <u>in which</u>
                          A
    they must <u>cooperate</u>, the hyena <u>employs</u>
            B   C
    subtle signs of dominance and submission
    <u>within</u> their groups. <u>No error</u>
     D   E

33. <u>When examining</u> the letters and tape
         A
    recordings from the Oval Office, the extent
    of <u>the deception</u> and <u>illicit</u> behavior of the
          B   C
    President <u>becomes</u> obvious. <u>No error</u>
           D   E

34. Meryl Streep <u>has avoided</u> vocal stereotyping,
              A
    so common <u>among</u> famous actors,
            B
    by <u>adapting</u> her voice with uncanny fluency
       C
    <u>to fit characters</u> with many different
        D
    nationalities. <u>No error</u>
           E

Directions for "Improving Paragraphs" Questions

Below is an early draft of an essay. It requires revision in many areas.

The questions that follow ask you to make improvements in sentence structure, diction, organization, and development. Answering the questions may require you to understand the context of the passage as well as the rules of standard written English.

Questions 35–39 pertain to the following passage.

(1) *When buying consumer goods, we rarely think beyond what we want and what they cost.* (2) *But there are two other important questions we should be asking: where did they come from? and where are they going?* (3) *Unlike long ago, when our consumer goods were usually made locally, we usually don't know the history of the things we buy.* (4) *And then, when we throw it out, or its packaging, we put it out of our minds.*

(5) *The manufacturers of some products, like paper and wood, employ unsustainable methods that destroy forests irrevocably.* (6) *This provides income for local workers, but then soon they must move on because they have rendered the environment unlivable.*

(7) *Other manufacturers employ slave labor, prison labor, or child labor to create cheap products like clothing or electronic equipment.* (8) *Some believe that producers should be permitted to search for the cheapest possible labor to make a good profit, but not if it means being inhumane to workers.*

(9) *Many consumer items contain dangerous chemicals that end up poisoning streams and groundwater.* (10) *In order to turn a short-term profit, manufacturers sometimes sacrifice whole ecosystems for generations to come.*

(11) *We cannot afford to be ignorant of where our consumer goods come from or where they are going.* (12) *As cogs in the machine of consumerism, we are as much responsible as the manufacturers themselves for the pollution and injustices that these items may cause.*

GO ON TO THE NEXT PAGE ▶▶▶

35. Which of the following is the best revision of the underlined portion of sentence 3 (reproduced below)?

Unlike long ago, when our consumer goods were usually made locally, we usually don't know the history of the things we buy.

(A) we don't hardly
(B) today we rarely
(C) the consumers of today don't usually
(D) it's less likely today that we
(E) it's not as likely to

36. In context, which of the following is the best version of sentence 4 (reproduced below)?
And then, when we throw it out, or its packaging, we put it out of our minds.

(A) We also rarely give much thought to where these items, or their packaging, will go when we discard them.
(B) Nevertheless, we also rarely think of where these items or their packaging will end up when we throw them out.
(C) We also rarely think about where it, or its packaging, goes when we throw it out.
(D) Then, when we throw them out, it's out of our minds.
(E) Throwing them out is what simply puts them out of our minds.

37. In context, which of the following is the best version of the underlined portion of sentence 6 (reproduced below)?
This provides income for local workers, but then soon they must move on because they have rendered the environment unlivable.

(A) (as it is now)
(B) This is good for some local workers in providing income, but bad in making them move because they have rendered
(C) Which provides income for local workers, but forces them to move because it has rendered
(D) Although providing income for local workers, it forces them to move by rendering
(E) Although such methods provide income for local workers, they also soon force the workers to move on by rendering

38. In context, which of the following is the best version of the underlined portion of sentence 8 (reproduced below)?
Some believe that producers should be permitted to search for the cheapest possible labor to make a good profit, but not if it means being inhumane to workers.

(A) (as it is now)
(B) but even though that means being inhumane to workers
(C) but sometimes this search leads to inhumane practices
(D) and that means being inhumane to workers
(E) but it shouldn't mean being inhumane to workers

39. Which of the following sentences, if placed before sentence 9 to begin the fourth paragraph, would provide the most logical transition?

(A) The low prices of such items hardly seem worth it.
(B) It really doesn't take much effort to become aware of some of the problems in manufacturing.
(C) Some consumers are becoming aware of these problems and changing their buying habits.
(D) We should consider not only the manufacture of consumer goods, but their disposal as well.
(E) Many manufacturers, however, are more responsible in their practices.

STOP

You may check your work, on this section only, until time is called.

ANSWER KEY

Section 1 Critical Reading	Section 3 Critical Reading	Section 2 Math	Section 4 Math	Section 5 Writing
☐ 1. A	☐ 25. D	☐ 1. C	☐ 21. D	☐ 1. D
☐ 2. C	☐ 26. A	☐ 2. C	☐ 22. B	☐ 2. B
☐ 3. E	☐ 27. C	☐ 3. A	☐ 23. D	☐ 3. C
☐ 4. B	☐ 28. E	☐ 4. B	☐ 24. A	☐ 4. D
☐ 5. E	☐ 29. D	☐ 5. E	☐ 25. E	☐ 5. E
☐ 6. B	☐ 30. E	☐ 6. A	☐ 26. E	☐ 6. B
☐ 7. A	☐ 31. C	☐ 7. E	☐ 27. C	☐ 7. E
☐ 8. A	☐ 32. B	☐ 8. B	☐ 28. C	☐ 8. A
☐ 9. E	☐ 33. E	☐ 9. D		☐ 9. B
☐ 10. B	☐ 34. A	☐ 10. B	# Right (A):	☐ 10. A
☐ 11. A	☐ 35. E	☐ 11. C		☐ 11. C
☐ 12. C	☐ 36. D	☐ 12. C	――――――	☐ 12. D
☐ 13. D	☐ 37. C	☐ 13. E	# Wrong (B):	☐ 13. E
☐ 14. C	☐ 38. B	☐ 14. A		☐ 14. B
☐ 15. C	☐ 39. D	☐ 15. E	――――――	☐ 15. C
☐ 16. E	☐ 40. A	☐ 16. D	# (A) $-\frac{1}{4}$ (B):	☐ 16. A
☐ 17. B	☐ 41. D	☐ 17. B		☐ 17. C
☐ 18. D	☐ 42. B	☐ 18. D	☐ 29. 1.6 or 8/5	☐ 18. E
☐ 19. A	☐ 43. E	☐ 19. B	☐ 30. 54	☐ 19. B
☐ 20. D	☐ 44. D	☐ 20. B	☐ 31. 44	☐ 20. A
☐ 21. C	☐ 45. A		☐ 32. 3/4 or .75	☐ 21. B
☐ 22. B	☐ 46. C		☐ 33. 43 or 78	☐ 22. D
☐ 23. D	☐ 47. D		☐ 34. 14	☐ 23. D
☐ 24. D	☐ 48. C		☐ 35. 1.5 or 3/2	☐ 24. A
			☐ 36. 27	☐ 25. B
			☐ 37. 8/5 or 1.6	☐ 26. C
			☐ 38. 2	☐ 27. E
				☐ 28. D
				☐ 29. A
				☐ 30. B
				☐ 31. E
				☐ 32. C
				☐ 33. A
				☐ 34. E
				☐ 35. B
				☐ 36. A
				☐ 37. E
				☐ 38. C
				☐ 39. D

# Right (A):	# Right (A):	# Right (A):	# Right (A):	# Right (A):
――――――	――――――	――――――	――――――	――――――
# Wrong (B):	# Wrong (B):	# Wrong (B):		# Wrong (B):
――――――	――――――	――――――		――――――
# (A) $-\frac{1}{4}$ (B):	# (A) $-\frac{1}{4}$ (B):	# (A) $-\frac{1}{4}$ (B):		# (A) $-\frac{1}{4}$ (B):

SCORE CONVERSION TABLE

How to score your test

Use the answer key on the previous page to determine your raw score on each section. Your raw score on any section is equal to the number of correct answers on that section minus 1/4 of the number of wrong answers, with the exception of the mathematical "grid-in" section, on which wrong answers are not deducted from your score. Remember to add the raw scores from Sections 1 and 3 to get your Critical Reading raw score, and to add the raw scores from Sections 2 and 4 to get your Math raw score. Write the three raw scores here:

Raw Critical Reading score (Section 1 + Section 3): _____

Raw Math score (Section 2 + Section 4): _____

Raw Writing score (Section 5): _____

Use the table below to convert these to scaled scores.

Scaled scores: Critical Reading: _____   Math: _____   Writing: _____

Raw Score	Critical Reading Scaled Score	Math Scaled Score	Writing Scaled Score	Raw Score	Critical Reading Scaled Score	Math Scaled Score	Writing Scaled Score
48	80			20	49	52	54
47	80			19	48	51	52
46	78			18	47	50	51
45	76			17	46	48	50
44	74			16	45	47	49
43	72			15	44	46	48
42	71			14	43	45	46
41	69			13	42	44	45
40	68			12	41	43	44
39	67		80	11	40	42	43
38	66	80	80	10	39	41	41
37	64	77	78	9	38	40	40
36	63	74	77	8	37	39	39
35	62	72	76	7	36	38	37
34	62	70	74	6	34	36	36
33	61	68	73	5	33	35	35
32	60	66	71	4	32	34	33
31	59	65	69	3	30	32	32
30	58	64	68	2	29	30	31
29	57	62	66	1	27	29	30
28	56	61	65	0	25	26	29
27	55	60	63	−1	22	23	28
26	54	59	62	−2	20	20	27
25	54	58	60	−3	20	20	25
24	54	57	59	−4	20	20	24
23	52	55	57	−5	20	20	22
22	51	54	56	−6	20	20	21
21	50	53	55	−7 or less	20	20	20

Detailed Answer Key

Section I

1. A If she was *aggressive* for *what seemed like days*, she must have been quite *tenacious*. *unrelenting* = stubbornly persistent; *reflective* = pensive, thoughtful; *stagnant* = showing no movement or progress for a long period of time.

2. C If the helmsman *steered the ship away from the rocks*, then clearly the disaster was *avoided*. If he had to be *quick-thinking*, the rocks must have emerged *suddenly*. *forestalled* = put off until a later time; *averted* = prevented; *dispelled* = halted the spread of a wrong idea; *passively* = without effort or action; *serenely* = calmly.

3. E If investors *expected [the stock's] value to remain [steady] for many months*, they would be surprised by a *rapid* decline. *volatile* = explosive, prone to rapid change; *improvised* = performed quickly and without planning; *uniform* = having a consistent, monotonous quality; *cumbersome* = burdensome; *liquid* = quickly convertible to cash; *precipitous* = steep and rapid.

4. B If the new manager does not make *sudden decisions without thinking*, she must be more *thoughtful*. *capricious* = inclined to act on a whim; *pensive* = thoughtful; *inexorable* = unstoppable

5. E Those who study human cultures are *anthropologists*. *herpetologists* = scientists who study reptiles; *oncologists* = physicians specializing in cancer; *ornithologists* = scientists who study birds; *agronomists* = scientists who study farming.

6. B If *those who were familiar with* Alicia's demeanor were *surprised* by something she did, then she must have done something out of character. Look for the word pair that describes opposite kinds of behaviors. *intrepid* = fearless; *stolid* = unemotional; *meticulous* = paying close attention to details; *flippant* = inappropriately jocular, prone to making jokes at the wrong times.

7. A If *truthfulness is...an impediment to success* in a certain field, then to be successful in that field one must learn to *avoid the truth*. *prevarication* = willful avoidance of the truth; *timidity* = shyness; *certitude* = certainty; *perseverance* = ability to remain committed to a task.

8. A Most people would consider *thousands of hours of volunteer work* to be *selfless* rather than *selfish*, but Gina obviously thinks differently. She does not consider herself a *paragon* (prime example) of *generosity*. *altruistic* = selfless; *magnanimity* = generosity; *egotistical* = self-centered; *placidity* = calmness; *diversity* = variation within a population.

9. E The passage states that one example of knowledge that can be *gained directly* is that something *looks orange and tastes sweet* (lines 7–8). Such knowledge can only be gained through the physical senses.

10. B The statement *believe nothing* (line 26) and what follows indicates that the author is advocating a skeptical attitude toward argumentation.

11. A Passage 2 states that *many argument maneuvers are not made consciously* (lines 30–31), thereby suggesting that those making arguments aren't always fully aware of their own reasoning.

12. C The author of Passage 1 states that *the vast bulk of human knowledge is based on reasoning* (lines 15–16), and that reasoning from direct knowledge is the *foundation on which all other beliefs are based* (lines 19–20); in other words, belief is the result of reasoning. The author of Passage 2, however, says *believe nothing* (line 26), and, although this is clearly a hyperbolic statement, the author intends us to regard our beliefs skeptically.

13. D The first paragraph states that *individuals have the right...to save their own lives...and countries have the right...to prevent their own destruction* (lines 4–8).

14. C By saying that *the slaying of an evildoer is lawful*, Aquinas clearly supports the death penalty.

15. C The passage states that we proclaim our special reverence for life by *reserving the ultimate penalty of death for those who wantonly kill* (lines 18–19).

16. E The argument being made here is that the increase in homicides between 1950 and 1980 was due to the *abandonment of the death penalty*; yet no alternative explanations for such a rise are considered. A refutation, then, would cite other possible reasons for this rise, such as a rise in population and the availability of weapons.

---

17. **B** Mr. van den Haag says that *life becomes cheaper as we become kinder to those who wantonly take it* (lines 71–72), thereby suggesting that life is honored as we become less kind to killers. Therefore, his attitude toward killers is harsh and uncompromising.

---

18. **D** These *reams* are the many *studies on the issue [of whether executions deter potential murders]* (lines 79–80). The author then goes on to say that these studies, save one that was *soundly refuted* (lines 82–83), show that no correlation exists.

---

19. **A** The *abolitionist states* (line 92) are contrasted directly with those that have capital executions; therefore abolitionst states are those that have abolished the death penalty.

---

20. **D** The author of Passage 2 states that *the death penalty is absolute and irrevocable.* This means that it cannot be taken back if it is rendered in error, as the author fears it may be.

---

21. **C** The author discusses the *moral foundation of a just society* (lines 73–74) in the first paragraph and the *just role of the state* (line 113) in the final paragraph.

---

22. **B** Passage 1, in lines 29–41, uses Ehrlich's research to support the thesis that executions are effective. Passage 2, however, states that this research was *soundly refuted* (lines 82–83).

---

23. **D** The two passages take clearly opposing views on the necessity of the death penalty to a just society. Passage 1 regards the death penalty as *clearly proclaiming our special reverence for life* (lines 20–21), while Passage 2 regards it as *murderous vengeance* (line 120) that must not be legitimized.

---

24. **D** The author of Passage 2 clearly would *attack this notion [of employing execution as sheer retribution]* and in fact does so by criticizing it as *murderous vengeance* (line 120).

Section 2

1. **C** This one is pretty straightforward. Simply double each number given in the choices. This gives 10, 12, 14, 16, and 18. The right answer will be a number that is two more than a multiple of 12, so subtract 2 from each one, getting 8, 10, 12, 14, and

16, and choose the multiple of 12. This gives an answer of (C).
(Chapter 8 Lesson 7: Divisibility)

---

2. **C** If the circle has an area of 16π square inches, just use the area formula for a circle (remember, it's in the reference information on every test) to find the radius:

$$16\pi = \pi r^2$$
Divide by π: $\qquad 16 = r^2$
Take the square root: $\quad 4 = r$

Then use the circumference formula to find the circumference: $c = 2\pi r = 2\pi(4) = 8\pi$.
(Chapter 11 Lesson 8: Circles)

---

3. **A** Write the equation: 4.5 zots = 1 zat

Divide by 4.5: $\qquad$ 1 zot $= 2/9$ zat
Multiply by 36: $\quad$ 36 zots $= 72/9$ zats $= 8$ zats

(Chapter 9 Lesson 1: Solving Equations)

---

4. **B** Think of the sequence of 20 terms as being 10 sets of 2 terms, (1, 2). Since each set as a sum of $1 + 2 = 3$, the sum of the 20 terms is $3(10) = 30$.
(Chapter 7 Reasoning Skill 3: Finding Patterns)

---

5. **E** This one is best done algebraically, although you can work backward from the answer choices, as well. If you do it algebraically, start by saying that Tom weighs t pounds and Carl weighs c pounds. If Tom weighs 20 pounds less than twice Carl's weight, then $t = 2c - 20$. If together they weigh 340 pounds, then $t + c = 340$. Since you are looking for Tom's weight, eliminate c from the system through substitution:

$$t + c = 340$$
Subtract t: $\qquad\qquad\qquad\qquad c = 340 - t$
Substitute $340 - t$ for c in the
first equation ($t = 2c - 20$): $\quad t = 2(340 - t) - 20$
Distribute: $\qquad\qquad\qquad\qquad t = 680 - 2t - 20$
Simplify: $\qquad\qquad\qquad\qquad\ t = 660 - 2t$
Add $2t$: $\qquad\qquad\qquad\qquad\quad 3t = 660$
Divide by 3: $\qquad\qquad\qquad\qquad\ t = 220$

Don't forget to check your answer. If they weigh 340 pounds altogether, then Carl must weigh $340 - 220 = 120$ pounds. Check that this satisfies the first condition, namely, that Tom weighs 20 pounds less than twice Carl's weight: $220 = 2(120) - 20$. Yes!
(Chapter 9 Lesson 7: Word Problems)

6. **A**   As always, be sure to mark up the diagram with the information you are given or can figure out.

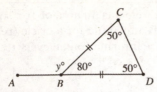

Since $BC = BD$, the two angles opposite those sides must be equal also, so $\angle BCD = 50°$. Since the sum of the angles in a triangle is always $180°$, $\angle CBD = 180 - 50 - 50 = 80°$. Since $\angle ABC$ is supplementary to $\angle CBD$ because they form a straight angle, then $y = 180 - 80 = 100$.
(Chapter 11 Lesson 1: Lines and Angles)

7. **E**   First evaluate *10. Since 10 is not a multiple of 3, *10 = 3(10) = 30. Now check to see which choice is also equivalent to 30. [Be careful not to jump right to choice (D) just because it contains a 30!] Following the instructions gives (A) *3 = 3/3 = 1, (B) *9 = 9/3 = 3, (C) *20 = 3(20) = 60, (D) *30 = 30/3 = 10, and (E) *90 = 90/3 = 30.
(Chapter 10 Lesson 1: New Symbol or Term Problems)

8. **B**   First notice that the shaded region consists of a right triangle and a rectangle, the areas of which you can find easily once you know the base and height of each. As always, mark up the diagram.

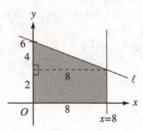

Remember that the slope of the line is simply the "rise" between two points divided by the "run" between those same two points. Consider line ℓ between the y-axis and the line $x = 8$. Clearly, the "run" here is 8. Since the slope of line ℓ is $-1/2$,

$$\text{rise}/8 = -1/2$$
$$\text{Multiply by 8:} \quad \text{rise} = -4$$

So line ℓ descends 4 units between the y-axis and the line $x = 8$, as shown in the diagram. Since line ℓ intercepts the y-axis at 6, the height of the rectangle

must be $6 - 4 = 2$. The area of the rectangle, then, is $(8)(2) = 16$, and the area of the right triangle is $(\frac{1}{2})(8)(4) = 16$. The area of the shaded region, then, is $16 + 16 = 32$.
(Chapter 11 Lesson 4: Coordinate Geometry)
(Chapter 11 Lesson 5: Areas and Perimeters)

9. **D**   You can use simple algebra or plug in simple values for x and d, whichever is easier. If each box contains x pencils, then 10 boxes contain $10x$ pencils, which you are told cost d dollars. Simply multiplying by 5 shows that $50x$ pencils cost $5d$ dollars.
Alternatively, you could just pick simple values like $x = 20$ and $d = 6$. This would mean that 10 boxes of 20 pencils cost 6 dollars, or $10 \times 20 = 200$ pencils cost 6 dollars. The question now becomes: how much do $50x = (50)(20) = 1,000$ pencils cost? A proportion might be handy:

$$\frac{200 \text{ pencils}}{6 \text{ dollars}} = \frac{1,000 \text{ pencils}}{y \text{ dollars}}$$
$$\text{Cross-multiply:} \quad 200y = 6,000$$
$$\text{Divide by 200:} \quad y = 30$$

Now, if you plug $x = 20$ and $d = 6$ into the answer choices, you will see that only choice (D) gives the value of 30.
(Chapter 9 Lesson 7: Word Problems)
(Chapter 8 Lesson 4: Ratios and Proportions)

10. **B**   First notice that this is a rate problem and remember the rate formula: *distance = rate × time*. Compare the real race with the "planned" race. Beth had planned to run at 6 mph and finish in t hours. Therefore, using the rate formula, you can express the distance of the race as $6t$ miles. But she actually ran the race at 7 mph and finished in $t - 1/6$ hours. (Remember that 10 minutes is $10/60 = 1/6$ of an hour.) So the race distance can also be expressed as $7(t - 1/6)$. Since the distance is the same in either case,

$$7(t - 1/6) = 6t$$
$$\text{Distribute:} \quad 7t - 7/6 = 6t$$
$$\text{Subtract } 6t: \quad t - 7/6 = 0$$
$$\text{Add } 7/6: \quad t = 7/6$$

Therefore, the distance is $6t = 6(7/6) = 7$ miles
(Chapter 10 Lesson 4: Rate Problems)

11. C   Since the map is drawn to scale, you can set up a proportion:

$$\frac{1.5 \text{ cm}}{2 \text{ miles}} = \frac{x \text{ cm}}{35 \text{ miles}}$$

Cross-multiply: $52.5 = 2x$

Divide by 2: $26.25 = x$

(Chapter 8 Lesson 4: Ratios and Proportions)
(Chapter 11 Lesson 6: Similar Figures)

12. C   Since comparing decimals is easier than comparing fractions, it's probably best to convert all the fractions to decimals with your calculator. Since the project requires $5/8 = .625$ meter of pipe, the correct answer must be no less than .625. To minimize the waste, we must find the smallest length that is greater than .625. "Decimalizing" the choices gives (A) .5625, (B) .6, (C) .75, (D) .8, and (E) .83. The smallest length greater than .625 is (C) .75.

(Chapter 10 Lesson 3: Numerical Reasoning Problems)

13. E   Just focus on one equation at a time to find the values of the unknowns:

$$4c = 24$$

Divide by 4: $c = 6$

$$2b = 24$$

Divide by 2: $b = 12$

$$\left(\frac{1}{2}\right)a = 24$$

Multiply by 2: $a = 48$

Therefore $a + b + c = 48 + 12 + 6 = 66$.
(Chapter 9 Lesson 1: Solving Equations)

14. A   Think about the statement $x^2 > 6$. Notice that both positive values, like $x = 5$, and negative values, like $x = -5$, satisfy this inequality. (Try them and see!) The square root of 6 is $\pm 2.449...$, so if x^2 is greater than 6, x must be either greater than $2.449...$ or *less* than $-2.449...$. Therefore x could equal 2.5, which shows that statement I is not necessarily true (because $|2.5|$ is not greater than 3). Also, x could be $-1,000,000$, because anything less than $-2.449...$ will work, so statement III is not necessarily true (because $-1,000,000 + 1,000$ is not greater than 0). Now, if you simply eliminate all of the answer choices containing statement I or statement III, you are left only with (A). So statement II must be true. If you want to be sure, a little algebra will show that statement II is equivalent to the

given statement and therefore must be true.

$$(x-2)(x+2) > 2$$

FOIL: $x^2 + 2x - 2x - 4 > 2$

Simplify: $x^2 - 4 > 2$

Add 4: $x^2 > 6$

(Chapter 9 Lesson 6: Inequalities, Absolute Values, and Plugging In)

15. E   As always, mark up the diagram with the information as you get it.

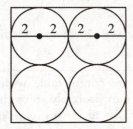

You are given the circumference of the circles, and asked to find the area of the square. So, you must find the relationship between the circles and the square. You can use the circumference formula to find the radius of each circle:

$$4\pi = 2\pi r$$

Divide by 2π: $2 = r$

Now notice that one side of the square has the length of 4 radii, as shown in the diagram. So the length of one side of the square is $(4)(2) = 8$. The area of the square is found by squaring the length of one side: $s^2 = 8^2 = 64$.

(Chapter 11 Lesson 8: Circles)
(Chapter 11 Lesson 5: Areas and Perimeters)

16. D   Since your task is to *maximize* the number of evens in this set, it is best to first ask whether they can *all* be even. Notice that this gives (even)(even) (even) + (even)(even) + (even). Remember that the product of an even number and any other integer is always even, and that the sum of two even numbers is always even. Therefore this expression reduces to (even) + (even) + (even), which necessarily yields an even number. This can't be, though, because we are told that the result must be odd. To get an odd result, all we would have to do is change the last number, g, to an odd number. (Check it and see!) Therefore, the maximum number of evens in this set is five.

(Chapter 10 Lesson 3: Numerical Reasoning Problems)

17. **B**   If the average of six numbers is 32, then their sum is $(6)(32) = 192$. Since this sum is fixed, then to maximize one of the numbers, you must *minimize* the sum of the other 5. You are told that the numbers are *different integers*, none of which is less than 10, implying that the least the other 5 can be is 10, 11, 12, 13, and 14. Therefore, if x is the greatest possible value of any of the numbers,

$$10 + 11 + 12 + 13 + 14 + x = 192$$

Simplify: $60 + x = 192$

Subtract 60: $x = 132$

(Chapter 10 Lesson 2: Mean, Median and Mode Problems)

18. **D**   If you are comfortable with your rules of exponents, you can probably solve the equation for n algebraically. If not, you can just "test" the choices by plugging them in for n until you find one that makes the equation true. Here's one of many ways to solve agebraically:

$$(1/4)^n = 2^{-3}$$

Simplify: $(1/4)^n = 1/8$

Cross-multiply: $4^n = 8$

Write with common base: $(2^2)^n = 2^3$

Simplify: $2^{2n} = 2^3$

Equate the exponents: $2n = 3$

Divide by 2: $n = 3/2$

(Chapter 9 Lesson 3: Working with Exponents)

19. **B**   Looking at the choices makes it pretty clear that writing out all of the possible numbers is going to take more than a little while. To simplify the counting, use the fundamental counting principal. First, notice that all of the integers between 100 and 1,000 have three digits, so "choosing" one of these integers involves specifying three digits. There are only 9 choices for the first digit, since it can't be 0. Once that first digit is chosen, there are 9 digits remaining for the second digit. (Remember that you can use 0 as the second digit, but you can't use the first digit again.) Then, since you can't use either of the first two digits again, there are only 8 digits remaining for the last digit. This give a total of $9 \times 9 \times 8 = 648$ such integers.
(Chapter 10 Lesson 5: Counting Problems)

20. **B**   Be sure to mark up the diagram with any given information and any information you can

deduce:

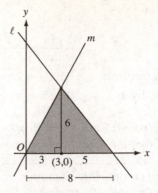

If line m has a slope of 2, then when the "run" is 3 (as it is from the origin to the point where the lines intersect), then "rise" must be $(2)(3) = 6$. Notice that this is also the height of the triangle. Since the area of the triangle is 24, you can use the triangle area formula to find the length of the base:

$$24 = (1/2)b(6)$$

Simplify: $24 = 3b$

Divide by 3: $8 = b$

Since the base is 8 units, the other part of the base is $8 - 3 = 5$, as shown in the diagram. This gives a "rise" and "run" for line ℓ, so the slope is $-6/5$.
(Chapter 11 Lesson 1: Lines and Angles)
(Chapter 11 Lesson 4: Coordinate Geometry)

Section 3

25. **D**   Editing a manuscript from 400 pages down to 250 pages is quite a *reduction. enhanced =* improved; *abridged* = shortened a text

26. **A**   The sentence contains a parallel structure that indicates that the first missing word should contrast *bland* and the second missing word should contrast *artistically daring. enchanting* = charming and delightful; *conventional* = ordinary; *innovative* = new and inventive; *tedious* = difficult to tolerate; *pedestrian* = ordinary; *trite* = overused

27. **C**   An *inveterate gambler* is one who gambles habitually. To disprove the assumption that *payoffs must be consistent* to support an addiction, one must show that the payoffs might be *given at irregular intervals. steadfast* = fixed or unchanging; *sporadic* = occurring at irregular intervals; *placid* = peaceful

28. **E**   If one is *surprised* by the finding that walking prolongs life, that person must have *denied a relationship between exercise and long life. mediation* = the

act of resolving a dispute between two or more other parties; *prosperity* = flourishing success; *correlation* = relationship; *longevity* = length of life

29. **D** The phrase *even to* suggests an element of surprise. Those who study something for a long time are expected to know a lot about it. It would be surprising, therefore, if they still found that subject *difficult to understand*. It would logically be *even more difficult to understand* for someone who did not study the subject. *forthcoming* = frank and honest; *daunting* = intimidating; *fallow* = unproductive; *cryptic* = hard to decipher; *inscrutable* = incapable of being comprehended; *fatuous* = foolishly stupid; *singular* = unique

30. **E** The passage states that *the current media environment* allows individuals to *offer messages inexpensively over the internet* so that they are no longer *constrained by cost*. In other words, the new media are more accessible to users.

31. **C** The passage does not take any controversial or emotional stance on the topic, mentioning only objective facts.

32. **B** This quotation states that *mathematics [needs] persons who . . . have a sense of the beautiful*. Therefore, an aesthetic sense is helpful to mathematical thought.

33. **E** John Conway is mentioned because he *cannot imagine he is doing anything but discovering* rather than inventing mathematical results. His quotation reinforces that point, saying that mathematical truths are as closed to interpretation as the truth that *pigs don't fly*.

34. **A** This passage, as a whole, praises newspapers for *their achievements in crusading*. Therefore, its overall tone is *laudatory*.

35. **E** The author states that it is *singular* (surprising and unique) *that newspapers . . . have made so little to-do about their achievements in crusading* (lines 1–3). In other words, the newspapers are not acknowledging one of their virtues.

36. **D** This *wealth of material* refers to the information about how newspapers have acted as *champions of reform . . . [and] protagonists of their communities* (lines 4–6). This means that they have acted to change their communities.

37. **C** In saying that the institution of newspapers *has discharged it [that is, crusading] for the most*

part admirably, the passage is saying that it has *performed or accomplished* this task well.

38. **B** The skeptics *deny that campaigns are ever undertaken for other than sordid motives*. In other words, they believe that newspapers only "crusade" for selfish purposes.

39. **D** In saying that *zeal . . . fires a crusading editor*, the author means that this zeal *inspires* or stimulates the editor.

40. **A** The final paragraph indicates that some campaigns result in a *loss of circulation and advertising* (line 53), which are the only sources of revenue for a newspaper.

41. **D** The overall purpose of the passage is to examine the art form of *cut and pasted paper* (lines 10–11) which was pioneered by Henri Matisse. Notice that every paragraph refers to *cut and pasted paper*, *collage*, or *decoupage*, which all refer to the same art form.

42. **B** The quotation indicates that Matisse was *afraid the young . . . will . . . [dispense] with certain efforts* (lines 6–9) because Matisse has tried to *never let . . . anyone know the labors* of his art. In other words, he is concerned that younger artists will think that his art is easier to make than it really is.

43. **E** This comment is made in the context of a discussion of how *lively and energetic* Matisse's art is, so the comment about Matisse's advanced age serves as a stark contrast.

44. **D** The *brilliant hues* of the paper are its *vibrant colors*. Therefore, *shining* is the best choice.

45. **A** Matisse is quoted to say that he has achieved a form that is *reduced to the essential* (lines 62–63) and is *no longer in the complexity of its space* (lines 63–64), in other words, his decoupage is pictorially simple.

46. **C** This *intimacy* describes the relationship between Matisse and the medium of decoupage, in which he is able to *select, place, and reposition the cut paper shapes* (lines 73–74).

47. **D** In lines 19–20, the passage states that Matisse's most famous work of decoupage shows *no three-dimensional modeling of the forms or shadows*. Elsewhere in the passage, however, the author describes the medium's relative ease of use (*less strenuous*, line 34), manipulability (*select*,

place, and reposition, lines 73–74), *pictorial strength* (lines 52–53), and vitality (*lively and energetic*, line 14).

---

48. **C**   The final paragraph states that Matisse *truly enjoyed*, indeed *relished*, his challenges, suggesting that he was enthusiastic. It also states that he had the *habit of hard work* (line 75), indicating that he was diligent.

Section 4

21. **D**   You might simply notice that 18/15 reduces to 6/5, making the answer obvious. If you want to use the "brute force" method, however, cross-multiply:

$$(18)(5) = 15x$$
Simplify: $90 = 15x$
Divide by 15; $6 = x$

(Chapter 8 Lesson 4: Ratios and Proportions)

---

22. **B**   Remember the formula for the area of a triangle, and simply plug in what you know:

$$A = \frac{1}{2}bh$$

Substitute: $24 = \frac{1}{2}(6)h$

Simplify: $24 = 3h$
Divide by 3: $8 = h$

(Chapter 11 Lesson 5: Areas and Perimeters)

---

23. **D**   Read the chart carefully and notice that each book represents 20,000 copies. Since the sales in 2003 are 2.5 "books" more than in 2002, the difference in copies is $2.5 \times 20,000 = 50,000$ copies.
(Chapter 7 Reasoning Skills 2: Analyzing)

---

24. **A**   What number is 24 less than 3 times itself?

Translate: $x = 3x - 24$
Subtract $3x$: $-2x = -24$
Divide by -2: $x = 12$

(Chapter 9 Lesson 1: Solving Equations)

---

25. **E**   You need to know the parallel lines theorem for this one. Because the two lines are parallel, angles 1 and 9 must be equal because they are "corresponding" angles. Angles 5 and 7 must be equal because they are "vertical" angles. Therefore, statements I and III are true. The only answer choice containing both I and III is (E), so that must be the correct

answer. As to statement II, angles 2 and 8 are not necessarily equal, because they do not share any common lines.
(Chapter 11 Lesson 1: Lines and Angles)

---

26. **E**   The average of 0, a, and b is $\frac{0+a+b}{3}$.

$$\frac{0+a+b}{3} = 2a$$
Multiply by 3: $a + b = 6a$
Subtract a: $b = 5a$

(Chapter 10 Lesson 2: Mean/Median/Mode Problems)

---

27. **C**   The prime factorization of 21 is 3×7, and the prime factorization of 39 is 3×13. Since b represents a common factor of 21 and 39 that is greater than 1, it must be 3. This means that a is 7 and c is 13. Therefore $b < a < c$.
(Chapter 10 Lesson 3: Numerical Reasoning)

---

28. **C**   You can solve this one algebraically or just test the choices. Recall that when you test the choices, it's usually best to start with (C) because it's the "middle" value. Begin by guessing that Rudy earns $8. Since Rudy earned $2.50 less than Charlene did, Charlene must have earned $8.00 + $2.50 = $10.50. If Charlene earned 3 times as much as David did, then David must have earned $10.50 ÷ 3 = $3.50. Check this by seeing if the total is $22.00, as the problem says: $8.00 + 10.50 + $3.50 = $22.00. Bingo!
Here we got lucky because the first choice we checked happened to be correct. The drawback to testing the choices is that you may need to do it more than once. To avoid this, you can set up an equation and solve directly. If Rudy earned r dollars, then Charlene must have earned $r + 2.50$ dollars, and David must have earned $(r + 2.50)/3$ dollars. Set up the equation:

$$r + (r + 2.50) + \frac{r + 2.50}{3} = 22$$

Multiply by 3: $3r + 3r + 7.50 + r + 2.50 = 66$
Simplify: $7r + 10 = 66$
Subtract 10: $7r = 56$
Divide by 7: $r = 8$

(Chapter 7 Lesson 6: Finding Alternatives)
(Chapter 9 Lesson 7: Word Problems)

29. 1.6 or 8/5 Recall that two-part ratios can be treated as fractions: $2.5/16 = .25/x$

Cross-multiply; $\quad 2.5x = 4$
Divide by 2.5: $\qquad x = 1.6$ or $8/5$

(Chapter 8 Lesson 4: Ratios and Proportions)

30. 54 Simply substitute the given numbers using the definition of the new symbol. Since $x \, \Delta \, y = (xy) - (x+y)$, then $12 \, \Delta \, 6 = (12 \times 6) - (12 + 6) = 72 - 18 = 54$
(Chapter 10 Lesson 1: New Symbol or Term Problems)

31. 44 Because the sum of the five angles is a straight angle, which measures $180°$, $x + x + y + y + y = 180$

Simplify: $\qquad\qquad\qquad 2x + 3y = 180$
Substitute 24 for x: $\quad 2(24) + 3y = 180$
Simplify: $\qquad\qquad\qquad 48 + 3y = 180$
Subtract 48: $\qquad\qquad\qquad 3y = 132$
Divide by 3: $\qquad\qquad\qquad\quad y = 44$

(Chapter 9 Lesson 1: Solving Equations)
(Chapter 11 Lesson 1: Lines and Angles)

32. 3/4 or 75 To simplify the problem, first notice that half of the cards in each deck are odd and half are even. Therefore, you only need to consider four possible outcomes from multiplying a number from one deck and a number from the other: (even)(even), (even)(odd), (odd)(even), and (odd)(odd). Each of these outcomes is equally likely, and the first three produce an even product. Therefore, the probability that the product is even is 3/4.
(Chapter 10 Lesson 6: Probability Problems)

33. 43 or 78 Since you only need to look at the integers between 40 and 80, listing them isn't so difficult. Since the number you want gives a remainder of 1 when it is divided by 7, start by listing the integers between 40 and 80 that are 1 more than a multiple of 7: $42 + 1 = 43$, $49 + 1 = 50$, $56 + 1 = 57$, $63 + 1 = 64$, $70 + 1 = 71$, and $77 + 1 = 78$. The only numbers in this set that give a remainder of 3 when divided by 5 are 43 and 78.
(Chapter 10 Lesson 3: Numerical Reasoning Problems)
(Chapter 8 Lesson 7: Divisibility)

34. 14 This question tests your ability to use the distributive law to multiply polynomials:

$$(2x^2 + 5x + 3)(3x + 1)$$

$$(3x)(2x^2 + 5x + 3) + (1)(2x^2 + 5x + 3)$$

$$(3x)(2x^2) + (3x)(5x) + (3x)(3) + 2x^2 + 5x + 3$$

$$6x^3 + 15x^2 + 9x + 2x^2 + 5x + 3$$

Combine like terms: $6x^3 + 17x^2 + 14x + 3$

Since c represents the coefficient of the "x" term, $c = 14$.
(Chapter 8 Lesson 2: Laws of Arithmetic)

35. 1.5 or 3/2 It may help to write out blank spaces to represent the unknown terms in the sequence. Since the fourth term is 12, the sequence looks like ------, ------, ------, 12. Now you need to "work backwards" to find the first term. Since each term is 4 less than 4 times the previous term, then each term must by 1/4 of the number that is 4 *greater* than the *next* term. (If this makes your brain hurt a bit, try it out and check.) In other words, the third term must be $(1/4)(12 + 4) = 4$. (Now check: notice that if you follow the rule to get the next term, you get 12!) Continuing gives you $(1/4)(4 + 4) = 2$ for the second term, and $(1/4)(2 + 4) = 1.5$ for the first term. Check one more time that the sequence follows the rule *forward*: 1.5, 2, 4, 12.
(Chapter 7 Reasoning Skill 3: Finding Patterns)

36. 27 One way to analyze this problem is to find the point where the two lines cross. This is the same as solving the system $y = 6$ and $y = (2/3)x$.

Set the ys equal: $\quad 6 = (2/3)x$
Multiply by 3/2: $\qquad\; = x$

So the point of intersection is $(9, 6)$, which means that the triangle has a "base" of 6 and a "height" of 9. (You might turn the diagram 90° to get a clearer picture.)

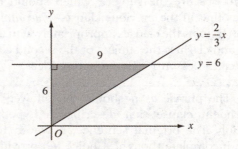

Therefore, it has an area of $(1/2)(9)(6) = 27$
(Chapter 9 Lesson 2: Systems)
(Chapter 11 Lesson 4: Coordinate Geometry)
(Chapter 11 Lesson 5: Areas and Perimeters)

37. **8/5 or 1.6** $\dfrac{2x+10}{5}+\dfrac{3x-2}{5}$

Add fractions: $\dfrac{(2x+10)+(3x-2)}{5}$

Simplify: $\dfrac{5x+8}{5}$

Distribute: $\dfrac{5x}{5}+\dfrac{8}{5}$

Simplify: $x+\dfrac{8}{5}$

Therefore, this expression is 8/5 greater than x.
(Chapter 8 Lesson 3: Fractions)

---

38. **2**

$$9\left(\dfrac{1}{3}\right)=3^m$$

Simplify: $9\left(\dfrac{1}{3^n}\right)=3^m$

Multiply by 3^n: $9=3^m \times 3^n$
Simplify: $9=3^{m+n}$
Write with common base: $3^2=3^{m+n}$
Equate exponents: $2=m+n$

(Chapter 9 Lesson 3: Working with Exponents)
(Chapter 9 Lesson 1: Solving Equations)

Section 5

1. **D**   The modifying phrase at the beginning of the sentence must be followed by the noun it modifies, *Francis*. Choice (C) uses *then* redundantly, and choice (E) is illogical.
(Chapter 13 Lesson 8: Other Misplaced Modifiers)

2. **B**   This is a run-on sentence because it joins two independent clauses with only a comma. The second clause is also unnecessarily vague. It uses the passive voice to obscure the subject, which should be the same as that in the previous clause—*paleontologists*. Choice (B) joins the clauses appropriately with a semicolon, and clarifies the subject of the second clause.
(Chapter 13 Lesson 15: Coordinating Ideas)

3. **C**   The phrase *as if* should be followed by an independent clause that describes a hypothetical condition. The original sentence, however, follows it with incomplete thought. Choice (C) provides the most logical phrasing. The past perfect subjunctive *had swum* must be used because the statement is hypothetical (or subjunctive), and because the action would have been completed before James

got out of the pool, and so is a "perfect" action.
(Chapter 13 Lesson 15: Coordinating Ideas)
(Chapter 13 Lesson 9: Tricky Tenses)
(Chapter 13 Lesson 14: The Subjunctive Mood)

4. **D**   The original sentence lacks parallel form and therefore reads awkwardly. The two clauses have the same subject and so should both be in the active voice. Choice (D) accomplishes this most concisely.
(Chapter 13 Lesson 3: Parallelism)

5. **E**   The subject and verb of the sentence are *a hurdle is*. What follows should be a noun (predicate nominative) that is equivalent to the *hurdle*. In the original phrasing, what follows is an independent clause rather than a noun phrase. Choices (B), (D), and (E) are all noun phrases, but (B) is illogical, and (D) uses the unidiomatic *expect being* instead of the correct *expect to be*.
(Chapter 13 Lesson 15: Coordinating Ideas)
(Chapter 13 Lesson 3: Parallelism)

6. **B**   The original phrasing is redundant and contains two problems: a lack of parallelism and a misplaced modifier. The two clauses have the same subject, so they should both be in the active voice. Also, the phrase *such as Woody Allen* should be closer to the noun it modifies, *humorists*. Choice (B) corrects both problems most concisely and effectively.
(Chapter 13 Lesson 3: Parallelism)
(Chapter 13 Lesson 12: Other Problems with Modifiers)

7. **E**   The original phrasing is awkward, wordy and unclear. The subject and verb *the fact is* do not convey the central idea of the sentence, and the modifying phrase at the end of the sentence is nonstandard. Choice (E) uses a much more effective and meaningful subject and verb: *Noam Chomsky discovered*.
(Chapter 13 Lesson 15: Coordinating Ideas)

8. **A**   The original phrasing is the most concise and logical.

9. **B**   The original sentence uses pronouns inconsistently. Since the first clauses uses *your*, the second clause should, also. Choice (B) is better than (C) because its phrasing is parallel with that of the first clause.
(Chapter 13 Lesson 5: Pronoun Agreement)
(Chapter 13 Lesson 3: Parallelism)

10. **A**   The original phrasing is best. The subject and verb of the sentence are *the reason was*.

Therefore, what follows should be a noun phrase that describes the *reason*. Choice (B) is not a noun phrase, and it uses the nonstandard construction *the reason was because*. The other choices are also not noun phrases.

---

11. **C**   The modifying phrase at the beginning of the sentence should be followed by the noun that it modifies, *the small company*. Choice (C) is the only one that repairs the dangling modifier.
(Chapter 13 Lesson 8: Other Misplaced Modifiers)

---

12. **D**   The phrasing in the original sentence is not parallel. Since it contains a list, the phrasing of the items should be similar. Choice (D) puts all three items in the same form: *adjective noun*.
(Chapter 13 Lesson 3: Parallelism)

---

13. **E**   In the original sentence, the phrasing of the two clauses is not parallel, and the pronoun *it* has no clear antecedent. Choice (E) might sound odd at first reading, because it uses *ellipsis*, that is, the omission of a phrase that is implied by the parallelism in the sentence. In other words, the sentence is equivalent to *Many visitors were impressed by the monument's sheer size; others [were impressed] by its solemn gravity*. The phrase in brackets can be omitted because it is implied by the parallel clause that came before.
(Chapter 13 Lesson 5: Pronoun Agreement)
(Chapter 13 Lesson 3: Parallelism)

---

14. **B**   The participial phrase beginning with *finding* should be followed by the noun it modifies, *the expedition leader*, since it was he who did the finding. Choice (D) appears to repair the dangling participle, but it does not create a complete sentence.
(Chapter 13 Lesson 7: Dangling and Misplaced Participles)

---

15. **C**   The original sentence phrases the comparison awkwardly. It is not clear what is being compared. Furthermore, the subject and verb of the sentence are *educators believe*, so what follows should be a noun phrase that describes what they believe. Choices (C) and (E) are both noun phrases, but only choice (C) shows a clear and logical comparison.
(Chapter 13 Lesson 4: Comparison Errors)

---

16. **A**   The original phrasing is correct.

---

17. **C**   The original phrasing is only a sentence fragment, because the main "clause" contains no verb. Choices (C) and (E) are the only ones that form complete sentences, but choice (E) is illogical.
(Chapter 13 Lesson 15: Coordinating Ideas)

---

18. **E**   The pronoun *its* has no clear antecedent in the sentence. Choices (D) and (E) clarify the noun by specifying it as *the claim*, but choice (D) uses the unidiomatic phrasing *of support to*.
(Chapter 13 Lesson 5: Pronoun Agreement)
(Chapter 13 Lesson 10: Idiom Errors)

---

19. **B**   The original comparison is illogical and not parallel. Choice (B) makes the comparison clearer and more logical through parallel phrasing—*on the advice of a friend* parallels *on my own analysis*.
(Chapter 13 Lesson 4: Comparison Errors)
(Chapter 13 Lesson 3: Parallelism)

---

20. **A**   This sentence is correct. It must use the subjunctive verbs *could not have completed* and *had not made* because it describes a hypothetical situation.
(Chapter 13 Lesson 14: The Subjunctive Mood)

---

21. **B**   The subject of the verb is *treats*, so the verb should be conjugated for a plural subject: *were*. This is a bit tricky because the sentence is "inverted"; that is, the subject comes *after* the verb.
(Chapter 13 Lesson 1: Subject-Verb Disagreement)
(Chapter 13 Lesson 2: Trimming Sentences)

---

22. **D**   This is an illogical comparison. The comparison should be between the *money* collected this year and the *money* collected last year, so the correct phrasing in (D) is *we collected last year*.
(Chapter 13 Lesson 4: Comparison Errors)

---

23. **D**   The idiomatic phrasing here should be *not only A but B as well*. Therefore (D) should be changed to *but*.
(Chapter 13 Lesson 3: Parallelism)
(Chapter 13 Lesson 10: Idiom Errors)

---

24. **A**   The word *before* indicates that the *seeing* would have been completed before the *being astonished*. To show the correct time sequence, choice (A) should use the perfect participle *never having seen*.
(Chapter 13 Lesson 9: Tricky Tenses)

---

25. **B**   *Precede* means *come before*. This usage is illogical here. The sentence clearly implies that the actress could not *proceed* (continue).
(Chapter 13 Lesson 11: Diction Errors)

26. **C**   The subject of the sentence is *Ricardo*. Since this is a singular subject, the verb conjugation should be *was*.
(Chapter 13 Lesson 1: Subject-Verb Disagreement)

27. **E**   The sentence is correct.

28. **D**   This phrase is not idiomatic. The correct idiom is *insights into*.
(Chapter 18 Lesson 10: Idiom Errors)

29. **A**   This modifies the verb *resembled*, so it should be the adverb *closely*.
(Chapter 13 Lesson 12: Other Problems with Modifiers)

30. **B**   This comparison is illogical. It should compare the *movies of Frank Capra* to the *movies of many modern directors*.
(Chapter 13 Lesson 4: Comparison Errors)

31. **E**   The sentence is correct.

32. **C**   The pronoun *they* requires a plural antecedent, so this phrase should read *hyenas employ*.
(Chapter 13 Lesson 5: Pronoun Agreement)

33. **A**   The participle *examining* dangles in the original sentence since its subject never appears. The best way to correct this problem is to rephrase it as *when one examines*.
(Chapter 13 Lesson 7: Dangling and Misplaced Participles)

34. **E**   The sentence is correct.

35. **B**   The word *unlike* indicates a comparison between *long ago* and some other time. This "other time" must be indicated for the comparison to be logical. Choice (B) corrects this problem by comparing *long ago* to *today*.
(Chapter 13 Lesson 4: Comparison Errors)
(Chapter 13 Lesson 8: Other Misplaced Modifiers)

36. **A**   The pronoun *it* does not have a proper antecedent. It seems to refer to *the things we buy* in sentence 3, but this is plural, not singular. Choices (A), (B), and (E) avoid this problem, but (B) shows an illogical contrast and (E) is awkward and vague.
(Chapter 13 Lesson 5: Pronoun Agreement)

37. **E**   The pronoun *this* has no clear antecedent, and the pronoun *they* is used to refer to two different antecedents, *workers* and *methods*. Choice (E) clarifies these references most effectively.
(Chapter 13 Lesson 5: Pronoun Agreement)

38. **C**   The clause *it means being inhumane* is extremely vague. Choice (C) clarifies the subject and verb and conveys the idea logically.
(Chapter 13 Lesson 15: Coordinating Ideas)

39. **D**   Choice (D) provides the most logical transition because it mentions the previous discussion about *the manufacture of consumer goods* and introduces a new, but related, discussion about *their disposal*.
(Chapter 13 Lesson 15: Coordinating Ideas)

PRACTICE TEST 3

ANSWER SHEET

Last Name: _____   First Name: _____

Date: _____   Testing Location: _____

Administering the Test

- **Remove this answer sheet** from the book and use it to record your answers to this test.
- This test will require **2 hours and 10 minutes** to complete. Take this test in one sitting.
- Use a stopwatch to time yourself on each section. The time limit for each section is written clearly at the beginning of each section. The first four sections are 25 minutes long, and the last section is 30 minutes long.
- Each response must **completely fill the oval. Erase all stray marks completely**, or they may be interpreted as responses.
- **You must stop ALL work on a section when time is called.**
- If you finish a section before the time has elapsed, check your work on that section. **You may NOT move on to the next section until time is called**.
- Do not waste time on questions that seem too difficult for you.
- Use the test book for scratchwork, but you will only receive credit for answers that are marked on the answer sheets.

Scoring the Test

- Your scaled score, which will be determined from a conversion table, is based on your raw score for each section.
- You will receive one point toward your raw score for every correct answer.
- You will receive no points toward your raw score for an omitted question.
- For each wrong answer on a multiple-choice question, your raw score will be reduced by 1/4 point. For each wrong answer on a numerical "grid-in" question (Section 4, questions 29–38), your raw score will receive no deduction.

SECTION 1 — Critical Reading — 25 minutes

Questions 1–24, answer choices A B C D E

Time: 25 minutes

Start: _____

Stop: _____

SECTION 2 — Math — 25 minutes

Questions 1–20, answer choices A B C D E

Time: 25 minutes

Start: _____

Stop: _____

SECTION 3 — Critical Reading — 25 minutes

Questions 25–48, answer choices A B C D E

Time: 25 minutes

Start: _____

Stop: _____

SECTION 4

Math

25 minutes

Time: 25 minutes

Start: _____

Stop: _____

21. Ⓐ Ⓑ Ⓒ Ⓓ Ⓔ   25. Ⓐ Ⓑ Ⓒ Ⓓ Ⓔ
22. Ⓐ Ⓑ Ⓒ Ⓓ Ⓔ   26. Ⓐ Ⓑ Ⓒ Ⓓ Ⓔ
23. Ⓐ Ⓑ Ⓒ Ⓓ Ⓔ   27. Ⓐ Ⓑ Ⓒ Ⓓ Ⓔ
24. Ⓐ Ⓑ Ⓒ Ⓓ Ⓔ   28. Ⓐ Ⓑ Ⓒ Ⓓ Ⓔ

29. 30. 31. 32. 33.

34. 35. 36. 37. 38.

SECTION 5

Writing Skills

30 minutes

Time: 30 minutes

Start: _____

Stop: _____

1. Ⓐ Ⓑ Ⓒ Ⓓ Ⓔ   14. Ⓐ Ⓑ Ⓒ Ⓓ Ⓔ   27. Ⓐ Ⓑ Ⓒ Ⓓ Ⓔ
2. Ⓐ Ⓑ Ⓒ Ⓓ Ⓔ   15. Ⓐ Ⓑ Ⓒ Ⓓ Ⓔ   28. Ⓐ Ⓑ Ⓒ Ⓓ Ⓔ
3. Ⓐ Ⓑ Ⓒ Ⓓ Ⓔ   16. Ⓐ Ⓑ Ⓒ Ⓓ Ⓔ   29. Ⓐ Ⓑ Ⓒ Ⓓ Ⓔ
4. Ⓐ Ⓑ Ⓒ Ⓓ Ⓔ   17. Ⓐ Ⓑ Ⓒ Ⓓ Ⓔ   30. Ⓐ Ⓑ Ⓒ Ⓓ Ⓔ
5. Ⓐ Ⓑ Ⓒ Ⓓ Ⓔ   18. Ⓐ Ⓑ Ⓒ Ⓓ Ⓔ   31. Ⓐ Ⓑ Ⓒ Ⓓ Ⓔ
6. Ⓐ Ⓑ Ⓒ Ⓓ Ⓔ   19. Ⓐ Ⓑ Ⓒ Ⓓ Ⓔ   32. Ⓐ Ⓑ Ⓒ Ⓓ Ⓔ
7. Ⓐ Ⓑ Ⓒ Ⓓ Ⓔ   20. Ⓐ Ⓑ Ⓒ Ⓓ Ⓔ   33. Ⓐ Ⓑ Ⓒ Ⓓ Ⓔ
8. Ⓐ Ⓑ Ⓒ Ⓓ Ⓔ   21. Ⓐ Ⓑ Ⓒ Ⓓ Ⓔ   34. Ⓐ Ⓑ Ⓒ Ⓓ Ⓔ
9. Ⓐ Ⓑ Ⓒ Ⓓ Ⓔ   22. Ⓐ Ⓑ Ⓒ Ⓓ Ⓔ   35. Ⓐ Ⓑ Ⓒ Ⓓ Ⓔ
10. Ⓐ Ⓑ Ⓒ Ⓓ Ⓔ   23. Ⓐ Ⓑ Ⓒ Ⓓ Ⓔ   36. Ⓐ Ⓑ Ⓒ Ⓓ Ⓔ
11. Ⓐ Ⓑ Ⓒ Ⓓ Ⓔ   24. Ⓐ Ⓑ Ⓒ Ⓓ Ⓔ   37. Ⓐ Ⓑ Ⓒ Ⓓ Ⓔ
12. Ⓐ Ⓑ Ⓒ Ⓓ Ⓔ   25. Ⓐ Ⓑ Ⓒ Ⓓ Ⓔ   38. Ⓐ Ⓑ Ⓒ Ⓓ Ⓔ
13. Ⓐ Ⓑ Ⓒ Ⓓ Ⓔ   26. Ⓐ Ⓑ Ⓒ Ⓓ Ⓔ   39. Ⓐ Ⓑ Ⓒ Ⓓ Ⓔ

Section 1

Time—25 minutes

24 Questions (1–24)

Each sentence below has one or two blanks, each blank indicating that something has been omitted. Beneath the sentence are five words or sets of words labeled A through E. Choose the word or set of words that, when inserted in the sentence, <u>best</u> fits the meaning of the sentence as a whole.

Example:

Medieval kingdoms did not become constitutional republics overning; on the contrary, the change was ------.

(A) unpopular
(B) unexpected
(C) advantageous
(D) sufficient
(E) gradual

1. The *varicella* virus, also know as the chicken pox virus, remains ------ in the nervous system, unbeknown to the host, and can reappear later in life as a condition known as "shingles."

    (A) lukewarm
    (B) dormant
    (C) solitary
    (D) active
    (E) aggressive

2. The ------ businessman ------ his unsuspecting partner of 15 years, embezzling large sums of money and secretly wiring it to his bank account in the Cayman Islands.

    (A) deceitful..swindled
    (B) duplicitous..supported
    (C) admirable..rebuked
    (D) ambidextrous..accommodated
    (E) ethical..duped

3. André showed a great ------ for computers as a child; he wrote his first program at the age of seven when most kids barely even knew what a computer was.

    (A) tolerance
    (B) atrophy
    (C) aptitude
    (D) skepticism
    (E) antagonism

4. While her camp friends thought it was natural for her to feel so ------ after she broke up with her boyfriend of three years, her incessant crying and ------ demeanor were starting to get on their nerves.

    (A) mystified..sanguine
    (B) elated..meticulous
    (C) jubilant..disheartened
    (D) irate..jocular
    (E) despondent..melancholy

5. "Rite of Spring" by twentieth-century Russian-American composer Igor Stravinsky is ------ masterpiece to the enthusiasts of his work; but many cannot believe that the ------ produced in this piece is anything more than dissonance set to irregular rhythms.

    (A) a sublime..harmony
    (B) a mortifying..dissonance
    (C) an abstract..benevolence
    (D) an aesthetic..cacophony
    (E) a trivial..punctiliousness

GO ON TO THE NEXT PAGE ▶▶▶

Each passage below is followed by one or two questions based on its content. Answer each question based on what is stated or implied in the passage introductory material preceding it.

This excerpt from a geological textbook discusses the broad effects of volcanoes.

Line Volcanoes are crucibles of change and are held
      in fascination mainly for their awesome powers
      of destruction. In the span of human life, they
      can change a landscape from jungle to desert,
5   degrade the global climate, induce great floods,
      and even bury entire cities. Yet, volcanoes are
      ultimately benevolent. The oceans in which life
      began, and the lakes, rivers, and groundwaters
      that renew and sustain life, are all condensed
10   volcanic steam that was produced during
      countless eruptions over billions of years. The
      very air we breathe is a store of volcanic vapors.
      Wondrously fertile volcanic soils yield
      sustenance for millions in tropical and
15   temperate regions. Volcanic geothermal
      systems that breach the surface as soothing hot
      springs are also clean, safe, and renewable
      sources of electrical energy. The tallest
      volcanoes wring moisture from passing clouds,
20   creating glaciers as well as tumbling rivers that
      endow us with hydroelectric power.

6. The passage indicates that the water on the earth's surface

(A) is one of the main causes of volcanic activity
(B) originated beneath the earth's surface
(C) diminishes in abundance as more volcanoes become active
(D) can temper the damaging effects of volcanoes
(E) is more toxic in areas around active volcanoes

7. The passage indicates that volcanic activity affects the abundance of all of the following EXCEPT

(A) atmospheric gases
(B) moisture in certain climates
(C) glaciers
(D) insects
(E) arable soil

The following is from a textbook on logic written in 1986.

Line What is reasoning? It is an inference, or chain
      of inferences. An inference is a mental state or
      process in which one or more beliefs support or
      lead to another belief. Thus I may observe that
5   Bob has a temperature, and infer that he is sick.
      From the fact that Bob is sick, I may infer
      further that he should rest. I have described two
      inferences which constitute a two-step
      reasoning process. Inferences can be expressed
10   in language in another way, as arguments. An
      argument is a sequence of statements some of
      which are offered as providing a sufficient
      reason to believe the others. The supporting
      statements are called premises; the statements
15   they support are called conclusions. An
      argument, therefore, is a linguistic unit in
      which premises are stated from which
      conclusions are drawn.

8. The main purpose of this passage is to provide

(A) a brief history of a phenomenon
(B) a humorous vignette
(C) a justification of a position
(D) a set of definitions
(E) a refutation of a common misconception

9. If the statements in lines 4–7 constitute a single argument, then which of the following represent all of the "premises" among these statements?

(A) None of these statements are premises.
(B) Bob has a temperature AND Bob is sick.
(C) Bob is sick AND Bob should rest.
(D) Bob has a temperature AND Bob should rest.
(E) Bob has a temperature AND Bob is sick AND Bob should rest.

First paragraph: from *Volcanoes: Crucibles of Change*, Richard V. Fisher, Grant Heiken, and Jeffrey Hulen. © 1997 Princeton University Press, Page xiii Second paragraph: *An Introduction to Logic*, Davis, Wayne, ©1986 Prentice-Hall. Reproduced courtesy of the author, Professor Wayne A. Davis.

GO ON TO THE NEXT PAGE ▶▶▶

The questions below are based on the content of the passage that precedes them. The questions are to be answered on the basis of what is stated or implied in the passage or in the introductory material that precedes the passage.

Questions 10–16 are based on the following passage.

The following passage is an excerpt from a story written by a German writer in 1966.

Line None of my friends can understand the care
with which I preserve a scrap of paper that has
no value whatever: it merely keeps alive the
memory of a certain day in my life, and to it
5   I owe a reputation for sentimentality which is
considered unworthy of my social position:
I am the assistant manager of a textile firm. But
I protest the accusation of sentimentality and
am continually trying to invest this scrap of
10   paper with some documentary value. It is a tiny,
rectangular piece of ordinary paper, the size,
but not the shape, of a stamp—it is narrower
and longer than a stamp—and although it
originated in the post office it has not the
15   slightest collector's value. It has a bright red
border and is divided by another red line into
two rectangles of different sizes; in the smaller
of these rectangles there is a big black R, in the
larger one, in black print, "Düsseldorf" and a
20   number—the number 634. That is all, and the
bit of paper is yellow and thin with age, and
now that I have described it minutely I have
decided to throw it away: an ordinary
registration sticker, such as every post office
25   slaps on every day by the dozen.

And yet this scrap of paper reminds me of a
day in my life which is truly unforgettable,
although many attempts have been made to
erase it from my memory. But my memory
30   functions too well.

First of all, when I think of that day, I smell
vanilla custard, a warm sweet cloud creeping
under my bedroom door and reminding me of
my mother's goodness: I had asked her to make
35   some vanilla ice cream for my first day of
vacation, and when I woke up I could smell it.

In the kitchen my mother was humming a
tune. It was a hymn. I felt very happy. Then I
heard my mother coming to listen at my door;
40   she crossed the hall, stopped by my door, it was
silent for a moment in our apartment, and I was

just about to call "Mother" when the bell rang
downstairs. My mother went to our front door,
and I heard a man's voice, and I knew at once it
45   was the mailman, although I had only seen him
a few times. It was very quiet for a moment, the
mailman said "Thanks," my mother closed
the door after him, and I heard her go back
into the kitchen.

50   Nobody will believe it, but my heart
suddenly felt heavy. I don't know why, but it
was heavy. I could no longer hear the coffee
mill. I put on my shirt and trousers, socks and
shoes, combed my hair and went into the
55   living room.

Mother came in from the kitchen carrying
the coffeepot and I saw at once she had been
crying. In one hand she was holding the
coffeepot, in the other a little pile of mail, and
60   her eyes were red. I went over to her, took the
pot from her, kissed her cheek and said: "Good
morning." She looked at me, said: "Good
morning, did you sleep well?" and tried to
smile, but did not succeed.

65   "Was there any mail?" I asked, a senseless
question, since Mother's small red hand was
resting on the little pile on top of which lay the
newspaper. "Yes," she said, and pushed the pile
toward me. I saw there was a post card, but
70   I had not noticed the registration sticker, that
tiny scrap of paper I still possess and to which
I owe a reputation for sentimentality. When
I reached for the post card I saw it had gone.
My mother had picked it up, she was holding
75   it up and looking at it, and I kept my eyes on
my half-eaten slice of bread, stirred my coffee
and waited.

I shall never forget it. Only once had my
mother ever cried so terribly: when my father
80   died; and then I had not dared to look at her
either. A nameless diffidence had prevented me
from comforting her.

I tried to bite into my bread, but my throat
closed up, for I suddenly realized that what was
85   upsetting Mother so much could only be
something to do with me. Mother said
something I didn't catch and handed me the
post card, and it was then I saw the registration
sticker: that red-bordered rectangle, divided by
90   a red line into two other rectangles, of which
the smaller one contained a big black R and the
bigger one the word "Düsseldorf" and the
number 634. Otherwise the post card was quite
normal, it was addressed to me and on the back
95   were the words: "Mr. Bruno Schneider: You are

GO ON TO THE NEXT PAGE ▸▸▸

required to report to the Schlieffen Barracks in Adenbrück for eight weeks of military training."

"Only eight weeks," I said, and I knew I was lying, and my mother dried her tears, said:

100 "Yes, of course," we were both lying, without knowing why we were lying, but we were and we knew we were.

10. The first paragraph establishes that the narrator regards his "scrap of paper" (line 2) with

(A) deep disgust
(B) sad nostalgia
(C) ambivalence
(D) light-hearted amusement
(E) fear

11. The narrator regards his "reputation for sentimentality" (line 5) as

(A) a positive trait that he inherited from his mother
(B) a useful quality in his work environment
(C) an unrealized goal
(D) a burden that he carries willingly
(E) an unwarranted attribution

12. The description in lines 10–20 ("It is a tiny . . . the number 634") primarily reveals the narrator's

(A) attempt to be objective
(B) uncertainty regarding the origin of the scrap of paper
(C) efforts to define an emotion
(D) desire to return to his youth
(E) depth of historical knowledge

13. The narrator mentions his heart in line 50 in order to

(A) dispute his reputation for sentimentality
(B) indicate a dramatic emotional shift
(C) demonstrate his emotional attachment to his childhood home
(D) reveal a secret that he had held for a long time
(E) show that he desired to leave his home to seek adventure

The Post Card, Heinrich Böll, McGraw-Hill ©1966 p 56–61.
Reprinted with the permission of the Permissions Company.

14. The narrator's question is "senseless" (line 65) because

(A) his mother cannot hear him
(B) he already knows the answer
(C) it is illogical and irrelevant
(D) he has already asked it
(E) he is using a term that his mother does not understand

15. The narrator indicates that he did not comfort his mother when his father died because he

(A) did not know his father well
(B) was far away from his mother at the time
(C) was angry with his mother
(D) lacked confidence
(E) resented his father

16. The narrator's comment to his mother after reading the post card in line 98 ("'Only eight weeks'") indicates his effort to

(A) repress a belief
(B) demonstrate his knowledge of the military
(C) express his wish to avoid military training
(D) protest a political injustice
(E) express unabashed pessimism

The questions below are based on the content of the passage that precedes them. The questions are to be answered on the basis of what is stated or implied in the passage or in the introductory material that precedes the passage.

Questions 17–24 are based on the following passage.

The following passage discusses the scientific debate regarding whether heredity or environment is a more important factor in human development.

Line   When Richard Mulcaster referred in 1581 to "that treasure . . . bestowed on them by nature, to be bettered in them by nurture," he gave the world a euphonious name for an opposition
5   that has been debated ever since. People's beliefs about the relative importance of

heredity and environment affect their opinions on an astonishing range of topics. Do adolescents engage in violence because of the way their parents treated them early in life? Are people inherently aggressive and selfish, calling for a market economy and a strong police, or could they become peaceable and cooperative, the state to wither and a spontaneous socialism to blossom? Is there a universal aesthetic that allows great art to transcend time and place, or are people's tastes determined by their era and culture? With so much seemingly at stake in so many fields, it is no surprise that debates over nature and nurture evoke more rancor than just about any issue in the world of ideas.

During much of the twentieth century, a common position in this debate was to deny that human nature existed at all—to aver, with José Ortega y Gasset, that "Man has no nature; what he has is history." The doctrine that the mind is a blank slate was not only a cornerstone of behaviorism in psychology and social constructionism in the social sciences, but also extended widely into mainstream intellectual life.

Part of the blank slate's appeal came from the realization that many differences among people in different classes and ethnic groups that formerly were thought to reflect innate disparities in talent or temperament could vanish through immigration, social mobility, and cultural change. But another part of its appeal was political and moral. If nothing in the mind is innate, then differences among races, sexes, and classes can never be innate, making the blank slate the ultimate safeguard against racism, sexism, and class prejudice. Also, the doctrine ruled out the possibility that ignoble traits such as greed, prejudice, and aggression spring from human nature, and thus held out the hope of unlimited social progress.

Though human nature has been debated for as long as people have pondered their condition, it was inevitable that the debate would be transformed by the recent efflorescence of the sciences of mind, brain, genes, and evolution. One outcome has been to make the doctrine of the blank slate untenable. No one, of course, can deny the importance of learning and culture in all aspects of human life. But cognitive science has shown that there must be complex innate mechanisms for learning and culture to be possible in the first place. Evolutionary psychology has documented hundreds of universals that cut across the world's cultures, and has shown that many psychological traits (such as our taste for fatty foods, social status, and risky sexual liaisons) are better adapted to the evolutionary demands of an ancestral environment than to the actual demands of the current environment. Developmental psychology has shown that infants have a precocious grasp of objects, intentions, numbers, faces, tools, and language. Behavioral genetics has shown that temperament emerges early in life and remains fairly constant throughout the life span, that much of the variation among people within a culture comes from differences in genes, and that in some cases particular genes can be tied to aspects of cognition, language, and personality. Neuroscience has shown that the genome contains a rich tool kit of growth factors, axon guidance molecules, and cell adhesion molecules that help structure the brain during development, as well as mechanisms of plasticity that make learning possible.

These discoveries not only have shown that the innate organization of the brain cannot be ignored, but have also helped to reframe our very conception of nature and nurture.

17. The author uses the quotation from Richard Mulcaster in lines 2–3 to emphasize the fact that

(A) many nonscientists are intrigued by biological discoveries
(B) a controversy has endured for many centuries
(C) many sixteenth-century beliefs have since been disproved
(D) adolescents have always been aggressive
(E) an important discovery was made by a relatively obscure researcher

18. The author uses the terms "wither" and "blossom" in lines 14–15 in order to

(A) imply that an idea is not as important as it was thought to be
(B) emphasize the fact that there is no such thing as human nature
(C) advocate a particular system of government
(D) criticize a long-standing biological claim
(E) draw a comparison between social phenomena and natural phenomena

19. It can be inferred that José Ortega y Gasset's notion of one's "history" (line 26) does NOT include

(A) voluntary actions
(B) reactions to music and art
(C) unpleasant experiences
(D) conversations with one's peers
(E) congenital behavioral tendencies

20. The passage indicates that "social constructionism" (lines 28–29) was based on an assumption that

(A) there is no such thing as human nature
(B) people are born with innate skills
(C) capitalism is the strongest economic system
(D) individuals of different ethnicities were likely to have different temperaments
(E) individuals preferred to remain in their own countries rather than immigrate to other countries

21. The passage indicates that the "blank slate" theory is appealing to some people because it

I. suggests that societies can develop without bound
II. undermines the basis of prejudice
III. reinforces the appropriateness of the current social order

(A) I only
(B) II only
(C) I and II only
(D) I and III only
(E) II and III only

22. The purpose of the sentence beginning on line 55 ("No one . . . human life") is to

(A) present a specific example of learning
(B) refute the theory of the blank slate
(C) cite the viewpoint of a biological authority
(D) qualify the central thesis of the passage
(E) support a claim with statistical evidence

23. The passage indicates that "fatty foods" (line 64) appeal to most modern humans because

(A) they are easier to find than low-fat options
(B) fat keeps modern humans warm in winter
(C) our ancestors benefited from eating such foods
(D) most regional cuisines require them
(E) they are advertised frequently in the media

24. The author suggests that "axon guidance molecules" (line 80) are

(A) recent discoveries that support the blank slate theory
(B) theoretical structures whose existence is in doubt
(C) components of human biochemistry that we do not share with our ancestors
(D) innate factors that contribute to cognition
(E) discoveries that inspired the work of Richard Mulcaster

STOP

You may check your work, on this section only, until time is called.

Section 2

Time—25 minutes

20 Questions (1–20)

Directions for Multiple-Choice Questions

In this section, solve each problem, using any available space on the page for scratchwork. Then decide which is the best of the choices given and fill in the corresponding oval on the answer sheet.

- You may use a calculator on any problem. All numbers used are real numbers.
- Figures are drawn as accurately as possible EXCEPT when it is stated that the figure is not drawn to scale.
- All figures lie in a plane unless otherwise indicated.

Reference Information

$A = \pi r^2$ $A = \ell w$ $A = \frac{1}{2}bh$ $V = \ell wh$ $V = \pi r^2 h$ $c^2 = a^2 + b^2$ Special Right Triangles

$C = 2\pi r$

The arc of a circle measures 360°.

Every straight angle measures 180°.

The sum of the measures of the angles in a triangle is 180°.

---

1. If $x^2 + 3x + 4 = x^2 + 3x + 4y$, what is the value of y?

(A) 0
(B) 1
(C) 2
(D) 3
(E) 4

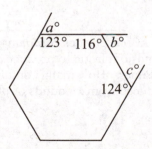

Note: Figure not drawn to scale.

2. In the figure above, what is the sum of $a + b + c$?

(A) 126
(B) 135
(C) 177
(D) 184
(E) 196

3. If $\dfrac{1}{w} = \dfrac{3}{16}$, then what is the value of w?

(A) $\dfrac{4}{3}$

(B) $\dfrac{5}{3}$

(C) $\dfrac{10}{3}$

(D) $\dfrac{16}{3}$

(E) $\dfrac{19}{3}$

---

4. A total of 350 signatures is needed for a petition to be considered by the town legislature. If 125 signatures have already been obtained, what percentage of the signatures needed must still be acquired for the petition to be considered?

(A) 32%
(B) 36%
(C) 55%
(D) 64%
(E) 68%

GO ON TO THE NEXT PAGE ▸▸▸

5. If p is a positive integer greater than 1, which of the following must be negative?

(A) $5 - p$
(B) $2p - 6$
(C) $1 - p$
(D) $-p + 3$
(E) $2p + 3$

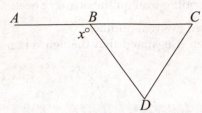

Note: Figure not drawn to scale.

6. In the figure above, the measure of $\angle CDB = 34°$ and $CD = BD$. What is the value of x?

(A) 34
(B) 73
(C) 94
(D) 107
(E) 146

---

7. If $a + b = 6$ and $a - b = 4$, what is the value of $2a + 3b$?

(A) 9
(B) 10
(C) 11
(D) 12
(E) 13

---

8. The average (arithmetic mean) of -4, 3, and x is 2. What is the value of x?

(A) 3
(B) 4
(C) 5
(D) 6
(E) 7

---

9. Which of the following ratios is equal to the ratio of 3 to 4?

(A) 6 to 12
(B) 9 to 16
(C) 12 to 16
(D) 12 to 20
(E) 15 to 25

---

10. A taxi cab fare starts at \$2.25, and \$0.25 is added after each whole mile driven. If a cab ride costs Michelle \$5.00, how many miles did she travel?

(A) between 9 and 10
(B) between 11 and 12
(C) between 13 and 14
(D) between 16 and 17
(E) between 20 and 21

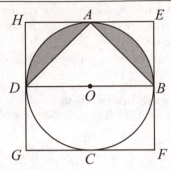

11. Circle O is tangent to square $EFGH$ at points A, B, C, and D. If A is the midpoint of side HE and the area of square $EFGH$ is 64, what is the area of the shaded region?

(A) $4\pi + 16$
(B) $8\pi - 16$
(C) $16\pi - 8$
(D) $16\pi - 4$
(E) $24\pi - 16$

---

12. If $q = p = 3t = 6$, what is the value of $3q - 4p + 2t$?

(A) -4
(B) -2
(C) 0
(D) 2
(E) 4

---

13. The ACME plastics company requires p pounds of plastic to produce c storage containers. How many containers can be produced from x pounds of plastic?

(A) $\dfrac{xc}{p}$

(B) $\dfrac{px}{c}$

(C) xcp

(D) $\dfrac{xp}{c}$

(E) $\dfrac{pc}{x}$

14. For all values of w and y, let $w \blacktriangleright y = \dfrac{wy}{w+y}$. If $6 \blacktriangleright z = 4$, what is the value of $z \blacktriangleright 6$?

(A) 2.4
(B) 2.8
(C) 3.2
(D) 3.6
(E) 4.0

15. The product of seven consecutive even integers is 0. What is the least possible value of any one of these integers?

(A) -14
(B) -12
(C) -10
(D) -8
(E) -6

16. The senior class at Weston High School has 40 fewer boys than girls. If the class has n boys, then what percent of the senior class are boys?

(A) $\dfrac{n}{2n+40}\%$

(B) $\dfrac{n}{2n-40}\%$

(C) $\dfrac{100n}{2n+40}\%$

(D) $\dfrac{100n}{2n-40}\%$

(E) $\dfrac{100n}{n+40}\%$

17. If x and y are positive integers and $(xy+x)$ is even, which of the following must be true?

(A) If x is odd, then y is odd.
(B) If x is odd, then y is even.
(C) If x is even, then y is odd.
(D) If x is even, then y is even.
(E) x cannot be odd

18. If $2^k \cdot 8^w = 2^{20}$, what is the value of $k + 3w$?

(A) 8
(B) 12
(C) 16
(D) 20
(E) 24

19. The fashion consultant at King's Department Store is given five dressed mannequins to arrange side by side in the display window. If the tallest of these mannequins is not allowed to be placed on either end of the display, how many different arrangements of the mannequins are possible?

(A) 18
(B) 36
(C) 72
(D) 96
(E) 120

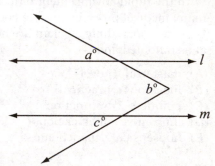

20. In the figure above, line l is parallel to line m. Which of the following is equal to c in terms of a and b?

(A) $b - a - 180$
(B) $180 + b - a$
(C) $180 - b - a$
(D) $90 + b - a$
(E) $b - a$

STOP

You may check your work, on this section only, until time is called.

Section 3

Time—25 minutes

24 Questions (25–48)

Each sentence below has one or two blanks, each blank indicating that something has been omitted. Beneath the sentence are five words or sets of words labeled A through E. Choose the word or set of words that, when inserted in the sentence, <u>best</u> fits the meaning of the sentence as a whole.

Example:

Medieval kingdoms did not become constitutional republics overnight; on the contrary, the change was ------.

(A) unpopular
(B) unexpected
(C) advantageous
(D) sufficient
(E) gradual

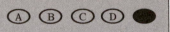

25. With the rapid advancement of technology, many medical procedures once considered ------ and incredibly efficient are now looked at as outdated and ------.

(A) masterful..novel
(B) ingenious..practical
(C) pointless..dysfunctional
(D) innovative..inefficacious
(E) nonsensical..inadequate

26. The concept that an atom is composed of minuscule charged particles was once ------ theory, but is now accepted as an undeniable truth.

(A) an incontrovertible
(B) a generous
(C) a contentious
(D) a hospitable
(E) an egotistical

27. If the rapid ------ of Africa's remaining rain forests persists, the rare and ------ creatures that make the region their home will soon become extinct.

(A) annihilation..engendered
(B) overgrowth..obstinate
(C) amelioration..vulnerable
(D) destruction..endangered
(E) cultivation..unyielding

28. *Stenocereus thurberi*, the organ pipe cactus, is famous for its ability to thrive in the Sonoran Desert in spite of the ------ climate, where water is so scarce.

(A) arid
(B) fervent
(C) lucid
(D) banal
(E) sweltering

29. The usually ------ store manager shocked her employees when she exploded into a vicious tirade full of expletives and insults.

(A) vexed
(B) intemperate
(C) belligerent
(D) vivacious
(E) tranquil

30. A feeling of ------, a sense of profound depression and obsession with death and gore, permeates the canvases of nineteenth-century painter Antonio Calvelli.

(A) notoriety
(B) lethargy
(C) pomposity
(D) morbidity
(E) humility

GO ON TO THE NEXT PAGE ▸▸▸

31. Her coworkers respect her because she is both
------ and ------; she refuses to compromise
her principles, and she never lies.

    (A) inexorable..forthright
    (B) capricious..candid
    (C) unrelenting..perfidious
    (D) intransigent..guileful
    (E) mercurial..veracious

32. Although the common practice among
scientists of the sixteenth century was to ------
the beliefs of the Church as law, Galileo Galilei
expressed ------ opinions that contrasted
strongly with this dogma and found himself
exiled to a life in prison.

    (A) discount..iconoclastic
    (B) endorse..orthodox
    (C) espouse..heretical
    (D) impugn..dissident
    (E) advocate..conformist

The following two passages are followed by
questions based on their content and the
relationship between the passages. Answer
each question based on what is stated or
implied in the passages.

**Questions 33–36 are based on the
following passages.**

*The following passages discuss life during the
Gold Rush of the mid-1800s, when thousands of
people migrated to California in search of gold.*

Passage 1

Line My father went prospecting north of
Haileybury when there was no such mining
field known as Kirkland Lake. I think it was
called Larder Lake. He had someone helping
5 him, and staked some claims, but a bear
climbed a tree and ate their bacon. That left
them short of supplies and they had to come
out and go back again with more supplies. If
you don't sell your claims you have to do thirty
10 days of assessment work per claim the first
year, and the second year sixty days and the
third year ninety days before you can get them
patented. That's rather expensive unless you
have money to begin with. So he didn't sell
15 those claims, and it became, I think, the Kerr-
Addison Mine. It's still producing gold. That's

the way it goes in the mining game. It's like
tossing coins to see who's lucky.

Passage 2

In spite of the hard conditions of life, the lack of
20 all the creature comforts, the business of child
bearing and rearing went on apace. Families
were large and the burden must have been well
nigh crushing, for gold mining was not always
profitable, and women knew what it was to be
25 obligated to help to fill the family larder.
Heaven alone knows how these women toiled
and silently suffered. Their hair is white now,
and their faces deeply graven with lines. They
say that wrinkles tell in cipher the story of a
30 woman's life, and these faces tell a noble story
that they who run may read.

33. Unlike Passage 2, Passage 1 conveys a tone of

    (A) hopefulness
    (B) jollity
    (C) horror
    (D) resignation
    (E) embarrassment

34. Both passages indicate that

    (A) gold mining was restricted to a small
        geographical region
    (B) women were often called upon to do
        mining work
    (C) gold miners often broke the law
    (D) mining claims could only be purchased
        by men
    (E) gold mining was often unsuccessful

35. The first sentence of Passage 2 characterizes
the women of the Gold Rush as

    (A) harsh
    (B) steadfast
    (C) creative
    (D) fortunate
    (E) intelligent

First paragraph: "I Hear your Home Town Is All Burned Up" from
Tell Me Another Story, Edith Macfie. ©1988 The McGraw-Hill
Companies
Second paragraph: *http://www.sfmuseum.org/hist5/foremoms.
html*

GO ON TO THE NEXT PAGE ▶▶▶

36. The statement "the burden must have been well nigh crushing" (lines 22–23) means that

(A) the task of mining for gold was very hard labor
(B) families often had to make long and difficult treks in search of gold
(C) raising families was difficult because income was not reliable
(D) mining supplies were often very expensive
(E) there were many governmental regulations that restricted the activities of miners

The passages below are followed by questions based on their content or the relationship between he passages. Answer the questions on the basis of what is stated or implied in the passages or the introductory material preceding them.

Questions 37–48 are based on the following passages.

The following passages discuss the issue of medical confidentiality, a physician's responsibility to keep a patient's medical information private.

Passage 1

Line   There are two primary philosophical arguments in favor of preserving medical confidentiality. The first argument is utilitarian and refers to possible long-term consequences.
5   The second argument is non-utilitarian and speaks of respect for the right of persons.
    The utilitarian argument for the preservation of medical confidentiality is that without such confidentiality the physician-
10   patient relationship would be seriously impaired. More specifically, the promise of confidentiality encourages the patient to make a full disclosure of his symptoms and their causes, without fearing that an embarrassing
15   condition will become public knowledge. Among medical professionals, psychotherapists have been particularly concerned to protect the confidentiality of their relationship with patients.
20   A second argument for the principle of medical confidentiality is that the right to a sphere of privacy is a basic human right. In

what is perhaps the classic essay concerning the right of privacy, Samuel Warren and Louis
25   Brandeis wrote in 1890 that the common law secured "to each individual the right of determining, ordinarily, to what extent his thoughts, sentiments, and emotions shall be communicated to others." Present-day
30   advocates of the right of privacy frequently employ the imagery of concentric circles or spheres. In the center is the "core self," which shelters the individual's "ultimate secrets"— "those hopes, fears, and prayers that are
35   beyond sharing with anyone unless the individual comes under such stress that he must pour out these ultimate secrets to secure emotional release." According to this image, the next largest circle contains intimate secrets
40   which can be shared with close relatives or confessors of various kinds. Successively larger circles are open to intimate friends, to casual acquaintances, and finally to all observers.
    The principle of medical confidentiality can
45   be based squarely on this general right of privacy. The patient, in distress, shares with the physician detailed information concerning problems of body or mind. To employ the imagery of concentric circles, the patient
50   admits the physician to an inner circle. If the physician, in turn, were to make public the information imparted by the patient—that is, if he were to invite scores or thousands of other persons into the same inner circle—we would
55   be justified in charging that he had violated the patient's right of privacy and that he had shown disrespect to the patient as a human being.
    These two arguments for the principle of medical confidentiality—the argument based
60   on probable consequences of violation and the argument based on the right of privacy— constitute a rather strong case for the principle.

Passage 2

    As professionals who wield enormous power
65   over their patients' lives, physicians are burdened with commensurate responsibilities. Certainly those responsibilities include maintaining a high level of skill in medical procedures and knowledge about new
70   medications and their side-effects. The commitment to such tasks constitutes not only a respect of the craft and science of medicine, but even more importantly a respect of the

Passage 1: *Biomedical Ethics*, Thomas A. Mappes, Jane S. Zembaty, McGraw-Hill ©1981 p 116–117

GO ON TO THE NEXT PAGE ▶▶▶

75 patient. Interwoven in this patient-physician relationship, and critical to its success, is the principle of confidentiality.

The word confidentiality derives from the Latin fidere, meaning to trust. Confidentiality, then, implies more than keeping secrets; it
80 implies being worthy of trust. It is acting always to inspire the patient that one has his or her best interests in mind. The issue of confidentiality, then, is more subtle and complicated than merely keeping medical
85 information private.

The Hippocratic oath is surprisingly unspecific about the issue of confidentiality, and the good physician must judiciously negotiate the sometimes tricky terrain of
90 professionalism and patient confidence. In many rural areas, for instance, physicians are responsible for the health care of entire families. A woman may have incurred a disease or trauma that renders her sterile, and wish to
95 keep this fact from her husband, perhaps in naive hope or to avoid a confrontation. The inability to conceive may induce the husband, at the same time, to express signs of depression and a sense of inadequacy which could be
100 alleviated by knowing the facts. How must a physician act when the confidences of different patients conflict? A responsibility to public health also constrains a physician's responsibility to confidentiality. The need to
105 avoid an epidemic usually outweighs a patient's desire to avoid the stigma associated with a highly communicable disease.

Perhaps the thorniest question concerning confidentiality is: what information is truly a
110 matter of confidence? Medical anecdotes are invaluable sources of professional knowledge (and, often, levity). Convention holds that patients in such anecdotes remain anonymous, but the unique features of the malady or
115 circumstance can reveal as much as identifying the patient by name. This is all the more true if the patient is already in the public eye.

The Hippocratic pledge to do no harm may raise more questions than it answers. Perhaps
120 the father of medicine intended physicians themselves to be as much philosophers as practitioners.

37. The purpose of the first paragraph of Passage 1 is to

(A) summarize a controversy
(B) present an individual's point of view
(C) indicate the existence of a popular misconception
(D) provide historical background to an issue
(E) introduce the reasoning behind a practice

38. In Passage 1, the author uses the term "utilitarian" to mean regarding

(A) the monetary costs of medical care
(B) the reputation of the medical profession
(C) the effectiveness of a physician's services
(D) the moral rights of a patient
(E) the education of physicians

39. In the second paragraph of Passage 1, psychotherapists are singled out as doctors who

(A) are exceptions to the rule of confidentiality
(B) do not use invasive procedures
(C) require more sophisticated diagnostic tools than do most doctors
(D) need extensive education before they can practice their specialty
(E) require the trust of their patients to be successful

40. The center of each of the "concentric circles" (line 31) is

(A) the patient
(B) the principle of confidentiality
(C) the physician
(D) the patient's closest friends
(E) any medical condition the patient might have

41. As it is used in line 55, the word "charging" most nearly means

(A) entrusting
(B) purchasing
(C) making an accusation
(D) attacking violently
(E) giving an order

GO ON TO THE NEXT PAGE ▸▸▸

42. The author of Passage 2 uses the term "interwoven" (line 74) to suggest that physician-patient confidentiality is

(A) extremely complicated
(B) part of a larger set of responsibilities
(C) not fully appreciated by patients
(D) the focus of a heated controversy
(E) often ignored in the medical community

43. The author of Passage 2 discusses the origin of the word "confidentiality" in order to

(A) indicate that a medical controversy has endured for centuries
(B) suggest that physicians have been misusing the term for a long time
(C) emphasize the importance of proper diction when a physician communicates with a patient
(D) reveal a shade of meaning that may sometimes be overlooked
(E) imply that physicians did not always have the responsibilities they have today

44. As it is used in line 81, "inspire" most nearly means

(A) energize
(B) fill
(C) persuade
(D) exalt
(E) cause

45. The "facts" mentioned in line 100 would most likely include information about

(A) new forms of therapy
(B) the medical condition of another person
(C) the limits of medical technology
(D) potentially dangerous drugs
(E) the personal life of the physician

46. The purpose of the question in lines 100–102 is to

(A) open a new line of investigation
(B) summarize the issue presented by the preceding example
(C) make a definitive statement in a rhetorical way
(D) mock a particular class of people
(E) indicate the weakness of a particular argument

47. The parenthetical remark in line 112 indicates that medical anecdotes are sometimes

(A) malicious
(B) hard to interpret
(C) violations of confidentiality
(D) humorous
(E) anonymous

48. Which of the following best summarizes the perspective of each passage on a patient's right to privacy?

(A) Passage 1 suggests that it is inviolable, while Passage 2 implies that it can be violated in certain circumstances.
(B) Passage 1 suggests that it is anachronistic, while Passage 2 indicates that it is still relevant.
(C) Passage 1 suggests that it is an issue that concerns philosophers more than physicians, while Passage 2 suggests that it is an issue that concerns physicians more than philosophers.
(D) Passage 1 suggests that it should be resolved on a case-by-case basis, while Passage 2 indicates that it must be codified in a set of standards.
(E) Passage 1 suggests that the courts have used it to impose an improper burden on physicians, while Passage 2 makes light of that burden.

STOP

You may check your work, on this section only, until time is called.

Section 4

Time—25 minutes
18 Questions (21–38)

Directions for Multiple-Choice Questions

In this section, solve each problem, using any available space on the page for scratchwork. Then decide which is the best of the choices given and fill in the corresponding oval on the answer sheet.

- You may use a calculator on any problem. All numbers used are real numbers.
- Figures are drawn as accurately as possible EXCEPT when it is stated that the figure is not drawn to scale.
- All figures lie in a plane unless otherwise indicated.

Reference Information

$A = \pi r^2$
$C = 2\pi r$
$A = \ell w$
$A = \frac{1}{2}bh$
$V = \ell wh$
$V = \pi r^2 h$
$c^2 = a^2 + b^2$
Special Right Triangles

The arc of a circle measures 360°.
Every straight angle measures 180°.
The sum of the measures of the angles in a triangle is 180°.

---

21. If $x - 3$ is 4 more than w, then x is how much more than w?

(A) 3
(B) 4
(C) 5
(D) 6
(E) 7

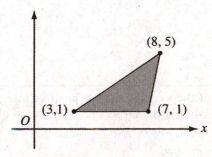

22. What is the area of the triangle in the figure above?

(A) 6
(B) 8
(C) 10
(D) 12
(E) 14

GO ON TO THE NEXT PAGE ▶▶▶

23. If $7b - 8 \geq 4b + 16$ and b is an odd integer, what is the least possible value of b?

(A) 8
(B) 9
(C) 10
(D) 11
(E) 12

26. If a triangle has two sides of length 6 and 10, what is the largest possible integer value of the length of the third side?

(A) 13
(B) 14
(C) 15
(D) 16
(E) 17

24. If the ratio of the area of circle A to the area of circle B is $2 : 1$, then how many times larger is the circumference of circle A than the circumference of circle B?

(A) $\sqrt{2}$
(B) 2
(C) $\sqrt{3}$
(D) 4
(E) 5

27. Two identical cubes, each with a volume of 64 cubic inches, are glued together by setting the face of one of the cubes on top of the face of the other cube to form a rectangular solid. What is the surface area of the newly formed solid?

(A) 64
(B) 112
(C) 128
(D) 160
(E) 192

25. If the average of four positive integers is 12, what is the largest possible value of one of those integers?

(A) 35
(B) 37
(C) 40
(D) 42
(E) 45

28. In the preliminary round of the Little League World Series, each of the six teams in a bracket plays every other team in the bracket exactly twice. How many games are played altogether in the preliminary round in one bracket?

(A) 12
(B) 15
(C) 21
(D) 30
(E) 46

GO ON TO THE NEXT PAGE ▶▶▶

Directions for Student-Produced Response Questions

Each of the questions in this section requires you to solve the problem and enter your answer in a grid, as shown below.

- If your answer is 2/3 or .666..., you must enter the most accurate value the grid can accommodate, but you may do this in one of four ways:

Start in first column · Grid result here

Start in second column

Grid as a truncated decimal

Grid as a rounded decimal

- In the example above, gridding a response of 0.67 or 0.66 is incorrect because it is less accurate than those above.
- The scoring machine cannot read what is written in the top row of boxes. You MUST fill in the numerical grid accurately to get credit for answering any question correctly. You should write your answer in the top row of boxes only to aid your gridding.
- Do not grid in a mixed fraction like $3\frac{1}{2}$ as $\boxed{3}\ \boxed{1}\ \boxed{/}\ \boxed{2}$ because it will be interpreted as $\frac{31}{2}$. Instead, convert it to an improper fraction like 7/2 or a decimal like 3.5 before gridding.
- None of the answers will be negative, because there is no negative sign in the grid.
- Some of the questions may have more than one correct answer. You must grid only one of the correct answers.
- You may use a calculator on any of these problems.
- All numbers in these problems are real numbers.
- Figures are drawn as accurately as possible EXCEPT when it is stated that the figure is not drawn to scale.
- All figures lie in a plane unless otherwise indicated.

---

29. The gas tank in car A holds 30% less gasoline than the gas tank in car B does. If car A can hold 21 gallons, how many gallons does the tank in car B hold?

30. Eric bakes a cake for his daughter's birthday party. He cuts the cake into 4 equal-sized pieces and then cuts each of the 4 pieces into 3 more equal-sized pieces. Hidden in one of the pieces is a golden coin. If he gives his daughter one of the slices chosen at random, what is the probability that she will get the piece containing the coin?

$$\begin{array}{r} 6A \\ +\,CB \\ \hline 1B7 \end{array}$$

31. In the correctly worked addition problem above, each of the three letters A, B, and C represents a different digit and $B + C = 14$. What is the value of A?

GO ON TO THE NEXT PAGE ▶▶▶

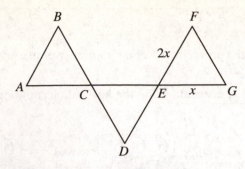

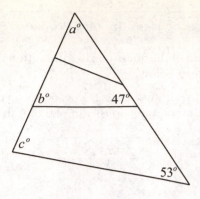

Note: Figure not drawn to scale.

Note: Figure not drawn to scale.

32. In the figure above, line segments *AB*, *BD*, *DF*, *FG* and *AG* are drawn to create three congruent isosceles triangles. If $\angle BAC = \angle ACB = \angle CED = \angle EGF$, and the sum of the perimeters of all three triangles is 45, what is the measure of length *AG*?

35. In the figure above, what is the value of $b - c$?

36. Eight students in a physics class of twenty students took the final exam and scored an average of 87. What is the average score for the remaining twelve students in the class if the average for the entire class was an 84?

33. If $bc = 4$, $cf = 6$, $fh = 12$, and $bh = 8$, what is the value of $b^2c^2f^2h^2$?

$$-4, 2, 4, -4, 2, 4, -4, 2, 4\ldots$$

37. The sequence above continues according to the pattern shown. What is the sum of the first 20 terms of this sequence?

$$X: \{2, 4, 6, 8, 10\}$$
$$Y: \{1, 3, 5, 7, 9\}$$

34. One number is to be chosen at random from set *X* and added to a number chosen at random from set *Y*. What is the probability that the sum will be an odd number?

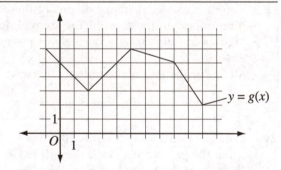

38. The figure above shows the graph of $y = g(x)$. If $g(m) = g(1) - 2$, where $0 \leq m \leq 11$, then what is the value of *m*?

STOP

You may check your work, on this section only, until time is called.

Section 5

Time—30 minutes

39 Questions (1–39)

Directions for "Improving Sentences" Questions

Each of the sentences below contains one underlined portion. The portion may contain one or more errors in grammar, usage, construction, precision, diction (choice of words), or idiom. Some of the sentences are correct.

Consider the meaning of the original sentence, and choose the answer that best expresses that meaning. If the original sentence is best, choose (A), because it repeats the original phrasing. Choose the phrasing that creates the clearest, most precise, and most effective sentence.

The children <u>couldn't hardly believe their eyes</u>.

(A) couldn't hardly believe their eyes
(B) would not hardly believe their eyes
(C) could hardly believe their eyes
(D) couldn't nearly believe their eyes
(E) could hardly believe his or her eyes

Ⓐ Ⓑ ● Ⓓ Ⓔ

---

1. With so much evidence to the contrary, it is difficult to understand why so many people still contend that, for tooth care, whitening creams are <u>as good, if not better, than</u> regular brushing and routine checkups.

    (A) as good, if not better, than
    (B) as good as, if not better than,
    (C) better than, not just as good as
    (D) as good, if not the best compared to
    (E) the best as compared against

2. Despite having sometimes dangerous side effects, <u>many people still prefer medication to exercise when attempting to lose weight.</u>

    (A) many people still prefer medication to exercise when attempting to lose weight
    (B) medication, rather than exercise, is still the preferred method of weight loss for many people
    (C) medication instead of exercise for weight loss is the method that is preferred
    (D) many people consider medication a better alternative to exercise when attempting to lose weight
    (E) medication, rather than exercise, being the most preferred method of weight loss by many people

3. The auditors sifted <u>meticulous through the old</u>
    <u>tax returns</u> in an effort to find any unpaid taxes.

    (A) meticulous through the old tax returns
    (B) through the old tax returns with meticulousness
    (C) meticulously through the old tax returns
    (D) through the old tax returns in meticulously fashion
    (E) the old tax returns in meticulous fashion

4. The news that the house was no longer for sale came <u>as a disappointment to him, in that he had been excited to have the opportunity</u> to buy the house for his wife as a wedding present.

    (A) as a disappointment to him, in that he had been excited to have the opportunity
    (B) as a disappointment to him; he having had the opportunity
    (C) to him as a disappointment; having been excited as to have had the opportunity
    (D) disappointed him; he had been excited
    (E) to him as a disappointment, in that he was excited for the opportunity

5. <u>Except for you and me, everyone bought</u> a ticket to the concert.

GO ON TO THE NEXT PAGE ▸▸▸

(A) Except for you and me, everyone bought
(B) Except for you and I, everyone bought
(C) With the exception of you and I, everyone bought
(D) Except for you and me, everyone have bought
(E) Everyone except you and I bought

6. As the first person in his family to attend college, <u>the need to become a successful professional is strongly felt by Gerard.</u>

   (A) the need to become a successful professional is strongly felt by Gerard.
   (B) Gerard feels a strong need to become a successful professional.
   (C) a successful professional is what Gerard feels the strong need to become.
   (D) Gerard's need to become a successful professional is strong.
   (E) it is the need to become a successful professional that Gerard feels strongly.

7. Before the school bus returned from the basketball game, <u>the snow began to fall,</u> making the trip home from the game slow and unpleasant.

   (A) the snow began to fall
   (B) was when the snow began falling
   (C) the snow begins to fall
   (D) when the snow began falling
   (E) snow is falling

8. Doctor Strathmore is <u>one of the professors who is planning</u> to speak at graduation.

   (A) one of the professors who is planning
   (B) one of the professors that is planning
   (C) one of the professors who are planning
   (D) the professor that is one planning
   (E) one professor of the ones that plan

9. The two candidates differ in their congressional <u>experience, the older candidate has</u> served for three times as many years as his younger opponent.

   (A) experience, the older candidate has
   (B) experience, and the older candidate having
   (C) experience; the older candidate has
   (D) experience; but the older candidate has
   (E) experience, because the older candidate having

10. <u>If you could have been present for your son's musical performance,</u> you would have witnessed firsthand the incredible progress he has made in the last year.

   (A) If you could have been present for your son's musical performance
   (B) If you were to have been present for your son's musical performance
   (C) You could have been present for your son's musical performance and
   (D) If you would have been present for your son's musical performance,
   (E) Had you been present at your son's musical performance,

11. <u>High school students today, unlike just 10 years ago,</u> face greater pressures in the college application process.

   (A) High school students today, unlike just 10 years ago,
   (B) Compared to their counterparts of just 10 years ago, high school students today
   (C) Unlike high school students 10 years ago; those today
   (D) Today's high school student, different from those of 10 years ago,
   (E) Different from a student of 10 years ago, today's high school student

12. <u>When one visits a car dealership to shop for a vehicle, you have to be careful</u> not to fall

GO ON TO THE NEXT PAGE ▸▸▸

victim to the ploys of the occasional devious salesperson.

(A) When one visits a car dealership to shop for a vehicle, you have to be careful
(B) When you visit a car dealership to shop for a vehicle, one must be careful
(C) If you visit a car dealership to shop for a vehicle, you must have been careful
(D) When one is visiting a car dealership to shop for a vehicle, you must be careful
(E) When you visit a car dealership to shop for a vehicle, you have to be careful

13. After skillfully managing the department for 18 months, the promotion to vice president of the company was offered to Lisa.

(A) the promotion to vice president of the company was offered to Lisa
(B) the promotion to vice president of the company had been offered to Lisa
(C) Lisa was offered the promotion to vice president of the company
(D) Lisa will have been offered the promotion to vice president of the company
(E) the offer to Lisa had been made for her to be the vice president of the company

14. It is important on the morning of the exam to make sure that you can eat a good breakfast, dress comfortably, getting to the school well before the test is scheduled to begin.

(A) dress comfortably, getting
(B) dress comfortably, and get
(C) dress comfortably, and will get
(D) dressing comfortably, and get
(E) dressing comfortably and getting

15. Despite having an impressively polished routine, the comedian was unable to illicit laughter from the unreceptive audience.

(A) the comedian was unable to illicit laughter from the unreceptive audience
(B) the comedian was unable to illicit laughter from the audience that was not receptive
(C) the comedian was unable to elicit laughter from the unreceptive audience
(D) the unreceptive audience had made it impossible for him to elicit laughter
(E) the comedian was not able to elicit from the unreceptive audience laughter

16. The tobacco company spent millions of dollars on research, the results that they then kept from the public because it had discovered that cigarettes could cause cancer.

(A) The tobacco company spent millions of dollars on research, the results that they then kept from the public because it had discovered
(B) Despite having spent millions of dollars on research, the tobacco company then kept their results from the public having discovered
(C) The tobacco company spent millions of dollars on research, the results of which it then kept from the public because it discovered
(D) Having spent millions of dollars on research, the tobacco company then kept its results from the public and it discovered
(E) Because they spent millions of dollars on research, the tobacco company kept its results from the public which discovered

17. Upon reviewing the videotape footage of the convenience store robbery, the verdict was clear; the members of the jury quickly agreed that the defendant was guilty.

(A) Upon reviewing
(B) Having been reviewing
(C) When they reviewed
(D) When reviewing
(E) Reviewing

18. By the time Christmas vacation arrives, I have finished all of my exams and my last term paper.

(A) I have finished all of my exams and my last term paper
(B) all of my exams and my last term paper have finished
(C) I will have been finishing all of my exams and my last term paper
(D) all of my exams and my last term paper have been finished
(E) I will have finished all of my exams and my last term paper

GO ON TO THE NEXT PAGE ▸▸▸

19. According to an outdated survey conducted in 2002 by a San Francisco-based consulting firm, <u>Pittsburgh ranked among the cleanest cities in the world.</u>

(A) Pittsburgh ranked among the cleanest cities in the world

(B) Pittsburgh ranks among the cleanest cities in the world

(C) Pittsburgh has been ranked among the cleanest cities in the world

(D) among the cleanest cities in the world is ranked Pittsburgh

(E) ranked among the cleanest cities in the world had been Pittsburgh

20. Portrayed as a power-hungry conqueror, Napoleon Bonaparte, a great military commander of the eighteenth and nineteenth centuries, <u>argues he was instead building a united federation of free people in Europe.</u>

(A) argues he was instead building a united federation of free people in Europe

(B) instead argued that he was building Europe into a united federation of free people

(C) argued he was instead building a united federation of free people in Europe

(D) will argue that he was building a united federation of free people's in Europe

(E) argued he was building, for Europe, a united federation of free people

---

Directions for "Identifying Sentence Error" Questions

The following sentences may contain errors in grammar, usage, diction (choice of words), or idiom. Some of the sentences are correct. No sentence contains more than one error.

If the sentence contains an error, it is underlined and lettered. The parts that are not underlined are correct.

If there is an error, select the part that must be changed to correct the sentence.

If there is no error, choose (E).

EXAMPLE:

By the time <u>they reached</u> the halfway point
        A
in the race, most <u>of the runners</u> <u>hadn't hardly</u>
    B   C   D
begun to hit their stride. <u>No error</u>
                            E

---

21. Frank Lloyd Wright, <u>who</u> was one of
                            A
America's <u>most influential</u> architects, is
              B
remembered for <u>his innovative</u> designs
                    C
and <u>boundless energy.</u> <u>No error</u>
        D   E

22. The teacher <u>warned</u> the students that,
                    A
<u>if any of them</u> intended to hand in <u>their</u>
    B   C
assignment after the due date, he or she

<u>should be prepared</u> to receive a substan-
        D
tially lower grade. <u>No error</u>
                    E

23. Although Raul Vazquez <u>is</u> working
                        A   B
<u>at the company</u> for <u>only</u> 16 months, he was
        C   D
promoted to Head of Operations last week.

<u>No error</u>
E

24. The twig caterpillar <u>is</u> a bug that escapes
                            A
<u>detection by</u> birds because of <u>their</u> striking
        B   C
ability to blend in with the <u>surroundings.</u>
                                D
<u>No error</u>
E

GO ON TO THE NEXT PAGE ▶▶▶

25.   Sitting on the porch <u>overlooking</u> the lawn
                            A
       below, I <u>could hear</u> Erica and Lydia laugh-
               B
       ing as <u>she</u> ran full-speed <u>through</u> the spray
              C   D
       of the sprinkler. <u>No error</u>
                          E

26.   <u>During</u> the Cold War, the Soviet Union and
       A
       the United States <u>seemed to be</u> <u>engaged in</u>
                         B   C
       a constant battle to see who was the

       <u>strongest</u> nation. <u>No error</u>
        D   E

27.   <u>In</u> my locker <u>was</u> a few textbooks and a bag
       A   B
       of sporting equipment <u>that</u> my friend
                              C
       <u>had forgotten</u> to take home with him.
        D
       <u>No error</u>
        E

28.   The senior members <u>of the law firm</u> were
                           A
       getting tired of <u>him</u> constantly leaving the
                        B
       office <u>early</u> on Fridays <u>to begin</u> his
              C   D
       weekend. <u>No error</u>
                 E

29.   <u>If not</u> in <u>peak</u> physical condition, running a
       A   B
       marathon <u>can have</u> devastating effects <u>on</u>
                 C   D
       one's leg muscles. <u>No error</u>
                           E

30.   A student protest <u>on</u> the social and political
                         A
       control <u>still held</u> by the communist party,
               B
       the Tiananmen Square demonstration of

       1989 <u>resulted</u> <u>in the deaths of</u> over 2,000
             C   D
       civilians. <u>No error</u>
                   E

31.   <u>Of the two</u> sophomores on the debate team,
       A
       Gilbert was the one <u>less</u> nervous
                           B
       about speaking in public <u>and was the one</u>
                                 C
       selected <u>to represent</u> the team in the state
                 D
       finals. <u>No error</u>
                E

32.   <u>In an effort</u> to <u>pull</u> the country <u>out of</u> a
       A   B   C
       recession, the President cut taxes,

       <u>increasing</u> spending, and lowered interest
        D
       rates. <u>No error</u>
              E

33.   Though many archaeologists

       <u>have concluded</u> that the ancient Egyptians
        A
       were morbidly <u>preoccupied in</u> death,
                      B
       others argue that the Egyptians

       <u>were instead</u> attempting to perpetuate a
        C
       good existence in the after-life

       <u>for the individual</u> that was buried. <u>No error</u>
        D   E

34.   Lavender, like <u>other</u> herbs that
                       A
       <u>can be dried</u>, <u>are</u> useful <u>as a salve</u> and
        B   C   D
       lotion. <u>No error</u>
               E

Directions for "Improving Paragraphs" Questions

Below is an early draft of an essay. It requires revision in many areas.

The questions that follow ask you to make improvements in sentence structure, diction, organization, and development. Answering the questions may require you to understand the context of the passage as well as the rules of standard written English.

Questions 35–39 refer to the following passage.

(1) *The nonspecific immune system is the nonspecific prevention of the entrance of invaders into the body.* (2) *Saliva contains an enzyme called lysozyme that can kill germs before they have a chance to take hold.* (3) *Lysozyme is also present in our tears, providing a nonspecific defense mechanism for our eyes.*

(4) *A nonspecific cellular defense mechanism is headed up by cells called phagocytes.* (5) *These cells, macrophages and neutrophils, roam the body in search of bacteria and dead cells to engulf and clear away.* (6) *Some assistance is offered to their cause by a protein molecule called complement.* (7) *This protein has the task of making sure that molecules, which need to be cleared will have some sort of identification for the displaying of the need for phagocyte assistance.* (8) *An antigen is a molecule that is foreign to our bodies and causes our immune system to respond.* (9) *Complement coats these cells, stimulating phagocytes to ingest them.* (10) *Cells involved in mechanisms that need cleanup assistance, such as platelets, have the ability to secrete chemicals that attract macrophages and neutrophils to places such as infection sites to help the elimination of foreign bacteria.*

(11) *A prime example of a nonspecific cellular response is inflammation.* (12) *Imagine that you pick up a tiny splinter in your finger as you grab a piece of wood.* (13) *Cells in the figure tissue, called mast cells, containing the signal histamine that is initiating the inflammation response.* (14) *Entrance of the splinter damages these mast cells, causing them to release histamine, which migrates through the tissue toward the bloodstream.* (15) *Histamine causes increased permeability and bloodflow to the injured tissue.* (16) *The splinter also causes the release of signals that call in the nonspecific phagocytic cells, which come to the site of the injury to clear away any debris or pathogens within the tissue.* (17) *The redness and warmth associated with inflammation occur because bloodflow increases to the area as a result of this process.*

35. Where is the best place to insert the following sentence?
The skin covering the entire body is a nonspecific defense mechanism; it acts as a physical barrier to infection.

(A) after sentence 2
(B) after sentence 3
(C) after sentence 4
(D) after sentence 5
(E) after sentence 7

36. Which of the following sentences contributes least to the unity of the second paragraph?

(A) sentence 6
(B) sentence 7
(C) sentence 8
(D) sentence 9
(E) sentence 10

GO ON TO THE NEXT PAGE ▶▶▶

37. Which of the following is the best way to combine sentences 6 and 7 (reproduced below)?

Some assistance is offered to their cause by a protein molecule called complement. This protein has the task of making sure that molecules, which need to be cleared will have some sort of identification for the displaying of the need for phagocyte assistance.

(A) Making sure that molecules which need to be cleared will have some sort of identification for the displaying of the need for phagocyte assistance, complement works to this end.

(B) Complement, a protein molecule, offers assistance to their cause by making sure that molecules, which need to be cleared will have some sort of identification for the displaying of the need for phagocyte assistance.

(C) Some assistance is offered to their cause by a protein molecule called complement; a protein that has the task of making sure that molecules to be cleared have some sort of identification for the displaying of this need.

(D) A protein molecule called complement helps these cells in this task by identifying those molecules that must be cleared.

(E) Complement offers assistance, as a protein molecule, by making sure that molecules, which need to be cleared, have some sort of identification that displays this need for clearance by phagocytes.

38. Which of the following is the best revision of sentence 13 (reproduced below)?

Cells in the figure tissue, called mast cells, containing the signal histamine that is initiating the inflammation response.

(A) Cells in the figure tissue, called mast cells, containing the signal histamine that is initiating the inflammation response.

(B) Cells in your finger tissue known as mast cells contain the signal histamine that will initiate the inflammation response.

(C) The inflammation response in the finger tissue is initiated when it is made to do so in the cell by histamine.

(D) Histamine, a signal in the cells of the finger tissue, will be initiating the inflammation response.

(E) Cells in your finger tissue are containing the signal histamine that will initiate the inflammation response.

39. Which of the following is the best sentence to insert after sentence 17?

(A) This immune process is nonspecific because the cells are not searching for a particular target; they are just looking for anything foreign to clear away.

(B) The immune system also contains defense mechanisms, which are quite specific.

(C) The mucous lining of our trachea and lungs prevent bacteria from entering cells and actually assists in the expulstion of bacteria by ushering the bacteria up and out with a cough.

(D) A vaccine is given to a patient in an effort to prime the immune system for a fight against a specific invader.

(E) Splinters can also cause a lot of pain, and the inflammation process can contribute to this pain.

 STOP

You may check your work, on this section only, until time is called.

ANSWER KEY

Section 2 Math	Section 4 Math	Section 1 Critical Reading	Section 3 Critical Reading	Section 5 Writing
☐ 1. B	☐ 21. E	☐ 1. B	☐ 25. D	☐ 1. B
☐ 2. C	☐ 22. B	☐ 2. A	☐ 26. C	☐ 2. B
☐ 3. D	☐ 23. B	☐ 3. C	☐ 27. D	☐ 3. C
☐ 4. D	☐ 24. A	☐ 4. E	☐ 28. A	☐ 4. D
☐ 5. C	☐ 25. E	☐ 5. D	☐ 29. E	☐ 5. A
☐ 6. D	☐ 26. C	☐ 6. B	☐ 30. D	☐ 6. B
☐ 7. E	☐ 27. D	☐ 7. D	☐ 31. A	☐ 7. A
☐ 8. E	☐ 28. D	☐ 8. D	☐ 32. C	☐ 8. C
☐ 9. C	# Right (A):	☐ 9. B	☐ 33. D	☐ 9. C
☐ 10. B		☐ 10. C	☐ 34. E	☐ 10. E
☐ 11. B	———————	☐ 11. E	☐ 35. B	☐ 11. B
☐ 12. B	# Wrong (B):	☐ 12. A	☐ 36. C	☐ 12. E
☐ 13. A		☐ 13. B	☐ 37. E	☐ 13. C
☐ 14. E	———————	☐ 14. B	☐ 38. C	☐ 14. B
☐ 15. B	# (A) - ¼ (B):	☐ 15. D	☐ 39. E	☐ 15. C
☐ 16. C		☐ 16. A	☐ 40. A	☐ 16. C
☐ 17. A	———————	☐ 17. B	☐ 41. C	☐ 17. C
☐ 18. D	☐ 29. 30	☐ 18. E	☐ 42. B	☐ 18. E
☐ 19. C	☐ 30. 1/12 or	☐ 19. E	☐ 43. D	☐ 19. A
☐ 20. E	0.083	☐ 20. A	☐ 44. C	☐ 20. B
	☐ 31. 2	☐ 21. C	☐ 45. B	☐ 21. E
	☐ 32. 9	☐ 22. D	☐ 46. B	☐ 22. C
	☐ 33. 2304	☐ 23. C	☐ 47. D	☐ 23. B
	☐ 34. 1	☐ 24. D	☐ 48. A	☐ 24. C
	☐ 35. 6			☐ 25. C
	☐ 36. 82			☐ 26. D
	☐ 37. 10			☐ 27. B
	☐ 38. 10			☐ 28. B
				☐ 29. A
				☐ 30. A
				☐ 31. E
				☐ 32. D
				☐ 33. B
				☐ 34. C
				☐ 35. B
				☐ 36. C
				☐ 37. D
				☐ 38. B
				☐ 39. A
# Right (A):	# Right (A):	# Right (A):	# Right (A):	# Right (A):
# Wrong (B):	———————	# Wrong (B):	# Wrong (B):	# Wrong (B):
———————		———————	———————	———————
# (A) - ¼ (B):		# (A) - ¼ (B):	# (A) - ¼ (B):	# (A) - ¼ (B):

Score Conversion Table

How to score your test

Use the answer key on the previous page to determine your raw score on each section. Your raw score on any section is equal to the number of correct answers on that section minus 1/4 of the number of wrong answers, with the exception of the mathematical "grid-in" section, on which wrong answers are not deducted from your score. Remember to add the raw scores from Sections 1 and 3 to get your Critical Reading raw score, and to add the raw scores from sections 2 and 4 to get your Math raw score. Write the three raw scores here:

Raw Critical Reading score: _____

Raw Math score: _____

Raw Writing score: _____

Use the table below to convert these to scaled scores.

Scaled scores: Critical Reading: _____   Math: _____   Writing: _____

Raw Score	Critical Reading Scaled Score	Math Scaled Score	Writing Scaled Score	Raw Score	Critical Reading Scaled Score	Math Scaled Score	Writing Scaled Score
48	80			15	44	46	48
47	80			14	43	45	46
46	78			13	41	44	45
45	76			12	40	43	44
44	74			11	39	42	43
43	72			10	38	41	41
42	71			9	37	40	40
41	69			8	36	39	39
40	68			7	34	38	37
39	67		80	6	33	36	36
38	66	80	80	5	32	35	35
37	64	77	78	4	30	34	33
36	63	74	77	3	29	32	32
35	62	72	76	2	27	30	31
34	62	71	74	1	25	29	30
33	61	70	73	0	22	26	29
32	60	68	71	−1	20	24	28
31	59	66	69	−2	20	21	27
30	58	64	68	−3	20	20	25
29	57	62	66	−4	20	20	24
28	56	61	65	−5	20	20	21
27	56	60	63	or below	20	20	20
26	54	59	62				
25	54	58	60				
24	53	57	59				
23	52	55	57				
22	51	54	56				
21	50	53	55				
20	49	52	54				
19	48	51	52				
18	47	50	51				
17	46	49	50				
16	45	47	49				

Detailed Answer Key

Section I

1. B   The virus remains inactive (*dormant*) in the host without the host being aware of it (*unbeknownst*). *lukewarm* = lacking enthusiasm, tepid; *dormant* = inactive; *solitary* = alone

2. A   The businessman *embezzled* (stole) large sums of money from his partner, and he *secretly* wired it to a bank account in the Caymen Islands. This shows that he is a *deceitful* individual who *steals* from his partner. *deceitful* = given to cheating; *swindle* = to steal; *duplicitous* = marked by deceptiveness; *rebuke* = to reprimand sharply; *dupe* = to trick

3. C   The fact that he *wrote his first program at the age of seven* suggests that he is very talented. The missing word should describe his *great skill* with computers. *atrophy* = a wasting away, deterioration; *aptitude* = talent, skill; *skepticism* = doubt; *antagonism* = contentiousness, a feeling of dislike

4. E   Since she had been with her boyfriend for three years before the breakup, it is *natural* for her to feel *unhappy* afterward. It can be inferred that she was upset and thus her demeanor was overly *melancholy* (marked by depression). *mystified* = puzzled; *sanguine* = cheerfully optimistic; *elated* = very happy; *meticulous* = attentive to detail; *jubilant* = very happy; *disheartened* = disspirited; *irate* = extremely angry; *jocular* = characterized by joking; *despondent* = lacking hope; *melancholy* = marked by depression or sadness

5. D   Stravinsky's *followers* are those who support his work. The sentence implies a contrast between his followers and *many others* who consider his music *unpleasantly harsh dissonance* and *irregular rhythms*. *sublime* = majestic; *mortify* = embarrass; *dissonance* = discord; a disagreeable combination of sounds; *abstract* = not concrete; difficult to understand; *benevolent* = kind; *aesthetic* = pertaining to beauty; *cacophony* = a combination of harsh sounds; *punctiliousness* = attention to detail

6. B   The passage indicates that *volcanic geothermal systems ... breach the surface as soothing hot springs* (lines 15–17), which indicates that these water sources originated beneath the surface.

7. D   Volcanic activity affects the abundance of each of the answer choices except (D), insects. *The*

very air we breathe [gases, choice (A)] can be found in line 12. In line 7–10, *The oceans ... and lakes, rivers, and groundwaters ... are all condensed volcanic steam* [moisture, choice (B)]. Answer choice (C), glaciers, can be found in line 20: *creating glaciers*. Answer choice (E), arable soil, can be found in line 13: *wondrously fertile vocanic soils....*

8. D   This short passage functions to introduce some concepts and to define some terms. It is not a *brief history of a phenomenon*, because there is no real phenomenon being discussed. It is not *a humorous vignette*, because there are no jokes being told. It is not a *justification of a position*, because it is not taking a side so much as objectively introducing *a set of definitions* to the reader. It is not a *refutation of a common misconception*, because there is no misconception introduced in the passage.

9. B   A *premise* (line 14) is a statement that *supports a conclusion*. The argument in lines 4–7 consists of three statements: Bob has a temperature, Bob is sick, and Bob should rest. A premise should *[provide] a sufficient reason to believe the others* (lines 12–13). The statement *Bob should rest* is a conclusion. Bob could need to rest for numerous reasons. Just saying that he should rest does not support the conclusion that he has a temperature or that he is sick. The other two statements, *Bob is sick* and *Bob has a temperature*, support the conclusion and provide evidence as to why *Bob should rest*. This makes them premises.

10. C   The ambivalence of the narrator toward the scrap of paper is clearly demonstrated by the conflict between his attachment to it and his desire to get rid of it. He mentions *the care with which I preserve* (lines 1–2) the paper because of its value in *[keeping] alive the memory of a certain day* (lines 3–4) on the one hand and his decision *to throw it away* (line 23) on the other hand.

11. E   The narrator says *I protest the accusation of sentimentality*, indicating that he does not think his reputation is warranted. He would not protest it if he carried it willingly or considered it a positive trait or a useful quality.

12. A   The description the narrator gives is starkly objective. He simply describes the scrap without any reference to emotion. He describes it to give it some *documentary value* (line 10) in order to dispute his reputation for sentimentality.

---

13. **B**   The statement *my heart suddenly felt heavy* (lines 50–51) stands in stark contrast to the mood the narrator conveyed in the previous paragraph when he said *I felt very happy* (line 38).

---

14. **B**   The narrator's question *"Was there any mail?"* is *senseless* (line 65) because he can see that *Mother's small red hand was resting on the little pile* (lines 66–67) of mail. Therefore, he already knows the answer to the question.

---

15. **D**   The narrator states that *a nameless diffidence had prevented me from comforting her* (lines 81–82). *Diffidence* mean *lack of self-confidence*.

---

16. **A**   The narrator is clearly repressing a belief because he says *I knew I was lying* (lines 98–99).

---

17. **B**   The quotation, which is over 300 years old, *provides the world a euphonious [nice sounding] name for an opposition that has been debated ever since* (lines 4–5). It is being used to indicate that the debate being discussed in this passage is centuries old.

---

18. **E**   The terms *wither* and *blossom* refer to plants, but they are here used to describe what might happen to certain social institutions. They are drawing a comparison between natural and social phenomena.

---

19. **E**   Ortega y Gassett asserts than *"Man has no nature..."* meaning that humans are not born with any innate tendencies. Therefore, his conception of *history* must not include congenital behavioral tendencies.

---

20. **A**   The passage states that social construction-ism depended on *the doctrine that the mind is a blank slate* (lines 26–27), which asserts that there is no such thing as human nature.

---

21. **C**   The appeal of the blank slate theory is dis-cussed in the third paragraph (lines 32–47), where the theory is said to hold out *the hope of unlimited social progress* (line 47) and to be *the ultimate safe-guard against racism, sexism, and class prejudice* (lines 42–43). The passage does not suggest that the blank slate theory reinforces the appropriateness of the current social order.

---

22. **D**   This sentence acknowledges the major argu-ment against the theory for *innate mechanisms*, namely the effectiveness of learning and culture, so it *qualifies*, or moderates, the thesis of the passage, which is stated in the next sentence, namely that *there must be complex innate mechanisms for learning and culture to be possible in the first place* (lines 57–60).

---

23. **C**   The passage states that our taste for fatty foods is one of the *psychological traits... [that is] better adapted to the evolutionary demands of an ancestral environment than to the actual demands of the current environment* (lines 63–67). In other words, the inclination for such foods helped our ancestors to survive.

---

24. **D**   These *axon guidance molecules* are men-tioned as examples of *mechanisms of plasticity that make learning possible*. That is, they are innate factors that contribute to cognition.

Section 2

1. **B**
$$x^2 + 3x + 4 = x^2 + 3x + 4y$$
Subtract $(x^2 + 3x)$: $4 = 4y$
Divide by 4: $1 = y$

(Chapter 9 Lesson 1: Solving Equations)

2. **C**

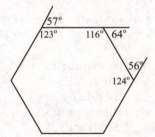

Remember there are 180° in a line. $123 + a = 180$
Subtract 123: $a = 57$
                              $116 + b = 180$
Subtract 116: $b = 64$
                              $124 + c = 180$
Subtract 124: $c = 56$
                           $a + b + c =$
Substitute: $57 + 64 + 56 = 177$

(Chapter 11 Lesson 1: Lines and Angles)

---

3. **D**
$$\frac{1}{w} = \frac{3}{16}$$
Cross-multiply: $16 = 3w$
Divide by 3: $5.33 = w = \frac{16}{3}$

(Chapter 8 Lesson 4: Ratios and Proportions)

4. D   First calculate how many signatures are needed: $350 - 125 = 225$.

225 is what percent of 350?

$$225 = \frac{x}{100}(350)$$

Simplify: $225 = 3.5x$

Divide by 3.5: $x = 64\%$

(Chapter 8 Lesson 5: Percents)

---

5. C   Just pick a value for p that fits the rules. Plug it into the answer choices and see which one works.

If $p = 3$,

(A) $5 - p = 5 - 3 = 2$ not negative
(B) $2p - 6 = 2(3) - 6 = 0$ not negative
(C) $1 - p = 1 - 3 = -2$
(D) $-p + 3 = -3 + 3 = 0$ not negative
(E) $2p + 3 = 2(3) + 3 = 9$ not negative

(Chapter 10 Lesson 3: Numerical Reasoning Problems)

---

6. D

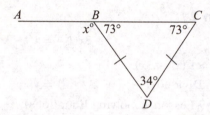

$\angle CDB = 34°$ and triangle BCD is isosceles with $BD = CD$. This means that $\angle CBD = \angle BCD = y$.

There are 180° in a triangle: $y + y + 34 = 180$
Subtract 34: $2y = 146$
Divide by 2: $y = 73$
There are 180° in a line: $73 + x = 180$
Subtract 73: $x = 107$

(Chapter 11 Lesson 2: Triangles)

---

7. E $a + b = 6$

Stack the equations and add: $+a - b = 4$
                                     $2a = 10$

Divide by 2: $a = 5$

                                     $a + b = 6$

Substitute 5 for a: $5 + b = 6$

Subtract 5: $b = 1$

                                     $2a + 3b =$

Substitute a and b: $2(5) + 3(1) = 13$

(Chapter 9 Lesson 1: Solving Equations)

---

8. E   Write an equation to find the average:

$$\frac{-4 + 3 + x}{3} = 2$$

Multiply by 3: $-4 + 3 + x = 6$
Combine like terms: $-1 + x = 6$
Add 1: $x = 7$

(Chapter 10 Lesson 2: Mean/Median/Mode Problems)

---

9. C   The ratio $3 : 4$ is equal to $3 \div 4$, or 0.75.

(A) $6 \div 12 = 0.50$
(B) $9 \div 16 = 0.5625$
(C) $12 \div 16 = 0.75$
(D) $12 \div 20 = 0.60$
(E) $15 \div 25 = 0.60$

(Chapter 8 Lesson 4: Ratios and Proportions)

---

10. B   The cab fare begins at $2.25. To figure out how many miles she went, first subtract out the starting price from the $5.00 total: $5.00 - $2.25 = $2.75. Divide $2.75 by $0.25 per mile: $2.75 \div $0.25 = 11$ miles. So, the cab has gone between 11 and 12 miles.

(Chapter 9 Lesson 1: Solving Equations)

---

11. B

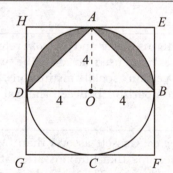

A square with an area of 64 has sides of length $\sqrt{64} = 8$. Since the side of the square is congruent to the diameter of the circle, which is twice the radius, the radius of the circle is 4. To find the area of the shaded region, find the area of half of circle O and subtract out the area of triangle ABD.

Area of circle O: $A = \pi r^2$

Substitute 4 for r: $A = \pi(4)^2 = 16\pi$

Divide by 2: $8\pi =$ half the circle

Find the area of $\triangle ABD$: $A = \frac{1}{2}(b)(h)$

Substitute: $A = \frac{1}{2}(8)(4) = 16$

Subtract the areas: $A_{\text{semicircle}} - A_{\text{triangle}}$

Substitute: $8\pi - 16$

(Chapter 11 Lesson 8: Circles)

12. **B**   If $q = p = 3t = 6$, then $q = 6$, $p = 6$, and $t = 2$.
$$3q - 4p + 2t$$
Substitute: $3(6) - 4(6) + 2(2) = -2$

(Chapter 9 Lesson 1: Solving Equations)

---

13. **A**   Set up a ratio to solve this problem.
$$\frac{c \text{ containers}}{p \text{ pounds}} = \frac{? \text{ containers}}{x \text{ pounds}}$$
Cross-multiply: $cx = p$

Divide by p: $\dfrac{cx}{p} = ?$

(Chapter 8 Lesson 4: Ratios and Proportions)

---

14. **E**   First, solve for z. Let $w \blacktriangleright y = \dfrac{wy}{w+y}$.

Plug in: $6 \blacktriangleright z = 4$ $\dfrac{6z}{z+6} = 4$

Cross-multiply: $6z = 4(z+6)$

Distribute: $6z = 4z + 24$

Subtract $4z$: $2z = 24$

Divide by 2: $z = 12$

Now solve: $z \blacktriangleright 6 = 12 \blacktriangleright 6 = \dfrac{(12)(6)}{12+6} = \dfrac{72}{18} = 4$

(Chapter 10 Lesson 1: New Symbol or Term Problems)

---

15. **B**   If the product of a set of integers is zero, then one of the numbers must be zero. To minimize the value of any one of them, let 0 be the *largest* of the integers. Do not miss the fact that they are consecutive *even* integers. They are $-12, -10, -8, -6, -4, -2, 0$.

(Chapter 10 Lesson 3: Numerical Reasoning Problems)

---

16. **C**   Because there are 40 more girls than boys, the number of girls is $n + 40$. If the class has n boys, then the total number of seniors is $n + 40 + n = 2n + 40$. Now find out what percent of $2n + 40$ is n.

n is what percent of $2n + 40$? $n = \dfrac{x}{100}(2n + 40)$

Divide by $(2n + 40)$: $\dfrac{n}{2n + 40} = \dfrac{x}{100}$

Multiply by 100: $\dfrac{100n}{2n + 40}\% = x$

(Chapter 8 Lesson 5: Percents)
(Chapter 9 Lesson 1: Solving Equations)

---

17. **A**   To solve this logic problem, first try an odd value for x and an odd value for y and see if you can obtain an even result for $xy + x$. Let's say $x = 3$ and $y = 5$. $xy + x = 3(5) + 3 = 18$. So when x is odd, y can also be odd. This eliminates answer choices (B) and (E). Let's say $x = 4$ and $y = 6$. $xy + x = 6(4) + 6 = 30$. So, when x is even, y can also be even. This eliminates answer choice (C). Now, let's say $x = 3$ and $y = 4$. $xy + x = 3(4) + 3 = 15$. This does not work because the solution must be even. So when x is odd, this means y must also be odd—answer choice (A) is thus correct. To prove (D) wrong, try $x = 4$ and $y = 3$. $xy + x = 4(3) + 4 = 16$.

(Chapter 10 Lesson 3: Numerical Reasoning Problems)

---

18. **D**   You can only compare exponents if they have the same base. Change 8^w into a base 2 exponential. Since $8 = 2^3$, you can substitute 2^3 in for 8.
$$2^k \times (2^3)^w = 2^{20}$$
Simplify: $2^k \times 2^{3w} = 2^{20}$

Combine: $2^{k+3w} = 2^{20}$

Eliminate bases: $k + 3w = 20$

(Chapter 9 Lesson 3: Working with Exponents)

---

19. **C**   The tallest mannequin cannot be placed on either end of the display. This means that there are only 4 choices for the first spot. The final spot is also restricted because the tallest mannequin cannot go there. With one mannequin already placed, this means there are only 3 choices for the final spot. Now you have the middle three positions to fill. There are 3 choices for the second spot, 2 choices for the third spot, and 1 choice for the fourth spot. There are $4 \times 3 \times 2 \times 1 \times 3 = 72$ possible arrangements.

(Chapter 10 Lesson 5: Counting Problems)

---

20. **E**

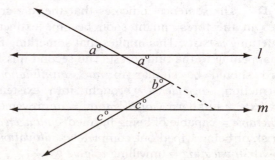

With a problem like this, don't be afraid to extend the line to make the diagram easier to use. The dotted line extends the diagram to form a triangle. Vertical angles for *a* and *c* have been filled in.

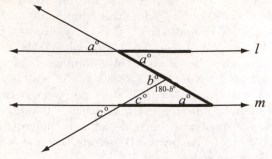

Since lines *l* and *m* are parallel, find the "Z" and locate the alternate interior angles that are equal, as shown in the diagram above. The final angle of the triangle can be filled in using linear pair, which says the two angles should be 180°. Use the fact that there are 180° in a triangle.

Set up an equation: $a + c + 180 - b = 180$

Subtract 180°: $a + c - b = 0$

Add *b*: $a + c = b$

Subtract *a*: $c = b - a$

(Chapter 11 Lesson 1: Lines and Angles)

Section 3

25. D   The parallelism of the contrast is the key to this sentence. Because technology is advancing rapidly and becoming more efficient and complex, procedures once considered *modern* and *efficient* are now looked at as *outdated* and *inefficient*. *novel* = new; *ingenious* = brilliant; *innovative* = new and fresh; *inefficacious* = ineffective

26. C   The phrase *now accepted as an undeniable truth* suggests that the concept was not that way before. Thus the missing word should be in contrast to *undeniable truth*. *incontrovertible* = unable to be disputed; *contentious* = controversial

27. D   The sentence indicates that the *rare* creatures in the forest might soon become extinct if something *persists*. This implies that something bad is happening to the rain forest. The second missing word should be similar to *rare*. *annihilation* = destruction; *engendered* = brought into existence; *obstinate* = stubborn; *amelioration* = improvement; *vulnerable* = capable of being harmed; *endangered* = at risk of being wiped out completely; *cultivation* = growth; *unyielding* = unwilling to give way

28. A   The cactus is able to survive in the desert despite the *dry* climate (*water is so scarce*). *arid* = extremely dry; *fervent* = showing great emotion; *lucid* = clear; *banal* = everyday, common; *sweltering* = oppressively hot and humid

29. E   The manager's explosion of *expletives* (profanities) and *insults* shocked her employees, so she must normally be a *calm, even-tempered* person. *vexed* = bothered, annoyed; *intemperate* = lacking moderation; *belligerent* = warlike; *vivacious* = full of life; *tranquil* = calm, even-tempered

30. D   A feeling of *profound depression and obsession with death ...permeates* (flows throughout) Antonio Calvelli's artwork. The missing word should relate to depression and death. *notorious* = famous for bad deeds or qualities; *lethargy* = a state of sluggishness; *pomposity* = pretentiousness; *morbidity* = relating to death or disease; *humility* = the quality of being humble or modest

31. A   The clause that follows the semicolon extends the idea in the first clause. Parallelism suggests that the two missing words should be similar to *uncompromising* and *truthful*. *inexorable* = unable to be swayed; *forthright* = honest; *capricious* = whimsical, acting without thought; *candid* = honest; *unrelenting* = unyielding; *perfidious* = treacherous; *intransigent* = refusing to compromise; *guileful* = deceitful; *mercurial* = constantly changing; *veracious* = truthful

32. C   The word *although* indicates a contrast between ideas in the sentence. The second half of the sentence indicates that Galileo's opinions *contrasted strongly with* the accepted views. Thus, it can be inferred that the *common practice* was to *support* or *follow the beliefs of the church as law*. It can also be inferred that since his opinions contrasted strongly with accepted views, they were *controversial*. *iconoclastic* = attacking traditional views; *endorse* = support publicly; *orthodox* = adhering strictly to teaching; *espouse* = give loyalty to; *heretical* = deviating starkly from tradition; *impugn* = attack as false; *dissident* = disagreeing; *advocate* = argue in favor of; *conformist* = deliberately conventional

33. D   The phrase *that's the way it goes* (lines 16–17) conveys an attitude of resignation, or reluctant acceptance of an unfortunate situation. Passage 2, on the other hand, uniformly praises the noble work of women during the Gold Rush.

34. **E**   Passage 1 states that *the mining game . . . is like tossing coins to see who's lucky* (lines 17–18), thereby indicating that success in gold mining was not always guaranteed. Passage 2 states that *gold mining was not always profitable* (lines 23–24) and that women in mining families often had to work hard to feed their families.

35. **B**   The first sentence states that *the business of child bearing and rearing went on apace* despite hardships. This indicates the women's steadfast commitment to maintaining their families.

36. **C**   The *burden* refers to the task of raising families during the difficult times of the Gold Rush, which is the focus of Passage 2.

37. **E**   This paragraph summarizes two *arguments*, or lines of reasoning, that support the practice of *medical confidentiality*. These two arguments do not conflict with each other, so they do not represent a *controversy*; in fact, at the end of the passage the author suggests that the two arguments should be taken together to argue for the principle of confidentiality. Also, neither is the point of view of just one individual; both are stated as general arguments. Lastly, the paragraph presents no *historical background*, nor does it discuss a *misconception*.

38. **C**   Line 3 refers to the *utilitarian* argument, which refers to *possible long-term consequences*, but does not specify the kinds of consequences. The second paragraph explains in more detail. It says that the utilitarian argument argues that *without such confidentiality the physician-patient relationship would be seriously impaired* (lines 9–11). In other words, by *utilitarian*, the author means *pertaining to the effectiveness of the physician-patient relationship*.

39. **E**   In summarizing the utilitarian argument for medical confidentiality, the author says that *psychotherapists have been particularly concerned to protect the confidentiality of their relationship with patients*. In the context of this paragraph, that can only mean that the success of psychotherapy depends in particularly large measure on the trust of their patients. Although psychotherapists do not use *invasive procedures* as surgeons do, and do require extensive training, these facts are not mentioned in the passage and are irrelevant to the discussion.

40. **A**   The center of these *concentric circles* is clearly the patient. The physician and the patient's close friends may be admitted into one or more of the inner circles, but this suggests that they could not have been at the center of these circles to begin with.

41. **C**   In saying that *we would be justified in charging that he had violated the patient's right to privacy*, the author means that we would be justified in *accusing* him of doing something wrong.

42. **B**   The term *interwoven* means *enmeshed with other things*. In this case, the other things are the *responsibilities* (line 67) that include *maintaining a high level of skill in medical procedures and knowledge about new medications*. In other words, the term *interwoven* suggests that confidentiality is one of many that the physician is burdened with.

43. **D**   The discussion of the origin of the word *confidentiality*, and particularly its relation to the Latin word *fidere*, serves to emphasize a particular shade of meaning within the word. In saying that the term *implies more than keeping secrets*, the author is cautioning the reader against a simplistic interpretation of the word. This caution does not suggest, however, that physicians have been *misusing the term*, but rather that the reader can better understand the nuances of the term by understanding its origin.

44. **C**   In saying that confidentiality implies *acting always to inspire the patient that one has his or her best interests in mind*, the author means that doctors should *persuade* their patients that they have their best interests in mind.

45. **B**   The *facts* in this discussion include the *fact* (line 95) of his wife's disease or trauma. The discussion does not mention any *therapy, limits of technology, drugs*, or the *personal life of the physician*.

46. **B**   This question summarizes the issue presented in the preceding several sentences, which describe a situation in which the confidences of two patients may be in conflict with each other. It does not *open a new line of investigation*, because a new, but related, topic is discussed in the next sentence. It does not make any *definitive statement* and certainly does not *mock* any class of people. It also does not *indicate the weakness of an argument*, because it does not refer to an argument at all, but simply a complicated issue that must be addressed.

47. **D**   The word *levity* means *light-heartedness or good humor*. In this context, it suggests that medical anecdotes can sometimes be humorous.

48. A Passage 1 discusses two arguments for medical confidentiality and indicates that confidentiality can *be based squarely on this general right to privacy.* It does not suggest that there are any exceptions to this right, and it argues that this right constitutes a *strong case* for confidentiality. Therefore, Passage 1 suggests that this right is absolute and inviolable. Passage 2, on the other hand, suggests that there are circumstances in which perhaps this right to privacy might have to be violated, for instance when *public health* (lines 102–103) is at stake.

Section 4

21. E Begin by converting the information into an equation:

$$x - 3 = 4 + w$$
$$\text{Add 3:} \quad x = 7 + w$$

Therefore x is 7 more than w
(Chapter 9 Lesson 1: Solving Equations)

22. B To find the area of this triangle, find the lengths of the base and the height of the triangle and use the formula $A = \frac{1}{2}bh$. To find the base, find the distance between (3, 1) and (7, 1). Since these points have the same y-coordinate, you can just subtract the x-values of the two coordinates to find the distance: $7 - 3 = 4$.

To find the height, find the distance from the base to the opposite vertex (8, 5). This is simply the vertical distance from $y = 1$ to $y = 5$. So the height is $5 - 1 = 4$.

$$\text{Area} = \frac{1}{2}(b)(h)$$
$$\text{Area} = \frac{1}{2}(4)(4) = 8$$

(Chapter 11 Lesson 5: Areas and Perimeters)

23. B

$$7b - 8 \geq 4b + 16$$
$$\text{Add 8:} \quad 7b \geq 4b + 24$$
$$\text{Subtract } 4b: \quad 3b \geq 24$$
$$\text{Divide by 3:} \quad b \geq 8$$

The question says that b must be an *odd* integer, so $b = 9$.
(Chapter 9 Lesson 6: Inequalities, Absolute Values, and Plugging In)

24. A Set up a ratio that relates the two areas:
$$\frac{\pi r_A^2}{\pi r_B^2} = \frac{2}{1}$$

$$\text{Simplify:} \quad \frac{r_A^2}{r_B^2} = \frac{2}{1}$$

$$\text{Take the square root:} \quad \frac{r_A}{r_B} = \frac{\sqrt{2}}{1}$$

$$\text{Cross-multiply:} \quad r_A = \sqrt{2}r_B$$

The circumference of circle A is $2\pi r_A = 2\pi\sqrt{2}r_B = \sqrt{2}(2\pi r_B)$, which is $\sqrt{2}$ times greater than the circumference of circle B.
(Chapter 11 Lesson 8: Circles)
(Chapter 11, Lesson 5: Areas and Perimeters)

25. E Begin by writing an equation to solve for the average of the four positive integers.

$$\frac{a + b + c + d}{4} = 12$$

Multiply by 4: $a + b + c + d = 48$
If you want to find the *largest* possible value of one of the integers, make the others as *small* as possible. The problem says that they must be *positive* integers, but it says nothing about them being *different* integers. Therefore you would make each of the three smallest integers 1. $\quad 1 + 1 + 1 + d = 48$
Subtract 3: $d = 45$
(Chapter 10 Lesson 2: Mean/Median/Mode Problems)

26. C The third side of any triangle must have a length that is between the sum and the difference of the other two sides. Since $10 - 6 = 4$ and $10 + 6 = 16$, the third side must be between (but not including) 4 and 16:
$4 < x < 16$
Therefore the largest possible integer value of the third side is 15.
(Chapter 11 Lesson 2: Triangles)

27. D

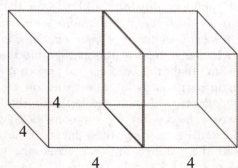

When the two cubes are joined together, two of the faces are lost because they are attached to each other. The surface area is just the sum of all the areas on the surface of the shape. Each face

of the shape is a square that has an area of $(4)(4) = 16$ square units. There are 10 faces, which gives a surface area of $10(16) = 160$ square units.
(Chapter 11 Lesson 7: Volumes and 3-D Geometry)

---

28. D
The general strategy is to find out how many games there are if each team plays each other team once and multiply that by 2.

Opponents:	# matches
Team 1: 2, 3, 4, 5, 6	5
Team 2: 3. 4. 5. 6	4
Team 3: 4, 5, 6	3
Team 4: 5, 6	2
Team 5: 6	1
Total head-to-head matchups:	15

Since they play each other twice, there is a total of $15 \times 2 = 30$ games.
(Chapter 10 Lesson 5: Counting Problems)

---

29. 30 Set up an equation that represents the information given: Tank A holds 30% less than tank B.

$$A = B - 0.30B = 0.70B$$

Substitute: $21 = 0.70B$

Divide by 0.7: $30 = B$

(Chapter 8 Lesson 5: Percents)

---

30. $\dfrac{1}{12}$ **or 0.08**

After the first cut into 4 pieces:

After the second cut:

There are 12 identical pieces after the second cut. This means that there will be a 1 out of 12 probability that she gets the coin.
(Chapter 10 Lesson 6: Probability Problems)

---

31. 2 Starting with the column on the far right:
$A + B = 7$ or $A + B = 17$

Moving on to the second column, we see that:

$$6 + C = B + 10$$

Subtract 6:	$C = B + 4$
Subtract B:	$C - B = 4$
	$+C + B = 14$
Add equations:	$2C = 18$
Divide by 2:	$C = 9$
	$C - B = 4$
Substitute for C:	$9 - B = 4$
Subtract 9:	$-B = -5$
Divide by -1:	$B = 5$
	$A + B = 7$
Substitute for B:	$A + 5 = 7$
Subtract 5:	$A = 2$

Note: $A + B \neq 17$ because since $B = 5$, A would have to be 12 and these letters must be **DIGITS**, not integers.
(Chapter 10 Lesson 3: Numerical Reasoning Problems)

---

32. 9 Recall that vertical angles are congruent, so all of the angles marked in the figure below must be congruent. Also, remember that, in a triangle, sides opposite congruent angles are also congruent. So your diagram should look like this:

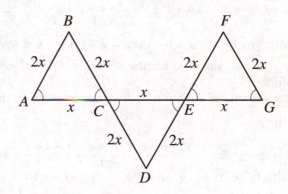

Because the sum of the perimeters is 45,

$$2x + 2x + x + 2x + 2x + x + 2x + 2x + x = 45$$

Simplify:	$15x = 45$
Divide by 15:	$x = 3$

Therefore, AG is $3 + 3 + 3 = 9$

(Chapter 11, Lesson 1: Lines and Angles)

(Chapter 11, Lesson 2: Triangles)

33. **2304**, To solve this problem, just multiply the expressions together:

$$bc \times cf \times fh \times bh = b^2c^2f^2h^2$$

Substitute: $4 \times 6 \times 12 \times 8 = b^2c^2f^2h^2$

Simplify: $2,304 = b^2c^2f^2h^2$

(Chapter 10 Lesson 3: Numerical Reasoning Problems)

34. **1** If you look at set X, all of the members are even. All of the members of set Y are odd. When an even number is added to an odd number, the result is always odd. Therefore the probability that the sum would be odd is 1.
(Chapter 10 Lesson 3: Numerical Reasoning Problems)

35. **6** There are multiple triangles in this problem. Set up equations for the two larger triangles and stack them.

$$a + b + 47 = 180$$
$$a + c + 53 = 180$$

Subtract: $b - c - 6 = 0$

Add 6: $b - c = 6$

(Chapter 11 Lesson 2: Triangles)
(Chapter 9 Lesson 2: Systems)

36. **82** Begin by setting up an equation that you can use to calculate the average of the first eight students.

$$\frac{a+b+c+d+e+f+g+h}{8} = 87$$

Multiply by 8: $a+b+c+d+e+f+g+h = 696$

This means the 8 students scored a total of 696 points.

Now set up an equation to find the average of the entire

20-student class: $\dfrac{a+b+c+\cdots+q+r+s+t}{20} = 84$

Multiply by 20: $a+b+c+\cdots+q+r+s+t$
$$= 1,680$$

The class as a whole scored 1,680 points.

Therefore, the remaining 12 students scored $1,680 - 696 = 984$ points. To find the average for those 12 students, divide their point total by 12: $984 \div 12 = 82$.
(Chapter 10 Lesson 2: Mean/Median/Mode Problems)

37. **10**
The first 9 terms are written out for you. Identify the repeating pattern: $-4, 2, 4\ldots$
The pattern repeats every 3 digits, and the sum of each repetition of the pattern is $-4 + 2 + 4 = 2$.
The pattern occurs $20 \div 3 = 6.67$ times, or 6 with remainder 2.
The 6 full repetitions have a sum of $6 \times 2 = 12$.
The nineteenth term is -4 and the twentieth term is 2, so the overall sum is $12 + (-4) + 2 = 10$.
(Chapter 10 Lesson 7: Sequences)

38. **10**

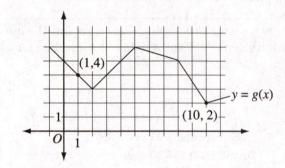

The first step is to evaluate $g(1)$, which is the y-value of the function when $x = 1$. The point on the graph that corresponds to $x = 1$ is the point $(1,4)$, so $g(1) = 4$. Substituting this value into the given equation gives $g(m) = g(1) - 2 = 4 - 2 = 2$. This means that m is the input, or x-value, of the function that yields an output, or y-value, of 2. The only point on the graph that has a y-value of 2 is the point $(10,2)$, therefore $m = 10$.

Section 5

1. B   The original sentence lacks the *as ... as* construction that should accompany this comparison. Answer choice (B) best corrects the error.
(Chapter 13 Lesson 4: Comparison Errors)

2. B   This contains a dangling modifier. The modifying phrase that begins the sentence describes the *medication*, not the *people* who prefer the medication.
(Chapter 13 Lesson 7: Dangling and Misplaced Participles)

3. C   The word *meticulous* is an adjective and can thus modify only a noun. But since it modifies the verb *sifted*, the adverb *meticulously* is needed here.
(Chapter 13 Lesson 12: Other Problems with Modifiers)

4. D   The two clauses are not properly coordinated. The semicolon is used to join two closely related independent clauses in a single sentence. (C) does not work because the second clause cannot stand alone.
(Chapter 13 Lesson 15: Coordinating Ideas)

5. A   The sentence is correct.

6. B   The original sentence begins with a dangling modifying phrase. Since this phrase clearly modifies *Gerard* and not *the need*, Choice (B) is the only option that keeps the phrase from dangling.
(Chapter 13 Lesson 8: Other Misplaced Modifiers)

7. A   The sentence is correct.

8. C   This question is tricky. The subject of the verb is the plural subject *professors*, not *Doctor Strathmore*. So the verb should be *are* and not *is*.
(Chapter 13 Lesson 1: Subject-Verb Disagreement)

9. C   The two clauses are not properly coordinated. A semicolon should be used to join the two independent clauses in a single sentence. (C) is the most concise, logical, and complete.
(Chapter 13 Lesson 15: Coordinating Ideas)

10. E   The original sentence is in the wrong mood. Answer choice (E) is clear and concise and appropriately conveys the conditional nature of the wish, since the event did not actually take place.
(Chapter 13 Lesson 14: The Subjunctive Mood)

11. B   The original phrasing contains a comparison error, comparing *high school students today* to *10 years ago*. Choice (B) best corrects the mistake.
(Chapter 13 Lesson 4: Comparison Errors)

12. E   When *one* is used as a subject in the beginning of a sentence, it is improper to then use *you* later on in that same sentence to refer to the same subject. It must either be *one* and *one* or *you* and *you*. Choice (E) corrects this mistake in the most concise and logical way.
(Chapter 13 Lesson 5: Pronoun Agreement)

13. C   This contains a dangling modifier. The participial phrase that begins the sentence describes *Lisa*, not the *promotion* she has been offered. Answer choice (C) is the most concise and logical correction of the error.
(Chapter 13 Lesson 7: Dangling and Misplaced Participles)

14. B   The sentence is not parallel. The first two items in the list establish the pattern, *eat, ... dress, ...* So the last item should be *get ...*
(Chapter 13 Lesson 3: Parallelism)

15. C   This is a diction error. *Illicit* means unlawful, which makes no sense here. The word should be *elicit*.
(Chapter 13 Lesson 11: Diction Errors)

16. C   The two clauses are not properly coordinated. A semicolon should be used to join the two independent clauses in a single sentence. (C) is the most concise, logical, and complete.
(Chapter 13 Lesson 15: Coordinating Ideas)

17. C   This is an error in word order. Choices (A), (B), (D), and (E) are incorrect because of a dangling participle. Answer choice (C) is the only one that eliminates this error.
(Chapter 13 Lesson 7: Dangling and Misplaced Participles)

18. E   The sentence suggests that Christmas vacation has yet to arrive. Answer choice (E) uses the future perfect tense and corrects this error in the most concise and logical way.
(Chapter 13 Lesson 9: Tricky Tenses)

19. A   The sentence is correct.

20. B   Napoleon Bonaparte lived in the eighteenth and nineteenth centuries. Thus his argument

obviously occurred in the past. This eliminates answer choices (A) and (D). Answer choice (B) is the most concise and clear choice and in the proper tense.
(Chapter 13 Lesson 9: Tricky Tenses)

---

21. **E**   The sentence is correct.

---

22. **C**   The pronoun *their* does not agree with its antecedent *anyone*, which is singular, and should be changed to *his or her*.
(Chapter 13 Lesson 5: Pronoun Agreement)

---

23. **B**   The verb *is* is in the wrong tense. It should be in the present perfect tense, *has been*, because he was promoted last week, which suggests that he is *still* working there.
(Chapter 13 Lesson 9: Tricky Tenses)

---

24. **C**   The pronoun *their* does not agree with its antecedent, *bug*, which is singular, and should be changed to *its*.
(Chapter 13 Lesson 5: Pronoun Agreement)

---

25. **C**   The pronoun *she* is an ambiguous pronoun. We cannot tell whether it is referring to Erica or Lydia as it is written. Correct the error by specifying whether it was Erica or Lydia who was laughing.
(Chapter 13 Lesson 5: Pronoun Agreement)

---

26. **D**   This is a comparison error. Because the sentence compares *two* nations, the comparative *stronger* should be used instead of *strongest*.
(Chapter 13 Lesson 4: Comparison Errors)

---

27. **B**   The subject of the verb is the plural *textbooks*. Hence, the verb should be *were* instead of *was*.
(Chapter 13 Lesson 1: Subject-Verb Disagreement)

---

28. **B**   *Leaving* is the object, so the pronoun should not be in the objective case, but rather in the possessive case, *his*.
(Chapter 13 Lesson 6: Pronoun Case)

---

29. **A**   This sentence contains a misplaced modifier. As written, this sentence suggests that the *marathon* is not in peak physical condition. The phrase *If not* should be changed to *If one is not* to remove the misplaced modifier error.
(Chapter 13 Lesson 7: Dangling and Misplaced Participles)

---

30. **A**   It would be a protest *against* the social and political control rather than a protest *on* the social

and political control.
(Chapter 13 Lesson 10: Idiom Errors)

---

31. **E**   The sentence is correct.

---

32. **D**   This sentence violates the law of parallelism. The President *cut* taxes and *lowered* interest rates. To create parallel sentence structure, it should be changed to *increased* spending.
(Chapter 13 Lesson 3: Parallelism)

---

33. **B**   The Egyptians would be preoccupied *with* death rather than preoccupied *in* death.
(Chapter 13 Lesson 10: Idiom Errors)

---

34. **C**   The subject of the verb is lavender. Since the subject is singular, the verb should be *is* instead of *are*.
(Chapter 13 Lesson 1: Subject-Verb Disagreement)

---

35. **B**   This sentence provides another example of a nonspecific defense mechanism, and so the most sensible place for the new example is after sentence 3 in between two other examples that are discussed in the passage.
(Chapter 13 Lesson 15: Coordinating Ideas)

---

36. **C**   This paragraph is discussing a nonspecific cellular defense mechanism involving cells called phagocytes. Sentence 8 introduces a definition of the term *antigen*, which is not mentioned again anywhere else in the passage. Removing this sentence would actually improve the passage.
(Chapter 13 Lesson 15: Coordinating Ideas)

---

37. **D**   Choice (D) provides the most logical, concise, and clear phrasing.
(Chapter 13 Lesson 15: Coordinating Ideas)

---

38. **B**   Choice (B) provides the most logical, concise, and clear phrasing.
(Chapter 13 Lesson 15: Coordinating Ideas)

---

39. **A**   Choice (B) is not a good fit because it would end the paragraph with an introduction to a new topic. Choice (C) would be out of place if written after sentence 17. Choice (D) discusses vaccines, which are not mentioned anywhere else in this passage. Choice (E) may well be a correct fact, but it does not function as a good conclusion to the passage. Choice (A) is the best choice because it sums up the immune process just discussed and explains why it is nonspecific.
(Chapter 13 Lesson 15: Coordinating Ideas)